HANDBOOK OF RELATIONAL DIAGNOSIS
AND DYSFUNCTIONAL FAMILY PATTERNS

HANDBOOK OF RELATIONAL DIAGNOSIS AND DYSFUNCTIONAL FAMILY PATTERNS

edited by

Florence W. Kaslow, PhD

John Wiley & Sons, Inc.

New York • Chichester • Brisbane • Toronto • Singapore

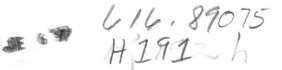

This text is printed on acid-free paper.

Copyright © 1996 by John Wiley & Sons, Inc.

All rights reserved. Published simultaneously in Canada.

This publication is designed to provide accurate and authoritative
information in regard to the subject matter covered. It is sold
with the understanding that the publisher is not engaged in
rendering professional services. If legal, accounting, medical,
psychological, or any other expert assistance is required, the
services of a competent professional person should be sought.

DSM and DSM-IV are trademarks of the American Psychiatric Association.

Library of Congress Cataloging-in-Publication Data:

Handbook of relational diagnosis and dysfunctional family patterns /
    edited by Florence W. Kaslow.
        p.   cm. — (Wiley series in couples and family dynamics and
    treatment)
      Includes index.
      ISBN 0-471-08078-0 (alk. paper)
      1. Problem families—Evaluation.   2. Communication in the family.
    3. Family—Mental health.   4. Family—Psychological aspects.
    I. Kaslow, Florence Whiteman.   II. Series.
    RC455.4F3H356   1996
    616.89′ 075—dc20   95-30113

Printed in the United States of America

10   9   8   7   6   5   4   3   2

Series Preface

Our ability to form strong interpersonal bonds with romantic partners, children, parents, siblings, and other relations is one of the key qualities that defines our humanity. These relationships shape who we are and what we become—they can be a source of great gratification or tremendous pain. Yet only in the mid-twentieth century did behavioral and social scientists really begin focusing on couples and family dynamics, and only in the last several decades have the theory and findings that emerged from those studies been used to develop effective therapeutic interventions for troubled couples and families.

We have made great progress in understanding the structure, function, and interactional patterns of couples and families—and made tremendous strides in treatment. However, as we stand poised on the beginning of a new millennium, it seems quite clear that both intimate partnerships and family relationships are in a period of tremendous flux. Economic factors are changing work patterns, parenting responsibilities, and relational dynamics. Modern medicine has helped lengthen the lifespan, giving rise to the need for transgenerational caretaking. Cohabitation, divorce, and remarriage are quite commonplace, and these social changes make it necessary for us to rethink and broaden our definition of what constitutes a family.

Thus, it is no longer enough simply to embrace the concept of the family as a system. In order to understand and effectively treat the evolving family, our theoretical formulations and clinical interventions must be informed by an understanding of ethnicity, culture, religion, gender, sexual preference, family life cycle, socioeconomic status, education, physical and mental health, values, and belief systems.

The purpose of the *Wiley Series in Couples and Family Dynamics and Treatment* is to provide a forum for cutting-edge relational and family theory, practice, and research. Its scope is intended to be broad, diverse, and international, but all books published in this series share a common mission—to reflect on the past, offer state-of-the-art information on the present, and speculate on, as well as attempt to shape, the future of the field.

FLORENCE W. KASLOW
Florida Couples and Family Institute

Preface

Relational diagnosis is a concept whose time has come. In fact, it is long overdue on the main stage of family and in the overall arena of mental health diagnoses. Throughout the world, those treating families have experienced a growing sense of urgency about the need to develop a typology or classification system for assessing distressed relationships in close interpersonal systems and for the individuals within those relationships.

The compelling case for a relational diagnostic schema stems, in no small part, from the basic need for a common language. A standardized nomenclature would allow us to impart clearly to clients/patients our evaluation of their system dynamics and problems. It also would enable us to communicate succinctly with our peers and the multitude of other professionals—including schoolteachers, public welfare and human services personnel, nurses and physicians, clergy, and attorneys—who play significant roles in a family's ecological context.

On a clinical level, a widely accepted relational diagnostic schema would permit us to clearly and accurately convey to other mental health professionals our assessment of our clients' problems and the rationale behind the treatment plan and interventions used. In addition, such a taxonomy would simplify the task of researchers seeking to mount or replicate a study involving relational dynamics and patterns. Only to the extent that we can agree upon a common vocabulary for assessing and depicting behavioral and interactional sequences can we begin to build consensus about what we are studying, observing, analyzing, interpreting, and concluding.

In addition to the communication advantages just described, other pragmatic factors support the need for relational diagnosis. In this era of managed health care and third-party payers, reimbursement is based largely on what diagnosis is made and whether the treatment plan emanates logically from, and is consistent with, the diagnosis. Family clinicians have not had the means to convey concisely their dynamic evaluation of relational difficulties—which has precluded a campaign to convince third-party payers that couples and family therapies are cost-effective treatments that produce positive outcomes. The few vague relational diagnoses included in the DSM-III-R and DSM-IV are listed as V codes—which are rarely reimbursable and not at all illuminating. It is time that this is remedied.

One purpose of this book is to offer a forum for a variety of conceptualizations regarding relational diagnosis. A second goal is to provide some actual diagnoses for consideration, field testing, and feedback. Although the book is as inclusive and comprehensive as we could make it at this time, it is not yet a definitive *Manual of Relational Diagnosis*. Much more research on the categories and proposed criteria sets needs to occur before we can get to that point. However, in undertaking this project, we wanted to foster ideas about relational classification and stimulate further dialogue leading toward such a manual.

By recording our formulations, we also hope to ensure that other diagnostic manuals will no longer relegate relational problems to second- or third-class status. Our efforts are congruent with those of other groups that have banded together recently to produce books and manuals that go beyond the somewhat narrow focus of the DSM-IV. It is perhaps unrealistic to expect that any single diagnostic volume can ever be so inclusive that everyone's needs are addressed. As alluded to earlier, when enough data is gathered to produce professional consensus, it may well be that the interests of our clients, and the field of couples and family therapy, would be best served by a free-standing, comprehensive *Manual of Relational Diagnosis*. But whatever the form and forum in which the information ultimately appears, what is most important is that it *does* appear. With this book, we hope to take the first concrete steps in that direction.

The concept of relational diagnosis has been gestating for some time, and in developing this volume I was fortunate to enlist the support of a number of prominent clinicians, theorists, and researchers who have been at the forefront of this debate. Many of the individuals who have been involved in the American Psychological Association's Division of Family Psychology (#43) Task Force on Diagnosis and Treatment and in the interorganizational Coalition on Family Diagnosis (founded in 1987 and 1988, respectively) were invited to prepare chapters for this volume. In organizing the book, I tried to assemble people with acknowledged expertise in their specific spheres who could bring together state-of-the-art information and insights into the phenomena being considered. Almost all of the individuals I asked to contribute to this effort readily agreed to do so. I am deeply grateful to the authors, who took on this huge task—despite the limited time allotted and the distinct possibility that a book on relational diagnosis might spark considerable controversy. Several other individuals who have done important work in the area of relational diagnosis were also invited to contribute to this book but were unable to do so because of other commitments. We regret their absence from this volume and hope that if there is a sequel, they will be able to take part.

Given that the family field is so vast and diverse, it seemed imperative in this volume to try to showcase the gamut of thinking regarding the subject of relational diagnosis. Thus, this book includes the work of several well-known social constructionists, who do not utilize or advocate diagnosis, as they believe that such labeling may be detrimental to the treatment process. This is a salient position and one that must be heard in any balanced discussion of relational diagnosis.

At the other end of the continuum, there are ground-breaking chapters that advocate very formal assessment and diagnostic procedures. Wherever possible, authors of these chapters were asked to develop criteria sets and provide guidelines on specific intervention paradigms. Since it is my contention that no one discipline has a monopoly on researching, understanding, and treating children, couples, and families, this book is intentionally interdisciplinary in terms of the background of the contributing authors, the scope of the syndromes and patterns being addressed, and the treatment strategies outlined. It is hoped that this multitude of perspectives has resulted in a book that will be of relevance to the entire field of family, as it is most broadly conceived.

Developing and editing a book intended to speak to such a wide audience is no easy task, and there are several people who deserve special acknowledgment. My thanks to Kelly Franklin and Herb Reich, editors at John Wiley & Sons, for inviting and encouraging me to embark on this project and for asking me to establish and edit the series in which this volume is being published. To Kelly, who has worked with me very closely, a special thanks for her incisive suggestions and wonderful sense of humor. To Gladys Adams, my loyal and supercompetent secretary, who has labored with me through the long birth process for this book, my continued admiration and appreciation. And, as always, my heartfelt gratitude for the patience and support of my husband Sol, who tolerated my worrying about deadlines and working long hours on nights and weekends when we could have been playing. Finally, to all of those who have served on and/or supported the work of the Coalition on Family Diagnosis and the Task Force on Diagnosis and Treatment, I express my profound appreciation for your shared commitment to making relational diagnosis a viable, living classificatory system.

FLORENCE W. KASLOW, PhD

September 1995

Foreword

The preparation and publication of the fourth edition of the Diagnostic and Statistical Manual of Mental Disorders (DSM-IV) has intensified interest in clinical classification among mental health researchers and practitioners throughout the world. As Florence Kaslow details in Chapter 1, family researchers and clinicians, and the many organizations of which they are members, made valiant efforts to clarify and promote concepts concerning the family for inclusion in the published version of DSM-IV. These efforts addressed two questions. First, is there common ground among family practitioners on issues of clinical classification? Second, can family researchers and family clinicians persuade the larger clinical community that they can make an important contribution to a comprehensive system of classification of disorders? The current volume represents the best effort to date to address these questions. As the writer of the Foreword, I want to assist readers in engaging the chapters by encouraging them to formulate and answer questions of their own as they read. Here I report some results of my own engagement.

IS THERE A CONSENSUS ON FAMILY CLASSIFICATION?

This volume divides this question into two parts. First, what concepts and methods are available as a foundation for classification of relationships and their disorders? Second, what are the merits and problems entailed in the process of clinical classification?

Consensus on an Approach to Classification of Relationships

Broadly speaking, the chapters in this book do not—collectively or singly—lay out an explicit system for classifying relationships and their disorders. However, a close reading of all of them suggest that a consensus is emerging nonetheless. Perhaps the most important theme cutting across all chapters is an increasing comfort by family clinicians with systems of classification that focus both on the individual and on relationship systems. For example, chapters on anxiety, dissociative, mood, and eating disorders are organized around concepts and assessments that focus first on the individual and then consider the impact of the individual's disorder on the family. At the same time, several chapters delineate subtle patterns of relationships and relationship disorders to be considered as clinical problems in their own right whether they are associated with classifiable disorders in individual members or not. Some of these family level systems, such as the Structural Analysis of Social Behavior, are exquisitely attentive to intrapsychic functioning.

Having all these chapters in one book helps us recognize the hub of a new consensus on clinical classification. This hub is a flexible system that can give emphasis to disorders of relationships in some cases and disorders of individuals in others and that can strike a relatively even balance between the two in still others. Moreover, the system should allow for changing emphases across the clinical life of a single clinical problem. Reading these chapters suggested to me that a flexible system like this one might be captured by a schema with four very broad categories. This schema might serve as a useful armature for collaborative research among family researchers and between family and other clinical researchers.

These categories can be arranged to form a series. The first category reflects the clinician's focus on relationship disorders as important in their own right; in using the last, the clinician focuses on the individual disorder, with family problems as a critical but subordinate concern. The other two categories have a mixture of the two. The four categories are: well-delineated disorders of relationships; well-delineated relationship problems associated with individual disorders; disorders that require relational data for their validity; and individual disorders whose evocation, course, and treatment are strongly influenced by relationship factors.

Well-Delineated Disorders of Relationships

The first category captures clinical problems where the clinician attends primarily to relation problems. Typically, these disorders are the focus of attention because they lead to severe psychological distress for one or more members, they involve physical battery, or they presage the disruptive breakup of the relationship. Because these are the primary focus of concern and are serious in nature, they are termed "relationship disorders."

This level of classification is probably used most frequently when a single individual or a dyad seeks treatment for a problem that they themselves perceive is a relational one and the clinician cannot detect a significant individual disorder in the individual members of that relationship. It is also used when the severity of the relationship disturbance is conspicuous whether the relationship members complain about it or not. The Relationship Conflict Inventory, described in Chapter 24, is one way to approach the assessment of severity. The Global Assessment of Relational Functioning, now located in Appendix B of DSM-IV and alluded to throughout this book, is another. The presence of violence, serious physical or psychological abuse or neglect, or the imminent breakup of the relationship are also clear indicators of a severe disorder of relationships whether they engender complaints or not. Again, in contrast to the next category, this level of classification is appropriate only if there are no discernible mental disorders in any individual involved in the relationship. A third form of clinical presentation for a relationship disorder is when a clinician reframes a disorder that is presented initially as residing within a single individual; this reframing may clarify for the whole family that the index patient's chief (and individual) complaint (or the complaints of others about the index) is embedded in a relational nexus. Chapters 5, 6, and 24 provide concepts and methods for detecting various forms of relationship disturbances.

To my knowledge, there is no reliable data on the incidence or prevalence of relationship disorders of this type. It is possible that severe relationship disorders without evidence of individual psychopathology are very rare, or they might be very common. Those who study individual disorders are now very familiar with the powerful techniques of epidemiology, but family researchers, in general, have been shy about using population-based or community-based epidemiology. This approach to research provides clear concepts, effective methods, and strong inferences about the incidence and prevalence of disorders as well as some of the likely causes of those disorders. Recent advances in epidemiology makes this approach especially suitable for developing and validating classification schemes for relationship disorders. First, epidemiology is focusing more on the social demands for adaptation required by particular communities and assessing individual capacities to respond to these particular demands. Second, a large number of common-use data sets are available to family researchers; increasingly, these contain already-collected data about individuals and their families. Third, tools have been developed to collect very high quality data on relationships in epidemiological studies; these include techniques for observing family interaction process in their own homes. Family-based epidemiology could answer many important questions about the co-occurrence of relationship and individual disorders and help flesh out the ideas advanced in this book and which are reflected in the simple scheme I am presenting here.

Well-Delineated Relationship Problems That Are Associated with Individual Disorders

The second category is used for clinical situations where the relationship is still the primary focus of treatment. The severity of the disturbance may be conspicuous or it may be subtler; relationship members may complain about it or be unaware of it. However, part of the importance of treating the relational problem stems from the likelihood that the problem is evoking or influencing serious disorders in one or more individual members. Clinicians use this level of analysis when they detect both a relationship and an individual disorder *and* the two are plausibly linked either by careful clinical analysis or by valid research data. By using this level of analysis, clinicians commit themselves to evaluate progress in treatment of the relational disorder, not only by monitoring the relationship itself but also by careful assessment of individual disorders even if they elect not to provide individual treatment, such as individual psychotherapy or pharmacotherapy, directed at these disorders. An example is the choice of marital therapy as the only mode of therapy for depression.

A variant in this domain is drawn from the literature on prevention. A relational problem may constitute not only a serious source of distress for individuals who are involved in the relationship but may be a risk for future individual psychopathology in those members or in another member of the family. An example is the treatment of marital conflict in parents of very young children. The children may show no manifest disorder at the time couple's therapy is begun. However, accumulating research data, some of it reviewed in Chapter 12 on childhood depression, suggests that there is a very high likelihood that, if not properly treated, marital conflict will evoke serious psychopathology in the children. By classifying a clinical problem in this broad level, the clinician is reminded to assess the status of these children while evaluating the effectiveness of the therapy directed at the marital couple.

Disorders That Require Relational Data for Their Validity

In this third category, an individual disorder is central in the presentation of the clinical problem to the clinician. However, a full clinical description of the disorder requires relational data. For disorders in this level, part of the set of criteria for reaching a classification decision requires knowledge about one or more key relationships of that individual. Chapter 14 provides interesting examples of this for conduct disorders. Early-onset conduct disorders, a particularly malignant condition if left untreated, probably cannot be adequately defined or classified unless data on the parent-child relationship is a criterion for making the classification. Research data suggest that the most likely characteristic of the parent-child relationship is inadequate parental monitoring and control of these children. This inadequacy does not reside "in" the parent since the conduct-disordered child very frequently is more difficult to monitor and control; nor does it reside "in" the child since parental behavior is such a critical part of the clinical picture. Children with serious conduct disturbances who are not embedded in these inadequate parent-child relationships are rare and may be considered to have a very different disorder. The same principle, of using relationship data as criterion for diagnosis, clearly applies to some forms of severe eating and sleep disorders in infants and toddlers.

Individual Disorders Whose Evocation, Course, and Treatment Are Strongly Influenced by Relationship Factors

Finally, there is a class where the individual disorder is a continuing and primary focus of clinical attention but additional treatment of the family is essential to promote rapid recovery, reduce morbidity, or prevent relapse. As in the case of relationship problems associated with individual disorders, this approach to classification is supported by abundant research data that link individual physical and psychiatric disorders to family functioning. Chapter 15 on children with life-threatening illness, Chapter 16 on anxiety disorders in adults, and Chapter 28 on adults with depression summarize a great deal of well-known research in this area. The current volume also has chapters exploring newer areas of inquiry in this domain, particularly the correlation of dissociative disorders, of childhood disorders, and of a range of personality disorders with relational processes.

The level 4 approach to classification differs from level 2 in that the individual disorder remains a central focus of concern and often is the explicit objective of individual-level somatic or psychological treatment. Research data supporting this approach would indicate that family therapy is necessary but not sufficient for patient recovery and for the prevention of relapse. That is why family interventions are important in the treatment plan but are rarely selected as the only mode of treatment. In contrast, if research data supports the effectiveness of the family therapy as sufficient for the adequate treatment of both the relationship and the individual disorder, then the disorder is more suitably located in level 2. Clinicians will vary, when working with problems at level 4, in how they assess the adaptive strengths or psychopathology of other family members as a criteria for the outcome of their interventions. This approach also differs from level 3 because the classification of the individual disorder that is the primary clinical focus, for example Recurrent Major Depressive Disorder, does not require an assessment of current relationships as part of the definition of the disorder itself.

Consensus on the Value of the Classification Process

Chapters 7 and 8 were included specifically to raise questions about the value of diagnostic classification in clinical work with families. In a book of 34 chapters, it might appear as if these chapters reflect a minority opinion. However, at least two more chapters—Chapters 10 and 11, which focus on culture and classification—provide additional cautionary notes on classifying either individuals or families. Culturally uninformed clinicians may be confused themselves and may injure their patients with cultural biases and distortions. I would guess that most experienced clinicians, whether they advocate classification systems or not, are concerned about some of the unintended side effects of classifying families or family process that are raised in these four levels. Thus, these cautionary chapters do not necessarily reflect a minority view but reflect the ambivalence most of us feel about assuming expert status and labeling the families with whom we work.

However, even though it is likely that these concerns about classification are widespread, there is very little research exploring the pros and cons of the process of classification within the interpersonal nexus of family therapy. Fortunately, there are successful precedents in the research literature for approaching this problem. For example, social psychology—and related disciplines—provides a repertoire of concepts and approaches that might be adapted to an important program of research in this area. The most notable line of research was on "experimenter expectancy effects" where hypotheses of researchers were shown to have their own strong influence on the behavior of research subjects. A range of other studies from this tradition documents the powerful affects of attributions, both those of self and those of others, on self-perceived confidence and competence. These approaches could be applied to the family therapy setting.

HAVE WE PERSUADED OUR CLINICAL COLLEAGUES ABOUT THE IMPORTANCE OF FAMILY ISSUES IN CLASSIFICATION?

Since the family field is only now defining a consensus on clinical classification, it may be premature to ask how persuasive we have been to other clinicians outside our field. Nonetheless, as I write this, DSM-IV will have passed the 500,000 mark in sales. It forms an important basis for treatment planning in inpatient and outpatient treatment programs throughout the world. It lies at the core of clinical record keeping, it structures training programs and textbooks, and it is a critical component of reimbursement systems and health care planning. Thus, the content of its text is a tempting yardstick to measure how seriously our work is regarded by our mental health colleagues. Were we to accept such a metric of our persuasiveness, we might note wistfully that in 886 pages of dense prose, families and relationships get only the briefest attention: A few paragraphs on family troubles are a part of "other conditions which may be a focus of clinical attention" and the Global Assessment of Relational Functioning is provided in an appendix presenting material for "further study."

Adding to our distress might be the long latency phase that will almost certainly precede the publication of DSM-V. It can now be recognized that DSM-III, III-R, and IV were all part of a relative short cycle of system construction where a classification scheme and specific inclusion and exclusion criteria were worked out. Although there is continuing disagreement on many of the decisions that were made in DSM-IV, its principal authors state that we will be well into the next millennium before a substantial overhaul of DSM-IV will be contemplated, much less carried out. Many of us seniors in the profession wonder if we will still be fit to serve as crew when DSM-V docks for a new load of ideas.

However, there are three good reasons to be cautious about using the volume of DSM-IV text space as a yardstick for measuring the impact of our ideas about relational classification on our colleagues. The first, as I have noted, is that consensus among us on this topic is only just emerging. The second reason is that there are clear limits and problems in DSM-IV. These are widely recognized and the subject of new research plans in which family clinicians and researchers can play a meaningful part. Third, while family therapy has contributed only a fraction of the total text to DSM-IV, it is widely practiced and widely taught. DSM-IV, has stimulated a broad interest in reliable and valid clinical classifications; family therapists and clinicians who work with them will certainly be avid consumers and useful critics of developing family classification schemes whether they are in DSM-IV or not or whether or not these diagnoses serve as a dependable basis for reimbursement.

The Limits of DSM-IV

While it reflects a prodigious achievement in research and clinical consensus, DSM-IV is best regarded as an important base for ongoing clinical research in classification. Its principal authors would almost certainly agree to this. What limits can we define now, what research is appropriate to address them, and where might improved approaches to family classification fit into this process? For illustrative purposes I will mention only three here, although the list of already-recognized shortcomings is much longer.

Classification vs. Diagnosis

First, DSM-IV—despite the big "D" in its initials—is a classification system, not a diagnostic system. Individuals are placed in categories but the underlying causes of their disorders are not systematically delineated by this system. The DSM-III, III-R, and IV cycle was an effort to use the best research available to define patterns of co-occurring symptoms or syndromes. These syndromes were an effort to represent the full range of clinical problems dealt with by the majority of American psychiatrists. During the preparation of DSM-IV, important efforts were made to extend the system beyond the discipline of psychiatry, by including other members of other disciplines on its panels. An important effort also was made to improve the validity of the system beyond the majority of American cultures by drawing on cross-national studies and by providing important information on how culture influences the clinical manifestation of most syndromes. In an appendix DSM-IV also provides a list of disorders that may be relatively unique to particular cultures. However, none of these efforts at extension were intended to address the central causes of the diagnostic syndromes, and in many cases, the causes are unknown or hotly disputed.

My own guess is that the authors of DSM-IV are right; DSM-V will be a long time in coming. However, I also sense that a long latency before its appearance increases the chances that

DSM-V will start a new cycle of manuals, one that reflects a mixture of careful classification, as they do now, but also a growing understanding of factors that influence the development, manifestations, and course of psychiatric disorders. In short, the manuals starting with DSM-V will more closely approximate a diagnostic system where the act of classifying patients is part of understanding the causes of their disorders and how to treat them. Here, family research can play a major role—particularly research that links family process to the development of psychopathology or to the definition of psychopathology itself. This research is likely to influence classification by providing new syndromes that are exclusively relational disorders, better definitions of existing syndromes by adding relational data to criteria sets, and by increasing clarity to diagnosis through clearer data on the family's role in pathogenesis.

Narrow vs. Broad Inquiries in the Classification Process

An important basis for consensus in DSM-IV is the very limited means that are required to make reliable classifications. A single structured diagnostic interview, lasting at most two hours, is all that is required. Two or three very well-developed interviews for adults and good ones for children have been field-tested for major collaborative studies of the epidemiology of childhood psychiatric syndromes. Moreover, for both adults and children in research settings, some of these interviews are designed to be conducted by interviewers with relatively little clinical training. Ironically, this major effort to professionalize the mental health discipline makes it possible for nonprofessionals to do a great deal of its business. As we move from classification to diagnosis, this rather anomalous situation cannot last. Diagnosis will almost certainly require much broader inquiry. Radiology and the clinical laboratory will almost certainly be involved not only to rule out "medical" diagnoses but to rule in certain "psychiatric" diagnoses with radiological or biochemical stigmata. Likewise relational data also will be crucial and must depend on highly skilled clinical observation of interaction patterns and, in all likelihood, more technical forms of data collection. Our field is defining more clearly where these data are crucial additions to the self-report that lies at the center of diagnostic interviews, particularly those conducted by nonprofessionals. The more we explore the importance of these data in reaching valid diagnoses of relational disorders, the more likely they are to be central requirements for a widely accepted diagnostic system.

Dimensional vs. Categorical Diagnosis

In her introductory chapter, Kaslow reports that the DSM-IV task force was concerned that research on family classification could not provide enough data to establish "thresholds" to distinguish illness from health. In Chapter 24, Bodin reports on his effort to design a scale that might indicate relationships which are "cases" because they exceed a conflict threshold. Indeed, the concept of thresholds is central to the DSM-III–IV series of manuals because they distinguish ill persons from the nonill. Family clinicians and researchers are uncomfortable with dichotomization. If they accept the concept of "illness" or "disorder" at all, they are much more likely to conceive of continua of difficulties rather than discrete categories. The Global Assessment of Relational Functioning provides assessment along single continuum of competence to disruption. Will family clinicians and research have to swallow the categorical pill to be included in DSM-V?

This seems unlikely. The categorical approach to diagnosis is already being challenged from two important lines of research. First, researchers oriented toward syndromes have become concerned about "subsyndromal" cases: People who are clearly suffering but fail to meet the DSM-IV thresholds. What should be done with them? One hypothesis was that these relatively mild disorders might be transient disturbances and that a high proportion would remit spontaneously. However, careful research suggests that this is not the case. Individuals in subsyndromal categories often remain the same or get worse unless they are treated; moreover, when one assesses their level of functioning in several spheres of life, they are quite impaired even though their criterial symptoms fail to meet minimum thresholds.

A second research tradition questioning simple dichotomies in classification are studies on the prevention of mental disorders. Here researchers have sought to identify individuals at highest risk for developing full-blown disorders so that preventive interventions can reach them before they fall ill. One strategy has been to identify prodromes of illness. This tactic has shown promise, for example, in preventing first episodes of full-blown schizophrenia in an initial field trial in England. As the enterprise of prevention expands, the search for reliable prodromes will continue. Chapter 14 reports, for example, evidence that the relatively mild disturbance of oppositional behavior in very young children is a reliable prodrome of a much more malignant conduct disorder. Prodromes will invariably be mild versions of the full-blown disorders, mild versions that over time shade continuously into full-blown disorders. Family researchers and clinicians may not have to distort their data and experience to fit into the dichotomous system of DSM-IV. Rather they can participate in an enlarging debate about when categories are appropriate and when continua more closely fit the clinical and research data.

Current Family Practice

It seems abstemious in the extreme for family clinicians and researchers to deny themselves the satisfaction of influencing their colleagues until the DSM-V boat arrives at the dock. The widening world of family therapy practice will have, I suspect, an increasing interest in valid classificatory schemes. Experienced family therapists will be badgered by reimbursement requirements and questioned by their students, and with all their reservations, they will be impressed that DSM-IV is a good tool both for reimbursement and clinical training. Concepts and approaches, such as those in this book, will form an attractive foundation for a systematic approach to classification that could receive wide interest and acceptance among family therapists.

But a deal should be struck. Family researchers should not formulate and disseminate systems of classification unless clinicians agree to participate in field trials of these systems. One can easily imagine that the authors of the chapters and their colleagues in the many organizations that sponsored the proceedings leading up to this book could continue work to develop a consensus document on a clinically important system of family classification. Extensive field trials would test the reliability and clinical utility of these systems. This pattern of transaction, within the family field, may be the most important factor in influencing clinicians practicing outside of it.

David Reiss

October 1995

Contents

Contributing Authors

All have lengthy resumes and many have numerous publications. We regret that only the briefest biographical sketches can be given here, and prior publications have been omitted.

James F. Alexander, PhD, is a professor of psychology and past director of clinical training at the University of Utah. He is a past president of the Division of Family Psychology and a fellow of the American Psychological Association. He has presented as a "master therapist" at the American Association for Marital and Family Therapy (AAMFT), is on the board of directors of the American Family Therapy Academy, and is a past recipient of that organization's Award for Contributions to Family Therapy Research. He has a grant from the National Institute of Drug Abuse as part of the multisite Center for Research on Adolescent Drug Abuse (CRADA) to study culturally sensitive and empirically based family therapy process and outcome with substance abusing adolescents.

Tom Andersen, MD, practices at the Institute of Community Medicine in Tromso, Norway. His teaching and writing about the use of language in creating meaning in psychotherapy and the use of reflecting teams has been influential in many countries.

Harlene Anderson, PhD, director of the Houston-Galveston Institute, has earned an international reputation at the leading edge of systems-oriented psychotherapy as a thinker, clinician, educator, and consultant. She serves on the Commission on Accreditation for Marriage and Family Education of the American Association for Marriage and Family Therapy.

Peter Ash, MD, a child and adolescent psychiatrist, is an assistant professor and director of the Psychiatry and Law Service at Emory University School of Medicine, Department of Psychiatry and Behavior Sciences, Atlanta, Georgia.

Joan C. Barth, PhD, is a family therapist in Doylestown, Pennsylvania, a member of the American Family Therapy Academy, the American Association for Marriage and Family Therapy, and the American Psychological Association, and is corresponding secretary of the International Family Therapy Association.

Lorna Smith Benjamin, PhD, is a professor of psychology at the University of Utah. A past president of the International Society for Psychotherapy Research and an advisor to the DSM-IV work group on personality disorders, she is the author of over 50 professional publications. She uses the Structural Analysis of Social Behavior, which she has been developing for over 20 years, to study psychopathological processes and train clinicians in the efficacious treatment of major mental disorders.

Arthur M. Bodin, PhD, FAClinP, is in independent practice and a senior research fellow, Mental Research Institute, Palo Alto, California; associate clinical professor of medical psychology, Department of Psychiatry, University of California, San Francisco School of Medicine, a past president, Division of Family Psychology of the American Psychological Association; and chair of the Coalition on Family Diagnosis. He was named Family Psychologist of the Year by the Division of Family Psychology in 1990 and Distinguished Practitioner in Psychology of the National Academics of Practice.

José M. Canive, MD, is an assistant professor of psychiatry at the School of Medicine, University of New Mexico, and is the director of the PTSD clinic at the Veterans Administration Medical Center in Albuquerque, New Mexico. He is treasurer of the American Society of Hispanic Psychiatrists and a board member of the Society for the Study of Psychiatry and Culture.

Israel W. Charny, PhD, is executive director, Institute on the Holocaust and Genocide; a professor of psychology and family therapy and director, Program for Advanced Studies in Integrative Psychotherapy, at the Martin Buber Center and Department of Psychology, Hebrew University of Jerusalem, Israel.

Lillian Comas-Díaz, PhD, is the executive director of the Transcultural Mental Health Institute and maintains a private practice in clinical psychology in Washington, DC. She is the editor-in-chief of *Cultural Diversity and Mental Health,* a journal published by John Wiley & Sons. She has published extensively on the topics of ethnocultural mental health, gender and ethnic factors in psychotherapy, treatment of torture victims, international psychology, and Latino mental health.

Jan L. Culbertson, PhD, is an associate professor of pediatrics and director of Child Neuropsychology Services at the University of Oklahoma Health Sciences Center, Oklahoma City. She has served as president of the American Psychological Association's Division of Children, Youth and Family.

José de la Gandara, MD, is a psychiatrist in private practice in West Palm Beach, Florida. He has a particular interest in psychopharmacology and neuropsychiatry research and is a co-principal investigator on several research projects. He is the director of research at the Memory Disorder Center at North Broward Neurological Institute and an associate professor of psychopharmacology of the University of Miami School of Medicine.

Catherine Gray Deering, PhD, RN, CS, is an assistant professor of psychology at Clayton State College in Morrow, Georgia. She is a consulting psychologist at the Atlanta Veterans Administration Medical Center and an adjunct assistant professor at Emory University School of Medicine, Department of Psychiatry and Behavioral Sciences.

Frank V. deGruy, MD, MSFN, is an associate professor and director of the Divisions of Research and Community Medicine in the Department of Family Practice and Community Medicine at the University of South Alabama College of Medicine. He has made substantial contributions to the literature on mental health problems in primary care; current research projects are on somatization and on collaborative management of subthreshold mental distress in rural primary care. He is a member of the work group that wrote the DSM-IV-PC and of the Collaborative Family Health Care Coalition.

Wayne H. Denton, MD, PhD, is board certified in psychiatry and has a PhD in marriage and family therapy. He is assistant professor and director of the Marital and Family Therapy Clinic in the Department of Psychiatry and Behavioral Medicine, The Bowman Gray School of Medicine, Wake Forest University in Winston-Salem, North Carolina.

Paul Florsheim, PhD, is an assistant professor of psychology at the University of Utah. His research focuses on the cross-ethnic study of adolescent development, psychopathology, and family relations. He uses the Structural Analysis of Social Behavior to examine interpersonal processes related to behavioral problems among inner-city youth and the parental practices of teen parents.

Kenneth J. Gergen, PhD, is the Frank and Gil Mustin Professor of Psychology at Swarthmore College, Pennsylvania. He is a leading voice in the social constructionist movement in the human sciences, a cultural critic, and a frequent contributor to dialogues on therapeutic process.

Cheryl Glickauf-Hughes, PhD, is an associate professor and associate director of training in the Department of Psychology at Georgia State University and an adjunct professor at Emory University School of Medicine. She has published a book and numerous articles on relational masochism and has a private practice in Decatur, Georgia.

Vicki L. Gluhoski, PhD, is a research fellow at Cornell University Medical College and a practicing psychologist at the Cognitive Therapy Center of New York. She completed her postdoctoral training with Aaron T. Beck and has published articles on diverse applications of cognitive therapy.

Jackie K. Gollan, MS, is a fourth-year graduate student in the Clinical Psychology PhD program at the University of Washington, Seattle. She is working with Neil S. Jacobson, PhD, researching the reciprocal relationship between dyadic interaction and depression.

Eric T. Gortner, MA, is a fourth-year graduate student in the Clinical Psychology PhD program at the University of Washington, Seattle. He has been working with Neil S. Jacobson, PhD, as a clinical interviewer and statistician on a Component Analysis of Cognitive Therapy for Depression project.

Michael C. Gottlieb, PhD, practices independently in Dallas, Texas. He is an ABPP Diplomate in Family Psychology, an APA Fellow, a past president of the American Board of Family Psychology, the Academy of Family Psychology, and the Texas Psychological Association. He is a member of the Adjunct Faculty at Texas Women's University.

William P. Henry, PhD, is an assistant professor of psychology at the University of Utah and a licensed clinical psychologist. Previously, he was research director at the Center for Psychotherapy Research at Vanderbilt University. His research has been in the areas of interpersonal processes in psychotherapy, training and outcome in time-limited dynamic psychotherapy, interpersonal assessment, and abnormal personality and Axis II disorders.

Lynn Hoffman, ACSW, has been at the forefront of innovative thinking in the field of family therapy for three decades. She teaches in the doctoral program of Smith College in Northampton, Massachusetts, and at the Family Therapy Program at St. Joseph's College in West Hartford, Connecticut. In 1988, she received the AAMFT Lifetime Achievement Award for Distinguished Contributions to the Field.

Neil S. Jacobson, PhD, is a professor of psychology at the University of Washington. Author of 200 articles and 9 books, Dr. Jacobson is one of the most widely cited family therapists in the world. He has received awards from both the American Family Therapy Academy and the American Association for Marriage and Family Therapy for his cumulative, distinguished, and lifetime contributions to family therapy research. He has also received MERIT and Research Scientist Awards from the National Institute of Health for his seminal contributions to mental health research. Dr. Jacobson is a past president of the American Association for Behavior Therapy and a designated master lecturer by AAMFT.

Florence W. Kaslow, PhD, is director of the Florida Couples and Family Institute, a visiting professor of medical psychology in psychiatry at Duke University Medical Center, Durham, North Carolina, and a visiting professor of psychology at Florida Institute of Technology in Melbourne. She is editor of the Wiley Book Series in Couples and Family Dynamics and Treatment and appears weekly on a Voice of America program, *The Parenting Corner.* Dr. Kaslow is the recipient of numerous APA, ABPP, and AAMFT awards, serves on many journal editorial boards, and is a past president of the Division of Family Psychology of the American Psychological Association and of the International Family Therapy Association.

Nadine J. Kaslow, PhD, is an associate professor at Emory University School of Medicine, Department of Psychiatry and Behavioral Sciences. She holds joint appointments in the Departments of Pediatrics and of Psychology. Dr. Kaslow also is chief psychologist, Emory University Department of Psychiatry and Behavioral Sciences at Grady Health System, in Atlanta, Georgia.

Anne E. Kazak, PhD, is an associate professor, Departments of Pediatrics and Psychiatry, University of Pennsylvania School of Medicine; director of Psychosocial Services, Division of Oncology, The Children's Hospital of Philadelphia; and on the Psychology Training Faculty, Philadelphia Child Guidance Center.

Gabor I. Keitner, MD, is a professor of psychiatry at Brown University, medical director for inpatient services, director of the Mood Disorders Program, and member of the Family Research Program at Butler Hospital, Providence, Rhode Island. He obtained his medical degree from Queen's University and did his psychiatric residency at McMaster University, both in Canada.

Diana A. Kirschner, PhD, and *Sam Kirschner, PhD,* are leading authorities on treating survivors of sexual abuse. They have co-authored several books and numerous articles on integrating individual, marital, and family therapy with different clinical populations. They are frequent faculty members for New England seminars and are in private practice in Gwynedd Valley, Pennsylvania.

Wilhelmina S. Koedam, PhD, is in private practice in North Miami Beach and Cooper City, Florida. She has authored articles on patients in Witness Protection Programs. Her other diverse areas of research interest are older couples starting families and dissociative identity disorders.

Joan D. Koss-Chioino, PhD, is a professor of anthropology at Arizona State University and an adjunct professor of psychiatry and neurology at Tulane Medical Center, New Orleans, Louisiana. She is a fellow of the American Association of Anthropologists, a trustee of the American Society of Hispanic Psychiatrists, and a board member of the Society for the Study of Psychiatry and Culture.

Paula Levine, PhD, is the director of both the Anorexia and Bulimia Resource Centers in Coral Gables, Florida. She is well known for her innovations and experience in the treatment of eating disorders and speaks regularly at national and local conferences. She has served as a consultant to the Renfew Center and is a past president of Eating Disorders Awareness & Prevention (EDAP), a national nonprofit organization dedicated to the prevention of eating disorders.

Don-David Lusterman, PhD, is in private practice in Baldwin, New York. He serves as an editorial consultant for the *Journal of Family Psychology* and is on the editorial board of the *American Journal of Family Therapy.* He is a recipient of the Family Psychologist of the Year Award from the Division of Family Psychology of the APA.

Susan H. McDaniel, PhD, is an associate professor of psychiatry (psychology) and family medicine at the University of Rochester School of Medicine and Highland Hospital in Rochester, New York. She is co-editor of the journal *Families, Systems, and Health,* a member of the Planning Group for the Collaborative Family Health Care Coalition, and on the board of the Division of Family Psychology of the APA.

Ivan W. Miller, PhD, is an associate professor, Department of Psychiatry and Human Behavior at Brown University, director of Psychology, and director of the Brown University Research Program at Butler Hospital, Providence, Rhode Island.

Dawn M. Niedner, PhD, is an associate professor of psychology in the Department of Behavioral Sciences at Purdue University, Calumet. As a clinical psychologist, she maintains a private practice in northwest Indiana.

William C. Nichols, EdD, is in private practice as a marital and family therapist at the Family Workshop in Atlanta, Georgia, an adjunct associate professor in the Department of Psychology and Behavioral Sciences at Emory University, an adjunct professor in the Department of Child and Family Development, University of Georgia in Athens, and editor of *Contemporary Family Therapy.*

David H. Olson, PhD, is a professor, Family Social Science Department, University of Minnesota, St. Paul. He is a fellow and clinical member of the American Psychological Association and the American Association of Marital and Family Therapy (AAMFT). He is a past president of the National Council on Family Relations and the Upper Midwest Association of Marital and Family Therapists. Over 500 studies have been done on the Circumplex Model of Marital and Family Systems, which he developed. Over 25,000 counselors have been trained on his PREPARE and ENRICH Inventories. He has written more than 20 books and 100 articles in the field of marriage and family.

Terence E. Patterson, EdD, is a licensed psychologist in private practice. He is also licensed as a clinical social worker and a marriage and family therapist in California. He is chair of the Counseling Psychology Program at the University of San Francisco, past chair of the Coalition on Family Diagnosis, editor of *The Family Psychologist,* and editor of the *Journal File* of the *American Journal of Family Therapy.*

Angela Pedraza, MD, is a psychiatrist in private practice in West Palm Beach, Florida. She has a particular interest in psychopharmacology and neuropsychiatry research and is a co-principal investigator on several research projects. She is associate director of the Memory Disorder Center at North Broward Neurologic Institute in Fort Lauderdale, Florida.

Christie A. Pugh, MA, is a graduate student in the Clinical Psychology PhD program at the University of Utah specializing in child and family psychology. Her research activities to date have been focused on the development and treatment of disruptive behavior disorders in young children. She is also involved in research on the process of family therapy funded by the National Institute of Drug Abuse.

Andrew Rosen, PhD, is a diplomate in clinical psychology, American Board of Professional Psychology, and has a certificate in psychoanalysis and psychotherapy from the Derner Institute for Psychoanalysis and Psychotherapy. He is founder and director of the Center for Treatment of Phobias and Anxiety Disorders in Delray Beach, Florida.

Christine E. Ryan, PhD, is an assistant professor in the Department of Psychiatry and Human Behavior at Brown University, associate director of the Brown/Butler Hospital Family Research Program, and assistant director of the Mood Disorders Program at Butler Hospital, Providence, Rhode Island.

Jane F. Silovsky, MA, is a doctoral candidate at the University of Alabama. Her PhD is anticipated for Fall 1995. She completed her clinical internship at the University of Oklahoma Health Sciences Center.

Steven Simms, PhD, is a psychologist in the Division of Oncology, Children's Hospital of Philadelphia; on the Psychology Training Faculty, Philadelphia Child Guidance Center; and an adjunct faculty member, Chestnut Hill College, Philadelphia.

Marion F. Solomon, PhD, is a psychologist in Los Angeles specializing in the problems of intimate relationships. She is coordinator of mental health training programs, Department of Humanities, Sciences and Social Sciences, UCLA Extension, and is on the faculty of California Graduate Institute.

William R. Stayton, ThD, is a clinical psychologist and a marital, sex, and family therapist. He has a private practice in Wayne, Pennsylvania. He has authored numerous articles on sexuality issues, is a professor in the human sexuality program at the University of Pennsylvania, and also teaches at La Salle University in the Pastoral Counseling Program. Dr. Stayton is an ordained American Baptist clergyman.

Terry S. Trepper, PhD, is director of the Family Studies Center and a professor of psychology and of family therapy at Purdue University, Calumet. A fellow in the American Psychological Association, he is the editor of the *Journal of Family Psychotherapy,* senior editor for the Haworth Marriage and the Family Series, and serves on numerous editorial boards.

Lenore E. A. Walker, EdD, is a clinical and forensic psychologist with offices in Denver, Colorado, and Miami Beach, Florida. She earned her diplomate in clinical psychology in 1979, is a fellow of the American Psychological Association, and is an elected member of the National Academies of Practice in Psychology. She has served as chair of the American Psychological Association's President's Task Force on Violence and the Family from 1994 to 1995. She has authored numerous books on the battered woman syndrome and on survivor therapy. She is founder and executive director of the international Domestic Violence Institute, and travels around the world lecturing and giving workshops on domestic violence.

Theodore G. Williams, MD, is a diplomate of the American Board of Psychiatry and Neurology, a captain in the U.S. Navy Medical Corps (retired), and an associate clinical professor, Neuropsychiatric Institute, UCLA School of Medicine. He is in the private practice of Psychiatry and Addiction Medicine, in Orange County, California, and medical director, Starting Point Hospital, Costa Mesa.

Jeffrey E. Young, PhD, is founder and director of the Cognitive Therapy Centers of New York and Fairfield County (Connecticut). He is a licensed psychologist, on the faculty in the Department of Psychiatry at Columbia University (College of Physicians and Surgeons). Dr. Young has written or edited several books. He also lectures throughout the world on schema-focused therapy for personality disorders.

PART I

The Context and
Models of Relational Diagnosis

CHAPTER 1

History, Rationale, and Philosophic Overview of Issues and Assumptions

FLORENCE W. KASLOW, PhD

Classification is at the core of any science (Barlow, 1991). Absent some system for ordering and labeling objects or experiences, investigators (and clinicians) lack the vocabulary to communicate with one another, and the level of knowledge does not advance. But when the subject matter is human behavior in general, and psychological disorders in particular, controversy surrounds all aspects of the endeavor, including the very issue of whether classification even ought to be attempted (Barlow, 1988).

The issues identified regarding individual diagnosis (e.g., Barlow, 1988, 1991) become even more complex when the focus is on relational diagnosis—a phenomenon comprised of more numerous variables that contribute to its being more multifaceted. Therefore, to date, mental health professionals working with family systems have lacked a nosological system. The situation is complicated further by the fact that leaders in the field of family therapy are far from unanimous regarding the need for such a classification system. In fact, the authors of Chapter 7 (Gergen, Anderson, & Hoffman) believe strongly that diagnosing is dangerous for therapist and client alike. Their arguments, which represent the growing postmodernist, social constructionist wing of the family therapy field, are compelling and warrant serious consideration. Nonetheless, the clear majority of the authors and myriad other family therapy practitioners have been pursuing the quest for a taxonomy of the variety of problems, syndromes, and interactive difficulties that can be subsumed under the broad rubric of dysfunctional family patterns. Some of the reasons for these endeavors were presented in the preface. More will emerge as the chapters unfold.

As Millon (1991) has indicated, concepts utilized in current nosological systems and diagnostic schemas are primarily descriptive. Initially all classification schemas are predicated on observeable phenomena and attempt to produce taxonomies that specify the symptoms or attributes that comprise a particular dysfunctional pattern.

It is hoped that the combined efforts presented in this volume will produce greater levels of agreement in most areas and will sharpen the areas of disagreement so that they can become part of a dialogue that ultimately leads us forward in establishing a viable, dynamic classification system of relational diagnoses that is open to periodic revision. In addition, any taxonomy promulgated now will need more clinical and empirical validation.

Before viewing some of the standards generally utilized in constructing classification systems, let us consider the history, rationale, and philosophy that have formed the foundation and overall conceptual framework for the efforts in the realm of relational diagnosis. The following account is based on notes and correspondence maintained by the author, telephone conversations with other mental health professionals involved in this endeavor, minutes of meetings of the Coalition on Family Diagnosis (hereafter Coalition); and the Task Force on Diagnosis and Classification of the APA Division of Family Psychology #43 (hereafter Division #43 Task Force); which have played a significant role recently in defining the tasks required for devising a relational diagnostic schema, creating several relevant instruments and a few diagnostic categories, and publicizing the importance of the concept of relational diagnosis.

THE IMPETUS IN CONTEXT

In 1987, when it was announced that various work groups had been convened and that preparation of DSM-IV had begun, many family systems therapists and clinical researchers were distressed by the realization that family diagnosis might again be, at the least, neglected or included peripherally (in V codes), or, at the worst, ignored completely. While a task force of family-oriented practitioners had been formed in the late 1970s to ready materials for inclusion in the third edition of the DSM (DSM-III), somehow this effort had gone awry. We believed one of the probabilities just listed would eventuate again and that such an outcome would exacerbate several serious problems generated by the DSM-III and the revised DSM-III-R systems for classifying disorders (American Psychiatric Association, 1980, 1987). First, there would continue to be no broad consensus about terminology for depicting relational difficulties. The lack of an agreed-upon nomenclature impedes communication between and among professionals involved with the same families, concurrently or sequentially, and makes it harder to discuss observations and hypotheses with clients in an effort to reach some agreement regarding the nature of their problems and the pathways toward resolution. We thought then, and believe even more strongly at the time of this writing, that evolving a typology of relational disorders predicated on empirical and clinical data and on an in-depth perusal of the literature that is definitive and sufficiently clear for inclusion in a handbook will augment the perceptions of the strength and credibility of the family systems field in the eyes of the larger mental and physical health communities, the legal and judicial world, the sprawling managed health care industry, and the public at large who are the consumers of our services.

Second, when clients/patients are couples and/or families, insurance reimbursement frequently is not available if a DSM-IV V-code diagnosis is assigned, yet individual diagnoses are not applicable given the assessment process and the treatment modality undertaken. Without reimbursement, many patients and potential patients cannot afford treatment.[1] For the therapist, the dilemma inherent in diagnosing accurately and also trying to maximize the likelihood of reimbursement poses complex ethical and legal dilemmas. For instance, if the therapist submits one or several different diagnoses for individual family members, he or she experiences great discomfort over misrepresenting the problems being addressed and the treatment methodology. Additionally, the therapist may be committing insurance fraud and violating his or her own professional Code of Ethics. Yet the clinician may know that if these patients are not covered by insurance,

---

[1] Throughout the book, different authors have referred to patients, clients, and consumers. The term selected varies, based on the setting in which therapy takes place, the nature of symptomatology, and the author's philosophic stance.

financially they may not be able to enter and/or sustain treatment. Some therapists rationalize that the practice of giving individual diagnoses is widespread, forced upon them by the system, and done in behalf of their patients. Some third-party payors knowingly foster this practice. Many practitioners yearn for a system that will compensate integrity rather than mislabeling and that will validate the existence of family diagnosis and treatment (Kaslow, 1993b). These and other related serious dilemmas led many family psychologists/psychiatrists/therapists to decide that something must be done, and a cadre of leaders banded together to take action.

THE COALITION ON FAMILY DIAGNOSIS

History and Organizational Structure—Several Mainstreams Merged

When the critical need began to emerge for devising a system of relational diagnosis, I was finishing my term as president of the Division of Family Psychology (#43) of the American Psychological Association in 1987. Thus I became involved in the establishment of a task force on (family) diagnosis and classification. Its goals were to research and formulate family diagnosis and press for their inclusion in DSM-IV. My successor as president of the Division of Family Psychology, Arthur Bodin, concurred and invited me to chair the task force. James Alexander was the original cochair (1987–1988), followed by David Olson, who continues, as I do, in this capacity (through 1995). We had little idea what a mammoth task we were undertaking, nor that it would be impossible to achieve without substantial funding and enormous investments of time from many people.

Shortly after this task force was created, we learned that the Group for the Advancement of Psychiatry's (GAP) Task Force on the Family had formed a committee with similar goals. I contacted the GAP committee chair, Herta Gutman. At our mutual urging, our respective groups agreed to collaborate, to the extent possible (GAP, 1989).

News of these developments traveled swiftly through the family therapy grapevine. In 1988, Robert Beavers, then president of the American Association for Marriage and Family Therapy (AAMFT) and a member of the GAP Task Force, encouraged AAMFT to participate. Additionally, he suggested that AAMFT become the umbrella organization, promoting and coordinating this potentially highly significant undertaking (Kaslow, 1993a). However, both APA groups insisted on a structure in which *all* participant organizations would be equal, and this is what eventuated.

The first interorganizational meeting was held in 1988. Various national professional mental health organizations with a major and sustained interest in the practice of family therapy were invited to send representatives. At this exciting meeting, the Coalition on Family Diagnosis was co-constructed; this name was chosen to convey that all member organizations were coequal. Our intent then and now was to be inclusive, so that any national organization wanting to be involved and contribute actively was, and is, welcome. We agreed that materials prepared should be disseminated for feedback from diverse sources.

As of 1994, the Coalition had expanded to include 15 member organizations. Their names reflect the broad range of disciplines interested in the realm of family diagnosis. Their combined memberships, after eliminating duplication, total over 400,000 people. If even half of these individuals are interested in utilizing relational diagnosis, a vast need and gap has to be filled. The following organizations are and/or have been represented.

Academy of Family Psychologists (AFP)

American Association for Marriage and Family Therapy (AAMFT)

American Association of Sex Educators, Counsellors and Therapists (AASECT)

American Family Therapy Academy (AFTA)

American Group Psychotherapy Association (AGPA)

American Orthopsychiatric Association (AOA)

American Psychiatric Nurses Association (APNA)

Division of Family Psychology (#43) of American Psychological Association (APA)

Group for the Advancement of Psychiatry of American Psychiatric Association (GAP)

International Association for Marriage and Family Counsellors (IAMFC)

National Association of Social Workers (NASW)

National Council on Family Relations (NCFR)

National Federation of Societies of Clinical Social Work (NFSCSW)

Society for Education and Research in Psychiatry/Mental Health Nursing

Society of Teachers of Family Medicine (STFM)

At the initial meeting, the following "officers" were elected: chairperson, Florence Kaslow; co-chair, Herta Gutman; secretary/treasurer, Mark Ginsberg, then executive director of AAMFT. The administrative structure purposefully was kept simple. Each participating organization has been asked to contribute $200.00 for operating costs. For several years, AAMFT underwrote some of the administrative costs not covered by the minimal assessment. Because of budget constraints, this stopped by 1993, and the Coalition has been wholly self-sustaining since then. Obviously, funds were never sufficient to support any research or writing projects.

The Coalition has met two to four times a year since 1988—always in conjunction with the American Psychological Association conference in August and usually with the AAMFT conference in October. Some years it has also been convened at the APA March mid-winter meeting and/or the AFTA June meeting. Representatives or designated alternates of most participating organizations' can attend these conferences.

Elections were held in March 1993 for an expanded slate of officers, and by-laws for the coalition were drafted and passed. Terry Patterson became the chair in August 1993 and was succeeded by Arthur Bodin in March 1995. I have remained actively involved as a member-at-large and a consultant to the chair(s).

Activities

At the beginning, a *mission statement* was developed, drafted by Wayne Denton (an AAMFT representative), with input from many others. It emphasized the rationale for the importance of the inclusion of relational diagnosis in DSM-IV. A segment of that document follows (Denton & Coalition members, 1989, p. 8):

> In DSM-III-R ". . . each of the mental disorders is conceptualized as a clinically significant behavioral or psychological syndrome or pattern that occurs *in a person* . . . it must currently be considered a manifestation of a behavioral, psychological, or biological dysfunction *in a person*" (1987, 1, p. xxii, emphasis added). Symptomatology is assumed to be due to a dysfunction within the individual.

This assumption is in contrast to one made by family systems theorists, researchers, and therapists. Although there are different approaches to family therapy, a common thread is an acknowledgment of the influence of general systems theory (e.g., Haley, 1976; Selvini-Palazzoli, Boscolo, Cecchin, & Prata, 1978). *Whereas in traditional psychopathology, the interest is in what symptoms tell us about the inner workings of the individual, in family systems approaches the interest is in what symptoms tell us about the interaction among family members.* For example, the family therapist assesses how the symptom helps stabilize the family (Minuchin, 1974), how the symptom regulates closeness and distance between the family members (Alexander & Parsons, 1982), or what nonverbal message the symptom might be communicating (Watzlawick, Bavelas, & Jackson, 1967). Family systems therapists conceptualize clinical problems in this manner whether they are seeing a family unit or just one family member (e.g., Fisch, Weakland, & Segal, 1982).

Defining the scope of the DSM as including only disorders representing the dysfunction within the individual constitutes a subtle, and probably unplanned, theoretical assumption which has great significance for family therapists. It excludes problems that emerge from disturbed relational patterns and systems.

The essential features of certain disorders described in DSM-IV involve relationships between persons. Such disorders are better diagnosed as relational disorders than as disorders of single individuals. Like all disorders appearing in Axis I and Axis II, these are clinically significant syndromes or patterns which are associated with distress, disability, or dysfunction or with a significantly increased risk of suffering, disability and/or loss of autonomy in one or more important areas. . . . Whatever the original cause, to be diagnosed the distress or disability must currently be manifest in the relationship between specific persons and exist for a minimum specified time period.

Diagnosable relational disorders may be either the principal focus of attention or treatment (to be listed as the principal diagnosis), or they may be a significant though secondary focus (listed as a secondary diagnosis). Often, relational disorders precede, accompany, or follow manifestations of other disorders coded on Axis I, II, or III. When a relational disorder and an individual disorder are concurrently present, both should be listed as diagnoses, the order depending on the one which is the principal focus of attention or treatment, rather than on a belief concerning the causal relationship between them. [See for example, Chapter 21.]

Many meetings were devoted to generating a list of diagnoses that might accurately describe various prevalent marital and family dysfunctional patterns. Delineating these dysfunctional interactive patterns and finding descriptive terminology for these patterns that could elicit widespread agreement among participants proved extremely difficult. There has been "consensus that we are concerned about severe and repetitive or chronic dissension in close, ongoing relationships—including within married couples and traditional families, and in various kinds of nonmarried couples and nontraditional families" (Kaslow, 1993b, p. 199). "Even though a shift in focus from the individual psychopathology to the more inclusive arena of relational diagnosis makes the task broader and more complex, those assembled concurred that this thrust was more consonant with our objectives" (p. 199).

During Phase I of the Coalition's existence, Lyman Wynne formulated the Global Assessment of Relational Functioning (GARF) instrument. Other Coalition members and associates, including William Doherty and Pauline Boss (NCFR), Don-David Lusterman (Division #43), critiqued and helped shape the GARF. The Medical School at the University of Rochester served as the home base and one of the main centers for field testing the GARF. Susan McDaniel (STMF) was centrally involved in the field testing conducted at Rochester. The GARF deliberately was constructed to be easy to administer by paraprofessionals as well as professionals in various settings, such as emergency rooms, outpatient clinics, and family service agencies. The inclusion of this instrument in the DSM-IV Options Book, (APA, 1991, pp. W:10–12) and in DSM-IV (APA, 1994, pp. 758–760) reflects some progress in terms of recognition of the salience of relational issues.

During this phase, Coalition members tentatively formulated a few diagnostic categories after literature reviews. These categories include:

Couples with borderline and narcissistic disorders (Marion Solomon, NFCSW)

Intrafamily child physical and sexual abuse (Terry Trepper, AASECT)

Oppositional defiant disorder (James Alexander, Division #43)

Postsexual abuse syndrome (Diana and Sam Kirschner, Division #43)

Each of the original conceptualizations has been refined and extended, and ultimately developed into chapters for this book.

During this period, Arthur Bodin began developing a Relationship Conflict Inventory (RCI) that could be utilized for assessing amount and severity of verbal and physical conflict. Various versions of questions and rating scales were discussed and edited by coalition and Division #43 Task Force members, field tested at the Mental Research Institute in Palo Alto and elsewhere, and are now ready for utilization. Bodin has chronicled the evolution of the RCI and what it measures in Chapter 24. We believe this instrument will prove valuable to many practitioners who wish to have a reliable and valid instrument for assessing the level of violence in couples and families so they can more accurately and rapidly diagnose, understand, and intervene to prevent and treat conflictual relational systems.

From the outset, we tried to have contact with the DSM-IV Task Force. For example, Thomas Widiger, research coordinator for the task force, attended a coalition meeting and offered constructive ideas on how to approach the research for family diagnosis. Theodore Millon served as a consultant to the Division #43 Task Force at one of its early meetings. Several members had periodic contacts with Allen Frances, chair of the DSM-IV Task Force. The channels of communication were fairly open. Unfortunately, the coalition's request to be designated as an official work group of the DSM-IV Task Force was turned down. Although we did request this some time after their structure was in place, some Coalition members do not believe this was the only reason for noninclusion.

Since its inception, Coalition leaders have endeavored to keep abreast of developments occurring in the rewriting of the International Classification of Diseases (ICD-10). For example, during 1990, we learned that the DSM-IV Task Force was considering how to respond to the Y and Z code items that were likely to be included in ICD-10. One response to some of the more family-oriented items was that the DSM-IV Task Force asked various respected researchers in the child and family field, broadly defined, to do extensive literature reviews on some family interactive patterns. We were invited to submit names of experts, some of whom subsequently were asked to prepare comprehensive reviews. These have been on such topics as expressed emotion, inadequate parental discipline, and family violence (Kaslow, 1993b, p. 200). Some Coalition members served as readers of these reviews, often recommending the inclusion of literature more focused on family systems interpretations of communications patterns, transactions, and behaviors, and less on sociological analyses.

By 1990, some representatives of member organizations urged that we concentrate more on the essential linkages between a nosology of relational disorders, its promulgation in a recognized diagnostic manual or other volume, and insurance reimbursement issues. Since then, the complex and mammoth political, economic, and professional/ethical ramifications of this vast dilemma have been dissected and deliberated. A subcommittee on insurance reimbursement, consisting mainly of Terrence Patterson and Don-David Lusterman (both Division #43), has begun investigating this area, and their thoughts and activities to date are summarized in Chapter 4. This is a gigantic endeavor, and a huge, long-term investment of time, money, and effort will be essential to accumulate sufficient data to document the comparative efficacy and cost effectiveness of couples and family therapy, based on outcome research studies, in an accurate and persuasive manner to present to insurance and managed care companies. Yet this is exactly what must be done in a very proactive manner. A beginning has been made; there is strong momentum to accelerate our activity and enlist the aid of our member organizations to mobilize their resources to mount an all-out campaign with third-party payers for reimbursement based on relational diagnosis.

We received a missive from Lyman Wynne (August 4, 1992, personal communication) entitled "Scales and Categories for Relational Problems in DSM-IV" that was circulated to coalition members and became the basis for discussion at our August 1992 meeting. The major points were that:

1. *Axis IV* was being rewritten and probably would be changed to include any contextual theme or issue that might be related to the targeted disorder being diagnosed; and the list would probably be taken from ICD-10 and would include a broader range of relational problems than had been previously present in the criteria for psychosocial stressors in Axis IV.

2. *Axis V* was still being debated; . . . in addition to several primary scales, additional ones would be listed . . . probably including the GARF . . . with the scale described in the Appendix; with the expectation that inclusion would encourage research so that the potential values of the scales could then be evaluated more fully.

3. There continued to be a hard core of Task Force members who are *individualistically and biologically oriented* and who *oppose any mention of relational problems*—positing that this is a manual just for *individual disorders.*

4. Some compromise might be reached in which the relational problems would be included under the heading "Other Clinically Significant Problems That May Be a Focus of Diagnosis and Treatment," with a glossary-type definition of each of the relational categories.

5. The DSM-IV Task Force thought that the *research* on relational problems/disorders had not yet reached the point of being able to set thresholds for severity that would enable practitioners to identify "cases" . . . particularly those alleging physical and sexual abuse. Some (unspecified) people from within the relational fields have asserted that there are difficulties when the criteria are both too narrow and too broad. If narrow, so that only the most severe examples are included, the concern is that there would be many false negatives and that such strict criteria would be useful mainly in forensic cases involving severe physical and sexual abuse, but not for prevention and treatment. If the criteria are relatively broad,

the category might be overused, with legal problems occurring from trivialization of categories.

6. Despite concerns that both extremes of usage might occur, the decision seemed to be that relational problems would be listed in the Appendix in order to stimulate research that might lead to clarification of ideas and to greater consensus regarding criteria and thresholds.

After pondering Wynne's letter, the coalition members felt reenergized and agreed to work toward either the inclusion of relational diagnoses in DSM-IV or toward a separate manual that reflects the following beliefs:

1. Relational diagnoses mark a philosophic shift to a system framework.
2. Our context for understanding the people we serve is a relational and biopsychosocial one.
3. A descriptive, flexible language of relational problems is essential for family systems theorists, researchers, therapists, and patients to communicate with one another and with professionals and other disciplines.
4. We want our submissions for insurance to be factually correct and ethical for us and for our clients. (Kaslow, 1992, p. 1; 1993b, p. 202).

Since then, we have continued to urge Coalition members (and the organizations they represent) to conduct research and to collect the necessary data to formulate clearly relational diagnoses and their accompanying criteria and thresholds, with the ultimate goal of organizing and seeing that a pilot manual is published. Sadly, we have not had at our disposal funding to support undertaking the research, field testing, writing up, editing, and administration of such a mammoth undertaking. Although several of the organizations represented have publications programs, our overtures to ascertain their willingness to underwrite and publish such a manual have not met with an enthusiastic, action-oriented approach. In addition constituent members wanted to avoid having the manual seem to belong to and become identified with only one organization.

Following the August 1992 meeting, I had further contact with Allen Frances. We both agreed that the pathway should be a parallel and complementary one, rather than a competitive one. He indicated (Frances, personal correspondence, September 9, 1992):

I think it is an excellent idea for you to develop a family diagnostic system. I would not underestimate the difficulty of the task—both conceptually and practically.

Frances stated that assistance from the DSM-IV Task Force in the form of literature reviews and the tentative criteria sets they have worked on was possible. We appreciated his encouragement and offers of a collaborative relationship.

CURRENT STATUS OF COALITION EFFORTS

By March 1993, Coalition member organizations were approached to determine what kind and level of commitment they wanted to make to Phase II of this endeavor. Most constituent groups were willing to continue to participate. Despite the fact that within the field there are theoretical schools such as social constructivism (see, e.g., Andersen, 1990) and brief solution-focused approaches (de Shazer, 1985) that are basically antidiagnosis, there is a huge groundswell of interest in the formulation of a language and a typology that can be utilized, with a high degree of consensus about descriptive definitions and criteria sets, by family therapists of various disciplines and theoretical persuasions worldwide.

Eight years after beginning work on this project, we have grasped the enormity of the task and still are proceeding, because we also are more convinced that we must continue to progress in Phase II of the Coalition's enterprise. Unfortunately, Coalition membership has changed frequently, since no one's attendance at these meetings nor research and writing time is subsidized; nonetheless, the group, as a Coalition, has survived.

Unfortunately, actual productive work by Coalition and Division #43 Task Force members has been minimal due to a lack of funding that would enable anyone to devote the time necessary to conduct research and do literature reviews, and no one has written a grant proposal to a funding agency, such as the National Institute of Mental Health (NIMH). Enthusiasm began to wane by mid-1993 but was regenerated slightly by late 1994 in both groups.

The small GAP Task Force on the family has continued its efforts, somewhat separately in the past two years, and may be developing some materials. (See Chapter 3, "Problems Encountered in Reconciling Individual and Relational Diagnosis" for a partial update on GAP activities.) We have had no definitive news from them in several years.

THE WILEY INITIATIVE

In August 1993, just when Coalition activity was at its lowest ebb, several editors from Wiley contacted me and arranged for a meeting at the American Psychological Association conference. Informally, they had been conducting their own survey to determine what type of book was most needed in the field, and the largest gap seemed to surround relational diagnosis. They were unaware of the preceding history; their decision to approach me was coincidental. It seemed clear that this might be the most viable way to conduct the work and disseminate the information we wished to convey. We had several reasons for proceeding in this way. First, clinicians and researchers are accustomed to doing the laborious work necessary to write book chapters, often unfunded, and publication by Wiley would (almost) guarantee that their work product would receive attention. Second, by working with a commercial publisher, we could avoid the thorny debate about which professional organization should do the publication, to the consternation of any others. Third, many others who were engaged in significant areas of work that merited inclusion but who had not represented any constituent organization could be invited formally to participate through writing a book chapter, thus expanding the depth and breadth of the deliberations. Finally, a book contract would provide the structure and time frame to mobilize the action needed. Nonetheless, before accepting Wiley's offer, it seemed essential to check with some Coalition and Division #43 Task Force members to see if they thought this was an appropriate solution or if they wanted to wait until a manual or book could be published under Coalition auspices. Those consulted unanimously concurred that I should accept the Wiley offer, and all approached agreed to submit chapters. Letters of invitation went out to prospective authors in 1994, indicating that this handbook is not intended to be an all-inclusive definitive manual of relational disorders but a volume to stimulate dialogue and research, in the United States and abroad, en route to a more definitive future work. To that end, all authors are interested in feedback from readers so they can refine and extend their own thinking. Any criteria sets proffered herein are meant to be tentative, are open to modification, and are not to be considered etched in stone. But they are intended to be working guidelines.

DSM-IV

In 1994, DSM-IV appeared (APA, 1994); it includes a few features that may be making it more useful for family therapists. These include:

1. The GARF, along with criteria sets and axes provided for further study.
2. Expansion of relational problems, highlighted in the section entitled "Other Conditions That May Be a Focus of Clinical Attention." This section includes:

Relational Problems

V61.9	Relational Problem Related to a Mental Disorder or General Medical Condition
V61.20	Parent-Child Relational Problem
V61.1	Partner Relational Problem
V61.8	Sibling Relational Problem
V62.81	Relational Problem NOS

The next group of diagnoses, from our perspective, also all occur in a dyadic (or triadic) relationship. To be more specific, abuse occurs between people and therefore warrants being coded as a relational diagnosis. The DSM-IV cites abuse or neglect as follows (APA, 1994, p. 20).

Problems Related to Abuse or Neglect

V61.21	Physical Abuse of Child (code 995.5 if focus of attention is on victim)
V61.21	Sexual Abuse of Child (The next two have same coding instructions as above.)
V61.21	Neglect of Child
V61.1	Physical Abuse of Adult (code 995.81 if focus of attention is on victim)
V61.1	Sexual Abuse of Adult (same coding as above)

Note that all of these have been assigned V codes; usually they were coded on Axis IV but now they can be coded on Axis I if the relational problem constitutes the primary disorder. Unfortunately, each diagnosis has received only a one-paragraph, vague description, which leaves them all innocuous; they certainly lack the kind of specificity essential for straightforward communication with patients and insurance companies. To illustrate, V61.8 Sibling Relational Problem reads as follows: "This category should be used when the focus of clinical attention is a pattern of interaction among siblings that is associated with clinically significant impairment in individual or family functioning or the development of symptoms in one or more of the siblings" (APA, 1994, p. 681).

3. Axis IV, entitled "Psychosocial and Environmental Problems," which is intended to provide somewhere to indicate the family and relational context in which Axis I and Axis II disorders present. (Chapter 21 herein elaborates on this topic.)

4. Volume 3 of the DSM-IV Source Book includes extensive literature reviews on relational problems.

Obviously, some inroads have been made and some ideas of family clinicians and researchers have been included, but in essence, much too little has been achieved in the DSM-IV.

As of April 1995, both the Coalition and the Division #43 Task Force have each written to request work group status when work commences for DSM-IV-R or DSM-V. However, I and others have come to realize and accept that no one manual can be all-inclusive and that the American Psychiatric Association and those funding the research for and preparation of the DSM manuals have every right to limit their locus of concern to mental disorders of individuals. Inherently, the theoretical foundations for diagnosing individual psychopathology and relational disorders are markedly different and may not be compatible. This position is similar to the original stance of many of the more biologically oriented members of the DSM-III and DSM-IV task forces. Assuming this might continue to be true, then it becomes imperative that we work toward a "separate but equal," parallel and complementary classification system of relational diagnoses that covers a different spectrum of the mental health/mental illness terrain.

OTHER CLASSIFICATION SYSTEMS

It is important to note that other groups apparently have reached the same conclusion, in that the DSM does not have to be, and probably should not be, the one and only diagnostic manual covering all mental and emotional disorders, disabilities, disturbances, and dysfunctions.

For example, in 1980, the International Classification of Impairments, Disabilities, and Handicaps (ICIDH) was promulgated by the World Health Organization (WHO) as a vehicle for the classification of consequences and implications of disorders on the lives of the individuals who are afflicted as well as on their significant others. It was revised and reissued in 1985, 1989, and 1993, and various international meetings on substantive themes have, or will, occur through 1997, when final agreements will be reached prior to the next revision. The ICIDH is particularly significant for mental health researchers and practitioners in that it delineates and describes the disorders and their consequences at three levels—impairments, disabilities, and handicaps. To illustrate (and most relevant to Chapter 13), a child with an attention deficit disorder may have a neurological *impairment* in brain functioning; this can lead to a learning *disability,* and if the child's frustrations lead to acting-out behavior or inability to concentrate and do his or her schoolwork, he or she is labeled a "problem student" with a learning *handicap.* The ICIDH includes a scale for measuring the severity of the disorder. This manual is quite comprehensive, as it includes sensorimotor, neurological, social-emotional, behavioral, and occupational disorders.

Given that the *International Classification of Disorders* (*ICD*) manuals are also produced under WHO auspices, the communication and interaction between the ICD and the ICIDH task forces are likely to be strong. (See van Goor Lambo, Orley, Poustka, & Rutter's paper, 1990, which argues that ICD-10 should use a multiaxial approach in the classification of child psychiatric disorders and that psychosocial factors play a central role in the etiology of many child psychiatric conditions. This emphasis on psychosocial factors is completely consonant with the position taken in this book.) Such diagnostic information is essential for planning appropriate education and therapeutic interventions and community rehabilitation facilities and services.

Sameroff and Emde (1989) have organized a book entitled *Relationship Disturbances in Early Childhood.* Based on their study and review of theories of infant and child development, they concluded that "the individual-based nosology for adult psychopathology could not easily be extended downward to early childhood" (p. vii) and decided that the classification of early childhood disorders might be approached more advantageously from the perspective of relationships and their disturbances. One of the premises that came to undergird their undertaking was perhaps there is no psychopathology in the baby; for developmental reasons, disorder can only exist in the infant-caregiver relationship. The model they evolved from this assumption closely parallels that held by the vast majority of systems theorists, who believe that even if a disorder is internalized and is presented as individual psychopathology, it has its origins within a relationship. For example, a person whose dissociative identity disorder began as a reaction to being abused (see Chapter 27) formed this defensive structure to someone else's behavior—that is, in an interpersonal transaction. As infants, children, and their parents/caregivers are parts of family units, the work of these authors is relevant to ours and vice versa, and perhaps we can bring about a real confluence in the future.

Sameroff and Emde (1989) classify relationship problems into three categories: relationship perturbation, relationship disturbance, and relationship disorder. According to them, the category into which a particular dysfunction falls is determined, among other factors, by intensity, duration, and rigidity of the pattern. Authors of various chapters in this book also selected these as three of the criteria in defining patterns or sets.

More recently, the National Center for Clinical Infant Programs has published a *Diagnostic Classification of Mental Health and Developmental Disorders of Infancy and Early Childhood* (1994) for ages birth to three years, which follows the DSM format. The contents page includes, among others, such items as:

Axis I: Primary Diagnosis

Traumatic Stress Disorder

Disorders of Affect

Anxiety Disorders of Infancy and Early Childhood

Mood Disorder

Childhood Gender Identity Disorder

Reactive Attachment Deprivation/Maltreatment Disorder of Infancy and Early Childhood

Regulatory Disorders

Impulsive, Motorically Disorganized

Sleep Behavior Disorder

Eating Behavior Disorder

Disorders of Relating and Communicating: Multisystem Developmental Disorder and Pervasive Developmental Disorder

Axis II: Relationship Disorder Classification

Overinvolved

Underinvolved

Anxious/Tense
Angry/Hostile
Verbally Abusive
Physically Abusive
Sexually Abusive

Appendixes

Parent-Infant Relationship Global Assessment Scale
Multisystem Developmental Disorder

The items in Axis II and the Parent-Infant Relationship Global Assessment Scale clearly reflect that a relational orientation has been utilized.

Several other typologies have come to our attention and bear mentioning here. Reiss-Brennan, Oppenheim, Ross, Vos, and Thompson (1995) have formulated a classification system of family relationship patterns for diagnosing and managing difficult families in psychotherapy. This system "assesses family relationship patterns across four domains: the family's engagement in the helping relationship, the therapist's response to the relationship with the family, the family's relationship history, and the family's ability to use support networks" (p. 12). The authors elucidate three common patterns found in families that roughly equate with dysfunctional, midrange, and functional (Lewis, Beaver, Gossett, & Phillips, 1976). Like numerous chapters in this volume, their nosology is influenced by attachment, object relations, and family systems theories. We believe both of these systems are useful as adjuncts to what we are trying to accomplish, but in and of themselves, they lack the criteria sets necessary for identifying specific dysfunctional relational patterns—which they were not intended to do.

The California Chapter of NASW produced a manual entitled "Person in Environment: A Coding System of the Problems of Social Functioning (PIE)" (1985). This manual recommends describing the individual client on four factors: social role dysfunction, environmental problems, mental disorders, and physical disorders. Here again, particularly in terms of problems of social role dysfunction, *severity* and *chronicity* must be evaluated and addressed. The authors' concern about taking physical disorders into account corresponds to what should be coded on Axis III, General Medical Conditions, in DSM-IV (American Psychiatric Association, 1994). Even though the lens might be focused from a different angle, most of the chapters in this volume consider these environmental issues as contextual or ecological concerns that must be addressed when patients are being assessed and throughout the course of treatment.

Apparently, when it became clear that relatively little was included on relational problems, a group of primary care physicians and others working closely with them organized and are writing a DSM-IV PC that focuses specifically on the common intertwining of physical illness and relational distress. Stressed in their work is the importance of collaboration among primary care physicians, nurses, and family therapists/psychologists. (See Chapter 9 for discussion of DSM-IV PC.)

The fact that these several more relationally based schemas have appeared independent of one another in the last dozen years seems to answer a query I posed recently in a commentary article, "Relational Diagnosis: An Idea Whose Time Has Come?" (1993a). Clearly the answer, in many quarters, is yes. Accurate differential diagnosis is widely believed to be necessary, because in addition to all the reasons already enumerated, effective treatment interventions are predicated on proper assessment and as full an understanding as can be achieved of what is transpiring, and why, in the relational system.

PRINCIPLES FOR CONSTRUCTING CLASSIFICATION SYSTEMS

In any classification attempt, it is imperative to recognize that the concepts and categories that scientists construct are merely optional tools to be used to guide the observation and interpretation of whatever segment of the world they are studying. Other scientists might construct alternative concepts and categories for studying the same subject matter (Schwartz, 1991). Millon underscores the "arbitrary nature of the task" and indicates that this is "why psychopathological states and processes may be classified in terms of any of several data levels, such as behavioral, intrapsychic, or phenomenological" (1991, p. 246). We would add interpersonal to the data levels, and insert the words "dysfunctional" and "relational" before processes to describe our perception of what is being encompassed herein. Millon posits further that no classification in psychopathology is an incontrovertible representation of the real world. Optimally, typologies serve as interim tools for advancing knowledge of human behavior, provide an organizing framework to give structure and meaning to our clinical experiences, and facilitate reaching therapeutic goals.

Various overlapping concepts seem inherent in the composition of a taxonomy, specifically clinical attributes, defining features, and diagnostic criteria, which usually are organized in sets. (See Millon, 1991, pp. 246–250, for fuller discussion on classificatory terminology and conceptual issues.) Typically, DSMs have considered the objective *signs* and the subjectively reported *symptoms* as well as specific personality *traits* to be relevant data needed for making a diagnosis.

Generally one of three taxonomic structures have prevailed: vertical or *hierarchical* models, which usually are arranged in taxonomic decision trees; horizontal or *multiaxial* models, which encourage consideration of relevant physical and contextual factors; and circular or *circumplical* models, which have been used as a structural tool for ordering interpersonal traits in conjunction with personality disorders and processes (Millon, 1991). Authors of chapters in this volume were not asked to stay within one specific model, so that all three are represented, either implicitly or explicitly. In a subsequent volume, which is more like a manual, a more uniform format might be selected, or we might decide to retain a great deal of latitude since this kind of flexibility is congruent with the openness and freedom that characterize the family field.

Because of the preliminary nature of some of the material contained in the chapters, this volume is a precursor to a definitive taxonomy of relational disorders. Not all of the categories fully meet the principles or standards that undergird "the construction and evaluation of taxonomic taxa and attributes" (Millon, 1991, pp. 258–259), namely, feature comparability, empirical reference, quantitative range, clinical relevance, representative scope, and concurrent robustness. Nonetheless, some do; all are strong on the variables of clinical relevance and representative scope, and great strides have been made already on the other four variables delineated in the literature.

ORGANIZATION OF THE HANDBOOK

In light of all of these considerations enumerated, this volume was divided into three parts. Part I is entitled "The Context and Models of Relational Diagnosis." Section

A provides an overview of relational diagnosis and discusses some of the most serious problems confronted by those who have and are attempting to make the paradigmatic shift to using systemic concepts in research, assessment, and treatment efforts. Section B includes chapters on two very important relational models, both primarily circumplical. Chapters 7 and 8 present the work of leading social constructionists who argue against formalizing any diagnostic nosology because they believe it is harmful to helping consumers of therapeutic services. Chapter 9 reminds us that families often seek services from their primary care physician and not from a family therapist, and looks at how to incorporate family therapy principles and strategies into primary care settings. Given that sensitivity to culturally diverse populations has become essential as many societies have become more pluralistic, the authors of Chapters 10 and 11 in Section C were invited to deal with cultural considerations in diagnosis and treatment. In essence, all of the chapters in Part I provide the foundation and context for Part II.

Part II is devoted to some of the various categories we deemed essential for inclusion. Given that these are relational in substance and conceptualization, many cannot be reduced to two or three words; in the next volume, more uniformity of working style probably will be sought. It is important to reiterate that the list of categories included is by no means exhaustive; nonetheless, we believe we have identified many of the most frequently presented relational disorders. Some categories could have been placed in various of the three sections of Part II—Child and Adolescent Focused; Couple Focused; and Family Focused. There is overlap across categories, and the decision as to where a diagnosis best fits is ultimately an arbitrary one. The choices for this volume were made jointly by the chapter author(s) and the book editor.

Several chapters take a unique, entirely new look at severely disturbed styles of relating and the devastating impact these have on everyone who comes into the person's orbit. Chapter 31, Charny's "Evil in Human Personality: Disorders of Doing Harm to Others in Family Relationships," best exemplifies this genre of contribution.

Part III, "The Future of Relational Diagnosis," consists of just one chapter. First it presents a summary of the major themes articulated in the handbook, and then it attempts to foresee where this mammoth endeavor and mission is likely to lead. While this volume constitutes a major leap into the immediate and the more distant future, much remains to be done before we can formalize a dynamic, flexible relational diagnosis system into a manual that has a high level of consensual validation.

REFERENCES

Alexander, J., & Parsons, B. V. (1982). *Functional family therapy.* Monterey, CA: Brooks/Cole.

American Psychiatric Association (1980). *Diagnostic and statistical manual of mental disorders* (3rd ed.). Washington, DC: Author.

American Psychiatric Association (1987). *Diagnostic and statistical manual of mental disorders* (3rd ed., rev.). Washington, DC: Author.

American Psychiatric Association (1991). *DSM-IV options book: Work in progress.* Washington, DC: Author.

American Psychiatric Association (1994). *Diagnostic and statistical manual of mental disorders* (4th ed.). Washington, DC: Author.

American Psychological Association (1987). *General guidelines for providers of psychological services.* Washington, DC: Author.

Anderson, T. (Ed.) (1990). *The reflecting team: Dialogues and dialogues about the dialogues.* West Germany: Borgmann.

Barlow, D. H. (1988). *Anxiety and its disorders: The nature and treatment of anxiety and panic.* New York: Guilford.

Barlow, D. H. (1991). Introduction to the special issue on diagnosis, dimensions, and DSM-IV: The science of classification. *Journal of Abnormal Psychology, 100*(3), 243–244.

Denton, W., and Coalition members. (1989). *Rationale for the inclusion of relational disorders with DSM-IV.* Photocopy paper. Coalition on Family Diagnosis.

de Shazer, S. (1985). *Keys to solution in brief therapy.* New York: Norton.

Fisch, R., Weakland, J. H., & Segal, L. (1982). *The tactics of change: Doing therapy briefly.* San Francisco: Jossey-Bass.

Group for the Advancement of Psychiatry Committee on the Family (1989). The challenge of relational diagnoses: Applying the biopsychosocial model in DSM-IV. *American Journal of Psychiatry, 146*(11), 1492–1494.

Haley, J. (1976). *Problem-solving therapy.* New York: Harper & Row.

Kaslow, F. W. (1992, August 26). Photocopied memoranda to Coalition of Family Diagnosis members.

Kaslow, F. W. (1993a). Relational diagnosis: An idea whose time has come? *Family Process, 32*(2), 255–259.

Kaslow, F. W. (1993b). Relational diagnosis: Past, present and future. *American Journal of Family Therapy, 21*(3), 195–204.

Lewis, J., Beavers, W. R., Gossett, J. T., & Phillips, V. A. (1976). *No single thread: Psychological health and the family system.* New York: Brunner/Mazel.

Millon, T. (1991). Classification in psychopathology: Rationale, alternatives, and standards. *Journal of Abnormal Psychology, 100*(3) 245–261.

Minuchin, S. (1974). *Families and family therapy.* Cambridge, MA: Harvard University.

National Association of Social Workers. (1985). *Person in environment: A coding system of the problems of social functioning (PIE).* Sacramento, CA: Author.

National Center for Infant Clinical Programs (1994). *Diagnostic classification of mental health and developmental disorders of infancy and early childhood.* Arlington, VA: Author.

Reiss-Brennan, B., Oppenheim, D., Ross, B. L., Vos, B., & Thompson, M. L. (1995, Winter). A classification system of family relationship patterns for diagnosing and managing difficult families in psychotherapy. *The Family Psychologist,* 12–16.

Sameroff, A. J., & Emde, R. M. (1989). *Relationship disturbances in early childhood: A developmental approach.* New York: Basic Books.

Schwartz, M. A. (1991). The nature and classification of the personality disorder. A re-examination of basic premises. *Journal of Personality Disorders, 5,* 25–30.

Selvini-Palazzoli, M., Boscolo, L., Cecchin, G., & Prata, G. (1978). *Paradox and counterparadox.* Northvale, NJ: Aronson.

van Goor Lambo, G., Orley, J., Poustka, F., & Rutter, M. (1990). Classification of abnormal psychosocial situations: Preliminary report of a revision of a WHO scheme. *Journal of Child Psychology and Psychiatry, 31*(2), 229–241.

Watzlawick, P., Bavelas, J. B., & Jackson, D. D. (1967). *Pragmatics of human communication: A study of interactional patterns, pathologies, and paradoxes.* New York: Norton.

World Health Organization (1980, 1985, 1989, & 1993). *International classification of impairments, disabilities, and handicaps (ICIDH).* Geneva, Switzerland: Author.

CHAPTER 2

Some Ethical Implications of Relational Diagnoses

MICHAEL C. GOTTLIEB, PhD

Ethics codes of the mental health professions provide standards for practitioners based on principles of biomedical ethics (e.g., Beauchamp & Childress, 1983). Typically, such codes are developed from reports of actual dilemmas faced by clinicians, and an extensive literature now exists on the application of these codes to practice. (See Haas & Malouf, 1989; Keith-Spiegel & Koocher, 1985.)

Unfortunately, these codes are based almost exclusively on the assumption that the patient is an individual rather than several persons being seen conjointly (Woody, 1990). As a result, such codes seldom are helpful when clinicians are confronted with ethical dilemmas arising from the treatment of couples and families.

Some research has been devoted to the development of conceptual schema and classification systems for understanding family functioning (Beavers, 1981; Olson, Sprenkle, & Russell, 1979). Unfortunately, there is still no formal, systemically based, diagnostic nosology. Instead, the most recent psychiatric diagnostic classification system, DSM-IV (American Psychiatric Association, 1994), has marginalized this relationally conceptualized work, continuing to adhere to a traditional medical model of individual diagnosis.

Consequently, if a clinician chooses to participate in the current insurance reimbursement system, an individual diagnosis, based on the prevailing DSM, is required. This limitation produces troublesome ethical dilemmas. For example, if a couple receives marital therapy, what is the consequence of the use of an individual diagnosis? While it may allow the couple to receive financial reimbursement for the service, it misleads the payor and may be illegal. More important, such a practice defeats the very purpose of systemically oriented therapy, which works to avoid notions such as the "identified patient." Were insurance companies to accept relational diagnoses, many such problems could be avoided. (See Chapter 4 for a different interpretation.)

On the other hand, if relational diagnoses were established, they would create other ethical dilemmas. This chapter speculates about those dilemmas and their implications for practice, and provides some initial recommendations for practitioners.

ASSUMPTIONS AND CRITERIA

A relational diagnosis may be indicated when there is a dysfunctional pattern of interaction between two or more people within a system that leads to a reduced level of functioning for at least one member of the system. The dysfunctional relationship pattern cannot be due to situational factors that may disrupt interpersonal interactions temporarily. Instead, there must be an ongoing pattern of dysfunctional relations. The degree of dysfunction may vary from mild to severe, and individual members of the system may be affected to varying degrees at different points in time.

Relational diagnoses should not be ruled out because an individual does not behave in similarly dysfunctional ways in other relational contexts. Nonetheless, such diagnoses may not be appropriate when an individual behaves dysfunctionally in the absence of a complementary response from others within or outside a particular system.

A relational diagnosis may be made in conjunction with or independent of an individual diagnosis. Conversely, the diagnosis of an individual family member does not presume or require a relational diagnosis.

This volume represents the progress that has been made in the development of a relationship-based diagnostic classification system. I assume that the system has received empirical support and that such diagnoses are accepted as legitimate alternatives for practitioners to consider.

Systems theory and relational diagnosis raise issues surrounding the question of individual versus collective responsibility (Searight & Merkel, 1991). From the former perspective, a relational diagnosis could be unethical if it risks diminishing individual responsibility and autonomy. This is a worthy argument, but such a debate is beyond the scope of this work, and I shall assume that relational diagnosis can be an ethical alternative in clinical practice.

When discussing ethics, issues inevitably blur into one another. Therefore, some issues have been placed, perhaps arbitrarily, under one heading when they could as easily have been placed under another.

BACKGROUND

Mental health professionals have been treating couples and families since the early 1950s (Hoffman, 1981), but isolated articles on the ethical dilemmas of this approach did not begin to appear until much later (e.g., Boszormenyi-Nagy & Krasner, 1980; Grosser & Paul, 1964; Hines & Hare-Mustin, 1978; Karpel, 1980; Nichols, 1973 & 1984; Rinella & Goldstein, 1980).

The particular ethical dilemmas unique to this work were first established by Margolin (1982), who isolated three issues: patient definition, confidentiality, and therapeutic neutrality. Shortly thereafter, O'Shea and Jessee (1982) added a fourth issue regarding the unique iatrogenic risks inherent in the procedure. These four basic dilemmas have been augmented recently by Gottlieb (1995a), who added two: a definition for change of format and ethical dilemmas associated with live supervision.

These six dilemmas arose from problems encountered by systems therapists in their daily work. Establishing a nosology of relational diagnoses would create a seventh set of ethical dilemmas unique to family work. The remainder of this chapter examines some of the problems that may arise if relational diagnoses are adopted.

PROFESSIONAL RESPONSIBILITY

A mental health professional's primary obligation is to his or her individual patient (Woody, 1990). Using a relational diagnosis raises basic questions about how to discharge professional responsibility to a couple or a family. On what basis should the therapist choose to use a relational diagnosis? To whom is the professional primarily responsible? How will a therapist maintain neutrality and avoid the risks of multiple relationships?

Choosing a Relational Diagnosis

There are three major areas one must consider before choosing a relational diagnosis. First, under what circumstances should a relational diagnosis be considered primary, and when should it be considered secondary to an individual one? On what basis is a clinician to decide? Will empirically based decision trees be developed, or will the choice rest on clinical judgment and/or theoretical orientation?

Second, what impact would there be from choosing either a relational diagnosis or an individual one? Making a relational diagnosis might bring needed focus to interpersonal issues, but it also might draw attention away from individual issues that require care. For example, systems therapists often have minimized individual difficulties, such as depression or learning disabilities, in favor of systemic constructions that allowed such conditions to go untreated. Conversely, systems theorists have justly criticized the exclusive use of an individual diagnosis when it diverted attention from relational issues that might be causing individual distress.

Third, what if both individual and relational diagnoses are made for the same family system? Will this be confusing to both therapist and family? How will treatment priorities be determined? Under what conditions will the treatment plan be altered, and who will be responsible for the decision? Furthermore, what problems might concurrent diagnoses create when a provider must obtain approval for treatment from an unsophisticated managed care company representative?

Defining the Patient

Margolin (1982) was the first to raise the question of who should be defined as the patient in marital therapy. Recently, the American Psychological Association (1992) revised its Ethical Principles of Psychologists and Code of Conduct and acknowledged that psychologists may have more than one patient at a time. The code states (p. 1605) that it is necessary to clarify, from the outset of treatment, which persons are patients and the relationship the psychologist will have with the other parties. This guideline also would apply when a relational diagnosis is made. Such clarification creates both advantages and disadvantages.

Using a relational diagnosis can foster greater clarity about the professional relationship. It also requires an explanation of the roles and responsibilities of all those involved, including the responsibility of the therapist to each family member.

Treatment effectiveness might be improved for several reasons. If the family accepts the relational diagnosis, each might feel more responsible for the problem, separately and jointly. Feeling more responsible could lead family members to be more cooperative with treatment and to exert greater effort toward change. When a family presents with an identified patient, the procedure might foster treatment by immediately confronting the scapegoating and help all to have a more realistic expectation of the requirements for change. Finally, using relational diagnoses could involve family members not previously seen who could facilitate movement toward the desired outcome(s).

Unfortunately, this procedure is not without its disadvantages. One problem is that explaining roles and responsibilities is time consuming. Utilizing time in such a manner is increasingly difficult to support when time spent with patients already has become so limited by the imposition of cost containment measures.

Another problem is that following the procedure risks disrupting the nascent professional relationship just at the precise time when joining or creating a therapeutic alliance generally is considered to be the most important activity.

And finally, a relational diagnosis may foster resistance in at least two different situations: families with rigid structures who blame one member for all of the family's problems may resist, and less sophisticated consumers might reject what appears to be counterintuitive treatment, presuming that the clinician was either inattentive to their complaints or simply ignorant.

Neutrality

In individual therapy, a clinician's primary obligation is to his or her patient (Woody, 1990). The patient enjoys the therapist's full attention, loyalty, and support. By assigning a relational diagnosis to a family system, some if not all family members become patients, and the practitioner becomes responsible to them equally. Systemically oriented therapists have been urged to maintain therapeutic neutrality to avoid being triangulated into family conflict (Margolin, 1982; Selvini, Boscolo, Cecchin, & Prata, 1980). While good advice, there is no consensus regarding how neutrality should be managed. There are four alternatives.

1. Maintain primary loyalty to each family member as if they were being treated as individuals and sometimes see them separately. Some patients may feel comfortable with this arrangement and divulge more information than they would in conjoint sessions. Unfortunately, in so doing the therapist accepts greater risk of conflict of interest by exposing him- or herself to having information that may not be shared with other family members to whom he or she is equally responsible.

2. Be responsible only to the system, refusing to align with any individual. This position generally will preclude questions of divided loyalty, but it risks reduced treatment effectiveness if information is withheld.

3. Declare loyalty to all, but shift alliances between individuals or subsystems during treatment sessions, as in the concept and use of multilateral partiality (e.g., Borszormenyi-Nagy & Spark, 1984). In this case neutrality is maintained, but more time and energy is required for patients to accept the therapist's neutrality.

4. Adhere exclusively to the stated therapeutic goal of the family. While conceptually more straightforward, this position requires a therapist who can operate from a value-free perspective, which generally is considered unlikely, if not impossible (Doherty & Boss, 1991).

The use of relational diagnoses will require a therapist to take a position regarding therapeutic neutrality. Doing so may have some advantages. First, the clinician will have an opportunity to intervene with more family members if he or she is not seen as aligned with an individual or subsystem. Second, it will be possible to gain a better understanding of the system by having relationships with more family members. And third, the use of a relational diagnosis itself may help keep the therapist neutral. For example, a family conflict arises in which the therapist becomes triangulated. Another family member may remind everyone of the therapist's neutral role, thereby helping the therapist to extricate him- or herself from a potentially harmful position.

Maintaining neutrality is a desirable goal, but there are numerous exceptions. A family member may complain of physical symptoms such as chronic and severe headache. While the symptoms may have systemic importance, the clinician cannot ignore the possible physical basis of the condition and should refer the family member to a physician. Neutrality also may be inappropriate in certain clinical situations. For example, Madanes (1981) has argued that when adolescents are acting out, the therapist should align with the parents to assist them in gaining control over out-of-control children. Finally, there are times when violation of neutrality is required, such as when child abuse must be reported (Margolin, 1982).

Multiple Relationships

Health professionals aspire to avoid dual relationships because of their potential harm to patients (Beauchamp & Childress, 1983). In recent years, the issue has received heightened attention among mental health practitioners due to the frequency of sexual exploitation of patients by therapists (Holroyd & Brodsky, 1977; Pope & Bouhoutsos, 1986; Sell, Gottlieb, & Schoenfeld, 1986).

Publicity surrounding the issue, while generally salutary for consumers, has caused many to fear that even benign extraprofessional contact could prompt an ethics complaint. Unfortunately, adhering to such an extreme position is not realistic for many practitioners in small or confined communities nor for academics, where "dual relations" are a daily occurrence.

As a result, some began to claim that all such relationships were not unethical per se (Haas & Malouf, 1989; Keith-Spiegel & Koocher, 1985). This thinking lead to a change in the next revision of the American Psychological Association's ethical principles (1992). While adhering to the principle of avoiding exploitation, it acknowledges that in certain situations "it may not be feasible or reasonable for psychologists to avoid social or other nonprofessional contact with persons such as patients" (p. 1601). It cautions that while such multiple relationships may not be harmful, the psychologists must refrain from them if he or she feels that doing so would impair objectivity or cause harm.

Multiple relationships occur when a person occupies more than one set of role expectations in relationship to another person. These situations arise naturally in daily life, but the risk of exploitation increases as role expectations diverge from one another and a power differential is created between the parties (Gottlieb, 1993a; Kitchener, 1988). Serving in the roles of both teacher and research supervisor involves similar expectations and poses minor risk to a student. Being a therapist and an employer of a patient involves highly divergent expectations and is fraught with danger.

Employing relational diagnoses may increase the likelihood of having multiple relationships. A typical example involves a couple that receives a relational diagnosis and proceeds with marital therapy. During the course of treatment, the husband requests individual treatment for personal issues from the therapist, but he and his wife do not want to interrupt the relationship therapy. If the therapist agrees to see the husband, he or she will play the dual roles of individual and relational therapist with the husband. If a clinician were to treat an entire family, the number of possible roles he or she could play increases dramatically.

Filling multiple roles with patients, is not unethical per se (American Psychological Association, 1992; Gottlieb & Cooper, 1990), but doing so entails greater risk since relationships are more complex, and there is increased room for misunderstanding. Such arrangements also risk potential feelings of divided loyalty on the part of patients and conflict of interest.

On the other hand, there are advantages to playing multiple roles. With regard to the example just given, the therapist already has much information about the husband. This information could allow a rapid and smooth transition to individual treatment and perhaps a more effective intervention. Transfer to another therapist would require time to collect clinical data and to establish a new relationship. In addition, the potential problem created by two therapists treating members of the same family system is eliminated. Also, the original therapist, by agreeing to see the husband alone, has the opportunity to gain additional information about his perspective, which could benefit the relational therapy.

Recommendations

- Practitioners should explain the nature of their professional responsibilities to all concerned, despite the amount of time required. While this procedure may disrupt development of the therapeutic relationship briefly, it is time well spent, and most patients will appreciate such efforts on their behalf.
- Careful consideration should be given to assigning individual and/or relational diagnoses. Once this decision is made, the clinician should explain his or her diagnostic impressions to the family, emphasizing that the diagnoses are fluid, not static. The diagnosis or diagnoses should inform the treatment plan and the relationship the therapist is to have with each family member.
- The practitioner should convey his or her policy regarding therapeutic neutrality and inform all concerned at the outset of treatment. This policy should be based on the diagnostic formulation of the case, including individual diagnoses when necessary, and thoughtful clinical judgment. The clinician must remain mindful of the advantages and disadvantages of the chosen policy as well as those circumstances when exceptions must be made. In cases where a clinician must align with a family member or subsystem, it may be necessary to reconsider the relational diagnosis, treatment plan, and policy regarding neutrality. Individual diagnoses should not be ignored simply to maintain therapeutic neutrality.
- In some cases the therapist may agree to play more than one role with a family member. This procedure is ethically acceptable but risks both real and perceived conflicts of interest. The clinician must remain alert to this possibility and insure that the multiple roles are not highly discrepant and that professional responsibilities are clarified as often as necessary.

CONFIDENTIALITY

When individuals seek psychotherapy, they expect the information they reveal to be kept in confidence. Although there are statutory exceptions to patient privilege in all jurisdictions, exceptions do not arise often, and confidentiality generally is maintained (American Psychological Association, 1992, p. 1606f).

Treating couples or families creates a different exception to confidentiality since, by common law, information revealed in the presence of a third party is not considered confidential. Therefore, when a relational diagnosis is made and a therapist is to have multiple patients, a specific policy for the management of confidential information must be established. The clinician has four options (Gottlieb & Cooper, 1990).

1. *Treat information disclosed individually as confidential.* This alternative has the same advantages and disadvantages as noted earlier regarding neutrality.

2. *Set a policy that no information is to be confidential.* This policy avoids the risks of being triangulated into family conflict. It also may lead family members to feel more comfortable when they know that the therapist is not withholding information from them.

Unfortunately, such a policy may create barriers to treatment and runs the risk that relevant information may be lost. For example, a child may be quite silent and self-contained during treatment to maintain the family secret of a father's abusive behavior. Or a family member who fears being confronted about drinking may resist the policy and try to sabotage treatment.

3. *Agree that certain information will be kept confidential as a matter of personal privacy.* For example, a therapist might agree not to reveal information about a wife's previous romantic relationships to her husband. While this notion seems reasonable, the therapist cannot know if the husband would consider such information vital to their relationship. Thus, while this alternative may seem appealing, it is impossible to know where to draw such lines in advance. Some experts on affairs, such as Pittman (1989), believe therapists should not protect this type of information.

4. *Agree to keep certain information confidential temporarily with the understanding that it will be disclosed at a later date.* For example, a partner learns that he is seropositive for HIV and wants to inform his lover but is fearful of rejection if he does so. Keeping the information confidential for a brief period, while working with the patient, might provide sufficient time for the infected partner to confront the issue and disclose the information. This choice also may be appropriate for practitioners who live in states that require such disclosure. On the other hand, the patient may renege and insist that confidentiality be maintained. The therapist now has information that is vital to the partner but which he or she cannot reveal without violating confidentiality. While such a choice could be highly beneficial in some clinical situations, it risks harming others to whom the therapist is equally responsible.

Recommendations

The use of relational diagnoses will require thorough consideration and discussion of how confidentiality will be managed at the outset of treatment. The therapist's policy and role with each family member must be clarified once a diagnosis and treatment plan are made. If certain information is to remain confidential, it should be understood as such from the outset. The practitioner must also remain mindful of the legal exceptions to confidentiality within his or her jurisdiction, explain them, and provide them in written form.

INFORMED CONSENT

The procedure of informed consent is derived from the ethical principle of respect for the autonomy of others (Beauchamp & Childress, 1983). It is intended to give patients information about what to expect from and during the course of treatment. Most ethics codes contain provisions requiring informed consent from a patient before initiating treatment, and some spell out the steps the therapist must follow. For example:

> ... informed consent generally implies that the person (1) has the capacity to consent, (2) has been informed of significant information concerning the procedure, (3) has freely and without undue influence expressed consent, and (4) consent has been appropriately documented. (American Psychological Association, 1992, p. 1605)

Procedures like these are written with the assumption that the clinician has a single patient. If the therapist makes a relational diagnosis, consent must be obtained from all patients who are competent to give it. Unfortunately, systems-oriented therapists face additional dilemmas that make unambiguous informed consent quite difficult. These include accurately predicting the course of treatment problems and record keeping.

Predicting the Course of Treatment

It is the clinician's responsibility to provide patients with information regarding the course of treatment to the best of his or her ability. This requirement is fairly straightforward when a pediatrician treats a child's ear infection. It is far more difficult to do when providing psychotherapy because numerous unpredictable events may alter the course of treatment. The task of predicting such events is even more difficult in a relational context because the therapist cannot predict how family members will behave or what effect their behavior will have on one another (Lakin, 1994).

For example, a couple requests marital therapy due to poor communications. The therapist agrees, makes a relational diagnosis, and treatment begins. Upon arrival for the third session the husband states that, despite his initial agreement to work on communication issues, he is really there to help his wife address her drinking. He admits that he used the communications issue as a ruse to get her into treatment but refuses to work on any issue other than her drinking. He claims that once she gains control of her drinking, all their other problems will be solved. The wife is shocked by his behavior and denies that she has such a problem.

What impact will this turn of events have on the wife? How could the therapist have predicted this outcome? Should therapists be expected to inform patients that such things may occur? If so, what should patients be told, and what guidelines can a therapist use in making such a disclosure?

Record Keeping

Practitioners are required to inform patients that records are kept, what information is recorded, and under what circumstances the information can be released (American Psychological Association, 1992, 1993). When a clinician concludes that some members of a family should be diagnosed individually, maintaining an individual record is a reasonable practice alternative, especially if the patient is to receive individual as well as relational treatment. But what if a relational diagnosis is the only one assigned, and the parties are to be seen conjointly?

Systemically oriented therapists are trained to keep a single, or comingled, treatment record based on the assumption that the system is being treated regardless of the number of people involved. This practice generally is considered clinically beneficial and ethically appropriate (Gottlieb, 1993b), but it challenges our legal tradition of confidentiality and professional responsibility to individuals.

A comingled record has the advantage of preserving rich interactional and contextual data, which can be invaluable to treatment planning. This data is lost when only individual records are kept. Additionally, by recording systemic interventions, the clinician has a chronology of the interventions attempted and their outcomes to aid him or her in treatment planning.

On the other hand, keeping comingled records has certain drawbacks. In a misguided effort to remain even-handed, would a clinician fail to record data that would lead to a diagnosis of individual psychopathology (Searight & Merkel, 1991)? Or might the therapist avoid assigning responsibility to a particular family member for his or her individual behavior when it was appropriate to do so?

Comingled records also present a problem when information is to be released to others. For example, a family is seen conjointly. One adult member chooses to obtain individual psychotherapy services elsewhere, the therapist agrees, and the other family members consent to a release of information. However, the person was seen only in a relational context, never as an individual. Since behavior is contextually based, how valuable will the information be to the new therapist who will see the patient individually (Gottlieb & McDowell, 1994)?

A far more serious situation occurs when conflict arises among family members. For example, a couple consults a family psychologist for marital counseling. The psychologist maintains a comingled record and informs them at the outset that both must consent before the record can be released. As part of the treatment contract, the therapist explains that he or she will not testify as an expert witness on behalf of either party in the event of a legal dispute over the custody of their children in a divorce action. Both agree to the terms and sign the contract containing this provision (F. Kaslow, personal communication, April 1, 1995). The counseling proceeds, but the couple eventually decides to divorce and to terminate treatment. Each then retains an attorney who requests the record, enclosing their client's signed release. The psychologist refuses to release the record in the absence of the other party's consent. The lawyers respond with subpoenas claiming that their clients' interests supersede the therapist's ethical concerns.

The psychologist is left with few attractive choices. Should he or she call the former patients, remind each of their agreement, indicate reluctance to testify because he or she believes it would be detrimental to them and ask them to rescind their requests? Could he or she call the attorneys, explain the situation, and ask them to persuade their clients to withdraw their requests? Or, being mindful that this has become an adversarial situation, should the therapist obtain his or her own legal advice?

Recommendations

When using a relational diagnosis, informed consent becomes a complex matter. Standard information should be reviewed with multiple patients just as it is with individuals. In addition, issues specific to the treatment format should be discussed, including: procedures to be followed, relevant law, and treatment options and their accompanying risks and benefits. When discussing systemically oriented treatment, the therapist should inform the family of his or her limited ability to control the behavior of individual family members and the effect their behavior may have on one another.

The clinician should take as much time as necessary to obtain the informed consent of all involved. Doing so respects autonomy and increases the likelihood of treatment effectiveness.

Informed consent does not end once treatment begins. A therapist should remain alert to the need for repeating or providing additional information, such as when a family member discloses feelings of coercion. When such feelings are divulged, they should be confronted promptly, and therapy should not proceed until such issues are resolved.

Some clinicians are prone to view informed consent procedures as an obstacle to be removed before treatment can begin. Instead, informed consent should be seen as a process (Packman, Cabot, & Bongar, 1994; Stone, 1990). When viewed in this manner, the clinician will understand that it should be interwoven throughout the therapy process as a matter of sound ethical decision-making and good clinical practice (Gottlieb & Handlesman, in preparation).

Maintaining comingled records is an ethical record-keeping option, but it requires that all competent adults be fully informed of the procedure at the outset. Specifically, all persons involved in treatment should be apprised of the advantages and disadvantages of keeping a record that reflects a conjoint process. They also should be told how and under what circumstances the record may be released.

If one party wishes records released and another is opposed, the record should not be released unless the therapist is ordered to do so by a court of competent jurisdiction. Under no circumstances should the clinician try to delete portions of the record that apply to the nonreleasing party. Data collected in an interactional context should not be released as if it were collected individually. The clinician should make every effort to resolve conflicts regarding the release of records informally. If such efforts fail, the therapist may wish to consult his or her own attorney or legal consultation services offered through professional organizations.

IATROGENIC RISK

O'Shea and Jessee (1982) were the first to note the iatrogenic risk specific to family treatment, that is, other members of a system may deteriorate even though they are not the focus of the treatment. Using relational diagnoses should reduce this type of iatrogenic risk for a number of reasons:

1. If family members understand the role each plays in the presenting problem, they may be more alert to potential adverse treatment reactions.
2. Understanding this danger may make individual family members more amenable to individual evaluation if they know that they too may be at risk.
3. Such a procedure may foster enhanced treatment effectiveness if all are more aware of the larger contextual factors that contribute to the presenting problem.

Unfortunately, the use of a relational diagnosis may produce iatrogenic risks. For example, a family member, not initially the focus of treatment, may decompensate once treatment is under way. If the therapist finds it necessary to shift focus temporarily and attend to the individual, a conflict of interest may arise. Will the therapist feel a sense of divided loyalty, having to turn away from the family's treatment temporarily in order to aid the individual? Will other family members feel neglected and accuse the therapist of providing them with less than adequate care? Or may they appreciate the sensitivity and flexibility of the therapist and find it a more useful style to emulate?

A more common risk may arise when a couple seen for marital therapy chooses to divorce. If only a relational diagnosis were made, one may be prone to view him- or herself as no longer having a problem now that the relationship has ended. If so, is the individual at risk for engaging in another similarly dysfunctional relationship?

There are at least three additional situations in which relational diagnosis may create iatrogenic risk: those in which a practice is restricted to one theoretical perspective, families with disabled and severely mentally ill members, and family violence.

Theory-Induced Risk

In certain clinical situations, an individual diagnosis may be the only one that is appropriate. Devoted systems therapists, disposed to see all personal issues as relational, run a risk if they overlook individual diagnoses. Consider the following. A couple is treated in marital therapy for chronic relational problems surrounding the husband's lack of enthusiasm, negativity, and lethargy. A relational diagnosis is made and treatment begins. During the treatment, the husband consults his physician and learns that he has an underactive thyroid. The condition is treated, the husband improves, and so does the relationship. The couple concludes that their relational problem was due to the undetected physical illness, which has been resolved.

Such examples challenge the systems theory assumption that symptoms are functional and a manifestation of disordered relationships. A zealous or inadequately trained systems therapist, who intervenes based on insufficient data, incurs great risk when he or she imposes theoretical assumptions on patients without ruling out other diagnostic considerations.

Families with Disabled and Severely Mentally Ill Members

Families with seriously mentally ill and/or disabled members often suffer under the burden of long-term care for their loved one (Backer & Richardson, 1989). Is it appropriate to use a relational diagnosis and presume systemic dysfunction when a family member is chronically ill, disabled, or schizophrenic?

In some circumstances, the answer may be in the affirmative. For example, parents may reorganize around a child's physical disability in a systemically dysfunctional manner (Barth, 1993; Gottlieb, 1995b). In such a situation, a relational diagnosis, in additional to the individual one, may be appropriate and helpful. Conversely, a relational diagnosis may be harmful in the case of a family with an adult child who is severely manic-depressive. If the parents already feel needlessly guilty for having caused what many consider a biological disorder, a relational diagnosis could exacerbate their feelings needlessly.

Family Violence

Another iatrogenic risk may arise when using a relational diagnosis in the treatment of family violence. Systems theory has been correctly criticized for arguing that family violence was a systemic problem and not advocating on behalf of victims (Hare-Mustin, 1978; Margolin, 1982; Walker, 1984). Would the use of a relational diagnosis in situations of family violence raise this criticism anew, and would it not be justified? Using a relational diagnosis could encourage an abusive husband to blame his wife for provoking him and feel that his behavior was justified. It also might prompt deterioration in the wife's condition if she feels responsible for her own victimization.

Conversely, might such a diagnosis increase the likelihood of treatment effectiveness? For example, a relational diagnosis, in conjunction with an individual one for the husband, might provide him greater latitude to confront his issues. It also might be of assistance to a wife who denies having any role in the couple's relational problems.

Recommendations

Diagnostic formulation should include consideration of both individual (intrapsychic) and relational (interpersonal) diagnoses. Examining for both will reduce the risk that either one will be missed. Considering both types of diagnoses should lead to a more accurate diagnostic formulation because individual, systemic, and contextual information is considered. If a relational diagnosis is made, all family members should be assured they will receive whatever individual treatment they may require, if the need arises.

It is necessary to offer patients the range of treatment options appropriate to their condition, based on current scientific knowledge. A clinician may jeopardize patient welfare when he or she rigidly adheres to a theoretical position that restricts treatment options.

In situations where families present with disabled or severely emotionally disturbed members, relational diagnoses should be considered most carefully. Diagnosis should be deferred until the clinician is able to differentiate between a dysfunctional system and one that labors under chronic interpersonal burden beyond the family members' control.

Family violence presents unique problems for systems-oriented practitioners. Relational diagnoses may be inappropriate in these circumstances and should be used with the utmost caution in order to protect victims.

SPECIAL CIRCUMSTANCES

In addition to the major ethical dilemmas just discussed, the use of relational diagnoses will create ethical problems in other clinical situations, including working with families from diverse cultural backgrounds, in hospital settings, and within the legal system. Space limitations prevent detailed exploration of these issues. Instead, each will be mentioned with some of the problems that may arise.

Cultural Issues

Mental health professionals are now working with an increasingly diverse population. Will relational diagnoses be helpful or harmful when working with families of different cultural backgrounds? For example, such diagnoses may be an advantage in working with Latin families. Latins view human behavior as more interdependent, and they do not draw boundaries between themselves as strictly as North Americans do. As a result, we can hypothesize that Latin families would be more receptive to relational diagnoses and that treatment effectiveness might be enhanced as a result. (See Chapter 11 for elaboration of this issue.)

On the other hand, the systemic assumption that behavior is contextually based may be met with resistance by Americans from an English tradition. These families value personal responsibility, independence, containment of affect, and greater emotional distance between themselves. How would such families respond to a relational diagnosis that contradicts such strong individualistic cultural traditions?

The Legal System

Systems thinking is based on specific assumptions. These include: (1) an individual's symptom represents familywide distress (Searight & Openlander, 1986); (2) because behavior is interdependent, it is not solely within the control of the individual (Nichols, 1984); (3) the family is not a group of individuals but an organic unit (Nichols, 1984); and (4) causality is best understood as a circular rather than as a linear process (Merkel, 1983).

Such assumptions contradict those of our legal system, which presumes individual responsibility. We do not hold systems legally responsible for the behavior of their members. How are we to resolve the ethical dilemma of upholding our legal standard of individual responsibility when there is substantial empirical evidence that behavior is contextually based, at least in some circumstances (Gottlieb & McDowell, in press; Searight & Merkel, 1991)?

One area of the law where relational diagnoses may be of significant value is that of child custody evaluation. When all members of the family system are evaluated, interactive diagnostic interpretations can be made that will help judges understand the personalities and responsibilities of all parties, reduce fault finding and oversimplified conclusions.

The Psychiatric Hospital

How can a systemically based relational diagnosis be used in a linear-based psychiatric hospital that insists on an individual diagnosis for each patient? Will using an individual diagnosis reinforce the family's notion that the hospitalized member is and should be the identified patient? What modifications would the hospital have to make in order to support a relational diagnosis?

If an individual family member is hospitalized and family therapy continues in the hospital setting, a comingled record has not been established in the hospital chart. How can the hospital respond to a release of information signed by the patient when the chart contains confidential information regarding other persons who did not sign a release and were not hospital patients (Gottlieb & Cooper, 1993)?

Recommendations

Therapists have an ethical obligation to understand the cultural background of the families they treat. It is important to consider the potential impact that a relational diagnosis will have on those whose cultural values are different from our own.

Systems orientations are based on assumptions that are contradictory to those of our legal system. Nevertheless, the use of relational diagnoses from a systemic perspective may be of great value, especially in the context of child custody evaluation, when employed by a mental health professional properly trained and experienced with the legal process.

Working from a systemic perspective within the hospital setting may enhance treatment effectiveness and reduce length of stay. Nevertheless, the hospital milieu may reinforce systemic dysfunction by focusing on an identified patient. The therapist must work against this notion and obtain the assistance of the hospital staff in doing so. If the therapist is to perform family therapy in the hospital, he or she must learn what procedures are needed in order for medical records to be released. Typically, the family should be informed that a release will be required of all who are competent and all who were seen in the hospital while the family member was there.

CONCLUSION

Why should we create a classification system of relational diagnoses when many will consider it an oxymoron? Focus on an individually based medical model leads to the loss of precious interactional data. A relational nosology is essential if we are to evaluate accurately and treat the interpersonal behavior we observe. Including relationships as diagnostic considerations expands traditional notions of psychopathology process producing a holistic and more realistic picture of the complexity of human interaction. Patient welfare will be improved by an enriched diagnostic process that yields a wider variety of treatment options.

Relational diagnoses will not and should not replace individual diagnoses. Rather, they represent a valuable augmentation to the process of diagnostic conceptualization with minimal additional risk. For those who are traditionally trained and/or individually oriented, the creation of relational diagnoses will contribute an additional perspective to their diagnostic armamentarium and may help them to think in a more contextually based manner. Systemically oriented practitioners, many of whom have eschewed diagnosis altogether, will benefit from being able to practice in a way that is more congruent with their theoretical orientation.

As I noted in the introduction, few ethical principles exist for the use of relational diagnoses at this time. Principles will be developed once a relational nosology is established and continues to evolve. Then the ethical dilemmas presented will be based on critical incidents in relational therapy. As this process occurs, a body of literature will develop to sharpen awareness of family dynamics, continuing the course charted by this volume.

REFERENCES

American Psychiatric Association. (1994). *Diagnostic and statistical manual of mental disorders* (4th ed.). Washington, DC: Author.

American Psychological Association. (1992). Ethical principles of psychologists and code of conduct. *American Psychologist, 47,* 1597–1611.

American Psychological Association. (1993). *Record keeping guidelines.* Washington, DC: Author.

Backer, T. E., & Richardson, D. (1989). Building bridges: Psychologists and family of the mentally ill. *American Psychologist, 44,* 546–550.

Barth, J. (1993). *It runs in my family: Overcoming the legacy of family illness.* New York: Brunner/Mazel.

Beauchamp, T. L., & Childress, J. F. (1983). *Principles of biomedical ethics.* New York: Oxford University Press.

Beavers, W. R. (1981). A systems model of family for family therapists. *Journal of Marital and Family Therapy, 7,* 299–307.

Boszormenyi-Nagy, I., & Krasner, B. (1980). Trust-based therapy: A contextual approach, *American Journal of Psychiatry, 137,* 767–775.

Boszormenyi-Nagy, I., & Spark, G. M. (1984). *Invisible loyalties.* New York: Brunner/Mazel.

Doherty, W. H., & Boss, P. G. (1991). Values and ethics in family therapy. In A. Gurman & D. Kniskern (Eds.), *Handbook of family therapy,* (vol. 2, pp. 606–637). New York: Brunner/Mazel.

Gottlieb, M. C. (1993a). Avoiding exploitive dual relationships. *Psychotherapy: Theory, research, practice and training, 30,* 41–48.

Gottlieb, M. C. (1993b). Co-mingling of patient records: What's a family psychologist to do? *The Family Psychologist, 9*, 19–20.

Gottlieb, M. C. (1995a). Ethical dilemmas for family psychologists and systems therapists: Change of format and live supervision. In R. H. Mikesell, D. Lusterman, & S. H. McDaniel (Eds.), *Integrating family therapy: Handbook of Family Psychology and Systems Theory* (pp. 561–570). Washington, DC: American Psychological Association.

Gottlieb, M. C. (1995b). Ethical issues in the treatment of families with chronically ill members. In S. McDaniel (Ed.), *Counseling families with chronic illness,* (pp. 69–84).

Gottlieb, M. C., & Cooper, C. (1990). Treating individuals and families together: Some ethical considerations. *The Family Psychologist, 6*, 10–11.

Gottlieb, M. C., & Cooper, C. (1993). Some ethical issues for systems oriented therapists in hospital settings. *Family Relations, 42*, 140–144.

Gottlieb, M. C., & McDowell, V. (1994, November). *Practical applications of family systems theory to child custody evaluations.* Paper presented at the annual meeting of the Texas Psychological Association, Houston.

Grosser, G., & Paul, N. (1964). Ethical issues in family group therapy. *American Journal of Orthopsychiatry, 34*, 875–884.

Haas, L. J., & Malouf, J. L. (1989). *Keeping up the good work: A practitioner's guide to mental health ethics.* Sarasota, FL: Professional Resource Exchange.

Hare-Mustin, R. T. (1978). A feminist approach to family therapy. *Family Process, 17*, 181–194.

Hines, P., & Hare-Mustin, R. (1978). Ethical concerns in family therapy. *Professional Psychology: Research and Practice, 9*, 165–171.

Hoffman, L. (1981). *Foundations of family therapy.* New York: Basic Books.

Holroyd, J. C., & Brodsky, A. M. (1977). Psychologists' attitudes and practices regarding erotic and nonerotic physical contact with patients. *American Psychologist, 32*, 893–899.

Karpel, M. (1980). Family secrets: I. Conceptual and ethical issues in the relational context. II. Ethical and practical considerations in therapeutic management. *Family Process, 19*, 295–306.

Keith-Spiegel, P., & Koocher, G. P. (1985). *Ethics in Psychology.* New York: Random House.

Kitchener, K. (1988). Dual role relationships: What makes them so problematic? *Journal of Counseling and Development, 67*, 217–221.

Lakin, M. (1994). Morality in group and family therapies: Multiperson therapies and the 1992 ethics code. *Professional Psychology: Research and Practice, 25*, 344–348.

Madanes, C. (1981). *Strategic family therapy.* San Francisco: Jossey-Bass.

Margolin, G. (1982). Ethical and legal considerations in marital and family therapy. *American Psychologist, 37*, 788–801.

Merkel, W. T. (1983). *Research implications of the new epistemologies.* Paper presented at the 41st annual conference of the American Association of Marriage and Family Therapy, Washington, DC.

Nichols, W. C. (1973). The field of marriage counseling: A brief overview. *The Family Coordinator, 22*, 3–13.

Nichols, W. C. (1984). *Family therapy: Concepts and methods.* New York: Gardner.

Olson, D. H., Sprenkle, D. H., & Russell, C. S. (1979). Circumplex model of marital and family systems: I. cohesion and adaptability dimensions, family types, and clinical applications. *Family Process, 18*, 3–28.

O'Shea, M., & Jessee, E. (1982). Ethical, value and professional conflicts in systems therapy. In L. L'Abate (Ed.), *Values, ethics, legalities and the family therapist* (pp. 1–22). Rockville, MD: Aspen Systems.

Packman, W. L., Cabot, M. G., & Bongar, B. (1994). Malpractice arising from negligent psychotherapy; Ethical, legal and clinical implications of Osheroff v. Chestnut Lodge. *Ethics and Behavior, 4,* 176–197.

Pittman, F. (1989). *Private lies.* New York: Norton.

Pope, K. S., & Bouhoutsos, J. C. (1986). *Sexual intimacy between therapists and patients.* New York: Praeger.

Rinella, V., & Goldstein, M. (1980). Family therapy with substance abusers: Legal considerations regarding confidentiality. *Journal of Marital and Family Therapy, 6,* 319–326.

Searight, H. R., & Merkel, W. T. (1991). Systems theory and its discontents: Clinical and ethical issues. *American Journal of Family Therapy, 19,* 19–31.

Searight, H. R., & Openlander, P. (1986). Assessment and treatment of social contexts: Toward an interactional therapy. *Journal of Social and Personal Relationships, 3,* 71–87.

Sell, J. M., Gottlieb, M. C., & Schoenfeld, L. S. (1986). Ethical considerations of social/romantic relationships with present and former clients. *Professional Psychology: Research and Practice, 17,* 504–508.

Selvini, M. P., Boscolo, L., Cecchin, G., & Prata, G. (1980). Hypothesizing-circularity-neutrality: Three guidelines for the conductor of the session. *Family Process, 19,* 3–12.

Stone, A. A. (1990). Law, science and psychiatric malpractice: A response to Klerman's indictment of psychoanalytic psychiatry. *American Journal of Psychiatry, 147,* 419–427.

Walker, L. E. (1984). *The battered woman syndrome.* New York: Springer.

Woody, J. D. (1990). Resolving ethical concerns in clinical practice; Toward a pragmatic model. *Journal of Marital and Family Therapy, 16,* 133–150.

CHAPTER 3

Problems Encountered in Reconciling Individual and Relational Diagnoses

WAYNE H. DENTON, MD, PhD

Interest in diagnosis has focused almost exclusively on the disorders of individuals despite the fact that family and relationship distress is the most common problem of people presenting for mental health Treatment (Veroff, Kulka, & Douvan, 1981). Attention to the diagnosis of relational problems is relatively recent and has come from different directions. Some investigators who are concerned primarily with individual disorders have turned toward an examination of relationships to better understand the individual disorder. Other professionals with a primary interest in relationships have tried to demonstrate the importance of relational functioning to individual health. These attempts at linkage have met with varied degrees of success. This chapter reviews some of the historical antecedents to our societal focus on the individual and the bias toward the individual in our official diagnostic systems. In addition, some of the major attempts to link individual and relational diagnoses as well as efforts at developing a separate nomenclature for relational diagnoses are addressed. The difficulties in attempting to link individual and relational disorders directly are discussed, and, finally, there is a call for more interactive approaches.

A HISTORICAL PERSPECTIVE

The Greek concept of "mind" as a powerful force that can create, abstract, and organize has been attributed to the pre-Socratic philosophers of the 6th and 5th centuries BC (Simon, 1978, pp. 159–160). These thinkers located the activity of the mind within the person. From the Latin word for mind sprang the word "mental," which came to refer to all matters "of or relating to mind." This began an enduring interest in the "mental" phenomenon of individuals in Western civilizations.

Individuals with "mental disturbances" (manifested by behavior considered abnormal) have inhabited the earth for as long as there have been people. While at different times they have aroused feelings of fear, humor, or pity, the unusual nature of their speech and actions have made them impossible to ignore. It is human nature to ask "why?" of such observed phenomenon that we do not understand. Historically there have been three basic explanations for these conditions: magic, the environment, or genetics.

The earliest view was that these unusual behaviors were the result of magic or the supernatural. It was typically believed that something had been " 'shot' into the body by a sorcerer or god . . ." (Alexander & Selesnick, 1966, p. 8). The magical/supernatural view continues to have its proponents today. For example, belief in voodoo is strong in Haiti (Campinha-Bacote, 1992), and some in our own society place more importance on the role of the supernatural in causal attributions for illness (Landrine & Klonoff, 1994). In the scientific community, however, the magical perspective has largely given way to other explanations of causality.

One view is that abnormal behavior is the result of forces outside of the individual (i.e., in the environment) acting on the mind. The other position is that such behavior is the result of forces within the individual but not part of the mind per se (e.g., genetics) acting on the mind. These are the two poles of the ever-present "nature versus nurture" debate. Formal attempts to tease out the contributions of nature and nurture date as far back as the thirteenth century (Kimble, 1993); the formal concept of "nature" and "nurture" has been traced to the sixteenth century (Teigen, 1984). Mulcaster wrote in 1582 regarding the child's natural endowment "Nature makes the boy toward; nurture sees him forward" (cf. Quick, 1929, p. 95) (that is, nature points the child while nurture moves the child forward).

The nature-nurture debate has impacted on most of the social sciences. Ironically, as Teigen (1984) points out, while Mulcaster's original intention seems to have been a demonstration of the harmony and interdependence of these two concepts, they have been used more commonly to describe an either/or dichotomy of attribution rather than a both/and inclusive interpretation.

Although family interactions often are perceived as a prominent part of "nurture," these relationships still are used to explain the abnormality in an individual person (nature/genetics). The "nature-nurture" debate is about how to explain peculiarities in individuals. The focus of interest is still a "mental" disturbance. Only its origins are explained differently.

BIAS TOWARD INDIVIDUAL DIAGNOSIS

This "mental" bias is reflected in the major diagnostic systems of mental disorders and/or conditions. Because the classifications are "mental" disorders, they are focused on individuals. This is clearly stated in the fourth edition of the *Diagnostic and Statistical Manual of Mental Disorders* (DSM-IV): "In DSM-IV, each of the mental disorders is conceptualized as a clinically significant behavioral or psychological syndrome or pattern that occurs *in an individual* . . . it must currently be considered a manifestation of a behavioral, psychological, or biological dysfunction *in the individual*" (American Psychiatric Association, 1994, pp. xxi–xxii).

The tenth revision of the *International Classification of Diseases* (ICD-10) is less specific in defining what "mental and behavioural disorders" mean. It explains that " 'disorder' is not an exact term, but . . . is used . . . to imply the existence of a clinically recognizable set of symptoms or behaviour associated in most cases with distress and with interference with personal functions" (World Health Organization, 1992, p. 5). The clear implication is still that these symptoms or behaviors have to do with an individual. Critical reviews of the current systems for diagnosis of mental disorders (e.g., Carson, 1991; Millon, 1991; Pichot, 1994) may disagree with all or part of the official classifications but do not question that the focus of the taxonomy should be *individuals*.

This focus on the individual is seen in nearly all alternative systems proposed to replace or supplement the official classificatory systems. Whether the focus is on classification of psychological distress in primary care settings (Goldberg, 1992), the seriously and persistently mentally ill (Hannah, 1993), substance abuse and mental disorders in the homeless (Struening, Padgett, Pittman, Cordova, & Jones, 1991), or for use in nursing care (O'Leary, 1991), the emphasis is on describing problems *within individuals.*

ATTEMPTS TO CORRELATE RELATIONAL AND INDIVIDUAL DISORDERS

Numerous attempts have been made to link specific relational disorders with specific individual disorders. There are several reasons for this. One is the hope that an understanding of family processes will assist in the prevention and treatment of individual disorders. As these conditions represent significant problems in and costs to our societies, every factor, including the family dynamics, has been explored in trying to understand them more completely.

Until recently not much value has been placed on relational problems and even less on relational diagnosis. Apart from marriage and family therapy training programs, most mental health training focuses on individual therapy. The developers of standard nomenclatures such as the DSM and ICD come nearly exclusively from an individual orientation. This is reflected in the diagnostic systems they produce and in their reluctance to include relational disorders in them. Family researchers might seek to increase the perceived value of their work by documenting how family interaction affects the development and course of individual problems. It seems reasonable to assume that if a relational condition can be shown to influence an individual disorder, the relational disorder might gain in importance by the connection.

There have probably been more efforts to link family processes with schizophrenia than with any other individual disorder. Some of these explanations will be chronicled in the next section as an example of the attempts to link individual and relational diagnoses.

Psychoanalytic theory began gaining prominence in the United States after Sigmund Freud delivered his famous series of lectures at Clark University in 1909. According to traditional psychoanalytic view, schizophrenia was the result of regression to a very primitive level of development (Cameron, 1963), to the extent that the person enters "a sort of dream world" (p. 615) where fantasy and reality can no longer be distinguished. Regardless of the validity of this untested assumption, it eventually became clear even to the most ardent devotees that psychoanalysis had little to offer in the treatment of schizophrenia.

Out of this failure, other ideas began to be considered. One focus was on family relationships. Some contributions along this line were made by neo-Freudian psychoanalysts. Fromm-Reichman's concept of the "schizophrenogenic mother" (1948) was one of the earliest attempts to show how family relationships affected the development of schizophrenia. Horney (1950) and Sullivan (1953) were other analysts who incorporated interpersonal ideas into theories of schizophrenia. These ideas, however, were primarily expansions of psychoanalytic theory. The focus was on how these familial influences shaped the processes developing within the given individual.

Groups of investigators interested in family processes began to take more unique approaches. Bateson and colleagues (Bateson, Jackson, Haley, & Weakland, 1956) broke with psychoanalytic theory by attempting to demonstrate that a specific and unique pattern of family communication (the "double bind") was associated with the development of schizophrenia in an individual.

They described "a communicational theory of the origin and nature of schizophrenia . . ." (Bateson et al., 1956, p. 251), using the concept of the double bind to explain the development of psychotic symptoms. They suggested that when the person who develops schizophrenia is presented repeatedly with a double bind, "it is better to shift and become somebody else, or shift and insist that he is somewhere else" (p. 255) and explained how double binds can result specifically in the paranoid, hebephrenic, and catatonic schizophrenic subtypes.

This then-novel approach to the understanding of families and schizophrenia produced much excitement and was one of the forerunners of the modern family systems movement (Guttman, 1991). In terms of linking a specific relational diagnosis with an individual diagnosis, it was not as successful. Evidence is lacking that double binds precede the development of schizophrenia or that their occurrence is unique in the lives of people with schizophrenia (Helmersen, 1983).

Bateson and colleagues were not the only family theorists during the 1950s and 1960s who tried to link specific patterns of family communication with schizophrenia in a family member. The concept of communication deviance was another attempt at such a reconciliation (Singer & Wynne, 1965a, 1965b). Communication deviance was defined as a situation in which a "listener is unable to construct a consistent visual image or a consistent construct from the speaker's words" (Singer et al., 1978, p. 500). Unlike the double-bind hypothesis, the measurements of communication deviance have proven able to distinguish families with a member having schizophrenia from those where no member has schizophrenia (Docherty, 1993; Miklowitz, 1994; Miklowitz & Stackman, 1992). However, communication deviance is apparently not *unique* to schizophrenia (Miklowitz et al., 1991).

More recently interest has focused on emotional expression in families with a member having schizophrenia. Brown, Birley, and Wing (1972) found that people with schizophrenia had a higher relapse rate if their parents were rated high on hostility, critical comments, and emotional overinvolvement, a constellation that has come to be known as "expressed emotion" (EE). These studies have been replicated (Vaughn & Leff, 1976; Vaughn et al., 1984), and the outcomes have been found to persist up to two years later (Falloon et al., 1985; Leff & Vaughn, 1981).

The related measure of Family Affective Style (AS) measures "the degree of criticism, intrusiveness, and/or guilt-inducing remarks parents make during an emotionally charged family discussion" (Doane & Diamond, 1994, p. 13). As with EE, it has been found that negative family AS is also a predictor of relapse in schizophrenia (Doane, Goldstein, Falloon, & Mintz, 1985).

However, it does not appear that either EE or AS can be directly or uniquely linked with schizophrenia. High EE also has been found to be associated with depression (Florin, Nostadt, Reck, Franzen, & Jenkins, 1992; Hooley, Orley, & Teasdale, 1986) while negative AS has been associated with bipolar disorder (Miklowitz et al., 1988). There is evidence that high EE also might be associated with relapse in medical conditions, such as diabetes (Koenigsberg, Klausner, Pelino, Rosnick, & Campbell, 1993).

The association of various other types of family distress with most of the other major individual mental disorders have been examined. Another individual disorder that has received much attention is depression. It has been found repeatedly that marital dissatisfaction has a significant association with depression (Beach, Jouriles, & O'Leary,

1985; Christian, O'Leary, & Vivian, 1994; Schmaling & Jacobson, 1990; Weissman, 1987) while having a partner in whom to confide can serve as a protection against depression (Brown & Harris, 1978). Depression and poor family functioning also are linked (Crowther, 1985; Keitner, Miller, & Epstein, 1986; Keitner, Miller, Epstein, Bishop, & Fruzzetti, 1987). In none of these cases, however, is there evidence that a specific and unique pattern of marital or family interaction is associated with the development of a course of depression.

The same situation exists for alcoholism. While there is an association between family interaction and the presence of alcohol dependence in one member (Bennett & LaBonte, 1993; Steinglass, 1980, 1981), it does not appear that a specific pattern of family interaction "causes" alcoholism.

To summarize, it seems clear after 40 years of family research that family interaction definitely has an association with the functioning of the individuals in a family. Conversely, it does not appear that any relational diagnosis is uniquely associated with a specific individual diagnosis. It is not possible to discuss "schizophrenic" or "depressed" families as families that always function and present in the same way.

THE SEARCH FOR DIRECT CAUSES

Although it might be convenient if individual mental disorders could be tied to specific relational disorders, clearly the interaction of relational and individual functioning is not so simple. Early family researchers (e.g., the Bateson group) may have been influenced by the "bacterial" model of disease in their attempts to understand the connection between relational and individual problems. This is explained further below.

The medical model arose in the early nineteenth century. Prior to that time, physical (as well as mental) disorders were attributed to magical or supernatural forces. Louis Pasteur, author of the "germ theory" of disease (Alexander & Selesnick, 1966), made one of the major contributions toward the birth of the medical model. Pasteur and other early microbiologists discovered that what came to be called the anthrax bacillus "caused" anthrax, that the tubercle bacillus "caused" consumption, the streptococcus "caused" puerperal fever, and so on (Wyngaarden, 1988) in a linear fashion (even though even here there are undeniable social factors at work, such as public sanitation).

Between 1935 and 1945, the introduction of antibiotics such as the sulfonamides and penicillin allowed many terrible diseases to be "cured" (Wyngaarden, 1988). Among these diseases are venereal diseases, which certainly have a relational component in their etiology. Given the dramatic, almost miraculous changes that these discoveries produced, it is not surprising that scientists and researchers set out to discover the "causes" of other major human afflictions so that a "cure" could be discovered for them as well.

Researchers soon turned toward the mental disorders. It was discovered that the "mental" disorder of general paresis (manifested by dementia and psychosis) was "caused" by syphilis (again transmitted by interpersonal sexual activity). Kraepelin (1904) and others hoped that the "cause" of other mental disorders would soon be discovered.

Unfortunately, further "causes" of mental and physical disorders generally were not unearthed. After infectious agents were discovered, the remaining medical conditions were not explained so simply or easily. This situation is perhaps best seen with cancer. After much search for its "cause," it is now recognized that there are many interacting (systemic) "causes" of cancer, and the search for a single "cancer bacillus" has been abandoned.

Much as early psychoanalysts sought to link specific intrapsychic conflicts to specific somatic illnesses, Bateson and colleagues were caught up (probably unaware) in a similar search for linear causality. Their theory was that a specific pattern of communication *caused* schizophrenia. They stated: "The psychosis seems, in part, a way of dealing with double bind situations to overcome their inhibiting and controlling effect" (Bateson et al., 1956, p. 261). (They do not indicate what the other parts might be.) Although this group made lasting contributions to the development of family therapy by focusing attention on patterns of familial interaction, they did not discover the "cause" of schizophrenia.

INTERACTIVE MODELS

Most practicing clinicians intuitively realize that the serious clinical problems individuals and families face are complex and the result of different types of forces, such as interactional, cultural, political, social, and physiological. It may primarily be academicians who can afford to be "purists."

It is more difficult to conceptualize circular interactions than linear ones, and a model is needed to help guide such thinking. Although not entirely satisfactory, the systemic model that has achieved the most acceptance in medicine is the "biopsychosocial" model. Engel (1980) turned to general systems theory as that best suited to provide "a conceptual framework within which both organized wholes and component parts can be studied" (p. 536). The biopsychosocial model conceptualizes nature as arranged on a hierarchical continuum ranging from molecules, through individuals, to families, to societies. While each system level interacts with those levels above and below it, each level also represents a "dynamic whole" in its own right (Engel, 1980).

A logical extension of this idea would be that each system level can have its own type of dysfunction. General systems theory (and the biopsychosocial model) maintains that dysfunction in one system level will impact the other system levels. However, for that impact to produce exactly the same result in every case would require that every system level have no heterogeneity. For example, suppose that an individual experiences a double bind in family communication. What the double-bind hypothesis failed to recognize is that there is more to a family than simply the fact that the members may convey double binds. Each family will have a host of strengths and weaknesses, which will in some ways distinguish it from other families that also might communicate in double binds. This hypothesis also ignored the fact that the individual on the receiving end of the double-bind message will have had a variety of learning experiences as well as a unique genetic makeup. Further, that individual will live in a specific community and culture that will be different from the ones in which other individuals who might experience communicational double binds reside. Thus, while coping with double-bind communication might be difficult and undesirable, it seems reasonable to assume that this type of interaction will affect different individuals differently and that all symptomatology has multiple causes, rather than only one.

RELATIONAL DISORDERS

Since each system level in the biopsychosocial model represents a dynamic whole, it is understandable that there would be unique methods of studying and understanding each level. Classifications of disorders specific to each system level are needed, and numerous proposals for family classifications have been offered. Relational (or individual) problems can be classified using a dimensional or a typological approach. Although there have been previous attempts at developing typologies of relational functioning (e.g., Fisher, 1977; Fleck, 1983), dimensional approaches have received greater attention. These have included the circumplex (Olson, 1986) and McMaster (Epstein, Bishop, Ryan, Miller, & Feitrer, 1993) models as well as the models of Reiss (1981) and Beavers (1989). These models continue to be important and deserving of further research, but none has been accepted universally by family therapists for clinical use.

There have been several proposals for including relational diagnoses within the DSM. The first published suggestion was to allow the modifier "With (or without) Significant Family Pathology" to be included with any of the diagnoses within the DSM (Bloch, 1977). A new diagnosis of "Adjustment Disorder with Disturbance of Family (or other primary interpersonal) Relationships" was proposed by Terkelsen (cited in Wynne, 1987). Others wanted to change the multiaxial system to create a place for relational assessment. It was suggested that Axis II (personality disorders) could place more emphasis on interpersonal features (Frances, Clarkin, & Perry, 1984) and that Axis IV (psychosocial stressors) (Wynne, 1987) or a new Axis VI (Frances, Clarkin, & Perry, 1984) could be used for relational assessment.

As the fourth edition of the DSM was being prepared, there were calls for relational diagnosis to be given a place in the manual (e.g., Group for the Advancement of Psychiatry [GAP] Committee on the Family, 1989). A multidisciplinary coalition of professionals interested in the family, under the title Coalition on Family Diagnosis, was organized partially to pressure for such inclusion (Kaslow, 1993). Both dimensional and typological approaches were considered, evaluated, and proposed by the coalition, as will be described.

ICD-10 (WHO, 1992) includes numerous codes for relational problems, such as "physical abuse" (Y07.01), "sexual abuse" (Y07.02), "problems in relationship with spouse or partner" (Z63.0), and "disruption of family by separation and divorce" (Z63.5). Unfortunately, these relational codes are scattered throughout the manual and thus cannot be utilized easily by clinicians. The GAP Committee on the Family (in press) used *ICD-10* codes to compile a typology of relational problems. With the support of both the GAP Committee and the Coalition on Family Diagnosis, some of these relational codes were included in the *DSM-IV Options Book* (American Psychiatric Association, 1991), which cataloged changes being considered for DSM-IV. Ultimately, however, the relational codes were not included in the DSM-IV.

A dimensional model for relational diagnosis was supported by the Coalition on Family Diagnosis and the GAP Committee. This dimensional model, the Global Assessment of Relational Functioning (GARF) scale, was included as an optional rating scale in DSM-IV (American Psychiatric Association, 1994). The GARF allows for an unidimensional assessment of relational functioning based on problem solving, organization, and emotional climate. It is simple enough for use by professionals who are not family therapists or even mental health care practitioners, such as emergency department and intake staff.

CONCLUSION

Relationship problems (such as violence, abuse, and other forms of family disruption) can have serious consequences regardless of whether anyone in the family has a diagnosable individual disorder. These relational problems are worthy of investigation in their own right. It is clear that relational disorders impact upon individuals and vice versa. The questions to be answered are to what extent, in what ways, and through what mechanisms. Further research is needed on the links between relational and individual functioning and disorders. It is hoped that the availability and further development of relational assessment instruments (e.g., the GARF) will further this goal.

The interaction between relational conflicts and individual medical disorders is also one that needs much further study. For example, the finding that marital discord is associated with a diminished level of immune function (Kiecolt-Glaser et al., 1987) points to a little-studied domain in which the understanding of relational disorders might help contribute to the understanding of general medical conditions.

We should not expect, however, that a specific relational disorder will necessarily be perfectly correlated with a specific individual disorder. The ultimate problem in such a reconciliation between relational and individual disorders is that they describe different and unique levels of organization of nature. There exist *interactions* between these levels, but the levels also function independently of each other. We should continue to try to understand these connective links but appreciate at the same time that it is unlikely that we will find simple, "linear" linkages between what goes on *within* and *between* people.

REFERENCES

Alexander, F. G., & Selesnick, S. T. (1966). *The history of psychiatry.* New York: Harper & Row.

American Psychiatric Association. (1991). *DSM-IV options book: Work in progress.* Washington, DC: Author.

American Psychiatric Association. (1994). *Diagnostic and statistical manual of mental disorders* (4th ed.). Washington, DC: Author.

Bateson, G., Jackson, D. D., Haley, J., & Weakland, J. (1956). Toward a theory of schizophrenia. *Behavioral Science, 1,* 251–264.

Beach, S. R. H., Jouriles, E. N., & O'Leary, K. D. (1985). Extramarital sex: Impact on depression and commitment in couples seeking marital therapy. *Journal of Sex and Marital Therapy, 11,* 99–108.

Beavers, W. R. (1989). Beavers systems model. In C. N. Ramsey (Ed.), *Family systems in medicine* (pp. 62–74). New York: Guilford.

Bennett, L. A., & LaBonte, M. (1993). Recent developments in alcoholism: Family systems. *Recent Developments in Alcoholism, 11,* 87–94.

Bloch, D. (1977). Notes and comments: DSM-III (continued). *Family Process, 16,* 511–512.

Brown, G. W., Birley, J. L.T., & Wing, J. K. (1972). Influence of family life on the course of schizophrenic disorders: A replication. *British Journal of Psychiatry, 121,* 241–258.

Brown, G. W., & Harris, T. (1978). *Social origins of depression: A study of psychiatric disorders in women.* New York: Free Press.

Cameron, N. (1963). *Personality development and psychopathology: A dynamic approach.* Boston: Houghton Mifflin.

Campinha-Bacote, J. (1992). Voodoo illness. *Perspectives in Psychiatric Care, 28,* 11–17.

Carson, R. C. (1991). Dilemmas in the pathway of the DSM-IV. *Journal of Abnormal Psychology, 100,* 302–307.

Christian, J. L., O'Leary, K. D., & Vivian, D. (1994). Depressive symptomatology in maritally discordant women and men: The role of individual and relationship variables. *Journal of Family Psychology, 8,* 32–42.

Crowther, J. H. (1985). The relationship between depression and marital maladjustment: A descriptive study. *Journal of Nervous and Mental Disease, 173,* 227–231.

Doane, J. A., & Diamond, D. (1994). *Affect and attachment in the family.* New York: Basic Books.

Doane, J. A., Goldstein, M. J., Falloon, I. R. H., & Mintz, J. (1985). Parental affective style and the treatment of schizophrenia: Predicting course of illness and social functioning. *Archives of General Psychiatry, 42,* 34–42.

Docherty, N. M. (1993). Communication deviance, attention, and schizotypy in parents of schizophrenic patients. *Journal of Nervous and Mental Disease, 181,* 750–756.

Engel, G. L. (1980). The clinical application of the biopsychosocial model. *American Journal of Psychiatry, 137,* 535–544.

Epstein, N. B., Bishop, D., Ryan, C., Miller, I., & Feitrer, G. I. (1993). The McMaster Model: View of healthy family functioning. In F. Walsh (Ed.), *Normal Family Processes* (2nd ed., pp. 138–160). New York: Guilford.

Falloon, I. R. H., Boyd, J. L., McGill, C. W., Williamson, M., Razani, J., Moss, H. B., Gilderman, A. M., & Simpson, G. M. (1985). Family management in the prevention of morbidity of schizophrenia: Clinical outcome of a two-year longitudinal study. *Archives of General Psychiatry, 42,* 887–896.

Fisher, L. (1977). On the classification of families. *Archives of General Psychiatry, 34,* 424–433.

Fleck, S. (1983). A holistic approach to family typology and the axes of DSM-III. *Archives of General Psychiatry, 40,* 901–906.

Florin, I., Nostadt, A., Reck, C., Franzen, U., & Jenkins, M. (1992). Expressed emotion in depressed patients and their partners. *Family Process, 31,* 163–174.

Frances, A., Clarkin, J. F., & Perry, S. (1984). DSM-III and family therapy. *American Journal of Psychiatry, 141,* 406–409.

Fromm-Reichmann, F. (1948). Notes on the development of treatment of schizophrenics by psychoanalytic psychotherapy. *Psychiatry, 11,* 263–273.

Goldberg, D. (1992). A classification of psychological distress for use in primary care settings. *Social Science and Medicine, 35,* 189–193.

Group for the Advancement of Psychiatry Committee on the Family. (1989). The challenge of relational diagnoses: Applying the biopsychosocial model in DSM-IV. *American Journal of Psychiatry, 146,* 1492–1494.

Group for the Advancement of Psychiatry Committee on the Family. (in press). *Beyond DSM-IV: A model for the classification and diagnosis of relational disorders. Psychiatric Services.*

Guttman, H. A. (1991). Systems theory, cybernetics, and epistemology. In A. S. Gurman & D. P. Kniskern (Eds.), *Handbook of Family Therapy* (vol. 2, pp. 41–62). New York: Brunner/Mazel.

Hannah, M. T. (1993). An empirical typology of seriously and persistently mentally ill patients using symptom and social functioning factors. *Journal of Clinical Psychology, 49,* 622–637.

Helmersen, P. (1983). *Family interaction and communication in psychopathology: An evaluation of recent perspectives.* London: Academic Press.

Hooley, J. M., Orley, J., & Teasdale, J. D. (1986). Levels of expressed emotion and relapse in depressed patients. *British Journal of Psychiatry, 148,* 642–647.

Horney, K. (1950). *Neurosis and human growth.* New York: Norton.

Kaslow, F. W. (1993). Relational diagnosis: An idea whose time has come? *Family Process, 32,* 249–253.

Keitner, G. I., Miller, I. W., & Epstein, N. B. (1986). The functioning of families in patients with major depression. *International Journal of Family Psychiatry, 7,* 11–15.

Keitner, G. I., Miller, I. W., Epstein, N. B., Bishop, D. S., & Fruzzetti, A. E. (1987). Family functioning and the course of major depression. *Comprehensive Psychiatry, 28,* 54–64.

Kiecolt-Glaser, J. K., Fisher, L. D., Ogrocki, P., Stout, J. C., Speicher, C. E., & Glaser, R. (1987). Marital quality, marital disruption, and immune function. *Psychosomatic Medicine, 49,* 13–34.

Kimble, G. A. (1993). Evolution of the nature-nurture issue in the history of psychology. In R. Plomin & G. E. McClearn (Eds.), *Nature, nurture, and psychology* (pp. 3–25). Washington, DC: American Psychological Association.

Koenigsberg, H. W., Klausner, E., Pelino, D., Rosnick, P., & Campbell, R. (1993). Extending the expressed emotion construct: EE and glucose control in insulin-dependent diabetes mellitus. *American Journal of Psychiatry, 150,* 1114–1115.

Kraepelin, E. (1904). *Lectures on clinical psychiatry,* rev. and ed. by T. Johnstone. London: Bailliere, Tindall & Cox.

Landrine, H., & Klonoff, E. A. (1994). Cultural diversity in causal attributions for illness: The role of the supernatural. *Journal of Behavioral Medicine, 17,* 181–193.

Leff, J., & Vaughn, C. (1981). The role of maintenance therapy and relatives' expressed emotion in relapse of schizophrenia: A two-year follow-up. *British Journal of Psychiatry, 139,* 102–104.

Miklowitz, D. J. (1994). Family risk indicators in schizophrenia. *Schizophrenia Bulletin, 20,* 137–149.

Miklowitz, D. J., Goldstein, M. J., Nuechterlein, K. H., Snyder, K. S., & Mintz, J. (1988). Family factors and the course of bipolar affective disorder. *Archives of General Psychiatry, 45,* 225–231.

Miklowitz, D. J., & Stackman, D. (1992). Communication deviance in families of schizophrenic and other psychiatric patients: Current state of the construct. *Progress in experimental personality and psychopathology research, 15,* 1–46.

Miklowitz, D. J., Velligan, D. I., Goldstein, M. J., Nuechterlein, K. H., Gitlin, M. J., Ranlett, G., & Doane, J. A. (1991). Communication deviance in families of schizophrenic and manic patients. *Journal of Abnormal Psychology, 100,* 163–173.

Millon, T. (1991). Classification in psychopathology: Rationale, alternatives, and standards. *Journal of Abnormal Psychology, 100,* 245–261.

O'Leary, C. (1991). A psychiatric patient classification system. *Nursing Management, 22,* 66.

Olson, D. H. (1986). Circumplex model VII: Validation studies and FACES III. *Family Process, 25,* 337–351.

Pichot, P. (1994). Nosological models in psychiatry. *British Journal of Psychiatry, 164,* 232–240.

Quick, R. H. (1929). *Essays on educational reformers.* London: Longmans, Green.

Reiss, D. (1981). *The family's construction of reality.* Cambridge, MA: Harvard University Press.

Schmaling, K. B., & Jacobson, N. S. (1990). Marital interaction and depression. *Journal of Abnormal Psychology, 99,* 229–236.

Singer, M. T., & Wynne, L. C. (1965a). Thought disorder and family relations of schizophrenics: 3. Methodology using projective techniques. *Archives of General Psychiatry, 12,* 187–200.

Singer, M. T., & Wynne, L. C. (1965b). Thought disorder and family relations of schizophrenics: 4. Results and implications. *Archives of General Psychiatry, 12,* 201–212.

Simon, B. (1978). *Mind and madness in ancient Greece.* Ithaca, NY: Cornell University Press.

Steinglass, P. (1980). A life history model of the alcoholic family. *Family Process, 19,* 211–226.

Steinglass, P. (1981). The alcoholic family at home: Patterns of interaction in dry, wet and transitional stages of alcoholism. *Archives of General Psychiatry, 8,* 441–470.

Struening, E., Padgett, D. K., Pittman, J., Cordova, P., & Jones, M. (1991). A typology based on measures of substance abuse and mental disorder. *Journal of Addictive Diseases, 11,* 99–117.

Sullivan, H. S. (1953). *The interpersonal theory of psychiatry.* New York: Norton.

Teigen, K. H. (1984). A note on the origin of the term "nature and nurture": Not Shakespeare and Galton, but Mulcaster. *Journal of the History of the Behavioral Sciences, 20,* 363–364.

Vaughn, C. E., & Leff, J. P. (1976). The influence of family and social factors on the course of psychiatric illness. *British Journal of Psychiatry, 129,* 125–137.

Vaughn, C. E., Snyder, K. S., Jones, S., Freeman, W., Falloon, I. R. H., & Lieberman, R. P. (1984). Family factors in schizophrenic relapse: Replication in California of British research on expressed emotion. *Archives of General Psychiatry, 41,* 1169–1177.

Veroff, J., Kulka, R. A., & Douvan, E. (1981). *Mental health in America: Patterns of help seeking from 1957 to 1976.* New York: Basic Books.

Weissman, M. M. (1987). Advances in psychiatric epidemiology: Rates and risks for major depression. *American Journal of Public Health, 77,* 445–451.

World Health Organization. (1992). *The ICD-10 classification of mental and behavioural disorders: Clinical descriptions and diagnostic guidelines.* Geneva, Switzerland: Author.

Wyngaarden, J. B. (1988). Medicine as a science. In J. B. Wyngaarden & L. H. Smith (Eds.), *Cecil Textbook of Medicine* (18th ed., pp. 5–7). Philadelphia: Harcourt Brace Jovanovich.

Wynne, L. C. (1987). A preliminary proposal for strengthening the multiaxial approach of DSM-III: Possible family-oriented revisions. In G. L. Tischler (Ed.), *Diagnosis and classification in psychiatry: A critical appraisal of DSM-III* (pp. 477–488). Cambridge: Cambridge University Press.

CHAPTER 4

The Relational Reimbursement Dilemma

TERENCE E. PATTERSON, EdD and DON-DAVID LUSTERMAN, PhD

The assumptions underlying the thesis of this chapter are that:

1. Practitioners of couple, family, and parent-child therapy frequently have a need to provide formal diagnosis for reimbursement, quality assurance, and other purposes.
2. V codes from the fourth edition of the *Diagnostic and Statistical Manual of Mental Disorders* (DSM-IV) (American Psychiatric Association, 1994) currently available for relational diagnosis are not acceptable to third-party payers.
3. A classification procedure that enables us to describe and code behavior easily is not so much antithetical to a systems description as it is incomplete.
4. Congruent assessment and procedural terminology with specification of functional outcomes are and will continue to be efficient and effective in meeting the needs of clients, practitioners, and the managed care insurance industry.
5. Specificity, directness, and assertiveness are essential skills in negotiating the current third-party payer system.

SCOPE OF THE DILEMMA: THE NEED FOR A PARADIGM SHIFT

Practitioners of relational therapies long have been familiar with the difficulties that arise when third parties are involved in reimbursement. Usually the problem begins with a notice of denial of claims for "parent-child," "couple," or "family" therapy, with the therapist blaming him- or herself for not having checked the coverage limitations of a client's policy. Investigation with the insurer often points to the discrepancy between the diagnosis and the procedural code, and at its simplest level, the problem may be resolved by explaining the type of treatment that actually occurred and its rationale.

Most often, however, the reason for denial is more difficult to pinpoint. In many instances, the insurer is uninformed about the nature of relational therapy. Other insurers do not grasp the concept of why a child would be included in conjoint sessions in the treatment of a parent-child problem, or why a parent would be included in therapy when there is a behavior problem in school. Even more difficult for the nonclinically trained

The authors wish to acknowledge the excellent research assistance provided by Tamara Monosoff, MA, of the Department of Counseling Psychology at the University of San Francisco in the preparation of this chapter.

managed care representative to comprehend can be the conjoint treatment of a couple for the depression of one spouse. Clinicians who are up-to-date on the professional literature that provides clear indications for conjoint treatment of various presenting problems should not overlook the low level of basic understanding on the part of insurance and managed care staff and the general public regarding relational diagnosis and treatment. The reality is that utilization review staff most often have little knowledge of, or training in, couple, family, or parent-child therapy.

In communicating with representatives of third-party payers about relational disorders, the provider must clearly and comprehensively specify: (1) the nature of the problem(s) being treated; (2) the methods that will be used to address the problem (in light of the research literature); and (3) functional outcomes that demonstrate resolution of the specified problems. In today's marketplace, the specified outcomes often must be achieved within the limits established by the insurer regarding cost, number of sessions, and the time that has elapsed between problem presentation and resolution. Many insurers and managed care organizations require that the presenting problem be specified in terms of a *Diagnostic and Statistical Manual of Mental Disorders-IV* (American Psychiatric Association, 1994) diagnosis; that the methodology be reported by the use of *Physicians Current Procedural Terminology* (CPT) (American Medical Association, 1993) codes; and that the outcome be described in terms of a diminution or resolution of the disorder. These limitations have imposed restrictions on the ability of clinicians to be creative, flexible, relevant, and cost effective in moving from problem presentation to resolution. Often therapy must be terminated prior to the attainment of patient and therapist treatment goals. Additionally, systemically oriented practitioners who accept third-party payments, have been compelled to regress from a contextual, functional paradigm back to an individual, medical one, with all of the accompanying theoretical and ethical compromises that this shift can require.

One common procedure has been for providers to submit V codes, which are not disorders in themselves but are the focus of treatment. Insurers view such codes as unreimbursable and logically question the necessity of treating a condition that is not, by definition, a mental disorder. One insurance company executive highlighted the issue as follows:

> A . . . problem is the willingness . . . to put an insurance-acceptable diagnosis on a condition that is not considered a covered diagnosis. Examples of this category include the problems of living: floundering marriages, trouble raising children . . . insurance was never intended to cover this type of 'non-psychiatric' problem. (Guillette, 1979, p. 32)

Similarly, insurers frequently also view adjustment disorders (e.g., reactions to divorce) as "stress reactions" to normal life events and often question these diagnoses. The remaining option, psychiatric diagnosis of an individual in the couple or family system, typically has been selected by many practitioners and combined with a relational procedure code as the basis of reimbursement for couple, family, or parent-child therapy. This method is acceptable to some insurers and poses no ethical dilemmas provided the individual diagnosis is accurate. It is often a simple matter to justify a diagnosis for an individual, although it is just as likely to be unnecessary and, in fact, questionable in light of the damaging effects it can have on the patient's acquisition of future insurance coverage. Packer (1988) has used the term "insurance diagnosis" (p. 19) to indicate the use of a DSM category that is not clinically warranted. Unquestionably, rationalizing the diagnosis of an individual in order to obtain reimbursement is antithetical to a systemic paradigm and can produce confusion on the part of clients and dissonance on the part of clinicians devising treatment plans. In practical terms, diagnosis of an index client can overemphasize the prominence of that individual's role in the systemic dysfunction, increase the focus on that person, and deemphasize a deleterious interactional process. Austad and Hoyt (1992) note the dissonance that is experienced by many health maintenance organization (HMO) practitioners: "that formal DSM-III-R diagnoses are often not as promising as they had assumed they would be in understanding and actually helping the patient" (p. 113). Kutchins and Kirk (1988) point to the unfulfilled expectation that DSM would closely connect diagnosis and treatment planning.

Denton (1989) indicates that additional harmful effects can accrue to clients because of the stigma attached to those who have been diagnosed with a mental disorder and who might be denied a job, refused insurance, or blocked in custody hearings or other legal proceedings. Certainly these adverse effects can apply to anyone who has been diagnosed, but "insurance diagnoses" should be particularly avoided for individuals being treated solely for relational problems. Kaslow (1991) emphatically underscores that "a relational schema is essential if the practice of family psychology is to be anchored in a standard classificatory system that is empirically tested and found to have high reliability and validity" (p. 4).

Individual practitioners, groups, and clinics that do not require the use of DSM and procedural codes, and enlightened insurers who have allowed the use of congruent diagnostic and procedural terminology have found such a policy to be efficient and clear for all concerned. An example of such congruence would be as follows: assessment: family dysfunction—moderate, enmeshment—chronic; treatment: weekly conjoint family therapy.

One argument set forth by the developers of DSM-IV in opposition to the establishment of Axis I relational disorders is that no evidence currently exists that relational disorders are discrete pathologies separate from individual disorders. Such opposition is consistent with the medical and psychodynamic model, which holds that psychopathology is internal to the individual. A lack of understanding, or perhaps a bias against the systemic model and against a patient unit of more than one person, is inherent in this view. An example that indicates the illogic of the position that all disorder resides solely within the individual is oppositional defiant disorder, a DSM-IV category that, according to the criteria, requires contextual, interactional assessment and treatment. (See Chapter 14.)

The Price of Mislabeling

Proponents of family therapy long have advocated its relative efficiency in comparison to other modalities of treatment. Separate treatment of those individuals who are affected primarily by dysfunctional systemic patterns decreases the impact that could occur with greater economy of time and effort were they seen in systemic therapy. Definitive research remains to be accomplished demonstrating the relative efficacy of systemic treatment (Gurman & Kniskern, 1992; Gurman, Kniskern, & Pinsof, 1986), and the need for such research becomes increasingly critical with the advent of managed care. Managed care will be discussed in detail later in this chapter, but additional comments are in order here in view of the inefficiency of individual treatment for dysfunction that is determined to be primarily systemic in nature.

A major guiding principle underlying managed care is the *accountability* of providers to consumers and payers. The concept of matching presenting problems and assessment protocols with interventions that are the most effective in the shortest period of time has gained new prominence. Given the reality that family therapy is generally of shorter duration than most forms of individual psychotherapy, family, couple, and parent-child interventions are all likely to demonstrate greater accountability and efficiency. As Coyne and Liddle (1992) state:

> Even if systems therapy were shown to be no more effective than individual therapy in terms of its impact on identified patients, would it nonetheless be more efficient in dealing with families in which there are multiple patients? If we construe therapy in terms of its impact on a social context, not just an individual, what are the implications of working only with an *individual* versus directly engaging significant others in the process of therapy? . . . the practical issue of the efficiency of systems therapy may prove to be an important one. (p. 46)

Indeed, with regard to the research linking individual symptoms such as depression to marital dysfunction (Fincham & Bradbury, 1993), the question can be raised as to whether the clinical and monetary costs of *not* providing conjoint therapy are prohibitive compared to offering individual therapy alone.

Congruence with Other Models

Systemic theorists, researchers, and practitioners typically are against diagnosis and labeling of individuals in relation to systemic treatment. Inherently, the systemic viewpoint, with its circular, correlational, interpersonal, contextual components, is opposed to the specification of dysfunction in a family, for example, as residing within, or *caused by,* an individual. The intervention may be targeted toward interactional sequences in addition to intrapsychic processes. The systemic perspective is congruent with models of psychotherapy that view assessment within an interactional framework and delineate therapy objectives on a functional basis.

The systemic and behavioral models, for example, share the view that dysfunction does not reside *within* the individual but rather is embedded in the social context. Behaviorism challenges the notion inherent in the medical model that abnormal behaviors are caused by mental disorders (Hickey, 1994). In their discussion of behavior therapy, Tanaka-Matsumi and Higgenbotham (1994) assert that a systemic approach including the factors of family, communication, and assimilation (among others) is essential in treatment across ethnic and cultural boundaries.

AN IDIOGRAPHIC ACCOUNT OF THE CURRENT DILEMMA

In the future, the careful use of diagnostic formulations and treatment codes will assume even greater importance as insurance companies and governmental authorities become increasingly interested in the cost efficiency of various means of treatment. Three manuals are essential for the clinician conducting assessment. The first, DSM, now in its fourth edition (APA, 1994), uses the coding system of the second manual, *International Statistical Classification of Diseases and Related Health Problems* (ICD-10), (World Health Organization [WHO], 1993), and sets up diagnostic criteria and a multiaxial system to describe disorders. The multiaxial assessment includes five axes: (1) Clinical Disorders and Other Conditions That May Be a Focus of Clinical Attention; (2) Personality Disorders and Mental Retardation; (3) General Medical Conditions; (4) Psychosocial and Environmental Problems; and (5) Global Assessment of Functioning. Scales included in addenda to the DSM-IV are important to the clinician who wishes to indicate clearly systemic and environmental aspects of the problem. The third important manual is the *Physicians Current Procedural Terminology, (CPT)* (AMA, 1993), which describes itself as "a systematic listing and coding of procedures and services performed by physicians," and includes a section entitled "Psychiatric Therapeutic Procedures" (pp. 555–558).

The term "bean-counting" is frequently heard in conversations with managed care administrators. This means the ability to track treatment efficacy by using computerized accounting procedures, without regard for human factors. The significance of this process is twofold. It probably will affect directly the provider's relationship with the company, because the company wants to know, in effect, if it is getting its "money's worth" from the provider. It is inevitable that, once the utilization review/management system is in place, the therapist will be judged by his or her record with insurers on such aspects as diagnostic categories used, average number of treatment sessions, and outcomes based on self-report by the client or therapist. The utilization review system and its categories will affect the future of systems treatment because ultimately this treatment will be judged not by formal outcome studies but by the statistics that will be collected by the health industry over time. Given this high probability, it is important that we accurately report what we are doing. Currently we make this information available through the use of the manuals just described.

At present, providers communicate with managed care companies about cases under treatment in a variety of ways. The simplest is the filing of an insurance form. At a minimum, this generally requires that the therapist name a specific patient, provide a diagnostic code for that patient from DSM, and specify (from CPT) a code that describes the means of therapy. Increasingly, the practitioner must receive prior authorization from some managed care companies. This involves some direct contact with an agent of the company, often a nontherapist, who gives approval for beginning therapy. Again, it is necessary to provide enough information to justify undertaking therapy and to indicate the tentative diagnosis and means of treatment.

A third type of contact between the provider and the insurer occurs when an Outpatient Treatment Report (OTR) is requested. The forms for such reports generally have followed the multiaxial assessment system from the revised third edition of the DSM (DSM-III-R), described earlier. As of this writing (December 1994), companies are retooling their reporting instruments to reflect DSM-IV changes.

One author (D-DL) has found it is wise to be thoroughly conversant with the DSM reporting system. Many argue that family psychology and systems thinking have tended to be opposed to diagnosis, because a diagnosis may be seen as the labeling of an individual member of the system rather than a description of the system. However, there is little doubt that most family therapists are directed toward the goal of behavioral change. Since the DSM purports to be antitheoretical, it hews very closely to behavioral descriptions of psychological disorders. It can be argued that a classification procedure that enables us to describe and code behavior easily is not so much antithetical to a systems description as it is incomplete. Aside from the philosophical issues, the simple fact is that third-party representatives tend to think in terms that fit well into their computerized operations, and these terms relate to numbers. We need to understand this so that we can communicate clearly and convincingly. It is also useful to think in diagnostic terms when a mediator or another outside arbitrator is used to help settle a dispute between an insurer and a provider.

A well-planned report can use the multiaxial DSM format and a relational treatment CPT code to fashion a description of the case in such a manner that the desirability of systems treatment can be clearly presented to third-party representatives in a language that is understandable to them and conforms to their expectations about reporting.

Let us imagine a sample telephone conversation in which the therapist's (TH) description is based on multiaxial thinking. We use "TPR" to refer to the third-party representative:

TH: I am calling to request an approval to undertake therapy with a 16-year-old boy who was referred today.

TPR: What is the reason for the referral?

TH: The boy is suffering from diabetes (Axis III: general medical conditions) and he is reported as being depressed (Axis I).

TPR: Has this been going on long?

TH: I spoke with the father this morning, and he indicated that the boy has become increasingly withdrawn over the past several months and has refused school on some days. (This is an Axis V issue.) He is also becoming more resistant to necessary medical treatment.

TPR: What would you estimate is his current Axis V?

TH: Probably around 60—and his axis DSM-IV looks like a 3.

TPR: Will he be seen more than once per week?

TH: I think at this point that one session per week will be enough, but there are complicating issues. The father indicated on the phone that he and his wife are at odds over how to proceed and that they have had difficulty in getting direction from the physician. For this reason, I am planning to meet with the family, so that I can directly attack these issues.

TPR: So the treatment will be family therapy?

TH: Yes, although there may be some individual sessions as well. I will also have some telephone contact with the physician.

The TPR general records such a conversation, so that when it is time for a next contact, the TPR's information includes the patient's name, the presenting problem, some indication of the intensity of the problem, the current stressors, and the mode of treatment. It probably also will include a note on the collateral contact with the physician. This simple example shows that, by speaking the TPR's language, a case can rapidly be made for a systemic treatment. The wise clinician also will make note of such conversations. Accurate notes will be important in follow-up telephone contacts with the TPR.

When a written Outpatient Treatment Review (OTR) is required, the clinician generally is asked to indicate the nature and severity of the problem, the mode and frequency of treatment, the expected duration of treatment, and a host of related questions. One managed care group, VBH (Value Behavioral Health), uses procedures that seem to be built for systemic reporting. In addition to requiring the usual multiaxial reporting information, the form asks for data about the patient's work, school, marital and familial situations, and social relationship system. It also requests information about concurrent therapeutic relationships, whether the person is involved in any form of self-help group, such as Alcoholics Anonymous, and whether the patient is on psychotropic medication. Such a reporting system enables the clinician to make a very clear case for systemic treatment. Further, VBH is amenable to treatment of multiple individuals by several providers when its appropriateness can be documented. An example would be a psychiatrist who is medicating a patient for depression, but feels that a family systems approach is also advisable and makes a referral to a family therapist.

There are times when an OTR may be questioned. This usually occurs in the form of a telephone call from the managed care group, requesting that the provider set aside some time for a telephone conference with a higher-level person within its organization, usually a psychiatrist. In such instances, it is important for the clinician to provide a clear message to the consultant indicating that he or she is on solid clinical and theoretical ground. Occasionally the provider must use his or her best assertive skills. The following case history serves as an example.

Case History

A family presented for treatment. The presenting problem was the depression of Mrs. O'Leary, a 62-year-old government employee. The treatment system included Mrs. O'Leary, her husband, a 65-year-old plumber, her 38-year-old son, a drug and alcohol abuser who had recently been released from prison, and his eight-year-old son, for whom the court had awarded Mrs. O'Leary custody. The child had no contact with the mother, who was a heavy drug user and had disappeared. Although Mrs. O'Leary's depressive symptoms were severe, she refused the possibility of medication. "I've always been a strong and successful person, and I've licked a lot of things—I'll lick this too." After the second OTR, in which the therapist indicated that there had been some important changes in the system and a moderate improvement in the patient's depression, the consulting psychiatrist called to question why the need for medication had not been pushed. The therapist reiterated his position, that it was important to respect the patient's self-definition, and further, that her depression, although severe, seemed certainly to be appropriate to the situation at hand. The psychiatrist agreed to hold off on a psychiatric consult until the next OTR.

About a week later, the patient received a letter from the insurer indicating that unless she had a psychiatric consultation, the therapy would be terminated. The woman was infuriated, as was the therapist. He immediately telephoned the consulting psychiatrist and told him in the clearest possible terms that this was an undue interference in the patient's life and in the therapy, not to mention that it completely contradicted the agreement made only a week earlier. The psychiatrist apologized for the "error" and rescinded the demand for a consult. The therapy was successfully concluded.

In the attempt to report systemic treatment in a clear and compelling manner, the addition of a new assessment procedure may prove helpful. Those familiar with the DSM-III are aware of the Axis V Global Assessment of Functioning Scale (GAF). A new scale that is relational in nature has been provided in the DSM-IV, although it does not appear in the Desk Reference to the DSM-IV that most clinicians use. This new scale, called the Global Assessment of Relational Functioning (GARF) Scale, is included under the heading of "Critical Sets and Axes Provided for Further Study" (AMA, 1994). It would be useful for all systems-oriented clinicians to familiarize themselves with this scale and to include it routinely in their reports as an addition to the GAF evaluation. This will serve as another indicator, along with the use of the proper CPT, to insure that the insurance industry becomes increasingly conscious of what we are doing in relational assessment and treatment, and why we are doing it.

At times one is met with a point-blank refusal to accept systemic treatment. Author D-DL has found it useful to compose a letter to the president of the insurance company, documenting his attempts to discuss this with lower-echelon personnel and then making a clear case for family therapy as a treatment modality. The following letter achieved the desired result.

Mr. XXX XXXXXX, President
XXXX XXXX Incorporated

Dear Mr. XXXXXX:

I am writing you concerning the approach your company is taking toward the treatment of patients requiring psychotherapy using the modality of family therapy. Let me begin by introducing myself. I am a psychologist who is a Diplomate of the American Board of Professional Psychology (specialization in Family). I have been a provider for your company for many years. Until recently, your mental health insurance form asked whether family members were included in treatment. When such was the case, I always so indicated, and included a brief rationale for the inclusion of family members. Some time last year, a new form was introduced, requiring a service code, including a family therapy category. At the time I was seeing an adolescent, sometimes alone and sometimes in a session including the family, because of severe family pathology. I so indicated on the new form, and received a full reimbursement of $30 per family session, as opposed to the $75 reimbursement for the individual meetings. Payment was received on 07/10/92. The payment seemed irrational to me, since the time-frame for the family sessions was identical to the individual meeting.

No statement accompanied this new billing system, so I called our local representative for clarification. He knew nothing of the new form or the reimbursement system, and I was given a New York number to call. In the end, I made a total of seven calls, and received no clear rationale, and many different explanations, including the thought that the payment was simply an error. I finally spoke with a young woman in the central office, I believe, who introduced herself only as Kirsten. She assured me that the $30 reimbursement was per each family member included in the session. I pointed out the irrationality of this, indicating that this meant that if there were six identifiably troubled members of this family (as there indeed were) the total fee for 45 minutes of family therapy would be $180. She assured me that this was indeed the case.

Feeling uncomfortable with the reliability of this information, I once again requested a policy statement and a written confirmation of our oral understanding. At that point I was told I should await a letter from the legal department. This shocked me, since a thoroughly ethical request for clarification appeared to be turning into an adversarial proceeding. However, such a confirmation never arrived, and a new spate of phone calls eventually resulted in a letter from Ms. XXX (copy enclosed, dated 9/14/92). At that time I contacted Mr. XXXXX (copy of his eventual reply, dated 12/3/93), following innumerable telephone calls and evasive responses as the matter was "looked into" over many months. Mr. XXXXX mentions in his reply a "contract," but I have never received a contract specifying anything whatsoever about a family therapy rate. In fact, by asking on your prior form whether family members would be included and then reimbursing me for many patients under the previous form, your company was indicating that family therapy was reimbursable at the same rate as individual therapy.

I am writing to you to inform you that family therapy is a highly recognized modality of treatment, in fact, one that frequently produces better, faster, and more economical results. It is a particularly effective modality when more than one member of a family is clinically disturbed. Further, many major insurance companies acknowledge this by a clearly stated policy of reimbursement. Among these are the Empire Blues, Metropolitan, and Champus. I would be more than happy to provide you with an extensive review of the literature concerning the modality of family therapy.

As a long-time provider, I would appreciate a response to this letter, and would welcome dialogue between appropriate policy setters at your company and members of the mental health community who are knowledgeable researchers and practitioners of family therapy.

As is evident from these examples, the policies (or lack of them) among and within insurers for reimbursement of systemic therapy are inconsistent and variable. Providers have the opportunity to be both ethical and legal by providing DSM codes for individuals and CPT codes for relational procedures, although numerous resubmissions and clarification may be necessary. In some instances, the theoretical congruence between systemic treatment and individual diagnosis remains questionable.

Confidentiality Issues

One major change associated with managed care is the insistence that the provider reveal information that previously has been considered confidential. Because of this development, it is important to indicate to patients at the outset of treatment that in order to obtain reimbursement, the provider will be required to divulge information to the insurer. When patients ask how this information will be used, the provider may state that while the insurer indicates that the information is used only to verify that the treatment is covered and for quality control, there is no guarantee as to how the information actually will be used. For example, despite initiatives under national health care reform concerning preexisting conditions, it remains possible that treatment information will be listed in a national medical database, possibly jeopardizing future insurability. Many practitioners make a note in their case records to indicate that they have informed their clients of these conditions; others require a signed formal release. The therapist also should keep notes on the nature and dates of every form submitted, and sign a statement indicating that all information is accurate and truthful. Given the multiple procedures and potential consequences involved in submitting claims, some clients prefer to pay out of pocket for psychotherapy. Most, however, accept these conditions.

RELATIONAL ASSESSMENT, TREATMENT, AND REIMBURSEMENT UNDER A UTOPIAN SYSTEM: HOW THEY WOULD LOOK

The leap from current procedures to one that would be efficient and integral with systemic theory and practice is not a great one. The efforts of groups such as the Coalition on Family Diagnosis[1] and others have provided models that would meet the needs of both clients and practitioners of relational therapy and would improve reimbursement procedures with insurers substantially.

Some insurers feel it is difficult to make a legal argument that benefits should be mandated for family therapy because individuals, not families, are the primary beneficiaries of coverage. For example, the largest private medical insurer in Massachusetts is Blue Cross/Blue Shield (BC/BS), which has an outpatient maximum of $500 per year

---

[1] A national organization established in 1988, consisting of 15 major mental health organizations, for the purpose of establishing relational disorders as major categories in DSM-IV. The coalition is described in Chapter 1.

for mental health services. White and Shields (1991) cite an example in which Massachusetts BC/BS was barred from prohibiting family therapy. BC/BS alleged that policyholders were trying to cover family therapy by "looping" claims—submitting for multiple individual mental health session within the same family when they actually had been seen conjointly. A rare model for reimbursement is the Harvard Community Health Plan (HCHP), in which each member is entitled to 20 outpatient sessions per year, and family and couple therapy is encouraged. Families may "loop" their claims to provide sequential coverage for more than 20 sessions on a graduated payment basis. Although this system works well in an HMO, it would have to be revised in a preferred provider organization (PPO) or for general indemnity coverage by a group insurer (American Psychiatric Association memorandum, February 3, 1992). Another effective system is that of Value Behavioral Health (VBH), mentioned earlier in this chapter.

The following approach, while not conducive to relational treatment, is suggested by Sharfstein and Goldman (1989):

> if office visits lasted only 20–30 minutes, this would increase the physician's hourly reimbursement. It would also increase access to care and might increase the volume of care when coupled with a policy of placing no special dollar or visit limits on office visits for the medical management of patients with mental disorders. In the effort to control costs, an office visit for medical management could be limited to 20 or 30 minutes, which would further discourage gaming. (p. 348)

Gurman and Kniskern (1992) argue for a flexible format that is highly conducive to family therapy:

> The "format" of therapy, defined as who is or should be present, will be more varied. Thus, family therapists will with the same clinical case find themselves moving about, for example, from an initial behavioral parent training arrangement with the parents of a noncompliant child to a brief series of individual sessions with each parent, in which continuing family of origin issues are explored, only to return to conjoint couples therapy in an effort to enhance marital intimacy. (p. 66)

In an ideal system, the acceptance of current V codes (Partner Relational Problem, Parent-Child Relational Problem) as Axis I disorders, and the addition of other relational disorders (e.g., Parental Inadequate Discipline) on Axis I would establish the primacy of relational disorders and allow them to be paired appropriately with relational procedural codes. This would not only allow for clarity and congruence within a systemic context but would permit reimbursement without having to designate an index client with an individual diagnosis. To date, the only improvement upon the relegation of relational disorders to V codes has been the addition of the Global Assessment of Relational Function (GARF) on Axis V in DSM-IV (Denton, 1993).

A utopian diagnostic classification scheme would sidestep the debate over causality that commonly exists when both individual and relational disorders are present. For example, the research of Fincham and Bradbury (1993) examines the presence of depression in partners (particularly women) in troubled marriages. The question of whether the depression or the marital distress came first is an empirical one, and the authors argue that the treatment of choice is often couples' therapy. Kaslow and Racusin (1990) argue for an integrated approach involving a systemic approach to the treatment of depressed children. Current reimbursement procedures require that the depression of the individual be diagnosed on Axis I. The chosen treatment is frequently antidepressant medication and/or individual psychotherapy. Such treatment often occurs contrary to current research indicating that conjoint marital treatment may be substantially more effective in the treatment of depression (Jacobson, Fruzzetti, Dobson, & Whisman, 1993; Johnston & Levis, 1987). In a study by Beach and O'Leary (1993):

> Marital relationship variables were found to be predictive of later depressive symptomatology for all spouses (241 couples), but a chronically dysphoric subsample was found to be more reactive to changes in marital adjustment. Results support the hypothesis that those who are chronically dysphoric are more vulnerable to stresses within the marital relationship. (p. 407)

Therefore, depression in couples would more likely be reduced by conjoint rather than individual therapy because of the need to address the interaction and communication between the couple in treating the depression. If the marital problem is the primary diagnosis and focus of treatment, greater clarity, consistency, and effectiveness (financial and clinical) may result. The systemic model typically emphasizes variables that correlate in treatment and research, rather than one problem causing another. In true systemic fashion, relational therapies are designed to set into motion feedback loops that address both marital and depressive disorders that reinforce each other in a closed system.

One of the most compelling arguments in the managed care debate today is that consumers should have the freedom to choose providers who will assist them in deciding on the most effective mode of treatment, primarily on a *clinical* rather than an administrative basis. In an ideal system, individuals, families, and couples would seek the services of a competent clinician who would assist them in: (1) determining whether individual or relational therapy or a combination of both is indicated; (2) establishing a primary diagnosis, either relational or individual; (3) providing information to the insurer, to include a primary diagnosis with a congruent procedural code, approximate number of sessions, and desired outcomes in operational terms; and (4) initiating treatment, whether with the primary clinician or with another specialist. Periodic two-way communication would occur between the insurer and the provider, with reimbursement based on congruent treatment of the actual primary diagnosis within a range of sessions appropriate to the nature and severity of the problem.

Under the current system, as described earlier, clinicians are required to combined the systemic model with the medical model, and consumers of services are limited to utilizing providers who are willing to follow an individual model of diagnosing and treating psychopathology. Treatment and reimbursement often are limited to paradigms and modalities indicated by the diagnosis of an individual, whether it is accurately supported by current scientific data or not. This system poses more of a dilemma for some clinicians than others; for example, those with a theoretical orientation that incorporates the concept of pathology residing within the individual find less dissonance than those who are purely systemic or behavioral. Providers must determine whether their approach to practice allows for incorporation of the DSM conceptualizations into their chosen theories and methods.

REALITIES AND ROUTINES: CAN WE LIVE WITH A NEW SYSTEM?

New ways always entail giving up some comfortable, familiar ones. What would these involve for psychologists, psychiatrists, clinical social workers, and marriage and family therapists? First would be some "betrayal," as it would be viewed by some, of the medical model. Burrell (1987) states that "when therapists accept health insurance as payment for psychotherapy they are defining their clients' problems and their actions as medical or quasi-medical in nature and support the concepts and institutions of the medical view" (p. 66). Therefore, the shift from the commitment to psychopathology inherent in the individual would be a major paradigm shift. It might at times involve a specific therapist not treating an individual whose depression is determined to be interactionally based when individual therapy would be contraindicated. This could entail the need for further training to learn how to intervene in relational disorders. It also might mean not being accepted by a preferred provider organization or health maintenance organization that does not reimburse for relational therapy. Adherence to such beliefs and methods can alienate therapists from medical-model colleagues.

Second, practitioners may have to learn to understand and live with capitations (usually involving a fixed fee per client regardless of actual treatment time). If the assumptions outlined earlier in this chapter regarding the primacy and efficiency of systemic models are applicable, then systems therapy may be easily integrated into the capitation system currently being promoted within managed care. For example, if insured employee Wilson presents with stress symptoms, her spouse has an eating disorder, and their preschooler has an attention deficit disorder, the clinician treating this family may determine that systemic treatment employing various modalities and combinations of individuals may be the most clinically effective, cost-beneficial method. In other words, seeing three individuals for an average of 12 sessions each at $100 per session (= $3,600) may be less effective and financially prohibitive compared to 18 conjoint sessions ($1,800) and perhaps some educational workshops. The likelihood of a "cap" on mental health treatment of the family of an insured under managed care may indeed dictate such an arrangement. According to Combrinck-Graham (1994), "The problem is that both mental health professionals and patients have not been attentive to cost issues" (p. 22). The premise here is that the DSM is not flexible enough to include nonmedical model forms of dysfunction, and insurers usually are not flexible enough to include multiple modalities of treatment. A paradigm shift to a new system of diagnosis and reimbursement would correct this discrepancy.

Although there was very limited success in having relational issues included in the DSM-IV (American Psychiatric Association, 1994)—the GARF is the main item—the effort must continue so that the primacy of these essential issues is realized. A shift to a relational paradigm as the basis for reimbursement may parallel the recent experience of health care reform: Only after much resistance and nearly universal acknowledgment that some change was needed have those accustomed to the current system begun to alter their ways of doing business, and thus practitioners have begun adapting to new forms of mental health service delivery. Whether similar entrenched resistance will apply to relational reimbursement may depend in large part on whether practitioners experience sufficient dissonance within the current system to actively seek and support the establishment of relational diagnoses as primary disorders.

REFERENCES

American Medical Association. (1993). *Physicians current procedural terminology.* Chicago: Department of Coding and Nomenclature.

American Psychiatric Association. (1987). *Diagnostic and statistical manual of mental disorders* (3rd ed.). Washington, DC: Author.

American Psychiatric Association. (1994). *Diagnostic and statistical manual of mental disorders* (4th ed.). Washington, DC: Author.

Austad, C. S., & Hoyt, M. F. (1992). The managed care movement and the future of psychotherapy. *Psychotherapy, 29*(1), 109–117.

Beach, S. R., & O'Leary, K. D. (1993). Marital discord and dysphoria: For whom does the marital relationship predict depressive symptomatology? *Journal of Social and Personal Relationships, 10*(3), 405–420.

Burrell, M. (1987). Psychotherapy and the medical model: The hypocrisy of health insurance. *Journal of Contemporary Psychotherapy, 17*(1), 60–67.

Combrinck-Graham, L. (1994). Managed care for marriage and family therapists. *Family Therapy News, 24*(2), 22.

Coyne, J. C., & Liddle, H. A. (1992). The future of systems therapy: Shedding myths and facing opportunities. *Psychotherapy, 29*(1), 44–50.

Denton, W. (1989). DSM-III-R and the family therapist: Ethical considerations. *Journal of Marital and Family Therapy, 15*(4), 367–377.

Denton, W. (1993, December). Assessment of relational functioning to be optional in DSM-IV. *Family Therapy News, 23*(12), 28.

Fincham, F. D., & Bradbury, T. N. (1993). Marital satisfaction, depression, and attributions: A longitudinal analysis. *Journal of Personality and Social Psychology, 64*(3), 442–452.

Guillette, W. (1979). Is psychotherapy insurable? *National Association of Private Psychiatric Hospitals Journal, 9,* 30–32.

Gurman, A. S., & Kniskern, D. P. (1992). The future of marital and family therapy. *Psychotherapy, 29*(1), 65–71.

Gurman, A. S., Kniskern, D. P., & Pinsof, W. M. (1986). Research on the process and outcome of marital and family therapy. In S. L. Garfield & A. E. Bergin (Eds.), *Handbook of psychotherapy and behavior change* (3rd ed., pp. 565–624). New York: Wiley.

Hickey, P. (1994). Resistance to behaviorism. *The Behavior Therapist, 17*(7), 150–152.

Jacobson, N. S., Fruzzetti, A. E., Dobson, K., & Whisman, M. (1993). Couple therapy as a treatment for depression: The effects of relationship quality and therapy on depression relapse. *Journal of Counseling and Clinical Psychology, 61*(3), 516–519.

Johnston, T. B., & Levis, M. (1987). Treatment of depression in a couple with systematic homework assignments. In L. L'Abate (Ed.), *Family psychology II: Theory, therapy, enrichment, and training* (pp. 167–178). Lanham, MD: University Press of America.

Kaslow, F. (1991). Organization and development of family psychology in the United States. *Family Therapy, 18*(1), 1–8.

Kaslow, N. J., & Racusin, G. R. (1990). Depressed children and their families: An integrationist approach. In *Voices in family psychology* (vol. 2). Newbury Park, CA: Sage Publications.

Kutchins, H., & Kirk, S. (1988). The business of diagnosis: DSM-III and clinical social work. *Social Work, 33*(3), 215–220.

Packer, P. (1988, October 3). Let's put a stop to the "insurance diagnosis." *Medical Economics,* 19–28.

Sharfstein, S. S., & Goldman, H. (1989). Financing the medical management of mental disorders. *American Journal of Psychiatry, 146*(3), 345–349.

Tanaka-Matsumi, J., & Higgenbotham, H. N. (1994). Clinical application of behavior therapy across ethnic and cultural boundaries. *The Behavior Therapist, 17*(6), 123–126.

White, K., & Shields, J. (1991). Conversion of inpatient mental health benefits to outpatient benefits. *Hospital and Community Psychiatry, 42*(6), 570–572.

World Health Organization. (1993). International classification of diseases (ICD-10). Geneva: Author.

CHAPTER 5

Clinical Assessment and Treatment Interventions Using the Family Circumplex Model

DAVID H. OLSON, PhD

A major issue in the fields of marital and family therapy centers around the advantages and limitations of doing assessment. While assessment also has been a controversial topic in both psychology and psychiatry, it becomes a more challenging issue today for family therapists. Table 5.1 presents a number of reasons for doing and not doing systematic assessment. Since many of these issues are self-explanatory, they are merely listed. While the first list of reasons for not doing assessment are presented rather simplistically, they actually are important issues family therapists have raised about family assessment.

The Circumplex Model of Marital and Family Systems was developed in an attempt to bridge the gap that typically exists among research, theory, and practice (Olson, Russell,

Table 5.1   Reasons for Doing and Not Doing Assessment

Top Ten Reasons for Not Doing Assessment (*à la* David Letterman)
  1. Assessment only confuses me.
  2. Assessment interferes with my intuitive instincts.
  3. Constructionists would feel that we are deconstructing.
  4. Assessment prevents me from seeing the truth.
  5. Assessment does not pay my bills.
  6. Assessment only raises new issues.
  7. Assessment represents too positivistic an approach.
  8. Who really wants to know anyway?
  9. Assessment is too much work.
 10. Assessment is needed only by novices.

Ten Reasons for Doing Assessment
  1. You cannot not do assessment.
  2. Assessment is a process, not an outcome.
  3. Assessment can identify strengths rather than only problems.
  4. Client and therapist can share a common language.
  5. Assessment can provide a comprehensive picture of the system.
  6. Assessment can generate dialogue on relevant issues.
  7. Assessment can help the therapist and client connect.
  8. Assessment can be therapeutic and empowering.
  9. Assessment can save time and increase effectiveness.
 10. Outcome-based assessment can identify the most effective and efficient interventions.

& Sprenkle, 1989). The Circumplex Model is particularly useful as a "relational diagnosis" tool because it is system focused and integrates three dimensions that have been considered highly relevant in a variety of family theory models and family therapy approaches: *Family cohesion, flexibility,* and *communication.* (See Table 5.2.) These three dimensions emerged from a conceptual clustering of over 50 concepts developed to describe marital and family dynamics. Although some of these concepts have been used for decades (e.g., power and roles), many of the concepts such as pseudomutuality, double binds, have been developed more recently by individuals observing problem families from a general systems perspective.

A variety of other theoretical models have focused independently on variables related to the cohesion, flexibility, and communication dimensions. Most of these models have been developed in the last ten years by individuals who utilize a family systems perspective. Support regarding the value and importance of these three dimensions is evidenced in the fact that these theorists have concluded independently that these dimensions were critical for understanding and treating marital and family systems.

Table 5.2 summarizes the work of 11 theorists who have worked on describing marital and family systems. General systems theory has strongly influenced most recent theorizing about family dynamics and intervention. Recent work has focused on describing both clinical and nonclinical families or has been concerned with clinical intervention with families.

MARITAL AND FAMILY COHESION (TOGETHERNESS)

Family cohesion is defined as *the emotional bonding that family members have toward one another.* Within the Circumplex Model, some of the specific concepts or variables that can be used to diagnose and measure the family cohesion dimensions are: *emotional bonding, boundaries, coalitions, time, space, friends, decision making* and *interests and recreation.* (See the Clinical Rating Scale in Appendixes 5A–C for how each concept is assessed.)

There are four levels of cohesion, ranging from *disengaged* (very low), to *separated* (low to moderate), *connected* (moderate to high), to *enmeshed* (very high). (See Figure 5.1.) It is hypothesized that the central levels of cohesion (separated and connected)

Table 5.2   Theoretical Models Using Cohesion, Adaptability, and Communication

	Cohesion	Flexibility	Communication
Beavers & Hampson (1990)	Stylistic dimension	Adaptability	Affect
Benjamin (1977)	Affiliation	Interdependence	
Epstein, Bishop et al. (1993)	Affective involvement	Behavior control	Communication
		Problem solving	Affective responsiveness
French & Guidera (1974)		Capacity to change	
		Power	
Gottman (1994)	Validation	Contrasting	
Kantor & Lehr (1975)	Affect	Power	
Leary (1975)	Affection	Dominance	
	Hostility	Submission	
Leff & Vaughn (1985)	Distance	Problem solving	
Parsons & Bales (1955)	Expressive role	Instrumental role	
Reiss (1981)	Coordination	Closure	

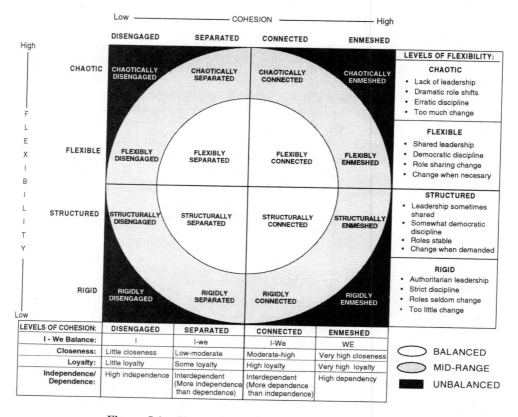

Figure 5.1 Circumplex Model: Couple and family map.

make for optimal family functioning. The extremes (disengaged or enmeshed) are generally seen as problematic.

In the model's balanced area (separated and connected), individuals are able to experience and balance these two extremes and also are able to be both independent from and connected to their families. Many couples and families that go for therapy often fall into one of the extremes. When cohesion levels are very high (enmeshed systems), there is too much consensus within the family and too little independence. At the other extreme (disengaged systems), family members "do their own thing," with limited attachment or commitment to their family.

Balanced couple and family systems (separated and connected types) tend to be more functional. More specifically, a *separated relationship* has some emotional separateness, but it is not as extreme as the disengaged system. While time apart is more important, there is some time together, some joint decision making and marital support. Activities and interests generally are separate but a few are shared. A *connected relationship* has emotional closeness and loyalty to the relationship. Time together is more important than time alone. There is an emphasis on togetherness. There are separate friends, but also friends shared by the couple. Shared interests are common with some separate activities.

Conversely, unbalanced levels of cohesion are at extremes (very low or very high). A *disengaged relationship* often has extreme emotional separateness. There is little involvement among family members, and there is a great deal of personal separateness and independence. Individuals often do their own thing; separate time, space, and interests predominate; and members are unable to turn to one another for support and problem-solving. In the *enmeshed relationship,* there is an extreme amount of emotional closeness, and loyalty is demanded. Individuals are very dependent on each other and reactive to one another. There is a lack of personal separateness, and little private space is permitted. The energy of the individuals is mainly focused inside the family and there are few outside individual friends or interests.

Based on the Circumplex Model, very high levels of cohesion (enmeshed) and very low levels of cohesion (disengaged) might be problematic for individual and relationship development in the long run. On the other hand, relationships having moderate scores (separated and connected) are able to balance being alone versus together in a more functional way. Although there is no absolute best level for any relationship, some may have problems if they function at either extreme of the model (disengaged and enmeshed) for too long.

MARITAL AND FAMILY FLEXIBILITY

Family flexibility is the amount of *change in a family's leadership, role relationships, and relationship rules.* The specific concepts include: *leadership* (control, discipline), *negotiation styles, role relationships,* and *relationship rules.* (See the Clinical Rating Scale in Appendixes 5A–C for how each concept is assessed.)

The four levels of flexibility range from *rigid* (very low), to *structured* (low to moderate), to *flexible* (moderate to high), to *chaotic* (very high). (See Figure 5.1.) As with cohesion, it is hypothesized that central levels of flexibility (structured and flexible) are more conducive to good marital and family functioning, with the extremes (rigid and chaotic) being the most problematic for families as they move through their life cycle.

Basically, flexibility focuses on the change in a family's leadership, roles, and rules. Much of the early application of systems theory to families emphasized the rigidity of the family and its tendency to maintain the status quo. Until the work of contemporary theorists, the importance of potential for change was minimized. Couples and families need both stability and change, and the ability to change, when appropriate, distinguishes functional couples and families from others.

Balanced couple and family systems (structured and flexible types) tend to be more functional over time. A *structured relationship* tends to have a somewhat democratic leadership with some negotiations, that include the children. Roles are stable with some sharing of roles. Rules are firmly enforced, and there are few rule changes. A *flexible relationship* has an equalitarian leadership with a democratic approach to decision making. Negotiations are open and actively include the children. Roles are shared and there is fluid change when necessary. Rules can be changed and are age appropriate.

Unbalanced marriages and families tend to be either rigid or chaotic. A *rigid relationship* is where one individual is in charge and is highly controlling. There tend to be limited negotiations with most decisions imposed by the leader. The roles are strictly defined and the rules do not change. A *chaotic relationship* has erratic or limited leadership. Decisions are impulsive and not well thought out. Roles are unclear and often shift from individual to individual.

Based on the Circumplex Model, very high levels of flexibility (chaotic) and very low levels of flexibility (rigid) might be problematic for individuals and for relationship development in the long run. On the other hand, relationships having moderate scores (structured and flexible) are able to balance some change and some stability in a more functional way. Although there is no absolute best level for any relationship, many relationships may have problems if they function at either extreme of the model (rigid and chaotic) for an extended period of time.

CIRCUMPLEX MODEL: A COUPLE AND FAMILY MAP

Another way to consider the model is as a descriptive map of 16 types of couple and family relationships. The Couple Map is used to describe 16 types of marriages; the Family Map is used to describe 16 types of families.

The *Family Map* is important because people often use their own family of origin as a reference for the type of marriage and family they either want or do not want. People often either re-create the type of family system they had or react by doing the opposite. If the members of a couple came from two quite different family systems or if they are predisposed to different types of family dynamics, it would be difficult for them to create a compatible relationship style that works for them. Thus, the *fit* between individuals is a critical variable in determining how functional and satisfying a relationship system is likely to be.

The Type of Marriage, as illustrated in the *Couple Map,* is important for individual and relationship development. Couples need to balance their levels of separateness-togetherness on cohesion and their levels of stability-change on flexibility. These levels can be adjusted by a couple to achieve a level that is acceptable to each individual.

An important distinction in the Circumplex Model is between balanced and extreme types of couple and family relationships. There are four balanced types that are "separated" or "connected" levels on cohesion and "structured" or "connected" on flexibility. Figure 5.1 illustrates the four balanced relationships and the four extreme or unbalanced relationships: chaotically disengaged, chaotically enmeshed, rigidly disengaged, and rigidly enmeshed.

THREE-DIMENSIONAL CIRCUMPLEX MODEL: FIRST-ORDER AND SECOND-ORDER CHANGE

A three-dimensional version of the Circumplex Model was developed in order to make a variety of improvements in the model's measurement and utility. (See Figure 5.2.) One advantage of the three-dimensional design is that it enables one to incorporate first- and second-order change more effectively into the Model, an idea that was suggested by Lee (1988).

First-order change is curvilinear in that too much or too little change is problematic. More specifically, either too much change (i.e., chaotic system) or too little change (i.e., rigid system) is related to a less functional pattern in families. In contrast, the two balanced types of flexibility are called "structured" and "flexible" because they represent more balanced levels of change.

Second-order change is change from one system type to another. It is "change of the system itself" and can be assessed only over time. Under stress these patterns become more apparent. Second-order change can occur in times of normative stress, such as the birth of a child, or nonnormative change, such as when a parent is injured in a car accident.

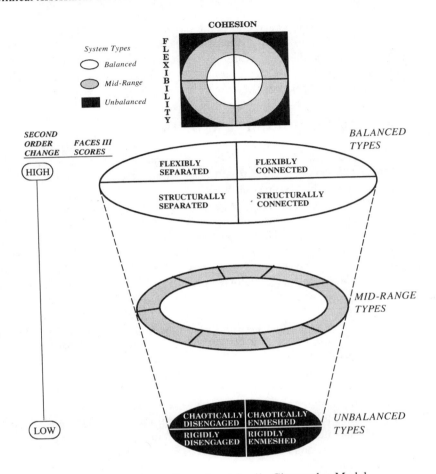

Figure 5.2   Three-dimensional family Circumplex Model.

Second-order change is linear with higher change in the balanced systems and the lowest level of change in unbalanced systems. In times of stress, balanced systems will tend to change to another system type to adapt, while unbalanced systems tend to stay stuck in their extreme pattern, which often can create more stress. Second-order change in this Model is thus similar to Beavers's concept of "competence" (Beavers & Hampson, 1990).

The three-dimensional model has the advantage of demonstrating more clearly the dynamic similarity of the types within the balanced, mid-range, and unbalanced types. This model more clearly illustrates that the four balanced types are more similar to each other dynamically in terms of second-order change than they are to any of the unbalanced types. Conversely, the four unbalanced types are similar to each other dynamically in that they are all low in second-order change. This clarifies the dynamic similarities within balanced or unbalanced types that often are lost when looking at the Circumplex Model when it is laid out in the two-dimensional (four levels by four levels) design.

Methodologically, the assessment scale called Family Adaptability and Cohesion Evaluation Scales (FACES III) (Olson, Portner, & Lavee, 1985) measures the three-dimensional model in a more effective way than it does the traditional flat four-by-four design. The various methodological studies and a review of the specific questions in FACES III show that high scores really measure balanced family types and low scores measure unbalanced family types, high scores on cohesion measure "very connected" families (balanced), and high scores on flexibility measure "very flexible" families (balanced).

Studies with FACES III should assume it is a *linear measure* with high scores representing balanced types and low scores representing unbalanced types. This revised conceptual approach to FACES III makes the three-dimensional model more similar to Beavers's System Model (see Beavers & Hampson, 1990) and McMaster's Family Model (see Epstein, Bishop et al., 1993). It also helps clarify why FACES III statistically is correlated in a linear way to the Self-Report Family Inventory (SFI) (Beavers & Hampson, 1990), the Family Assessment Measure (FAM III) (Skinner, Santa-Barbara, & Steinhauer, 1983), and the McMaster Family Assessment Device (FAD) (Epstein, Bishop et al., 1993).

MARITAL AND FAMILY COMMUNICATION

Family communication is the third dimension in the Circumplex Model and is considered a facilitating dimension. Communication is thought to be critical for facilitating movement on the other two dimensions. Because it is a facilitating dimension, communication is not graphically included in the model along with cohesion and flexibility. (See the Clinical Rating Scale in Appendixes 5A–C for more details.)

Family communication is measured by focusing on the family as a group with regard to their listening skills, speaking skills, self-disclosure, clarity, continuity tracking, and respect and regard. In terms of listening skills, the focus is on empathy and attentive listening. Speaking skills include speaking for oneself and not speaking for others. Self-disclosure relates to sharing feelings about self and the relationship. Tracking is staying on topic, and respect and regard relate to the effective aspects of the communication and problem-solving skills in couples and families. Balanced systems tend to have very good communication, whereas unbalanced systems tend to have poor communication.

HYPOTHESES DERIVED FROM THE CIRCUMPLEX MODEL

One of the assets of a theoretical model is that hypotheses can be deduced and tested in order to evaluate and further develop the model. The following are hypotheses derived from the Circumplex Model:

- **Couples and families with balanced types (two central levels) cohesion and flexibility generally will function more adequately across the family life cycle than those at the unbalanced (extreme) types.**

  An important issue in the Circumplex Model relates to the concept of *balance*. Individuals and family systems need to balance their separateness versus togetherness on cohesion and balance their level of stability versus change on flexibility. Even though a balanced family system is placed at the two central levels of the model, these families do not always operate in a "moderate" manner. Being balanced means that a family system can experience the extremes on the dimension when appropriate, but they do not typically function at these extremes for long periods of time.

Families in the balanced area of the cohesion dimension allow their members to experience being both independent from and connected to their family. On flexibility, balance means maintaining some level of stability in a system with openness to some change when it is necessary. Extreme behaviors on these two dimensions might be appropriate for certain stages of the life cycle or when a family is under stress, but they can be problematic when families are stuck at the extremes.

Unbalanced types of family systems are not necessarily dysfunctional, especially if a family is under stress or it belongs to a particular ethnic group (i.e., Hispanic, Southeast Asian) or religious group (i.e., Amish, Mormon). If a family's expectations support more extreme patterns, it then will operate in a functional manner as long as all the family members like the family that way. Ethnicity is a central trait of families and needs to be considered seriously in assessing family dynamics. What might appear to be an "enmeshed" family of color to a white outsider may, in fact, be functional for some ethnic groups.

- **Positive communication skills will enable balanced types of couples/families to change their levels of cohesion and flexibility.**

In general, positive communication skills are seen as helping family systems facilitate and maintain a balance on the two dimensions. Conversely, poor communication impedes movement in the unbalanced systems and increases the chances these systems will remain extreme.

- **To deal with situational stress and developmental changes across the family life cycle, families will modify their cohesion and adaptability to adapt to the stress.**

This hypothesis deals with the capacity in the family system (second-order change) to cope with stress or to accommodate changes in family members, particularly as family members change their expectations. The Circumplex Model is dynamic in that it assumes that couples and families will change types and it hypothesizes that change can be beneficial to the maintenance and improvement of family functioning.

When one family member's desires change, the family system must somehow deal with that request. For example, increasing numbers of wives want to develop more autonomy from their husbands (cohesion dimension) and also want more power and equality in their relationships (flexibility dimension). If their husbands are unwilling to understand and change in accordance with these expectations, the marriage probably will experience increasing levels of stress and dissatisfaction. Another common example of changing expectations occurs when a child reaches adolescence. Adolescents often want more freedom, independence, and power in the family system. These pressures by one member to change the family system can facilitate change in the family, despite its resistance to change.

CHANGES IN A COUPLE SYSTEM IN EARLY MARRIAGE

The Circumplex Model allows one to integrate systems theory and family development theory, a proposal made more than two decades ago by Reuben Hill (1970). Building on the family developmental approach, it is hypothesized that the stage of the family life cycle and composition of the family will have considerable impact on the type of family system (Carter & McGoldrick, 1988).

It is posited that at any stage of the family life cycle, there will be a diversity in the types of family systems described in the Circumplex Model. These ideas are developed more fully in a national study of 1,000 families across the family life cycle described in *Families: What Makes Them Work* (Olson, McCubbin, Larsen, Muxen, & Wilson, 1989). In spite of this diversity, it is predicted that at different stages of the family life cycle, many families will cluster together into some types more frequently than others.

The model is dynamic in that it assumes that changes can occur in family types over time (Olson et al., 1989). Families can move in any direction that the situation, stage of the family life cycle, or socialization of family members may require. The Circumplex Model can be used to illustrate developmental change of a couple as they progress from dating to marriage, to pregnancy, childbirth and child rearing, raising and launching adolescents, and moving into life as a couple again. (See Figure 5.3.)

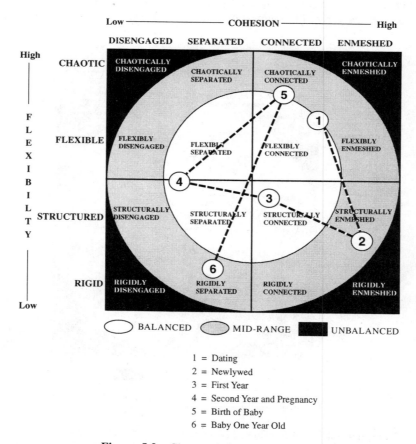

1 = Dating
2 = Newlywed
3 = First Year
4 = Second Year and Pregnancy
5 = Birth of Baby
6 = Baby One Year Old

Figure 5.3 Changes in early marriage.

FAMILY SYSTEM RELATED TO FAMILY STRESS

Although some hypotheses have been developed relating family systems as described by the Circumplex Model and family stress (Olson, Russell, & Sprenkle, 1989), little research has been done about the changes that take place in family processes related to physical and emotional illness. Short-term longitudinal studies are needed if we are to better understand the changes that occur in the family system, with comparisons between those individuals who recover more quickly and those who have difficulty recovering.

An example of second-order change is where the family changes its type of system to adapt to the major stressor. One hypothesis from the Circumplex Model is that balanced types of families will do better than unbalanced types because they are able to change their system in order to cope more effectively with the illness in a family member.

An example of how the Circumplex Model can be used in both understanding and graphing the changes in a family system over time is a family where the husband, Peter, age 53, had a heart attack. His wife, Martha, was a homemaker, and they had three teenagers living at home, one of whom was attending college.

The changes in this family system are illustrated in Figure 5.4. Before the heart attack (point A), the family was structurally separated, which was generally appropriate for that stage of the family life cycle. Once the heart attack occurred, however, the family quickly shifted to becoming more chaotically enmeshed (point B). Very high levels of closeness, characterized by enmeshment, occurred because the illness brought the

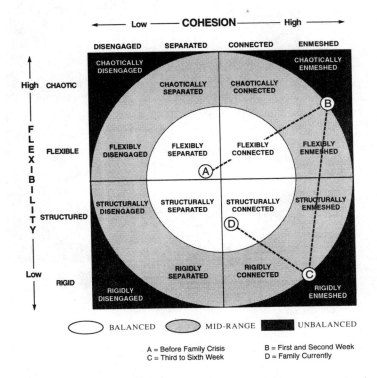

Figure 5.4   Family change before and after husband's heart attack.

family closer together emotionally. It also created chaos in the family because members needed to shift many of their daily routines dramatically.

From about the third to sixth week, the family continued to be enmeshed but became more rigid in its structure. In an attempt to stabilize the chaos by reorganizing some of the routines in their family system (point C), the family became rigid. Six months later the family was functioning as a structurally connected family (point D). Some of the rigidity and extreme cohesion decreased, but it remained a close family with a more structured system because of Peter's disability.

In summary, because of Peter's heart attack, this family's system changed several times over the course of the next six months as they adapted to this family crisis. It started as a balanced system (flexibly separated), moved to two extreme types (chaotically enmeshed and structurally enmeshed), before ending up once again as a balanced system (structurally connected).

It is expected that family systems will change in response to a crisis. As hypothesized in the Circumplex Model, the balanced families would have the resources and skills to shift their system in an appropriate way to cope more effectively with a crisis. In contrast, it is hypothesized that unbalanced families will not have the resources that are needed to change their family and, therefore, will have more difficulty adapting to a crisis. Balanced families are higher in second-order change because they are able to alter their family system to adapt to family crises.

Change in Family Systems

A few generalizations can be made about how relationships successfully change as time passes.

1. An intimate relationship is able to balance between too much change (chaos) and too little change (rigidity).
2. Too much change leads to a lack of predictability and chaos, while too little change leads to too much predictability and rigidity.
3. Those in an intimate relationship are able to change their system type when appropriate (second-order change).
4. Staying unbalanced (extreme system type) too long can create problems in an intimate relationship.

STUDIES VALIDATING THE CIRCUMPLEX MODEL

Balance versus Unbalanced Families

A central hypothesis derived from the Circumplex Model is that balanced couples/families will function more adequately than unbalanced couples/families. This hypothesis is built on the assumption that families extreme on both dimensions will tend to have more difficulties functioning across the life cycle. It assumes a curvilinear relationship between family functioning and the dimensions of cohesion and flexibility. Too little or too much cohesion or flexibility is seen as dysfunctional to the family system. However, families that are able to balance between these two extremes seem to function more adequately.

To test the major hypothesis that balanced family types are more functional than unbalanced types, various studies have focused on a range of emotional problems and symptoms in couples and families. A study by Clarke (1984) focused on families with schizophrenics, with neurotics, families that had completed therapy sometime in their past, and a no-therapy control group. (See Figure 5.4.) Using FACES II, a self-report scale that assesses family cohesion and flexibility, Clarke found a very high level of unbalanced families in the neurotic and schizophrenic groups compared to the no-therapy group. Conversely, he found a significantly higher level of balanced families in the no-therapy group compared to the other groups.

Figure 5.5 illustrates the differences in the levels of cohesion and flexibility between these groups. While the percentage of unbalanced family types decreased dramatically from the symptomatic to no-therapy groups (neurotic, 64 percent; schizophrenic, 56 percent; completed therapy, 38 percent; no therapy, 7 percent), the percentage of balanced families increased (neurotic, 8 percent; schizophrenic, 12 percent; completed therapy, 38 percent; no therapy, 48 percent) as hypothesized.

Carnes (1989) used FACES II to investigate the family systems in sex offenders and found high levels of unbalanced family types in both their family of origin and their current families. (See Figure 5.6.) While 49 percent had unbalanced family types in their family of origin and 66 percent of their current families were unbalanced types, only 19 percent of the nonoffender families were unbalanced. Conversely, while only 11 percent of their family of origin and 19 percent of their current families were balanced types, 47 percent of the nonoffender families were balanced.

These studies of clinical samples clearly demonstrate the discriminate power of the Circumplex Model in distinguishing between problem families and nonsymptomatic families. There is a strong empirical support for the hypothesis that balanced types of families are more functional than unbalanced family types. There is, however, a lack of evidence that any of these symptoms is linked specifically with a specific type of family system—for example, chaotically enmeshed. Such a linkage was a misplaced hope of

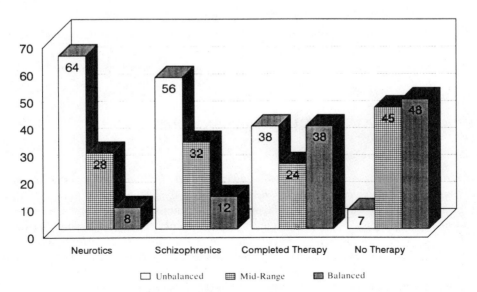

Figure 5.5   Problem families and the Circumplex Model.

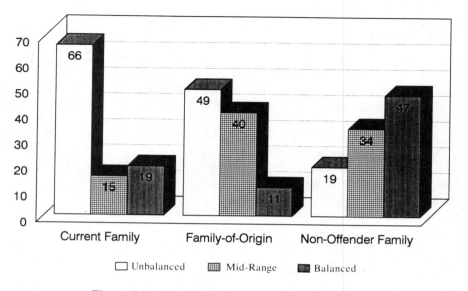

Figure 5.6   Sex offenders and the Circumplex Model.

early family research linking family symptoms (a schizophrenic offspring) and family systems (Walsh & Olson, 1989).

Balanced Families and Communication

Another hypothesis is that balanced families will have more positive communication skills than unbalanced families. Communication can be measured at both the marital and family levels using data from a national survey of 1,000 families, in which Barnes and Olson (1986) investigated parent-adolescent communication and family functioning. Using "nonproblem" families, the hypothesis that balanced families would have better communication skills was supported when relying on data from the parents' reports. Rodick, Henggler, and Hanson (1986) also found strong support for the hypothesis that balanced families have more positive communication skills. Using observational measures of mother-adolescent interaction, they found that mothers in the balanced group had significantly higher rates of supportive communication, explicit information, and positive affect than did mothers in the unbalanced type with the majority of problem dyads (chaotically enmeshed).

UPDATE ON INVENTORIES FOR FAMILY ASSESSMENT

In order to adequately assess the three major dimensions of the Circumplex Model and other related concepts, Olson and colleagues (1986) developed a variety of self-report instruments. The self-report instrument called the *Circumplex Assessment Package (CAP)* provides the insider's perspective, whereas the *Clinical Rating Scale (CRS)* provides the outsider's perspective. Both perspectives are useful, but they often yield apparently conflicting data. Used together, however, they help capture the complexity of marital and family systems.

Assessment Criteria: Multimethod, Multiperson, Multitrait, and Multisystem Levels

Multimethod assessment utilizes self-report scales that provide an "insider's perspective" on family members' own relationships, and the therapists' or observers' ratings, which provide an "outsider's perspective" on that same system. Because these two approaches often provide different perspectives, it appears important that both approaches should be used in work with families (Olson, 1986).

Multiperson assessment is also valuable because family members often do not agree with each other in describing their family system (Olson et al., 1989). Assessment using multiple family members, therefore, provides a more complete picture of how each family member views the system and the level of agreement or disagreement between members.

Multitrait assessment is based on the three central dimensions of the Circumplex Model: cohesion, flexibility, and communication. Although other traits can be incorporated into couple and family assessment, these three dimensions provide the foundation and central core of these relationship systems.

Multisystem assessment ideally focuses on the individual, the marital system, the parent-child system, and the total family—including extended family relationships. One important question to ask family members is whom they each consider to be members of their family. It is surprising to us how often family members disagree regarding who is currently in their family system. This raises important questions about boundary issues and who is psychologically and/or physically present in a given family system (Boss & Greenberg, 1984) and is especially important given the increasing diversity of family forms, particularly the changes accompanying divorce and remarriage.

Circumplex Assessment Package and Clinical Rating Scale

The *Circumplex Assessment Package (CAP)* is the latest in a series of self-report assessments based on the Circumplex Model. This procedure is multidimensional in that it assesses the three Circumplex dimensions. It also includes the satisfaction dimension, which focuses on each person's satisfaction with various aspects of the family system. It is the multisystem level in that procedures focus on both the marital system and the family system. More specifically, each of the four dimensions are assessed at the couple and family levels. Two-parent families (nuclear or blended) would complete both the marital and family scales. Single-parent families would complete the family scales and the marital scales if the single parent has a significant other. Couples (married or cohabitating) would complete the couple scales.

FACES III is an acronym for *Family Adaptability and Cohesion Evaluation Scales* (Olson, Portner, & Lavee, 1985), and MACES III is an acronym for *Marital Adaptability and Cohesion Evaluation Scales*. The communication dimension is assessed at the couple level using a subscale from the *Evaluating and Nurturing Relationship Issues, Communications and Happiness* (ENRICH) instrument (Olson, Fournier, & Druckman, 1986), and family communication is based on the Parent-Adolescent Communication Scale (Barnes & Olson, 1986). The satisfaction dimension is assessed at the couple level using a subscale from the ENRICH instrument, and the Family Satisfaction Scale (Olson & Wilson, 1986) is based on the Circumplex dimensions.

For clinical work with premarital and married couples, two comprehensive inventories that can be used are PREPARE and ENRICH respectively (Olson, Fournier, &

Table 5.3   Circumplex Assessment Package (CAP): Reliability

	Internal Consistency	Test/Retest
FACES III (Family)		
Cohesion	.84	.83
Adaptability	.79	.80
MACES III (Marital)		
Cohesion	.82	.83
Adaptability	.78	.80
Communication		
Couple (ENRICH)	.82	.90
Parent-Adolescent	.88	.88
Satisfaction		
Couple (ENRICH)	.86	.86
Family	.92	.81
Average	.84	.83

Scales are contained in the *Family Inventories* by Olson and colleagues (1985).

Druckman, 1986). *Premarital Personal and Relationship Evaluation,* (PREPARE), for premarital couples, has been found to predict which couples will divorce with 80–85% accuracy. ENRICH is designed for married couples and is able to discriminate happy, nonclinical pairs from clinical couples with 90 percent accuracy. Both PREPARE and ENRICH inventories contain 14 content categories, are computer scored, and have norms based on over 100,000 couples.

The reliability of these scales has been evaluated in a variety of studies. The most comprehensive summary is provided in *Family Inventories* (Olson et al., 1986). As indicated in Table 5.3, both the internal consistency and test-retest reliability of these scales is consistently high ($r = .80$). Therapists and researchers have evaluated the items in terms of face validity and find that they meet acceptable criteria. The scales also demonstrated having discriminate validity in that they distinguish between clinical and nonclinical families (Olson, 1986).

The Clinical Rating Scale (CRS) was developed by Olson (1990) in order to do clinical assessment on cohesion, adaptability, and communication. It describes specific indicators for each level of the three dimensions. This scale is a useful training device for helping individuals learn more about the Circumplex Model and is useful for family assessment and for planning treatment intervention. Appendixes 5A–C contain a list of the key concepts in the CRS.

GOALS OF FAMILY THERAPY USING THE CIRCUMPLEX MODEL

While family therapists have as a central goal reduction of the presenting problems and symptoms of family members, this is achieved by intervention focused on changing a dysfunctional type of couple and/or family system. The basic assumption is that the current family system dynamics are helping to maintain symptomatic behaviors. Thus, the current pattern of interaction in the family needs to be changed before the symptoms or presenting problems will be alleviated. (See Olson, Russell, and Sprenkle, 1989, for a full discussion.)

Table 5.4 summarizes the specific goals of family therapy based on the Circumplex Model. The first goal is ultimately to reduce any problems and symptoms. Since most dysfunctional families coming for therapy represent mid-range or unbalanced types, change often involves trying to shift the system one level on cohesion and one level on adaptability toward the balanced levels as it is typically assumed that the family will function more adequately if the family system is moved toward the balanced types.

Because the model is dynamic, intervention on cohesion or adaptability often has a ripple effect in that it influences the system on the other dimension. In terms of cohesion, problems in families often occur because of their inability to balance separateness (autonomy) and togetherness (intimacy). In couples coming for therapy, often there is a difference in the amount of separateness and togetherness the two partners experience or desire. For example, in disengaged couples, one or both individuals have emphasized looking out for themselves, and thus, they have not maintained their emotional bond of intimacy.

In families, the dynamics on cohesion often are more complicated. One type of problem family might have an enmeshed mother-adolescent coalition with a disengaged father. In this case, the marital dyad would not be emotionally close. Increasing their marital/parental collaboration is an effective strategy for breaking up the strong parent-child coalition.

In terms of flexibility, couples and families with problems often have difficulty balancing stability and change. These relationships are either too rigid or too chaotic. With rigid systems, often their behavioral repertoire is very narrow. When they are confronted with increasing stress, family members tend to become more rigid and inflexible. These families often can benefit from learning and using more democratic decision-making and better problem-solving skills. On the other hand, chaotic relationships often need increasing structure, and they also can benefit from improved problem-solving skills.

Increasing the positive communication skills of couples and families can facilitate system change as well. Individuals in problem families often need to learn how to be more assertive in expressing their wants and desires. They usually can gain from learning how to express their feelings in a constructive manner and how to listen and give empathic feedback to each other.

However, improving the communication skills in a family is a necessary but not sufficient condition for change on the dimensions of cohesion and adaptability.

Table 5.4   Goals of Marital and Family Therapy Based on the Circumplex Model

Goal Regarding Symptoms
- Reduce presenting problems and symptoms.

Goals Regarding System (Marital and/or Family)
- Change system one level on cohesion and adaptability toward balanced types.
- On cohesion, balance separateness and togetherness.
- On adaptability, balance stability and change.
- Improve communication skills.

Meta-Goal Regarding System (Preventive)
- Increase family members' ability to negotiate system change over time.

Communication skills can help increase awareness of current needs and preferences. System change on cohesion and adaptability is more difficult and complex. Having good communication skills enables families to express more clearly the type of relationship they would like to have on cohesion and adaptability.

One desirable goal of couple and family therapy is ultimately to teach the couple not only to deal with their current issues, but to provide them with the necessary skills to negotiate system change over time. It is an assumption of the model that couples and families need to alter their system as their individual needs and preferences change. Being able to articulate and negotiate these changes on cohesion and adaptability will also enable the couple or family to cope more adequately with stress and the other problematic issues that they encounter over time. This is an important preventive goal that moves beyond dealing with the current and presenting symptoms. Unfortunately, this meta-goal is rarely achieved in therapy because most families, and even some therapists, are too focused on only reducing the current presenting problems.

Treatment Planning Using the Circumplex Model

The Circumplex Model is a valuable resource in assessment-based treatment planning with severely dysfunctional families. A major task for outcome research is to determine which elements of intervention are most appropriate and effective with which presenting problems and with which elements of family functioning. The Circumplex Model and accompanying self-report scale (FACES III) and Clinical Rating Scale (CRS) offer an empirically based family assessment tool that can be used for treatment planning and outcome evaluation (Walsh & Olson, 1989).

The model provides a conceptual framework for assessing family system functioning on two fundamental dimensions of family organization: cohesion and flexibility. This descriptive typology of transactional patterns can be used to determine a family's current level and style of functioning on each dimension and to guide treatment planning to strengthen particular components of functioning toward clearly specified and realistic objectives. Thus, family therapy is not limited to reduction or interruption of extreme dysfunctional patterns but is directed systematically toward promotion of more functional patterns.

For families assessed at either extreme on the dimensions, intervention strategies can be targeted to fit their particular pattern of organization and to guide change, in a stepwise progression, toward a more balanced system. In most cases of severe and chronic dysfunction, a reachable therapeutic goal would be the achievement of higher functioning at the next, adjacent pattern, such as a shift from disengaged to separated or from enmeshed to connected. It would be unrealistic to attempt to change family patterns to a quite different type of organization, such as pushing a disengaged family to be strongly connected or an enmeshed family to become separated. Such goals might even be inappropriate to a family's values relative to their socioeconomic or ethnic context or to demands in their life cycle stage. A common therapeutic error with severely dysfunctional families is to assume either that patterns are unchangeable or that change toward the opposite pattern is necessary and desirable.

Severely dysfunctional families often assume such extreme all-or-none positions regarding change. They are likely to alternate between feelings of hopelessness that any change can occur and unrealistic expectations for goals that are unlikely to be met. They commonly fluctuate between extremes of enmeshed/disengaged and extremes of rigidity/chaos. An enmeshed family may resist a clinician's efforts to promote physical separation, such as leaving home at launching of the child, when they hold catastrophic expectations that any separation will result in a total cutoff.

Opposite extremes also may be found in different family subsystems. In many enmeshed families, some siblings may disengage completely from the family in order to avoid fusion, assuming positions of pseudoautonomy that dissolve in contact with the family. Clinicians must be cautious not to collude with presuppositions of either all-or-none position. Fears of runaway change or loss of patterns considered to be essential to individual or family survival are common sources of "resistance" to change and therapy dropout. Clinicians need to be alert to prevent extreme family oscillation that can occur much like a "shortcircuiting" process.

A therapist must be active in structuring and monitoring family interaction to block or interrupt the all-or-none tendency in these families to flip to the other extreme from their current organizational pattern. In work with families with unbalanced patterns, it is essential to set modest, concrete objectives to be reached through small increments of change in order to reduce anxiety to a manageable level, to prevent extreme fluctuations, and to help the family to modulate and moderate changes that can be maintained over time.

REFERENCES

Barnes, H., & Olson, D. H. (1986). Parent-adolescent communication scale. In D. H. Olson, H. I. McCubbin, H. Barnes, A. Larsen, M. Muxen, & M. Wilson (Eds.), *Family Inventories* (pp. 51–67). St. Paul, MN: Family Social Science, University of Minnesota.

Beavers, W. B., & Hampson, R. B. (1990). *Successful families: Assessment and intervention.* New York: Norton.

Benjamin, L. S. (1977). Structural analysis of a family in therapy. *Journal of Counseling Clinical Psychology, 45,* 391–406.

Boss, P. G., & Greenberg, J. (1984). Family boundary ambiguity: A new variable in family stress theory. *Family Process, 23,* 535–546.

Carnes, P. (1989). *Contrary to love: Helping the sexual addict.* Minneapolis, MN: CompCare Publications.

Carter, B., & McGoldrick, M. (Eds.). (1988). *The changing family life cycle.* New York: Gardner.

Clarke, J. (1984). *The family types of neurotics, schizophrenics and normals.* Unpublished doctoral dissertation. *Family Social Science,* University of Minnesota, St. Paul, MN.

Constantine, L. (1986). *Family paradigms.* New York: Guilford.

Epstein, N. B., Bishop, D. S., Ryan, C., Miller, I., & Keiter, G. (1993). The McMaster Assessment Device (FAD). In F. Walsh (Ed.), *Normal family processes* (pp. 138–160). New York: Guilford.

French, A. P., & Guidera, B. J. (1974). *The family as a system in four dimensions: A theoretical model.* Paper presented at the American Academy of Child Psychology, San Francisco.

Gottman, J. M. (1994). *Why marriages succeed or fail.* New York: Simon and Schuster.

Hill, R. (1970). *Family development in three generations.* Cambridge, MA: Schenkman.

Kanton, D., & Lehr, W. (1975). *Inside the family.* San Francisco: Jossey-Bass.

Leary, T. (1957). *Interpersonal diagnosis of personality.* New York: Ronald Press.

Lee, C. (1988). Theories of family adaptability: Toward a synthesis of Olson's Circumplex Model and Beavers' systems model. *Family Process, 27* (2), 73–85.

Leff, J., & Vaughn, C. (1985). *Expressed emotion in families.* New York: Guilford.

Olson, D. H. (1986). Circumplex Model VII: Validation studies and FACES III. *Family Process, 25,* 337–351.

Olson, D. H. (1990). Clinical rating scale for Circumplex Model. St. Paul: Family Social Science, University of Minnesota.

Olson, D. H. (1993). Circumplex Model of marital and family systems. In F. Walsh (Ed.), *Normal family processes.* (2nd ed., pp. 104–137). New York: Guilford.

Olson, D. H., Fournier, D. G., & Druckman, J. M. (1986). *PREPARE, PREPARE-MC and ENRICH inventories* (2nd ed.). Minneapolis: PREPARE/ENRICH, Inc.

Olson, D. H., McCubbin, H. I., Barnes, H., Larsen, A., Muxen, M., & Wilson, M. (1986). *Family inventories.* St. Paul: Family Social Science, University of Minnesota.

Olson, D. H., McCubbin, H. I., Barnes, H., Larsen, A., Muxen, M., & Wilson, M. (1989). *Families: What makes them work* (2nd ed.). Los Angeles: Sage.

Olson, D. H., Portner, J., & Lavee, Y. (1985). *FACES III.* St. Paul: Family Social Science, University of Minnesota.

Olson, D. H., Russell, C. S., & Sprenkle, D. H. (1989). *Circumplex Model: Systemic assessment and treatment of families.* New York: Haworth.

Olson, D. H., & Wilson, M. (1986). Family satisfaction. In D. H. Olson, H. I. McCubbin, H. Barnes, A. Larsen, M. Muxen, & M. Wilson (Eds.), *Family inventories.* (pp. 43–50). St. Paul: Family Social Science, University of Minnesota.

Parsons, T., & Bales, R. F. (1955). *Family socialization and interaction process.* Glencoe, IL: Free Press.

Reiss, D. (1981). *The family's construction of reality.* Cambridge, MA: Harvard University Press.

Rodick, J. D., Henggler, S. W., & Hanson, C. L. (1986). An evaluation of family adaptability, cohesion evaluation scales (FACES) and the Circumplex Model. *Journal of Abnormal Child Psychology, 14,* 77–87.

Skinner, H. A., Santa-Barbara, J., & Steinhauer, P. D. (1983). The family assessment measure. *Canadian Journal of Community Mental Health, 2,* 91–105.

Walsh, F., & Olson, D. H. (1989). Utility of the Circumplex Model with severely dysfunctional family systems. In D. H. Olson, C. S. Russell, & D. H. Sprenkle (Eds.), *Circumplex Model: Systemic assessment and treatment of families.* (2nd ed., pp. 51–78). New York: Haworth.

Appendix 5A Family cohesion.

Couple/Family Score	Disengaged (1, 2)	Separated (3, 4)	Connected (5, 6)	Enmeshed (7, 8)
EMOTIONAL BONDING	Extreme emotional separateness. Lack of family loyalty.	Emotional separateness. Limited closeness. Occasional family loyalty.	Emotional closeness. Some separateness. Loyalty to family expected.	Extreme emotional closeness. Little separateness. Loyalty to family demanded.
FAMILY INVOLVEMENT	Very low involvement or interaction. Infrequent affective responsiveness.	Involvement acceptable. Personal distance preferred. Some affective responsiveness.	Involvement emphasized. Personal distance allowed. Affective interactions encouraged and preferred.	Very high involvement. Fusion, over-dependency. High affective responsiveness and control.
MARITAL RELATIONSHIP	High emotional separateness. Limited closeness.	Emotional separateness. Some closeness.	Emotional closeness. Some separateness.	Extreme closeness, fusion. Limited separateness.
PARENT-CHILD RELATIONSHIP	Rigid generational boundaries. Low p/c closeness.	Clear generational boundaries. Some p/c closeness.	Clear generational boundaries. High p/c closeness.	Lack of generational boundaries. Excessive p/c closeness.
INTERNAL BOUNDARIES	**Separateness dominates.**	**More separateness than togetherness.**	**More togetherness than separateness.**	**Togetherness dominates.**
TIME (Physical & Emotional)	Time apart maximized. Rarely time together.	Time alone important. Some time together.	Time together important. Time alone permitted.	Time together maximized. Little time alone permitted.
SPACE (Physical & Emotional)	Separate space needed and preferred.	Separate space preferred. Sharing of family space.	Sharing family space. Private space respected.	Little private space permitted.
DECISION-MAKING	Individual decision-making. (Oppositional)	Individual decision-making, but joint possible.	Joint decisions preferred.	Decisions subject to wishes of entire group.
EXTERNAL BOUNDARIES	**Mainly focused outside the family.**	**More focused outside than inside family.**	**More focused inside than outside family.**	**Mainly focused inside the family.**
FRIENDS	Individual friends seen alone.	Individual friendships seldom shared with family.	Individual friendships shared with family.	Family friends preferred. Limited individual friends.
INTERESTS	Disparate interests.	Separate interests.	Some joint interests.	Joint interests mandated.
ACTIVITIES	Mainly separate activities.	More separate than shared activities.	More shared than individual activities.	Separate activities seen as disloyal.
Global Cohesion Rating (1-8)	Very Low	Low to Moderate	Moderate to High	Very High

Couple/Family Score	Rigid		Structured		Flexible		Chaotic	
	1	2	3	4	5	6	7	8
LEADERSHIP (Control)	Authoritarian leadership. Parent(s) highly controlling.		Primarily authoritarian but some equalitarian leadership.		Equalitarian leadership with fluid changes.		Limited and/or erratic leadership. Parental control unsuccessful. Rebuffed.	
DISCIPLINE (For families only)	Autocratic "law & order." Strict, rigid consequences. Not lenient.		Somewhat democratic. Predictable consequences. Seldom lenient.		Usually democratic. Negotiated consequences. Somewhat lenient.		Laissez-faire and ineffective. Inconsistent consequences. Very lenient.	
NEGOTIATION	Limited negotiations. Decisions imposed by parents.		Structured negotiations. Decisions made by parents.		Flexible negotiations. Agreed upon decisions.		Endless negotiations. Impulsive decisions.	
ROLES	Limited repertoire. Strictly defined roles. Unchanging routines.		Roles stable, but may be shared.		Role sharing and making. Fluid changes of roles.		Lack of role clarity. Role shifts and role reversals. Few routines.	
RULES	Unchanging rules. Rules strictly enforced.		Few rule changes. Rules firmly enforced.		Some rule changes. Rules flexibly enforced.		Frequent rule changes. Rules inconsistently enforced.	
Global Cohesion Rating (1-8)	Very Low		Low to Moderate		Moderate to High		Very High	

The global rating is based on your overall evaluation, not a sum score of the subscale.

Appendix 5B Family flexibility.

79

Low ←———— **Facilitating** ————→ **High**

Couple/Family Score	1	2	3	4	5	6
LISTENER'S SKILLS Empathy Attentive listening	Seldom evident Seldom evident		Sometimes evident Sometimes evident		Often evident Often evident	
SPEAKER'S SKILLS Speaking for self Speaking for others* *Note reverse scoring	Seldom evident **Often evident**		Sometimes evident **Sometimes evident**		Often evident **Seldom evident**	
SELF-DISCLOSURE	Infrequent discussion of self, feelings and relationships.		Some discussion of self, feelings and relationships.		Open discussion of self, feelings and relationships.	
CLARITY	Inconsistent and/or unclear verbal messages. Frequent incongruences between verbal and non-verbal messages.		Some degree of clarity, but not consistent across time or across all members. Some incongruent messages.		Verbal messages very clear. Generally congruent messages.	
CONTINUITY/ TRACKING	Little continuity of content. Irrelevant/distracting non-verbals and asides frequently occur. Frequent/inappropriate topic changes.		Some continuity, but not consistent across time or across all members. Some irrelevant/distracting non-verbals and asides. Topic changes not consistently appropriate.		Members consistently tracking. Few irrelevant/distracting non-verbals and asides. Facilitative non-verbals. Appropriate topic changes.	
RESPECT AND REGARD	Lack of respect for feelings or message of other(s). Possibly overtly disrespectful or belittling attitude.		Somewhat respectful of others, but not consistent across time or across all members. Some incongruent messages.		Consistently appears respectful of other's feelings and messages.	
Global Family Communication Rating (1-6)						

The global rating is based on your overall evaluation, not a sum score of the subscale.

Appendix 5C Family communication.

CHAPTER 6

Integrating Individual and Interpersonal Approaches to Diagnosis: The Structural Analysis of Social Behavior and Attachment Theory

PAUL FLORSHEIM, PhD, WILLIAM P. HENRY, PhD, and LORNA SMITH BENJAMIN, PhD

The topic of relational diagnosis raises a fundamental theoretical question, namely, why do human beings show such a strong propensity to form and maintain interpersonal relationships, often at the cost of considerable suffering? Any attempt to categorize relational dysfunctions from an interpersonal perspective first must address the basic problem of why relationships endure even when maladaptive. We believe that attachment theory (Bowlby, 1982) provides a compelling theoretical answer to this central question regarding the basis of interpersonal motivation. Additionally, it provides a framework for defining normal and abnormal relational processes, which is a necessary prerequisite of a coherent theory-guided nosology.

In this chapter, we sketch the outlines of how such an alternative, relationally based diagnostic system might be constructed, using the theoretical foundation of attachment theory, as operationalized and refined by Benjamin's three-level interpersonal circumplex model, the Structural Analysis of Social Behavior (SASB; Benjamin, 1974). Such a system is based on the general proposition that early disturbances in relational processes form the basis of interpersonal and/or intrapsychic structures that then disturb future relationships. The distinctions that serve as a basis for making relational diagnoses involve the specific types of interpersonal processes in which these disturbances become manifest between individuals.

OVERVIEW OF ATTACHMENT THEORY

Until relatively recently, it was widely held that affectional bonds are secondary to the primary drives of hunger (particularly in dependent children) and sex (particularly in adults) (Freud, 1940). However, Lorenz (1965) and Harlow (1958) provided convincing evidence that animals seek attachments and form the equivalent of relational bonds even in the absence of these "primary" reenforcers. In the development of attachment theory, Bowlby (1977, 1988) used these works to support his hypothesis that seeking interpersonal attachments is a primary goal of development. In broad strokes, Bowlby (1977) described attachment theory as a way of conceptualizing "the propensity of human beings to make strong affectional bonds to particular others and of explaining the many forms of emotional distress and personality disturbance . . . to which unwilling separation and loss give rise" (p. 201).

Bowlby (1977) described attachment behavior as "any form of behavior that results in a person attaining or retaining proximity to some other differentiated and preferred individual" (p. 201). This proximity-seeking component of the child's psychological makeup is referred to as the "attachment system," which Bowlby (1982) defined as an organized set of behaviors oriented to establish a "secure" bond with a protective caregiver from whom the child draws a sense of "felt security." Bowlby (1988) explains that

> attachment behavior is organized by means of a control system . . . analogous to the physiological control systems that maintain . . . blood pressure and body temperature within set limits. Thus, the theory proposes that . . . the attachment control system maintains a person's relation to his attachment figure between certain limits of distance and accessibility, using increasingly sophisticated methods of communication for doing so. (p. 123)

Once the child has established a secure base, other normative and developmentally appropriate activities become possible. Specifically, Bowlby (1982, 1988), identifies exploration as a second basic activity of the human infant, defined as the propensity to venture forth and examine the world beyond the protective domain of the attachment figure.

There are two primary reasons why attachment theory provides such an important theoretical base for relational diagnosis. First, the theory establishes the drive for interpersonal bonding as primary; hence maladaptive disruptions in the successful accomplishment of this drive are by definition pathological (Bowlby, 1977, 1982). Second, it describes two broad classes of normative activity that alternate in a balanced fashion in healthy development: attachment seeking or affiliation, and exploration or autonomous differentiation (Bowlby, 1982). As we will discuss more fully in a subsequent section, these two types of behavior form the basis of a relational diagnostic scheme.

INTERPERSONAL AND INTRAPSYCHIC PROCESSES RELATED TO ATTACHMENT

In addition to providing a primary motivational framework for human relatedness, attachment theory explains how and why specific patterns of interpersonal behavior emerge and endure (Bowlby, 1977, 1982, 1988). Based on differences in environmental contingencies, individuals become attached in particular ways (Ainsworth, Blehar, Waters, & Wall, 1978). As the infant interacts with primary caregivers, his or her expectations of self and other become patterned. These patterns are internalized and function as prototypes for relationships, guiding the child in how he or she relates and responds to other significant people.

The concept of internalized working models of self and others is a central component of attachment theory (Bowlby, 1973, 1988). A child's internalized representations of self and other usually reflect his or her experience of being cared for, responded to, and protected by the primary attachment figure(s). Bowlby (1973) explains that the child's confidence that an attachment figure will be responsive depends on "(a) whether or not the attachment figure is judged to be the sort of person who in general responds to calls for support and protection; [and] (b) whether or not the self is judged to be the sort of person towards whom anyone, and the attachment figure in particular, is likely to respond in a helpful way" (p. 238). Although not all subsequent relationships necessarily replicate primary attachments, these attachments create the basis for what the individual expects of self and others. Working models influence the way in which people approach and develop new relationships and cope with the transformation of old ones throughout the life cycle. An individual's attachment style functions like a set of interpersonal behavioral rules for engaging with others. They operate largely outside of consciousness and are resistant, but not impervious, to change; current relationships confirm and/or modify the nature of our working models.

CLASSIFICATION OF ATTACHMENT TYPES

Some attachment theorists maintain that attachment classifications describe an individual's behavioral response to a specific relational context, which elicits attachment behavior, rather than a personality trait (Ainsworth, 1990). This point underscores the fact that the development of an attachment behavioral system is heavily influenced by contextual factors and is responsive to changes in the interpersonal environment. Nevertheless, Bowlby and others (Bowlby, 1977, 1988; Hazan & Shaver, 1994a; Pilkonis, 1988) have clearly stated that these patterns of attachment behavior often persist over time and across contexts in ways that have profound effects on how a person experiences him- or herself and relates with others. While it may be true that a person's "attachment system" is not continuously active in all interpersonal contexts, the quality of that system is a defining characteristic of his or her significant relationships (Bowlby, 1982, 1988). Bowlby (1988) has written that as an attachment pattern develops and stabilizes, that "pattern becomes increasingly a property of the child himself, which means that he tends to impose it, or some derivative of it, upon new relationships" (p. 127).

The current systems for classifying attachment types are based on the assessment of behavior (Ainsworth et al., 1978) and/or working models (Bartholomew & Horowitz, 1991; Main & Goldwyn, 1985). Child-oriented attachment researchers tend to classify attachment behaviors on the basis of how a child reacts to being separated from and then reunited with his or her primary caregiver after being exposed to a stranger (Ainsworth et al., 1978; Sroufe, 1988). For example, a child described as anxious-avoidant will respond to the mother's departure and return with indifference, showing no overt signs of being upset by her absence or comforted by her presence.

Recently, a flurry of research activity has focused on the assessment of working models, which can be based on self-reports (Bartholomew & Horowitz, 1991) and/or interview data (Main & Goldwyn, 1985). These methodologies have helped researchers to describe the quality of adolescent and adult attachments to their parents, peers, and partners (Armsden & Greenberg, 1987; Bartholomew & Horowitz, 1991; Hazan & Shaver, 1994a). Generally, these methodologies classify attachment types based on a person's description of his or her relationships, expectations of self and other, and capacity to discuss interpersonal experiences openly and to describe important relationships coherently (Main & Goldwyn, 1985).

The varying approaches to studying attachment have resulted in the development of a number of schemas for delineating attachment types or styles (Ainsworth et al., 1978; Bartholomew & Horowitz, 1991; Main & Solomon, 1990; West & Sheldon, 1988). Table 6.1 lists and describes selected examples of current attachment classifications. The distinctions among these categories of attachment style involve: (1) whether a person views others positively (expects nurturance), negatively (expects abandonment or hostile

Table 6.1   Classifications of Attachment

Attachment Type	Description
Child to Parent	
Secure attachment	This child is confident that the parent figure will be responsive, available, comforting, and protective, particularly under distressful circumstances. This assurance enables the securely attached child to explore the environment and test his or her developing abilities (Ainsworth et al., 1978).
Anxious-ambivalent attachment	This child is uncertain whether the parent will be responsive, available, or protective when needed. Anxious-resistant children tend to be clingy, greatly distressed by separation, and often fearful of their environments. This pattern is associated with inconsistency in parental availability and threats of abandonment (Ainsworth et al., 1978).
Anxious-avoidant attachment	This child has no confidence that the parent will be responsive, caring, or protective and expects to be ignored or rebuffed. Such a child will attempt to live life without the love and support of others. Conflicts regarding dependency needs are hidden (Ainsworth et al., 1978; Bowlby, 1988).
Disorganized/ disoriented attachment	This child behaves erratically and inconsistently, often sending opposing messages at the same time. These children appear confused and engage in "incomplete or undirected movements or expression" (Main & Solomon, 1990, p. 122). These children were often found to be victims of abuse/neglect or their parental figure was grossly preoccupied with own problems (Crittendon, 1988; Main & Solomon, 1990).
Adult to Adult	
Secure attachment	The secure person has a positive view of self and others, a moderate to high level of intimacy and autonomy, and a moderate to low level of dependency (Bartholomew & Horowitz, 1991).
Preoccupied attachment	An interpersonally preoccupied person strives for self-acceptance "by gaining the acceptance of valued others" (Bartholomew & Horowitz, 1991, p. 227). Experience is characterized by a sense of unworthiness juxtaposed against a positive view of others.
Dismissive attachment	A dismissive person has a positive view of self and a negative view of others (Bartholomew & Horowitz, 1991; Main & Goldwyn, 1985). A dismissive person protects the self against disappointment by "avoiding close relationships and maintaining a sense of independence and invulnerability" (Bartholomew & Horowitz, 1991, p. 227).
Fearful-avoidant	A fearful-avoidant person has a negative attachment view of self and others and anticipates betrayal, rejection, and criticism. Such a person is likely to protect him- or herself from rejection or attack by avoiding involvement with others (Bartholomew & Horowitz, 1991).
Compulsive self-reliant	A compulsive, self-reliant person avoids turning to others for comfort, attachment support, or affection and places a high premium on self-suffiency. However, this form of avoidance is motivated by a counterdependent need to be self-sufficient, rather than by outright disdain for others (Bowlby, 1977; West & Sheldon, 1988).

Table 6.1   *(continued)*

Attachment Type	Description
Compulsive caregiving	A compulsive caregiver insists on taking the caretaker role in all relationships, never allowing others to reciprocate. These people's own needs are met by caring for others, thus they insist on providing help whether it is requested or not. Attachment is associated with feelings of self-sacrifice and self-neglect (Bowlby, 1977; West & Sheldon, 1988).
Compulsive care-seeking	A compulsive care seeker experiences a constant need to confirm the availability and responsiveness of attachment figures. These people have a heightened sense of vulnerability to loss, they tend to define their attachment in terms of receiving care, and feel unequipped to take responsibility for themselves (West & Sheldon, 1988).
Angry-withdrawn attachment	An angry withdrawn person is likely to react to responsiveness and unavailability with anger and defensiveness (West & Sheldon, 1988).
Obsessive-compulsive personality	An obsessive-compulsive personality style is characterized by excessive differentiation and a rigid adherence to a vision of how things should be. Such a person regards relationships as secondary to work and productivity, and prefers not to discuss problems and feelings with others (Pilkonis, 1988).
Lack of interpersonal sensitivity	An interpersonally insensitive person is unaffected by external feedback, is oblivious to the effect of his or her actions on others, tends to engage in antisocial behavior without guilt or remorse, and resents being held back by external demands (Pilkonis, 1988).

control), or ambivalently (is not sure what to expect) and (2) the type of interpersonal behavior used to reduce anxiety (i.e., clingy dependency, avoidance, dismissiveness, anger, control, etc.).

Several classifications of child and adult attachment have been omitted from Table 6.1, because they overlap in significant ways with those listed (Crittendon, 1988; Pilkonis, 1988). For example, in addition to the "obsessive compulsive" and "lack of interpersonal sensitivity" categories described in Table 6.1, Pilkonis (1988) proposed several other personality prototypes (e.g., defensive separation, excessive dependency, borderline features) that bear a close resemblance to those proposed by West and Sheldon (1988) and Bartholomew and Horowitz (1991). The lack of a consistent methodology and/or a common language for describing types of attachment behavior has led to the proliferation of overlapping and sometimes redundant systems.

TOWARD A RELATIONAL MODEL OF ATTACHMENT BEHAVIOR AND DYSFUNCTION

In this section we review issues relevant to the development of a more comprehensive, relationally based model of attachment and illustrate a schema for assessing interactive processes between attachment systems.

The Problem of Flexibility and Specification

Recent advances in attachment research have led attachment theorists to address the limitations of their current methodologies (Cicchetti, Cummings, Greenberg, & Marvin, 1990). As attachment theory has evolved, more attachment types have been identified and incorporated into Ainsworth's original classification system (Ainsworth et al., 1978), such as the "disorganized/disoriented" attachment type (Crittendon, 1988; Main & Solomon, 1990). While such developments contribute to the vitality of attachment theory, the introduction of new attachment types has required researchers to rethink their criteria for previously identified classifications. (See Ainsworth, 1990, and Main & Solomon, 1990, for a discussion of this issue.) Researchers also have begun to study the development of attachment relationships over the life cycle (Hazen & Shaver, 1994a). There has been considerable interest in how basic modes of attachment become more complex, differentiated, and specific (Sroufe, 1988; Cicchetti et al., 1990). For example, it seems possible that some infants classified as anxious-avoidant will develop into avoidant personalities, whereas others will become antisocial, paranoid, depressed, or narcissistic. However, there is no established system for delineating how such a process of developmental specification might unfold. Moreover, how a person's early attachments influence his or her peer relations and romantic liaisons has raised questions about how to assess the quality of attachment behavior as the target of these attachments change (Hazen & Shaver, 1994a).

These developments underscore the need for a more flexible, comprehensive, and systematic approach for assessing the quality of attachment behavior across situations and over the life cycle (Greenberg, Cicchetti, & Cummings, 1990). Such an approach would require a common metric: a clearly delineated set of specific terms for describing the components of attachment systems and types of attachment behaviors in their various manifestations, across interpersonal contexts and developmental stages. In subsequent sections we will discuss how the Structural Analysis of Social Behavior (SASB) fulfills this basic requirement.

The Need for a More Interpersonally Oriented Attachment Theory

Bowlby recognized that "the development of the child's attachment system is profoundly influenced by the way his parents (or parental figures) treated him (1988, p. 123). He was clear in stating that attachment behavior is the property of an individual rather than a relationship (Bowlby, 1982). As such, attachment researchers have focused on the study of individual behavioral systems and intrapsychic mechanisms rather than the matrix of relationships in which individual attachment systems develop.

Recently, several attachment theorists have addressed the importance of developing a more systematic understanding of the links between the intrapersonal, interpersonal, and systemic-contextual processes implicated in the development of attachments (Crittendon, 1988; Marvin & Stewart, 1990). How a person engages with and responds to others is a function of his or her attachment system and the systems to which he or she is attached. Moreover, a person establishes different attachments with several significant others (Hazen & Shaver, 1994b; Marvin & Stewart, 1990), and the quality of each is influenced by the relational matrix in which each person is embedded.

As it stands, attachment theory lacks a framework for assessing how individual attachment systems interact with one another (Cicchetti et al., 1990; Greenberg et al., 1990). The assessment of attachment systems is oriented toward the measurement of intrapsychic structures and individual behaviors. Most current coding schemes focus on only one participant in the relational dyad, assessing individual perceptions of or responses to attachment figures rather than the process of interpersonal exchange. Current descriptions of various attachment styles emphasize traitlike qualities, in that they imply the persistence of a particular interpersonal stance toward generalized others. While individuals may have tendencies to perceive and respond to others in certain ways, depending on the nature of their attachment system, this fact must be reconciled with the observation that individuals vary in their relationships with other people. For the purpose of relational diagnosis, the basic principles of attachment theory must be articulated in a way that permits an understanding of how different relationships emerge out of different combinations of attachment styles.

A Schema for Assessing the Interaction between Attachment Systems

A classification system that combines interpersonal and intrapersonal aspects of psychopathology would need to account for the fact that every relationship consists of at least three components: the individual psychological functioning of each participant (two or more) and the quality of the relationship between them. The components of such a model are outlined in Figure 6.1, which illustrates the primary interactions that can occur between two attachment systems. In this schema, working models of self and other derive from the treatment of early attachment figures and are composed of two primary components that influence the individual's attachment behavior. One component of the internal model of self is determined by a person's experience of him- or herself in relation with significant others (P1 → P2). The second component of the self consists of the person's treatment of him- or herself (P1 → P1). Similarly, a person's working model of other consists of his or her perception of the attachment figure's caretaking behavior (P2 → P1) as well as the attachment figure's treatment of him or her (P2 → P2). In a subsequent section, a dyad, the simplest version of a system, is analyzed to show how a relational diagnostic system based on this approach would work. Diagnosing larger systems (i.e., families) would be more complicated but would follow the same principles.

A relational diagnostic system must be able to describe the quality of a relationship, described by Figure 6.1 as existing somewhat separately from the prototypical attachment behavior of its individual participants. Although the quality of any relationship largely depends on the psychological makeup of its participants, what occurs when two or more people become intimately engaged cannot be described adequately as a simple combination of individual attachment systems. The quality of the internal working models of both individuals influences and is influenced by the interactive process. Attachment theory posits that through the process of forging new relationships, internal working models evolve, facilitating the development of new attachment systems (Ainsworth, 1990; Bowlby, 1988). Whether a relationship confirms or disconfirms expectations of self and other depends on several ephemeral factors, including each participant's: (1) ability to perceive the other as more than an extension of the self or the reflection of figures from the past; (2) capacity for disengaging from and redirecting the routine flow of negative exchanges, and (3) capacity for allowing him- or herself to be enticed into more positive exchanges.

A clinically useful relational diagnostic system would need to attend to the fact that the development of a relationship is an emergent process, potentially able to move in several interpersonal directions. A systematic analysis of the interpersonal and intrapersonal

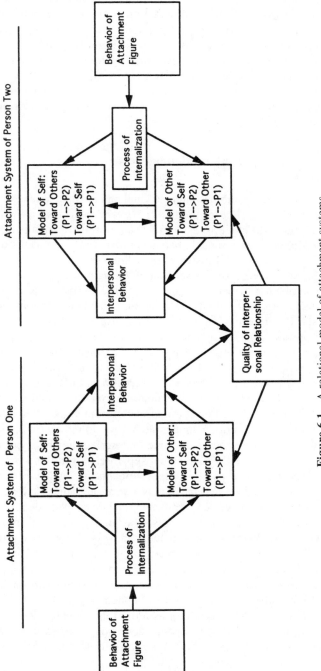

Figure 6.1 A relational model of attachment systems.

processes illustrated in Figure 6.1 could delineate how different combinations of attachment types lead to different types of relational outcomes. Such an analysis is contingent on the development of a common metric for describing the various components of the intrapsychic-behavioral-relational matrix, including: (1) the interpersonal behavior of individual participants; (2) the intrapsychic correlates of that behavior; (3) the quality of the relationship, defined both in terms of the dynamic between the two attachment systems (i.e., the balance of power, the degree of warmth, the level of differentiation) and in terms of its potential for facilitating or blocking the psychological well-being of its participants (i.e., the predicted positive and negative trajectories). The Structural Analysis of Social Behavior (SASB) model (Benjamin, 1974, 1993b), to be discussed next, provides a conceptual framework and methodology for assessing and diagnosing normal and abnormal processes in a way that integrates intrapsychic, interpersonal, and systemic levels of functioning.

THE STRUCTURAL ANALYSIS OF SOCIAL BEHAVIOR, ATTACHMENT THEORY, AND RELATIONAL DIAGNOSIS

In this section, the SASB model is introduced as a common metric for the development of a relationally based system for diagnosing attachment disorders. We will address how the SASB model defines and operationalizes normality and abnormality and provides an established measurement technology for assessing attachment systems and integrating existing schemas of attachment types. A case study is presented to illustrate how SASB can be used to delineate the relationship between intrapsychic and interpersonal processes.

Description of the SASB Model

The SASB model is based on a set of interrelated interpersonal and intrapsychic circumplexes developed by Benjamin (1974) and derived from the work of Sullivan (1953), Murray (1938), Leary (1957), and Schaefer (1971). The original interpersonal circumplex (Leary, 1957) was based on the axes of *affiliation* (love-hate) and *control* (dominance-submission), which a large body of evidence has confirmed as the basic dimensions of interpersonal behavior (Wiggins, 1982). As a methodological tool, the SASB model is able to capture specific, clinically meaningful aspects of interpersonal and intrapsychic processes (Pinsof, 1989). The utility of the model has been demonstrated by researchers who have used SASB to investigate a broad range of clinical phenomena, including family processes (Florsheim, Tolan, & Gorman-Smith, in press; Humphrey, 1989), mother-infant interaction (Benjamin & Gelfand, 1992), couples interaction (Brown & Smith, 1992), and psychotherapeutic processes (Henry, Schacht, & Strupp, 1986).

Benjamin (1974) refined the original interpersonal circumplex in two ways. First, she recognized that Leary's model was incomplete because its dominance-submission axis represented only one form of interpersonal control, namely, exchanges involving enmeshment. A model that encompasses both enmeshment and differentiation in human relations requires two separate control or interdependence axes. Drawing on the work of Schaefer (1971), Benjamin (1974) developed a circumplex model in which the opposite of dominance is autonomy-granting and the opposite of submission is differentiation/autonomy-taking.

SASB incorporates these four poles (dominance, submission, autonomy-granting, and autonomy-taking) by introducing the concept of interpersonal focus, which yields two complementary interpersonal surfaces and one intrapsychic surface. On all surfaces, the horizontal axis describes the degree of affiliation, ranging from extremely attacking or rejecting on the left, to extremely approaching or loving on the right. (See Figure 6.2.)

The first circumplex surface, Focus on Other, describes transitive actions that are directed outward toward another individual. The vertical dimension ranges from extremes of control at the bottom, to freeing or autonomy-granting at the top. The second surface, Focus on Self, describes intransitive behaviors focused on the self; these are generally reactive to another person. The vertical dimension ranges from submission at the bottom, to separation or autonomy-taking at the top. The third surface, Introject, is an intrapsychic surface that reflects the Sullivanian notion of the self as the reflexive appraisal of others (Sullivan, 1953). The introject surface describes actions directed by the self toward the self, and represents the internalization of behaviors directed toward the self by important others (such as attachment figures). The vertical dimension of this surface runs from control at the bottom, to freeing at the top.

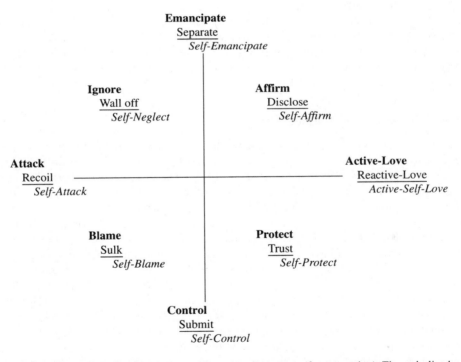

Labels in **bold print** describe actions directed at another person (focus on other). The <u>underlined</u> labels describe reactions to another person's (perceived) initiations (focus on self). Adjacent **boldfaced** and <u>underlined</u> labels mark complementary pairings. Labels in *italics* show what happens if a person treats himself or herself just as important as others have treated him or her (introject). Adapted from Benjamin (1993b, p. 54).

Figure 6.2   The SASB simplified cluster model, all three surfaces.

Three decisions are required to place a given interpersonal behavior in its SASB location. First, it must be decided whether the communication is focused on self or others. Next a determination is made about how much affiliation or disaffiliation is present, and then the degree of interdependence is assessed. Finally, the affiliation and interdependence ratings are used as coordinates to place the communication into one of eight cluster segments on the appropriate surface. SASB may be used to map the interpersonal process between interactants, the interpersonal content of spoken dialogue, or an individual's intrapsychic structure. SASB assessment can be based on coded transcripts or tapes of observed behavior, coded interviews, and/or self-report questionnaires (Benjamin, 1988).

Based on the analysis of a SASB-coded interaction, a relational process can be described as complementary, concordant, or antithetical. Complementarity describes the process in which one person's behavior complements the behavior of the other in terms of affiliation, interdependence, and focus, as in the case of the child who trusts his or her mother when she behaves protectively. Concordance refers to the process in which one person replicates how he or she has been treated by the other. For example, a husband's blame may be matched by his wife's counterblame. An antithetical process is the opposite of a complementary process, exemplified by a son who reacts to his father's controlling behavior by separating and asserting. Antithetical processes tend to occur in unstable relationships, in which the participants are working at cross-purposes and engaging in behavior that reflects very different personal agendas.

Defining Normal and Abnormal Interpersonal Patterns

The traditional interpersonal view derived from Leary's (1957) original circumplex conceives of normal and abnormal behavior as poles on a single continuum. In this quantitative view, abnormal behavior differs primarily in intensity, being an extreme variant of normal behavior. The SASB model proposes that normality is qualitatively distinct, not a milder variant of abnormal behavior (Benjamin, 1994a). This definition of normality is based on Bowlby's (1977, 1988) postulate that there are two fundamental and normative developmental processes: attachment-seeking (positive enmeshment) and exploration (friendly differentiation). In order to achieve these basic aims, an individual's baseline interpersonal behavioral pattern must incorporate a moderate degree of both enmeshment and differentiation (Henry, 1994). In the SASB model this is represented by a balance of behaviors in cluster two, three, and four, referred to as the attachment group (AG) (Benjamin, 1994a; Henry, 1994). An individual whose relationships are typified primarily by these clusters demonstrates the ability to behave in a friendly and moderately submissive manner while retaining the flexibility to act with a healthy and moderate degree of autonomy. Conversely, relationships marked by a transactional baseline pattern containing clusters six, seven, and eight are considered abnormal. These clusters, referred to as the disrupted attachment group (DAG), are so defined because they violate the interpersonal conditions through which secure attachments and normative differentiation are achieved.

As noted by Bowlby (1982), all individuals are thought to possess the same underlying motives for forming attachments, causing them to seek or wish for the sort of interpersonal conditions represented by the AG and avoid or fear those represented by the DAG. However, the conditions in which people form attachments vary tremendously, such that individuals actually may engage in abnormal behaviors while trying to adapt

Table 6.2   Attachment Types as Described by SASB Codes, Based on Observed Behavior and Self-Descriptions

Attachment Type	Basic Modes of Interpersonal Behavior	
	Experience of Other	Response to Other
Child		
secure	protect, love, affirm	trust, love, disclose
anxious/ambivalent	protect + ignore	trust + wall off, sulk + love sulk + trust
anxious/avoidant	ignore, wall off	wall off, submit + wall off
chaotic/disoriented	ignore, attack, blame	trust + wall off, love + sulk love + wall off, recoil
Adult		
secure	love, affirm, disclose protect, trust	affirm, disclose, love protect, trust
preoccupied attachment	ignore, wall off, free	control + trust, control + love
dismissive attachment	ignore, trust	wall off, separate
fearful	attack, blame	sulk
compulsive-self reliance	separate, ignore	separate
compulsive caregiving	trust, self-ignore	protect, control
compulsive care-seeking	ignore, wall off, free, separate	trust, control + trust
angry withdrawn	ignore, attack, blame	wall off
obsessive-compulsive	control, blame	wall off, separate
lack of interpersonal sensitivity	blame, ignore	blame, wall off

to dysfunctional interpersonal circumstances. That is, they may behave maladaptively while seeking normal adaptive ends (i.e., attachment and differentiation) if the people to whom they become attached manifest baseline DAG behaviors.

The SASB definition of relational pathology focuses on the pattern of emergent interpersonal behavioral processes. In the broadest possible terms, dysfunctional relationships could be described as pathological because they are hostile and/or out of balance by virtue of being either excessively enmeshed or excessively differentiated (or alternating between these extremes). For example, individuals categorized as anxious-ambivalent or preoccupied would likely engage in relationships that were overly enmeshed. Individuals typed as dismissive, fearful-avoidant, or compulsively self-reliant would be seen as too differentiated. Based on these general principles for defining normality and abnormality, the SASB model is able to describe attachment types and processes at a high level of specificity. For example, in Table 6.2 SASB codes were used to describe the various attachment types in terms of their specific intrapsychic and interpersonal components.

Components of Working Models		
Self to Self	Interpersonal Fear	Interpersonal Wish
affirm, love, protect	ignore, attack, blame	protect, love, affirm
blame, ignore	ignore, attack, blame	protect, love, affirm
ignore	attack, blame, control	affirm, free, love
ignore, attack, blame	attack, ignore	protect
protect, love, disclose	ignore, attack, blame	love, affirm, disclose protect, trust
blame	assert, free, ignore, wall off	protect, love
ignore, free, disclose	protect, control, blame	free
blame, ignore	blame, ignore, attack	protect, love, accept
ignore, disclose	blame, control, nurture	free
ignore	separate, wall off	trust + affirm
blame	free, ignore	protect
ignore	blame, attack	affirm
control, blame	control, blame	free
free	control, blame	free

RELATIONAL DIAGNOSIS: THE STRUCTURAL ANALYSIS OF ATTACHMENT BEHAVIOR

The SASB model provides a coherent and relationally based organizing framework for the diagnosis of attachment disorders, leading to more specific, developmentally oriented understanding of the interactions between attachment systems. In addition to describing the current attachment classifications, outlined in Table 6.2, in terms of their intrapersonal and interpersonal components, the flexibility and specificity of the SASB model system would facilitate the identification of new attachment types and lead to several theoretical refinements.

A More Specific Delineation of the Attachment Behavior

As indicated earlier, the behavior of the developing child's primary caregiver(s) largely determines the quality of his or her developing attachment system, including how he or she responds to others and his or her nascent experience of self. Based on the SASB model, the behavior of attachment figures (and the child's response) can be delineated more clearly, facilitating the establishment of a more complex and more coherent system for defining attachment types. For example, an attachment figure can be hostile, unavailable, and unresponsive in a variety of ways, each of which ultimately may lead to the development of very different types of attachment systems. Moreover, attachment theorists have identified "ambivalence" as a core component of the anxious attachment classification. While ambivalence usually is defined generically, there are several distinct types of ambivalence, which express different sets of mixed feelings. Ambivalence might express mixed messages of blame and understanding (blame + affirm) or neglect and nurturance (ignore + protect). The lack of clarity between different types of interpersonal ambivalence has posed problems for attachment researchers interested in fine-tuning current classifications (Crittendon, 1988). Based on the SASB model, mixed messages, and the ambivalences they create, can be assessed very specifically, allowing researchers to clarify the differences between distinct types of ambivalent attachments.

A Clearer Definition of Working Models

How a child experiences, defines, and behaves toward him- or herself depends on the process of internalization (Benjamin, 1993b; Henry, 1994). Bowlby and several of his psychoanalytic predecessors (Fairbairn, 1952; Greenberg & Mitchell, 1983) suggest that the normal developmental process involves the internalization of others, who function as psychologically potent abstract representations. Benjamin refers to these "working models" of others as "important people and their internalized representations," or IPIRs. Consistent with the principles laid out by Bowlby, Benjamin has written that how a person feels about and behaves toward him- or herself and others largely depends on the quality of his or her IPIRs (Benjamin, 1993a, in press).

The SASB model provides a methodology for describing these internalized representations of self and other. Using SASB language, the working model of other (the IPIR) consists primarily of a person's experience of the attachment figure's "focus on other" (transitive) behavior and secondarily of the attachment figure's "focus on self" behaviors (his or her anticipated reactions), and the attachment figure's behavior toward him or her. (See Figure 6.2, surface three.) Conversely, the working model of self consists of a person's prototypic behavior toward significant others, his or her prototypical reactions to significant others, and how he or she behaves toward the self.

These internalized representations of other can be "identified with" (copied as a model for self-action), "internalized" (reacted to as expectations), and/or "introjected" (resulting in treatment of the self that mirrors the treatment by others). For example, whether the child of an abusive parent becomes aggressive or depressed will depend on whether he or she identifies with or introjects the behavior of the attachment figure. The child who identifies with the attachment figure will learn to treat others as he or she has been treated (e.g., the child of abusive parents becomes a violent adolescent and abusive husband), or the child will experience the self as the product of how he or she was treated (i.e., the child of abusive parents experiences the self as fundamentally fearful, submissive, and deserving of punishment). Alternately, a child may try, either adaptively or maladaptively, to get others to provide him or her with the sort of treatment that was denied or unavailable (i.e., the child of neglectful parents becomes a compulsive care seeker). Whichever process dominates in a given interpersonal situation will determine the dynamic quality of the relationship between a person's internal self and internal other and influence how the child behaves toward others (Benjamin, in press). How this process unfolds may be heavily influenced by differences in temperment; an innately active child is likely to respond to aggression differently than an innately passive child.

A SASB-Based Link between Attachment Theory and DSM

Attachment theory proposes that a maladaptive working model in early childhood potentiates the development of psychopathology (Bowlby, 1977, 1988; Sroufe, 1988). Several attachment researchers have examined how early attachment relates to the development of psychopathology (Greenberg, Speltz, & DeKlyen, 1993; Sroufe, 1988). Although some have established a clear link between attachment problems in high-risk infants to the occurrence of generalized behavioral problems in childhood and beyond (Greenberg et al., 1993; Sroufe, 1988), the pathways leading from specific early attachment problems to specific types of psycholopathology, defined in DSM terminology, have not been delineated.

SASB provides a framework for delineating the relationship between attachment disorders and various types of psychopathology defined and described by DSM. Benjamin (1993b) has demonstrated that the current DSM-IV criteria for each of the ten personality disorders can be articulated and accounted for using a SASB-based formulation of: (1) developmental contingencies; (2) intrapsychic wishes, fears, and expectations; and (3) modes of relating. This framework highlights the relationship between early interpersonal experiences and the qualitative nature of particular types of psychopathology. The overarching principle is that the interpersonal dimensionality of early experiences correspond with the dimensionality of adult disorders. Since various attachment styles also can be described according to their SASB dimensionality, this provides a uniform theoretical and measurement link between attachment theory and DSM-style disorders.

Using SASB to translate the components of various attachment systems into specific interpersonal/intrapsychic coordinates (Table 6.2), we can begin to build a relationally based model of assessment, which integrates the symptom-based, individual-centered and the developmental-interpersonal approaches to diagnosis. Formulating a relational diagnosis begins with the classification of each participant's attachment system, translated into SASB language. It also includes assessing the following aspects of the relationship: (1) the dynamic quality of the match between attachment types (i.e., do the attachment systems operate in a complementary, concordant, or antithetical fashion?); (2) the balance of interpersonal control, affiliation, and differentiation; (3) whether the process of interpersonal exchange is reciprocal (rather than one participant being the primary focus of the other's attention); and (4) the potential for positive and negative interpersonal developments, based on a systematic analysis of the primary patterns of exchange.

In the following care history we provide an example, drawn from a study of interpersonal processes between teen parents, which illustrates how the SASB model describes the interaction between intrapsychic and interpersonal processes.[1]

---

[1] To apply this model to a larger relational system, such as an entire family, SASB codes would be used to describe each dyadic subsystem, how each participant behaves in relation to the system as a whole, and the implied interpersonal processes that occur when, for example, a husband and wife discuss how to punish their son.

Case History: Pete and Sandy

Sandy is a 16-year-old pregnant teenager with a history of drug abuse, conduct disorder, and depression. In Sandy's case, these psychological problems could be SASB-coded[2] as hostile avoidance (WALL OFF), SELF-IGNORE, and SELF-BLAME. She is highly conflicted about her involvement with others, typical of an anxious-ambivalent pattern of attachment. She feels that she needs support and nurturance, but characteristically experiences others as hurtful, BLAMING, CONTROLLING and/or intrusive.

Sandy is a middle child in a sibship of 12. She describes her mother as LOVING and accepting, but woefully relates that her mother is often busy with other things (IGNORE) and overly deferential to her father, whom she describes as extremely CONTROLLING, self-preoccupied, and quick to anger (BLAMING). She sees herself as a rebel in this staunchly religious family, engaging in self-destructive behavior to elicit concern from her mother and irritate her father. She was sexually abused by an older brother, whom she describes as the person in her family with whom she feels closest (LOVING and AT-TACKING).

Pete grew up under a different set of difficult circumstances. As the oldest child, he took care of his mother, who was depressed and engaged in a series of relationships with abusive men (SULK, SELF-IGNORE). Pete's response to his mother's inability to function in a caregiving role (IGNORE) was to self-identify as the head of the household (PROTECT, CONTROL).

Based on her internal-interpersonal blueprint (outlined in Figure 6.3), Sandy constructs a relational world in which she feels CONTROLLED by others. She evokes controlling behavior in Pete in three ways: (1) engaging in neglectful, destructive behaviors that elicit his concern and criticism (i.e., she smokes and hasn't been gaining weight, despite the fact that she's pregnant); (2) engaging in SUBMISSIVE and/or SULKY behaviors that encourage him to take more CONTROL; and (3) explicitly telling him to take control (CONTROLLING him into controlling her).

In response, Pete vacillates between being BLAMING/CONTROLLING and PROTECTIVE/AFFIRMING. When he tries to CONTROL her, Sandy resents it and responds by either WALLING herself OFF with passive compliance (SUBMIT) or by becoming SELF-BLAMING, which tends to elicit his concern (PROTECT). The fact that he is willing to take charge allows her to: (1) not take responsibility for herself (SELF-IGNORE); (2) resent him for controlling her (SULK); and (3) become emotionally disengaged when she feels stressed by the relationship (WALLOFF). The intrapsychic and interpersonal components of this dynamic, summarized by SASB codes, are schematized in Figure 6.3.

It is through a systematic analysis of individual and interpersonal patterns that we can begin to understand how:

1. Early experiences influence expectations of self and other (e.g., Sandy's self-experience as deprived, helpless, and victimized derive from her attachments to her loving yet unavailable mother, her hostile, controlling father, and her abusive brother).

2. Perceptions of self and other influence interpersonal behavior (e.g., Pete's caregiving behavior derives from his complementary identification with his dependent, self-destructive mother. (See Figure 6.3 for clarification.) This image of himself in relation to others attracts him to Sandy.

[2] SASB codes are presented in uppercase letters.

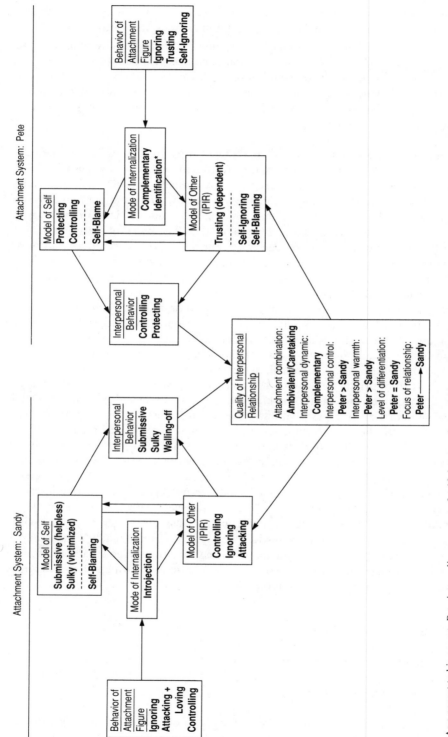

Figure 6.3 A relational model of attachment revisited: Sandy and Pete.

*As a parent to his parent, Pete internalizes a sense of self that complements his mother's identity.

97

3. Interpersonal behavior reinforces a person's self-perception (e.g., Sandy engages Pete in ways that confirm her self perception as weak and victimized.

4. Interpersonal behavior can shape the response of others, thereby confirming the IPIR (e.g., in addition to eliciting his care and concern, Sandy entices Pete into controlling and blaming her, confirming her belief that others are essentially intrusive and critical. Pete's involvement with Sandy seems motivated by a need to replicate his own family experience by caring for a woman who is withdrawn, self-destructive, and needy).

This interpersonal system could be characterized as a variation on the theme of hostile enmeshment. Using the categories of attachment currently available, Pete would be described as a compulsive caregiver; his protective, controlling behavior is based on a need to replicate his attachment experience with his mother. Sandy's tendency to vacillate between sulky, submissive behavior and avoidant, distancing behavior could be characterized as anxious-ambivalent. The dynamic between them is essentially complementary; Pete pursues and controls Sandy, who entices and/or reinforces his use of control through the complementary behavior of hostile submission. This pattern justifies Sandy's resentful defiance and verifies her self-image as incompetent, weak, and blameworthy.

There is a clear power differential in this relationship, in which Pete engages in far more controlling behavior than Sandy. Nevertheless, Sandy's hostile, self-focused behavior dominates the tone of their exchange; her anger elicits hostility in Pete, and her submissiveness sets him up to take control and behave as an authority figure. Sandy and Pete's relationship is nonreciprocal, in the sense that the focus of their interactions does not shift from person to person, as it would if they were more mutually engaged. Clearly defined roles are rigidly maintained, often at the expense of interpersonal growth. The potential for a negative interpersonal trajectory seems to originate with Sandy's sulky, self-abusive behavior, which elicits a hostile response from Pete with increasing frequency. While Pete does not seem characteristically hostile, his early experience of being neglected and seeing his mother abused suggests that under the right set of circumstances, the potential for hostile engagement (BLAME) or hostile disengagement (IGNORE) exists. On the other hand, the potential for a positive interpersonal trajectory seems to originate with Pete's protective, affirmative behavior, which occasionally pierces Sandy's defenses and elicits a trusting, relying response. While the presence of a DSM diagnosis helps to specify the nature of Sandy's maladaptive behavior, it does not fully describe the interpersonal or intrapsychic attributes of these individuals, nor does it help to characterize their relationship, which many clinicians would see as the primary target of intervention.

CONCLUSION

The example of Pete and Sandy represents the relational diagnostic process derived from the merger of attachment theory and SASB. This process is based on the following steps for differentiating between types of relationships:

1. The assessment of working models of self and other (IPIR) contained in each participant's attachment system.

2. The relevant internal processes by which the IPIRs manifest themselves in the current relational behavior of each participant (identification, internalization, and/or introjection.

3. The interpersonal principle that guides the sequence of problematic behaviors (complementary, concordant, antithetical).

4. The balance of enmeshment-differentiation and hostility-warmth exhibited by the participants.

5. The prototypical interpersonal focus of each participant.

6. The delineation of interpersonal triggers that initiate healthy and problematic relational sequences.

The current model is an attempt to apply the theoretical principles of attachment theory and interpersonal theory, as represented by SASB, to the problem of relational diagnosis. Although we have not explored the links between this model and the individual-centered, symptom-based DSM approach to diagnosis, such links exist, have been discussed elsewhere (Benjamin, 1993b, 1994b), and could be developed in ways that are explicitly relevant to attachment theory.

In this chapter, we describe the theoretical underpinnings of a relational model of attachment and delineate a process for diagnosing relationally based attachment disorders. Clearly, at this time we cannot provide an alternative, relationally based nosology per se. However, we believe that the empirical study of a large number of relational diagnoses, conducted according to the processes we describe, would yield a manageable number of prototypical clusters or patterns. These prototypical patterns, representing categorical outcomes of the interactions of participants' attachment systems, would serve as the basis for a relational nosology composed of a theoretically coherent set of relational disorders, which complement but does not obscure the benefits of the individual, symptom-based approach outlined in DSM-IV (Benjamin, 1993b, 1994b). Unlike the DSM, such an approach could provide clear guidelines for treatment. Benjamin (1993b) has applied the principles that underlie the SASB-based diagnostic system to the treatment of personality disorders. The application of these principles to the treatment of dysfunctional attachment systems would mark an important step in the further development of the proposed model.

REFERENCES

Ainsworth, M. D. S., Blehar, M. C., Waters, E., & Wall, S. (1978). *Patterns of attachment: A psychological study of the strange situation.* Hillsdale, NJ: Erlbaum.

Ainsworth, M. D. S. (1990). Some considerations regarding theory and assessment relevant to attachments beyond infancy. In M. T. Greenberg, D. Cicchetti, & E. Mark Cummings (Eds.), *Attachment in the preschool years: Theory, research and intervention* (pp. 463–488). Chicago: University of Chicago Press.

Armsden, G. C., & Greenberg, M. T. (1987). The inventory of parent and peer attachment: Individual differences and their relationship to psychological well-being in adolescence. *Journal of Youth and Adolescence, 16*, 427–454.

Bartholomew, K., & Horowitz, L. M. (1991). Attachment styles among young adults: A test of a four category model. *Journal of Personality and Social Psychology, 61*, 226–244.

Benjamin, L. S. (1974). The structural analysis of social behavior. *Psychology Review, 81,* 392–425.

Benjamin, L. S. (1988). *The short form INTREX user's manual, Part I.* Salt Lake City: University of Utah.

Benjamin, L. S. (1993a). Every psychopathology is a gift of love. *Psychotherapy Research, 4,* 1–24.

Benjamin, L. S. (1993b). *Interpersonal diagnosis and treatment of personality disorders.* New York: Guilford.

Benjamin, L. S. (1994a). Good defenses make good neighbors. In H. Conte and R. E. Plutchik (Eds.), *Ego defenses: Theory and research.* New York: Wiley.

Benjamin, L. S. (1994b). SASB: A bridge between personality theory and clinical psychology. *Psychological Inquiry, 5,* 273–316.

Benjamin, L. S. (in press). An interpersonal theory of personality disorders. In J. Clarkin (Ed.), *Major Theories of Personality.* New York: Guilford.

Benjamin, L. S., & Gelfand, D. M. (1992). *Possible transmission of depression through patterns of mother-infant interaction.* Progress report to John D. and Catherine T. MacArthur Foundation Mental Health Research Network on the Psychobiology of Depression and other Affective Disorders.

Bowlby, J. (1973). *Attachment and loss: Vol. 2. Separation: Anxiety and anger.* New York: Basic Books.

Bowlby, J. (1977). The making and breaking of affectional bonds. I. Aetiology and psychopathology in light of attachment theory. *British Journal of Psychiatry, 130,* 201–210.

Bowlby, J. (1982). *Attachment and loss: Volume 1. Attachment* (2nd ed.). New York: Basic Books.

Bowlby, J. (1988). *A secure base: Parent-child attachment and healthy human development.* New York: Basic Books.

Brown, P. C., & Smith, T. W. (1992). Social influence, marriage, and the heart: Cardiovascular consequences of interpersonal control in husbands and wives. *Health Psychology, 11,* 88–96.

Cicchetti, D., Cummings, E. M., Greenberg, M. T., & Marvin, R. (1990). An organizational perspective on attachment beyond infancy: Implications for theory, measurement and research. In M. T. Greenberg, D. Cicchetti, & E. M. Cummings (Eds.) *Attachment in the preschool years: Theory, research and intervention* (pp. 463–488). Chicago: University of Chicago Press.

Crittendon, P. M. (1988). Relationships at risk. In J. Belsky and T. Nezworski (Eds.), *Clinical implications of attachment theory* (pp. 136–174) Hillsdale, NJ: Erlbaum.

Florsheim, P., Tolan, P., & Gorman-Smith, D. (in press). *Family processes and risk for externalizing behavior problems among African-American and Hispanic boys.*

Fairbairn, W. R. D. (1952). *An object relations theory of personality.* New York: Basic Books.

Freud, S. (1940). An outline for psycho-analysis. *The standard edition of the complete psychological works of Sigmund Freud* (vol. 23, pp. 138–207). London: Hogarth Press.

Greenberg, J., & Mitchell, S. (1983). *Object relations in psychoanalytic theory.* Cambridge, MA: Harvard University Press.

Greenberg, M. T., Cicchetti, D., & Cummings, E. M. (1990). History of a collaboration in the study of attachment. In M. T. Greenberg, D. Cicchetti, & E. M. Cummings (Eds.), *Attachment in the preschool years: Theory, research and intervention* (pp. xiii–xix). Chicago: University of Chicago Press.

Greenberg, M. T., Speltz, M., & DeKlyen, M. (1993). The role of attachment in the early development of disruptive behavior problems. *Development and Psychopathology, 5,* 191–214.

Harlow, H. (1958). The nature of love. *American Journal of Psychology, 13,* 673–685.

Hazen, C., & Shaver, P. R. (1994a). Attachment as an organizational framework for research on close relationships. *Psychological Inquiry, 5,* 1–22.

Hazen, C., & Shaver, P. R. (1994b). Deeper into attachment theory. *Psychological Inquiry, 5,* 68–79.

Henry, W. P. (1994). Differentiating normal and abnormal personality: An interpersonal approach based on the Structural Analysis of Social Behavior. In S. Strack & M. Lorr (Eds.), *Differentiating normal and abnormal personality* (pp. 316–340). New York: Springer.

Henry, W. P., Schacht, T. E., & Strupp, H. H. (1986). Structural analysis of social behavior: Application to a study of interpersonal process in differential psychotherapeutic outcome. *Journal of Consulting and Clinical Psychology, 54,* 27–31.

Humphrey, L. L. (1989). Observed family interactions among subtypes of eating disorders using Structural Analysis of Social Behavior. *Journal of Consulting and Clinical Psychology, 54,* 190–195.

Leary, T. (1957). *Interpersonal diagnosis of personality.* New York: Ronald Press.

Lorenz, K. (1965). *The evolution and modification of behavior.* Chicago: University of Chicago Press.

Main, M., & Goldwyn, R. (1985). *An adult attachment classification system.* Unpublished manuscript, University of California at Department of Psychology.

Main, M., & Solomon, J. (1990). Procedures for identifying infants as disorganized/disoriented during the strange situation. In M. T. Greenberg, D. Cicchetti, & E. M. Cummings (Eds.), *Attachment in the preschool years: Theory, research and intervention* (pp. 121–160). Chicago: University of Chicago Press.

Marvin, R. S., & Stewart, R. B. (1990). A family systems framework for the study of attachment. In M. T. Greenberg, D. Cicchetti, & E. M. Cummings (Eds.), *Attachment in the preschool years: Theory, research and intervention* (pp. 51–86). Chicago: University of Chicago Press.

Murray, H. A. (1938). *Explorations in personality.* New York: Oxford University Press.

Pilkonis, P. (1988). Personality prototypes among depressives: Themes of dependency and autonomy. *Journal of Personality Disorders, 2,* 144–152.

Pinsof, W. (1989). A conceptual framework and methodological criteria for family therapy process research. *Journal of Consulting and Clinical Psychology, 57,* 53–59.

Schaefer, E. S. (1971). Development of hierarchical, configurational models for parent behavior and child behavior. In J. P. Hill (Ed.), *Minnesota Symposium on Child Psychology* (vol. 5, pp. 130–161). Minneapolis: University of Minnesota Press.

Sroufe, A. (1988). The role of infant-caregiver attachment in development. In J. Belsky & T. Nezworski (Eds.), *Clinical implications of attachment theory* (pp. 18–40). Hillsdale, NJ: Erlbaum.

Sullivan, H. S. (1953). *The interpersonal theory of psychiatry.* New York: Norton.

West, M., & Sheldon, A. (1988). Classification of pathological attachment patterns in adults. *Journal of Personality Disorders, 2,* 153–159.

Wiggins, J. S. (1982). Circumplex models of interpersonal behavior in clinical psychology. In P. C. Kendell & J. N. Butcher (Eds.), *Handbook of research methods in clinical psychology* (pp. 183–221). New York: Wiley.

CHAPTER 7

Is Diagnosis a Disaster?
A Constructionist Trialogue

KENNETH J. GERGEN, PhD, LYNN HOFFMAN, MSW, and HARLENE ANDERSON, PhD

For some time, the three of us have been deeply engaged in exploring the implications of a social constructionist view of knowledge for therapeutic practice. From a constructionist standpoint, our languages for describing and explaining the world (and ourselves) are not derived from or demanded by whatever is the case. Rather, our languages of description and explanation are produced, sustained, and/or abandoned within processes of human interaction. Further, our languages are constituent features of cultural patterns. They are embedded within relationships in such a way that to change the language would be to alter the relationship. To abandon the concepts of romance, love, marriage, and commitment, for example, would be to alter the forms of cultural life; to obliterate the languages of consciousness, choice, or deliberation would render meaningless our present patterns of praise and blame, along with our courts of law. By the same token, as we generate new languages in our professions and disseminate them within the culture, so do we insinuate ourselves into daily relations—for good or ill. It is against this backdrop that the three of us wish to consider the issue of diagnosis in general and relational diagnosis in particular. We opt for the trialogic conversation as a means of vivifying in practice (as well as in content) the constructionist emphasis on meaning through relationship.

KJG: I find myself increasingly alarmed by the expansion and intensification of diagnosis in this century. At the turn of the century our system for classifying mental disorders was quite rudimentary in terminology and not broadly accepted. However, as the century has unfolded, the terminology has expanded exponentially, and public consciousness of mental deficit terminology has grown acute. In the 1929 publication of Israel Wechsler's *The Neuroses,* a group of approximately a dozen psychological disorders were identified. With the 1938 publication of the *Manual of Psychiatry and Mental Hygiene* (Rosanoff, 1938), some 40 psychogenic disturbances were recognized. (It is interesting to note that many of the terms included therein, such as paresthetic hysteria and autonomic hysteria, have since dropped from common usage, and some of them—such as moral deficiency, vagabondage, misanthropy, and masturbation—now seem quaint or obviously prejudicial.) In 1952, with the American Psychiatric Association's publication of the first *Diagnostic and Statistical Manual of Mental Disorders* (APA, 1952), some 50 to 60 different psychogenic disturbances were identified. By 1987, only 20 years later, the manual had gone through three revisions. With the third revised edition (DSM-III-R) (APA, 1987), the number of recognized illnesses more than tripled (hovering between 180 and 200, depending on choice of definitional boundaries). The fourth edition (DSM-IV) expands the list even further (APA, 1994).

At the present time, one may be classified as mentally ill by virtue of cocaine intoxication, caffeine intoxication, the use of hallucinogens, voyeurism, transvestism, sexual aversion, the inhibition of orgasm, gambling, academic problems, antisocial behavior, bereavement, and noncompliance with medical treatment. Numerous additions to the standardized nomenclature continuously appear in professional writings to the public. Consider, for example, seasonal affective disorder, stress, burnout, erotomania, and the harlequin complex. What, we might ask, are the upper limits for classifying people in terms of deficits?

As these terminologies are disseminated to the public—through classrooms, popular magazines, television, and film dramas they become available to people for understanding of self and others. They are, after all, the "terms of the experts," and if one wishes to do the right thing, they become languages of choice for understanding or labeling people (including the self) in daily life. Terms such as depression, paranoia, attention deficit disorder, sociopathic, and schizophrenia have become essential entries in the vocabulary of the educated person. And when the terms are applied in daily life, they have substantial effects—in narrowing the explanation to the level of the individual, stigmatizing, and obscuring the contribution of other factors (including the demands of economic life, media images, and traditions of individual evaluation) to the actions in question. Further, when these terms are used to construct the self, they suggest that one should seek professional treatment. In this sense, the development and dissemination of the terminology by the profession acts to create a population of people who will seek professional help. As more professionals are required—as they have been in increasing numbers over the century—so is there pressure to increase the vocabulary. Elsewhere (Gergen, 1994) I have called this a "cycle of progressive infirmity."

LH: Ken's thinking has been most helpful in my particular struggles to find a way out of the naming bind, which is the belief that in order to be helpful about a complaint, you have to describe it and name it. The describing and naming makes it real. Medical practitioners have been so successful in creating a taxonomy of physical distress that psychological professionals have sought to follow suit.

There is an implicit contradiction between the nonessentialist stance of social construction theory and this volume on relational diagnosis. If social construction theory challenges psychobiological naming systems, it also challenges the descriptive truth of a relational syllabary. None of these self-confirming systems of naming provides a comfortable resting place for the social constructionist. At the same time, what is to become of the profession of family therapy if it does not join in the practice of naming? Our way of life is threatened with extinction.

Trying to think why I was drawn to social constructionism, I reflected that I had been through several "diagnostic worldviews" in my lifetime, each more convincing than the last, and was beginning to see this as evidence of a very relativistic and joking cosmic God. As far as psychology was concerned, I had come of age in total innocence. The community of left-wing artists I grew up in had their own brand of qualifying phrases: reactionary, fascist, businessman, Republican, Philistine. Only when I got to college did I find out about neuroses and psychoses and "mental illness." My earlier worldview took a hit; also, I found that many of the new terms could describe me. My discovery of the family therapy movement, which took the onus off the person and put it on the "system," was therefore a great relief.

I felt pleased with myself as the family systems movement gathered speed. Then I was challenged again. I discovered an article by a scholar from Ontario, Gerald Erickson (1988), who attacked systemic thinking from a postmodern point of view. As I scrambled to read about these new ideas, I realized that all of the models in the family therapy field had great failings. They were all modernist and mistaken. There were no systems out there, no patterns that connect, no levels, no structures waiting to be observed. For me this kind of thinking put an end to diagnostics of any kind.

This is a bit tongue in cheek, but I assure you that each epistemological earthquake leaves enormous damage in its wake. Every time you build a world of ideas or join one, it is like a screening device that limits you from seeing other worlds. Out of sight are those you left behind or those you uneasily suspect may lie ahead. There is also a gathering coherence that seems to go with the territory. As time passes, this coherence may become increasingly well defined and more fully knit. That is why it is necessary to damage only one piece of a world to bring down many related structures.

Nevertheless, these worlds have enormous resiliency. In my lifetime, in the field I am in, I have been shaken by earthquakes several times. I have tended to move on to a new community, but many of the inhabitants of the old ones have rebuilt and gone on as before. It takes an earthquake that strikes at a deep structure level, such as finances, to mark historic change. The health care upheaval, for better or worse, has given one of the cities in my field a mandate to be the capital. Gathered under the medicalized roof of DSM-IV, we find an attempt to enumerate and describe all existing problems of behavior: life problems, death problems, mind problems, disease problems, poverty problems, class problems, violence problems, sex problems, work problems, love problems. We see the proliferation of pathological titles Ken has talked about, and there seems no upper limit on what can be absorbed into the system of naming.

At the same time, I think this may be the good fortune of family therapists. Conditions that are "merely" relational have been exempted from inclusion in DSM-IV, except for a brief nod to a relationship-oriented axis that may not even be reimbursed. So perhaps we have been rescued from the "rage to order." Harlene Anderson (1994) and Ken Hardy (1994) were recently asked to answer the charge that family therapy would be marginalized unless it became more identified with the "major disciplines" in mental health (Shields, Wynne, & Gawinski, 1994). So much the better, they said. Only by remaining the one health industry that does not give people labels or diagnose conditions can family therapy represent an important stream of evolution in the field. That is my position too.

HA: The passionate plea for the inclusion of relational diagnoses in the DSM-IV locates family therapy within psychiatric discourse, with its medical heritage, its aspiration to mimic natural sciences, and its modernist, positivist disposition. This is understandable. As Ken suggests, diagnostic systems give a sense of legitimacy, confidence, and predictability both to the professional and to the client. In both psychotherapy and the broader culture, a diagnosis implies that the object of inquiry and the method of inquiry are based on stable assumptions like those in the biomedical realm. It operates as a professional code that has the function of gathering, analyzing, and ordering waiting-to-be-discovered data. As similarities and patterns are found, problems are then fitted into a deficit-based system of categories. In a larger sense, this framework is based on the assumption that language is representational and can accurately depict "reality." When I think of diagnosis, I think of cybernetician Heinz von Foerster's remark, "Believing is seeing."

Implicit in the DSM-IV is the assumption that psychotherapy is a relationship between an expert who has knowledge and a nonexpert who needs help. The public, the profession, and the state have given authority to the therapist to collect information about the client and place it on a predetermined therapist map from which the diagnosis is then derived and the treatment plan decided. This process reduces uncertainty by telling the therapist what he or she ought to do and suggesting how the client ought to change in order to get well.

From a postmodern perspective, a relational or "between-persons" diagnosis is no different from an individual or "within-the-person" diagnosis. The inclusion of family therapy criteria for "behavioral health" simply would place a new layer of labels upon an old one. For political, economic, and legitimation reasons, this would be a great step forward for family therapy, but in terms of family therapy's heritage as an alternative explanatory view, it constitutes a great step back. Simply to assume that the issue is a question of an individual versus a relational classification is to oversimplify a set of complex, ever-changing human dynamics.

If one approaches these questions from a postmodern social constructionist perspective, they are no longer relevant. Social constructionism frees one to think in terms of individuals-in-relationship rather than an individual-relationship dichotomy. It also locates psychological knowledge in a sociohistorical context and treats it as a form of discursive activity (Danziger, 1990; Gergen, 1973, 1985; Luria, 1971). "Discursive activity" refers to Wittgenstein's (1953) challenge to see language as representational—an expression of the nature of things—and his alternative idea that we generate descriptions and explanations as the means of coordinating ourselves with each other. It is the language that constructs what we take to be the person and the relationship. Diagnoses, for instance, are socially constructed meanings put forth by the dominant professional culture. A diagnosis is an agreement in language to make sense of some behavior or event in a certain way. But a social constructionist perspective warns us that this kind of agreement may mislead us into holding the diagnosis to be true. Is it the diagnostic reality we should be treating in therapy?

Social constructionism invites alternative questions: What is the intent of a diagnosis? What questions are believed to be answered by diagnosis? What information is thought to be gained? What do we want a diagnosis to communicate and to whom? If there are many ways to think about, to describe what may be thought of as the same thing (i.e., behaviors, feelings), how can we respect and work within all realities? Should we consider the possibility of multiple diagnoses? How can we bring the client into the process? How can, and is it possible for, a diagnosis to be meaningful for all involved? How can it be collaborative, tailored to the individual, useful? What other words can we use? If we reject diagnostic terms, should we try to persuade the helping system to change its nosology? How do we develop a way in which multiverses can coexist?

If one views life as dynamic, unstable, and unpredictable, then inquiry about it must be ever active. If one views knowledge as socially created and knowledge and knowers as interdependent, then it makes sense to include the client in the diagnostic process. This moves diagnosis from the realm of a private discourse to a shared inquiry in which it becomes a mutual discovery process.

In a serendipitous way clients have become involved in creating their own diagnoses and ideas about treatment. Our culture-bound human nature compels us to want to know what is wrong and to have a name for a problem. With the help of the media, diagnostic language and preferred treatments have leaked into the public domain. We all have clients who come in with self-diagnoses such as "codependent" and "adult child of an alcoholic" and clients who request Prozac for depression or a 12-step group for dealing with addiction. I question, however, whether these self-diagnoses do not often yield unworkable problems for both the client and the professional. Diagnoses, official and unofficial, often concretize identities that limit people; they create black boxes with few, obscure exits; and they form obstacles to more viable and liberating self-definitions (Anderson, 1992).

I recently talked with a couple who had appeared on a television talk show focused on gender issues in couples. The show's guest expert had diagnosed the husband as "irresponsible" (an individual description), the wife as an "adult survivor of childhood incest" (an individual description), and the couple as "codependent" (a relational description). When I saw them they were embroiled in a battle to make him responsible, to promote her "survivorhood," and to make them independent of each other. They were prisoners of diagnosis-created unworkable problems. Or, as Ken Gergen suggests, every move they made was dysfunctionalized. This is the tyranny of diagnosis.

Thinking of therapy and diagnosis from a postmodern social constructionist perspective redefines the therapist-client relationship and challenges professional knowledge. It moves therapy from a relationship between a knower and one who is ignorant to a collaborative partnership in which the deciding of, the exploring of, and the "solving" of problems is a process of shared inquiry in which the diagnosis is not fixed and the problem may shift and dissolve over time. It invites the client's voice and his or her expertise on lived experiences. Bringing in the client's voice—the words and terms that have significance for the client—gives productive life to everyday language. The yield is a more jointly created and thus more cooperative language that generates more possibilities than professional vocabularies—based on pre-knowledge that produces lifeless, sterile lookalikes—and suppresses the uniqueness of the individual client's narrative (Anderson, 1992). A constructionist stance favors a more mutual, personalized knowledge. This view of therapy and diagnosis entails uncertainty; while some might question this ethic of uncertainty, I question the ethic of certainty.

This is why I do not favor adding a "relational diagnosis" to the one already in use. Kaslow (1993) envisages the "formulation of a language and a typology that can be utilized, with a high degree of consensus about definitions and criteria sets, based on solid research findings, by family therapists emanating from many disciplines and theoretical persuasions," which would eventuate in a "validated nosology of relational disorders." There are many reasons, both theoretical and practical, for doubting that this is possible; and there are many reasons for arguing against such an end. Like Ken and Lynn, I suggest that rather than talk about a relational diagnostic system, we need to consider new and more promising directions for family therapy and psychology.

Of course this leaves us shaken. Many questions are left hanging. What do therapists do with their professional knowledge and past experience? How do we then communicate with professional colleagues, clients, and insurance companies? The ethical questions that face us in this new era of managed health care are far broader and more daunting, for instance, than simply whether submissions for insurance reimbursement are factually correct.

KJG: As I have been deliberating on your comments, Lynn and Harlene, I have been trying to take the role of an essentialist, diagnostician, and asking myself what questions I would raise. One of these is a question I often have faced myself, and it concerns the existence of what we would generally take to be "the real world." In more homely fashion, one asks, "Isn't there something these terms refer to, and aren't these kinds of behaviors deeply problematic both for the individuals (or families) as well as the society? We must have some way to talk about these patterns within our profession, some way to share our knowledge of effective treatment. So don't we require just these forms of terminology?" And, such an interrogator might add, we need such terms even if we agree with the constructionist argument that they may not be the only or the most accurate ways of describing such actions.

I would view this as a reasonable question, granting that we spend most of our time in cultural traditions where the "real world" counts. However, granting in this sense that there is "something these terms refer to," the question becomes, as you suggest, Harlene, whether and for what we require the professional labels. At the outset, the argument simply does not hold that the diagnostic terms describe observable behaviors. None of our terms, either from DSM-IV or from the newly developing vocabulary of relational diagnosis, actually refers to the specific movements of people's bodies through time and space, the sounds they emit, the liquids or smells they exude—or anything else we could assess with a set of mechanical instruments. Rather, all the terms refer to hypothetical processes, mechanisms, or purposes lying behind or served by a set of behaviors. If I say an individual is "depressed," based on a set of items from a depression inventory, it is not the check marks on the paper to which I am referring but to what these check marks suggest about a state of mind. Yet I have no access to a state of mind; this I presume a priori (or, you might say, because of the particular myths about the mind that I inherit from cultural history). In the same way, I don't as a therapist observe dysfunctional behavior. I observe behavior that I label a dysfunctional given a set of values I hold about what is functional. To be sure, these are academic arguments simply designed to deflate the presumption that professional labels have unambiguous referents. (See also Sarbin & Mancuso, 1980; Wiener, 1991.) However, soon I will propose that because of this problem, the therapeutic community stands in great danger.

Now, if our labels are but scantily tied to observables, the question of "why label?" takes on new dimensions. We cannot say that we need the labels to communicate professionally about the cases we confront, because there are no grounds to believe that what one person means (in terms of specific behavior) by "oppositional defiant disorder" or "partner relational problem" is the same thing that anyone else means; and should we agree, there is no means of substantiating this conclusion outside our local agreement. Thus, the diagnostic terms help us to think that we are all working on the same phenomena, but this creates a false sense of security. Do the professional diagnoses then help the client? Surely this is the most significant question we should be asking. There is reason for debate here, for some clients may indeed prefer the security of a professional term to replace what they feel are their own floundering attempts to comprehend. The availability of the diagnosis suggests that such cases are possibly common, well known, well understood, and quite effectively treatable. And while to give a diagnosis under such conditions would be an act of bad faith on the therapist's part, there might be ameliorative placebo effects.

At this point I am drawn to the wisdom of Harlene's comments concerning the ever-shifting character of daily activity, the communal construction of meaning, and the ways in which languages function in daily life. For, it might be asked, in the long run is it not a greater contribution to the lives of our clients (and indeed to our own) if we have multiple ways of understanding our activities, if we can see how different groups might describe what we do, if we understand how these various descriptions add or subtract from life's quality? Most of us are fully aware that we ourselves are too complex to slot into categories, that relationships are subject to infinite interpretation, that the same actions and the same descriptions may mean different things at different times and with different consequences. Would we not wish our clients to take advantage of these forms of cultural wisdom? In whose service do we "freeze the frame"?

Earlier I mentioned the possibility of danger. Both Lynn and Harlene endorse a field of family therapy that is unique in its avoidance of a professional nosology, a field that in my opinion would thus be at the cultural forefront. In the long run there is reason to believe that the other helping professions will follow suit. Much grassroots antipathy is developing for the kinds of diagnoses to which patients have been exposed over the years; organizations of ex-mental patients who feel they have been ill-served by the practices of the mental health professions have arisen (Chamberlin, 1990), as have feminist groups that feel women to be victims of the existing nosologies. (See, for example, Caplan, 1987, 1991.) And there are professionals from around the globe who (like us) feel that diagnostics are more injurious than helpful. The day will soon come (and indeed I will lend my efforts to the outcome) when those who require assistance for their problems will bring formal litigation against those who diagnose. When diagnostic categories become part of one's permanent records, and when such records become available for various evaluative purposes, the mental health profession will have no legitimate grounds on which to defend the practice of diagnosis.

LH: I agree with your warnings, Ken and Harlene, about the harmfulness of diagnostic labeling, or what I call "psychiatric hate speech." To find out what is actually experienced as hateful, I have been experimenting with consultations in workshops. I will talk with a therapist about a family situation (I have abandoned the term "case") while the family is sitting there overhearing us. I will then ask the family to comment on our conversation. Next I will ask the audience, in small groups, to arrive at some ideas to reflect back to the family. The groups take turns telling me their ideas, which I write down on a flip chart, but only after these are filtered through family members' reactions. This has been a very interesting procedure, in that we create a family-sensitive set of descriptions rather than the usual professional ones imposed from outside. I remember one incident involving a stormy couple who couldn't stay together and couldn't stay apart. One audience group had commented that the couple seemed to have an addiction to crisis. Another group, referring to a local spot that was known as the Bungee Capital of North America, likened their relationship to a pair of married bungee jumpers. The couple objected to the first idea but warmly accepted the second. Operations like this replace the usual expert model for diagnosis with a less pejorative one.

In doing homework for this piece, I found myself examining some of the more relational schemes for diagnosis. One that actually made it into the DSM-IV (1994), at least into the appendix, is family psychiatrist Lyman Wynne's Global Assessment of Family Functioning Scale (GARF), which parallels the Global Assessment of Functioning Scale (GAF) for individuals, reported under Axis V. GARF reflects the early thinking about family therapy that was based on the idea that the family is a "system," that is, a unit composed of subparts acting interdependently upon each other. This analogy was apparently contributed by Talcott Parsons (1951), whose normative model for family functioning was once a powerful image in the field.

Another effort to create a relational framework for diagnosis has been offered by Karl Tomm (1991), a psychiatrist from Canada. Tomm believes that a family in which there is a patient is one in which the communication is dominated by harmful patterns. These patterns are not produced by the family system per se but are a result of vicious cycles in which efforts to stop the pattern only reinforce it. Tomm calls these sequences Pathological Interpersonal Patterns (PIPs) and sees therapy as a matter of replacing them with Healing Interpersonal Patterns (HIPs). As a constructionist, I find both Wynne's and Tomm's formulations an improvement on DSM-IV's categories in that they are not so unkind to the individual, but I still feel uncomfortable with their assumption of an ontologically transparent pathology.

Fortunately, the recent jump to a narrative analogy has put diagnosis on a new track that jettisons the notion of an objective assessment of pathology, preferring to think of these formulations as stories or forms of discourse. In one swift shift of metaphor, we are catapulted into a postmodern universe where "reality" is placed in quotes. White and Epston (1990), among others, shoved the canoe from the bank by opposing the "problem-saturated" story and joining forces with the family to find a new, more hopeful one. A kindred soul to White is Chris Kinman of British Columbia. In working with First Nations youth, Kinman has been very much concerned with helping to create alternatives to the usual stereotyped pictures of problematic teens. While trying to come up with a narrative-based set of diagnostic tools, he has been experimenting with the term "discourse," using it to frame the situation of a young client by locating it under headings such as "Discourses of Youth and Peers" or "Discourses of Youth and School" (Kinman & Sanders, 1994). These descriptions are arrived at by conversations with the individual in question and with other people in the family or community.

I mention these efforts because even though many of us deplore the psychiatric profession's extraordinary attempt to cover all bases in a grab for territory, the appearance of DSM-IV has acted as a most important gadfly. The field of family therapy seems to have been preparing itself for this fight in view of the increasingly swift acceptance of a social constructionist and narrative point of view.

I would like to make one last point: This constructionist view is congruent with the movement toward user-friendliness in family therapy (Reimers & Treacher, 1995). A recent news report on malpractice suits against medical practitioners found that the number of suits correlated with a poor "bedside manner": Those who take time with their patients, listen attentively to them, and show kindness are sued far less often than their brusquer counterparts. In an era of managed care, the client's story is going to be listened to more carefully, and there will be a move toward including the user in the conversation, especially the conversation around diagnosis.

At the same time, even when I disagree with a position, I like to join with what is already in place. In this respect, I find that the structuring of diagnosis around axes of varying hues offers a useful starting point. It is easy to imagine this format transforming into a Roshomon-like array of differing perspectives. Customers could have a special axis to themselves or a separate place to comment on each axis. Since the process of definition is the primary framing act of any kind of therapy or consultation, it deserves as much time as is needed. Attention to this aspect seems to me crucial, not only in exposing the bedrock nature of therapy as a political as opposed to a medical event, but in allowing all parties to have their day in court.

HA: I am particularly captured by Ken's and Lynn's interest in the client's voice—the ways in which some clients either jointly through organized associations or singularly through the courts are securing an arena for the consumers' sentiments and grievances. Ken speaks of the days of litigation to come. I think they have already begun. Media reports of patients suing therapists (and winning) are no longer an anomaly. We read reports of patients who sued therapists for creating false memory syndromes and multiple personalities. Recently parents sued their 16-year-old daughter's therapist for not thoroughly investigating her accusations of sexual abuse. Such actions threaten the false sense of security that diagnosis gives the professional and highlight the complexity of human behavior and interactions. Likewise, such actions shout the importance of guaranteeing the consumer's voice, be it client, insurance company, managed health care agent, or therapist.

Like Lynn, I am drawn to the hope that a narrative perspective can provide a possible relief from the deficiency and illness language in the mental health field. Narrative understanding takes into account the beliefs and intentions and the narrative histories and contexts that underpin, shape, and give significance to those actions. As such, narrative understanding offers the possibility of understanding and, equally important, not understanding the actions of others.

I would like to echo Goolishian's comment in his plenary paper for the Houston Galveston Institute's conference, the Dis-diseasing of Mental Health, held in October 1991. He said, "We must rely on the capacity that people have for the narrative construction of their life and we must redefine therapy as a skill in participating in that process. . . . It will take more than relational language. . . . We must develop a language of description that moves us out of the linguistic black hole in which we are now captured." Inspired by Wittgenstein's words in *Culture and Value* (1980)— Nobody can truthfully say of himself that he is filth. Because if I do say it, though it can be true in some sense, this is not a truth by which I myself can be penetrated; otherwise I should have to go mad or change myself—Goolishian continued, "Our languages of description are not only normative but they have, over the years, ended up forcing socially constructed self-narratives on our clients of uselessness and filth. Is it possible that as a result they often select the option 'to go mad'?"

KJG: One hope that the three of us shared in this effort was that the trialogue as a form of writing would itself demonstrate some of the advantages of a constructionist orientation to relational diagnosis. What happens if we depart from monologue (which parallels the singular voice of diagnostic labeling practices) and approach a multivocal conversation (favored by the constructionist)? In some degree I think we have made good on this hope, inasmuch as each of us has brought a unique voice to the table, drawing from different experiences, relationships, and literatures. Our case is richer by virtue of our joint participation. At the same time, because there is so much general agreement among us, the trialogic form hasn't blossomed to its fullest degree. We have not yet cashed in on its catalytic potential.

To explore this possibility, I want to focus on a point of disagreement. How can we treat conflict within this conversational space in a way that is different from a monological orientation (where the interlocutor typically shields internal conflicts in favor of achieving full coherence)? The fact is that in the case of diagnostics, I do not favor Lynn's preference for joining "what is already in place." As she points out, "the process of definition is the primary framing act of any kind of therapy or consultation," and, by virtue of our various critiques, she proposes to multiply the range of definitions, even to include those of the clients themselves. Perhaps I feel more critical toward diagnosis, but I ask, if it is injurious to our "clients," why join what is in place? Why should we accept the process of definition as a primary feature of therapy or consultation?

Now, I realize that it is perhaps easier for me to take this strong position, because I am not a therapist and do not depend on maintaining the therapeutic traditions for my livelihood. I need not be so concerned with what is already in place because I have fewer worries about what it does to my relationships within the tradition (and my family) should I deviate sharply from it. And also, we already have seen Lynn's concern that the profession maintain itself in a realistic world of competition with the more diagnostically prone mental health professionals. Thus, as a constructionist I must understand the intelligibility of Lynn's preferences in terms of the relational matrix in which she lives. And vice versa. But where does such recognition take us? And, to play out the parallels with professional-client relations, what might follow if both the professional and the client realized the parochial nature of various diagnostic labels, respecting each other but realizing that such understandings represent only one tradition among many?

There is no single answer to these queries. The more general question of how to go on in a world of multiple and conflicting realities is as profound as it is complex. However, let me suggest that at least one possibility in the present instance is to locate an alternative intelligibility with which we both can live comfortably. I am thinking here primarily in terms of clinical practices. It seems to me that we might share in the belief that the process of labeling may sometimes have value, that it is sometimes injurious, but that it is not essential to the process of therapy. That is, therapeutic efficacy does not depend chiefly on slotting clients into a set of predetermined and publicly acknowledged categories. If we could agree on this assumption, then we might ask whether it would be possible to establish some form of "no-fault" insurance coverage for therapy. Such policies have been a major boon to divorce courts, where establishing the original source of marital problems has proven impossible. We enter much the same thicket in attempting to diagnose "the problem" in cases of most human suffering. If insurance companies no longer required diagnoses for third-party therapy billings, then diagnosis could become optional—available when useful but not essential for treatment. If every insured party in a given insurance plan had the right to a limited number of consultations, then the fact that the individual (or family) felt their suffering was severe enough to demand professional attention might be sufficient. Might we explore the possibilities together of instituting such policies across the mental health professions?

Reflexively speaking, it seems to me that our present trialogue has now managed to press our joint thinking on these topics forward—so that the three of us are changed during the course of our conversation. I am not in precisely the same place I was when I entered the conversation. If this is so, is there not a lesson here for the traditional tendency in the profession toward monologue? Diagnostic labeling has a way of "stopping the conversation." The professional announces "you are X" or "Y," and there is no obvious means of the diagnosis being transformed by the subsequent conversation with the client. Monologue insulates itself from change; diagnostics radically truncate the possibilities for therapeutic transformation.

HA: Ken suggests that our trialogue has not created the catalytic potential that he hoped to achieve. For me, it has created more thoughts than my written words reveal. I have more of a dialogue in my head about diagnosis, and I frequently bring the issues of diagnosis into my conversations with colleagues and students. As in therapy, is the catalytic potential ever visible? Can our words on paper further the dialogue about diagnosis for others? I hope so.

I will tell a story about a case that vividly illustrates the complexities of human problems and how diagnosis and diagnosis-driven treatment can oversimplify and exacerbate them: "I asked my daughter, why do you have this exotic white woman's disease?" These words were spoken by the exasperated father of Joan, a 16-year-old Afro-American girl who, in her efforts to control her weight, was starving herself to death. She met the essential criteria for anorexia nervosa. Joan was hospitalized a year ago at a private psychiatric hospital where her treatment included individual, family, and adolescent group therapy. She was discharged after 30 days when her psychiatric hospitalization insurance benefits were exhausted and admitted to a private hospital medical unit where her problem was diagnosed as a mental disorder. She was discharged after one week when the insurance company challenged the medical diagnosis, having determined it was a preexisting psychiatric diagnosis, and therefore denied coverage.

The hospital physician urged the family to commit their daughter to a county charity psychiatric hospital where she could receive psychiatric care for 30 days at no charge. The family refused. The physician said that Joan was "the most difficult" and "the most devious anorectic" that he had treated. He feared she would "slip through the cracks" if she did not receive continuous inpatient psychiatric treatment. His fear was corroborated by her and the family's behaviors. In talking about the family he said in frustration, "We're not on the same page of the book. No, we're not even in the same book." He believed that the father's responses did not match the daughter's life-threatening illness, and his belief was validated each time the father, who was a minister, talked about spirituality and expressed his faith in his daughter's "finding her way" and "trusting the process." The physician was also frustrated with and puzzled by the family's insincerity and by a family in which the father was more absorbed with the daughter's eating disorder than the mother. As he described the father carrying his limp daughter into the hospital emergency room, the physician said the father's calmness was "bizarre."

Two weeks after the medical hospital discharge, Joan drank a bottle of syrup to induce vomiting and began vomiting uncontrollably. Her parents took her to the county charitable hospital, where she was admitted because the staff thought she was suicidal. Joan insisted that she was not trying to kill herself. In the county hospital she had individual therapy and was discharged after two weeks with the condition that her family agree to engage in intensive family therapy. She was referred to a private psychiatric clinic where the intake screened her out because the insurance benefits were exhausted. The private clinic, in turn, referred Joan to a nonprofit counseling center. The referral was made to a specific therapist-in-training whom the intake person knew had personal experience with an eating disorder. Joan's parents took her to see the therapist. It was agreed that the therapist would continue to see Joan and that the parents would meet with the therapist whenever the therapist, Joan, or the parents felt it necessary.

The family continued to consult their family physician, who felt Joan's problem was out of his realm of expertise. He referred Joan—simultaneous with the referral to the nonprofit counseling center—to a private practice therapist who specialized in eating disorders. The family took Joan to the specialist, who added the diagnosis Major Depression, Single Episode, and initiated individual therapy for Joan and family therapy for her and her parents. He, too, said that the family was "the most bizarre family I have ever seen." He felt that Joan had "too much power over her parents" and was "victim" of and in turn was "acting out her parent's estrangement and conflict." When he found out that the parents had authorized a home-bound school program for Joan, he warned the counseling center therapist that "Joan must go to school . . . don't you know that anorectics manipulate and isolate?" He saw the school decision as evidence that Joan had too much power over her parents and now the counseling center therapist and her supervisor.

The private therapist continued to see Joan and the family and the counseling center therapist continued to see Joan, sometimes twice a week, and occasionally to meet with members of her family in different combinations. Who came to the sessions depended on what was being talked about and who wanted to come. The counseling center therapist thought the parents were cooperative. They always kept their appointments and often requested additional ones. The father usually brought Joan to the sessions because the mother worked and went to college.

Joan talked with the counseling center therapist frequently about the people who were "bugging" her by trying to be helpful. Referring to a previous therapist, Joan said, "He thought he knew all about me just because I'm an anorectic." She talked about how he confronted her and accused her of being secretive, isolating, and dishonest. She wished people would let her be herself.

The therapist asked curiously, "How do I treat you?" Joan said, "I like working with you because you don't treat me like I'm an anorectic. You let me be myself." Joan talked about how she wanted to be a teenager with teenage problems, how she was worried about the way she expressed her anger, and how ill at ease she was with what her peers were doing. She expressed anxiety about social awkwardness, boys, the dark, being lonely, expectations at home that she should take care of her younger brothers, taking up slack for chores her sister did not do, and wanting a job to earn some money. She said she felt like an "ugly duckling" and that people always commented on how pretty her sister was. She said, "I want to be an individual where others cannot copy me." Joan expressed concern about her parent's relationship, worrying that they were "so distant" and that "Mom buries herself in her work" and described how her mother's "stacks of paper had taken over the house." She expressed her worry about how her parents get "so stirred up" when they talk with the eating disorder therapist.

The therapist's curiosity about the father's question, "Why do you have this exotic white woman's disease?" led her to learn that the family lived in an all-white neighborhood and that all of Joan's friends were white. (Joan did not see the racial issue as a problem the way her father and brother did.) She learned that the father was a prominent black minister and that the mother was a devout Catholic. The daughter went to church with the mother and the son went to church with the father. The father, persuaded by his religious beliefs, felt that the daughter's illness was "the work of the devil." "All things happen for a purpose . . . God is testing her strength," he said, and he backed up his belief with biblical quotes. He was firm in his belief that "This is something she is working out . . . I trust her that she will work through this . . . trust her to make decisions about what is best for her . . . to find her own way."

The mother seemed genuinely concerned: "I want Joan to feel that I am here for her." (Of course, Joan thought the mother was "intrusive.") The mother hoped that the therapist could "help Joan with her emotions" and could "help Joan talk with the family about what is really bothering her." Joan's sister, like her mother, thought it would be helpful "if she would just talk to us about it."

Joan's older brother pinpointed the stressful relationship between Joan and her younger sister as the culprit. He felt strongly that if they were in a school where the majority of students were black, Joan, and her sister as well, would not have problems or the split between them because "In an all-black school you have to stick together to protect yourself." He had several other thoughts about Joan's problem—all relating to cultural issues. He agreed with the father that "Black girls don't have anorexia."

In reflecting on her work with Joan and her family, the counseling center therapist said, "At first I took the diagnosis that the family and I had inherited seriously. I believed it. Influenced by my preconceptions of anorectics as rigid, controlling, isolating perfectionists, I did not question the psychiatrist's and the eating disorder specialist's opinions and recommendations. I tried hard to help Joan and her family. I tried to talk with them about the diagnosis and convince them of the experts' opinions on the individual and family dynamics associated with anorexia nervosa. The harder I tried, the worse Joan became, and the more upset and worried I became."

Like the others before her, the more the therapist tried to treat the diagnosis, the more family members acted in ways that verified her preconceptions about anorectics and their families and hence confirmed the diagnosis. Frustration mounted until, as the therapist put it, "As I got to know Joan and her family, I gradually realized that I was getting to know another Joan, another mother, and another father. My interest in what they were concerned about led to conversations in which Joan and her family found causes and answers that were meaningful to them. To my surprise, I, too, was beginning to trust that Joan would find her answers and her own way. I realized that I was seeing and hearing the person, not an anorectic and a dysfunctional family."

Through the therapist's inquisitiveness about each person's ideas, she learned far more about the family and its members than simply pursuing what the diagnosis permits. The dysfunctional nonsense of their actions and beliefs now made sense. As the therapy with Joan and her family illustrates, there are as many definitions of "a problem," including what caused it and its imagined solutions, as there are people in conversation about the problem. And these ideas can change over time.

As I think about Joan and her family, I keep returning to the notions of monologue and dialogue that Ken mentioned. Embedded in my earlier comments is a bias toward the process, or the essence, of therapy as a dialogue. Diagnosis is part of this dialogue. Preconceptions can lead a therapist to an inner monologue and can lead to dueling monologues between client and therapist—and among professionals. The therapist's ability to question and not hold onto her preconceptions allowed her to be open and curious about others. Joan and her family and the therapist joined in dialogue—a conversational process involving a shared inquiry that led to shifts in the "problem" and new possibilities for all of them. This leads me to Lynn's comment on joining.

I am not sure if by joining Lynn means agreeing with or using as a starting point for conversation. Nevertheless, I do not believe that diagnosis or problem-defining necessarily needs to be part of the therapy, although clients usually do want to talk about their problem. That is why they come. How problems and solutions emerge and dissolve through dialogue, however, is beyond the scope of this trialogue. (See Anderson, 1995; Anderson & Goolishian, 1988.)

I agree that thinking of diagnosis in terms of either-or oversimplifies and clouds. Several questions have been intimated in this discussion on diagnosis that I think are worth highlighting. If there is a diagnostic process, toward what aim and who determines that aim? What meaning does the diagnosis have for each person involved? Most important, what meaning does it have for the client? Is it a useful meaning? Is it respectful? Does it allow for the opening of doors—the creation of potentials—or does it close doors and restrict possibilities? Does it perpetuate the problem? Does it create new problems? These are the questions we should confront prior to developing yet a new range of diagnostics.

Lynn mentioned managed health care. I think that managed health care will further marginalize the client's voice. This industry is already dictating and policing diagnoses. It is not unusual for a managed health care company to refuse to authorize any services except those for treating the diagnosis assigned by their case manager. Therapy is not only a political and medical event but also an economic one. But this leads us to another topic.

LH: It does seem that the conversation is now taking us into new spaces. The question I have is whether the shift would have happened if I had not "joined the opposition" or if Ken had not chosen to "disagree"? If we had used a debate format from the outset, with each person taking a different side, could we have reached this point earlier? Catherine Bateson said at a recent conference that to have the kind of improvisational conversation she finds useful, people first have to establish that they have a common code. So perhaps it is a matter of stages. What do the two of you think?

In response to Harlene's last comments, it seems to me that therapists struggling to find a niche in managed care apparently see no other way out but to stay within the diagnostic framework. Although I have opted out of this framework, I felt that I should put myself back in to represent their "side." But I think Harlene is right to say that this shift toward the medical metaphor not only distances us from our customers but makes us less effective. Then, since no one admits to the metaphor, we throw in mystification as well. I am glad, Harlene, that you included such a vivid story to illustrate the dilemma.

I also greatly liked Ken's idea of "no-fault" psychotherapy. With this suggestion, he has put himself in the category of "causal agnostic." I got this term from a recent Nobel prize winner, the economist Ronald Coase (Passell, 1991), who pioneered the idea that you didn't have to establish cause in cases of conflict over, say, responsibility for pollution. If you left it to the parties themselves to figure out, they would probably come up with a more workable solution on their own. The idea of exchanging air rights is an example. Coase's kind of thinking, like Ken's, starts to give everybody breathing room.

What is especially interesting here is that what Ken is advocating is already coming to pass. The cutting edge of family therapy is moving away from a concern with problems and their causes. The brief solution-oriented approaches that have gained such popularity and the narrative approach of Michael White are future-oriented, except for ways in which the past predicts what White (1989) calls "unique out-comes." An even more extreme version of that position, of course, is the "not-know-ing" stance of the late Harry Goolishian and Harlene. The therapist who takes that stance does not concern herself with causes except to the degree that they form part of different people's stories. She assumes that the complaint would not have come to her attention if it had been embedded in ways of talking that were helpful. The focus is therefore as much on changing the style of the conversation as on what the conversation is about.

Another idea that I think might shake things up is to divest ourselves of the corpus of thought known as modern psychology or the study of the "psyche." The idea of the psyche is useful because "it" is presented as a representation of an entity sitting inside the person like a tiny fetus. This makes it easy to think of "it" as susceptible to failure, breakdown, or distortions in growing. However, during psychology's period of supremacy in this modernist century, it has failed to present any classification of disorders equal to that which medical research and practice has come up with. The most cursory look at DSM-IV shows it to be built on cobwebs. This is because "invisible illnesses," as I call them, are not analogous to disorders expressed in the body and are not, therefore, susceptible to category and measurement. It is an exercise in absurdity to claim that they are.

It is interesting to think of getting rid of the whole extended family: "psychology," "psychiatry," "psychotherapy," and the like. Ken already has done a brilliant job in contesting many of these concepts, together with their assumptions about the reality of the "self." For instance, he has suggested that psychology, in its explanation for emotional distress, is wedded to a dubious belief in the stages a so-called psyche must go through to be properly mature. Psychiatry, when it is not being as medical as possible, continues to subscribe to this idea of an intrapsychic unit, even though it is no more persuasive than Descartes' little homunculus. As for psychotherapy, the word and what it has represented are undergoing rapid change. Since the middle of this century, I have been watching the course of what I call the social therapies (based on ideas about relational difficulties) as opposed to the psychological therapies (based on assumptions of intrapsychic dysfunction). It may well be that counseling, assuming that it is not stamped out by managed care, eventually will end up in the social camp, leaving psychiatry and psychology to the material world of memory, chemical imbalance, and genes.

Calling counseling a "social therapy" at least enlarges its scope. This widening process started with the antipsychiatry movement of the mid-twentieth century, for which we may thank rebel philosophers such as Thomas Szasz (1974) and R. D. Laing (Laing & Esterson, 1971). Family therapy, the bastard mutant that came into being around the same time, has been another source of change. There have been successive widenings since that original impulse, representing an effort to include progressively more of the social context. One could say that family therapy was only stage 1; stage 2 highlighted the professional context; throwing gender into the ring moved us to the level of the society; and now the concern with multicultural issues is pushing us to include intersocietal issues worldwide.

There is still a conservative element in the family field that has kept a version of developmental theory on which to base its ideas about dysfunction and cure. By this I mean the life stage template on which various versions of what I call "family repression theory" have been played out. This theory includes all explanations for emotional distress supposedly caused by repressed or unresolved memories. Family therapy orientations that locate reasons for problems in losses that have not been grieved, anger that has been suppressed, or untold family secrets fall into that category. This psychodynamic template also is enshrined in widespread folk beliefs about the relationship between expressing emotions and mental health. But the free radicals in family therapy always have been those who rejected the emotional repression theories for a more interpersonal focus on communication and exchange.

In any case, the three of us represent the position of a growing number of relational therapists and researchers who are willing to challenge the use of labels for mental disorder and the expansionist push to medicalize the whole enterprise. Our hit list includes all and any diagnostic systems—biological, psychological, or relational—that have been proposed. If we could but cease our psychologizing, perhaps the discipline of therapeutic conversation could be released from the grip of Newtonian science and placed under the aegis of language arts, where we believe it belongs.

REFERENCES

American Psychiatric Association. (1952). *Diagnostic and statistical manual for mental disorders*. Washington, DC: American Psychiatric Association.

American Psychiatric Association. (1987). *Diagnostic and statistical manual for mental disorders* (3rd ed. revised). Washington, DC: American Psychiatric Association.

American Psychiatric Association. (1994). *Diagnostic and statistical manual for mental disorders* (4th ed.). Washington, DC: American Psychiatric Association.

Anderson, H. (1992). *C* therapy and the *F* word. *American Family Therapy Association Newsletter, 50,* 19–22.

Anderson, H. (1994). Rethinking family therapy: A delicate balance. *Journal of Marital and Family Therapy, 20,* 145–150.

Anderson, H. (1995). Collaborative language systems: Toward a postmodern therapy. In R. Mikesell, D. D. Lusterman, & S. McDaniel (Eds.), *Integrating family therapy: Handbook of family psychology and systems therapy* (pp. 27–41). Washington, DC: American Psychological Association.

Anderson, H., & Goolishian, H. A. (1988). Human systems as linguistic systems: Preliminary and evolving ideas about the implications for clinical theory. *Family Process, 27,* 371–393.

Anderson, H., & Goolishian, H. A. (1992). The client is the expert: A not-knowing approach to therapy. In S. McNamee & K. Gergen (Eds.), *Therapy as Social Construction*. London: Sage.

Caplan, P. J. (1987). *The myth of women's masochism*. New York: Signet.

Caplan, P. J. (1991). What's happening these days with the DSM? *Feminism and Psychology, 1,* 317–319.

Chamberlin, J. (1990). The ex-patients' movement: Where we've been and where we're going. *Journal of Mind and Behavior, 11,* 323–336.

Danziger, K. (1990). *Constructing the subject: Historical origins of psychological research*. New York: Cambridge University Press.

Erickson, G. (1988). Against the grain: Decentering family therapy. *American Journal of Marital and Family Therapy, 14,* 225–236.

Gergen, K. J. (1973). Social psychology as history. *Journal of Personality and Social Psychology, 26,* 309–320.

Gergen, K. J. (1985). The social constructionist movement in modern psychology. *American Psychologist, 40,* 266–275.

Gergen, K. J. (1994). *Realities and relationships, soundings in social construction.* Cambridge, MA: Harvard University Press.

Hardy, K. (1994). Marginalization or development? A response to Shields, Wynne, and Gawinski. *Journal of Marital and Family Therapy, 20,* 139–144.

Kaslow, F. W. (1993). Relational diagnosis: An idea whose time has come? *Family Process, 32,* 255–259.

Kinman, C., & Sanders, C. (1994). *Unraveling addiction mythologies.* Sardis, BC: Valley Education and Therapy Services.

Laing, R. D., & Esterson, A. (1971). *Sanity, madness and the family.* New York: Basic Books.

Parsons, T. (1951). *The social system.* Glencoe, IL: Free Press.

Passell, P. (1991, October 2). For a common-sense economist, a Nobel Prize—And an impact on the law. Profile of economist Ronald Coase, "The Week in Review," *New York Times* p. 2.

Reimers, S., & Treacher, A. (1995). *Introducing user-friendly family therapy.* London: Routledge.

Rosanoff, A. J. (1938). *Manual of psychiatry and mental hygiene.* New York: Wiley.

Sarbin, T., & Mancuso, J. (1980). *Schizophrenia: Medical diagnosis or verdict?* Elmsford, NY: Pergamon.

Shields, C., Wynne, L., & Gawinski, B. (1994). The marginalization of family therapy: A historical and continuing problem. *Journal of Marital and Family Therapy, 20,* 117–139.

Szasz, T. (1974). *The myth of mental illness.* New York: Harper & Row.

Tomm, K. (1991). Beginning of a "HIPs" and "PIPs" approach to psychiatric assessment. *The Calgary Participator, 1,* 21–24.

Weschler, I. (1929). *The neuroses.* Philadelphia: Saunders.

White, M. (1989). *Selected Papers.* Adelaide, Australia: Dulwich Centre Publications.

White, M., & Epston, D. (1990). *Narrative means to therapeutic ends.* New York: Norton.

Wiener, M. (1991). Schizophrenia: A defective, deficient, disrupted, disorganized concept. In W. Flack, D. Miller, & M. Wiener (Eds.), *What is schizophrenia?* New York: Springer-Verlag.

Wittgenstein, L. (1953). *Philosophical investigations.* Oxford: Blackwell.

Wittgenstein, L. (1980). *Culture and value.* Oxford: Blackwell.

CHAPTER 8

Language Is Not Innocent

TOM ANDERSEN, MD

This chapter probably represents a minority position compared to the views held by most of the authors and readers of this book. It is connected to certain basic assumptions that also might be minority ones compared to those enunciated in the wider context that this book addresses. I believe that this book will be of great interest to professional therapists, politicians and administrators, the public, and maybe even more.

Let us first turn our attention to the word "assumptions" now and its context, the hermeneutic circle.

THE HERMENEUTIC CIRCLE

The hermeneutic circle is a concept usually related to two German philosophers, Martin Heidegger and Hans Georg Gadamer (Wachthauser, 1986; Warncke, 1987). Basically this concept refers to the idea that we live our lives within the frames of the life we have already lived. Heidegger says that life, or in his words, being-in-the world, is a constant search for meanings—meanings about how we can understand ourselves and our surroundings. What we thereby come to understand will influence how we relate to the surroundings as well as to those persons who are there.

What we come to understand is related to what we see and hear. And what we see and hear are related to what we look for and listen to. We do not see what we do not look for, and we do not hear what we do not listen to. Since life is so rich and so full, there is always, in any situation, much more to see than we are able to see and much more to hear than we are able to hear. It gets even more complex as the life we as therapists are particularly interested in comprises meanings and feelings that shift all the time; they are there for a second and have passed by the next second. In order to be able to grasp a meaning of what is going on, we actually have to select what we shall look at and listen to. In this act of creating meanings, we also perform an act of limitation both as ordinary persons and as therapists and scientists. We thereby also choose what we shall *not* look at and *not* listen to. Gadamer says that this act of limitation, namely what we include and what we exclude, is governed by our prejudices (Wachthauser, 1986). We have beforehand, more or less being aware of it, an understanding of what it is worthwhile to look for and listen to. The main point here is that we are prejudiced. We cannot *not* be. Heidegger (Wachthauser, 1986) uses another word for prejudice, namely preunderstanding. These basic assumptions of what we shall pay attention to and how that attention should be given are shaped and reshaped by the way we live our lives. Since the lives of various people are so different, we probably begin with different preunderstandings.

What we come to understand is more person-bounded and less general than we might want it to be. However, when we want or need to understand something particular, we might see and hear something we never saw or heard before. This new experience might feed back on our preunderstanding and subtly change it. This circular relationship between the more general preunderstanding and the special understanding is called the hermeneutic circle. Our prejudices are formed by the way we live our lives.

REFLECTING PROCESSES

As a therapist, many uneasy feelings followed my attempts to be in charge, to know what to talk about and how to do so, and to instruct the clients how they should live their lives. Working based on such therapeutic ideals will easily put the therapist on the top in a hierarchical relationship. And within a hierarchical relationship, the meanings easily are ranked as better or worse, useful or useless, wise or unwise, and the like. At least that happened when I tried to be a therapist who was expected to know and to tell what was best. The presented interventions tended to be "better" ideas than what the families had themselves. When families dared to speak up and tried to defend their ideas, battles between them and us, the therapists, about "either you are wrong or we are," broke out.

The reflecting processes became a solution to the hierarchical unpleasantness (Andersen, 1991, 1992). Letting our ideas about the families come out in the open, as the families let their ideas come to the fore, made us more equal. The hierarchical *either/or* tendencies declined, and we shifted into the frame of *both/and.*

Needless to say, we had come to a point where clients and therapists worked and talked *together.* Both parts had significant influence; the clients' influence was based on their own personal experiences, and ours was derived from our general experiences of working with many clients. Interventions and problem solutions are no longer the focus for our work, unless the clients ask for them. The talks we have together seem to bring out the alternative the clients themselves find useful—an alternative way of *being-in-the-world.*

Outer and Inner Talks

The reflecting processes can be described as shifts between talking with others about various issues and sitting back and listening to others talking about the same issues (Andersen, 1987, 1991, 1992, 1993). The talk with others is an *outer talk,* and that which one has with oneself (when listening to others' talk) is an *inner talk.* These two kinds of talking seem to deal differently with the same issue. What happens in the outer talk will be a perspective for the inner talk and vice versa. According to Bateson's assumption (1980), multiple perspectives of the same issue, when shared, will create new ideas and meanings.

BEING-IN-THE-WORLD IS BEING-IN-LANGUAGE AND BEING-IN-CONVERSATIONS

Following the Other

Being in these open talks and being in a both/and perspective makes it feel more natural to *follow the client*—literally. The client is given the freedom to decide what to talk about in whatever manner as long as necessary. The client who talks undisturbed, not interrupted, often will start and pause and start again and stop and start again in order to find better words and expressions. Talking can be seen as a search through language to find the best words to utter exactly what one wants to utter.

To Listen Is Also to See

The listener (the therapist) who follows the talker (the client), not only hearing the words but also seeing how the words are uttered, will notice that every word is part of the moving of the body. Spoken words and bodily activity come together in a unity and cannot be separated.

Words Are Touching and Moving

The listener who sees as much as he or she hears will notice that the various spoken words "touch" the speaker differently. The speaker is touched by the words as they reach his or her own ears. Some words touch the speaker in such a way that the listener can see him or her be moved. Sometimes these movements are small, sometimes, big. The listener might see a shift in the face, a change in the eyes, a moving on the chair, a cough. The words that prompt these movements are the ones that particularly attract my interest.

One example may clarify this.

A woman who had felt sad for a long while related that she could never ask for help, even when she was sick. Help had to be given by others, not asked for by her. "Because," she explained, "independence was the big word in my family. We were supposed to be independent." A shift in her face and a drop in the voice when she uttered the word "independent" indicated the meaningfulness of the word. When she was asked: "If you looked into that word 'independence,' what might you see?" she first said that she did not like the word very much. Asked what she saw that she did not like, she put her hands to her face and said, weeping: "It is so hard for me to talk about loneliness . . . yes, it means staying alone." As she told how hard it had been to stay alone in order to fulfill all expectations of being independent, she cried and the body sank in resignation. She talked for a long while without interruption and started to wonder if she would be able to fulfill those expectations. Being more and more eagerly involved in her own discussion, her voice raised, her neck and shoulders raised, and she talked more and more angrily as the idea of being-in-the-world as independent were forcefully challenged.

Asked what her mother would see in the word, she replied that she would see strength; her father also would see strength, but of another kind. Her sister and grandmother would see what she did.

Answers to these kinds of questions have taught me that there are always emotions in words, other words in words, sometimes sounds and music, sometimes whole stories, sometimes whole lives.

Others have put the same strong emphasis on conversations and language in their clinical and research work. This is particularly true of those at the Houston Galveston Institute, who have inspired me a great deal (Anderson, Goolishian, & Winderman, 1986; Anderson & Goolishian, 1988), and two of the therapists at the Ackerman Institute for Family Therapy in New York (Penn & Frankfurt, 1994).

SOME ASSUMPTIONS

We Are *in* Movements, *in* Feelings, and *in* Language

I used to think that we have movements and feelings and language inside us. Conversations such as the one just referred to have made me come to think the opposite way. We are *in* them: in the movements, in the feelings, and in the language. And we do not shape them, they shape us. Wittgenstein's work (Grayling, 1988) seems to support this assumption.

Talking Is Informing and Forming

Talking has an informing part as both the person him- or herself and others hear what he or she is thinking. Talking also has a forming aspect, as the person, by searching through language, reaches a meaning. When a person does this search, he or she forms not only a meaning but a being-in-the-world in that moment. Assuming that talking is a bodily activity, the whole body is formed or re-formed in the moment of an utterance. My utterances constitute my many selves. We do not have one self but many selves as our utterances change. This assumption already has been voiced by many others, such as Hans Georg Gadamer (Warncke, 1987), Ludwig Wittgenstein (Shotter, 1993), and Mikhail Bakhtin (Bakhtin, 1993; Shotter, 1993). Bakhtin takes this point further by saying that one's life is changing all the time; it is like small events tied together to a lifeline. Life is therefore "composed" of small events, which each happen only once. This is very different from those who assume that we are stems from "inner" or "deeper" structures, as Freud purported.

When I listen to a client, there is nothing behind or under the words to be interpreted and nothing behind the person's behavior. There is nothing more than what he or she says and does. Nothing more. In this framework then, there is no diagnosis!

Words Are Like Hands

Language and words are like searching hands. One might say that language is a sense organ. But words are more. Like a hand, they grasp on to meanings. So, the words we select influence the meanings we come to reach.

Words are not innocent. I used to think that the thought came first, then it was conveyed through words to others. Now I think differently. We search through words in order to find the thought. As the highly respected theoretician and clinician Harry Goolishian used to say: "We don't know what we think before we have said it."

If one accepts this assumption, it becomes critical to ask: Through which language is the person to search in order to form him- or herself? What happens if we, the professionals, require the therapeutic talks to be in our professional language and our professional metaphors? What happens if that professional language is a so-called deficit or incompetence language, a language that comprises words that describe failures and shortcomings? What kind a persons are thereby formed? Gergen (1990) has expressed grave concern about this possibility. I strongly second his concern.

With his colleague Harlene Anderson, Goolishian arranged a conference on these issues in San Antonio, Texas, shortly before he died in 1991. The announcement to the conference reads:

The central theme of this conference will be the exploration of the Wittgensteinian concept that the limits of the reality that can be known are determined by the language available to us to describe it. This theme will permit us to dialogue around the implications of the "deficiency language" of the mental health field and the effect these words have on our theoretical, clinical, and research work. This theme will also address the pragmatic distinction to be made between the concepts of constructivism and social constructionism.

It is our impression that over the last century of the mental health movement we have contributed thousands of words to the vocabulary of the world. Unfortunately, most of these contributed and constructed words reflect some sense of deficiency. It seems that in many ways the deficiency language has created a psychological and theoretical reality that can be metaphorically described as a black hole out of which there is very limited escape for meaningful clinical and research activity. . . .

I believe that words in the language of pathology are constraining, and I am critical of this and concerned. One concern is that the verb to be leaves out time. When we say that he or she is this or that, that expression makes us think that the person is like that and will be like that. No person, however, is static. It is our talking about the person that makes him or her appear static.

Let me give two examples.

It is not uncommon to say something like this: "He is resistant," or "He has a character of resistance."

One could easily practice language differently and say instead: "He resists." Which makes me ask: "What makes him resist?" Perhaps *I* said or did something he did not like and therefore resisted. And since I believe that the only person in the world I can change is myself, I rather do or say something differently that he does not have to resist (me).

It also often happens that persons are described as depressed or as having a depression. That language usage conveys a particular understanding of the person, and that understanding contributes to how we relate to her. Why not rather let her find her own words, which most probably would be: "I am sad." If she was asked what she tells herself in her inner talks, we might learn that that talk is filled with blaming words: "You are not good enough," or "You are not kind enough"—a monologue of blaming. That might make us discuss whether there could be space for an additional inner voice speaking more friendly words (Penn & Frankfurt, 1994).

Neither individuals nor families *are* a certain way. They change all the time. In some periods a family is enmeshed, in others, disconnected. In some contexts, isolating, in others, social. Families are changing all the time. As therapists, it is easy to make a family that appears happy feel guilty, ashamed, and angry, if we want that. (I hope few do.) It is easy to make a family that appears angry feel sad. And it is not impossible to make a family that appears sad feel happy. I try to be a therapist who does not concentrate on what the family is but one who finds out, together with them, how they might live their lives differently.

Another concern is the strong effect labeling might have on the forming of the labeled person's future. One woman who had been hospitalized at a mental hospital for a year finally came to family therapy. Besides herself and her family and the family therapist, the doctor-in-chief at the hospital and her nurse contact at the ward were present. When she was asked if she had been given any diagnoses, she said: "a manic-depressive psychosis." When she was asked if that diagnosis made any difference, she said it changed her life. She could no longer laugh and be happy nor be sad and cry, because she could see on the faces of those around her that they thought that she might go manic or she might become depressed. She therefore had a new inner voice speaking to her all the time: "Don't be happy and don't be sad! Don't laugh and don't cry!"

SOME OTHER ASSUMPTIONS

The fields of psychotherapy and family therapy certainly contain other preunderstandings. Many assume, as I already have indicated, that what a person says and does stems from an inner "core," that is, either a biological or a psychological structure. Others assume that what a person says and does is related to his or her position in sociological structures—the family. Many assume that such structures (biological, psychological, sociological) are stable over time, in fact, so stable that they can be described in terms of diagnoses. Some even assume that such structures are measurable and therefore can be measured. Those who hold such assumptions—the majority of the therapists—will do clinical practice and research according to them. Yet labels rarely take into account the flux in the human's being-in-the-world.

Politicians, Administrators, and the Public

Those outside the field of therapy will most probably be convinced of the majority assumptions of specialists, and probably will find diagnoses a good way to describe and categorize human fellows. I must accept that.

So what will I do if an insurance company requires a diagnosis in order to pay for my work? I would let that be part of the conversations with the client(s). *Together* we have to select which diagnosis best characterizes the situation and which one the client(s) best can be-in-the-world with. If the client(s) asks me what I think about this diagnostic bit of the work, I would say: "I don't like it, but for us to be able to work together, we have to do it." I would say *we*, not I.

CONCLUSION

Some words have helped me greatly. They relate to me and others and also to those who hold assumptions that are incompatible to mine. The words are: "You shall do what you believe in, and you shall not do what you do not believe in."

In closing, I sincerely hope that we, as therapists and researchers, can let those we meet with be-in-the-world in their own language and own images. That is important for them and for ourselves.

REFERENCES

Andersen, T. (1987). The reflecting team: Dialogue and meta-dialogue in clinical work. *Family Process, 26,* 415–428.

Andersen, T. (1991). *The reflecting team.* New York: Norton.

Andersen, T. (1992). Relationship, language and pre-understanding in the reflecting processes. *Australian & New Zealand Journal of Family Therapy, 13*(2), 87–91.

Andersen, T. (1993). See and hear, and be seen and heard. In S. Friedman (Ed.), *The new language of change* (pp. 303–322). New York: Guilford.

Anderson, H., & Goolishian, H. (1988). Human systems as linguistic systems: Preliminary and evoking ideas about implications for clinical theory. *Family Process, 27*(1), 371–394.

Anderson, H., Goolishian, H., & Winderman, L. (1986). Problem-determined system. Toward transformation in family therapy. *Journal of Strategic and Systemic Therapies, 5*(4), 1–11.

Bakhtin, M. M. (1993). *Toward a philosophy of the act.* Austin: University of Texas Press.

Bateson, G. (1980). *Mind and nature: A necessary unity.* New York: Bantam.

Gergen, K. J. (1990). Therapeutic professions and the diffusions of deficit. *Journal of Mind and Behavior, 11*(3), 353–368(4), 107–122.

Grayling, A. C. (1988). *Wittgenstein.* New York: Past Masters, Oxford University Press.

Penn, P., & Frankfurt, M. (1994). Creating a participant: Writing, multiple voices, narrative multiplicity. *Family Process, 33*(3), 217–232.

Shotter, J. (1993). *Cultural politics of everyday life.* Buckingham, UK: Open University Press.

Wachthauser, B. R. (1986). History and language in understanding. In B. R. Wachthauser (Ed.), *Hermeneutics and modern philosophy.* Albany, NY: State of New York Press.

Warncke, G. (1987). *Gadamer, hermeneutics, tradition, and reason.* Stanford, CA: Stanford University Press.

CHAPTER 9

Relational Disorders in Primary Care Medicine

SUSAN H. McDANIEL, PhD and FRANK V. deGRUY, MD, MSFN

The primary health care system has been characterized as the hidden mental health network (Schurman, Kramer, & Mitchell, 1985) or the de facto mental health services system, because over half of the patients with an identified mental health problem visit primary care physicians as their only source of care for this problem (Regier, Narrow, et al., 1993). Moreover, about half of all visits to primary care physicians are for symptoms for which no biomedical disease can be detected (Miranda, Perez-Stable, Hargreaves, & Henke, 1991); most of these visits involve psychosocial problems, and many involve relational disorders.

This chapter describes how mental and relational disorders present in primary care, the advantages and disadvantages of the DSM-IV and the new DSM-IV-PC (Primary Care, 1995), the frequent association of relational disorders with physical illness, and the importance of collaboration between family therapists/psychologists and primary care physicians and nurses. We begin with an example all too familiar to the primary care physician.

Case History

Ms. Sharon Brown is a 29-year-old woman who came to see Dr. deGruy, her family physician, because of severe abdominal pain. The initial workup for this complaint revealed no physical cause for her pain, and she initially reported that she had no significant mental or relational difficulties. Her symptoms worsened, and he ordered a CT scan of the abdomen, a barium enema, and an upper gastrointestinal X-ray study—tests that are expensive, invasive, and uncomfortable, but sensitive at detecting intraabdominal pathology. Since these tests were all normal, Dr. deGruy referred her to a surgeon for an exploratory laparoscopy. This is a "minor" surgical procedure wherein a hollow, lighted tube is inserted into the abdominal cavity in a search for disease; it is done under general anesthesia. This likewise did not reveal any reason for Ms. Brown's ongoing pain.[1]

The presence of pain with no known etiology poses a difficult clinical problem for both patient and doctor, but it is by no means unusual in a primary care medical setting. At this point, many surgeons and primary physicians would consider their work done, having ruled out serious intraabdominal pathology. But there is more to this story.

---

[1] The cases in this chapter are real; details of the people and their situations have been changed to protect anonymity.

Case History Continued

Ms. Brown did not recover from this procedure as expected but had a marked worsening of her pain, requiring high doses of narcotics for relief. This caused her to remain in the hospital much longer than anticipated. Even when these symptoms had subsided somewhat, she said that she would be unable to care for herself at home and requested more hospital time to recover. She was tearful and agitated, and reported that everyone would be better off if she were dead. Dr. deGruy reassessed her mental state, added Major Depressive Episode and Somatoform Pain Disorder to her problem list, discharged her from the hospital, and arranged a follow-up visit for early the next week. At follow-up, the physician noticed fresh contusions on her neck and back, inquired, and learned that she had been beaten by her husband. At this visit she related the onset of her abdominal pain to another beating during which she was kicked repeatedly in the abdomen. Dr. deGruy revised his diagnoses to Physical Abuse of an Adult and Complex Post Traumatic Stress Disorder, contacted a local woman's shelter, arranged a referral to a family therapist with expertise in domestic violence, and scheduled her for a return visit to his office in two days.

This case report illustrates several important points.

1. Primary care physicians are generally the first—and sometimes the only—professionals patients will see if they have a mental or relational problem.
2. Patients with mental or relational problems often will present to their primary care physician with a physical complaint and may initially deny the existence of emotional or relational difficulties. (This denial rarely persists after a trusting relationship is established.)
3. This presentation, together with the training of the physician and structure of primary care, results in primary care physicians often missing the fundamental relational diagnosis. In fact, they often miss traditional mental diagnoses.
4. Traditional individual mental diagnoses, while sometimes useful and appropriate in primary care, may fail to properly characterize the problems patients bring to their physicians.
5. The consequences of these missed diagnoses are expensive, both in terms of inappropriate monetary expenditures as well as exposure of patients to risky, invasive procedures that may be unnecessary.
6. Collaboration with a therapist who understands how to work with relationship problems is helpful for both the patient and physician and often results in more appropriate care.

MENTAL HEALTH DIAGNOSES IN PRIMARY CARE SETTINGS

In contrast to the mental health care setting, most primary care patients with a mental or relational diagnosis present with a physical complaint (Kroenke et al., 1994), as illustrated by Ms. Brown. The National Ambulatory Medical Care Survey (NAMCS) data indicate that the number of patients who describe the reason for their visit to a primary care physician as mental or relational is exceedingly small, much less than 0.1 percent (Schappert, 1992). Although most mental and relational problems have concomitant physical symptomatology, medical education is organized around physical disease, and physicians are trained to "see" and deal with physical symptoms. At the same time, physical symptoms are more acceptable to most primary care patients than are emotional difficulties, so they may offer medical practitioners physical symptoms as "the problem."

While some physicians provide excellent biopsychosocial care to their patients, others do not have the time, the training, or the inclination to look beyond the patient's presentation of physical complaints. In fact, even the most common and well-characterized mental diagnosis in this setting—depression—is overlooked about half the time (Schulberg, Saul, McClelland, Gangule, Christy, & Frank, 1985; Wells, Hays, Burnham, Rogers, Greenfield, & Ware, 1989). The rate of diagnosis of other mental disorders is lower than the rate for depression, and the rate of diagnosis of relational disorders is lower still (Schappert, 1989). (Some of this is no doubt attributable to the fact that these have not been codified or available for utilization prior to this volume's publication.) Of course, there are some primary care physicians who consistently inquire about relational issues and incorporate this material into their clinical strategies, but that is exceptional rather than usual clinical behavior.

Apart from rough estimates of the prevalence of childhood and adult abuse (Lechner, Vogel, Garcia-Shelton, Leichter, & Steibel, 1993), we are aware of no research documenting the frequency of relational problems in the primary care setting. This gap is particularly interesting in light of the fact that many or most of the problems seen by the primary care physician have a conspicuous psychosocial, or explicitly relational, component.

Relationships, when they are healthy, can contribute to a successful physical outcome for the patient.[2] For example, Coyne and Schwenk (1992) have shown that men with congestive heart failure have better medical outcomes if their wives are supportive and participate in their rehabilitation programs. Medalie, Snyder, Groen, Neufeld, Goldbourt, and Riss (1973) showed that the occurrence of angina among 10,000 Israeli men was related to whether they believed their wives loved and supported them. These are but two examples from a substantial literature that demonstrates the health-protective effects of positive social relationships (Callaghan & Morrissey, 1993).

Problematic relationships can have a negative effect on illness and disease. Minuchin and colleagues, in a series of studies, demonstrated the correlation between family functioning and blood sugar control among diabetic children (Baker, Minuchin, Milman, Liebman, & Todd, 1975), asthma attacks among asthmatic children (Liebman, Minuchin, & Baker, 1974b), and eating behavior among children with anorexia nervosa (Liebman, Minuchin, & Baker, 1974a). A number of adverse health outcomes, such as tuberculosis (Holmes, 1956), hypertension (Strogatz & James, 1986), and mortality from all causes (Berkman & Syme, 1979), have been shown to be correlated to relational problems. Coe, Wolinsky, and Miller (1955) documented that elderly patients who have lost their important family relationships use more medical services. Examples of this nature abound. Thus we have compelling evidence that attenuated or problematic relationships have definite health consequences (Burman & Margolin, 1992). Moreover, at least one study has documented that a high proportion of psychiatric outpatients have significant relational problems: deFigueiredo, Boerstler, and O'Connell (1991) studied all patients admitted to an outpatient psychiatric clinic for two years and learned that over half had a codable family problem. Of these, one-third had no mental diagnosis at all, and the other two-thirds had both a family problem *and* a mental diagnosis.

---

[2] For a review of the literature on families and health, see T. L. Campbell (1988), in W. J. Doherty and T. L. Campbell (Eds.), *Families and Health,* Family Study Series, Beverly Hills, CA: Sage.

The consequences of missing relational diagnoses are illustrated by the case history cited earlier. Anyone working in the primary care setting who is sensitive to relational conflicts recognizes this story as a recurrent one; to our knowledge, however, there is no research data documenting or even estimating the cost—in suffering and in the cost of unnecessary medical care—of missed relational diagnoses. We do know that patients with somatoform complaints—physical symptoms with no detectable physical explanation—use an inordinate amount of medical resources (Smith, Monson, & Ray, 1986; deGruy, Columbia, & Dickinson, 1987) and have a significantly higher proportion of negative medical workups as compared to matched patients without somatoform complaints (deGruy, Crider, Hashimi, Dickinson, Mullins, & Troncale, 1987), but we do not know whether this is also true of relational problems.

DSM AND PRIMARY CARE

The fact that primary care physicians do not diagnose relational problems does not mean that primary care medicine is devoid of attention to these problems. Indeed, much of the content of primary care—family medicine in particular—is concerned with problems having a conspicuous relational component: prenatal and perinatal care; pediatric developmental and behavioral issues; accidents, injuries, and violence perpetrated by one person against another; contraception and conception; somatization; behavioral and mental problems; chronic illness; and terminal care. Once one begins to think this way, it follows that most (if not all) problems seen in the primary care setting have a prominent relational dimension.

However, most medical practitioners do not conceptualize these problems systemically. When they are addressed, it is from the perspective of the individual patient rather than his or her relational system. Medical schools and primary care residency training programs generally organize the psychosocial material in their curricula around the diagnostic constructs used in psychiatry, that is, the DSM. In many cases, this has led to clear-cut improvement in the health and well-being of primary care patients. In addition, some practitioners have found the recently published DSM-IV (American Psychiatric Association, 1994)—compared to its earlier versions—to have improvements that make it more useful in primary care. Axis I, for example, now includes common diagnoses in primary care such as relational problems due to a medical condition, abuse, neglect, noncompliance, bereavement, and acculturation problems. Axis II includes maladaptive defense mechanisms such as idealization, acting out, apathetic withdrawal, help-rejecting complaining, and passive-aggressive behavior, all commonly seen in primary care. Axis IV includes a simpler way of characterizing psychosocial stressors. And the axes now facilitate a biopsychosocial description of a patient (Nowlis, personal communication, 1994). Nevertheless, even with these improvements, a number of problems arise when one attempts to apply a psychiatric nosology, and the management strategies implicit within it, to the practice of primary care medicine.

The first set of problems is theoretical: As the case history clearly illustrates, DSM diagnoses do not always adequately characterize the problem. It helps to understand that Ms. Brown is depressed—this is an improvement over simply regarding her as having abdominal pain that has been inadequately worked up—but regarding depression and somatoform pain as her "problems" are grossly inadequate characterizations of her predicament: The relational diagnoses are central to understanding her, and must be considered.

The second set of problems is epidemiological. The DSM criteria do not adequately characterize mental disorders as they appear in the primary care setting. Here patients tend to present somatized or masked forms of mental disorders; they tend to have subthreshold conditions that do not meet full diagnostic criteria but nevertheless cause significant functional impairment; and they tend to have several conditions concurrently (deGruy, Dickinson, Dickinson, & Hobson, 1994).

The third set of problems is practical. Traditional mental health care is organized and delivered differently from primary medical care and cannot be transferred without translation. For example, a typical psychiatric visit might last almost one hour, whereas the typical primary care visit lasts 13.5 minutes and almost always includes attention to more than one problem (Cypress, 1978). Furthermore, primary care physicians often are reimbursed poorly or not at all for visits having to do with mental health care, and therefore have a monetary incentive to formulate their patients' problems along other lines. For example, Ms. Brown's insurance carrier will not reimburse a primary care physician for managing depression but will reimburse him or her for managing abdominal pain.

In 1988 the National Institute of Mental Health and the American Psychiatric Association recognized that the DSM classification system was not being used in the primary care setting and organized several conferences on classification of mental disorders in primary care. One outgrowth was the formation of a work group to develop a specific classification system. This manual is called the DSM-IV-PC; as of August 1994, the first draft was complete and undergoing field tests. A publishable document should be available by early 1995. This manual should offer several advantages: diagnostic criteria often are simplified, and categories are collapsed; in some cases mixed and subthreshold syndromes are described; and the manual is organized algorithmically by presenting symptoms for easy navigation to a diagnostic end point.

Relational diagnoses are included in the DSM-IV-PC (and the DSM-IV), although they appear as V codes in the section entitled "Other Conditions That May Be a Focus of Clinical Attention." This secondary status of relational diagnoses in the DSM-PC, together with the fact that primary care physicians are frequently not reimbursed for attending to problems coded as relational, may result in relational diagnoses continuing to be a neglected set of categories. However, the DSM-PC will be revised as its shortcomings are recognized and as research augments our knowledge. Should this knowledge include the demonstration that relational diagnoses are common and important in the primary care setting, they undoubtedly will assume a more prominent place in subsequent revisions. It is hoped that this current work will constitute a resource for primary care physicians in refining their thinking and revising the DSM-IV-PC.

RELATIONAL DISORDERS ASSOCIATED WITH PHYSICAL ILLNESS

Thus, we see that relational diagnoses are a large, hidden component of primary medical care. Primary care medicine can accommodate the incorporation of relational work into its clinical agenda, but traditional medical training and primary care clinical practice are structured and financed in a way that hampers this effort. Despite these obstacles, primary care physicians frequently engage in the management of relational problems, and they do so with varying degrees of skill and training. The following sections will provide several illustrations.

Primary care physicians and nurses frequently take care of patients' relational disorders at the same time as they care for their individual disorders. Most commonly, this manifests as the relational adjustment disorders that are associated with the diagnosis of a new disease or a change in a family members's disease process. Consider the following example.

Case History

Mr. Lubovsky had his first heart attack at age 55. Mrs. Lubovsky was very distressed. When her father died at age 60 of a sudden heart attack, she had begged her husband to stop smoking, change his diet, and have a physical exam. These pleas went unheeded. While the heart attack acted as a "wake-up call" for Mr. Lubovsky, for his wife it was a devastating confirmation of her inability to prevent the men she loved from dying.

At first, Mr. Lubovsky was quite receptive to the rehabilitation suggested by his physician. However, Mrs. Lubovsky was so anxious that she pushed and nagged her husband every day about reforming his diet, beginning an exercise program, and "relaxing." The more she nagged, the more resistant Mr. Lubovsky became to the outpatient treatment plan. The day before Mr. Lubovsky was discharged from the hospital, Dr. Smith realized the extent of the problem when she was unable to secure a commitment from Mr. Lubovsky to attend the rehabilitation program. She asked Mrs. Lubovsky to join them the next day for a discharge planning meeting.

At that meeting, Dr. Smith validated both Mrs. Lubovsky's concerns and need for additional support, as well as Mr. Lubovsky's desire to be in charge of his treatment plan. In a 20-minute session, she negotiated a treatment contract that Mr. Lubovsky approved and signed. She also got Mrs. Lubovsky to agree not to remind her husband about his rehabilitation tasks, in exchange for a commitment from her husband for a nightly "communication hour" in which both partners discussed their successes and concerns with regard to rehabilitation and other nonillness events of the day.

This example of primary care counseling improved marital functioning and increased the patient's likelihood of a successful biomedical outcome. While the example illustrates a family meeting in the hospital setting (McDaniel, Campbell, & Seaburn, 1990), such meetings also can be useful with outpatients.

Case History

Mrs. Pryor was a community activist until she was diagnosed with Alzheimer's disease. As often happens with this illness, coming to terms with the diagnosis was a protracted process. It began with her husband and daughter noticing deterioration in her memory and other loss of functioning. Before the illness, the Pryor family functioned well, but the adult children (especially the sons) rarely called their parents. "We raised them to be independent," Mrs. Pryor said. As Mrs. Pryor's disease progressed, her husband became more fatigued and depressed. Dr. Bell suggested a family meeting to discuss Mrs. Pryor's illness.

The 30-minute meeting consisted of the patient, her husband, her three sons and their partners, and her single daughter. It began with Mrs. Pryor describing her experience of the illness, and Dr. Bell answering questions about prognosis. Soon the topic of caregiving emerged, and the sons heard about how their father was coping (or not coping) with the burden of this illness. Much of the problem revolved around the value this family placed on independence. What worked when family members were healthy resulted in a relational adjustment disorder when a key member became ill. Dr. Bell helped this family to negotiate a caregiving plan that included weekly visits by the adult children to help with caring for their mother. Six weeks later, the family met again with Dr. Bell. Mrs. Pryor's physical condition was unchanged, but her husband's depression was much

Table 9.1 Relational Disorders Commonly Seen in Primary Care Counseling

- Adjustment to the diagnosis of a new illness
- Adjustment to a change in functioning or prognosis in a chronic illness (such as entering the terminal phase)
- New onset of parent-child behavior problems
- New onset of marital problems
- New onset of workplace problems
- Uncomplicated grief reactions

Source: Adapted from S. H. McDaniel, T. L. Campbell, and D. Seaburn, "When and how to refer primary-care patients to mental health specialists," in *Family-oriented Primary Care: A Manual for Medical Providers,* p. 358. New York: Springer-Verlag, 1990.

improved and the adult children reported satisfaction in the role they played in caring for their mother.

In addition to relational disorders directly related to illness, many primary care physicians also meet and counsel parents about common childhood behavior problems, mild marital problems, and interpersonal problems at the workplace. (See Table 9.1.) This counseling may occur in the context of a brief medical visit or an extended (30- to 45-minute) visit that more closely matches the practice of mental health providers.

COLLABORATION BETWEEN PRIMARY CARE CLINICIANS AND FAMILY THERAPISTS

Primary care clinicians also regularly encounter people with psychosocial problems that benefit from consultation or referral to a mental health specialist such as a family therapist. For therapists who work in a medical setting, many opportunities occur for primary care providers to consult on preventive strategies or ongoing treatment of patients whose problems do not require referral. Once a referral is made (see Table 9.2), the family therapist first must develop a relationship that will form the foundation of collaboration with

Table 9.2 Relational Disorders Commonly Referred from a Primary Care Physician to a Mental Health Specialist

- Sexual or physical abuse
- Homicidal ideation
- Moderate to severe marital and sexual problems
- Multiproblem family situations
- Families coping with serious mental illness
- Substance abuse

Source: Adapted from S. H. McDaniel, T. L. Campbell, and D. Seaburn, "When and how to refer primary-care patients to mental health specialists," in *Family-oriented Primary Care: A Manual for Medical Providers,* p. 358. New York: Springer-Verlag, 1990.

the referring primary care physician. This may include an initial phone conversation to understand: the physician's reason for referral, his or her perspective on the patient's problem, the extent of the physician's involvement, and the format and frequency of feedback desired from the therapist. The therapist also needs to inform the physician about how he or she may be reached (McDaniel, Hepworth, & Doherty, 1992).

Once a relationship is formed between a therapist and a physician, the former therapist can aid the latter in making the difficult referrals by offering to consult before the referral is discussed with the patient. These brief consultations can explore the patient's motivation for psychotherapy and the best timing for and framing of the referral.

Close, collaborative care is most helpful to patients with problems at the interface of mind and body. These include patients such as Ms. Brown, who had a somatoform pain disorder related to possible childhood and documented spousal abuse. It is very likely that the standard referral process would not have worked with Ms. Brown for several reasons. First, she is apt to be distrustful of authority figures, given her history of abuse. Second, she speaks the language of the body rather than the mind. Her distress, both physical and emotional, is expressed through bodily symptoms. Physicians, not therapists, take care of bodily symptoms. If she could express herself emotionally, as is the expectation in psychotherapy, she probably would not have a somatoform disorder. For these reasons Ms. Brown, like many other primary care patients, is likely to resist a standard referral to a psychotherapist. Here is what happened when Dr. deGruy tried to make the referral.

DR. DEG: I understand now that you have both physical and emotional pain. You have been to the hospital three times for injuries your husband inflicted. I'd like you and him to see a therapist. If he won't go, I'd like you to go alone.

PT: Okay, Doctor. I know you're right. I'll go, but my husband will never go.

Ms. Brown made an appointment with a therapist at the mental health center, then did not keep it. She wanted the doctor to cure her pain but felt her husband would never allow her to see a therapist.

This kind of scenario is far too common in the practices of primary care physicians. When collaboration with a family therapist is available, the therapist can help the physician bridge the gap between his or her desire to refer a family with a relational disorder and that patient and family's acceptance of the referral. Two strategies are useful for the therapist who works closely with primary care physicians:

1. *Practice on-site with the physician.* This strategy offers many advantages and overcomes countless barriers of time allocation and distance. The patient has easy access to the therapist. The therapist is readily available and can participate in hallway consultations and team meetings with the rest of the medical team.

2. Even if it requires travel, *offer to meet with the patient and family at the physician's office when the physician makes the referral.* With hesitant or resistant families, this joint session allows the therapist and family together to hear why the physician wishes to make the referral. The patient and family witness the teamwork of the physician and the therapist, teamwork that can symbolize an integration of the mind-body split and model healthy relational functioning. It

allows the patient and family to observe the therapist and decide, before making a commitment, if he or she might be able to help them. This approach is a powerful investment in the future treatment of the family and can overcome the high no-show rate for patients referred by physicians.

CONCLUSION

To conclude, let us revisit the case of Ms. Brown, this time in the setting of a joint session to make the referral.

DR. DEG: Ms. Brown, I'm very worried about your pain. The medication we are using isn't helping you very much. I'd like to ask my colleague, Dr. McDaniel, to step in. She is a psychologist who has a special interest in patients and families with difficult pain problems. Would that be okay?

PT: I don't want to see a psychologist, Dr. deGruy. This pain isn't in my head.

DR. DEG: Ms. Brown, I believe your pain is very real, and I'd like you to get the best possible treatment for your pain. Why don't you just meet her today, and next week I could see you again with her and we could discuss the pain you've been having.

PT: Well, okay. I suppose it doesn't hurt to just meet her.

After Dr. McDaniel is introduced and Dr. deGruy explains his concerns about Ms. Brown, Dr. McDaniel makes a suggestion:

DR. MCD: Ms. Brown, I can see that you and Dr. deGruy have been working very hard to decrease your pain. I wonder if you'd be willing to keep a symptom diary for us over the next week. Please record all episodes of pain and how intense it is on the left-hand side of the page. Then record your feelings and other events that might be happening at the same time on the right-hand side of the page. Perhaps together we can study the diary for any clues about your pain. By the way, what does your husband think about your pain?

PT: He's grown very tired of it. And he's angry that Dr. deGruy hasn't cured it yet. He doesn't like doctors much.

DR. MCD: Well, I wonder if he might be willing to come with you to see Dr. deGruy next week, just so we can get his perspective on your pain.

In this way, with one five-minute interaction, followed by a 30-minute joint session, the therapist established a relationship with a mistrustful patient and her defensive husband. The third contact continued the investigation of the pain and was held with the patient and the husband without Dr. deGruy being present. The therapy first focused on the pain and, once trust was established, moved on to deal with the spousal abuse and both partners' histories of childhood abuse. Of course, not all primary care patients with relational disorders require this labor-intensive approach to make a referral. However, close collaboration increases the number of patients who will accept and benefit from a mental health referral. Successful treatment of patients like Ms. Brown can decrease expensive and inappropriate medical visits and procedures and provide them with relief, understanding, and new coping skills to deal with emotional pain.

Primary care providers and mental health professionals have much work ahead if we are to identify and treat relational disorders early and effectively in the primary care setting. Along with research that documents the prevalence, nature, and consequences of relational diagnoses in primary care and discovers the most effective treatments, the highest priority is to train both kinds of professionals to diagnose and collaborate in this treatment. We are confident that once that is accomplished, relational disorders will become core content for the training of primary care physicians and mental health professionals.

REFERENCES

American Psychiatric Association. (1994). *Diagnostic and statistical manual of mental disorders, 4th ed.* Washington DC: Author.

American Psychiatric Association. (1995). *Diagnostic and statistical manual of mental disorders, 4th ed. Primary care version.* Washington, DC: American Psychiatric Association.

Baker, L., Minuchin, S., Milman, L., Liebman, R., & Todd, T. (1975). Psychosomatic aspects of juvenile diabetes mellitus: A progress report. In *Modern Problems in Pediatrics, 12.* White Plains, NY: Karger.

Berkman, L., & Syme, S. (1979). Social networks, host resistance, and mortality: A nine-year followup study of Alameda County residents. *American Journal of Epidemiology, 109,* 186–204.

Burman, B., & Margolin, G. (1992). Analysis of the association between marital relationships and health problems: An interactional perspective. *Psychological Bulletin, 112,* 39–63.

Callaghan, P., & Morrissey, J. (1993). Social support and health: A review. *Journal of Advances in Nursing, 18,* 203–210.

Coe, R., Wolinsky, F., & Miller, D. (1985). Elderly persons without family support networks and use of health services: A followup report on social network relationships. *Research on Aging, 7,* 617.

Coyne, J., & Schwenk, T. (1992, April). The effect of supportive relationships on men with congestive heart failure. Paper presented at the Society of Teachers of Family Medicine Annual Conference on the Family in Family Medicine, Amelia Island, FL.

Cypress, B. K. (1978). *Patterns of ambulatory and family practice. The National Ambulatory Medical Care Survey, United States. January 1980–December 1981.* Series 13, No. 73, ed. Washington, DC: National Center for Health Statistics.

deFigueirido, J., Boerstler, H., & O'Connell, L. (1991). Conditions not attributable to a mental disorder: An epidemiological study of family problems. *American Journal of Psychiatry, 148,* 780–783.

deGruy, F., Columbia, L., & Dickinson, W. (1987). Somatization disorder in a family practice. *Journal of Family Practice, 25,* 45–51.

deGruy, F., Crider, J., Hashimi, D., Dickinson, W., Mullins, H., & Troncale, J. (1987). Somatization disorder in a university hospital. *Journal of Family Practice, 25,* 579–584.

deGruy, F., Dickinson, L., Dickinson, W., & Hobson, F. (1994, September), NOS: Subthreshold conditions in primary care. *Proceedings of the Eighth Annual NIMH International Research Conference of Mental Health Problems in the General Health Care Sector.*

Holmes, T. (1956). Multidiscipline studies in tuberculosis. In P. Sparer (Ed.), *Personality, stress, and tuberculosis.* Baltimore: International University Press.

Kroenke, K., Spitzer, R., Williams, J., Linzer, M., Hahn, S., deGruy, F., & Brody, D. (1994). Physical symptoms in primary care: Predictors of psychiatric disorders and functional impairment. *Archives of Family Medicine, 3,* 774–779.

Lechner, M., Vogel, M., Garcia-Shelton, L., Leichter, J., & Steibel, K. (1993). Self-reported medical problems of adult female survivors of childhood sexual abuse. *Journal of Family Practice, 36,* 633–638.

Liebman, R., Minuchin, S., & Baker, L. (1974a). An integrated treatment program for anorexia nervosa. *American Journal of Psychiatry, 131,* 432–436.

Liebman, R., Minushin, S., & Baker, L. (1974b). The use of structural family therapy in the treatment of intractable asthma. *American Journal of Psychiatry, 131,* 535–540.

McDaniel, S. H., Campbell, T. L., & Seaburn, D. (1990). *Family-oriented primary care: A manual for medical providers.* New York: Springer-Verlag.

McDaniel, S. H., Hepworth, J., & Doherty, W. (1992). *Medical family therapy: A Biopsychosocial approach to families with health problems.* New York: Basic Books.

Medalie, J. H., Snyder, M., Groen, J. J., Neufeld, N. H., Goldbourt, U., & Riss, E. (1973). Angina pectoris among 10,000 men: 5 year incidence and univariate analysis. *American Journal of Medicine, 55,* 583–594.

Miranda, J., Perez-Stable, E., Munoz, R., Hargreaves, W., & Henke, C. (1991). Somatization, psychiatric disorder, and stress in utilization of ambulatory medical services. *Health Psychology, 10*(1), 46–51.

Regier, D., Narrow, W., Rae, D., Manderscheid, R., Locke, B., & Goodwin, F. (1993). The de factor U.S. mental health and addictive disorders service system. *Archives of General Psychiatry, 50,* 85–94.

Schappert, S. M. (1992). National ambulatory medical care survey: 1989 summary. *Vital Health Statistics, 13*(110).

Schulberg, H. C., Saul, M., McClelland, M., Gangule, M., Christy, W., & Frank, R. (1985). Assessing depression in primary medical and psychiatric practices. *Archives of General Psychiatry, 42,* 1164–1170.

Schurman, R., Kramer, P., & Mitchell. (1985). The hidden mental health network. *Archives of General Psychiatry, 42,* 89–94.

Smith, G., Monson, R., & Ray, D. (1986). Patients with multiple unexplained symptoms. *Archives of Internal Medicine, 146,* 69–72.

Strogatz, D., & James, S. (1986). Social support and hypertension among blacks and whites in a rural southern community. *American Journal of Epidemiology, 124,* 949–955.

Wells, K. B., Hays, R. D., Burnam, M. A., Rogers, W., Greenfield, S., & Ware, J. E. (1989). Detection of depressive disorder for patients receiving prepaid or fee-for-service care: Results from the Medical Outcome Study. *Journal of the American Medical Association, 262,* 3298–3302.

CHAPTER 10

Cultural Issues in Relational Diagnosis: Hispanics in the United States

JOAN D. KOSS-CHIOINO, PhD and JOSÉ M. CANIVE, MD

INTRODUCTION

Those authors who have described the family across cultures view it as the basic sociocultural unit. It usually is defined as a social group characterized by common residence, economic cooperation, and reproduction (Stephens, 1963) or as the main social unit that fulfills the basic emotional, physical, and intellectual needs of the members of a society (Yorburg, 1983). However, because the structure and function of the family in any culture is shaped by related economic, political, and social factors, a definition that is applicable to all families across cultures, considered both diachronically and synchronically, is difficult. Our focus in this chapter will be on understanding how these factors relate to family structure and function and their impact on formulating relational diagnoses.

What Constitutes "Family?"

There has been considerable debate about the universality of "the family" and the validity of a culturally relativistic approach. Given extensive variability of the cultural (including ethnic) record (McGoldrick, Pearce, & Giordano, 1982; Tseung & Hsu, 1991), perhaps all that can be said is that the family as a social unit must fulfill certain culturally defined affective and instrumental needs of its members. Although these needs may be universal (i.e., rearing children or economic cooperation), the form and extent to which they are met clearly depends on the mores and values of a particular society. Cultural anthropologists have described how the organization of the family unit is highly variable (i.e., distinct marriage rules, descent systems, postmarital residence choice, and household structure). Moreover, the meanings associated with the family's needs—for example, why a child should be nurtured or the eventual consequences of lack of nurturing—are culturally constructed (Shweder, 1991).

Although the unfolding of the life cycle in biological terms is universal (with some differences in the timing of adolescence and old age), conceptualization of the process of individual and family development also is tied to the meanings given to developmental processes. This extends to the stages of development and their timing, including rituals that mark transitions between these stages and carry a symbolic load of traditional meanings. Further, stages of individual and family development are not necessarily determined by the bearing and raising of children, as is usually true in postindustrial societies. Where families are extended due to patterns of polyandry related to the need for economic cooperation (e.g., the Toda tribe in India and among Tibetans), or where marriage is a loosely defined unstable arrangement (e.g., in the Marshall Islands), family development takes a different course with much less focus on child rearing. Even in Western societies, increased longevity and birth control, as well as changed values about sexuality and mating, are creating alternative patterns of family life. While formerly the norm appeared to be nuclear families in urban environments and extended families in rural settings, diversity in family structure and organization is now much more the rule in both settings. In the United States, and particularly in ethnic minority communities, mother-headed families are becoming as frequent as two-parent families. Families are likely to be extended and to include someone from the grandparent generation.

Because our own developmental needs have been met by a particular type of family unit, and because that expectation is part of our view of the world, as family researchers or therapists we need to adopt "a culturally oriented understanding of the family, utilizing broad perspectives which go beyond the typical family pattern we are familiar with" (Tseung & Hsu, 1991). Unfortunately, there is a tendency to overgeneralize about the pattern of family life in a culture that differs from our own, even though anthropologists caution us about intracultural variation. In intervening with families, stereotypes may become masks that disguise acceptable strategies to solve problems or even hide the problems themselves (Lopez & Hernandez, 1986; Montalvo & Gutierrez, 1983). The solution for the therapist in diagnosing a family is to ask about associated behavior and meanings, relying on descriptions from the literature only for hypotheses. Therefore, careful consideration should be given to the assessment of family function across cultures, especially when utilizing models indigenous to professional sectors of Euroamerican culture.

DIMENSIONS OF FAMILY FUNCTION AND RELATIONAL DIAGNOSIS

Family structure and organization will vary across different societies and will be subject to intracultural patterning. How a family functions must respond to the biological, social, and psychological needs of its members; satisfying these needs can be described as the "adaptive" function of family life. This may be the one universal aspect of the family unit, no matter how that unit is structured. The needs of both individuals and families as social units and the ways in which they are satisfied are determined by the meanings ascribed to them by cultural norms and traditions.

Investigators of family functioning construct models that emphasize different dimensions. Whether the typology is theoretically or empirically derived (i.e., through cluster analysis), there are built-in biases in both approaches (Christiansen & Arrington, 1987). If the model is theoretically driven, it usually is based on concepts about family in the family systems' literature that are clinically oriented, such as the work of Minuchin (1974) and Haley (1976). Such constructs become part of the theoretical basis of the family therapy school itself and are then regarded as informed "truths." Similarly, if observations have been made on families within only one U.S. subculture (usually majority Anglo-Americans), then empirically deriving the constructs that guide the model of family functioning is invalid for families of other subcultures or those that are culturally diverse. This is the case in many popular self-rating scales.

Topologies have different tasks, among them to differentiate between normal and abnormal family functioning. According to Christiansen and Arrington (1987): "Although some systems such as Olson's (Olson, McCubbin, Barnes, Larsen, Muxen, & Wilson, 1982; Olson, Portner, & Bell, 1982) and Reiss' (1981) have had some success in differentiating normal from abnormal systems, only research on a wide variety of populations (across racial, ethnic and class lines) can confirm a taxonomy's functioning in this area" (p. 274).

Models and Cultural Difference: Some Examples

Are commonly used models of family functioning valid across cultures or ethnic groups? A number of authors raise this issue and answer it in similar ways, in part by describing a theory of core value orientations as underlying clinically important cultural characteristics of clients and families (Ibrahim, 1985; Szapocznik, Scopetta, Aranalde, & Kurtines, 1978). Sue and Sue (1990), for example, present a value orientation model adapted from Ibrahim (1985), who adapted it from Kluckhohn and Strodtbeck (1961). The model poses four dimensions as universal to human beings: time focus, human activity, social relations, and relationship with nature. Each of these dimensions has three major variations. For example, time orientation can be past, present, or future. Several family theorists, seeking models of cultural difference, hold that the profile of value orientations directs the selection of behavior. Values also are cited as determinants of how family members think and feel about themselves and their relationships (Spiegel, 1982). Kurtines and Szapocznik (in press) relate their choice of therapeutic approach (structural family therapy) for Cubans to the need for a therapist to take a "directive, present-oriented leadership role" as appropriate to paternal authority in Cuban families and necessary to deal with adolescents with behavior problems.

The value orientation approach suggests some transcultural correspondences as well as the charting of differences. It is a way to develop hypotheses about the patterning of family relationships and explain the potential content of specific cultures and familial patterns within them. That the profiles are idealized patterns for everyone in a specific population can be questioned; more important, it must be observed that given a particular pattern of values that provide idealized guidelines, human behavior is likely to be characterized by a wide range of variations based on what can be conceptualized as "culture as context."

This distinction has been drawn by Koss-Chioino and Vargas (1992). Cultural *content* refers to the specific meanings through which social phenomena are constructed, deconstructed, and reconstructed. It includes guidelines for specific behaviors and interpersonal interactions, beliefs about gender and role, definitions of identity, body, and sexuality, and world and self views. Cultural *context* refers to the nature and organization of local worlds as shaped by key historical, social, and economic forces. Forces that shape the local worlds of ethnic groups, for example, are directly related to the processes of migration, immigration, and acculturation as well as the general composition of society in terms of interaction with other ethnic groups. Ethnic groups' socioeconomic position in the social hierarchy and how these positions impact upon their social environments are salient factors.

As is described later, a schema based on these three distinctions—transcultural frame, cultural content, and cultural context—has greater power to approach the condition of behavioral variation that can be found within specific, even relatively small populations.

A number of studies have examined the effect of acculturation on family variables (Spiegel, 1982; Szapocznik, 1994), but relatively few examine the effects of prior acculturation at earlier historic periods. A case in point is that of two Hispanic subcultures in New Mexico: Hispanic New Mexicans and Mexican Americans. There are variations between these groups because their culture histories are very different. Hispanic New Mexicans are the descendants of Spanish adventurers and American Indian tribal peoples in the Southwest. They do not identify as "Mexican" because they did not experience the particular cultural changes attendant upon the process of "mestizoization" when Spanish colonists mixed with Central American Indians with highly developed cultures and then became newly created citizens of a mestizo nation that combined these specific cultural streams and traditions.

Few models of family functioning take culture as content or context into account. The McMaster model of family function focuses on six dimensions: problem solving, communication, roles, affective responsiveness, affective involvement, and behavioral control (Epstein, Bishop, & Levin, 1978). In contrast, the circumplex model (Olson, Portner, & Bell, 1982; Olson et al., 1982) is focused around the intersection of two curvilinear dimensions of cohesion (emotional bonding between family members) and adaptability (ability of family systems to reorganize in response to situational and developmental stresses). These in turn are divided into 16 sectors representing types of marital and family systems. Communication is viewed as a dimension that facilitates movement along the major orthogonal dimensions. Are these dimensions valid for cultures other than that of mainstream Anglo Americans?

If we take the McMaster model as a point of departure and examine various Hispanic subcultures to which we (the authors) belong and with whom we have worked, we might examine the dimensions one by one. With regard to "affective involvement" in Puerto Rican families, it would appear that most families could be described as "overinvolved," which this model judges to be the least adaptive way of functioning. In fact, using a similar dimension, Canino and Canino (1982) looked at enmeshment (as defined by Minuchin, 1974) in Puerto Rican families in the United States. They refute the idea that enmeshment in these families is dysfunctional, as a number of theoretical models of family functioning assume. Bernal (1982, pp. 197–198), referring to Cuban families in the United States and using a related dimension, dependency, discusses how "conflicting value orientations related to dependence versus independence" can lead to " . . . misattributions on the part of therapists" since "healthy interdependence" may appear as pathological.

Another dimension of the McMaster model, "communication," is described as most effective if "clear and direct." In our experience with Cuban, Puerto Rican, and Mexican American families, communication is largely indirect and conveyed by nonverbal, affectively oriented gestures and signs. Communication style is dependent on role relationships; for example, communication will be less direct when younger family members address older authority figures in parental roles. Further, a popular communication pattern both within and without families is that of gossip ("*chismes*"—Puerto Rico and Cuba; "*bochinches*"—malicious gossip in Puerto Rico; and "*mitotes*"—New Mexico). Not only are these examples of indirect communication, but they are widely approved social patterns. In addition, a great deal of interaction takes place around metaphoric expressions commonly referred to as *dichos* (sayings), which could be construed as "masked communication."

In regard to family roles, the McMaster model talks about accountability and "clear allocation" in terms of distributing role-related tasks in the family setting. This is allied to attitudes toward development. In the Anglo view, the individual develops slowly and progressively attains adult status. In the traditional Hispanic view, there is a clear differentiation between child and adult roles and status. Roles are formally defined, hierarchical in nature, and determined by gender and age. For example, in traditional Mexican families parents rarely appear to set rules for their sons' behavior outside of the home (as contrasted with daughters) and seldom insist that teenage sons respect a curfew. In Mexican American families, acculturation to U.S. mainstream values intertwines with the dilemma of parent-adolescent conflict in that parents expect youths to be responsible for themselves and to others, but the teenage subculture focuses more around freedom of expression and self-satisfaction.

With regard to behavioral control, the model specifies several styles but implies that a "flexible" style of control is more desirable. In traditional Hispanic families, however, norms for behavior are rigidly adhered to and there is little recognition that individuals have different needs.

Considering another dimension, problem solving, the model categorizes problems as "instrumental" or "affective." Instrumental problems must be solved first. Poor Hispanic families have more instrumental problems but frequently express an acceptance of their problems with expressions such as "God wanted it that way" ("*Dios lo quiso*") or "If God wills it" ("*Si Dios lo quiere*"). Given this situation for Hispanic families in the United States, diagnosis and treatment might emphasize affective problems that may be of more interest to them, but this should be ascertained by questioning family members.

The McMaster model divides emotions into two large categories: "welfare" emotions (expressions of well-being) and "emergency" emotions (responses to distress such as anger or pain). In general, Hispanic families are open and quick to express welfare emotions but closed to the expression of emergency emotions. Expressing anger, for example, is taboo. Even in the bosom of the family, emergency emotions are likely to be "backstage" ones rather than "front stage" or openly expressed.

Although these observations about the premises of the McMaster model and their application to Hispanic families are based on our own clinical experiences and subject to the same criticisms with which we began this discussion, they do illustrate the problem of whether the proposed dimensions of family structure and functioning are culturally responsive. We can only suggest that careful empirical data are required for a definitive analysis of family processes across subcultures in the United States. We and other family therapy researchers are actively engaged in planning this type of investigation.

Assessments of Family Functioning

Knight, Yun Tien, Shell, and Ross (1992) bring up the important issue of whether family interaction measures assess the same underlying constructs across cultural groups. In examining the Family Adaptibility and Cohesion Evaluation Scales (FACES) II (Olson, Portner, & Bell, 1982; Olson et al., 1982), Knight's group found that there may not be item equivalence for some items on the cohesion and adaptability subscales when comparing responses of Hispanic and Anglo American mothers. This fact then "suggested" nonequivalence of measures. However, these researchers claimed that the subscales containing these items do have "functional equivalence." In our opinion, this begs the question of equivalence of meaning in central constructs. The position that we will describe is that individual items and measures can differ greatly in terms of degree of *meaningful* equivalence. This raises the question of whether any commonly used family assessment instrument is equivalent across ethnic groups in the United States or across cultures.

One approach to understanding meaningful differences among ethnic cultures is to attempt to translate the instrument into the respondents' native language. This was a necessary step in the Hispanic Family Project, a National Institute of Drug Abuse (NIDA) funded treatment outcome study in Arizona (5-R01-DA-07381-03). Thirty-seven percent of the parents of adolescents enrolled in the study preferred to complete the Family Assessment Measure (FAM) in Spanish. The process of translating the FAM (and other instruments) comprised four steps:

1. For the first translation into Spanish, a panel of five bilingual staff members discussed all items.
2. A bilingual staff member who was not familiar with the FAM then back-translated the instrument into English.
3. This version was then compared systematically to the original English version and discrepancies were resolved.
4. The final version was compared to a Spanish-language version utilized by Szapocznik and his group in Miami (Szapocznik & Kurtines, 1989).

Translating the FAM was a laborious and sometimes frustrating task. The panel of staff members found words that occasioned day-long debates. For example, one of the items is: "When someone in our family is upset, we don't know if they are angry, sad, scared or what." In Spanish there is no word that specifically connotes the concept of "upset." In searching for an adequate translation, the panel considered two words, *molesto* and *enojado*. However, *molesto* implies being bothered, and *enojado* connotes being angry. Both words express specific feelings rather than a general notion of distress. Such observations made during the translation process raised questions about the cross-cultural equivalence of the items identified as most difficult to translate. The issue central to the problem is that of *conceptual equivalence,* not only of items but also of the scales and of the measure itself (Straus, 1969).

As part of the Hispanic Family Project, a study by Canive and Buki (1994) examined the conceptual/functional equivalence of the FAM. They selected a panel of 36 bilingual Hispanics of whom 56 percent were females and 58 percent had master's degrees or above. All lived in the United States but 31 percent were born in a Latin American country or in Spain. Utilizing four different questionnaires, the participants were asked to identify the underlying construct central to each item included in five of the scales of the FAM: role performance, communication, denial/defensiveness, affective involvement, and values and norms. The questionnaires were designed to identify the construct in both English and Spanish, in a forced-choice or multiple-choice format. The participants' task was to identify whether the items signified the construct underlying the scale.

Preliminary Results

Most of the items pertaining to the "communication" scale were easily identified by the majority of panel members. For example, the English version of the item "When I ask someone to explain what they mean, I get a straight answer" was identified as measuring communication by 100 percent of the participants, and the Spanish version of the item by 92 percent. In contrast, the construct "affective involvement" was more difficult to identify. The English version of the item "You don't get a chance to be an individual in our family" was identified as signifying "affective involvement" by 9 percent of the sample and the Spanish version by 4 percent.

Major differences appeared in the participants' ability to discern the underlying construct in some of the items when comparing the English and Spanish versions. For example, the concept "communication" was identified twice as often in the Spanish version compared to the English (68 percent versus 37 percent) in relation to the item "We argue about who said what in our family." Similarly, the item "We don't really trust each other" labeled in the FAM as "affective involvement" was correctly identified by 32 percent of the panel in the English version and by 16 percent of the sample in the Spanish version. Clearly the ease of identification of the construct varies with language. Bilingual persons cannot always correctly identify the item with the construct label when it is in its original language. This conundrum needs to be explained.

Although the study is still in progress, we have developed some hypotheses to understand preliminary results. First, the more specific the item is, the more likely it will be identified with the original construct. Specificity depends on defining a behavioral target. As described, the item "When I ask someone to explain what they mean, I get a straight answer" elicits an identification with the construct "communication" whatever the language. However, if the item does not have a behavioral target, the identification with the construct will depend on key words. If the connotation of the key word is similar to that of the construct that labels the scale, then regardless of language, the respondent will be likely to identify the original construct. The problem arises when key words in different languages have different connotations. For example, in the item "We don't really trust each other," the word "trust" in English connotes reliability. The translation of "trust" in Spanish is *confianza* which has the connotation of trust plus familiar intimacy as well as hope and belief. Hypothetically, it seems that the cognitive schemata that these words represent are different enough to elicit different levels of identification.

HISPANICS IN THE UNITED STATES: ISSUES AROUND FUNCTION AND DYSFUNCTION

The following section looks at both the commonalities and the differences in family structure and function among Hispanic ethnic populations in the United States including Mexican/Mexican Americans, Cubans, and Puerto Ricans. Our selection reflects most of the existing literature and our own experiences with these populations. The literature is largely anecdotal, generally lacking the requisite systematic study. To quote Vega (1992), "Given the non-comparability of most contemporary findings about the Hispanic family, and the lack of consistent conceptual grounding it is difficult to develop hypotheses about cultural similarities or differences in family processes that may exist among Cubans, Puerto Ricans, or Mexican Americans" (p. 499). The reader might consider the following as a hypothetical guide rather than a demonstrated set of facts.

Commonalities

Despite Vega's (1992) stance, he too recognizes that Hispanic families, when compared with non-Hispanic white families, have more face-to-face interactions and are more supportive of one another. The central role of the family in the lives of almost all individuals of Hispanic origin and the ubiquitous presence of extended family is echoed by a host of authors (Escobar & Randolph, 1982; Murillo, 1971; Ruiz, 1982). This especially high value on family, both nuclear and extended, appears to be the continuation of traditions adaptive to small-scale agrarian economies, the Iberian heritage of all Latin Americans. This heritage was augmented by the two major additional culture streams that mixed with Hispanics in the new world, Africans, and American Indians.

Marin and VanOss Marin (1991) include under the characteristic "familism" three types of value orientations: (1) family members are expected to provide material and emotional support to each other; (2) they expect to rely on other family members; and (3) they perceive relatives as examples of proper conduct and good attitudes. However, given various changes in economic context and lifestyle in the United States, the result of migration, immigration, urbanization, acculturation, and intrafamilial conflicts, familism remains an ideal that may be countermanded by the realities of postindustrial, urban life. What Hispanics still seem to hold in common is the expectation (if not always the reality) of reliance on family for emotional and other support throughout their lives (Keefe, 1984). This underlies the various descriptions of Hispanic family life as "interdependent" in nature, with the needs of the family taking precedence over individual needs. These formulations have appeared in studies of Puerto Ricans in the United States (Canino & Canino, 1982; Glazer & Moynihan, 1975), Cubans (Bernal, 1982; Szapocznik, Kurtines, & Fernandez, 1980), and Mexican Americans (Alvirez & Bean, 1976; Keefe, 1984).

Another commonality is the value placed on spirituality, defined as a sense of wholeness, inner peace, interconnection, and reverence for life (Cervantes & Ramirez, 1992; Vaughan, 1986). These values may be expressed through organized religions and belief in a higher power (particularly through Catholicism) but also are expressed through personal ideologies and folk religions. Spirituality summarizes the ideals that family life must fulfill.

Differences among Hispanics

Variations among Hispanic ethnic subcultures generally have been described as due to the effects of adaptation to life in the United States (Marin & VanOss Marin, 1991). However, there also are differences that can be ascribed to the culture history of each group, including the intermixing of cultures and genetic characteristics. The following sections compare some of the variations in family life patterns in the three Hispanic ethnic minority cultures on which we have chosen to focus. We approach these ethnospecific patterns from the perspective of their potential for functional or dysfunctional family processes. Our approach follows the distinction we noted earlier between culture as content and culture as context. Within each of these categories there are many possible themes that pattern family life, some of which we discuss. The distinction between content and context is heuristic, but it can be useful in the service of relational diagnosis. In actual fact, these dimensions are interrelated, given the fact that culture is an adaptive tool for both individuals and families.

Culture as Context

Socioeconomic Status, Education, and Immigrant Status

The three groups differ along all of these dimensions. Cubans in the United States tend to be wealthier and have more education. These conditions appear related to the fact that they have more intact families and a lower fertility rate (Vega, 1992). Puerto Ricans in the United States are the poorest of the three Hispanic groups and have greater numbers of mother-headed families and disrupted marital relationships. Mexican-descent families are intermediate in socioeconomic status, educational level, and family organization but have the highest rates of fertility and the largest families. While father-absence is implicated to a greater extent in adolescent behavior problems in Mexican American and Puerto Rican families, this syndrome among Cuban youths appears to be related more to intergenerational conflict due to asymmetrical acculturation (Szapocznik, 1994). Among Cubans and Mexican Americans, the higher the educational level, the greater the marital instability; the reverse is true among Puerto Ricans (Frisbie, 1986). Intervening variables may be the level of acculturation and economic status.

Culture History

As indicated earlier, all of these groups have had very different cultural histories, which have affected their patterns of family life. If we look selectively at how past history has affected current life conditions, it is clear that Cuba became much more divided along class lines due to its favored economic position in the Spanish colonial empire and a type of economy that imported African slaves to become ancestors of the poorer, lower classes. Except for the Mariel boat lift in 1985, Cubans who immigrated to the United States are largely white and middle class and devoted to a success ideology supported by the U.S. government.

In contrast, Puerto Rico was always a poorer place in which class distinctions were not as widespread, and Spanish and African genes and traditions mingled more freely. Different migrant streams brought largely lower-class, impoverished peoples to the United States. Even though acculturation has proceeded relentlessly toward assimilation, the back-and-forth journeys to the island have helped maintain the Spanish language and many traditions, especially among first-generation families.

Mexican Americans are the descendants of Mesoamerican Indians and Spaniards who have struggled to come to the United States for economic survival, a process that continues today among undocumented families. Although ties with Mexico are maintained to some extent, extended families are more often separated. Moreover, the Indian heritage contributes different family values, such as emphases on larger families and extended kinship (both lateral and horizontal as well as fictive kin) for social and economic support. When poor Mexican families are isolated in the United States, significant supportive ties with extended families often are lost as they are to those families where the father has died or abandoned his wife and children.

Acculturation and Ethnic Identity

There is extensive research on the impact of acculturation on mental health (Rogler, Cortes, & Malgady, 1991). However, relatively few studies of the effect of acculturation on family function have been conducted. Using clinical observations, Szapocznik, Kurtines, and Fernandez (1980) pointed to the ways greater acculturation to U.S. lifestyles and values lead to disharmony between Cuban American parents and their children when the hierarchy of authority is disrupted. These findings have been replicated in clinical studies of many types of minority families (Ho, 1987; Koss-Chioino & Vargas, 1992; Vargas & Koss-Chioino, 1992). Mirowsky and Ross (1987) describe how acculturation has the potential to unbalance the significant relationship between control and support as Mexican immigrants became more individualistic in their desire to retain control over personal resources. As younger members seek their fortunes in the United States, patterns of family need being placed above individual need become disrupted.

These types of dysfunction pertain more to first-generation immigrant families than to the whole spectrum of acculturation in families. A potent source of dysfunction in second-generation families is that of asymmetrical loss of ethnic identity between parents and youths. Hispanic youths often pursue conflict-generating activities, such as joining gangs that engage in antisocial behaviors in relation to the larger community but that offer a way to establish or confirm ethnic self-reference (Vigil, 1990). The most recent instruments to measure acculturation (see Cuellar, Arnold, & Maldonado, 1994) recognize the need for a multidimensional approach by measuring cultural orientation toward Anglo and Mexican culture simultaneously. This situation of biculturalism naturally leads to questions regarding ethnic identification. With regard to relational diagnosis, the important question is "How do families acculturate?" This question then leads to the need to explore how the role of ethnic identification impacts on family functioning.

Culture as Content

Ethos and Family Life

Relational diagnosis should not only consider family dynamics from structural and/or behavioral perspectives but should also examine the affective style that characterizes families. Although there are intracultural variations among Hispanic groups, in general, each Hispanic subculture has its own pattern of expressive style, one aspect of its own cultural scripts about emotions. Among Cubans there is a tendency toward high expressiveness characterized by flamboyance, exaggeration, and a love for a rich material life. Distress may not be disclosed until there is a relationship of trust (*confianza*) established, but once this exists, distress often is communicated as a prolonged litany of despair, particularly by women.

Bernal (1982) describes the sense of "specialness" that Cubans convey not only verbally but also in music, art, and literature. This privileged position relates to the "geopolitical importance that Cuba has had in relation to powerful nations throughout its history" (p. 157) and also to the influence of its African heritage. Within the same heritage, Puerto Ricans have a similar exuberant expressive style but a much humbler approach to life. This is probably attributable to Puerto Rico's lesser historical importance on the international scene and its many years of political domination. In contrast, Mexicans are more reserved, given their Indian heritage and a constant struggle to maintain their distinct cultural identity in a situation of close proximity to a powerful nation. Mexican Americans are less reserved but prefer to keep their deeper feelings, both euphoric and dysphoric, confined to an inner circle of confidants. Initial diagnostic workups are unlikely to tap these hidden feelings, which emerge only when familiarity and trust develop.

Role Relationships

Given the commonality of a rigid definition of hierarchy according to age and gender in Hispanic families in general (Falicov, 1982), the most important role relationships are father-child and husband-wife. The extent of marital discord (often pushed by acculturative stress and discrimination in job opportunities) varies according to the socioeconomic potential that life in the United States offers to these three groups, with Puerto Ricans suffering the most family disruption. A result of marital discord is the more frequent abandonment of children by fathers. Such losses disrupt the balanced power relationships structured by the ideal of a family hierarchy and lead to multiple types of family dysfunction. Among the more serious of these is loss of control over preteen and teenage youth, who are increasingly at risk for delinquency and substance abuse. Mexican American and Puerto Rican women as single mothers with little education, even if they are the sole support of their children, are seldom empowered to exercise authority.

Conflict and Harmony

The *ideal* across Hispanic families is the fostering of conflict-free relations among all family members (Marin & VanOss Marin, 1991). Aggressive behavior is both taboo and feared. Many families will avoid discussion of conflictual situations even if directly confronted. However, given the stresses of poverty, discrimination, and occupational frustrations, more acculturated Mexican American men (and some, but fewer, Mexican men) readily disinhibit when drinking, rage against and abuse spouses, and also sometimes abuse children. Some Puerto Rican men follow a similar pattern; perhaps they have little practice at learning how to titrate negative emotional states.

NORMALITY AND ABNORMALITY: THE CENTRAL ISSUE IN RELATIONAL DIAGNOSIS IN THE CONTEXT OF CULTURE

To this point we have examined the role of culture in diagnosing families by taking family systems theory as our point of departure. The overall measures we have used as a basis for discussion are "function" and "dysfunction"; we have inquired into the many ways in which variations in cultural patterns require that these terms be considered within a relativistic framework. However, as we acknowledged earlier, the family as a social unit has certain adaptive requirements that are transcultural in nature, but ethnospecific patterns of family behavior show relative emphases regarding these requirements and also how they are to be met. Given this perspective, we argue that "dysfunction" is not isomorphic with "abnormality." When socially accepted normative patterns (ideal or actual) are transgressed (always considering a range of variation in departures from the norm), family dynamics may be considered "abnormal" from the perspective of the family or its sociocultural referents. However, by definition, "dysfunction" refers to a family's failure to meet the needs of one or more of its members and implies a partial causative role in the development of symptomatic or asocial behavior in these individuals.

In sum, we are advocating a diagnostic approach quite different from that of the Diagnostic and Statistical Manual of Mental Disorders (DSM), which describes and categorizes individual psychopathology. Even the recent attempts to include the variable of culture in the fourth edition of the DSM (DSM-IV) do not change its basic emphasis on psychopathology as rooted within individuals. Culture, however defined, is an interpersonal and/or interactive phenomena. A system to diagnose families must share this attribute. The problems that arise when individual versus relational perspectives are brought to bear on understanding how families affect individual lives can be illustrated by the study of expressed emotion (EE) across cultures.

Brown, Birley, and Wing (1972) developed the "expressed emotion" (EE) construct from their work with families of the mentally ill in Great Britain. As formulated, EE is determined through a semistructured interview (the Camberwell Family Interview; see Brown, Birley, & Wing, 1972), which ascertains the level of criticism, hostility, and overinvolvement in relatives of a mentally ill family member. Results from many studies show that persons with schizophrenia, mania, or depression who live with high-EE relatives have higher rates of relapse at one-year follow-up.

The EE index had to be altered to reach predictive validity in most studies. In Milan, for example (Bertrando et al., 1992), EE did not predict relapse when utilizing the standard emotional overinvolvement cut-off score. The "warmth" scale of the interview was used to add to the predictive validity of the index of "overinvolvement." Those patients who lived with "cold" overinvolved relatives relapsed more frequently. Further, the prevalence of high EE appears to vary with cultural setting. In a comparative study of Anglo and Mexican American families, Karno et al. (1987) found that in the former, 67 percent could be categorized as high EE, while in the latter, only 41 percent could be thus categorized. The prevalence of high-EE families varies across study sites: 54 percent in London (Vaughan et al., 1984); 23 percent in Chandigarth (Wig et al., 1987); 58 percent in Madrid (Arevalo & Vizcarro, 1989); and 48 percent in Valencia (Montero et al., 1992).

Thus, the EE studies illustrate how culturally patterned differences in affective style in families can have differential effects on individual members. Knowing what ideal or mean patterns are prevalent can enhance measures to prevent or treat those families that develop dysfunctional behavior. In these efforts, relational diagnosis assumes a place of central importance.

CONCLUSION: NEXT STEPS

This chapter has reviewed some of the major issues in regard to the task of making a system of relational diagnoses culturally responsive. Because the subject is complex, we have not covered a number of relevant issues, such as the impact on family functioning of parents who are ethnically (and/or racially) different and sometimes even speak different languages (Sciarra & Ponterotto, 1991; the novel by Hijuelos, 1993, describes these family dynamics delightfully). Another complex issue is that of accounting for the network of interactions in communities where families reside. The social context affects many of the variables mentioned, from economic opportunity to experience of discrimination, and how these in turn can affect problems around differential acculturation and ethnic identity. Szapocznik and Kurtines (1993) have eloquently described the "embeddedness" of families in communities as necessary to a contextual understanding of them. By examining families in the context of culturally pluralistic communities, we can attend to the "local worlds" in which they exist and interact. This also permits the researcher/clinician to avoid stereotypes derived from a too-narrow conceptualization of culture.

It is perhaps the final irony that current news media are now highlighting how U.S. culture has become more individualized and less organized into family units. Some argue that this is a wave of culture change that will yield new types of family groupings as adaptive to the changing conditions of the twenty-first century, while others view one-parent and single-parent families and isolated one-person households as highly dysfunctional. Regardless of the problem of accurately summarizing cultural patterns due to intracultural variability, scores of studies of Hispanic cultures clearly show the high value placed on two-parent and extended family units and on family life in general. One of the results of the development of a culturally responsive system of relational diagnosis would be to understand the types of dysfunctions that characterize those Hispanic families that are no longer based on traditional norms and values but have adapted to the pattern of Anglo families in the United States. The transitions of Hispanic families from familism to individualistic types of social units are much more recent; the processes can be recaptured more readily. The establishment of a system of relational diagnosis that responds to cultural content and context could lead to this important direction for research and clinical development.

REFERENCES

Alvirez, D., & Bean, F. D. (1976). The Mexican American family. In C. Mindel & R. Habenstein (Eds.), *Ethnic families in America* (pp. 271–291). New York: Elsevier.

Arevalo, J., & Vizcarro, C. (1989). "Emocion expresada" y curso de esquizofrenia en una muestra espanola. *Analisis y Modificacion de Conducta, 15,* 275–316.

Bernal, G. (1982). Cuban families. In M. McGoldrick, J. Pearce, & J. Giordano (Eds.), *Ethnicity and family therapy* (pp. 187–207). New York: Guilford.

Bertrando, P., et al. (1992). Expressed emotion and schizophrenia in Italy: A study of an urban population. *British Journal of Psychiatry, 161,* 223–229.

Brown, G. W., Birley, J. L. T., & Wing, J. K. (1972). Influence of family life on the course of schizophrenic disorders: A replication. *British Journal of Psychiatry, 121,* 241–258.

Canino, G., & Canino, I. A. (1982). Culturally syntonic family therapy for migrant Puerto Ricans. *Hospital and Community Psychiatry, 33,* 299–303.

Canive, J., & Buki, L. P. (1994, August 12–16). *Evaluating test equivalence of a family assessment measure.* Paper presented at the 102nd annual convention of the American Psychological Association, Los Angeles.

Cervantes, J. M., & Ramirez, O. (1992). Spirituality and family dynamics in psychotherapy with Latino children. In L. A. Vargas & J. Koss-Chioino (Eds.), *Working with culture* (pp. 103–128). San Francisco: Jossey-Bass.

Christiansen, A., & Arrington, A. (1987). Research issues and strategies. In T. Jacob (Ed.), *Family interaction and psychopathology: Theories, methods, and findings* (pp. 259–296). New York: Plenum.

Cuellar, I., Arnold, B., & Maldonado, R. (1994). *Acculturation rating scale for Mexican Americans. II: A revision of the original ARSMA scale.* Unpublished manuscript, Department of Psychology and Anthropology, University of Texas-Pan-American, Edinburg, TX.

Epstein, N. B., Bishop, D. S., & Levin, S. (1978). The McMaster model of family functioning. *Journal of Marriage and Family Counseling, 4,* 19–31.

Escobar, J. I., & Randolph, E. T. (1982). The Hispanic and social networks. In R. Becerra, M. Karno, & J. Escobar (Eds.), *Mental health and Hispanic Americans: Clinical perspectives* (pp. 41–57). New York: Grune & Stratton.

Falicov, C. J. (1982). Mexican families. In McGoldrick, J. Pearce, & J. Giordano (Eds.), *Ethnic and family therapy* (pp. 134–163). New York: Guilford.

Frisbie, W. P. (1986). Variation in patterns of marital instability among Hispanics. *Journal of Marriage and Family Counseling, 48,* 99–106.

Glazer, N., & Moynihan, D. (1975). *Ethnicity: Theory and experience.* Cambridge, MA: Harvard University.

Haley, J. (1976). *Problem-solving therapy.* San Francisco: Jossey-Bass.

Hijuelos, O. (1993). *The fourteen sisters of Emilio Montez O'Brien.* New York: Harper Collins.

Ho, M. K. (1987). *Family therapy with ethnic minorities.* Newbury Park, CA: Sage.

Ibrahim, F. A. (1985). Effective cross-cultural counseling and psychotherapy: A framework. *The Counseling Psychologist, 13,* 625–638.

Karno, M., Jenkins, J. H., Lopez, S., & Mintz, J. (1987). Expressed emotion and schizophrenic outcome among Mexican-American families. *Journal of Nervous and Mental Diseease, 15,* 143–151.

Keefe, S. E. (1984). Real and ideal extended familism among Mexican Americans and Anglo Americans: On the meaning of "close" family ties. *Human Organization, 43,* 65–70.

Kluckhohn, F. R., & Strodtbeck, F. L. (1961). *Variations in value orientations.* Evanston, IL: Row, Patterson.

Knight, G. P., Yun Tien, J., Shell, R., & Ross, M. (1992). The cross-ethnic equivalence of parenting and family interaction measures among Hispanic and Anglo-American families. *Child Development, 63,* 1392–1403.

Koss-Chioino, J. D., & Vargas, L. A. (1992). Through the cultural looking glass: A model for understanding culturally responsive psychotherapies. In L. A. Vargas & J. D. Koss-Chioino (Eds.), *Working with culture: Psychotherapeutic interventions with ethnic minority children and adolescents* (pp. 1–22). San Francisco: Jossey-Bass.

Kurtines, W. M., & Szapocznik, J. (in press). Cultural competence in assessing Hispanic youths and families: Challenges in the assessment of treatment needs and treatment evaluation for Hispanic drug abusing adolescents. In E. Rahdert (Ed.), *Adolescent drug abuse: Clinical assessment and therapeutic interventions.* Bethesda, MD: National Institute on Drug Abuse.

Lopez, S., & Hernandez, P. (1986). How culture is considered in evaluations of psychopathology. *Journal of Nervous and Mental Disease, 176,* 598–606.

Marin, G., & VanOss Marin, B. (1991). Research with Hispanic populations. *Applied Social Research Methods Series* (vol. 23). London: Sage.

McGoldrick, M., Pearce, J., & Giordano, J. (1982). *Ethnicity and family therapy.* New York: Guilford.

Minuchin, S. (1974). *Families and family therapy.* Cambridge, MA: Harvard University.

Mirowsky, J., & Ross, C. E. (1987). Support and control in Mexican and Anglo cultures. In M. Gaviria & J. D. Arana (Eds.), *Health and behavior: Research agenda for Hispanics* (pp. 85–92). Chicago: University of Illinois Publications Services.

Montalvo, B., & Gutierrez, M. (1983). A perspective for the use of the cultural dimension in family therapy. In J. C. Hansen & C. J. Falicov (Eds.), *Cultural perspectives in family therapy* (pp. 15–32). Rockville, MD: Aspen.

Montero, I., Gomez-Beneyto, M., Ruiz, I., Puche, E., & Adam, A. (1992). The influence of family expressed emotion on the course of schizophrenia in a sample of Spanish patients. *British Journal of Psychiatry, 161,* 217–222.

Murillo, N. (1971). The Mexican-American family. In C. A. Hernandez, M. J. Haug, & N. N. Wagner (Eds.), *Chicana: Social and psychological perspectives* (pp. 155–170). St. Louis: C. V. Mosby.

Olson, D. H., McCubbin, H. I., Barnes, H. L., Larsen, A., Muxen, M. J., & Wilson, M. (1982). *Family inventories: Inventories asked in a national survey of families across the family life cycle.* St. Paul: Family Social Science, University of Minnesota.

Olson, D. H., Portner, J., & Bell, R. (1982). FACES II: Family adaptability and cohesion evaluation scales. In D. H. Olson et al. (Eds.), *Family inventories: Inventories asked in a national survey of families across the family life cycle* (pp. 5–23). St. Paul: Family Social Science, University of Minnesota.

Reiss, D. (1981). *The family's construction of reality.* Cambridge, MA: Harvard University.

Rogler, L. H., Cortez, D. E., & Malgady, R. G. (1991). Acculturation and mental health status among Hispanics: Convergence and new directions. *American Psychologist, 46,* 585–597.

Ruiz, P. (1982). The Hispanic patient: Sociocultural perspectives. In R. Becerra, M. Karno, & J. Escobar (Eds.), *Mental health and Hispanic Americans: Clinical perspectives* (pp. 17–27). New York: Grune & Stratton.

Sciarra, D. T., & Ponterotto, J. G. (1991). Counseling the Hispanic bilingual family: Challenges to the therapeutic process. *Psychotherapy, 28,* 473–479.

Shweder, R. A. (1991). *Thinking through cultures: Expeditions in cultural psychology.* Cambridge, MA: Harvard University Press.

Spiegel, J. (1982). An ecological model of ethnic families. In M. McGoldrick, J. Pearce, & J. Giordano (Eds.), *Ethnicity and family therapy* (pp. 31–51). New York: Guilford.

Stephens, W. N. (1963). *The family in cross-cultural perspective.* New York: Holt, Rinehart and Winston.

Straus, M. A. (1969). Phenomenal identity and conceptual equivalence of measurement in cross-national comparative research. *Journal of Marriage and Family, 31,* 233–239.

Sue, D. W., & Sue, D. (1990). *Counseling the culturally different: Theory and practice.* New York: Wiley.

Szapocznik, J. (Ed.) (1994). *A Hispanic family approach to substance abuse prevention.* Rockville, MD: Center for Substance Abuse Prevention.

Szapocznik, J., & Kurtines, W. M. (1989). *Breakthroughs in therapy with problem behavior youth.* New York: Springer.

Szapocznik, J., & Kurtines, W. M. (1993). Family psychology and cultural diversity: Opportunities for theory, research, and application. *American Psychologist, 48,* 400–407.

Szapocznik, J., Kurtines, W. M., & Fernandez, T. (1980). Bicultural involvement and adjustment in Hispanic American Youths. *International Journal of Intercultural Relations, 4,* 353–366.

Szapocznik, J., Scopetta, M. A., de los Angeles Aranalde, M., & Kurtines, W. M. (1978). Cuban value structure: Treatment implications. *Journal of Consulting and Clinical Psychology, 46,* 961–970.

Tseung, W., & Hsu, J. (1991). *Culture and family: Problems and therapy.* New York: Haworth Press.

Vargas, L. A., & Koss-Chioino, J. D. (1992). *Working with culture: Psychotherapeutic interventions with ethnic minority children and adolescents.* San Francisco: Jossey-Bass.

Vaughn, C. E., Snyder, K. S., Jones, S., Freeman, W. B., & Falloon, I. R. (1984). Family factors in schizophrenics' relapse. *Archives of General Psychiatry, 41,* 1169–1177.

Vaughan, F. (1986). *The inward arc: Healing and wholeness in psychotherapy and spirituality.* Boston: Shambhala Press.

Vega, W. A. (1992). Hispanic families in the 1980s: A decade of research. In A. S. Skolnick & J. H. Skolnick (Eds.), *Family in transition: Rethinking marriage, sexuality, child rearing, and family organization* (pp. 490–504). New York: Harper Collins.

Vigil, J. D. (1990). Cholos and gangs: Culture change and street youth in Los Angeles. In C. R. Huff (Ed.), *Gangs in America* (pp. 116–128). Newbury Park, CA: Sage.

Wig, N. N., Menon, D. K., Ghosh, A., Kuipers, L., Leff, J., Korton, A., Day, R., Sartoruis, N., Ernberg, G., & Jablensky, A. (1987). Expressed emotion and schizophrenia in North India. I. Cross-cultural transfer of ratings of expressed emotion. *British Journal of Psychiatry, 151,* 156–173.

Yorberg, B. (1983). *Families and societies: Survival or extinction?* New York: Columbia University Press.

CHAPTER 11

Cultural Considerations in Diagnosis

LILLIAN COMAS-DÍAZ, PhD

Culture has been recognized as a pivotal factor in mental health diagnosis and treatment (Comas-Díaz & Griffith, 1988; Gaw, 1993). Indeed, the American Psychiatric Association (APA) has formally acknowledged the significance of cultural issues in its diagnostic manual (DSM-IV) (APA, 1994). A group on culture and diagnosis composed of cultural experts was sponsored by the Office for Special Populations of the National Institutes of Mental Health, in collaboration with the DSM-IV Task Force of the APA, to examine the cultural validity of the DSM-IV with culturally diverse populations in the United States and internationally (Mezzich et al., 1993). On the basis of this group's input, DSM-IV now includes an introductory section placing cultural issues in a clinical context, a subsection per diagnostic category with relevant cultural treatment issues, and an appendix (appendix 1) with an outline for cultural formulations in diagnosis, along with a glossary of culture-bound syndromes recognized in other cultures that are not included in the main text (APA, 1994).

The American Psychological Association also has paid attention to cultural and ethnic factors affecting mental health (Comas-Díaz, 1990; Goodchilds, 1991), developing guidelines for providers of psychological services to ethnic, linguistic, and culturally diverse populations. These guidelines recognize ethnicity and culture as significant parameters in understanding psychological processes; acknowledge that socioeconomic and political factors have a significant impact on the psychosocial, political, and economic development of culturally diverse groups; recognize the need to help clients to understand, maintain, and resolve their ethnocultural identification; and recognize the need to understand the interaction of culture, gender, and sexual orientation on behavior (APA, 1993).

Notwithstanding these efforts by organized mental health organizations, we need to continue enhancing the cultural sensitivity and suitability of the mental health diagnostic process and nosology. In this chapter I review some problems in diagnosing culturally diverse clients given current diagnostic practices. Then, I examine the need for contextualizing the diagnostic process for culturally diverse clients. Finally, I propose relational diagnosis as a framework for contextualizing behavior and as a relevant format for culturally diverse populations.

The author gratefully acknowledges Florence Kaslow, Ph.D., for her insightful editorial suggestions; and David Wellman, Ph.D., and Frederick M. Jacobsen, M.D., for their stimulating discussions on mental health diagnosis.

CULTURE AND MENTAL HEALTH DIAGNOSIS

The systematic examination of psychopathological manifestations in different cultures has yielded two types of general findings. One suggests that the same major disorders occur in a variety of different cultures (Draguns, 1985). The other asserts that culture significantly influences the expression, course, and outcome of psychological disorders. Indeed, with the possible exception of organic brain disorders and substance abuse, empirical evidence seems to support the assertion that only four mental health diagnoses are distributed worldwide: schizophrenia, bipolar disorder, major depression, and a group of anxiety disorders (panic anxiety, obsessive compulsive disorder, and certain phobias) (Kleinman, 1993). The integration of these two types of findings strongly suggests that cultural variations in psychopathology occur around a detectable core of universal features of psychological dysfunction (Draguns, 1985). However, given the multiple determinants of human behavior, how can we discern what is individually, family, group, and/or culturally based? This question continues to pose a challenge for the diagnostician working with culturally diverse populations.

Sociopolitics in Mental Health Diagnosis

Psychological and psychiatric practices tend to reflect the cultural values and inherent biases of the majority society (Trimble, 1990). In discussing cultural bias, Hall (1981) argues that the cultural context structures reality by processing information through the designation of what we pay attention to and what we ignore. Likewise, culture affects the diagnostic patterns of clinicians as much as it influences the forms and patterns of disorder, individual coping mechanisms, and the strategies that families engage in to cope with the afflicted members (Kleinman, 1993).

Many diagnostic formulations tend to reify normative aspects of culture, race, ethnicity, gender, and class membership as forms of psychopathology (Brown, 1992). Diagnosing certain beliefs and behaviors as diseases tends to support dominant sociopolitical systems, institution, and interests (Wellman, 1993), and punish dissidents. For example, a report by a delegation of U.S. psychiatrists to the former Soviet Union investigated the charges of involuntary psychiatric hospitalization of political and religious dissidents who showed no signs of psychopathology by U.S. standards (Rathe, 1989). The report indicated that Soviet psychiatrists developed the diagnosis of "sluggish schizophrenia," characterized by symptoms of "delusion of reformism" or "heightened sense of self-esteem." The report identified other types of Soviet psychopathology, such as unitary activity (related to a high level of commitment to a single cause such as political reform) and failure to adapt to society, operationalized as individuals' inability to live in society without being subjected to arrest for their behavior. Thus, anti-Soviet behavior was diagnosed as "sluggish schizophrenia." Moreover, the report recognized the pharmacological treatment for patients who suffered from "sluggish schizophrenia" as being punitive instead of therapeutic. As an illustration, along with the antipsychotics used to treat patients for delusions of reformism and anti-Soviet behavior, sulfazine (a drug that causes severe pain, immobility, fever, and muscle necrosis) was used without proof of its efficacy (Rathe, 1989).

In the United States, mental health diagnosis historically has carried negative connotations and outcomes for culturally diverse populations, such as people of color. For example, during the nineteenth century two mental health disorders were identified as being prevalent among Black slaves in the South. A prominent New Orleans physician, Dr. Samuel W. Cartwright, discovered "drapetomania," or what he sometimes called "dysaethesia aethiopica" (Stampp, 1956). These conditions were characterized by the African slaves' uncontrollable urge to escape slavery, destroy property on the plantation, be disobedient, talk back, fight with their masters, and refuse to work. Cartwright attributed these behaviors to African slaves' "stupidity of mind and insensibility of the nerves caused by the disease." Consequently, slaves' desire for freedom was diagnosed as a disease in order to maintain the Southern system of slavery. More recently, Homma-True, Greene, López, and Trimble (1993) reviewed the mental health literature and provided evidence supporting the charges of differences in diagnosis and treatment given based on race, for example, assignment to group versus individual psychotherapy; over-diagnosis of schizophrenia; involuntary admission rates; and greater use of medication and restraints among patients of color. Indeed, the use of psychopharmacology with people of color often has been identified as a controlling and oppressive mechanism (Jacobsen, in press).

In investigating the politics of diagnosing personality disorders, Landrine (1989) empirically found that the gender distribution of personality disorders stems from the resemblance between each personality disorder and the role or role stereotype. In other words, she found that research participants were more likely to ascribe psychopathology to personality diagnoses that resemble female-gender behaviors (such as histrionic, borderline, or dependent personality disorders) than those that described male-gendered behaviors (such as obsessive compulsive and narcissistic personality disorders).

Iwamasa, Larrabee, and Merrit (1995) found empirical support for ethnic and gender bias in diagnosing personality disorders. Using a cardsort analysis, these authors ascertained that research participants diagnosed African Americans with antisocial and personality disorders, while Asian Americans were diagnosed with schizoid personality disorder and Native Americans were assessed to have schizotypal personality disorder. Latinos were not diagnosed with any of the DSM-III-R diagnoses used in the investigation. Regarding gender bias, males were diagnosed with antisocial, schizoid, and passive aggressive personality disorders by the majority of the research participants, while females were diagnosed with histrionic, dependent, paranoid, borderline, and avoidant personality disorders.

In a clinical situation, Loring and Powell (1988) empirically found that the gender and race of both the patient and the clinician can influence diagnosis. The influence of gender and race on diagnostic outcome can occur even when clear-cut diagnostic criteria are presented, as reflected in two case studies representing actual patients receiving psychiatric treatment for undifferentiated schizophrenic disorder with a dependent personality disorder. The researchers found that when the patient was described as a White male or when no gender or racial data were provided, 56 percent of the psychiatrists chose undifferentiated schizophrenia as the diagnosis. However, when the patient was identified as either an African American woman, White woman, or African American man, the proportion of psychiatrists who diagnosed undifferentiated schizophrenia ranged from 21 percent to 23 percent. The clinicians' judgment also varied according to their own gender. For example, male psychiatrists were biased toward giving a diagnosis of recurrent depression to female patients regardless of race, and used histrionic personality disorder when diagnosing White female patients.

Similarly, López (1989) asserted that because diagnosis relies on judgment, stereotypes might influence clinical judgments that affect mental health diagnosis. He stated that patient variables such as gender, race, and class contribute to overpathologizing (inappropriately perceiving patients as more disturbed), minimizing (inappropriately judging symptomatology as normative for members of a group), overdiagnosing (inappropriately applying a diagnosis as a function of group membership), and underdiagnosing (inappropriately avoiding application of a diagnosis as a function of group membership).

Clinicians who rely solely on clinical judgments can misdiagnose. Practitioners need to expand their assessment beyond the use of clinical judgment. A contextual and a comprehensive approach is required, including information provided by significant others, culturally relevant standardized psychological and neuropsychological testing, as well as screening for physical illnesses with symptoms similar to certain mental health illnesses (e.g., thyroid malfunctioning and depression can have similar symptoms). One means of addressing the problems inherent in our current diagnostic process is by contextualizing behavior.

Behavior, Context, and Diagnosis

To remedy some of the cultural biases and stereotypes, it has been recommended that the diagnostician be trained to take the context into account before arriving at a specific diagnosis (Kleinman, 1993). Required diagnostic methods should focus on the entire context, open to multiple, interacting influences, and thus provide more flexibility. The absence of a contextual orientation often negates the complexity and diversity of human experience.

One way of incorporating cultural relevance and validity into the diagnostic process is through the concept of relativism. Within this view, cultures are conceptualized as being fundamentally different and coequal. Using relativism within the diagnostic process affirms cultural diversity because it is problematic to define health and illness or adaptive and maladaptive behavior based solely on the normative standard of the dominant (most powerful) cultural group. Nonetheless, relativism also has significant limitations. For example, if there are multiple realities and they are all equally valid, how do we critically compare and evaluate them? The lack of comparability in cultural paradigms leads to an absence of common standards for diagnosis. Therefore, without sufficient commonality to facilitate discussion, cultural disagreements are handled through power and domination. This results in the hegemony of the dominant group's worldview over those worldviews of subordinate and underrepresented groups.

In a relativistic diagnostic nosology, the absence of rational criticism needed for evaluation precludes us from developing orientations relevant to all individuals, from effectively diagnosing human behavior, and from designing effective treatment interventions to change behavior. To remedy this limitation, Shweder and Bourne (1982) propose the model of holism as a paradigm for understanding and managing cultural diversity by considering context. These authors assert that holism is a relativistic theory of the context-dependent self and that holism emphasizes the functional interdependence of the part-whole relationship (unit-part changes when isolated from the unitwhole). Reality then is contextualized, that is, it cannot be understood in isolation, and behavior is seen in a context, as part of a larger whole. Similarly, evaluations and diagnosis do not occur in a vacuum, but within a context.

Thus, in a clinical situation, behavior can be assessed within its contextual framework (i.e., an individual's behavior is examined within the family's context) and its functionality or dysfunctionality is evaluated according to its specific and/or changing context. Given that behavior is dependent on its context, the diagnosis of the same behavior could differ according to different or varying contexts. For example, running amok (Malayan folk illness involving a dissociative state in which people act out violent impulses and attack others indiscriminately) (Gaw, 1993) was an accepted, normative, and condoned behavior in ancient societies, but it was condemned and perceived as dysfunctional when societies became modernized (Linton, 1956).

A clinical application of holism in the assessment of culturally different clients comes about by using relational diagnosis.

RELATIONAL DIAGNOSIS: THE I AND THE WE

The Cultural Self

Culture profoundly influences cognitions, feelings, and self-concept (Parron, Kleinman, Fabrega, Good, & Mezzich, 1993). As an internal representation with its own form of unconsciousness, culture shapes our concept of self (Comas-Díaz & Jacobsen, 1991; Gehrie, 1979). Consequently, the "cultural self" is embodied in a relative context that is in constant dynamic transformation.

Although there are psychological universals, there are also psychological variations affecting the cultural self. Definitions of this self vary along a continuum between egocentric and sociocentric orientations. The egocentric self, best exemplified in Western industrialized societies, characterizes the self as individualistic, solid, separate, and autonomous (Shweder & Bourne, 1982). This orientation tends to encourage individualism, competition, mastery of and control over the environment, and dualistic thinking. Within this view, the locus of the self is quintessentially the individual body, an idea compatible with the biomedical model (Twemlow, 1995).

The sociocentric self, found in many non-Western societies, views the self as fluid, interdependent, and interconnected (Comas-Díaz, 1992). It depicts the person in relational terms, as part of an interdependent collective, defined by kinship (Geertz, 1984). This object-relational view focuses on individuals actualizing themselves through others and through interpersonal interaction (Twemlow, 1995). As such, it tends to value cooperation, cohesiveness, group identity and solidarity, harmony with the environment, and holistic thinking (Ho, 1987).

In discussing the differences between British (egocentric) and Japanese (sociocentric) value orientations and their applications to therapy, Tamura and Lau (1992) assert that British individuals tend to value separateness, have a dualist (Cartesian split) worldview, and view differentiation and individuation as developmental change agents. These authors argue that such an orientation requires a mode of therapy that is verbal, works through, and effects change by externalizing—moving from the unconscious to the conscious. On the contrary, the Japanese tend to value connectedness, have a holistic worldview, and value integration as a developmental change agent. Tamura and Lau (1992) further state that this value orientation requires a therapeutic mode that acknowledges nonverbal communication, values meditation (and other internal states), and effects change by internalizing—moving from the conscious to the unconscious.

Many people of color in the United States have a sociocentric sense of self. In discussing the differences between European Americans and people of color, Richardson (1980) asserts that many African Americans tend to place the highest value on interpersonal relationships; many Asian Americans tend to value group membership and cohesiveness; while many American Indians view the tribal unity and sharing as integral for their survival. Likewise, many Latinos value group membership and interpersonal relationships. The Spanish philosopher José Ortega y Gasset (1958) asserted "I am me and my circumstances"—thus, emphasizing the connection between self and context (circumstances). Indeed, the cultural self of many people of color often is related to one's ties to ancestral, kinship, community, religious, and occupational groups (Comas-Díaz, 1992). In other words, the cultural self is placed within relational contexts: "The I is the we." For instance, the African cultural value of collectivity is illustrated in the saying: "I am because we are" (Akbar, 1985). The person of color's affiliation with the social and interpersonal worlds results in a specific web of connections binding people into contextual groups (Bankart, Koshikawa, Nedate, & Hakuri, 1992).

The emotional realities of many people of color also are arranged within a sociocentric and relational matrix (Toussignant, 1984). Therefore, psychological status is not solely an intrapsychic phenomenon. Manson and Good (1993) argue that diagnostic criteria that depend on eliciting individualistically oriented, contentless self statements (such as "I feel blue"; or "I fear things that I do not normally fear") may be constrained intrinsically from discovering other ways of feeling and expressing the same emotions among sociocentrically oriented individuals. Therefore, an effective and relevant diagnostic nosology for culturally diverse clients needs to acknowledge those orientations that attribute a greater focus to the social and interpersonal world. Consequently, in working with culturally diverse populations, the diagnostician is advised to seek a convergent evidence from other sources apart from the client, such as significant others (Mezzich et al., 1993). If we examine this advice, we see that relational diagnosis can be an effective avenue for examining the mental health functioning of many people of color.

Relational Diagnosis and Its Cultural Relevance

Among the general population, numerous emotional dysfunctions are associated with interpersonal problems rather than or besides intrapsychic distress. Thus, the inclusion of relational diagnoses in the DSM-IV has been proposed (Kaslow, 1993). Although there has been some acknowledgment of the importance of the relational context in mental health, the prevailing emphasis of the DSM-IV is still an individual and biological approach to psychopathology. Based on the concept of the cultural sociocentric self, such a limited and constricted approach can be ineffective and even unethical in addressing the needs of many culturally diverse clients.

The individualistic approach to diagnosing negates the realities not only of people of color but of members of other minority groups as well. For example, in discussing women as members of an oppressed group, several feminist writers (Brown, 1986; Jordan, Kaplan, Miller, Stiver, & Surrey, 1991; Lerner, 1988) have advocated contextualizing women's behavior. Similarly, the self-in-relation model of female development postulates that women tend to develop and organize their sense of identity, find meaning, become motivated, and achieve a sense of coherence and continuity within the context of a relationship (Jordan & Surrey, 1986).

For many culturally diverse clients, the context is a relational and a collective orientation. For many people of color, the cultural self is an extended (sociocentric) self that is validated only by its functioning in relationship and in harmony with the collective whole (Nobles, 1980). People of color often perceive themselves as being individuals within a collective and nonlinear context and, therefore, their relationships to others—family (multigenerational), community, history (ethnocultural and racial), and universe—are central to their well-being and sense of meaning and continuity. The sociocentric extended self values interdependence among individuated group members with an emphasis on connectedness and collective responsibility (Greene, 1990; McGoldrich, García-Preto, Hines, & Lee, 1989; Nobles, 1980). It functions as an adaptive and survival strategy within an oppressive and hostile environment because it often protects the group by subordinating the individual's needs to those of the collective (Comas-Díaz, 1994).

Several cultural values dominant among many people of color further attest to the centrality of the relational context in their lives. The extended family system or kinship network is still prevalent among many African Americans, American Indians, Asian Americans, and Latinos (Ho, 1987; McGoldrick, Pearce, & Giordano, 1982), whether they live in close geographical proximity or not. Similarly, *familismo*[1] involves the Latino extension of kinship relationships beyond the nuclear family boundaries. Familismo refers to the tendency to extend kinship relationships beyond the nuclear family boundaries, leading to emotional proximity, affective resonance, interpersonal involvement, and cohesiveness (Falicov, 1982). As a relational value, familismo emphasizes interdependence over independence, affiliation over confrontation, and cooperation over competition. Many American Indians tend to have collateral relationships with others in which the family and group take precedence over the individual (Attneave, 1982).

The Japanese concept of amae positively emphasizes the feeling of filial dependence (Doi, 1962) and parental indulgence (Bradshaw, 1990). Likewise, among many Filipino Americans, family welfare takes precedence over individual economic and social mobility, where the code of utang na loob (debt of gratitude) cements such relational value (Santos, 1983). Among some Asian groups, individual behavior is a function of family status. For example, the relational value of jang encourages older children to model good behavior for younger siblings (Ho, 1987), thus facilitating fraternal solidarity. The Japanese giri (social obligation) (Shon & Ja, 1982) and the Chinese concepts of hsiao (filial piety) and pao (reciprocity in social relationships) are virtues that emphasize the subordination of the individual's needs to those of the family or group (Kleinman, 1980).

Personalismo is the Latino preference of personal contacts over impersonal or institutional ones, thus contextualizing behavior within a personal relationship. The Indian dharma, a duty or code of behavior toward family and community, in addition to total cosmic responsibility (Tharoor, 1989) stresses the individual's responsibility and obligation toward others. Behaving according to karma, destiny, and fate is an acceptable response among many people of color (Comas-Díaz, 1992). The glossary presents several cultural values prevalent among people of color that highlight the centrality of relational contexts in their lives. (For fuller discussion of these cultural values, consult Comas-Díaz and Griffith, 1988; Gaw, 1993; Ho, 1987; McGoldrick, Pearce, and Giordano, 1982; and Powell, Yamamoto, Romero, and Morales, 1983.)

Infractions of and transgression to the relational codes of behavior among people of color often result in distress and emotional problems because violations of the relational

---

[1]See the glossary of terms at the end of this chapter.

canon can lead to psychopathology. Indeed, within systemic approaches, psychopathology is conceptualized as an interactional process between or among family members and/or significant others (Prochaska & Norcross, 1994). For many people of color, psychopathology is related to disturbances in the cultural extended self and disruptions in the relational context. For instance, among some Latinos illness is perceived as a family affair (Canino & Canino, 1982) and, thus, requires a family intervention for its cure. Only in the past decade has the emerging field of family systems medicine in the United States begun to promulgate ideas about illness as a family affair (Doherty & Baird, 1987) and of chronic illness as affecting all family members (Barth, 1993); the schism in the different belief systems is perhaps beginning to narrow.

The use of relational diagnosis with people of color is not only culturally congruent and effective but is also ethical. Relational and family-centered approaches to problem solving and treatment for emotional disturbances, including marital stress and difficulties in parenting, are central for treating people of color (Ho, 1987). Moreover, the transgenerational emphasis in some family therapy approaches (Bowen, 1978) is consistent with the multigenerational focus, sense of continuity, and need for collective survival prevalent among individuals with a sociocentric cultural self. Likewise, group and family therapy approaches are culturally relevant for many people of color due to their strong sense of connectedness, collectiveness, and belonginess. Network therapy, a Native American form of family therapy, involves re-creating the network to mobilize a family's kin and social support system to help an individual (LaFromboise, Berman, & Sohi, 1994). Among many Native Americans the family network represents a relational field characterized by intense personal exchanges that have lasting effects on an individual's behavior and life (Speck & Attneave, 1974). Thus, network therapy helps individuals by confirming the structural and cultural integrity of the extended family.

Regardless of theoretical orientations, clinicians working with people of color with a sociocentric worldview need to include relational variables within their assessment and treatment. Several experts on culturally relevant and gender sensitive mental health assessment (Brown, 1986; Comas-Díaz, 1994; Jacobsen, 1988; Westermeyer, 1993) recommend the gathering of the following contextual information.

- Ethnocultural heritage
- Racial and ethnic identities
- Gender and sexual orientation
- Socioeconomic class
- Physical appearance; ability/disability
- Religion when being raised and what now practicing; spiritual beliefs
- Biological factors (genetic predisposition to certain illness, etc.)
- Age cohort
- Marital status; sexual history
- History of (im)migration and generations from (im)migrations
- Acculturation and transculturation levels
- Family of origin and multigenerational history
- Family scripts (roles of women and men; prescriptions for success/failure, etc.)
- Individual and family life cycle development

- Client's languages and those spoken by family of origin
- History of individual abuse and trauma (physical, emotional, sexual, political including torture, oppression, and repression)
- History of collective trauma (slavery, colonization, Holocaust)
- Gender-specific issues such as battered wife syndrome
- Recreations and hobbies, avocations and special social roles
- Historical and geopolitical history of ethnic group and relationship with dominant group

This partial listing of variables that need to be assessed when working with culturally diverse clients emphasizes the relevance of the relational context. Regardless of ethnocultural background, these assessment areas provide a useful framework for obtaining data leading to a more comprehensive mental health assessment.

CLINICAL APPLICATIONS: BIRDS OF A FEATHER DON'T FLY TOGETHER

To examine the applicability of the thesis proposed in this chapter, two cases are discussed involving similar clinical symptoms, but requiring different diagnostic frameworks and, therefore, different therapeutic interventions.

Amber and Dawn had no previous individual or family psychiatric histories. Although the variables of socioeconomic class, gender, sexual orientation, religion, and education were similar, Amber and Dawn differed in ethnocultural and racial backgrounds. They were both treated by the same therapist—a Latina clinical psychologist. (Identifying data have been altered to protect clients' confidentiality.)

In a color-blind society, Amber and Dawn would be mirrored reflections of each other. However, in our racist society, they walked parallel paths, never converging in the same reality. Amber and Dawn were "birds of a feather"; however, they did not fly together. Amber, a 22-year-old African American woman, presented to therapy with complaints of concentration and attention problems affecting her academic performance. Dawn, a 22-year-old white Anglo-Saxon Protestant, presented with similar complaints. They were referred by their physician after a medical evaluation. Coincidentally, both women were first-year medical students and were attending the same medical school.

Case Histories

Amber: I Need to Be We

As presenting complaints, Amber reported anxious mood, plus sleeping, concentration, and attention difficulties. When asked about the etiology of her symptoms, Amber replied that she was having difficulties managing the multiple demands on her as a daughter, granddaughter, sister, student, girlfriend, friend, and member of a church community. She expressed fears that if she did not maintain her grade point average, she was not going to graduate from medical school. Moreover, she manifested additional stress at being one of the few African American medical students. Amber reported having a boyfriend and several good friends, but stated that she received most of her support from her family.

An examination of Amber's family configuration revealed that she was the oldest of three offspring. She behaved as a parental child toward her younger brother and sister.

Amber was living at home because she liked obtaining and providing family support. Additionally, her family lived close to their church, and its community was important to Amber. During the initial assessment, the client expressed concerns about disappointing her family due to her potential poor academic performance. She worried about setting the wrong example for her siblings and church community. The therapist took at face value Amber's worries about the consequences of her behavior on her family. She then recommended a family session as part of the assessment. In response to this recommendation, Amber requested that her maternal grandmother also be included.

The family session documented its members' adherence to sociocentric and relational orientations. Amber's family identified her problems as resulting from her trying to "do too much while attempting to please everyone." The family seemed to function as an enmeshed unit. Indeed, in discussing her academic difficulties, Amber stated: "I need to be we" as a means of expressing her feelings of interdependence, connectedness, and collective responsibility. The therapist avoided pathologizing the family's enmeshment and instead looked for its adaptive and functional aspects. As an illustration, among many African American families, enmeshment is correlated positively with healthy ego development in their adolescents (Watson & Protinsky, 1988).

Given Amber's family's fusion and not being a member of the family, the therapist utilized an ethnocultural psychotherapy approach to examine the cultural differences between herself and her clients (Comas-Díaz & Jacobsen, in press). In discussing these issues, Amber's family acknowledged the cultural differences but also acknowledged the sociopolitical similarities between many African Americans and Latinos with the common denominator of being people of color. This therapeutic intervention was consistent with Tamura and Lau's (1992) assertion that the therapist's role in working with a sociocentrically oriented family is to establish connection with its members. Additionally, this intervention seemed to facilitate the development of trust and credibility in the therapist's healing qualities.

During the session, Amber's grandmother made an observation connecting Amber's symptoms with the family life cycle expectations. She stated that Amber's mother was 22 years old when the client was born. This revelation unfolded an issue underlying gender family expectations. Amber revealed that she was feeling pressured to become a doctor, a wife, and a mother simultaneously. In other words, Amber's symptoms responded to the female role family script of becoming a mother at age 22. With the family's active participation, the therapist introduced a reframing of Amber's family role expectation. Amber was offered alternative ways of mothering involving her completion of medical school and subsequent work as a physician. This type of "family solution" to an "individual" problem seemed to be consistent with the client(s)' belief system.

The therapist utilized a "family therapy with one person" orientation in treating Amber individually. Family sessions were scheduled as needed. Systems theory and ethnocultural approaches were utilized in helping Amber cope with racial and gender issues in medical school. Given the relevant role that religion played in the client's life, the minister's collaboration was solicited during a network therapy session.

Dawn: I Did It My Way

Dawn reported anxious mood, sleeping, concentration, and attention problems. She expressed concern about her academic performance. Dawn was the oldest of three children, with a younger brother and sister. She indicated that she had a good relationship with her parents and was especially close to her father. However, she did not communicate her difficulties to them. Although Dawn had a boyfriend and a few good friends, she did not seek their help during this episode nor did she disclose that she was seeing a therapist.

Dawn saw herself as self-reliant, self-determined, assertive, and competent. She had a strong internal locus of control and need for achievement. Indeed, she stated "I always

On the contrary, Dawn saw her problem as solely individual, congruent with an egocentric cultural self. Her self-reliance, self-determination, and self-sufficiency were threatened by her crisis. Dawn's treatment needs involved an individual orientation aimed at strengthening her independence and autonomy. A cognitive behavioral approach within a psychodynamic perspective was consistent with her needs and value orientation.

Developmentally, both Amber and Dawn appeared to be coping with entering the early adult transition stage (Levinson et al., 1978). However, most adult developmental theories are based on an Eurocentric white middle-class orientation in which issues of differentiation, individuation, and separation from family of origin are viewed as the ideal norm. Consequently, the expression of these developmental needs was colored and shaped by each woman's ethnocultural background. According to Levinson and associates (1978), the person entering the adult world period must change the center of gravity of life from being a child in his or her family (connectedness) to a position of novice adult with a new home base that is more truly his or hers (separateness).

Dawn's development and clinical presentation appeared to be more consistent with Levinson's theory. Although she had a good relationship with her family, she was in the process of differentiation and individuation. Conversely, Amber's developmental needs revolved around integration and connection to her support network. Moreover, African American women's centrality in families and community organizations not only provides them with a high degree of support but also with a particular female way of knowing (Collins, 1991). Amber's family appeared to have significantly more fusion than Dawn's. Fusion may represent a culturally sanctioned way of being and/or an adaptive response to the pressure of racial oppression for many people of color (Hardy & Laszloffy, 1994). The therapist used the value of family fusion to foster added family support for Amber's problems and to reframe family scripts, thus effecting change. Dawn, who stressed her individuation, did not communicate her emotional difficulties to her family, nor did she want them involved in her treatment.

Dawn was treated with therapeutic approaches that emphasize the individual self over the social self. Thus, she was encouraged to tap into her individual resources and to continue her adult developmental tasks. Her motto, "I always did it my way," guided the treatment process. On the other hand, Amber was supported in her strong sense of belonging and connecting to her family ("I want to be we"); thus, a sociocentric orientation guided her treatment. Although cognitive behavioral techniques can be used with women of color, they have to be culturally relevant in order to be effective (Lewis, 1994). Ethnospecific egocentric psychotherapeutic interventions aimed at increasing separateness from significant others tend to be irrelevant for individuals with a sociocentric orientation (Comas-Díaz, 1992).

CONCLUSION

Culture provides an all-encompassing, pervasive context that infuses meaning to behavior. Because human behavior is expressed in a context, diagnostic practices that focus solely on individual and biological factors are often exclusive and constricted. Relational variables such as family, group, community, minority group membership, and sociopolitical realities are central to the lives of many people of color. The use of relational approaches to diagnosis provides a comprehensive assessment, one that is culturally congruent, effective, and ethical for many culturally diverse clients.

GLOSSARY

Amae   Japanese concept emphasizing filial dependence where the individual gains selfhood through reciprocal obligation to others.

Compadrazgo   Extended Latino family system based on the relationship resulting from baptizing the children. The baptismal compadres (coparents) become the child's padrinos (godparents) and as such the surrogate parents. Thus, compadre is the cofather and the child's godfather, while comadre (comother) is the godmother.

Confianza   Trust that requires a long time to develop. Latino personal relations are based on *confianza*. Therapist/patient relationships work better when confianza is developed.

Dharma   Hindu established order where each person's behavior is determined by contextual factors such as life cycle stage, plus caste and social class, thus resulting in identity being based on relationships with others (Tharoor, 1989).

Dignidad   (dignity) Fundamental traditional Latino value that emphasizes honesty, particularly within interpersonal transactions.

Enryo   Japanese expectation of an individual's modesty and humbleness in behavior, showing appropriate hesitation and unwillingness to intrude on another's time, energy, or resources.

Extended self   The identity of the person of color is validated only by its functioning in relationship and in harmony with the collective whole.

Familismo   (familism) The tendency to extend kinship relationships beyond the Latino nuclear family boundaries, emphasizing interdependence over independence, affiliation over confrontation, and cooperation over competition. (See *kinship network*.)

Giveaway   A ceremony during which the American Indian who is being honored gives gifts to others rather than receiving gifts. This is an example of the concept of ownership, which focuses on caretaking, sharing, and acknowledgment of kinship ties. Giveaways also take the forms of potluck suppers and pow wows.

Giri   Japanese social obligation.

Hsiao   Chinese filial piety.

Jang   Chinese value emphasizing the oldest offspring's responsibility to model appropriate behavior for the benefit of younger siblings.

Kenshin   Japanese expectation of submission and devotion to group interests and purposes.

Kinship network   Communal support that stresses the bonds beyond the biological ones, providing parenting, support, and alternative role models to children. (See *familismo*.)

Machismo   Traditional Latino sex role stipulating that males have authority by virtue of their gender. Culturally it means that males are responsible for others and are the financial and emotional providers of the family.

Marianismo   Traditional female sex role based on the Catholic cult of Mary, who is both a virgin and a madonna. It predicates that women are spiritually superior to men and therefore expected to sacrifice their individual needs in favor of their children's and families' needs.

Namesakes Supportive network for many Native American children who undergo a naming ceremony. Namesakes assume major social responsibilities for children ranging from frequent personal contact, role modeling, to caring for them.

Oya-koko Japanese filial piety to parents requiring an offspring's sensitivity, obligation, and unquestionable loyalty to patrilineage.

Pao Chinese reciprocity in social relationships.

Personalismo (personalism) The Latino tendency to prefer personal contacts over impersonal or institutional ones.

Respeto (respect) Latino concept governing all positive reciprocal interpersonal relationships, dictating the appropriate deferential behavior toward others on the basis of age, socioeconomic position, sex, and authority status.

Simpatía Latino interpersonal style that emphasizes maintaining a pleasant demeanor, aimed at lowering conflict and promoting agreement.

Utang na loob (debt of gratitude) Filipino code of valuing family welfare over individual economic and social mobility.

REFERENCES

Akbar, N. (1985). Our destiny, authors of a scientific revolution. In H. McAdoo & J. McAdoo (Eds.), *Black children* (pp. 17–31). Newbury Park, CA: Sage.

American Psychiatric Association. (1994). *Diagnostic and statistical manual of mental disorders* (4th ed.). Washington, DC: Author.

American Psychological Association. (1993). Guidelines for providers of psychological services to ethnic, linguistic, and culturally diverse populations. *American Psychologist, 48*, 45–48.

Attneave, C. (1982). American Indians and Alaska Native families: Emigrants in their own homeland. In M. McGoldrick, J. K. Pierce, & J. Giordano (Eds.), *Ethnicity and family therapy*. New York: Guilford.

Bankart, C. P., Koshikawa, F., Nedate, K., & Haruki, Y. (1992). When West meets East: Contributions of Eastern traditions to the future of psychotherapy. *Psychotherapy, 29*, 141–149.

Barth, J. (1993). *It runs in my family*. New York: Brunner/Mazel.

Bowen, M. (1978). *Family therapy in clinical practice*. New York: Jason Aronson.

Bradshaw, C. K. (1990). A Japanese view of dependency: What can *amae* psychology contribute to feminist theory and therapy? *Women & Therapy, 9*, 67–86.

Brown, L. S. (1986). Gender-role analysis: A neglected component of psychological assessment. *Psychotherapy, 23*, 243–248.

Brown, L. S. (1992). A feminist critique of the personality disorders. In L. S. Brown & M. Ballow (Eds.), *Personality and psychopathology: Feminist reappraisals* (pp. 206–228). New York: Guilford.

Canino, G., & Canino, I. (1982). Culturally syntonic family therapy for migrant Puerto Ricans. *Hospital & Community Psychiatry, 33*, 299–303.

Collings, P. H. (1991). *Black feminist thought: Knowledge, consciousness, and the politics of empowerment*. New York: Routledge.

Comas-Díaz, L. (1990). Ethnic minority mental health: Contributions and future directions of the American Psychological Association. In F. C. Serafica, A. I. Schwebel, R. K. Russel, P. D. Isaac, & L. B. Myers (Eds.), *Mental health of ethnic minorities*. New York: Praeger.

Comas-Díaz, L. (1992). The future of psychotherapy with ethnic minorities. *Psychotherapy, 29*(1), 88–94.

Comas-Díaz, L. (1994). An integrative approach. In L. Comas-Díaz & B. Greene (Eds.), *Women of color: Integrating ethnic and gender identities in psychotherapy* (pp. 287–318). New York: Guilford.

Comas-Díaz, L., & Jacobsen, F. M. (1991). Ethnocultural transference and countertransference in the therapeutic dyad. *American Journal of Orthopsychiatry, 61,* 392–402.

Comas-Díaz, L., & Jacobsen, F. M. (in press). *Ethnocultural psychotherapy.* New York: Basic Books.

Comas-Díaz, L., & Griffith, E. H. E. (Eds.). (1988). *Clinical guidelines in cross cultural mental health.* New York: Wiley.

Davis, D., & Padesky, C. (1989). Enhancing cognitive therapy with women. In A. Freeman, K. M. Simon, L. E. Beutler, & H. Arkowitz (Eds.), *Comprehensive handbook of cognitive therapy* (pp. 535–557). New York: Plenum.

Doherty, W. J., & Baird, M. A. (1987). *Family-centered medical care: A clinical casebook.* New York: Guilford.

Doi, T. (1962). *Amae*—a key concept for understanding Japanese personality structure. In R. J. Smith & R. K. Beardsley (Eds.), *Japanese culture.* Chicago: Aldine.

Draguns, J. (1985). Psychological disorders across cultures. In P. Pedersen (Ed.), *Handbook of cross-cultural and counseling therapy* (pp. 55–62). Westport, CT: Greenwood.

Falicov, C. J. (1982). Mexican families. In M. McGoldrick, J. K. Pearce, & J. Giordano (Eds.), *Ethnicity and family therapy* (pp. 134–163). New York: Guilford.

Gaw, A. (Ed.). (1993). *Culture, ethnicity & mental illness.* Washington, DC: American Psychiatric Press.

Geertz, C. (1984). For the native's point of view: On the nature of anthropological understanding. In R. Shweder and R. Levine (Eds.), *Culture theory: Essays on mind, self, and emotion.* Cambridge, MA: Cambridge University Press.

Gehrie, M. J. (1979). Culture as an internal representation. *Psychiatry, 42,* 165–170.

Goodchilds, J. D. (Ed.). (1991). *Psychological perspectives on human diversity in America.* Washington, DC: American Psychological Association.

Greene, B. (1990). What has gone before: The legacy of racism and sexism in the lives of Black mothers and daughters. *Women & Therapy, 9,* 207–230.

Hall, E. T. (1981). *Beyond culture.* Garden City, NY: Anchor Books.

Hardy, K. V., & Laszloffy, T. A. (1994). Deconstructing race in family therapy. *Journal of Feminist Family Therapy, 5,* 5–33.

Ho, M. H. (1987). *Family therapy with ethnic minorities.* Newbury Park, CA: Sage.

Homma-True, R., Greene, B., López, S., & Trimble, J. E. (1993). Ethnocultural diversity in clinical psychology. *Clinical Psychologist, 46,* 50–63.

Iwamasa, G. Y., Larrabee, A. L., & Merritt, R. D. (1995, August). *Are personality disorders ethnically and gender biased?* Poster presented at the annual meeting of the American Psychological Association, New York.

Jacobsen, F. M. (1988). Ethnocultural assessment. In L. Comas-Díaz & E. H. E. Griffith (Eds.), *Clinical guidelines in cross-cultural mental health* (pp. 135–147). New York: Wiley.

Jacobsen, F. M. (in press). *Psychoactive medications in mental health practice: A handbook for therapists.* New York: Wiley.

Jordan, J. V., Kaplan, A., Miller, J. B., Stiver, I., & Surrey, J. L. (Eds.). (1991). *Women's growth in connection: Writings from the Stone Center.* New York: Guilford.

Jordan, J. V., & Surrey, J. L. (1986). The self-in-relation: Empathy and the mother-daughter relationship. In T. Bernay & D. W. Cantor (Eds.), *The psychology of today's woman: New psychoanalytic visions.* Hillsdale, NJ: Analytic.

Kaslow, F. W. (1993). Relational diagnosis: Past, present and future. *American Journal of Family Therapy, 21,* 195–204.

Kleinman, A. (1980). *Patients and healers in the context of culture: An exploration of the borderland between anthropology, medicine, and psychiatry.* Berkeley: University of California Press.

Kleinman, A. (1993). How culture is important for DSM-IV? In J. Mezzich, A. Kleinman, H. Fabrega, B. Good, G. Johnson-Powell, K.-M. Lin, S. Manson, & D. Parron (Eds.), *Cultural proposals and supporting papers for DSM IV* (pp. 14–33). Rockville, MD: National Institute of Mental Health.

LaFromboise, T. D., Berman, J. S., & Sohi, B. K. (1994). American Indian women. In L. Comas-Díaz & B. Greene (Eds.), *Women of color: Integrating ethnic and gender identities in psychotherapy* (pp. 30–71). New York: Guilford.

Landrine, H. (1989). The politics of personality disorder. *Psychology of Women Quarterly, 13,* 325–340.

Lerner, H. G. (1988). *Women in therapy.* New York: Harper & Row.

Levinson, D. J., Darrow, C. N., Klein, E. B., Levinson, M., & McKee, B. (1978). *The seasons of a man's life.* New York: Ballantine.

Lewis, S. (1994). Cognitive behavioral approaches. In L. Comas-Díaz & B. Greene (Eds.), *Women of color: Integrating ethnic and gender identities in psychotherapy* (pp. 223–238). New York: Guilford.

Linton, R. (1956). *Culture and mental disorders.* Springfield, IL: Charles C Thomas.

López, S. (1989). Patient variable biases in clinical judgment: Conceptual overview and methodological considerations. *Psychological Bulletin, 106,* 184–203.

Loring, M., & Powell, B. (1988). Gender, race and DSM-III: A study of the objectivity of psychiatric diagnostic behavior. *Journal of Health and Social Behavior, 29,* 1–22.

Manson, S., & Good, B. (1993). Mood disorders. In J. Mezzich, A. Kleinman, H. Fabrega, B. Good, G. Johnson-Powell, K.-M. Lin, S. Manson, & D. Parron (Eds.), *Cultural proposals and supporting papers for DSM IV* (pp. 100–133). Rockville, MD: National Institute of Mental Health.

McGoldrick, M., García-Preto, N., Hines, P. M., & Lee, E. (1989). Ethnicity and women. In M. McGoldrick, C. M. Anderson, & F. Walsh (Eds.), *Women in families: A framework for family therapy.* New York: Norton.

McGoldrick, M., Pearce, J. K., & Giordano, J. (Eds.). (1982). *Ethnicity and family therapy.* New York: Guilford.

Mezzich, J. E., Kleinman, A., Fabrega, H., Good, B., Johnson-Powell, G., Lin, K.-M., Manson, S., & Parron, D. (Eds.). (1993). *Cultural proposals and supporting papers for DSM IV.* Rockville, MD: National Institute of Mental Health.

Nobles, W. (1980). Extended self: Rethinking the so-called Negro self-concept. In R. H. Jones (Ed.), *Black psychology.* New York: Harper & Row.

Ortega y Gasset, J. (1958). *Man and crisis.* New York: Norton.

Parron, D., Kleinman, A., Fabrega, H., Good, B., & Mezzich, J. (1993). Introduction to the manual. In J. Mezzich, A. Kleinman, H. Fabrega, B. Good, G. Johnson-Powell, K.-M. Lin, S. Manson, & D. Parron (Eds.), *Cultural proposals and supporting papers for DSM IV* (pp. 7–9). Rockville, MD: National Institute of Mental Health.

Powell, G. J., Yamamoto, J., Romero, A., & Morales, A. (Eds.). (1983). *The psychosocial development of minority group children.* New York: Brunner/Mazel.

Prochaska, J. O., & Norcross, J. C. (1994). *Systems of psychotherapy: A transtheoretical analysis* (3rd ed.). Pacific Grove, CA: Brooks/Cole.

Rathe, D. (1989, September). Delegation reports psychiatry is still abused in U.S.S.R. *Psychiatric Times/Medicine & Behavior,* 23–27.

Richardson, E. H. (1980). Mental health for Native Americans. In D. Martinez & J. Martinez (Chairs), *Biomedical research and its impact on the Hispanic and Indian communities.* Albuquerque, NM: Society for the Advancement of Chicanos and Native Americans in Science.

Santos, R. A. (1983). The social and emotional development of Filipino-American children. In G. J. Powell, J. Yamamoto, A. Romero, & A. Morales (Eds.), *The psychosocial development of minority group children* (pp. 131–146). New York: Brunner/Mazel.

Shon, S., & Ja, D. Y. (1982). Asian families. In M. McGoldrick, J. K. Pearce, & J. Giordano (Eds.), *Ethnicity and family therapy.* New York: Guilford.

Speck, R. V., & Attneave, C. L. (1974). *Family networks.* New York: Vintage.

Stampp, K. (1956). *The peculiar institution.* New York: Vintage.

Shweder, R. A., & Bourne, E. J. (1982). Does the concept of person vary cross culturally? In A. J. Marsella & G. M. White (Eds.), *Cultural conceptions of mental health and therapy.* Dordrecht, Holland: Reidel.

Tamura, T., & Lau, A. (1992). Connectedness versus separateness: Applicability of family therapy to Japanese families. *Family Process, 31,* 319–340.

Tharoor, S. (1989). *The great Indian novel.* London: Viking Penguin.

Trimble, J. E. (1990). Prefatory notes on the enculturation of American psychology. *FOCUS, 4,* 1.

Toussignant, M. (1984). Pena in the Ecuadorian sierra: A psychoanthropological analysis of sadness. *Culture, Medicine, and Psychiatry, 8,* 381–398.

Twemlow, S. W. (1995, January). DSM-IV from a cross-cultural perspective. *Psychiatric Annals, 25,* 46–52.

Watson, M. F., & Protinsky, H. D. (1988). Black adolescent identity development: Effects of perceived family structure. *Family Relations, 37,* 288–292.

Wellman, D. (1993). *Portraits of white racism* (2nd Ed.). New York: Cambridge University Press.

Westermeyer, J. (1993). Cross-cultural psychiatric assessment. In A. Gaw (Ed.), *Culture, ethnicity, and mental illness* (pp. 125–144). Washington, DC: American Psychiatric Press.

PART II

Various Relational Diagnoses:
A Leap into the Future

did it my way." Due to Dawn's egocentric cultural self, she felt individually responsible for and guilty about her problems. The precipitating event to her anxiety was failing a test in anatomy class. This event appeared to have shattered Dawn's self-concept.

The therapist decided to utilize a cognitive behavioral approach to be congruent with Dawn's cultural self-concept of mastery and reliance. The immediate goals were to restore Dawn's competent functioning and feelings of control. She was encouraged to understand her problem, develop skills, and try out new behaviors and/or ways of thinking. To achieve these goals, deep muscle relaxation, guided imagery, and cognitive restructuring (challenging irrational beliefs and changing dysfunctional cognitive patterns) were used. The process of identifying Dawn's irrational beliefs yielded the following negative thoughts: "I failed the test, therefore I am going to fail medical school. I am a total failure." Disputing her negative thinking involved challenging her irrational beliefs and reframing her test failure as an opportunity for knowledge and growth. Rather than viewing the failure incident as a catastrophe, it was presented as a normal negative event with which a significant percentage of medical students had to cope. This failure was used as a metaphor for dealing with adversity and for learning to change her dysfunctional reactions, thus increasing her sense of mastery and control. Learning such techniques was empowering and congruent with Dawn's needs of autonomy and competence.

Dawn's anxiety was reinterpreted as an indicator of a developmental crisis rather than an overwhelming state. She was encouraged to work on her developmental tasks of establishing her place in society as an adult (Levinson, Darrow, Klein, Levison, & McKee, 1978). Furthermore, she was encouraged to examine her adult developmental stage of early adulthood more as a process and less as a product. This stage usually is characterized by numerous separations, losses, and transformations (Levinson et al., 1978). The contextual meanings of failure and success were examined, revealing a conflict between Dawn's needs for competency and nurturance.

Dawn responded well to the cognitive behavioral approach. Her success with the techniques restored her self-confidence and sense of mastery. The client-therapist relationship was important in Dawn's treatment. Consistent with the cognitive behavioral therapy tenet of examining both client's and therapist's belief systems (Davis & Padesky, 1989), the client-therapist dyad's cultural differences were introduced at the beginning of treatment. Dawn reacted by saying that she appreciated the examination of the topic, commenting on differences and similarities. She stated, however, that the cultural differences did not matter to her. Although such a reaction could be interpreted as an ethnocultural denial, Dawn's tacit acknowledgment of differences and similarities suggested receptivity to the issue and appeared to cement the therapeutic alliance.

Discussion: Lives in Black and White

Amber's and Dawn's cases illustrate the effects of cultural and racial differences on mental health assessment and treatment. Both clients appeared to be struggling with the manifestation of their instrumental and expressive needs. Both women were bright, hardworking, responsible, persistent, strong, creative, and resourceful. Although these strengths were reclaimed in therapy, Amber and Dawn expressed them in different ways.

Amber's problems were presented in a contextualized relational manner. Consistent with her sociocentric self, she was concerned about the effect of her individual problems on the family as a whole. Therefore, her cultural extended self required a family systems intervention. Amber not only agreed to this recommendation but also requested the participation of her extended family with the therapeutic involvement of her grandmother and church minister.

CHAPTER 12

Relational Diagnosis of Child and Adolescent Depression

NADINE J. KASLOW, PhD, CATHERINE GRAY DEERING, PhD, RN, CS, and PETER ASH, MD

A relational paradigm for conceptualizing childhood depression is supported by research documenting the interpersonal contributions to, and consequences of, depression in individuals across the life span. (For review, see Kaslow, Deering, & Racusin, 1994; Keitner & Miller, 1990; McCauley & Myers, 1992.) This chapter proposes criteria for a relational diagnosis of child and adolescent depression. For depression to be considered a relational disturbance, the child must be depressed and the family and/or social network should manifest specified interactional patterns.

This chapter reviews childhood depression and associated risk factors, interactions of families with a depressed youngster, and familial and nonfamilial features that promote and maintain depression. An integrative perspective on a relational diagnosis of childhood depression is offered. It is not our intention to present an etiological theory, as a relational perspective implies reciprocal influences among the behavior of the child, family, and social environment. Although causal statements may appear to be made, this reflects the paucity of data from a systemic perspective and highlights the need for research that combines genetic and psychosocial factors.

CHILDHOOD DEPRESSION

Historically, theorists argued that depression in children could not exist. Even as clinicians and researchers acknowledged its existence, childhood depression continued to be ignored by significant people in the child's world (Kaslow & Racusin, 1990). Parents, teachers, and pediatricians often overlook children's depression, as their behavior typically does not cause problems for others, unless it is severe.

Childhood depression persists, recurs, and is associated with increased risk for other psychopathology and interpersonal difficulties in childhood, adolescence, and adulthood (Kovacs, 1989). An estimated 2 to 5 percent of youth meet criteria for a depressive disorder. By age 18, 20 percent of adolescents experience at least one depressive episode. Although there is a 1:1 female-to-male ratio of depression in prepubertal youth, depression is more prevalent among adolescent girls than boys, a finding attributable to biological and psychosocial factors (Nolen-Hoeksema & Girgus, 1994).

Depression in children and adolescents often is comorbid with other psychiatric problems, notably anxiety, attention deficit, and conduct/oppositional defiant disorders (Angold & Costello, 1993). Depression presents with myriad psychological symptoms that differ depending on the child's developmental stage and may interfere with interpersonal, affective, cognitive, and biological functioning (Kaslow & Racusin, 1990).

Risk Factors

The literature reveals a number of risk factors for childhood depression (Downey & Coyne, 1990; Gelfand & Teti, 1990; Hammen, 1991). A family history of mood disorders is the most prominent risk factor due to the interaction of genetic predisposition, marital discord, impaired parenting skills, and maladaptive family interaction patterns (Petersen et al., 1993). Other forms of family pathology associated with depression in youngsters include substance abuse, anxiety disorders, and antisocial personality disorder (Keitner & Miller, 1990).

Family Risk Factors

Family structure and family-environmental stressors also may be contributory risk factors. Children residing in single-parent and divorced families evidence higher levels of depression and a more protracted recovery than do youth from intact families (Feldman, Rubenstein, & Rubin, 1988; Hoyt, Cowen, Pedro-Carroll, & Alpert-Gillis, 1990).

Acute and chronic negative life events, notably losses by death, separation, divorce, or abandonment, are significant risk factors (Beck & Rosenberg, 1986; Weller, Weller, Fristad, & Bowes, 1991). The occurrence of these losses, the disrupted attachments, and the means by which parents help the child to cope contribute to the risk for depression. Other negative life events associated with increased rates of childhood depression include neglect and abuse, poverty and parental unemployment, exposure to violence, natural disasters, moves, and illness (Freeman, Mokros, & Poznanski, 1993; Gibbs, 1985). The presence of a depressed parent adds to the child's vulnerability to depression (Conger, Ge, Elder, Lorenz, & Simons, 1994). Social support may moderate the relation between negative life events and the development and maintenance of the youth's depression (Friedrich, Reams, & Jacobs, 1988). Additions to the family (remarriage of a parent, blending two families, birth of a sibling) also increase stress and thus serve as risk factors for depressive reactions.

RELATIONAL DIAGNOSTIC CRITERIA

Depressive disorders in children and adolescents may be primarily biologically based, intrapsychic in origin, or predominantly situationally and/or interpersonally based. Thus, there is a continuum of the extent to which relational factors are associated with depressive disorders. In addition, a number of interactional patterns have been associated with the development and maintenance of childhood depression (Kaslow, Deering, & Racusin, 1994; McCauley & Myers, 1992; Oster & Caro, 1990). Two categories of interactional patterns can be identified: (1) maladaptive styles of family relating and (2) nonfamilial social relationship problems. These interactional patterns have different consequences depending on the age and developmental stage of the depressed youth.

The following set of criteria can be used as a guideline for viewing childhood depression as a relational disturbance.

A. The index person must be less than 18 years of age and must meet criteria from the fourth edition of the *Diagnostic and Statistical Manual of Mental Disorders*

(DSM-IV) (American Psychiatric Association [APA], 1994) for at least one of the following:

1. major depressive disorder
2. dysthymic disorder
3. adjustment disorder with depressed mood
4. other adjustment disorder subcategory that includes depression
5. reactive attachment disorder
6. depressive personality disorder (APA, 1994; Benjamin, 1993) (proposed)
7. minor depressive disorder (proposed)
8. recurrent brief depressive disorder (proposed)
9. mixed anxiety-depressive disorder (proposed)

B. At least one of the following relational patterns is present.
  1. Family relational patterns
     a. attachment problems (e.g., insecure attachment)
     b. low cohesion and low support
     c. child maltreatment
     d. inappropriate levels of family control
     e. high levels of family conflict and ineffective conflict resolution
     f. difficulties with affect regulation
     g. impaired communication patterns
     h. transmission of depressive cognitions
     i. poorness of fit between the child's temperament and the family's style of relating
  2. A relationship pattern with peers, teachers, or other significant adults that continues over time and is characterized by social isolation, rejection, or criticism of child, and which is associated with
     a. low social self-esteem, and/or
     b. difficulties in interpersonal problem solving

MALADAPTIVE FAMILY RELATIONAL PATTERNS IN CHILDHOOD DEPRESSION

This section delineates commonly discussed family relational patterns that meet criteria for a relational diagnosis of childhood depression. Empirical support of each interaction pattern is reviewed.

Attachment Problems

The internalization of early attachments sets the stage for the development of depression via its impact on one's sense of self and the reenactment of depressogenic interpersonal patterns. Insecure parent-child attachment has been linked with the development of childhood depression (Hammen, 1992); an inverse relation between severity of depressive symptoms and security of attachment has been reported (Armsden, McCauley, Greenberg, Burke, & Mitchell, 1990; Kobak, Sudler, & Gamble, 1992).

One common attachment pattern is alternating overprotection/overcontrol and rejection by the parents toward the child (Parker, 1979). This inconsistent parental style is associated with an insecure parent-child attachment, whereby the child experiences relationships as uncontrollable. This perception may lead to helplessness and depressogenic cognitions that interfere with the development of positive nonfamilial relationships (Armsden et al., 1990). The type of depressive symptoms may be determined in part by the nature of the parent-child attachment (Blatt & Homann, 1992). Anaclitic depression (i.e., preoccupied with loss, dependent on others, feelings of helplessness) has been linked with anxious or ambivalent insecure attachments; introjective depression (i.e., prominent concerns about self-worth, feelings of inferiority and guilt) has been associated with an avoidant insecure attachment (Blatt & Homann, 1992).

The child's age and gender, life stress, and maternal behavior mediate the relation between attachment and childhood depression. Infants and young children are most vulnerable to disruptions in attachment and to an avoidant, anxious/ambivalent, or disorganized/disoriented attachment bond (Ainsworth, Blehar, Waters, & Wall, 1978; Main & Solomon, 1990). Boys tend to respond to insecure attachments with anger and sadness, while girls tend to exhibit depression (Kobak et al., 1992). Negative life stress and angry and dominant maternal behavior contribute to an increased vulnerability to depression among youth with insecure attachments (Kobak et al., 1992).

An insecure parent-child attachment reflects a reciprocal interaction between child and parent variables. This view is supported by findings that maternal dysphoria is associated with insecure mother-child attachment (Radke-Yarrow, Cummings, Kuczynski, & Chapman, 1985), and, as a child's depression remits, a more secure attachment is reported (Armsden et al., 1990).

Low Cohesion and Low Support

Family relationships lacking in cohesion (closeness) and social support (positive reinforcement, emotional availability) predict depression in youth (Cole & McPherson, 1993; Cumsille & Epstein, 1994; Garrison, Jackson, Marstellar, McKeown, & Addy, 1990; Prange et al., 1992). Some studies show that a low level of cohesion is the family variable that contributes most to the development of depression in a young family member (Garrison et al., 1990). Conversely, a cohesive family structure serves as a protective factor against depression (Reinherz et al., 1989). The correlation between cohesion and intimacy in the marital dyad and an adolescent's level of depressive symptoms is mediated by the degree of cohesion in the mother-adolescent and father-adolescent dyads (Cole & McPherson, 1993).

A key aspect of family support is positive reinforcement. Parents of depressed children provide low rates of positive reinforcement and positive affect (Cole & Rehm, 1986; Field et al., 1987). Depressed children's relatively low rates of positive communications contribute to these low levels of family support (Cook, Asarnow, Goldstein, Marshall, & Weber, 1990).

Child Maltreatment

Research reveals an association between child maltreatment (physical and sexual abuse, neglect) and depressive symptoms, especially among children with a psychiatrically disturbed or drug-dependent parent and/or those who experience multiple out-of-home placements (Downey & Walker, 1992; Kaufman, 1991). Compared to nonabused and emotionally neglected peers, physically abused children evidence more depressive symptoms (Allen & Tarnowski, 1989; Kaufman, 1991; Toth, Manly, & Cicchetti, 1992). There is a trend toward greater depressive symptoms among sexually abused children than nonsexually abused children (Elliot & Tarnowski, 1990), particularly for older survivors and those whose mothers do not comply with treatment (Wozencraft, Wagner, & Pellegrin, 1991). Although a concurrent association between parental neglect and depressive symptoms has yet to be documented (Toth et al., 1992), parental rejection is associated with depression later in life (Lefkowitz & Tesiny, 1984).

These results suggest that child maltreatment may contribute to the interactional cycle that produces and maintains childhood depression. The association between child abuse and depression is not surprising given that the use of harsh punishment (i.e., physical abuse) and the fear of abuse may foster feelings of helplessness, which in turn lead to depression (Kashani, Shekim, Burk, & Beck, 1987). Conversely, an internal locus of control for positive events and high self-esteem serve as protective mechanisms against depression for victims of maltreatment (Moran & Eckenrode, 1992). If the depression experienced during youth persists into adulthood, it places previously abused individuals at risk for maladaptive parenting of their own children.

Inappropriate Levels of Family Control

Parents of depressed youth tend to be controlling, autocratic, and likely to use coercive behavior (Amanat & Butler, 1984; Dadds, Sanders, Morrison, & Rebgetz, 1992; Friedrich et al., 1988; Stark, Humphrey, Crook, & Lewis, 1990). Typical oppressive behaviors include attempting to control their children's life goals and relationships, suppressing self-expressiveness, and not allowing age-appropriate input into the decision-making process (Amanat & Butler, 1984). Although this stance initially may foster compliant behavior, it interferes with the development of autonomy and engenders feelings of helplessness and incompetence in the child (Amanat & Butler, 1984; Racusin & Kaslow, 1991). In turn, the depressed child's passivity and low levels of spontaneous communication may elicit or perpetuate the parents' controlling behavior.

Family Conflict and Ineffective Conflict Resolution

Parent-child, family, and marital conflicts, particularly regarding child rearing (Burbach & Borduin, 1986; Forehand et al., 1988) and difficulties with conflict resolution (Sanders, Dadds, Johnston, & Cash, 1992) characterize many families of depressed children. During attempts to solve family problems, depressed youth manifest dysphoric affect and negative cognitions (Sanders et al., 1992) and report verbal and physical aggression during conflicts (Kashani, Burbach, & Rosenberg, 1988).

Difficulties with Affect Regulation

A failure to regulate affect effectively is seen in depressed youth (Cole & Kaslow, 1988; Garber, Braafladt, & Zeman, 1991). Depressed children may feel overwhelmed by dysphoric affects and become profoundly sad, or they may suppress positive feelings and thus experience pervasive anhedonia. Pessimism about the efficacy of their emotion regulation strategies may cause them to doubt their ability to alter their negative affective states (Garber et al., 1991).

Difficulties with affect regulation emerge in a social context. For example, depressed mothers have problems with the regulation of their own negative affect and are less responsive to their children's displays of negative emotions (Garber et al., 1991). In response, their offspring often manifest the anxious-sad and downcast affects seen in their mothers and may be reluctant to seek social support when distressed (Garber et al., 1991; Radke-Yarrow, Nottelmann, Belmont, & Welsh, 1993).

Interpersonal components of affect regulation receiving empirical attention include expressed emotion (EE) (family members' reports of the emotional aspects of their communication patterns) and affective styles (the behavioral manifestation of the emotional atmosphere of the family). A follow-up study of depressed child psychiatric inpatients found that youngsters returning to homes characterized by high expressed emotion (i.e., critical, hostile, and emotionally overinvolved) manifested a more protracted course of depression than did youth residing in homes with lower levels of EE (Asarnow, Goldstein, Tompson, & Guthrie, 1993). Similarly, children of depressed mothers who evidence high levels of EE have an increased risk for mood and conduct problems and substance abuse (Schwartz, Dorer, Beardslee, Lavori, & Keller, 1990). Depressed children reside in families characterized by higher levels of EE than do children with schizophrenia spectrum disorders and normal controls, suggesting some specificity in the association between EE and child psychopathology (Asarnow, Tompson, Hamilton, Goldstein, & Guthrie, 1994).

Maternal negative affective style is a stronger predictor of the child's coping style than either child or maternal diagnostic status (Hamilton, Hammen, Minasian, & Jones, 1993). Children of depressed mothers tend to respond to parental affectively charged communications by being critical toward their parent (Hamilton et al., 1993). These findings underscore the importance of examining child and parent variables and interactional processes to capture fully the family environments of depressed children.

Impaired Communication Patterns

Mothers of depressed youth communicate less with their children than do mothers of comparison children (Puig-Antich et al., 1985a). The affective tone of these parent-child communications has been characterized as hostile, tense, and punitive (Puig-Antich et al., 1985a). This negative tone improves upon remission of the child's depressive episode.

Communication patterns between depressed youth and significant others may present a more complex picture than a pervasive negative communication style. Significant others may express an admixture of anger and rejection, concern and support. This combination of positive and negative responses has been observed among primary caregivers of depressed pregnant adolescents (Sacco & Macleod, 1990). Depressed adolescents' confusion about these mixed messages may increase their feelings of helplessness and decrease their capacity to accept the care offered, thus prolonging their depressive state.

Transmission of Depressive Cognitions

Studies have begun to differentiate the cognitive patterns of depressed youth and their families from other pathogenic family structures (Stark, Humphrey, Laurent, Livingston,

& Christopher, 1993). Families with a depressed member manifest a distinct pattern of cognitive distortions that involves negative statements about self, others, the world, and the future. These depressive schemas are established early in life as a consequence of family relationships, particularly maladaptive attachment patterns, and are reinforced by later interpersonal difficulties (Beck, Rush, Shaw, & Emery, 1979; Blatt & Homann, 1992; Hammen, 1992). Once activated, experiences filtered through these negative schemata lead to depression and maladaptive interpersonal behaviors (Beck et al., 1979; Hammen, 1992). This negative sense of self and problematic interpersonal functioning is exacerbated by negative life events and may even increase the likelihood of their occurrence (Hammen, 1992). Thus, there is a complex interplay among maladaptive cognitions, negative life events, and interpersonal behavior in the development of childhood depression within a family context (Hammen, 1992).

There are a number of potential mechanisms for the transmission of depressive cognitions within the family system:

1. Parental modeling. Depressed parents verbalize negative perceptions about themselves, the world, and the future, and their children adapt a similar cognitive stance.

2. Instruction. Depressed or nondepressed parents criticize their children and may communicate, overtly or covertly through withdrawal and disengagement, negative parental perceptions. Their children internalize these negative perceptions and develop low self-esteem (Inoff-Germain, Nottelmann, & Radke-Yarrow, 1992).

3. Repeated experiences of noncontingent response-outcome patterns. These experiences within the family may lead children to develop a sense of helplessness and hopelessness (Seligman, 1975).

A number of adult models (Feldman, 1976; Teichman & Teichman, 1990) that integrate Beck's (1967) cognitive model and family systems theory inform our understanding of the transmission of depressive cognitions within family systems. When applied to parent-child dynamics, these models suggest that the depressed child acts helpless to gain parental reassurance. This helplessness triggers the nondepressed parents' schema of omnipotence and reassurances of the child, further enhancing the parents' self-esteem. This parental behavior, however, subtly reaffirms the child's inadequate sense of self, exacerbating the child's depressive cognitions and reinforcing the child's depression. As a result, the child becomes more hostile and withdrawn in interactions with parents, engendering feelings of rejection and a cognitive schema of depreciation in the parents. To manage their feelings, parents may engage in depression-inducing behaviors toward their child (e.g., criticism), exacerbating the child's sense of weakness and sustaining the depressive cycle. This cycle is complicated further when the depressed child resides with a depressed parent whose critical and negative parental posture is exacerbated by child's emotional problems (Conrad & Hammen, 1989; Hammen, 1992).

Poorness of Fit

In some cases, family coping patterns may not be inherently pathological. However, a child may develop a depression in response to a poor fit between his or her temperament or personality, parenting style, and the relational patterns of the family. This "poorness of fit" occurs when the demands and expectations of the family environment are discrepant with the child's capacities, motivations, and behavioral style (Chess & Thomas, 1984). "Poorness of fit" is apt to arise in families characterized by significant parental pathology, conflict, losses, or maltreatment.

Data suggest that depressive symptoms in adolescents are associated with the following temperamental variables: negative mood, withdrawal in new situations, rigidity in approaching tasks and situations, irregularity in daily habits, and distractibility and low persistence in tasks (Windle et al., 1986). These temperamental characteristics are not problematic inherently, but may increase a child's vulnerability to depression if the family expects him or her to adapt easily to novel situations. If the child's temperamental style elicits feelings of helplessness and a lowered sense of efficacy in his or her parents (Teti & Gelfand, 1991), this may increase further the likelihood that the child will develop emotional and social difficulties.

NONFAMILIAL SOCIAL RELATIONSHIPS

A relational diagnostic perspective acknowledges the impact of interpersonal relationships outside of the family system (e.g., peers, teachers, other significant adults) on the child's depression. Additionally, positive social relationships outside the immediate family may serve a protective function against depression in youth at risk for depression based on their family environment (Huntley & Phelps, 1990).

A burgeoning literature documents the pervasive nature of interpersonal deficits among depressed youth during a depressive episode and after recovery (Bell-Dolan, Reaven, & Peterson, 1993; Puig-Antich et al., 1985b; Rudolph, Hammen, & Burge, 1994). Depressed youngsters have a negative social self-concept and report difficulties in interpersonal problem solving (Altmann & Gotlib, 1988; Sacco & Graves, 1984). Compared to nondepressed youth, they are more inept socially, less active socially and more isolated, less assertive and more submissive, less likely to engage in positive social behaviors, and more impulsive (Altmann & Gotlib, 1988; Bell-Dolan et al., 1993; Cole, 1990; Peterson, Mullins, & Ridley-Johnson, 1985). They are perceived as less attractive and likable, are less popular (Jacobsen, Lahey, & Strauss, 1983; Peterson et al., 1985; Strauss, Forehand, Smith, & Frame, 1986), and a subgroup is rejected by their peers (Cole & Carpentieri, 1990; Rudolph et al., 1994). The most marked social difficulties are seen in depressed youth with comorbid externalizing behavior problems who tend to be aggressive in their interactions (Cole & Carpentieri, 1990; Rudolph et al., 1994).

Many depressed youth sabotage their own efforts at attaining social support by exhibiting behaviors that cause others to withdraw (Mullins, Peterson, Wonderlich, & Reaven, 1986; Peterson et al., 1985). Others experience their interpersonal behaviors as negative and feel increased anxiety and depression. In turn, potentially supportive others become rejecting, thereby validating depressed children's negative social self-concepts and heightening their feelings of unlikability and unworthiness. Their negative view of self becomes consistent with others' perceptions. These findings support Coyne's (1976) interactional theory, which posits that depressed individuals elicit negative social responses that in turn exacerbate the depressive symptoms. This cycle intensifies with repeated experiences.

The findings discussed in this section suggest that interpersonal difficulties in nonfamilial interactions may indicate a relational diagnosis of depression. Children who exhibit depressive symptoms and a continuing relationship pattern with peers, teachers, or other significant adults that is characterized by social isolation, rejection, or criticism and is associated with low social self-esteem or interpersonal problem-solving difficulties may meet criteria for a relational diagnosis of child or adolescent depression.

INTERACTIONAL DYNAMICS AND CHILDHOOD DEPRESSION

The following discussion is an effort to synthesize the relational diagnostic criteria just enumerated into potential systemic formulations of child and adolescent depression. The aforementioned research on the interaction between childhood depression and interactional patterns reflects a complex and subtle reciprocity between these variables.

The interaction between child depression and family dysfunction may operate in several ways: (1) family turmoil may trigger depression in a biologically and genetically predisposed child; (2) a family may have difficulty coping with a child's emotional and behavioral problems or temperamental style and respond in ways that foster or exacerbate depression; or (3) parenting styles associated with parental depression may promote depression in one or more child (Kaslow et al., 1994; Keitner & Miller, 1990; Oster & Caro, 1990). The complex interplay among child variables, family interactional patterns, and external events produces an every-changing picture of depression in the child.

Constitutionally susceptible children are those with a positive family history for mood, anxiety, and/or substance use disorders. Other variables that may contribute to a biological vulnerability to depression include perinatal complications, slow-to-warmup or difficult temperament, central nervous system difficulties, and impaired physical health. Children biologically or genetically vulnerable to depression may be at risk for a mood disorder when confronted with negative life events or psychosocial stressors, particularly those associated with loss or maltreatment.

Children at increased risk for depression due to biological and/or environmental factors may be sensitive to disruptions in the family milieu and have problems regulating their negative affects in response to such difficulties. Their parents may be limited in their capacity to help them modulate these intense, distressing affects. At-risk children are prone to depression if they do not feel attached securely, do not perceive their families as cohesive and supportive, or experience their families as rigidly controlling and inhibiting age-appropriate separation. Their perceptions of the quality of their attachments may be biased by negative cognitive styles, such that they focus on evidence of rejecting and critical parental attitudes and fail to attend to their parents' positive and nurturing qualities. This process is complicated further by the fact that their parents may model and/or reinforce negative cognitive styles, a process particularly prominent in families with parental mood disorders.

Family communication patterns that may perpetuate a child's depression include low levels of spontaneous positive communication, ineffective conflict resolution, and high levels of hostility, criticism, and parental overinvolvement alternating with rejection. Children's depressive symptoms are exacerbated in the face of controlling and oppressive parenting styles that instill a sense of helplessness in the child. In turn, the child's expressions of helplessness may increase the likelihood of parental controlling responses, further perpetuating the depressive cycle. Similarly, a child's depressed behavior often is associated with low levels of spontaneous communication and interaction, leaving parents with little positive behavior to reinforce. As this cycle intensifies, the parents may become more critical and angry, further contributing to the child's depressive cognitions and behaviors.

Depressogenic parent-child interaction patterns are compounded by sibling conflicts. Conversely, positive sibling attachments may decrease the impact of negative parent-child interactions on family members most prone to depression (Jenkins & Smith, 1990). Difficulties with significant persons outside the family may increase a child's feelings of low self-esteem, helplessness, and hopelessness, resulting in a depressive symptom picture. Conversely, positive relationships with peers and significant adults may buffer a vulnerable child from becoming depressed.

Depressed children challenge their parents, requiring flexibility and ingenuity in parenting styles. While some parents may be able to adjust the environmental expectations to accommodate these children's needs, other family environments fail to provide a "goodness of fit" for the child's adaptive capacities and behavioral style. The family environment may set the stage for an increased vulnerability for depression in a child who otherwise would not be biologically predisposed.

A depressed parent further intensifies the maladaptive relational patterns associated with childhood depression, as depressed parents have difficulties in parenting effectively (Hammen, 1992). Because they are focused on their own internal distress and dysphoria, depressed parents often are insensitive to their children's needs and find parenting stressful. Depressed parents tend to be critical and negative, a parenting style that may contribute to a child's feelings of worthlessness and helplessness. In families with both a depressed child and parent, the overall family climate may be characterized by such a preponderance of negative affect that each family member may be vulnerable increasingly to an intensification of their depressive symptoms, and recovery from a depression may seem impossible.

CONCLUSION

This chapter presents our evolving conceptualization of a relational diagnosis of child and adolescent depression. Interpersonal variables and interaction patterns are not the sole or primary contributory factors in the etiology and course of childhood depression. Rather, there is a need for multifactorial causal models in which family, developmental, social, and biological factors are investigated (McCauley & Myers, 1992). More comprehensive models will enable clinicians and researchers to ascertain a fuller picture of the relative contributions of biological, psychological, and social factors to the onset and maintenance of mood disorders in children and adolescents.

When assessing and treating children with mood disorders, it is essential to consider the social context. Depressive affects and cognitions are embedded in the interpersonal environment and cultural context within which the depressed child lives, and thus interventions must address the child's interactions within the nuclear and extended family, at school, and in the community.

Current research lays the groundwork for developing criteria for a relational diagnosis of childhood depression. Further empirical investigation from a systemic perspective is needed to clarify processes central to a depressive family environment and patterns that differentiate families with a depressed child from families with other child psychopathology. It is important to ascertain family and child characteristics that differentiate depressed and nondepressed children within the same family.

We hope that the relational diagnostic criteria proposed facilitate research efforts elucidating interpersonal processes associated with childhood depression, in turn leading to refinement of the criteria. As research accumulates on the relational patterns associated with child emotional and behavioral difficulties, we build a stronger case for developing a classification system that incorporates individual, family, and interpersonal variables and the sociocultural context.

REFERENCES

Ainsworth, M. D. S., Blehar, M. C., Waters, E., & Wall, S. (1978). *Patterns of attachment: A psychological study of the Strange Situation.* Hillsdale, NJ: Erlbaum.

Allen, D. M., & Tarnowski, K. J. (1989). Depressive characteristics of physically abused children. *Journal of Abnormal Child Psychology, 17,* 1–11.

Altmann, E. O., & Gotlib, I. H. (1988). The social behavior of depressed children: An observational study. *Journal of Abnormal Child Psychology, 16,* 29–44.

Amanat, E., & Butler, C. (1984). Oppressive behaviors in the families of depressed children. *Family Therapy, 11,* 65–75.

American Psychiatric Association (1994). *Diagnostic and statistical manual of mental disorders* (4th ed.). Washington, DC: Author.

Angold, A., & Costello, E. J. (1993). Depressive comorbidity in children and adolescents: Empirical, theoretical, and methodological issues. *American Journal of Psychiatry, 150,* 1779–1791.

Armsden, G. C., McCauley, E., Greenberg, M. T., Burke, P. M., & Mitchell, J. R. (1990). Parent and peer attachment in early adolescent depression. *Journal of Abnormal Child Psychology, 18,* 683–697.

Asarnow, J. R., Goldstein, M. J., Tompson, M., & Guthrie, D. (1993). One-year outcomes of depressive disorders in child psychiatric in-patients: Evaluation of the prognostic power of a brief measure of expressed emotion. *Journal of Child Psychology and Psychiatry, 34,* 129–137.

Asarnow, J. R., Tompson, M., Hamilton, E. B., Goldstein, M. J., & Guthrie, D. (1994). Family-expressed emotion, childhood-onset depression, and childhood-onset schizophrenia spectrum disorders: Is expressed emotion a nonspecific correlate of child psychopathology or a specific risk factor for depression? *Journal of Abnormal Child Psychology, 22,* 129–146.

Beck, A. T. (1967). *Depression: Clinical, experimental and theoretical aspects.* New York: Hoeber.

Beck, A. T., Rush, A. J., Shaw, B. F., & Emery, G. (1979). *Cognitive therapy of depression.* New York: Guilford.

Beck, S., & Rosenberg, R. (1986). Frequency, quality, and impact of life events in self-rated depressed, behavioral-problem and normal children. *Journal of Consulting and Clinical Psychology, 54,* 863–864.

Bell-Dolan, D. J., Reaven, N. M., & Peterson, L. (1993). Depression and social functioning: A multidimensional study of the linkages. *Journal of Clinical Child Psychology, 22,* 306–315.

Benjamin, L. S. (1993). *Interpersonal diagnosis and treatment of personality disorders.* New York: Guilford.

Blatt, S. J., & Homann, E. (1992). Parent-child interaction in the etiology of dependent and self-critical depression. *Clinical Psychology Review, 12,* 47–91.

Burbach, D. J., & Borduin, C. M. (1986). Parent-child relations and the etiology of depression: A review of methods and findings. *Clinical Psychology Review, 6,* 133–153.

Chess, S., & Thomas, A. (1984). *Origins and evolution of behavior disorders from infancy to early adult life.* New York: Brunner/Mazel.

Cole, D. A. (1990). Relation of social and academic competence to depressive symptoms in childhood. *Journal of Abnormal Psychology, 99,* 422–429.

Cole, D. A., & Carpentieri, S. (1990). Social status and the comorbidity of child depression and conduct disorder. *Journal of Consulting and Clinical Psychology, 58,* 748–757.

Cole, D. A., & McPherson, A. E. (1993). Relation of family subsystems to adolescent depression: Implementing a new family assessment strategy. *Journal of Family Psychology, 7,* 119–133.

Cole, D. A., & Rehm, L. P. (1986). Family interaction patterns and childhood depression. *Journal of Abnormal Child Psychology, 14,* 297–314.

Cole, P. N., & Kaslow, N. J. (1988). Interactional and cognitive strategies for affect regulation: Developmental perspective on childhood depression. In L. B. Alloy (Ed.), *Cognitive processes in depression* (pp. 310–342). New York: Guilford.

Conger, R. D., Ge, X., Elder, G. H., Lorenz, F. O., & Simons, R. L. (1994). Economic stress, coercive family process, and developmental problems of adolescents. *Child Development, 65,* 541–561.

Conrad, M., & Hammen, C. (1989). Role of maternal depression in perceptions of child maladjustment. *Journal of Consulting and Clinical Psychology, 57,* 663–667.

Cook, W. L., Asarnow, J. R., Goldstein, M. J., Marshall, V. G., & Weber, E. (1990). Mother-child dynamics in early-onset depression and childhood schizophrenia spectrum disorders. *Development and Psychopathology, 2,* 71–84.

Coyne, J. C. (1976). Toward an interactional description of depression. *Psychiatry, 39,* 28–40.

Cumsille, P. E., & Epstein, N. (1994). Family cohesion, family adaptability, social support, and adolescent depressive symptoms in outpatient clinic families. *Journal of Family Psychology, 8,* 202–214.

Dadds, M. R., Sanders, M. R., Morrison, M., & Rebgetz, M. (1992). Childhood depression and conduct disorder II. An analysis of family interaction patterns in the home. *Journal of Abnormal Psychology, 101,* 505–513.

Downey, G., & Coyne, J. C. (1990). Children of depressed parents: An integrative review. *Psychological Bulletin, 108,* 50–76.

Downey, G., & Walker, E. (1992). Distinguishing family-level and child-level influences on the development of depression and aggression in children at risk. *Development and Psychopathology, 4,* 81–95.

Elliot, D. J., & Tarnowski, K. J. (1990). Depressive characteristics of sexually abused children. *Child Psychiatry and Human Development, 21,* 37–48.

Feldman, L. B. (1976). Depression and marital interaction. *Family Process, 15,* 389–395.

Feldman, S. S., Rubenstein, J. L., & Rubin, C. (1988). Depressive affect and restrain in early adolescents: Relationships with family structure, family process and friendship. *Journal of Early Adolescence, 8,* 279–296.

Field, T. M., Sandberg, D., Goldstein, S., Garcia, R., Vega-Lahr, N., Porter, K., & Dowling, M. (1987). Play interactions in interviews of depressed and conduct disorder children and their mothers. *Child Psychiatry and Human Development, 17,* 213–234.

Forehand, R., Brody, G., Slotkin, J., Fauber, R., McCombs, A., & Long, N. (1988). Young adolescents and maternal depression: Assessment, interrelations and family predictors. *Journal of Consulting and Clinical Psychology, 56,* 422–426.

Freeman, L. N., Mokros, H., & Poznanski, E. O. (1993). Violent events reported by normal urban school-aged children: Characteristics and depression correlates. *Journal of the American Academy of Child and Adolescent Psychiatry, 32,* 419–423.

Friedrich, W. N., Reams, R., & Jacobs, J. (1988). Sex differences in depression in early adolescents. *Psychological Reports, 62,* 475–481.

Garber, J., Braafladt, N., & Zeman, J. (1991). The regulation of sad affect: An information-processing perspective. In J. Garber & K. A. Dodge (Eds.), *The development of emotion regulation and dysregulation* (pp. 208–240). New York: Cambridge University Press.

Garrison, C. Z., Jackson, K. L., Marstellar, F., McKeown, R. E., & Addy, C. (1990). A longitudinal study of depressive symptomatology in young adolescents. *Journal of the American Academy of Child and Adolescent Psychiatry, 29,* 581–585.

Gelfand, D. M., & Teti, D. M. (1990). The effects of maternal depression on children. *Clinical Psychology Review, 10,* 329–353.

Gibbs, J. T. (1985). Psychosocial factors associated with depression in urban adolescent females: Implications for assessment. *Journal of Youth and Adolescence, 14,* 47–60.

Hamilton, E. B., Hammen, C., Minasian, G., & Jones, M. (1993). Communication styles of children of mothers with affective disorders, chronic medical illness, and normal controls: A contextual perspective. *Journal of Abnormal Child Psychology, 21,* 51–63.

Hammen, C. (1991). *Depression runs in families: The social context of risk and resilience in children of depressed mothers.* New York: Springer-Verlag.

Hammen, C. (1992). Cognitive, life stress, and interpersonal approaches to a developmental psychopathology model of depression. *Development and Psychopathology, 4,* 189–206.

Hoyt, L. A., Cowen, E. L., Pedro-Carroll, J. L., & Alpert-Gillis, L. J. (1990). Anxiety and depression in young children of divorce. *Journal of Clinical Child Psychology, 19,* 26–32.

Huntley, D. K., & Phelps, R. E. (1990). Depression and social contacts of children from one-parent families. *Journal of Community Psychology, 18,* 66–72.

Inoff-Germain, G., Nottelmann, E. D., & Radke-Yarrow, M. (1992). Evaluative communications between affectively ill and well mothers and their children. *Journal of Abnormal Child Psychology, 20,* 189–212.

Jacobsen, R. H., Lahey, B. B., & Strauss, C. C. (1983). Correlates of depressed mood in normal children. *Journal of Abnormal Child Psychology, 11,* 29–40.

Jenkins, J. M., & Smith, M. A. (1990). Factors protecting children living in disharmonious homes: Maternal reports. *Journal of the American Academy of Child and Adolescent Psychiatry, 29,* 60–69.

Kashani, J. H., Burbach, D. J., & Rosenberg, T. K. (1988). Perception of family conflict resolution and depressive symptomatology in adolescents. *Journal of the American Academy of Child and Adolescent Psychiatry, 27,* 42–48.

Kashani, J. H., Shekim, W. O., Burk, J. P., & Beck, N. C. (1987). Abuse as a predictor of psychopathology in children and adolescents. *Journal of Clinical Child Psychology, 16,* 43–50.

Kaslow, N. J., Deering, C. G., & Racusin, G. R. (1994). Depressed children and their families. *Clinical Psychology Review, 14,* 39–59.

Kaslow, N. J., & Racusin, G. R. (1990). Childhood depression: History, current status, and future directions. In A. S. Bellack, M. Hersen, & A. E. Kazdin (Eds.), *International handbook of behavior modification and therapy* (2nd ed.) (pp. 649–667). New York: Plenum.

Kaufman, J. (1991). Depressive disorders in maltreated children. *Journal of the American Academy of Child and Adolescent Psychiatry, 30,* 257–265.

Keitner, G. I., & Miller, I. W. (1990). Family functioning and major depression: An overview. *American Journal of Psychiatry, 147,* 1128–1137.

Kobak, R. R., Sudler, N., & Gamble, W. (1992). Attachment and depressive symptoms during adolescence: A developmental pathways analysis. *Development and Psychopathology, 3,* 461–474.

Kovacs, M. (1989). Affective disorders in children and adolescents. *American Psychologist, 44,* 209–215.

Lefkowitz, M., & Tesiny, E. P. (1984). Rejection and depression: Prospective and contemporaneous analyses. *Developmental Psychology, 20,* 776–785.

Main, M., & Solomon, J. (1990). Procedures for identifying infants as disorganized/disoriented during the Ainsworth Strange Situation. In M. Greenberg, D. Cicchetti, & E. M. Cummings (Eds.), *Attachment in the preschool years* (pp. 121–160). Chicago: University of Chicago.

McCauley, E., & Myers, K. (1992). Family interactions in mood-disordered youth. *Child and Adolescent Psychiatric Clinics of North America, 1,* 111–127.

Moran, P. B., & Eckenrode, J. (1992). Protective personality characteristics among adolescent victims of maltreatment. *Child Abuse and Neglect, 16,* 743–754.

Mullins, L. L., Peterson, L., Wonderlich, S. A., & Reaven, N. M. (1986). The influence of depressive symptomatology in children on the social responses and perceptions of adults. *Journal of Clinical Child Psychology, 15,* 233–240.

Nolen-Hoeksema, S., & Girgus, J. S. (1994). The emergence of gender differences in depression during adolescence. *Psychological Bulletin, 115,* 424–443.

Oster, G. D., & Caro, J. E. (1990). *Understanding and treating depressed adolescents and their families.* New York: Wiley.

Parker, G. (1979). Parental characteristics in relation to depressive disorders. *British Journal of Psychiatry, 134,* 138–147.

Petersen, A. C., Compas, B., Brooks-Gunn, J., Stemmler, M., Ey, S., & Grant, K. E. (1993). Depression in adolescence. *American Psychologist, 48,* 155–168.

Peterson, L., Mullins, L. L., & Ridley-Johnson, R. (1985). Childhood depression: Peer reactions to depression and life stress. *Journal of Abnormal Child Psychology, 13,* 597–609.

Prange, M. E., Greenbaum, P. E., Silver, S. E., Friedman, R. M., Kutash, K., & Duchnowski, A. J. (1992). Family functioning and psychopathology among adolescents with severe emotional disturbances. *Journal of Abnormal Child Psychology, 20,* 83–102.

Puig-Antich, J., Lukens, E., Davies, M., Goetz, D., Brennan-Quattrock, J., & Todak, G. (1985a). Psychosocial functioning in prepubertal major depressive disorders. I. Interpersonal relationships during the depressive episode. *Archives of General Psychiatry, 42,* 550–607.

Puig-Antich, J., Lukens, E., Davies, M., Goetz, D., Brennan-Quattrock, J., & Todak, G. (1985b). Psychosocial functioning in prepubertal major depressive disorders II. Interpersonal relationships after sustained recovery from an affective episode. *Archives of General Psychiatry, 42,* 511–517.

Racusin, G. R., & Kaslow, N. J. (1991). Assessment and treatment of childhood depression. In P. A. Keller & S. R. Heyman (Eds.), *Innovations in clinical practice: A Sourcebook* (vol. 10) (pp. 223–243). Sarasota, FL: Professional Resource Exchange.

Radke-Yarrow, M., Cummings, E. M., Kuczynski, L., & Chapman, M. (1985). Patterns of attachment in two- and three-year olds in normal families and families with parental depression. *Child Development, 36,* 884–893.

Radke-Yarrow, M., Nottelmann, E., Belmont, B., & Welsh, J. D. (1993). Affective interactions of depressed and nondepressed mothers and their children. *Journal of Abnormal Child Psychology, 21,* 683–695.

Reinherz, H. Z., Stewart-Barghauer, G., Pakiz, B., Frost, A. K., Moeykens, B. A., & Holmes, W. M. (1989). The relationship of early risk and current mediators to depressive symptomatology in adolescence. *Journal of the American Academy of Child and Adolescent Psychiatry, 28,* 942–947.

Rudolph, K. D., Hammen, C., & Burge, D. (1994). Interpersonal functioning and depressive symptoms in childhood: Addressing the issues of specificity and comorbidity. *Journal of Abnormal Child Psychology, 22,* 355–371.

Sacco, W. P., & Graves, D. J. (1984). Childhood depression, interpersonal problem solving, and self-ratings of performance. *Journal of Clinical Child Psychology, 13,* 10–15.

Sacco, W. P., & Macleod, V. A. (1990). Interpersonal responses of primary caregivers to pregnant adolescents differing on depression level. *Journal of Clinical Child Psychology, 19,* 265–270.

Sanders, M., Dadds, M. R., Johnston, B. M., & Cash, R. (1992). Childhood depression and conduct disorder: I. Behavioral, affective, and cognitive aspects of family problem-solving interactions. *Journal of Abnormal Psychology, 101,* 495–504.

Schwartz, C. E., Dorer, D. J., Beardslee, W. R., Lavori, P. W., & Keller, M. B. (1990). Maternal expressed emotion and parental affective disorder: Risk for childhood depressive disorder, substance abuse, or conduct disorder. *Journal of Psychiatric Research, 24,* 231–250.

Seligman, M. E. P. (1975). *Helplessness: On depression, development, and death.* San Francisco: Freeman.

Stark, K. D., Humphrey, L. L., Crook, K., & Lewis, K. (1990). Perceived family environments of depressed and anxious children: Child's and maternal figure's perspective. *Journal of Abnormal Child Psychology, 18,* 527–547.

Stark, K. D., Humphrey, L. L., Laurent, J., Livingston, R., & Christopher, J. (1993). Cognitive, behavioral, and family factors in the differentiation of depressive and anxiety disorders during childhood. *Journal of Consulting and Clinical Psychology, 61,* 878–886.

Strauss, C. C., Forehand, R., Smith, K., & Frame, C. L. (1986). The association between social withdrawal and internalizing problems of children. *Journal of Abnormal Child Psychology, 14,* 525–535.

Teichman, Y., & Teichman, M. (1990). Interpersonal view of depression. *Journal of Family Psychology, 3,* 349–367.

Teti, D. M., & Gelfand, D. M. (1991). Behavioral competence among mothers of infants in the first year: The mediational role of maternal self-efficacy. *Child Development, 62,* 918–929.

Toth, S. L., Manly, J. T., & Cicchetti, D. (1992). Child maltreatment and vulnerability to depression. *Development and Psychopathology, 4,* 97–112.

Weller, R., Weller, E., Fristad, M., & Bowes, J. (1991). Depression in recently bereaved prepubertal children. *American Journal of Psychiatry, 148,* 1536–1540.

Windle, M., Hooker, K., Lenerz, K., East, P. L., Lerner, J. V., & Lerner, R. M. (1986). Temperament, perceived competence, and depression in early and late adolescents. *Developmental Psychology, 22,* 384–392.

Wozencraft, T., Wagner, W., & Pellegrin, A. (1991). Depression and suicidal ideation in sexually abused children. *Child Abuse and Neglect, 15,* 505–511.

CHAPTER 13

Learning Disabilities and Attention Deficit Hyperactivity Disorders: Their Impact on Children's Significant Others

JAN L. CULBERTSON, PhD and JANE F. SILOVSKY, MA

Both learning disabilities (LD) and attention deficit hyperactivity disorder (ADHD) are among the most studied disorders in children, and they account for frequent referrals to child mental health clinics and private practitioners today. Most referrals initially focus on determining if there is a diagnosis of LD and/or ADHD and, if so, then moving toward recommendations for treatment. In the context of discussions about treatment, questions inevitably emerge regarding the impact of these disorders on the child's (or adolescent's or adult's) relationships with family members, teachers, peers, or key people in the school setting. Whereas there is a vast literature regarding special education treatment strategies for LD and medical or behavioral interventions for ADHD, issues concerning the impact of these disorders on the child's relationships with significant others have been neglected. There is a need to discuss the relational issues that play an important role in the child's adjustment to LD and/or ADHD. This chapter reviews the definitions and clinical features of LD and ADHD and the typical interventions employed, before moving to a discussion of relational symptomatology, using both existing DSM-IV (American Psychiatric Association [APA], 1994) relational categories and proposed new relational categories. The chapter concludes with empirical questions that need to be addressed regarding existing and proposed categories for relational diagnoses related to LD and ADHD. Despite the increasing knowledge regarding the impact of these difficulties during the adult years, it is beyond the scope of this chapter to address these issues fully. The term "child" is used to encompass the preschool, elementary, and adolescent ages.

DEFINITIONS, CLINICAL FEATURES, AND MANAGEMENT OF LD AND ADHD

Learning Disability (LD)

Definition

The most widely accepted definition of LD is found in the federal law mandating a free, appropriate public education for all children with handicaps (the Education for All Handicapped Children Act of 1975; PL 94-142). The following official definition has been criticized for being too general, as lacking operational criteria, and for treating LD as a single disorder rather than a multifaceted one (Hooper & Willis, 1989).

Education for all Handicapped Children Act of 1975 (PL 94-142)

Specific learning disability means a disorder in one or more of the basic psychological processes involved in understanding or using language, spoken or written, in which the disorder may manifest itself in an imperfect ability to listen, think, speak, read, write, spell, or to do mathematical calculations. The term includes such conditions as perceptual handicaps, brain injury, minimal brain dysfunction, dyslexia, and developmental aphasia. The term does not include children who have learning problems which are primarily the result of visual, hearing, or motor handicaps, or mental retardation, or emotional disturbance, or of environmental, cultural, or economic disadvantage. (U.S. Office of Education, 1977, p. 65083)

Subsequent definitions by professional organizations concerned with LD have broadened the original definition by recognizing its multifaceted nature (thus providing a conceptual foundation for subtyping) and acknowledging the neurobiological basis presumed to underlie disorders of learning (Hammill, Leigh, McNutt, & Larsen, 1981) and by introducing the chronic nature of LD and the pervasive impact that it may have on an individual's academic and nonacademic functioning (Association for Children with Learning Disabilities [ACLD], 1985).

There is ongoing controversy regarding the criteria for diagnosis of LD (Algozzine & Ysseldyke, 1986; Heath & Kush, 1991), but the regulations provided for implementing PL 94-142 are widely accepted. According to this law, the diagnosis of LD is made based on:

1. Whether a child does not achieve commensurate with his or her age and ability when provided with appropriate educational experience
2. Whether the child has a severe discrepancy between achievement and intellectual ability in one or more of seven areas relating to communication skills and mathematical abilities (Rules and Regulations Implementing Education for all Handicapped Children Act of 1975, 1977, p. 655082).

The term "severe discrepancy" has been defined numerous ways, but usually involves a discrepancy of 1.5 to 2 standard deviations between the child's actual achievement level and his or her expected achievement level, with expected achievement determined through a regression model (Heath & Kush, 1991). This regression model uses a prediction equation based on the correlation between the child's IQ and achievement scores, and assumes that the expected achievement level will regress toward the mean. The child's achievement is not compared directly to IQ because there is an imperfect correlation between IQ and achievement tests—typically in the range of .50 to .65 (Heath & Kush, 1991).

In contrast to the definitions just discussed, the DSM-IV (APA, 1994) refers to "learning disorders" instead of using the term "learning disability" and indicates that the diagnosis is made "when the individual's achievement on individually administered, standardized tests in reading, mathematics, or written expression is substantially below that expected for age, schooling, and level of intelligence" (p. 46). The DSM-IV diagnostic criteria specify that the disturbance must interfere with academic achievement or activities of daily living that require the respective academic skills (i.e., reading, mathematics, or written expression), and that this interference must be over and above that related to any possible sensory impairment that may exist. The DSM-IV specifies four different types of learning disorders: reading disorder, mathematics disorder, disorder of written expression, and learning disorder not otherwise specified (NOS). The DSM-IV criteria are much less specific and therefore less accepted in the educational community than the criteria discussed earlier.

For the purposes of this chapter, the term "learning disability" is used synonymously with the DSM-IV term "learning disorder" and is considered a generic term inclusive of disorders of reading, writing, spelling, arithmetic, listening, thinking, talking, and social perception. This term is inclusive of subtypes of LD involving reading (dyslexia), mathematics (dyscalculia), written expression (dysgraphia), and social-emotional disorders (social-emotional LD). The clinical features of these subtypes are discussed in the next section.

Clinical Features

Because of the heterogeneous nature of LD, the clinical features may vary tremendously, ranging from verbal, to motor, perceptual, academic, social, or behavioral features. The presentation of LD symptoms depends on the age and developmental level of the child. In the preschool years, the diagnosis of LD often is not made, but precursors of LD may be apparent in deficits in expressive or receptive language abilities, perceptual functioning, gross and fine motor coordination, and behavioral symptoms. The child may have an immature vocabulary for his or her age, misunderstand verbal directions, or have a delay/disorder in the development of articulation skills. In the perceptual area, the child may confuse similar-sounding words, have difficulty matching or discriminating colors or shapes, or have poor construction ability (as in building objects or designs from blocks). The presence of these precursors indicates that there are developmental delays that may be indicative of a diagnosis of LD at school age (Culbertson & Edmonds, in press).

During the school-age years, the child with LD typically will present with academic problems in one or more specific areas such as spelling, writing, reading, or mathematics. Underlying the academic problems may be auditory perceptual difficulties in associating the correct phonetic sound to letters, with resulting problems in reading and spelling; visual discrimination problems that result in confusion about the orientation and sequencing of letters for reading, spelling, and writing; or problems in listening comprehension and oral expression. It is not uncommon for children with LD to present to mental health professionals with primary behavioral symptoms, such as refusal to complete classroom or homework assignments, disruptive or oppositional behavior at school, or extremely withdrawn or anxious behavior (Culbertson & Edmonds, in press). For example, a second grader with problems reading may try to cover his or her disability by distracting the teacher and other students through "clowning" or being otherwise disruptive in class. Likewise, a fourth-grade child with LD in written expression may be overwhelmed when presented with large amounts of writing assignments. The child's speed of writing production may be slower than that of peers, and there may be significant hurdles to overcome with spelling, grammatic usage, and remembering rules of punctuation when completing written assignments. Faced with the laborious task of finishing homework tasks that may take the child hours longer than peers, such a child often gives up and "shuts down" rather than battling to keep up with assignments. The frustrated parents then present with complaints about "laziness, lack of motivation, and noncompliance" rather than a primary complaint of writing problems. It is important for the clinician to distinguish between behavioral symptoms as a primary diagnosis versus being secondary to a primary learning disorder such as LD.

The clinical presentation during the teen years may be obscured by the compensatory techniques learned by adolescents to mask their symptoms. From a positive perspective, compensatory strategies may be an excellent way for adolescents to recognize and correct their academic errors (e.g., errors in spelling, failure to attend to the operational sign in mathematics problems, etc.). From the negative perspective, the compensatory strategies may mask the problem, resulting in misdiagnosis or failure to diagnose the LD, thus reducing access to special education services. Often the adolescent with good compensatory skills may turn in homework with few errors, but this may obscure the "struggle behavior" involving additional time and effort to prevent or to correct mistakes in this work (Culbertson & Edmonds, in press). Another problem noted with LD adolescents is increasing academic difficulty as they advance in school. This occurs due to the cumulative problems with achievement that have persisted over many years and that result in a widening gap between current and expected achievement levels. Thus, the clinical expression of LD must be viewed in the context of the child's developmental level and the academic expectations for that child at a given time.

Research during the past ten to 15 years has brought attention to a type of LD with significant social and behavioral ramifications. Termed variously "social emotional learning disability" (Denckla, 1983, 1989), "right hemisphere deficit syndrome" (Voeller, 1986), and "nonverbal learning disability syndrome" (Rourke, 1988a, 1988b, 1989), this disorder presumes a neurologically based deficit in social perception that leads to pervasive social relationship and behavioral adjustment problems. For our purposes, the term "social-emotional LD" will be used. The literature on this disorder suggests several common characteristics.

Social and Behavioral Characteristics Associated with Social-Emotional LD
- Peer rejection and social isolation
- Failure to respond to normative behavior of peer group
- Abnormal affective expression
- Difficulty interpreting emotional cues of others
- Poor eye contact
- Impaired ability to engage in interactive play
- Problems with interpersonal space
- Hyperverbal
- Poor pragmatic communication skills
- Obsessed with narrow topics/interests
- Poor adaptation to novel situations
- Decreased appreciation for humor or metaphor
- Inappropriate use of gesture

Johnson and Myklebust (1967) described children with social-emotional LD as having difficulty learning the meaning of actions of others, so that they cannot pretend or anticipate, are unable to understand the unspoken rules of games, and fail to learn the implications of facial expressions, gestures, and other nonverbal manifestations of attitude. These children fail to learn through experience, unless they are taught by someone who verbalizes the unspoken rules for them. The primary deficit appears to be in the ability to interpret the behaviors of others from observation and conversely to understand the impact of their own behavior on others. Voeller (1990) described two general patterns of behavior among children with social-emotional LD. One group was described as withdrawn, remote, unrelated, with little eye contact, limited range of affective expression, and monotonous, "robotlike" speech. The other group was described as overly and inappropriately friendly, with a tendency to invade the space of others by standing too close and touching too much, being hyperverbal, and using clichés or automatic phrases inappropriately.

In addition to these social and behavioral characteristics, such children also are reported to have a pattern of both neuropsychological dysfunction and assets (Rourke, 1988b). Deficits are seen in tactile and visual attention, tactile and visual memory skills, concept formation, and abstract reasoning. Academically, difficulty is seen in mechanical arithmetic, mathematics reasoning, and reading comprehension. Strengths are noted in rote verbal memory, auditory/verbal attention, learning through the auditory modality, basic word decoding (in reading), spelling, and writing (Rourke, 1988b).

Although children with social-emotional LD sometimes are diagnosed as having primary psychiatric disorders (such as Pervasive Developmental Disorder NOS, Schizoid or Schizotypal personality disorder, high functioning Autistic Disorder, Asperger's Syndrome, ADHD, or affective disorder), it is important to remember that the primary deficit is presumed to be a neurologically based social perception problem that leads to social interaction deficits. The primary problems may lead also to secondary emotional manifestations, such as affective disorders due to the isolation and peer rejection that is commonly experienced by children with social-emotional LD. An important distinguishing factor is that these children seem genuinely confused about why others reject them and do not understand what they can do to help their social interactions. They desire friendships and acceptance but seem to be "out of sync" with their peers in many ways that prevent the social relationships from forming.

The previous discussion illustrates the multifaceted nature of LD and suggests many examples of how relational problems may develop between children with LD and their significant others. Only now are children with social-emotional LD beginning to be diagnosed with regularity in clinics, due to the recent emergence of more specific literature on the nature of this disorder (Denckla, 1989; Rourke, 1988a, 1988b, 1989; Voeller, 1986). Information about effective treatment modalities is limited, and it is unclear how often children with this syndrome receive mental health services.

Management of LD

The traditional interventions for children with academic manifestations of LD are through special education services provided by the public schools. Federal legislation (PL 101-476: Individuals with Disabilities Education Act) ensures that children with LD will have an educational program that is individualized and appropriate for their educational needs, ranging from total inclusion (full-time placement in the general education classes with monitoring by the special education teacher), to self-contained special education placement (a full-day LD class for all academic subjects). Most children diagnosed with LD have some brief periods of special education assistance per area of disability. Current provisions in the public law have mandated transition services for students with LD who are age 16 years and older, to assist with their transition from high school to postsecondary education or vocational training (O'Leary, 1993). Adolescents and young adults with LD are now guaranteed legal rights based on the Rehabilitation Act of 1973 (PL 93-112) that protects them from discrimination in employment or training (e.g., college). Some youth have been able to access special education services at the college level through this legislation (Gajor, 1992).

Whereas the special educational interventions have been widely accepted and used in treating children with LD, attention to their social/emotional adjustment and relationships with significant others have received less attention. A number of possible risk factors associated with LD may impact the child's close interpersonal relationships (Abrams & Kaslow, 1976). Primary among these are the stressors related to the child's academic underachievement that impact such things as self-esteem, the child's place within his or her social network of peers and within the family structure, the child's perception of acceptance/rejection by significant others, and the practical or functional problems inherent in the child's struggle to "keep up" with expected performance (Kaslow & Cooper, 1978). Secondarily, risk factors that relate to the specific nature of a child's LD, such as language/communication problems, nonverbal perceptual problems, or organization and time management problems, may impact relationships as well. Finally, added to these factors are the risks and/or buffers associated with the social context of the child's environment (e.g., family, school, peer social network). The interaction of all these variables influences the quality of the child's relationships with significant others.

Attention Deficit Hyperactivity Disorder

Definitions

The changes in definition and diagnostic criteria for ADHD through the various revisions of the *Diagnostic and Statistical Manual* (APA, 1968, 1980, 1987) are considerable and generally reflect the empirical validation of this disorder over time. The DSM-IV conceptualization of ADHD recognizes the empirical support for three primary subtypes: Predominantly Inattentive Type, Predominantly Hyperactive-Impulsive Type, and Combined Type. It also goes further than previous versions of the DSM in recognizing the pervasiveness of the disorder and the clinically significant adjustment problems often associated with ADHD.

The essential feature of ADHD, according to the DSM-IV, is a "persistent pattern of inattention and/or hyperactivity-impulsivity that is more frequent and severe than is typically observed in individuals at a comparable level of development" (p. 78). The DSM-IV criteria are an improvement over previous criteria in requiring that symptoms be present in at least two settings (e.g., home, school, etc.) and clear evidence of interference with developmentally appropriate social, academic, or occupational functioning (APA, 1994).

ADHD has been subtyped not only according to the dimensions of *inattention, hyperactivity,* and *impulsivity* but also according to the presence or absence of aggression or conduct disorders comorbid with ADHD. Various researchers have reported that 50 percent to 65 percent of clinic-referred children with ADHD also meet criteria for an Oppositional Defiant Disorder (see Chapter 14), characterized by disturbance of mood (hostile/angry and negative temperament) and defiant, resistant, oppositional behavior

(Barkley, DuPaul, & McMurray, 1990; Barkley, Fischer, Edelbrock, & Smallish, 1990; Loney & Milich, 1982). The importance of this subtyping relates not only to the development of effective intervention strategies but also to the individual's prognosis for improvement in functioning.

Clinical Features

The primary clinical features of ADHD include inattention, behavioral disinhibition, hyperactivity, deficient rule-governed behavior, and variability in task performance. Inattention includes a variety of dimensions such as levels of alertness, arousal, sustained attention, selectivity of attentional focus, distractibility, and span of attention (Hale & Lewis, 1979). Children with ADHD appear to have poor persistence of effort in responding to tasks that have little appeal or have few immediate consequences for completion (Barkley, 1990). The dimension of behavioral disinhibition involves acting impulsively, having difficulty delaying gratification and working for long-term goals, and generally displaying poor regulation and inhibition of behavior (Barkley, 1990). Hyperactivity refers to the "motor driver" quality of these children, who have excessive and unnecessary gross bodily movements that often seem irrelevant to the task or situation at hand or seem purposeless (Barkley, 1990; Stewart, Pitts, Craig, & Dieruf, 1966). Routh (1978) has suggested that the impairment may not lie so much in the level of activity as in the failure of the child to regulate his or her activity level to the setting or to task demands. Deficient rule-governed behavior has been suggested as one of the primary deficits of ADHD (Barkley, 1981, 1982, 1990; Kendall & Braswell, 1984). The child who has deficient rule-governed behavior may have difficulty following rules in the environment and may be described as not listening, failing to comply with instructions, or having problems following directions associated with a particular task (Barkley, 1990).

Finally, children with ADHD often display variability in task performance. This may be due to variability in environmental demands for inhibition; situational requirements for organization, planning, and use of executive functions; fatigue factors; or it may be related to the person in the environment who is providing the directions. The variability often leads teachers and parents to suspect that the child with ADHD could be more attentive, less active, and more goal directed "if only he or she wanted to." The child may be misperceived as lazy, unmotivated, or oppositional because the variability in performance is not commonly understood as a primary clinical feature of ADHD (Culbertson & Krull, in press). Not surprisingly, clinical features of ADHD often lead to relational problems for the child in the family, school, and social environments in which he or she lives.

Management of ADHD

Various treatment approaches are used to manage the symptoms of ADHD. Educational and school interventions include provision of special education services (under the category "Other Health Impaired") for those children whose ADHD symptoms significantly interfere with their academic functioning, curriculum modifications, changes in teaching strategies to increase the child's optimal performance, other changes in the structure of the classroom environment (e.g., to limit distractions, provide increased feedback to the child), and behavioral management programs designed to provide consistent reminders, rewards, and punishments for appropriate behavior.

Parent training and support groups also have been shown to be useful for instructing parents on how to manage the symptoms of ADHD (Barkley, 1987). These programs help to educate parents about the causes of child misbehavior, ways to improve their child's attentional skills, how to use social rewards such as their attention to encourage compliance, and how to use time-out procedures for dealing with noncompliance. Other forms of psychotherapy, such as family therapy or individual child therapy, also may be beneficial.

Stimulant medications, such as methylphenidate (Ritalin) or pemoline (Cylert), also have been used effectively to treat the primary symptoms of ADHD, with studies showing that about 70 to 80 percent of children with ADHD have a positive response (i.e., reduction of disruptive, hyperactive, and impulsive behavior) (Barkley, 1990). Concerns about stimulant medication extend to the common side effects that may occur, including decreased appetite and possible growth interruption, insomnia, anxiety, irritability, and a possible increased risk of tics (Barkley, McMurray, Edelbrock, & Robbins, 1990; Golden, 1988). The side effects are reported to be mild in most cases, but the use of stimulants always should be based on the severity of the current symptoms, the level of disruptiveness of the ADHD symptoms to the child's school and/or family functioning, and the absence of internalizing symptoms (i.e., anxiety, fearfulness, or psychosomatic disturbances) in the child (Barkley, 1990). Stimulant medication usually is not effective in treating the oppositional or conduct problems that may be comorbid with ADHD, and in most cases, medication should not be the sole treatment. Barkley (1990) recommends that a combination of educational and parent interventions, in conjunction with psychostimulant medication, may lead to the best outcome.

As with LD, greater attention has been given to interventions such as psychostimulant medication and psychotherapeutic treatment of the child's behavior problems with less attention paid to the issue of relational problems experienced by children with ADHD and their parents, siblings, peers, and teachers. Numerous factors produce relational problems for children with ADHD. Primary among these is the disruptive nature of the child's behavior and the frequency with which it is "out of sync" with the contextual demands of the environment. Due to the child's difficulty maintaining rule-governed behavior, he or she often is "in trouble" with significant others and experiences much negative feedback regarding behavior. The likelihood for adjustment problems is apparent. When one considers other problems that may be comorbid with ADHD (conduct problems, academic performance problems, social skills deficits, emotional immaturity, etc.), the probability of adjustment problems is compounded. For those children who have the predominantly inattentive subtype of ADHD, stressors related to academic underachievement, disorganization, and problems with focused attention may be the primary risk factors for relational problems rather than disruptive behavior problems. Secondarily, ADHD is a disorder that often is misconstrued, and failure to obtain an accurate diagnosis may be problematic. Relational problems may evolve from lack of understanding of the nature and etiology of the child's disruptive behavior and/or inattentive problems. Finally, risk and supportive factors within the larger social context of the child's environment also influence whether relational problems will develop.

The next section explores the rationale for developing and strengthening relational diagnoses when LD and/or ADHD are present.

RATIONALE FOR STRENGTHENING RELATIONAL DIAGNOSES

The most relevant current DSM-IV relational diagnoses for children with LD and ADHD are "Parent-Child Relational Problem" and "Sibling Relational Problem" (APA, 1994, p. 681). However, both are extremely limited in their descriptions of the range and impact of relational impairment, and they have vague criteria. As currently stated, these diagnoses offer little in the way of constructive implications for treatment.

Furthermore, a relational problem with peers—which has received the most attention in the literature on LD and ADHD—is not included as a specific diagnosis in DSM-IV, unless coded under the "Relational Problem NOS" category, which is even more vague than the parent-child and sibling diagnoses. Many relational problems of children with LD and ADHD occur in the school setting and involve teachers or other school personnel. This area of relational difficulties is ignored in the DSM-IV nosology.

Therefore, the problems with the existing DSM-IV relational diagnoses include vague descriptors of adjustment problems and lack of operational criteria for severity of impairment or "clinically significant" symptoms in the parent, sibling, or child. As noted earlier, the existing relational diagnoses do not adequately cover the broad areas in which children with LD and ADHD have relational problems. There is a definite need for relational diagnostic criteria in areas related to peers and school settings.

Development of clear operational criteria for relational diagnoses would accomplish several important goals. First, it would assist the collection of reliable data on the prevalence, severity, and chronicity of relational problems. This information would be important in building an empirical literature to examine etiological factors, the efficacy of different treatment methods, the association of relational problems with other disorders, and the long-term outcome regarding relational issues. Second, refinement of treatment goals could be enhanced by specific and clear operational criteria for relational diagnoses. For example, the focus of treatment for a child with ADHD may be quite different depending on the presence and severity of a relational component to the presenting problem. Parent-Child Interaction Therapy (PCIT) (Eyberg & Boggs, 1989; Eyberg & Robinson, 1982) is a commonly used parent training program that includes both relationship enhancement as well as behavior management aspects. With the child with ADHD who has a parent-child relational problem as the basis of current Oppositional Defiant Disorder (ODD) symptoms, the therapist may wish to emphasize the relationship enhancement components of PCIT relative to the behavioral management components. This refinement of treatment goals would become more systematic once relational diagnoses were more clearly delineated.

Related to the issue of more refined treatment goals is the need for assessment methods for relational diagnoses. Currently there are few reliable and valid methods of assessment for relational disorders. Sociometric techniques for peer relations are the exception to the rule, but to date they have not led to a corresponding diagnostic category of "peer relational diagnoses." With other types of relational problems (i.e., parent-child, sibling), assessment methods often are limited to interview and/or observation of behavior. With such methods, one could expect a high degree of variability and subjectivity among clinicians with regard to the "clinical significance" of the symptomatology.

Fourth, better understanding of the nature of relational problems would provide a stronger rationale for early intervention and possibly prevention. The opportunity to provide treatment at an earlier stage of development of relational problems may be useful in preventing the emergence of Axis I mental disorders. Current literature provides evidence that children with ADHD often may have comorbid emotional and/or other disruptive behavioral disorders. A large epidemiological study by Szatmari, Offord, and Boyle (1989) revealed that up to 44 percent of children with ADHD have at least one other psychiatric disorder, 32 percent have two disorders, and 11 percent have at least three other disorders. Several studies have reported that children with ADHD have more symptoms of anxiety, depression, and low self-esteem than either normal children or LD children without ADHD (Breen & Barkley, 1983, 1984; Margalit & Arieli, 1984). There is abundant research regarding the comorbidity of aggressive, oppositional, defiant, and even antisocial characteristics in children with ADHD. Approximately 40 percent of children and 65 percent of adolescents with ADHD will meet full diagnostic criteria for Oppositional Defiant Disorder (Barkley, DuPaul et al., 1990; Barkley, Fischer et al., 1990). Further, as many as 21 to 45 percent of children and 44 to 50 percent of adolescents with ADHD will meet diagnostic criteria for Conduct Disorder (CD). Mental or disruptive behavioral disorders such as Major Depressive Disorder or ODD often are associated with relational problems. By implication, treatment of the relational problems may serve a preventive function with regard to the primary mental or behavioral disorders.

A fifth rationale for strengthening relational diagnoses is to enhance the status of relational diagnoses. This would bring much-needed attention to problems that often are neglected. Also, establishment of relational diagnoses would help to justify treatment to payers who provide reimbursement for mental health services and therefore would make treatment more readily accessible to children and families.

Based on this rationale, the next two sections focus on elaboration of relational symptomatology using existing DSM-IV categories and propose new categories for incorporation in future diagnostic systems.

RELATIONAL SYMPTOMATOLOGY WITH LD AND ADHD USING EXISTING DSM-IV RELATIONAL CATEGORIES

The following sections discuss a variety of relational problems that may develop between parents and children who have LD and ADHD. The comments are not meant to suggest that all children with LD and ADHD have relational problems, but rather to delineate the range of potential problems that may develop. In fact, family support may be the most important buffer to the child with LD or ADHD in dealing with the stressors inherent to the disorders. As in all clinical situations, it is important to assess the balance between family supports and conflicts in order to determine the presence and severity of a relational problem.

Parent-Child Problems in Relation to LD

Parent-child relational problems that evolve from LD may be apparent in various aspects of family interaction, including cognitive aspects (e.g., understanding vs. misperceptions of the disorder), affective aspects (emotional responses of the parents and/or child with LD), family boundary and hierarchy aspects, specific characteristics of the child and/or parent that impact the parent-child relationship, and increased demands on the caregiver related to the functional aspects of living with a child who has LD.

Cognitive and Affective Aspects

From the child's perspective, both cognitive and affective issues must be considered. Children with LD may be confused about the nature and implications of their disorder and may have misperceptions about their own abilities and self-worth. Providing developmentally appropriate information to the child is an important first step in fostering his or her adaptation. Children's affective response to learning about their LD may take various forms, from a sense of relief at finally learning about the reason for their academic struggles, to a sense of embarrassment at being different or perceiving themselves as deficient, to feelings of anger related to the difficulties caused by the LD. Such children may employ a variety of defense mechanisms to protect themselves from the painful aspects of their disability; these may range from denial, social withdrawal, avoidance of academic work, and overdependence, to disruptive, defiant, or clowning behavior. The presence of strong defensive reactions and/or parental misinterpretation of their child's defensive behavior may lead to relational problems.

Parental expectations may be appropriate or inappropriate based on their understanding of the information available to them about their child's LD, their affective response to that information, and their ability to act upon and utilize the information (i.e., the operative response). At the cognitive level of understanding, it is essential that a diagnostic evaluation be obtained to provide not only an accurate diagnosis but also a clear description of the potential impact of LD on various aspects of the child's functioning. For instance, the child with a language-based LD may have difficulty in understanding and/or remembering verbal instructions as well as in reading and spelling. These and other implications of the diagnosis must be explained to parents in such a way that they can understand and adequately integrate the information into their daily interactions with their child. The second level of understanding is more affective than cognitive; it relates to the parents' emotional response to the information about their child's LD. At this level, the parents' idealized perception of their child must be reformulated to incorporate the information about LD and the implications of possible lowered achievement and/or vocational accomplishments. The parents' emotional response may include grieving the loss of their idealized child and may involve use of a variety of defenses, such as anger, denial, or projection, that interfere with adaptation. The parents' cognitive understanding and affective response to the diagnosis of LD in turn influence their operative response, or their ability to act on the information in a variety of ways, such as modifying the amount of help they give the child on homework assignments, taking the child for tutoring twice a week, and so on. Difficulty in parental response at any of the three levels may lead to inappropriate expectations (i.e., expecting too little or too much of their child) and ultimately parent-child relational problems. Parental adaptation to their child's disability is not a one-time occurrence. The adaptation is ongoing over the child's life span, changing as a function of the child's developmental stages and life experiences and the child's acquisition of compensation skills. The process of parental grieving over the loss of the idealized child is not pathological, but it may become so if a parent becomes "stuck" at a level of reaction (e.g., anger, denial) and is unable to move forward toward adaptation.

Family Boundary and Hierarchy Aspects

Inappropriate parental expectations, characteristics inherent within the child (e.g., immaturity, anxiety regarding academic performance), or the interaction of these factors may lead to problems in separation/individuation or boundary issues. Thus, the parental role in relation to the child or the child's behavior in relation to the parent may be adversely affected by the impact of the child's learning disability. For instance, the child with LD may be immature or delayed in development of age-appropriate independent functioning. The natural tendency is for the parent to compensate by being overprotective or providing too much assistance for the child. The most extreme example of this problem could be characterized as enmeshment, with the result that the separation/individuation of the child would be further compromised. Conversely, the parent may show frustration toward the child for his or her inability to learn or develop at a more normal rate, and the child may respond with anger or anxiety. At the other end of the spectrum, the parent whose affective response to the diagnosis involves disappointment or shame may disengage emotionally from the child. Enmeshment and disengagement are extreme examples of dysfunctional family relations well addressed in the family therapy literature (Bowen, 1978; Minuchin, 1974). Other less extreme examples of disrupted parent-child relationships described in this chapter need to receive attention as well. Structural family therapy theory would suggest that the middle ground (in which the parent has flexible expectations appropriate to the child's ability and functioning level) is the most adaptive for a healthy relationship (Lewis, Beavers, Gossett, & Phillips, 1976; Walsh, 1982).

The child with LD may have a lower status within the family system by virtue of his or her deficits in learning and achievement and possibly deficits in communication and social skills. The child may perceive siblings who do not have LD as having higher status. Conversely, the sibling may perceive the child with LD to have higher status because that child receives more parental attention. Parents may try to enhance the status of the child with LD artificially via special privileges or attention, in an attempt to compensate. The sibling who does not have LD may feel neglected by virtue of the parents' behavior toward the special child. This sets up a situation in which the parents are in a "double bind" with regard to the competing needs of their children. Concerning family interactional patterns, issues of how decisions get made and who has more relative influence over family activities and interactions must be considered. Communication patterns between and among various members of the family system both reflect and influence the balance of power within the family. The child with LD may have less competence in communication and/or social skills and therefore less influence in the family hierarchy. These family systems issues indirectly affect the parent-child relationship and may contribute to relational problems.

Characteristics of the Child That Impact the Parent-Child Relationship

There may be problems within the child that make social relationships and/or interaction difficult. Children with language-based LD may have problems with a wide spectrum of receptive and expressive communication skills, including the ability to understand multistep oral directions, formulate their ideas and express them in coherent sentences, and remember verbal information. These communication problems are a "setup" for misunderstanding between parent and child, unless the adult has a good understanding of the nature of the child's problems and takes care to adapt to the difficulty in communication.

The child with LD may have social perception problems that make it hard to read the nonverbal social cues of others and function adaptively in the environment. These children may have difficulty with time perception, organization, and understanding and remembering the rules for daily functioning in the family. Social perception and social interaction problems are core symptoms found in children with Social-Emotional LD. They often are severe enough to lead to extreme social rejection and isolation among peers, and also may interfere significantly with interaction within the family. The deficits associated with Social-Emotional LD make the child extremely difficult to live with, because of his or her poor perception of others' feelings/attitudes/moods, problems reading nonverbal cues that transmit information about the impact of his or her behavior on others, and poor ability to benefit from parental teaching about appropriate or expected social behavior. These deficits often engender frustration and confusion within the parents, with a resulting negative impact upon the parent-child relationship.

Functional Impact of LD

Increased caregiver demands are common in families that have a child with LD. Functional problems related to daily homework assignments, studying for tests, and the child's organization and study habits (or lack thereof) increase the burden of care for parents who must monitor the child's performance and provide practical assistance. Homework may become a focal point for a nightly battle between parents who try to provide assistance and children who feel frustrated. Parents may not have the expertise to provide instruction in a way that the child with LD can learn—yet schools often expect parents to do so. The child often encounters stressors within the school environment in relations with teacher(s) and peers, and parents inevitably become involved when their child is frustrated. Stressors related to the school environment may increase the demands on the parent, which in turn may influence the parent-child relationship. The increased demands on the parent related to functional stressors associated with LD may lead to increased parental frustration—and therefore impact the parent-child relationship.

In sum, a number of aspects of the parent-child relationship may be severely strained due to stressors associated with LD. However, in assessing the clinical significance of these aspects, it is critical to view the conflicts and stressors within the context of family support and strengths. Weighing the balance between risk and resilience factors in parent-child relationships is critical to determining whether a clinically significant parent-child relational problem exists.

Parent-Child Problems in Relation to ADHD

Many of the parent-child relational issues discussed with LD also pertain to ADHD. The similarities are pointed out briefly, but an effort is made in the following sections to discuss illustrations that are unique to the child with ADHD and his or her parents.

Cognitive and Affective Aspects

Children with ADHD may be aware that others are unhappy with them but may lack an understanding of what makes them act without thinking, fidget and move about too much, or have trouble paying attention. Their parents have many challenges in understanding the disorder. The many changes in definition and conceptualization of ADHD over the past 20 years have created problems in consistency among professionals who diagnose and treat the disorder, and this has led to confusion for parents. The predominantly inattentive type of ADHD may be misunderstood even more than the hyperactive/impulsive type, because the problems these children encounter are less obvious. Children with attention disorders may look as if they are reading or paying attention to the teacher, but their attention is focused elsewhere. Finally, the variability that is so common in presentation of ADHD symptoms creates confusion for parents and others. Children who are "bouncing off the walls" one day and calmer the next day run the risk of being mislabeled as having behavioral or motivational problems that are presumed to be within their control. Thus, children with ADHD face many obstacles inherent in the understanding of their disorder.

Their parents need more than just an understanding of the core symptoms of the disorder; they also need to comprehend how to structure the environment in such a way as to enhance their child's ability to compensate for the symptoms. Parental expectations for their child must be altered to incorporate their child's problems with organization, remembering rules for appropriate behavior, and tendency toward impulsive responding. For example, the child with ADHD may function better in an environment that has a consistent routine for doing homework, eating meals, going to bed, and completing necessary chores as opposed to a chaotic, disorganized environment. Parents who lack understanding of their child's need for structure or, for other reasons—perhaps related to their affective response to their child's disorder or an erratic work schedule—are unable to provide the needed structure, may be frustrated because their child's behavior is so often problematic. An added problem relates to the frequency with which ADHD is found in one or both parents also. This often inherited disorder may result in the parents exhibiting the same symptoms as their child. When this occurs, the home environment often is not well organized, and parents have difficulty helping their child manage time, responsibilities, and impulsivity. Parents with ADHD symptoms may find that they react impulsively when frustrated with their child's behavior, and this may exacerbate their child's anger and frustration. It is easy to see how these situations may lead to parent-child relational tensions.

Affective responses of parents to having a child with ADHD are similar to those of parents whose children have other types of disabilities. As noted earlier, issues of parental grief and adaptation are salient throughout their child's developmental years. Even when the parents have a good cognitive understanding of the disorder, their tolerance for the disruptive and annoying aspects of their child's behavior may be limited. Parents who originally may have developed a compassionate and tolerant understanding of their child's problems may "wear down" over time due to the constant demands on their time, energy, and patience. Mash and Johnston (1983) reported that parents of older children with ADHD cite significantly lower self-esteem related to their knowledge and parenting skills than parents of younger children with ADHD, suggesting a possible cumulative effect of "unsuccessful childrearing experiences" (p. 95).

Added to the stressors for parents is the problem with finding substitute caregivers such as baby-sitters or extended family members who will provide occasional respite by caring for the child with ADHD. The child's often demanding behavior may be overwhelming or irritating to others, and substitute caregivers often are reluctant to take on this responsibility. The implications for parents are increased fatigue and little time for themselves or for their other children. The implication for the child with ADHD may be a feeling of rejection.

Family Boundary and Hierarchy Issues

ADHD may place a child at greater risk for being labeled the "bad child" in the family compared to siblings because his or her behavior more often is out of synchrony with the demands of the environment. This situation may evolve into a "self-fulfilling prophecy" for the child, who may organize his or her behavior around the self-concept of being the "bad kid." The child with ADHD who has problems with impulsivity may not be included in family decision making because of his or her problems with careful thinking and consideration of details. From a family systems perspective, other family problems (e.g., marital conflicts) may be displaced upon the child with ADHD, whose behavior is a focal point of family attention. Conversely, the stressors associated with having such a child may lead to increased marital problems. Literature on families of children with ADHD has noted a higher incidence of marital dysfunction than in families of normal children (Befera & Barkley, 1985).

Characteristics of the Child That Impact the Parent-Child Relationship

Frequent characteristics include poor regulation and inhibition of behavior, excessive and unnecessary movement, deficient rule-governed behavior, and inattention and distractibility—all of which may lead to conflictual interactions with parents and others. Children with ADHD are more negative, less compliant, and more often off-task than children without ADHD, and their mothers are more negative, give more directives, and are less responsive to their child's positive and neutral communications than are mothers of normal children (Cunningham & Barkley, 1979). Even when adults who are not the parents are observed interacting with children who have ADHD, they exhibit negative, controlling, and directive behavior that is similar to the behavior of the parents (Cunningham & Siegel, 1987; Whalen, Henker, & Dotemoto, 1980). Barkley and others have demonstrated that when children with ADHD are placed on psychostimulant medication, the behavior of their caregiver toward them changes dramatically in terms of less disapproval and a lower level of control and number of commands (Barkley & Cunningham, 1979; Barkley, Karlsson, Strzelecki, & Murphy, 1984; Cunningham & Barkley, 1978; Humphries, Kinsbourne, & Swanson, 1978). These various lines of evidence provide ample support for the assertion that the characteristics of the child with ADHD have a negative impact on the parent and others.

Children with the hyperactive/impulsive type of ADHD may be at increased risk for poor self-concept due to the frequent negative feedback related to their disruptive behavior. They often experience increased restrictions on their actions and exasperation from tired and frustrated parents; this may impact the child's self-esteem, even at a very young age. Likewise, children with the inattentive subtype of ADHD may receive negative feedback from the environment because they are perceived as deliberately noncompliant or inattentive. Barkley (1990, p. 113) reported that self-esteem problems are common in children with ADHD by late childhood, yet they tend to blame others for their difficulties because of their limited self-awareness. Their poor insight and tendency to externalize blame often preclude resolution of the problem.

The frequent comorbidity of ODD and Conduct Disorder (CD) in children with ADHD complicates the relational picture. When oppositional, aggressive, or delinquent behavior are added to the symptom complex of overactivity, poor impulse control, and poorly focused attention, interactional problems with every aspect of the child's environment (e.g., parents, siblings, school, peers) are compounded. Longitudinal studies with clinic-referred children have shown that by adolescence, 43 to 45 percent meet criteria for Conduct Disorder in addition to ADHD (Barkley, 1990, p. 122; Gittleman, Mannuzza, Shenker, & Bonagura, 1985) and engage in antisocial acts such as stealing, thefts outside the home, and fire setting. Mannuzza, Gittleman, Konig, and Giampino (1989) have shown that this subgroup of adolescents is at risk for adult criminal behavior and that the adolescent antisocial behavior is a stronger predictor of adult criminality than the ADHD. Thus, the comorbidity of ODD and CD become an important prognostic indicator suggesting poor outcome.

Sibling Relational Problems

With sibling relational problems, the focus of clinical attention is on the pattern of sibling interaction that may be associated with clinically significant impairment in either individual or family functioning. Impairment of individual functioning can occur in the child with LD or ADHD, and/or it can occur in one or more siblings (DSM-IV; APA, 1994, p. 681).

Cognitive and affective issues are sometimes neglected in siblings of children with ADHD and/or LD. Parents may seek diagnostic information, and the child with the disability may receive an explanation, but siblings often are not included in this process. They may continue to be confused or have misattributions regarding their sibling's problems because the disability is not fully explained. Siblings' affective response to the disability may range from shame to defensiveness or protectiveness. At times, they may feel a sense of superiority compared to their siblings with LD or ADHD—with implications for status conflicts within the family. Or they may feel neglected because the sibling with a disability gets more parental attention. Particularly in the case of ADHD, behavioral problems may be a focus of family attention, with the ADHD child being perceived as a "bad child" and the non-ADHD sibling being perceived as a "good child" by parents, extended family, friends, and others. Even parents who are aware of these issues sometimes have difficulty influencing the perceptions of those external to the family.

The behavioral aspects of ADHD often result in children being reprimanded or punished more than their siblings, and this may result in feelings of guilt among the siblings. Siblings of an LD child may make better grades in school but may inhibit their excitement at home or diminish their accomplishments in deference to their sibling. Parents also are caught in the dilemma of wanting to praise the child who performs well but avoid embarrassment to the child with LD. It is particularly difficult when a younger sibling surpasses the achievement of the child with LD. During homework sessions, the child with LD may stumble over pronunciation of a word while the younger sibling readily volunteers the correct response. Some parents feel a need to protect the child with a disability from painful experiences or embarrassment, and this may suggest to the sibling that his or her feelings and accomplishments are devalued. The goal for adaptation is to foster a sense of personal acceptance of both the sibling with a disability and the sibling who is not disabled, with acceptance of each one's special attributes and weaknesses.

Families that have children both with and without LD or ADHD are confronted with the dilemma of how to address the often conflicting needs. Siblings may feel that they are prevented from experiencing "normal" family activities because of the child with the disability. For instance, families may avoid going to a restaurant if the child with ADHD cannot remain seated long enough to finish a meal, or avoid going to a movie theater if the child is excessively disruptive. Often even shopping trips are curtailed because the child with ADHD cannot inhibit his or her activity level in a large store or mall. Relational tensions between siblings may develop from this situation.

The sibling reactions discussed here are not necessarily uncommon or pathological, but they can lead to relational problems if they are not addressed. It is important to foster awareness and identification of these relational issues so they can become the focus of appropriate intervention.

PROPOSED NEW RELATIONAL CATEGORIES

Teacher/School Relational Problems

Children with LD and ADHD spend many of their waking hours throughout the week in the school environment. Many of the problems encountered by these children in adapting to their disability are handled by teachers and other school personnel. Yet relational problems in the school environment have been virtually neglected as diagnoses. With teacher/school relational problems, the focus of clinical attention is a pattern of interaction between the teacher (or other school personnel) and the child that is associated with clinically significant impairment or symptoms in the child's functioning (e.g., school phobia, secondary emotional reactions or defensive behaviors that are used to detract from the primary disability, primary emotional problems such as one of the depressive or anxiety disorders, or adjustment disorders that impact emotional functioning, behavior, and/or school achievement). Cognitive, affective, and practical management issues with LD and ADHD may lead to teacher/school relational problems.

The need for a clear diagnosis is as important for the teacher and other school personnel as for parents and the individual child. Teachers' attributions regarding a child's behavior or functioning level may need to be corrected, as in the case of a child with LD or ADHD (Predominantly Inattentive Type) who is perceived as "lazy" or unintelligent, or a child with ADHD (Combined Type) who is perceived as deliberately trying to annoy the teacher by not following the class rules. Teacher affective responses to these disabilities may vary along a number of dimensions, depending on the teacher's experience and tolerance for dealing with special needs children. Due to increased demands (e.g., time, attention, specialized teaching strategies) associated with instruction of children with LD or ADHD, teachers may have less time and energy to devote to their nondisabled students. Teachers can develop frustration and a sense of guilt about their inability to meet the diverse needs of all their students. Concerns about professional competence also may develop when teachers interact with children who have LD or ADHD—from the perspective of both self-evaluation and also evaluation from school administrators and/or parents. For example, the failure of various teaching strategies to produce success in academic achievement with the LD child, or failure to manage the disruptive "motor-driven" behavior of a child with ADHD, may lead the teacher to be perceived as less competent. This may result in the teacher feeling guilty or defensive or diverting blame to the child—thus setting the stage for potential relational problems.

The degree of organization and structure in the classroom learning environment can impact the child with LD and ADHD significantly. Relational problems in this instance are associated with the nature of the environment more than interpersonal variables. Sometimes it is difficult to achieve the proper balance in classroom structure and to avoid either an overly rigid or a chaotic learning environment. The "climate" of the classroom is determined in part by the personal style of the teacher, the expectations of the school administration, and the makeup of the individual children in the class. For instance, teachers who have several children with ADHD must provide more reminders about expected behavior, monitor on-task and off-task behavior, and help the children with organizational tasks such as finding their pencils, remembering to turn in their assignments, and the like. Teachers who are frustrated and overwhelmed may handle these tasks in a rigid, harsh, or punitive manner, thus setting up a tense and negative classroom climate. Other teachers may have the ability to juggle the diverse and sometimes conflicting needs of students in a flexible and supportive manner, remembering to notice when students are behaving appropriately and to use their sense of humor. The latter classroom climate is more positive and conducive to learning. Also, classrooms with only one energetic, rambunctious child with ADHD will be less chaotic than classrooms with five of six such children.

School environments also differ with regard to the level of expectations for achievement among their students and willingness to modify those expectations for a child with a disability. Schools with extremely high academic standards may be less willing to tolerate the needs of the child with LD or ADHD, or may try to exclude these children from more advanced curriculum tracks. Conversely, some schools are ill equipped to provide the necessary specialized instruction, so that some children "fall through the cracks." In schools with special education classes, children with LD/ADHD and their parents often perceive a stigma associated with the diagnosis and with referral for special education. Relational problems may develop when referred children feel ostracized or perceive that they have a lower status within the classroom/school environment because of their need for special education.

Peer Relational Problems

The category of relational problems should be used when the focus of clinical attention is a pattern of interaction among peers that is associated with clinically significant impairment in individual or group social functioning. Peer relational problems associated with LD or ADHD may have a pervasive impact on the child's functioning within the neighborhood, in sports groups, scouts, church, and other social activities.

There is an abundant literature indicating problems in peer social interaction among children with LD and/or ADHD. Children with LD have been found to have more negative peer interactions, to be more aggressive, more immature, to have more internalizing personality problems, and fewer appropriate interpersonal behaviors than children without LD (Gresham & Elliott, 1990; Gresham & Reschly, 1986; Swanson & Malone, 1992). There is ample evidence that children with LD are less accepted and more often rejected by their peers than children without LD (Gresham, 1992; La Greca & Stone, 1990). Likewise, 50 to 60 percent of children with ADHD experience some form of social rejection from their peers (Guevremont, 1990, p. 540). During the preschool years, the behavior of children with ADHD often is characterized by aggressiveness, destructiveness, and attempts to dominate peers. During the early elementary years, peer rejection often is associated with disruptive and inattentive classroom behavior, arguing, noisy or obnoxious behavior, and physical and/or verbal aggression. Researchers have noted that children with ADHD also show age-inappropriate and immature development of prosocial skills (Guevremont, 1990, p. 541). Disturbed peer relations have been shown to be predictive of adolescent and adult mental health problems, such as juvenile delinquency, school dropout, police contacts, job termination, bad conduct discharges from the military, and psychiatric hospitalization. (See Parker & Asher, 1987, for a review.) Thus, early peer relational problems not only indicate concurrent difficulty for the child but also serve as an "at-risk" marker for later emotional and behavioral disturbance (Landau & Milich, 1982; Landau & Moore, 1991). This fact underscores the importance of early recognition and intervention with peer relational problems.

Other factors related to LD and ADHD may influence the development of peer relational problems. First, learning problems are not only apparent in the classroom, but also are apparent in extracurricular activities that require academic skill (e.g., in Scouts, earning merit badges may involve reading, writing, or other skills directly affected by the LD). Second, children who are struggling in school may spend so much time on homework that they have less opportunity to be involved in organized social activities, such as clubs or sports. This results in social isolation and less opportunity for developing social skills. Children with ADHD may find that their distractibility precludes their participation in organized sports because they have trouble remembering the rules of the game, or become distracted on second base and forget to watch for the fly ball coming toward them. Often they are viewed as intrusive and annoying to their peers because they are unable to inhibit their impulsive behavior. When this occurs, peers may have less incentive or motivation to be understanding than family members and therefore may choose to reject the child with ADHD.

Social status among peers is subject to a hierarchy similar to that found in families—with some children playing leadership roles and having more influence in decision making, and other children being relegated to less important roles. Children with lower status often feel neglected or rejected, and this may lead to peer relational problems.

RELATIONAL DIAGNOSTIC CRITERIA

Both LD and ADHD are considered to be neurologically based disorders, yet the effects of each can have profound influence on children and their relationships with significant others. The delineation of clear diagnostic criteria for parent-child, sibling, teacher/school, and peer relational disturbances awaits further empirical research; however, based on the foregoing, suggestions can be made for areas to consider in making a relational diagnosis associated with either LD or ADHD.

Parent-Child Relational Problem

A. The index person must meet DSM-IV (APA, 1994) criteria for one of the types of ADHD and/or one of the Learning Disorders.

B. At least one of the following relational patterns is present:
1. Parent-Child Relational Patterns
   a. Inappropriate parental expectations for achievement and/or behavior
   b. Impaired parent-child communication patterns
   c. Inappropriate levels of family control
   d. Interactional pattern in which the child with LD or ADHD feels devalued or perceives that he or she has lower status within the family by virtue of the problems associated with their disability
   e. High levels of parent-child conflict related to the functional problems associated with LD and ADHD (i.e., academic achievement, homework assignments, or behavioral control)
2. A relational pattern with parents that is characterized by overprotection, rejection, or criticism of the child, and that is associated with:

a. Low self-esteem in the child, and/or

b. Difficulty in interpersonal problem solving

Sibling Relational Problem

A. The index person must meet DSM-IV (APA, 1994) diagnostic criteria for one of the types of ADHD and/or one of the Learning Disorders.

B. At least one of the following relational patterns is present:

1. Sibling Relational Patterns

    a. Sibling rejection or neglect of the index person due to shame, anger related to the effects of the LD or ADHD, or a sense of superiority compared to the index child

    b. Sibling devaluation of their own accomplishments to an excessive degree in an attempt to protect the feelings of the index child

    c. Interactional pattern in which the child with LD or ADHD feels devalued or perceives that he or she has lower status within the family by virtue of the problems associated with their disability

    d. Impaired sibling-child communication patterns

2. A relational pattern with siblings that results in either the index child or the sibling having low self-esteem or difficulty in interpersonal problem solving

Teacher/School Relational Problem

A. The index person must meet DSM-IV (APA, 1994) diagnostic criteria for one of the types of ADHD and/or one of the Learning Disorders.

B. At least one of the following relational patterns is present:

1. Teacher/School Relational Patterns

    a. Inappropriate teacher/school expectations for achievement and/or behavior

    b. Impaired teacher-child communication patterns

    c. Classroom environment that is overly rigid and controlled or overly lax and chaotic

    d. Inappropriate levels of structure/organization in the classroom environment, which has a resulting negative impact on the child's functioning

    e. High levels of teacher-child conflict related to the functional problems associated with LD and ADHD (i.e., academic achievement, completion of assignments, following class rules, or behavioral control)

    f. Interactional pattern in which the child with LD or ADHD feels devalued or perceives that he or she has lower status within the classroom or school environment by virtue of the problems associated with their disability

2. A relational pattern with teachers or other school personnel that is characterized by social isolation, rejection, or criticism of the child, and which is associated with:

    a. Low self-esteem, and/or

    b. Difficulty in interpersonal problem solving

Peer Relational Problem

    A. The index person must meet DSM-IV (APA, 1994) criteria for one of the types of ADHD and/or one of the Learning Disorders.

    B. At least one of the following relational patterns is present:

        1. Peer Relational Patterns

           a. Peer rejection or neglect of the index child

           b. Interactional pattern in which the social skills of the index child interfere with positive and/or appropriate peer relations

           c. Impaired peer-child communication patterns

           d. Interactional pattern in which the child with LD or ADHD feels devalued or perceives that he or she has lower social status in the peer group by virtue of the problems associated with the disability

           e. Social isolation (and/or extremely diminished involvement in age-appropriate social activities) of the index child by virtue of the problems associated with their disability

        2. A relational pattern with peers that results in the index child having low self-esteem or problems in interpersonal problem solving

CONCLUSION

The suggestions for relational diagnostic criteria must stand up to the test of empirical research and clinical field trials before they can be used with confidence by practitioners. However, in the spirit of this text, they are offered for consideration and debate as an initial step in broadening our understanding of the vast relational issues associated with LD and ADHD.

REFERENCES

Abrams, J. C., & Kaslow, F. W. (1976). Learning disability and family dynamics: A mutual interaction. *Journal of Clinical Child Psychology, 5,* 35–40.

Algozzine, B., & Ysseldyke, J. (1986). The future of the LD field: Screening and diagnosis. *Journal of Learning Disabilities, 19,* 394–398.

American Psychiatric Association. (1968). *Diagnostic and statistical manual of mental disorders* (2nd ed.). Washington, DC: Author.

American Psychiatric Association. (1980). *Diagnostic and statistical manual of mental disorders* (3rd ed.). Washington, DC: Author.

American Psychiatric Association. (1987). *Diagnostic and statistical manual of mental disorders* (3rd ed., rev.). Washington, DC: Author.

American Psychiatric Association. (1994). *Diagnostic and statistical manual of mental disorders* (4th ed.). Washington, DC: Author.

Association for Children with Learning Disabilities. (1985). ACLD offers new definition. *Special Education Today, 2,* 19.

Barkley, R. A. (1981). *Hyperactive children: A handbook for diagnosis and treatment.* New York: Guilford.

Barkley, R. A. (1982). Specific guidelines for defining hyperactivity in children (Attention Deficit Disorder with Hyperactivity). In B. Lahey & A. Kazdin (Eds.), *Advances in clinical child psychology* (vol. 5, pp. 137–180). New York: Plenum.

Barkley, R. A. (1987). *Defiant children: A clinician's manual for parent training* (pp. 33–37). New York: Guilford.

Barkley, R. A. (1990). *Attention deficit hyperactivity disorder: A handbook for diagnosis and treatment.* New York: Guilford.

Barkley, R. A., & Cunningham, C. E. (1979). Stimulant drugs and activity level in hyperactive children. *American Journal of Orthopsychiatry, 49,* 491–499.

Barkley, R. A., DuPaul, G. J., & McMurray, M. B. (1990). Comprehensive evaluation of attention deficit disorder with or without hyperactivity as defined by research criteria. *Journal of Consulting and Clinical Psychology, 58*(6), 775–789.

Barkley, R. A., Fischer, M., Edelbrock, C. S., & Smallish, L. (1990). The adolescent outcome of hyperactive children diagnosed by research criteria: I. An 8 year prospective follow-up study. *Journal of the American Academy of Child and Adolescent Psychiatry, 29*(4), 546–557.

Barkley, R. A., Karlsson, J., Strzelecki, E., & Murphy, J. (1984). Effects of age and Ritalin dosage on the mother-child interactions of hyperactive children. *Journal of Consulting and Clinical Psychology, 52,* 750–758.

Barkley, R. A., McMurray, M. B., Edelbrock, C. S., & Robbins, K. (1990). Side effects of methylphenidate in children with attention deficit hyperactivity disorder: A systemic placebo-controlled evaluation. *Pediatrics, 86*(2), 184–192.

Befera, M., & Barkley, R. (1985). Hyperactive and normal boys and girls: Mother-child interaction, parent psychiatric status, and child psychopathology. *Journal of Child Psychology and Psychiatry, 26,* 439–452.

Bowen, M. (1978). *Family therapy in clinical practice.* New York: Aronson.

Breen, M., & Barkley, R. A. (1983). The Personality Inventory for Children (PIC): Its clinical utility with hyperactive children. *Journal of Pediatric Psychology, 8,* 359–366.

Breen, M., & Barkley, R. A. (1984). Psychological adjustment of learning disabled, hyperactive, and hyperactive-learning disabled children as measured by the Personality Inventory for Children. *Journal of Clinical Child Psychology, 13,* 232–236.

Culbertson, J. L., & Edmonds, J. E. (in press). Neuropsychological assessment of children, adolescents, and adults with learning disabilities. In R. A. Adams, O. Parsons, J. L. Culbertson, & S. J. Nixon, *Neuropsychology for clinical practice.* Washington, DC: American Psychological Association.

Culbertson, J. L., & Krull, K. R. (in press). Attention deficit hyperactivity disorder. In R. A. Adams, O. Parsons, J. L. Culbertson, & S. J. Nixon, *Neuropsychology for clinical practice.* Washington, DC: American Psychological Association.

Cunningham, C. E., & Barkley, R. A. (1978). The effects of Ritalin on the mother-child interactions of hyperkinetic twin boys. *Developmental Medicine and Child Neurology, 20,* 634–642.

Cunningham, C. E., & Barkley, R. A. (1979). A comparison of the interactions of hyperactive and normal children with their mothers in free play and structured tasks. *Child Development, 50,* 217–224.

Cunningham, C. E., & Siegel, L. S. (1987). Peer interactions of normal and attention-deficit disordered boys during free play, cooperative tasks, and simulated classroom situations. *Journal of Abnormal Child Psychology, 15,* 247–268.

Denckla, M. B. (1983). The neuropsychology of social-emotional learning disability. *Archives of Neurology, 40,* 461–462.

Denckla, M. B. (1989). Social learning disabilities. *International Pediatrics, 4,* 133–136.

Eyberg, S. M., & Boggs, S. R. (1989). Parent training for oppositional-defiant preschoolers. In C. E. Schaefer & J. M. Briesmeister (Eds.), *Handbook of parent training: Parents as cotherapists for children with behavior problems.* New York: Wiley.

Eyberg, S. M., & Robinson, E. A. (1982). Parent-child interaction training: Effects on family functioning. *Journal of Clinical Child Psychology, 11,* 130–137.

Gajor, A. (1992). Adults with learning disabilities: Current and future research priorities. *Journal of Learning Disabilities, 25*(8), 507–519.

Gittleman, R., Mannuzza, S., Shenker, R., & Bonagura, N. (1985). Hyperactive boys almost grown up. *Archives of General Psychiatry, 42,* 937–947.

Golden, G. S. (1988). The use of stimulants in the treatment of Tourette's Syndrome. In D. J. Cohen, R. D. Bruun, & J. F. Lechman (Eds.), *Tourette's syndrome and tic disorders: Clinical understanding and treatment* (pp. 317–327). New York: Wiley.

Gresham, F. M. (1992). Social skills and learning disabilities: Causal, concomitant, or correlational? *School Psychology Review, 21,* 348–360.

Gresham, F. M., & Elliott, S. N. (1990). *Social skills rating system.* Circle Pines, MN: American Guidance Service.

Gresham, F. M., & Reschly, D. J. (1986). Social skills and low peer acceptance of mainstreamed learning disabled children. *Learning Disability Quarterly, 9,* 23–32.

Guevremont, D. (1990). Social skills and peer relationship training. In R. A. Barkley (Ed.), *Attention deficit hyperactivity disorder* (pp. 540–572). New York: Guilford.

Hale, G. A., & Lewis, M. (1979). *Attention and cognitive development.* New York: Plenum.

Hammill, D. D., Leigh, J. E., McNutt, G., & Larsen, S. C. (1981). A new definition of learning disabilities. *Learning Disability Quarterly, 4,* 336–342.

Heath, C. P., & Kush, J. C. (1991). Use of discrepancy formulas in the assessment of learning disabilities. In J. E. Obrzut & G. W. Hynd (Eds.), *Neuropsychological foundations of learning disabilities* (pp. 287–307). San Diego: Academic.

Hooper, S. R., & Willis, W. G. (1989). *Learning disability subtyping: Neuropsychological foundations, conceptual models, and issues in clinical differentiation.* New York: Springer-Verlag.

Humphries, T., Kinsbourne, M., & Swanson, J. (1978). Stimulant effects on cooperation and social interaction between hyperactive children and their mothers. *Journal of Child Psychology and Psychiatry, 19,* 13–22.

Individuals with Disabilities Education Act. (1990). Code of Federal Regulations: Title 34; Education; Parts 300 to 399. U.S. Government Printing Office, Washington, DC 20402.

Johnson, D. J., & Myklebust, H. R. (1967). Nonverbal disorders of learning. In D. J. Johnson & H. R. Myklebust (Eds.), *Learning disabilities: Educational principles and practices* (pp. 272–306). New York: Grune & Stratton.

Kaslow, F. W., & Cooper, B. (1978). Family therapy with the learning disabled child and his/her family. *Journal of Marriage and Family Counseling,* 41–49.

Kendall, P. C., & Braswell, L. (1984). *Cognitive-behavioral therapy for impulsive children.* New York: Guilford.

LaGreca, A., & Stone, W. (1990). Children with learning disabilities: The role of achievement in their social, personal, and behavioral functioning. In H. L. Swanson & B. Keogh (Eds.), *Learning disabilities: Theoretical and research issues* (pp. 333–352). Hillsdale, NJ: Erlbaum.

Landau, S., & Milich, R. (1982). Assessment of children's social status and peer relations. In A. M. La Greca (Ed.), *Through the eyes of a child: Obtaining self-reports from children and adolescents* (pp. 259–291). Boston: Allyn and Bacon.

Landau, S., & Moore, L. A. (1991). Social skill deficits in children with attention-deficit hyperactivity disorder. *School Psychology Review, 20,* 235–251.

Lewis, J. M., Beavers, W. R., Gossett, J. T., & Phillips, V. A. (1976). *No single thread: Psychological health in family systems.* New York: Brunner/Mazel.

Loney, J., & Milich, R. (1982). Hyperactivity, inattention, and aggression in clinical practice. In D. Routh & M. Wolraich (Eds.), *Advances in developmental and behavioral pediatrics* (vol. 3, pp. 113–147). Greenwich, CT: JAI Press.

Mannuzza, S., Gittelman, R., Konig, P. H., & Giampino, T. L. (1989). Hyperactive boys almost grown up: VI. Criminality and its relationship to psychiatric status. *Archives of General Psychiatry, 46,* 1973–1979.

Margalit, M., & Arieli, N. (1984). Emotional and behavioral aspects of hyperactivity. *Journal of Learning Disabilities, 17,* 374–376.

Mash, E. J., & Johnston, C. (1983). Parental perceptions of child behavior problems, parenting self-esteem, and mothers' reported stress in younger and older hyperactive and normal children. *Journal of Consulting and Clinical Psychology, 51,* 68–99.

Minuchin, S. (1974). *Families and family therapy.* Cambridge, MA: Harvard University Press.

O'Leary, E. (1993). Transition services and IDEA: Issues for states and local programs. *South Atlantic Regional Resource Center Newsletter, 2,* 1–11.

Parker, J. G., & Asher, S. R. (1987). Peer relations and later personal adjustment: Are low-accepted children at risk? *Psychological Bulletin, 102,* 357–389.

Rehabilitation Act of 1973, P.L. 93-112, Section 504 (Non-Discrimination under Federal Grants). Code of Federal Regulations: Title 34; Education; Parts 100 to 106. U.S. Government Printing Office, Washington, DC 20402.

Rourke, B. P. (1988a). Socioemotional disturbances of learning disabled children. *Journal of Consulting and Clinical Psychology, 56,* 801–810.

Rourke, B. P. (1988b). Syndrome of nonverbal learning disabilities: Developmental manifestations in neurological disease, disorder and dysfunction. *The Clinical Neuropsychologist, 2,* 293–330.

Rourke, B. P. (1989). *Nonverbal learning disabilities: The syndrome and the model.* New York: Guilford.

Routh, D. K. (1978). Hyperactivity. In P. Magrab (Ed.), *Psychological management of pediatric problems* (pp. 3–48). Baltimore, MD: University Park Press.

Rules and Regulations Implementing Education for All Handicapped Children Act of 1975. PL 94-142. 42 *Federal Register* 42474 (1977).

Stewart, M. A., Pitts, F. N., Craig, A. G., & Dieruf, W. (1966). The hyperactive child syndrome. *American Journal of Orthopsychiatry, 36,* 861–867.

Swanson, H. L., & Malone, S. (1992). Social skills and learning disabilities: A meta-analysis of the literature. *School Psychology Review, 21,* 361–374.

Szatmari, P., Offord, D. R., & Boyle, M. H. (1989). Ontario child health study: Prevalence of attention deficit disorder with hyperactivity. *Journal of Child Psychology and Psychiatry, 30,* 219–230.

U.S. Office of Education. (1977). Assistance to states for education of handicapped children: Procedures for evaluating specific learning disabilities. *Federal Register, 42* (250), 65082-65085.

Voeller, K. K. S. (1986). Right hemisphere deficit syndrome in children. *American Journal of Psychiatry, 143,* 1004–1009.

Voeller, K. K. S. (1990). Right hemisphere deficit syndrome in children: A neurological perspective. *International Pediatrics, 5*(2), 163–170.

Walsh, F. W. (1982). *Normal family processes.* New York: Guilford.

Whalen, C. K., Henker, B., & Dotemoto, S. (1980). Methylphenidate and hyperactivity: Effects on teacher behaviors. *Science, 208,* 1280–1282.

CHAPTER 14

Oppositional Behavior and Conduct Disorders of Children and Youth

JAMES F. ALEXANDER, PhD and CHRISTIE A. PUGH, MA

SIGNIFICANCE OF THE BEHAVIOR DISORDERS

Disruptive behaviors and conduct problems constitute the most common reasons that parents, schools, and courts refer young children and adolescents to mental health care professionals (Kazdin, 1991; Rutter, 1981). Indeed, it appears that serious acting-out behaviors are so prevalent that up to one-half of all clinical referrals of children and adolescents are based on reports of disruptive behaviors (Kazdin, 1987; Robins, 1981). Presenting problems may represent a wide range of behaviors, including varying degrees of the behaviors found in the DSM-IV criteria for diagnosis of Oppositional Defiant and Conduct Disorders, delinquency, the impulse-control problems typical of Attention Deficit Hyperactivity Disorder, and substance abuse problems, all of which are often included under the heading of Disruptive Behavior Disorders (Costello & Angold, 1993). While we recognize this vast heterogeneity in presentation of behavior disorders and the significant degree of comorbidity with other disorders, this chapter will focus on Oppositional Defiant Disorder and Conduct Disorder.

There are many reasons for clinicians and researchers to be concerned about conduct disorders. Sheer numbers aside, in many cases the behaviors and problems associated with these disorders appear to continue throughout the life span, causing difficulties in many contexts (Loeber, 1991). Oppositional and aggressive behaviors in early childhood are associated with poor peer relations, underachievement in school, and increased risk of later violence and delinquency. The latter "advanced" disruptive behavior disorders are costly to the individuals who are victims of violent or antisocial acts. They are also extremely costly to the general public who end up paying for therapy and incarceration for offenders, and they are costly in terms of the actual structural damage often perpetrated by aggressive and antisocial individuals (Kazdin, 1993; Reid, 1993). In addition to these severe antisocial outcomes, early behavior problems also are associated with increased risk of the serious adulthood problems of alcoholism, drug abuse, marital disruption, chronic unemployment, physical

This chapter was prepared while both authors were supported in part by a National Institute of Drug Abuse Center Grant (DA07697): Center for Treatment Research on Adolescent Drug Abuse, Howard Liddle, Temple University, Primary Investigator, James F. Alexander, University of Utah, Site Primary Investigator.

disorders, and persistent social and psychiatric impairment (Kazdin, 1985; Reid, 1993; Robins, 1978). Also, poor peer relations put children at additional risk for a variety of poor outcomes and increase risk even in children who do not demonstrate behavior problems (Dodge, 1983). Finally, disruptive and aggressive behaviors appear to put the child at increased jeopardy of being abused by parents (Reid, Taplin, & Lorber, 1981), possibly adding residuals from abuse to the lengthy list of associated problems.

GOALS FOR THIS CHAPTER

In this chapter we do not intend to provide a complete review of the vast body of current research regarding the developmental trajectories and proposed developmental models, presentations and comorbidity issues, and suggested modes of treatment of behavior disorders. These topics have been responsibly and thoroughly covered in other publications (Cicchetti & Nurcombe, 1993, including several major articles contained therein; Kazdin, 1987; Webster-Stratton & Herbert, 1994). Rather, we will utilize current research, liberally citing references to direct a discussion of the problems that our current system of diagnosis (DSM-IV) poses for responsible assessment and effective treatment of behavior disorders. We also recommend potential solutions to these problems, identified as a "more responsible Relational Diagnostic System" for disruptive behaviors of children and youth.

DSM-IV CLASSIFICATION

Oppositional Defiant Disorder (ODD) and Conduct Disorder (CD) are categories of classification used in the DSM-IV to diagnose children and adolescents whose acting-out behaviors are disruptive to others. While DSM-IV criteria provide convenient and relatively concrete criteria for the diagnosis of ODD and CD, the narrowly defined behaviors contained in the DSM-IV fail to capture the richness of the construct(s) underlying these diagnoses. As Morey (1991) points out, underlying constructs may include "implications about etiology, course, prognosis, treatment, and interrelations with other constructs" that are clinically and scientifically important but beyond the current scope of the DSM.

The following behaviors are used to classify an individual as having Oppositional Defiant Disorder (DSM-IV criteria):

1. Often loses temper.
2. Often argues with adults.
3. Often actively defies or refuses to comply with adults' requests or rules.
4. Often deliberately annoys people.
5. Often blames others for his or her mistakes or misbehavior.
6. Is often touchy or easily annoyed by others.
7. Is often angry and resentful.
8. Is often spiteful or vindictive.

The DSM-IV Diagnostic Criteria for Conduct Disorder are as follows:

1. Often bullies, threatens, or intimidates others.
2. Often initiates physical fights.
3. Has used a weapon that can cause serious physical harm to others (e.g., a bat, brick, broken bottle, knife, gun).
4. Has been physically cruel to people.
5. Has been physically cruel to animals.
6. Has stolen while confronting a victim (e.g., mugging, purse snatching, extortion, armed robbery).
7. Has forced someone into sexual activity.
8. Has deliberately engaged in fire setting with the intention of causing serious damage.
9. Has deliberately destroyed others' property (other than by fire setting).
10. Has broken into someone else's house, building, or car.
11. Often lies to obtain goods or favors or to avoid obligations (i.e., "cons" others).
12. Has stolen items of nontrivial value without confronting a victim (e.g., shoplifting, but without breaking and entering; forgery).
13. Often stays out at night despite parental prohibitions, beginning before age 13 years.
14. Has run away from home overnight at least twice while living in parental or parental surrogate home (or once without returning for a lengthy period).
15. Is often truant from school, beginning before age 13 years.

The DSM-IV has made some advances over DSM-III-R in recognition of environmental contributions by warning against applying the diagnosis of Conduct Disorder when these behaviors "make sense" in the context in which the individual has lived. However, the system does not suggest how to classify or treat children in these circumstances. According to DSM-IV, the diagnosis of CD should be given only "when the behavior in question is symptomatic of an underlying dysfunction within the individual and not simply a reaction to the immediate social context" (p. 88). Such warnings are not given for Oppositional Defiant Disorder. While warnings of this type appear to provide recognition of environmental influences, they actually may serve to place further emphasis on the idea that "diagnosable" ODD and CD are the products of an individual suffering from a mental disorder and are essentially acontextual in nature. However, as the research to be cited indicates, such a stance is both conceptually and empirically untenable, especially in the case of ODD and late-onset CD. While methods of classification must necessarily lose some clinical richness in order to be useful, especially when these classification schemes are touted as "atheoretical," simplification to the degree found in the DSM-IV can cause a disorder to be artificially punctuated in such a way that the criteria only provide a narrow view of the actual clinical presentation. As Kazdin, Siegel, and Bass (1992) have pointed out, while a diagnosis of Conduct Disorder is based on symptoms the child presents, the clinical reality of the disorder presents as a package that includes the family and socioeconomic factors in which the child dysfunction is embedded.

We posit herein that recognition of the different developmental trajectories of disruptive behavior disorders is a necessary prerequisite to accurate diagnosis and effective treatment of these disorders. The DSM-IV criteria include only limited recognition of this point by requiring that CD be specified as Early or Late Onset type. Further, it will be suggested that consideration of the role of parents, peers, schools, and other "environmental" factors in the development and/or maintenance of disruptive behavior disorders is central to accurate description of the disorder and effective treatment planning and therefore should be included directly in the diagnostic process.

DEVELOPMENTAL CONSIDERATIONS

Questions of etiology and maintenance of disruptive behavior disorders and other disorders of childhood are intertwined with the delineations of the developmental trajectories these disorders appear to follow. The literature suggests several developmental routes and a long list of factors that have been found to be potential contributors to the development and maintenance of disruptive behavior disorders. As a result, great heterogeneity characterizes the clinical presentations of these disorders. In addition, the manifestations of disruptive behavior disorders change and develop as the child grows older, further complicating the diagnostic picture (Hinshaw, Lahey, & Hart, 1993). While this complexity can cause even the most tenacious clinician or researcher to feel overwhelmed, it can be represented schematically in a coherent, heuristic way. Figure 14.1 is a representation of a heuristic framework that has been developed based on current developmental and clinical research and will be used throughout this chapter to help organize current findings and potential diagnostic and treatment strategies for Oppositional Defiant Disorder and Conduct Disorder.

The vast body of current literature devoted to the topic of disruptive behavior disorders generally supports the conclusion that at least two major pathways may lead to the development of the serious behavior problems that contribute to a diagnosis of CD (Hinshaw et al., 1993; Loeber, 1991; McGee, Feehan, Williams, & Anderson, 1992; Robins, 1966). The first has been called the aggressive/versatile or childhood-onset path (Loeber, 1991). Children who follow this trajectory typically develop disruptive, often aggressive behaviors as early as the preschool years and demonstrate at least some of the more serious behavior problems prior to the onset of adolescence.

Although the early-onset pathway is not as prevalent as the adolescent-onset pathway, it is of particular concern because of the severity and stability of the behaviors demonstrated by children who follow this trajectory (Hinshaw et al., 1993). It is estimated that while individuals who fit the profile of early-onset behavior problems represent only 3 to 5 percent of the population, they are responsible for over half of the crimes committed by children and adolescents (Elliott, Huizinga, & Ageton, 1985). Children on this trajectory are likely to be markedly more aggressive and to have more academic problems and comorbid hyperactive and impulsive behaviors, and behaviors are far more likely to persist into adulthood than those of children with a later onset of behavior problems (Hinshaw et al., 1993). Aggression in particular appears to be a marker of this constellation, with onset of patterns of physical aggression occurring prior to adolescence in most cases (Loeber, 1991).

The typical behavioral progression in cases of childhood-onset disruptive behaviors involves a move from oppositional-type behaviors to more serious conduct-disordered

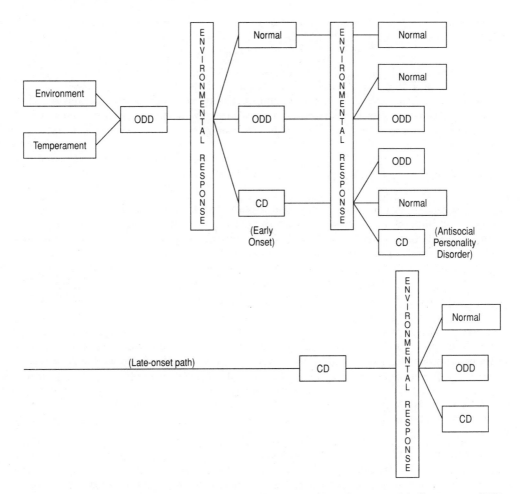

Figure 14.1   Differential pathways, timing of onset, and environmental influence on ODD and CD.

behaviors, with less serious problem behaviors appearing as a precursor to the eruption of more serious problem behaviors (Lahey et al., 1990; Loeber, 1991). Oppositional behaviors frequently are manifested as early as during the preschool years, and signs of more serious physical aggression may appear prior to admission to kindergarten.

It should be noted that many of the children who receive a diagnosis of ODD in childhood *do not progress* to more serious behavior problems. Some continue to meet criteria for ODD, and some no longer meet criteria for any behavior disorder (Lahey et al., 1990). Thus, while nearly all children who meet criteria for CD previously met criteria for ODD, a diagnosis of ODD is not a specific predictor of later CD; the aforementioned presence of aggression has been identified as a possible method of identifying those children who are more likely to progress from ODD to CD.

The second (late-onset) pathway to CD typically consists of behaviors that emerge during early adolescence. These behaviors include more concealing, nonaggressive problems, such as delinquency and shoplifting. Typically these are adolescents who, during childhood, did not demonstrate the behaviors or experience the maladjustment in peer and family relationships that are typical of ODD (Hinshaw et al., 1993). A larger percentage of adolescents in this category are female compared to the great predominance of males in the early-onset trajectory (McGee et al., 1992). While adolescents who follow this developmental trajectory tend to have as many police contacts during adolescence as do those who show an early onset, they are far less aggressive and much more likely to desist after adolescence (Lahey, Loeber, Quay, Frick, & Grimm, 1992; Robins, 1966).

From the previous section it should be apparent that the DSM-IV categories of ODD and CD do not adequately address the constructs underlying disruptive behavior disorders. Further evidence comes from findings that, while ODD is strongly correlated with early-onset CD, it is not correlated significantly with adolescent-onset CD (Lahey et al., 1992). Thus, our discussion of the relational processes involved in these disorders will focus on the two pathways supported by the research (and their many potential outcomes) rather than the two disorders currently listed in the DSM-IV.

RELATIONAL CONSIDERATIONS

Disruptive behavior disorders may be caused by any number of factors, in any number of combinations. These disorders demand consideration of relational influences to a greater degree than do many other types of disorders, for several reasons. First, it may be noted that disruptive behaviors, at least in the early-onset form, are demonstrably more prevalent in children who are exposed to certain maladaptive parenting contexts, including abuse, neglect, and multiple foster care placements (Famularo, Kinscherff, & Fenton, 1992; Graziano & Mills, 1992; McIntyre & Keesler, 1986). Further, research has identified potential mechanisms, in the form of specific maladaptive patterns of interactions between children and caregivers, that cause and/or maintain disruptive behaviors in children (Patterson & Dishion, 1988; Vuchinich & Patterson, 1992). Finally, and most important, in many cases children with disruptive behavior problems can be relieved of their symptoms without any individual treatment; the literature is replete with indices of successful treatment either through parent training or through family therapy. In fact, individual treatment of behavior disorders has proven to be notably ineffective in comparison to more relational treatment modes (Dodge, 1993). Clearly, none of these points rules out the real likelihood of multiple causality, including biological and/or genetic influences, or the further likelihood that etiology differs from child to child. However, in many cases relational processes are closely tied to the development and maintenance of disruptive behavior patterns. Therein lies the danger with diagnostic systems such as the DSM; through their focus on the "underlying individual mental disorder" responsible for disruptive behaviors, such systems will tend to perpetuate an inappropriate and often blaming attitude toward the child. Subscribing to this perspective can lead to ignorance of the suffering of the child as well as the rather dismal end result of avoiding more effective modes of treatment in favor of the individual-based treatments. There is also the strong possibility that, in cases where the environmental contribution to the child's behavior is marked, mental health professionals will be tempted to place children inappropriately in those diagnostic categories that do include recognition of environmental input, such as Post-Traumatic Stress Disorder (PTSD) or the Adjustment Disorders. A viable system of classification that recognizes the relational nature of behavior disorders would alleviate these serious problems inherent in the current system; the formulation of such a nosology is the mission of this book.

GENERIC APPLICATION OF A RELATIONAL MODEL TO EARLY-ONSET CD

For reasons just stated, early-onset conduct disorder is of particular concern to researchers and clinicians. Research has identified a large number of potential etiological factors in the development of this disorder. In the current model, these causal mechanisms have been broken down into two groups. The first group of factors includes environmental influences that may play a part in the development of ODD in early childhood and may increase the likelihood of progression to CD. Aggression in particular may be fostered through maladaptive early relationships with adults (Hinshaw et al., 1993), with the most obvious and direct factor being that of poor parenting practices. Additional factors may include any number of family and social problems such as divorce, parental psychopathology, socioeconomic disadvantage, and other stresses that influence parenting practices negatively and in turn affect the child indirectly (Reid, 1993). Disruptions in the child-caregiver relationship during the preschool years have been associated with behavior disorders (Loeber, 1991). Influences of the extended family, peers and neighborhood, schools, churches, and larger cultural institutions are included in this category as well.

The second group of factors includes those that are attributable to the intraorganismic makeup of the child (Costello & Angold, 1993), including genetic, anatomical, physiological, and neuropsychological factors, temperament, and any other individual causes of early childhood behavior. Comorbidity with other disorders, in particular ADHD, fall into this area of influence. There is evidence that these intraorganismic factors are particularly important in early-onset CD and may not have much influence in cases of later-onset CD (Hinshaw et al., 1993; Moffitt, 1993).

These two groups of factors may act singly or together to produce serious behavior problems. Research evidence suggests that while many children develop serious behavior disorders as a result of difficulties in only one of the two groups of factors, children who suffer both intraorganismic deficits and maladaptive environments are more likely to progress to CD and engage in serious aggressive behaviors (Hinshaw et al., 1993; Susman, 1993). However, while early child troublesomeness is a strong predictor of later conduct problems, poor parental discipline (including poor monitoring, harsh and ineffective discipline, and low involvement) is a better predictor (Loeber & Dishion, 1983; Farrington, 1991; Reid, 1993). Thus, child intraorganismic factors may have an important role in the development and maintenance of some behavior problems, but extensive research literature suggests that maladaptive parenting is a necessary, if not sufficient, factor in determining whether the child continues on the trajectory toward serious conduct problems.

Note that the phrase "maladaptive parenting" does not necessarily imply inherently "bad" conduct (e.g., abuse, neglect) on the part of the parent(s); it may instead represent an inability to respond constructively to certain temperamental tendencies in some children, and/or an inability to provide "Positive Parenting Process" (Alexander, Pugh,

Gunderson, & DeLoach, 1994) due to overwhelming extrafamilial stressors. Nonetheless, the final behavioral outcome of ODD or CD represents a relational, or systemic, problem rather than a singular "underlying dysfunction" in the child.

Regardless of the etiology of a particular young child's ODD, parents and others who come in contact with him or her will respond in ways that will help determine the child's behavioral condition during middle childhood. (See Figure 14.1.) The environmental response may consist of any number of behaviors, including appropriate and useful referral for parent training or family therapy, heightening of parents' maladaptive ways of responding to their child, secondary labeling and stereotyping in the school, constructive support from the extended family, or rejection by extended family members. While most literature has focused on the influence of environmental factors impinging on the child, it is clear that disruptive children also behave in ways that tend to influence the environment negatively (Alexander et al., 1994; Patterson, 1986; Reid, 1993). The response of the context to this influence can be reactive, reciprocally negative, and contributory to further child disruption (Patterson, 1986). In contrast, the child's misbehavior can initiate constructive environmental responses through such avenues as school-based programs and parent training. Thus, environmental responses to the onset of disruptive child behavior may be equally or more important than the variables that contribute to the initiation of the problem behavior patterns. Once again, DSM-IV tends to divert our focus from such developmental and systemic variables, which in turn decreases our understanding of the dynamics involved in these behavioral patterns.

Further, research literature and common sense suggest that behavior problems are more malleable early in their development and that Oppositional Defiant behaviors are more frequently successfully treated than CDs (Loeber, 1991; Loeber, Lahey, & Thomas, 1991). Reid (1993) and others suggest that the preschool period is the best time to target intervention toward those oppositional children who appear to be at risk for development of CD. When a child displays aggressive and/or noncompliant behaviors in the school setting, peers and teachers develop enduring attitudes toward the child that can help keep him or her locked into maladaptive patterns of behavior and can propel him or her toward peer groups that will promote further behavioral deviance. It appears that the most efficacious interventions for behavior problems target not only the identified patient but also the various members of the child's contexts that may exert influence on his or her patterns. During the preschool years the family is by far the context of greatest influence. Thus, treatment during this time typically need focus only on the child and parent(s), and parent training alone often is sufficient to alleviate a preschool child's maladaptive behaviors (McNeil, Eyberg, Eisenstadt, Newcomb, & Funderburk, 1991; Webster-Stratton, 1991). In fact, parent training may be an effective intervention regardless of whether there is comorbid hyperactivity, though severe hyperactivity may warrant additional pharmacological intervention (Barkley, 1989; Reid, 1993). In cases involving traumatized children, programs that include more intensive child-focused interventions in addition to parent training may prove most effective (Webster-Stratton & Herbert, 1994).

As a result of whatever environmental responses are made to the preschooler or young child with ODD, the child enters early and middle childhood on one of three levels of functioning. Whether due to therapy, good parenting or strong intraorganismic factors, positive early school experiences, lack of aggressiveness, or simple maturation, a number of children who demonstrate ODD at a young age either remain ODD (failing to progress to the behaviors indicative of CD), or they no longer even qualify for a diagnosis of ODD (Lahey et al., 1990). Other children begin to demonstrate more serious behavior problems and may meet criteria for a diagnosis of CD by middle childhood. While it is easy to react with some degree of hopelessness to children who display severe behavior problems at this age, behavior disorders along this trajectory remain relatively malleable at least through the age of 12 years (Loeber, 1991). However, if children who fall into this category continue to engage in coercive and aggressive family interactions with parents who continue to utilize ineffective parenting strategies, during this stage of development parental failure to monitor becomes predictive of later antisocial behavior (Loeber & Dishion, 1983; Patterson, Reid, & Dishion, 1992; Reid, Taplin, & Loeber, 1981). Aggressive children also experience rejection by well-adjusted peers and, to some degree, teachers, and instead may find acceptance by maladjusted peers. Because of the strong bidirectional influence that failure in each of these three domains can exert, the optimal treatment approach will target multiple settings (Reid, 1993). It is also likely at this time that interventions with the individual child may become a more necessary aspect of thorough treatment. For example, behavior-disordered children in this developmental stage have demonstrated consistent cognitive processing problems, especially in the realms of social information and affective attributions (Dodge, Pettit, McKlaskey, & Brown, 1986; Kendall, 1985).

Fortunately, interventions do exist that appear to be relatively successful in the treatment of each of these separate domains involved in the disruptive behavior process. Treatments that simultaneously focus on family interactions and children's cognitions have proven especially effective with young CD children (Kazdin et al., 1992). Classroom management techniques can improve classroom behavior significantly (Barrish, Saunders, & Wolf, 1969), and the various techniques that exist for reducing playground aggression (Walker, Hops, & Greenwood, 1981) hold hope of improving peer relations. Studies currently are being conducted on interventions that target high-risk children in the early grades of school and apply treatment across the contexts of family, school, and peer relationships (Coie & Jacobs, 1993; Reid, 1993). It is hoped that these multifaceted approaches will prove more effective than interventions aimed at individual areas in the life of the behavior-disordered child.

Again dependent on environmental reactions to the child during early and middle childhood, the child enters adolescence on one of a large number of potential levels. (See Figure 14.1.) Of particular concern at this point is the child who remains on the CD trajectory. At this point in development, it is likely that the CD involves a stable pattern of severe aggressive and overt problem behaviors, and the likelihood of continued development toward a diagnosis of Antisocial Personality Disorder is high (Loeber et al., 1991). At some point during adolescence the child who has followed the early-onset trajectory to CD demonstrates such consistent and stable delinquent behavior that it becomes appropriate to view the disorder as it is intended in the DSM-IV, as an individual mental disorder. At this point, it is likely to be as difficult to treat CD as it is to treat Antisocial Personality Disorder, and the distinction between the two disorders actually may consist of no more than the rather arbitrary DSM age requirement for the diagnosis of a personality disorder. The extant data fails to provide clear guidance as to the most appropriate form of intervention for children whose CD behaviors have progressed to this level of severity and stability. Family-based programs (e.g., Functional Family Therapy—see Barton, Alexander, Waldron, Turner, & Warburton, 1985) with seriously

offending adolescents have generated promising data but have failed to differentiate between early- and late-onset CD, the latter possibly representing the majority of successfully treated cases.

RELATIONAL PROCESSES AND LATE-ONSET CD

Adolescents who follow the late-onset trajectory in the development of delinquency and
CD typically do not experience similar early environments or intraorganismic factors
that are present in early-onset children. These adolescents tend to engage more in delinquent behaviors and less in aggressive or overt problem behaviors. It is suggested that
in a number of these cases, delinquent and problem behaviors emerge in the context of
disruptions in family functioning and increased reliance on peers to dictate behavioral
limits. Dysfunctional family relationships are not distinguishable from normal ones
until the advent of adolescence, when parenting styles may not be flexible enough to
appropriately deal with the emerging independence and stereotypically annoying adolescent behaviors and perhaps the parents' own relational difficulties (e.g., "midlife
crises"). A high percentage of cases of this nature appear to be particularly well suited
for certain types of family therapy (Alexander & Barton, 1995; Alexander, Holtzworth-
Munroe, & Jameson, 1993). Others may benefit from combinations of family and individual cognitive treatments (Kazdin, Siegel, & Bass, 1992). While these adolescents do
not typically appear to develop adult behaviors of the same severity as those with early-
onset CD, this in no way indicates that treatment of adolescents with late-onset CD is
not necessary or beneficial. Therapy may save the adolescent's relationships with other
family members and may keep the adolescent from acquiring a police record or from
being injured or killed while engaging in dangerous behaviors. Further, family therapy
can reduce the chances that a younger sibling subsequently will demonstrate delinquent
or conduct-disordered behaviors (Klein, Alexander, & Parsons, 1976).

TOWARD A RESPONSIBLE SYSTEM OF CLASSIFICATION

In an attempt to maintain the "atheoretical" nature of the DSM-IV, its framers again
have demonstrated how tightly they cling to the outdated idea that emotional and behavioral problems occur within the vacuum of the individual. Clinicians and researchers
who are convinced of the importance of parents, schools, peers, and abusive and neglectful environments in the development and maintenance of behavior disorders have
been relegated to the less influential world of V codes and Axis IV descriptors. This
does not imply that V codes and Axis IV descriptors are not important notations for
many DSM disorders, rather that in the case of behavior disorders, these "additional
environmental factors" are so thoroughly intertwined in development, maintenance, and
responsible treatment that they need to be included as part of the Axis I diagnosis. As
mentioned earlier, refusal to recognize the importance of relational factors results in a
diagnostic system that encourages individual treatment of behavior disorders (largely ineffective) and intentional misdiagnosis of disorders such as PTSD in order to accord
some recognition to environmental factors in a child's diagnosis. A more responsible diagnostic system might rely more heavily on current research and include references to

aid professionals in effective treatment based on more accurate diagnoses. A simple expansion of current DSM-IV labels to improve the richness of information added to diagnoses of the categories of ODD and CD, and inclusion of proper developmental information, would represent an important first step.

AN EXAMPLE OF A MORE RESPONSIBLE RDS (RELATIONAL DIAGNOSTIC SYSTEM)

Collection of information needed to properly assess the condition of a preschooler referred for oppositional behaviors might encompass the following steps:

1. Determine whether the preschooler meets the current DSM-IV criteria for ODD.
2. Determine whether the preschooler clearly demonstrates behaviors indicative of ADHD.
3. Assess the parenting procedures used with this child (reports and observations of specific instances of parent-child interactions).
4. Assess whether aggressive behaviors are present.
5. Determine whether the child has suffered trauma stemming from abuse or neglect. (Depending on the circumstances of the maltreatment, this may or may not be related to the current parent figure's ability to parent.)

Utilizing this system, two preschool children might be diagnosed this way: Child 1: ODD with maladaptive parenting, aggressive type, comorbid ADHD; and Child 2: ODD with adaptive parenting, aggressive type, sex abuse.

Child 1 presents with symptoms of ODD and ADHD. Aggressive symptoms are present and parenting patterns are coercive and possibly aggressive. Abuse is not reported. Child 2 presents oppositional and aggressive symptoms and has suffered sexual abuse outside the home. The parent engages in appropriate parenting practices.

Two very different treatment programs may be suggested by these diagnoses. Child 1 is at high risk for continued oppositional behaviors and progression toward early-onset type conduct disorder. Potential to be abused is high, and parent training/ family therapy is strongly indicated. Pharmacological interventions may be considered due to the comorbidity with ADHD, and attendance at a child therapy group or structured preschool with an emphasis on reducing the child's aggressive behaviors may be a useful collateral intervention.

Child 2 is more likely to require some type of individual or group treatment to eliminate aggression and deal with sexual abuse issues. The parent(s) in this case might require more support than training as a result of the guilt involved with having a child suffer abuse, assuming of course that the parent was not involved in the abuse. In this case special consideration should be given to identifying the "functional" nature of the ODD behaviors. These might include behaviors that serve to replicate certain sensations involved in the prior sexual abuse or, conversely, to create conditions that will ensure (as much as possible) its nonrecurrence. The ODD behavior may serve to elicit parental monitoring that previously occurred at a lower rate, or it may provoke frustration that serves as punishment by the child for what he or she perceived as lack of protection.

For older children, assessment of the interactions of peer and school factors needs to be added to the five areas of assessment used for preschoolers. With adolescents, responsible assessment needs to include determination of the developmental trajectory that has led to a diagnosis of a behavior disorder and further assessment based on developmental findings. Webster-Stratton and Herbert (1994) provide in-depth examples of a thorough assessment procedure for children with conduct disorder and their families. Numerous possibilities exist, but the important point is that *the "diagnosis" represents an edifying step in a careful relational assessment, not a final "label" that in and of itself implies the nature of treatment.*

CONCLUSIONS AND IMPLICATIONS FOR TREATMENT

Unlike many Axis I categories, the Relational Diagnosis System for ODD (and at least some expressions of CD) inherently prescribes the general nature of intervention. Most of the studies cited earlier clearly demonstrate the importance of family and other environmental factors in the development and maintenance of behavior disorders, and suggest intervention techniques based on their findings. The data patterns presented in the currently available observational and treatment studies that have served as a basis for creating the diagnostic formula also serve to prescribe intervention. What is clear from a review of currently available treatment methods is the demonstrated superior efficacy of relational treatment approaches over those that treat only the individual who has been given the role of the identified patient. Parent training appears to be one of the most effective (and least costly) interventions available for parents of young children, and often it is effective as a sole intervention for the parents of preschool children with ODD (Patterson, 1986; Webster-Stratton & Herbert, 1994). For preschool children who have experienced trauma, and for older children who demonstrate behaviors indicative of CD, collateral treatment of parent(s) and children may produce the best results (Kazdin et al., 1992; Webster-Stratton & Herbert, 1994). Family therapy has proven highly effective with adolescents who demonstrate patterns of late-onset CD and substance abuse problems (Alexander et al., 1994), and innovative approaches that focus on larger social influences such as peers and school systems show promise with older children and adolescents.

The Relational Diagnostic System proposed in this chapter provides mental health professionals with an empirically supported method of classification that promotes thorough assessment and effective treatment of behavior disorders. It is not intended to replace current diagnostic models; however, it *is* designed to render them more complete, appropriate, and useful. Without an empirically based strategy to guide our assessment and treatment decisions, we face the consequences of continued high rates of referrals and treatment responses that are far too costly and inefficient to be maintained in the current Zeitgeist of limited services and inadequate funding. It is our stance that in addition to these economic considerations, we as a field must assume a *moral* stance of providing the most appropriate, timely, and effective intervention to the children and families that experience the disruptions we identify as ODD and CD. The research literature strongly asserts that such intervention should be based on the relational considerations identified in this chapter, not the more limited perspective of current DSM-IV categorizations.

REFERENCES

Alexander, J. F., & Barton, C. (1995). Family therapy research. In R. H. Mikesell, D. D. Lusterman, & S. McDaniel (Eds.), *Family psychology and systems therapy: A handbook*. Washington, DC: American Psychological Association.

Alexander, J. F., Holtzworth-Munroe, A., & Jameson, P. B. (1993). Research on the process and outcome of marriage and family therapy. In A. E. Bergin & S. L. Garfield (Eds.), *Handbook of psychotherapy and behavior change* (4th ed., pp. 595–630). New York: Wiley.

Alexander, J. F., Pugh, C., Gunderson, D., & DeLoach, C. (1994, October). *Family disintegration and behavior disorders of youth: An inevitable cycle?* Paper presented at the William J. and Dorothy K. O'Neill Conference. Cleveland, OH.

American Psychiatric Association. (1994). *Diagnostic and statistical manual of mental disorders* (4th ed.). Washington, DC: Author.

Barkley, R. A. (1989). Attention deficit-hyperactivity disorder. In E. J. Mash & R. A. Barkley (Eds.), *Treatment of childhood disorders* (pp. 39–72). New York: Guilford.

Barrish, H. H., Saunders, M., & Wolf, M. M. (1969). Good behavior game: Effects of individual contingencies for group consequences on disruptive behavior in a classroom. *Journal of Applied Behavior Analysis, 2,* 119–124.

Barton, C., Alexander, J. F., Waldron, H., Turner, C. W., & Warburton, J. (1985). Generalizing treatment effects of functional family therapy: Three replications. *American Journal of Family Therapy, 13*(3), 16–26.

Cicchetti, D., & Nurcombe, B. (1993). Special issue: Toward a developmental perspective on conduct disorder. *Development and Psychopathology, 5,* 1–344.

Coie, J. D., & Jacobs, M. R. (1993). The role of social context in the prevention of conduct disorder. *Development and Psychopathology, 5,* 263–275.

Costello, E. J., & Angold, A. (1993). Toward a developmental epidemiology of the disruptive behavior disorders. *Development and Psychopathology, 5,* 91–101.

Dodge, K. A. (1983). Behavioral antecedents of peer social status. *Child Development, 54,* 1386–1399.

Dodge, K. A. (1993). The future of research on the treatment of conduct disorder. *Development and Psychopathology, 5,* 311–319.

Dodge, K. A., Pettit, G. S., McKlaskey, C. L., & Brown, M. M. (1986). Social competence in children. *Monographs of the Society for Research in Child Development, 51* (2, Serial No. 213).

Elliott, D. S., Huizinga, D., & Ageton, S. S. (1985). *Explaining delinquency and drug use*. Newbury Park, CA: Sage.

Famularo, R., Kinscherff, R., & Fenton, T. (1992). Psychiatric diagnoses of maltreated children: Preliminary findings. *Journal of the American Academy of Child and Adolescent Psychiatry, 31,* 863–867.

Farrington, D. P. (1991). Childhood aggression and adult violence: Early precursors and later-life outcomes. In D. J. Pepler & K. H. Rubin (Eds.), *The development and treatment of childhood aggression* (pp. 5–29). Hillsdale, NJ: Erlbaum.

Graziano, A. M., & Mills, J. R. (1992). Treatment for abused children: When is a partial solution acceptable? *Child Abuse & Neglect, 16,* 217–228.

Hinshaw, S. P., Lahey, B. B., & Hart, E. L. (1993). Issues of taxonomy and comorbidity in the development of conduct disorder. *Development and Psychopathology, 5,* 31–49.

Kazdin, A. E. (1985). *Treatment of antisocial behavior in children and adolescents*. Homewood, IL: Dorsey.

Kazdin, A. E. (1987). Treatment of antisocial behavior in children: Current status and future directions. *Psychological Bulletin, 102,* 187–203.

Kazdin, A. E. (1991). Effectiveness of psychotherapy with children and adolescents. *Journal of Consulting and Clinical Psychology, 59,* 785–798.

Kazdin, A. E. (1993). Treatment of conduct disorder: Progress and directions in psychotherapy research. *Development and Psychopathology, 5,* 277–310.

Kazdin, A. E., Siegel, T. C., & Bass, D. (1992). Cognitive problem-solving skills training and parent management training in the treatment of antisocial behavior in children. *Journal of Consulting and Clinical Psychology, 60,* 733–747.

Kendall, P. C. (1985). Toward a cognitive-behavioral model of child psychopathology and a critique of related interventions. *Journal of Abnormal Child Psychology, 13,* 357–372.

Klein, N. C., Alexander, J. F., & Parsons, B. V. (1976). Impact of family systems intervention on recidivism and sibling delinquency: A model of primary prevention and program evaluation. *Journal of Consulting and Clinical Psychology, 45*(3), 469–474.

Lahey, B. B., Loeber, R., Quay, H. C., Frick, P. J., & Grimm, J. (1992). Oppositional defiant and conduct disorders: Issues to be resolved for DSM-IV. *Journal of the American Academy of Child and Adolescent Psychiatry, 31,* 539–546.

Lahey, B. B., Loeber, R., Stouthamer-Loeber, M., Christ, M. G., Green, S., Russo, M. F., Frick, P. J., & Dulcan, M. (1990). Comparison of DSM-III and DSM-III-R diagnoses for prepubertal children: Changes in prevalence and validity. *Journal of the American Academy of Child and Adolescent Psychiatry, 29,* 620–626.

Loeber, R. (1991). Antisocial behavior: More enduring than changeable? *Journal of the American Academy of Child and Adolescent Psychiatry, 30,* 393–397.

Loeber, R., & Dishion, T. (1983). Early predictors of male delinquency: A review. *Psychological Bulletin, 94,* 68–99.

Loeber, R., Lahey, B. B., & Thomas, C. (1991). Diagnostic conundrum of oppositional defiant disorder and conduct disorder. *Journal of Abnormal Psychology, 100,* 379–390.

McGee, R., Feehan, M., Williams, S., & Anderson, J. (1992). DSM-III disorders from age 11 to age 15 years. *Journal of the American Academy of Child and Adolescent Psychiatry, 31,* 50–59.

McIntyre, A., & Keesler, T. Y. (1986). Psychological disorders among foster children. *Journal of Clinical Child Psychology, 15,* 297–303.

McNeil, C. B., Eyberg, S., Eisenstadt, T. H., Newcomb, K., & Funderburk, B. (1991). Parent-child interaction therapy with behavior problem children: Generalization of treatment effects to the school setting. *Journal of Clinical Child Psychology, 20,* 140–151.

Moffitt, T. E. (1993). The neuropsychology of conduct disorder. *Development and Psychopathology, 5,* 135–151.

Morey, L. C. (1991). Classification of mental disorders as a collection of hypothetical constructs. *Journal of Abnormal Psychology, 100,* 289–293.

Patterson, G. R. (1986). Performance models for aggressive boys. *American Psychologist, 1,* 432–444.

Patterson, G. R., DeBaryshe, B. D., & Ramsey, E. (1989). A developmental perspective on antisocial behavior. *American Psychologist, 44,* 329–335.

Patterson, G. R., & Dishion, T. J. (1988). Multilevel family process: Traits, interactions and relationships. In R. A. Hinde & J. Stevenson-Hinde (Eds.), *Relationships within families: Mutual influences* (pp. 283–310). Oxford: Oxford University Press.

Patterson, G. R., Reid, J. B., & Dishion, T. J. (1992). *Antisocial boys.* Eugene, OR: Castalia.

Patterson, G. R., & Stouthamer-Loeber, M. (1984). The correlation of family management practices and delinquency. *Child Development, 55,* 1299–1307.

Reid, J. B. (1993). Prevention of conduct disorder before and after school entry: Relating interventions to developmental findings. *Development and Psychopathology, 5,* 243–262.

Reid, J. B., Taplin, P. S., & Lorber, R. (1981). A social interactional approach to the treatment of abusive families. In R. Stuart (Ed.), *Violent behavior: Social learning approaches to prediction, management, and treatment* (pp. 83–101). New York: Brunner/Mazel.

Robins, L. N. (1966). *Deviant children grow up: A sociological and psychiatric study of sociopathic personality.* Baltimore: Williams & Wilkins.

Robins, L. N. (1978). Sturdy childhood predictors of adult antisocial behavior: Replications from longitudinal studies. *Psychological Medicine, 8,* 611–622.

Robins, L. N. (1981). Epidemiological approaches to natural history research: Antisocial disorders in children. *Journal of the American Academy of Child Psychiatry, 20,* 566–580.

Rutter, M. (1981). Epidemiological/longitudinal strategies and causal research in child psychiatry. *Journal of the American Academy of Child Psychiatry, 20,* 513–544.

Susman, E. J. (1993). Psychological, contextual, and psychobiological interactions: A developmental perspective on conduct disorder. *Development and Psychopathology, 5,* 181–189.

Vuchinich, S., & Patterson, G. R. (1992). Parenting, peers, and the stability of antisocial behavior in preadolescent boys. *Developmental Psychology, 28,* 510–521.

Walker, H. M., Hops, H., & Greenwood, C. R. (1981). Recess: Research and development of a behavior management package for remediating social aggression in the school setting. In P. S. Strain (Ed.), *The utilization of classroom peers as behavior change agents* (pp. 261–303). New York: Plenum.

Webster-Stratton, C. (1991). Annotation: Strategies for helping families with conduct disordered children. *Journal of Child Psychology and Psychiatry, 32,* 1047–1062.

Webster-Stratton, C., & Herbert, M. (1994). *Troubled families, problem children.* Chichester, England: Wiley.

CHAPTER 15

Children with Life-Threatening Illnesses: Psychological Difficulties and Interpersonal Relationships

ANNE E. KAZAK, PhD and STEVEN SIMMS, PhD

This chapter presents the relationships among serious childhood illness, families, and psychosocial issues pertinent to relational diagnosis. Social ecological theory is utilized to organize relevant research guiding our knowledge of ill children within a broader family and systems perspective. The roles that relational diagnosis can play in childhood illness are developed with a practice-oriented perspective. Case presentations conclude the chapter to illustrate the themes presented.

Serious and/or chronic pediatric health problems are relatively common. Fortunately, recently there has been an increased appreciation of the fact that families face many psychosocial issues and crises over the course of diagnosis and treatment (Kazak, Segal-Andrews, & Johnson, 1995). The experience is, in most cases, an unexpected, lengthy, difficult, and bumpy journey for children, families, and clinicians.[1] However, long-standing associations of serious illness with psychopathology have been weakened with studies that illustrate the adaptive normality of families and fail to substantiate the presence of serious disturbances (Cadman, Rosenbaum, Boyle, & Offord, 1991; Kazak & Marvin, 1984). While psychiatric diagnoses are applicable to a subset of seriously ill children and their families, psychological adaptation is always central to the illness process.

Family/systems perspectives on development and relationships provide a framework pertinent to competent functioning over the course of serious childhood illness. We outline ways in which illness, development, and family functioning can be understood as loss and adaptation in a relational diagnostic framework. From a systemic perspective, the information also guides the therapeutic process toward enhancing the collaborations among pediatric and mental health specialists in helping children and families cope with these processes of loss and adaptation.

---

[1] We use the analogy of a journey, including maps and associated images of terrain, throughout the chapter to illustrate relevant points. Other authors in this field have used similar analogies (e.g., Rolland, 1994), which we have found useful in describing work with families and illness.

SOCIAL ECOLOGICAL MODEL

Social ecology examines relationships between the developing individual and his or her adaptation to relationships, settings, and contexts (Bronfenbrenner, 1979). It provides a template for understanding how childhood illness reciprocally impacts individuals and systems internal and external to the family (Kazak, 1989). The child is at the center of nested concentric spheres. (See Figure 15.1.)

The first level is the microsystem, or "patterns of activities, roles, and interpersonal relations experienced by the developing person," including the immediate family. Social ecology emphasizes the importance of individual development and the implications of developmental processes for coping and adapting. The disease itself is part of the microsystem as it places demands on child and family, and can be addressed by "putting the illness in its place" (Reiss, Gonzalez, & Cramer, 1986, p. 69).

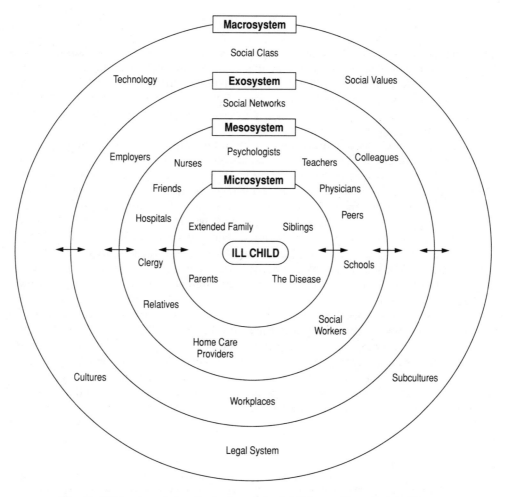

Figure 15.1   A social ecological model of children with pediatric illness.

Mesosystems are interrelated microsystems—for example, the relationships between families and both schools and hospitals. Families with an ill child often have particular educational needs that accentuate the importance of family/school relationships. Moreover, the long-term relationships with the health care team evolve and change with the nature and demands of treatment.

The exosystem is an environment that does not affect the child directly but has profound indirect effects. Given the importance of caregiving for chronically ill children and its provision by parents, understanding the social context in which parents perform this role is critical. For example, health care needs of children can demand parental work absences. The flexibility of the parents' employers may affect the child indirectly via parental work stress.

At the outermost level is the macrosystem or subculture, culture, and general belief patterns. Although frequently not considered within the realm of psychological intervention, neglect of these systems can result in a dangerously myopic view of families. For example, local, state, and federal laws and policies have direct implications for services available.

The Disease

The disease and its treatment warrant careful consideration in understanding how families cope with childhood illness. Frameworks that have been advanced for understanding the impact of the illness include a noncategorical approach (Stein & Jessop, 1982), psychosocial parameters of illness (Rolland, 1984), and the contribution of physiologic factors (Wood, 1993).

The Ill Child

While a higher incidence of psychiatric problems has been reported in children with chronic diseases (cf. Cadman, Boyle, Szatmari, & Offord, 1987), such disturbances are not inevitable. Some research fails to confirm the presence of depression and anxiety in pediatric samples and, paradoxically finds extremely low rates (Greenberg, Kazak, & Meadows, 1989; Worchel et al., 1988). These findings have been interpreted in three ways: (1) that resilience, coping skills, and support may eradicate depression; (2) that depression may be denied; and (3) that self-report scales fail to assess the types of depression experienced by children with cancer. Consideration of anxiety in children with pediatric conditions often has been limited primarily to situational anxiety related to medical procedures and has evaluated behavioral interventions to lessen these episodes of acute distress. As with depression, generalized anxiety may be denied.

For many conditions (e.g., prematurity, cancer, cystic fibrosis, muscular dystrophy), prognoses have changed favorably. The medical sequelae of increased survival and the resultant morbidity associated with intense medical interventions are more apparent. Thus, the meaning attributed to survival is likely to become increasingly important as more children survive serious pediatric conditions and grow up, with or without disabling conditions associated with their initial disease. In cancer, for example, the impact of variables such as learning problems, gender, or the lingering perceptions of traumatic memories in understanding long-term adaptation are areas worthy of further research (Kazak, Christakis, Alderfer, & Coiro, 1994; Stuber, Christakis, Houskamp, & Kazak, 1995).

Siblings

While parents worry about the impact of the illness on other children, siblings have received little attention. Early studies evaluated responses to the death of a sibling or assessed the impact of having a severely mentally retarded sibling. Serious psychiatric or behavioral disorders tended to be used as outcome measures. A systemic orientation toward understanding the impact of childhood health problems on siblings requires more complex designs and more specific types of questions than previously asked. For example, in a study of preschool siblings of children with cancer and a matched comparison group, Horwitz and Kazak (1990) examined the ways in which mothers viewed siblings as alike or different from the ill child. The mothers were more likely to view the sibling like the child with cancer than comparison mothers rating well children.

Parents

The increased caregiving that often falls upon mothers may contribute to increased burden and ultimately to psychological distress (cf. Breslow, Staruch, & Mortimer, 1982; Kazak, 1987a). Mothers' concerns with the long-term burdens of parenting also are salient. For example, mothers of autistic children showed a profile of stress that related specifically to the child's present and future dependence (Koegel et al., 1992). In a small study of fathers of autistic, developmentally delayed, and developmentally normal children, the results support the general findings of competence among parents, while identifying specific stressors that impinge upon family functioning (Rodrique, Morgan, & Geffken, 1992).

A development affecting parental caregiving demands is the increased use of home care, through highly sophisticated technology introduced into the home, with home care staff training parents and monitoring patients. The impact of home care on families has been documented, with clear benefits and its own set of stressors (cf. Crutcher, 1991; Jessop & Stein, 1991). The issue of parents providing increased medical care at home is inextricably involved with the broader systems issues that must be considered.

The Marital Relationship

Although one of the most frequently heard comments related to the potentially destructive impact of childhood illness on family functioning concerns the possibility of increased marital conflict and likelihood for divorce, there is evidence of no differences in overall rates of marital satisfaction between families with and without affected children (cf. Kazak, Reber, & Snitzer, 1988; Sabbeth & Leventhal, 1984). In their prospective research on infants at risk for asthma, Klinnert, Gavin, Wamboldt, and Mzarek (1992) provide data that supports similarities between families with and without a medically involved child. That is, marital satisfaction in their sample declined after the child's birth.

While encouraging, the data does not suggest that marital strain is unimportant. Indeed, the marital relationship is a central one in family functioning and inevitably is affected by the losses experienced when there is a serious childhood illness. The ways in which adaptive coping and marital functioning interact warrant further consideration in learning to support families throughout their illness experiences.

The Family

Much of the literature comparing families with and without a child with a health problem assumes that those families who have such a child will be different from those without. The difference often has been assumed to be in the direction of greater family dysfunction. A strong early tradition in research on family adjustment to chronic illness is the comparison of families with and without an affected child. This design serves an important function but also has some unintended effects and potential complications. To select measures that are applicable to both groups, important questions about the very experience (illness!) often cannot be asked.

In response to illness, family rules and organizing principles may look different. In a study using audiotaped family interaction tasks with families of adolescent diabetics and families with a recent, acute illness, more enabling behaviors (focusing, problem solving) were found for mothers of children with diabetes than for the control group (Hauser et al., 1986). The extent to which group differences like these are associated with adjustment of individuals within the family (e.g., parents, patients) and with long-term outcome is important information awaiting longitudinal studies.

For healthy functioning, flexibility is needed to meet the changing needs of the individuals and the family as a unit. Normal developmental changes of children and families require alterations in boundaries and closeness. An adolescent may ask for more privacy and less emotional closeness from parents than when younger. Those with chronic illness may experiment with identity issues through the medical management of their disease. For example, less proximity may take on a very different meaning to the family when an adolescent is not taking responsibility. Additionally, an adolescent who has struggled with an illness for a long time may be expected to experience identity issues later than a child without a medical history because of a longer period of dependency and uncertainty, with possible long-term implications for personality and coping styles. Children and adolescents with sickle cell disease have been shown to have elevated levels of depressive symptomatology, with evidence that maladaptive attributional styles can ensue (Brown et al., 1993).

There may be distinct family developmental tasks that may be "normal" within the context of a chronic illness. For example, the period of launching children with chronic illnesses from home may be different from nonill children due to negotiating issues such as continuity of medical management, concerns about physical safety, and emotional security.

Schools

Serious illness immediately disrupts children's and adolescents' participation in routine school activities, with potentially adverse effects on academic achievement and social development. Besides these short-term issues, there are longer term ones. That is, parents and schools need collaborative partnerships in assessing difficulties, ascertaining if problems are treatment-related, and charting an educational program over time. Thus, learning problems and educational progress and placement can be considered long-term stressors that build on the initial stressors associated with diagnosis and treatment.

The importance of considering and involving other systems in the care of ill children is well illustrated by the example of school collaboration. Excessive absences can be minimized by working with school personnel to individualize the child's program.

If the child is encouraged to be as functional as possible, the school will need to accommodate to his or her special needs to facilitate regular school attendance and to help him or her function less as a "patient" and more as a normal child with special needs.

Systemically, building a partnership with school personnel is key in working with families with an ill child. Power and Bartholomew (1987) describe five types of interaction styles between schools and families (avoidant, competitive, merged, one-way, collaborative) that provide helpful models for understanding these partnerships. O'Callaghan (1993) presents a model of ecosystems consultation in which a competence enhancing, multisystems model can be used for empowering families and resolving school-based problems in a manner consistent with systems theory.

The Health Care System

The ways in which health care systems interface with family systems have been largely unexplored. When a family with a child with a pediatric health problem interfaces with these larger systems, social ecological and general systems models predict that characteristics of these systems will affect one another. Research has looked at unidirectional aspects of these systems, such as what parents think or feel about medical care (Chesler & Barbarin, 1984; Mulhern, Crisco, & Camitta, 1981; Patno, Young, & Dickerman, 1988), but has not addressed these issues over time or described attributes of the systems themselves.

Surprisingly, data on linkages between pediatric and mental health care systems and professionals points to a general lack of referral of children and families for mental health services, despite understanding of the potential for psychological difficulties (Sabbeth & Stein, 1990; Weiland, Pless, & Roghmann, 1992). Although mental health professionals in pediatric centers offer a great deal of diverse assistance to families, much of their work is directed at crisis intervention and/or referral. Many significant mental health needs and opportunities for therapeutic frameworks are obscured.

Other issues that have been described primarily at the level of the individual child or family can be understood as broader systems concerns. For example, treatment compliance can reflect, in part, the fit between family and the health care system (Stein & Pontius, 1985) and includes more obvious family interactions that can influence compliance. This framework allows for consideration of ethnic differences and provokes examination of the fit among families, professionals, and settings.

Another practical treatment concern that has been investigated primarily at the level of the individual child is the pain and anxiety associated with invasive medical procedures. Behaviorally oriented interventions have proven effective in decreasing child distress. However, linkages between behavioral distress in a specific treatment situation (procedures) with family adaptation are just beginning to be acknowledged (Kazak et al., 1995).

Parental Social Support Networks.

Concerns about social isolation in families facing serious chronic illness have been long acknowledged. The potentially overwhelming demands of caring for medically involved or chronically ill children can result understandably in decreased interaction with others and less inclination to use external resources. In recent years, the recognition and acknowledgment of families of chronically ill children as a group has promoted a sense of identity. Legal rights and funding of research and interventions for this group appear to have strengthened a sense of community for parents of children with serious health needs. However, despite the potential for empowerment evident within a group defined by common interests and goals, the risk of marginalization and alienation still remains. For these reasons, the investigation of social support allows for a detailed understanding of the types of persons available to parents for support, the ways in which help is provided, and the potential for aiding in the adjustment to serious childhood illness (Krahn, 1993).

Research that examines social support networks in families with and without children with disabilities suggests that general differences in network size are not apparent, although professionals (members of the child's health care team) comprise a significant portion of the network (cf. Kazak, 1991; Quitner, Glueckauf, & Jackson, 1990). The indirect effect of parental networks on child outcome is an area in need of further research, as there is evidence that network structure may affect child behavior differentially (Barakat & Linney, 1992).

Other network characteristics such as density (the extent to which members of the network know each other and interact) and the timing of support offered have been identified as important components of social support (Hobfoll & Lerman, 1988; Kazak, 1991). Networks of parents of children with spina bifida, phenylketonuria, and mental retardation tend to be more dense than those of matched control parents, and these denser structures are related to less successful parental adjustment (Kazak, 1988; Kazak, Reber, & Carter, 1988; Kazak & Wilcox, 1984). Highly dense networks resemble very cohesive family systems and could limit the individual's ability to act independently or to express disagreement. Alternatively, in a study of families of developmentally delayed children selected for their successful coping styles, Trute and Hauch (1988) found that highly dense networks were characteristic of these highly functioning families.

With respect to intervention, it is possible to enhance the provision of social support. Relationships with extended family members, old friends, new friends, and utilization of community resources are ways in which social support can be mobilized, within the context of figuring out strategies that are acceptable to a particular family. In addition to informal sources of support (e.g., family, friends), there are many formal sources of support (e.g., mental health professionals, hospital staff, community agencies, clergy). Despite concerns about social isolation from informal support, many families of children with serious health concerns have a broad formal support network available. Yet many issues emerge with regard to how to access, utilize, and sometimes help coordinate the components of the formal support network (Kazak, 1987b).

THE ROLES OF DIAGNOSIS

This chapter has highlighted how psychosocial adjustment reciprocally influences relationships at multiple levels. In the next section we translate this broad theoretical frame into a focused clinical perspective. In doing so, the linkages and continuities between "normal" psychological adaptation to illness and loss and less adaptive, psychopathological outcomes (e.g., psychiatric diagnoses) are clarified. The basic goal is to provide direction in constructing and promoting relational diagnosis, given the stressors associated with serious childhood illness. Three issues are salient: First, psychosocial issues related to an ill child are viewed as concrete landmarks linked to processes of loss and adaptation. Second, responses from others are viewed as positive, neutral, or negative in their influence on psychosocial adjustment. Finally, loss remains the central psychological response, with acknowledgment that this can flare up in the form of more severe symptomatology.

"Clinical maps" provide a structure akin to an initial assessment in which information is gathered to understand treatment needs and to diagnose. In the section entitled "Illness as Transitional Events" we encourage consideration of illness and treatment as a series of stressors, with the goal being to monitor their process and responses. The section "Illness Disrupting Mastery" introduces the developmental component into the diagnostic process. In "Coping as an Interpersonal Process," we lay out a plan for working with the child and family to create change. Finally, in "Behavioral Patterns and Psychosocial Symptoms," we emphasize that maladaptive behavior is always a possibility, and we provide a legend for understanding and managing it.

Clinical Maps

If the clinician can quickly and accurately detect visible landmarks on the pediatric illness terrain (e.g., grief, distress), he or she is positioned strategically to assist throughout the course of illness (Miller & Swartz, 1991). By anticipating illness-related events and offering an alternative, the clinician creates new meanings of the illness experience, with solvable problems, rather than contributing to inflexibility and blaming interpersonal patterns.

Illnesses as Transitional Events

When a child is diagnosed with a serious illness, this is a transition for the child and family (Colapinto, 1982). The transitions are associated with loss and adaptation processes. Ill children experience many losses. Unique aspects of the physical, psychological, and social self are altered and may not be regained. The trailhead marks a lifelong path that impacts psychological development and changes the child's social role in the family, school, and community. The family's foothold in "normal" family life cycle and "normal" family functioning is irretrievably lost. As in the changes in the child developmental path, the family is thrust into a new and unwanted path of development characterized by unremitting illness-related demands and shattered dreams (Rolland, 1994). Grieving lost aspects of the self and the family is a lifelong process. The child and family must live with this pain and struggle with how it will be evidenced in their daily lives.

While enduring grief, the child learns to cope. Psychological resources are rediscovered, expanded, and used to navigate around the illness-related barriers. New adaptive roles at home and school that the family never imagined are possible. The family begins the artful juggling of resources and discovers new and unforeseen sources of support.

The grief and adaptation processes are irreversible. Each family shows a unique indelible emotional mark created by the illness experience. Each also displays its own set of survival skills. The clinician's role is to help anticipate features of the terrain, to begin defining these in terms of grief and adaptation, and to respond with an orientation for survival and, perhaps, growth.

Illness Disrupts Mastery

During the illness process, the child begins to confront barriers. In the psychological domain, the illness insults the naturally unfolding developmental process of learning and skill acquisition. Psychological tools that facilitate task completion, problem solving, and maintaining relationships are compromised. This learning and problem-solving process that promotes mastery of the psychological and expanding interpersonal world is disrupted. As a result, the child with an illness is derailed from a normal developmental course.

The clinician should remain vigilant for changes in the child's behavior that are best viewed as the child's response to this developmental derailment. These behavioral patterns colored by emotional features such as fear, anger, and sadness further highlight this thwarted mastery. Here the clinician should assume that the child possesses the resiliency to adapt but is always at risk to become stuck.

The developmental process is flexible enough to allow many children with an illness to discover new solutions to illness-imposed barriers. For example, the child with diabetes quietly detours to the nurse's office each day before lunch for a blood sugar level reading. The procedure and injection are concluded in a matter of minutes. The child is seen running to catch up with classmates in the school cafeteria. However, when resources are drained and coping skills are not expanded, the child with an illness is at risk for psychosocial difficulties. Here the clinician sees and attends to an inflexible, repetitive, and maladaptive behavior pattern. The child trapped in this pattern may signal the stuck position with an emotional reaction that may be the basis for a referral for a future psychiatric evaluation (Simms, 1995).

Coping as an Interpersonal Process

When a child with an illness shows fear, anger, anxiety, and depression, this is an expected event on the therapeutic map that should be read as a normative reaction to the illness experience. Rather than the clinician focusing exclusively on this worrisome reaction, this signal is an opportunity for him or her to broaden the clinical focus. Instead of attempting to eliminate or control this expected and unavoidable emotional aspect of the illness experience, each family health care and school team member is oriented to develop a two-step response.

Step 1 reads the child's emotional signal. The adult offers acceptance and understanding of the distress over thwarted mastery. Step 2 focuses on a partnership. The adult takes a collaborative stance in an unrelenting search for a developmentally appropriate coping response. The question "Are you thinking of a way to help yourself feel better, or do you want me to give you an idea?" is an excellent starting point for many children and adolescents. This two-step process reduces the child's isolation in the grief process and maximizes his or her potential to adapt.

Many families utilize this two-step process. When this naturally occurs, the clinician is in a position to highlight the family's success. The clinician's punctuation of the family experience highlights survival of the illness experience (Colapinto, 1982). When families do not utilize this two-step process, the well-oriented clinician will be prepared for the inevitable crisis.

Behavioral Patterns and Psychosocial Symptoms

The barriers created by illness and the resultant family patterns may, in some cases, lead to maladaptive behavior. The clinician can recognize the terrain and see the pitfalls that create a mental health disaster. The child may become locked in a cycle of responding to thwarted mastery with fear or anger. When the child directs all attention to the illness-related barriers, he or she may become "blinded" to other "healthy" aspects of the self. Similarly, parents or health care providers focusing on the child's unremitting or escalating emotional responses also become "blinded" to the child's and their own resources. Trapped in this complementary pattern, the child's normal reaction to stymied developmental mastery and the family, school, or health care team's failure to help may escalate into clinical distress or seriously impaired functioning in the family, hospital, school, or community. This pattern of focusing on symptomatic aspects and missing the adaptive aspects of the self may become inflexible and crystallized (Simms, 1995).

Case Histories

The first case is of a ten-year-old boy (B) with a serious illness. The health care team first approached his compelling psychosocial difficulties as a Separation Anxiety Disorder (APA, 1994). The diagnosis seemed appropriate and warranted a referral for family therapy. Consistent with the diagnosis, B's history of excessive anxiety concerning separation from his mother was evidenced by persistent school refusal, stomachaches when challenged to attend school, and excessive distress at school. Despite an excellent response to medical treatment and improved physical health, he and his family responded as if he were "sick" and relapse was imminent.

After several family therapy sessions, it became evident that addressing B's symptoms from a psychiatric diagnostic perspective was not having an impact on the problem and was, in fact, creating an artificial dichotomy between medical and psychological issues. The insurance company's denial of family therapy charges highlighted the disagreement; the rejection was because "B doesn't have a mental problem, he has a physical illness."

B's ongoing psychosocial difficulties then were framed in relational terms. The locus of the intervention was the inflexible interactional pattern that evolved in the social ecology that included B, the illness, family, school, health care team, and insurance company. Each team member focused on approaching the family in a "different" way. Conversations with the family were structured to acknowledge the losses B suffered (e.g., lost opportunities for friendships) *and* highlight adaptation, such as his return to active family life. Each outpatient visit was concluded with a written "health report card." In order to intervene with his developmental derailment, the team member interacted with B as if he were "ten years old." Thus, when B was discovered in his mother's lap in the waiting room, the "five-year-old" side was ignored and a "ten-year-old" request was made.

When the family accrued several health report cards documenting worry over loss (gastrointestinal [GI] distress), barriers to development (missed school due to GI distress), and improving health, their physician challenged the parents to devise a plan for B's return to school. Surprisingly, B's parents presented a concrete plan. B's father would take him to school each day. If B required medical care at school, the school nurse would call B's clinic nurse to review nursing interventions. The clinic nurse would then call B's mother to apprise her of his status and treatment. By framing B's psychosocial difficulties as linked to loss and adaptation, highlighting developmental barriers, and connecting the levels of the social ecology differently, the symptoms resolved and B returned successfully to school.

The second case is P, a 25-year-old woman who had a serious illness as an adolescent. As an adult, she met criteria for Borderline Personality Disorder (BPD). Rather than sidestep her serious mental health issues, we viewed her ongoing difficulties in relational terms and examined the inflexible interactional patterns among her illness, P, the family, and the health care system that had crystallized over time.

Consistent with BPD, P's history revealed poor relationships, lack of success in school or work (she had never returned to school after diagnosis at age 13), suicide attempts, and a history of multisubstance abuse. Additional issues included bulimia, much sexual activity and cigarette use, and compounded ongoing medical problems secondary to her disease and treatment (e.g., poor lung function, GI disorders, gynecologic abnormalities). Although her medical treatment ended years before our consultation, P spoke as if she were currently in treatment. Despite her young-adult developmental status, she refused referral to an adult facility. When the health care team attempted to "force the issues," she increasingly became physically symptomatic with strong emotional overlays of anger and blame.

P lived with her mother, who had a history of depression. Although her parents were still married, her father lived in another city with a "secret" paramour. Her parents remained attentive at her bedside during hospitalizations, catered to her demands, and treated her like "a 13-year-old." When the staff pushed for "adultlike" behavior, her parents defended her demands and histrionic behavior. A symptomatic cycle was evident that revealed a young-adult woman "stuck" at the developmental stage at which she became ill. Her illness-related issues and personality disorder combined in a complex web as barriers to "growing up." The health care team responded with impatience and anger to the impressive list of symptoms. When "blinded" by a narrow view and isolated from the social ecology, the team inadvertently fueled the symptomatic cycle.

Our treatment with P was consistent with that suggested by her psychiatric diagnosis—structured sessions with limit setting, patience during episodes of adulation and anger, and a psychiatric hospitalization. This treatment approach, however, was linked to a developmental interpersonal frame. We focused on promoting developmental skills specifically linked to helping P transition to adult care. In addition to assisting her with "adult" goals, we remained connected with her through an active collaborative partnership of guiding, supporting, and pulling for adaptive behaviors. The process was at times excruciatingly slow and frustrating for all. By reinforcing the notion that transfer to an adult physician was not "abandonment" and by establishing a concrete multistep contract with P that all members of the social ecology supported, she was able to let go of remaining a pediatric patient.

P is not "cured." Indeed, her psychological difficulties persist, and she requires ongoing assistance to maintain an adaptive coping style. However, her case is an example of applying a developmental, relational perspective in the presence of serious psychopathology. Ideally, this approach is advocated for patients at diagnosis. Working with the relationships among P, her parents, health care team, and school when she was a young teenager ideally would have altered the patterns that were deeply entrenched by the time we were consulted. Also, while her medical illness is no longer a direct health threat, P does have substantial health concerns. Our goals included helping her accept these as "adult problems" and guiding her to master them in ways that will be productive. As a result, she gradually accepted an adult role, which helped loosen her self-image as a "sick child." The critical component to P's "individual" growth was the cultivation of a broad therapeutic interpersonal frame (particularly with the health care team) so that her "team" was oriented to help her navigate a more adaptive course.

CONCLUSION

Serious childhood illnesses have the potential to thwart the developmental course of children and families. Although most pediatric patients and their families cope well with the demands of illness and its treatment, the risk of more serious psychological problems must be acknowledged and appreciated. A social ecological perspective provides a map by which the processes of loss and adaptation can be understood, for children and families. It supports a framework for relational diagnosis. The model also provides a means by which interactions among systems (e.g., families, schools, workplaces, health care settings) can be understood with regard to their role in processes of adjustment to serious childhood illness.

REFERENCES

American Psychiatric Association. (1994). *Diagnostic and statistical manual of mental disorders* (4th ed.) Washington, DC: American Psychiatric Association.

Barakat, L., & Linney, J. (1992). Children with physical handicaps and their mothers: The interrelation of social support, maternal adjustment, and child adjustment. *Journal of Pediatric Psychology, 17,* 725–739.

Breslow, N., Staruch, K., & Mortimer, E. (1982). Psychological distress in mothers of disabled children. *American Journal of Diseases of Childhood, 136,* 682–686.

Bronfenbrenner, U. (1979). *The ecology of human development.* Cambridge, MA: Harvard University Press.

Brown, R., Kaslow, N., Doepke, K., Buchanan, I., Eckman, J., Baldwin, K., & Goonan, S. (1993). Psychosocial and family functioning in children with sickle cell syndrome and their mothers. *Journal of the American Academy of Child and Adolescent Psychiatry, 32,* 545–553.

Cadman, D., Boyle, M., Szatmari, P., & Offord, D. (1987). Chronic illness, disabilities and mental and social well-being: Findings of the Ontario Child Health Study. *Pediatrics, 79,* 805–813.

Cadman, D., Rosenbaum, P., Boyle, M., & Offord, D. (1991). Children with chronic illness: Family and parent demographic characteristics and psychosocial adjustment. *Pediatrics, 87,* 884–889.

Chesler, M., & Barbarin, O. (1984). Relating to the medical staff: How parents of children with cancer see the issues. *Health and Social Work, 9,* 59–65.

Colapinto, J. (1982). Structural family therapy. In A. H. Horne & M. M. Olson (Eds.), *Family counseling and therapy* (pp. 112–140). Itasca, IL: Peacock.

Crutcher, D. (1991). Family support in the home: Home visiting and Public Law 99–457. *American Psychologist, 46,* 138–140.

Greenberg, H., Kazak, A., & Meadows, A. (1989). Psychological adjustment in 8 to 16 year old cancer survivors and their parents. *Journal of Pediatrics, 114,* 488–493.

Hauser, S., Jacobson, A., Wertlieb, D., Weiss-Perry, B., Follansee, D., Wolfsdorf, J., Herskowitz, R., Houlihan, J., & Rajapark, D. (1986). Children with recently diagnosed diabetes: Interactions within their families. *Health Psychology, 5,* 273–296.

Hobfoll, S., & Lerman, M. (1988). Personal relationships, personal attributes, and stress resilience: Mothers' reactions to their child's illness. *American Journal of Community Psychology, 16,* 565–589.

Horwitz, W., & Kazak, A. (1990). Family adaptation to childhood cancer: Sibling and family systems variables. *Journal of Clinical Child Psychology, 19,* 221–228.

Jessop, D., & Stein, R. (1991). Who benefits from a pediatric home care program? *Pediatrics, 88,* 497–505.

Kazak, A. (1987a). Families with disabled children: Stress and social networks in three samples. *Journal of Abnormal Child Psychology, 15,* 137–146.

Kazak, A. (1987b). Professional helpers and families with disabled children: A social network perspective. *Marriage and Family Review, 11,* 177–191.

Kazak, A. (1988). Stress and social networks in families with older, institutionalized mentally retarded children. *Journal of Social and Clinical Psychology, 6,* 448–461.

Kazak, A. (1989). Families of chronically ill children: A systems and social ecological model of adaptation and challenge. *Journal of Consulting and Clinical Psychology, 57,* 25–30.

Kazak, A. (1991). The social context of coping with childhood chronic illness: Family systems and social support. In A. LaGreca, L. Siegel, J. Wallender, & C. E. Walker (Eds.), *Advances in pediatric psychology: Stress and coping with pediatric conditions* (pp. 263–278). New York: Guilford.

Kazak, A., Boyer, B., Brophy, P., Johnson, K., Scher, C., Coleman, K., & Scott, S. (1995). Procedure related distress and family adaptation in childhood leukemia. *Children's Health Care, 24,* 143–158.

Kazak, A., Christakis, D., Alderfer, M., & Coiro, M. (1994). Young adolescent cancer survivors and their parents: Adjustment, learning problems and gender. *Journal of Family Psychology, 8,* 1–11.

Kazak, A., & Marvin, R. (1984). Differences, difficulties, and adaptation: Stress and social networks in families with a handicapped child. *Family Relations, 33,* 67–77.

Kazak, A., Reber, M., & Carter, A. (1988). Structural and qualitative aspects of social networks in families with young chronically ill children. *Journal of Pediatric Psychology, 13,* 171–182.

Kazak, A., Reber, M., & Snitzer, L. (1988). Chronic childhood disease and family functioning: A study of phenylketonuria. *Pediatrics, 81,* 224–230.

Kazak, A., Segal-Andrews, A., & Johnson, K. (1995). Pediatric psychology research and practice: A family/systems approach. In M. Roberts (Ed.), *Handbook of Pediatric Psychology* (pp. 84–104). New York: Guilford.

Kazak, A., & Wilcox, B. (1984). The structure and function of social networks in families with handicapped children. *American Journal of Community Psychology, 12,* 645–661.

Klinnert, M., Gavin, L., Wamboldt, F., & Mrazek, D. (1992). Marriages with children at medical risk: The transition to parenthood. *Journal of the American Academy of Child and Adolescent Psychiatry, 31,* 334–342.

Koegel, R., Schreibman, L., Loos, L., Dirlich-Wilhelm, H., Dunlop, G., Robbins, F., & Plienis, A. (1992). Consistent stress profiles of mothers of children with autism. *Journal of Autism and Developmental Disorders, 22,* 205–216.

Krahn, G. (1993). Conceptualizing social support in families of children with special health care needs. *Family Process, 32,* 235–248.

Miller, T., & Swartz, L. (1991). Clinical psychology in general hospital settings. *Professional Psychology: Research and Practice, 21,* 48–53.

Mulhern, R., Crisco, J., & Camitta, B. (1981). Patterns of communication among pediatric patients with leukemia, parents, and physicians: Prognostic disagreements and misunderstandings. *Journal of Pediatrics, 99,* 480–483.

O'Callaghan, J. (1993). *School-based collaboration with families.* San Francisco: Jossey-Bass.

Patno, K., Young, P., & Dickerman, J. (1988). Parental attitudes about confidentiality in a pediatric oncology clinic. *Pediatrics, 81,* 296–300.

Power, T., & Bartholomew, K. (1987). Family-school relationship patterns: An ecological perspective. *School Psychology Review, 16,* 498–512.

Quitner, A., Glueckauf, R., & Jackson, D. (1990). Chronic parenting stress: Moderating versus mediating effects of social support. *Journal of Personality and Social Psychology, 59,* 1266–1278.

Reiss, D., Gonzales, S., & Cramer, N. (1986). Family process, chronic illness, and death. *Archives of General Psychiatry, 43,* 795–804.

Rodrique, J., Morgan, S., & Geffken, G. (1992). Psychosocial adaptation of fathers of children with autism, Down syndrome, and normal development. *Journal of Autism and Development Disorders, 22,* 249–263.

Rolland, J. (1984). Towards a psychosocial typology of chronic and life threatening illness. *Family Systems Medicine, 2,* 245–262.

Rolland, J. (1994). *Families, illness, and disability.* New York: Basic Books.

Sabbeth, B., & Leventhal, J. (1984). Marital adjustment to chronic childhood illness. *Pediatrics, 73,* 762–768.

Sabbeth, B., & Stein, R. (1990). Mental health referral: A weak link in comprehensive care of children with chronic physical illness. *Developmental and Behavioral Pediatrics, 11,* 73–78.

Simms, S. (1995). A protocol for seriously ill children with severe psychosocial symptoms: Avoiding potential disasters. *Family Systems Medicine, 13,* 245–259.

Stein, R., & Jessop, D. (1982). A noncategorical approach to childhood chronic illness. *Public Health Reports, 97,* 354–362.

Stein, H., & Pontius, J. (1985). Family and beyond: The larger context of noncompliance. *Family Systems Medicine, 3,* 179–189.

Stuber, M., Christakis, D., Houskamp, B., & Kazak, A. (1995). Post trauma symptoms in childhood leukemia survivors and their parents. *Psychosomatics.*

Trute, B., & Hauch, C. (1988). Social network attributes of families with positive adaptation to the birth of a developmentally disabled child. *Canadian Journal of Community Mental Health, 7,* 5–15.

Weiland, S., Pless, I., & Roghmann, K. (1992). Chronic illness and mental health problems in pediatric practice: Results from a survey of primary care providers. *Pediatrics, 89,* 445–449.

Wood, B. (1993). Beyond the "psychosomatic family": A biobehavioral family model of pediatric illness. *Family Process, 32,* 261–278.

Worchel, F., Nolan, B., Willson, V., Purser, J., Copeland, D., & Pfefferbaum, B. (1988). Assessment of depression in children with cancer. *Journal of Pediatric Psychology, 13,* 101–112.

CHAPTER 16

Anxiety Disorders as They Impact on Couples and Families

ANDREW ROSEN, PhD

DEFINITIONS OF ANXIETY

Anxiety affects everyone at one time or another during the course of a lifetime. It may be situational, in that a person may be going through a particular incident or issue, such as a job problem or financial strain, or it may be somewhat more ongoing or phase related, such as in adolescent dating worry or grave concern related to pregnancy. Whether situational or life-phase related, feelings of anxiety are a necessary part of life in that these help people prepare for important situations and alert them to potential danger. May (1979) proposed that

> [anxiety is] the apprehension cued off by a threat to some value that the individual holds essential to his existence as a personality. The threat may be to physical life (threat of death) or to psychological existence (the loss of freedom, meaninglessness) or the threat may be to some other value which one identifies with one's existence (patriotism, the love of another person, "success," etc.). (p. 180)

In our society, individuals spend billions of dollars each year to reduce their anxiety. People in the United States actually see their doctor more often for anxiety symptoms than for colds or infections (Marsland, Wood, & Mayo, 1976). Many people get prescriptions for tranquilizers, such as Xanax (Alprazolam) or Valium (diazapam). Many patients experience only the physical manifestations of anxiety, such as chest pain, headaches, joint pain, or gastrointestinal discomfort, and seek their physician's care, while being totally unaware that they are anxiety-ridden; that is, they do not "feel anxious," they just experience physical distress. Such people may go from doctor to doctor for years searching for the solution to their physical discomfort, when in fact the cause may be "anxiety" related. Others may have a clear ongoing problem with a particular type of anxiety.

For example, a person may be a worrier or one who has panic attacks, or may experience excessive fears going to certain places. Whatever the case may be, theoreticians and clinicians generally have focused on how the individual experiences and copes with anxiety, either of the "normal" variety or the "incapacitating" type. Many theories have been proposed about how anxiety develops and how it affects individuals' psychological and physical well-being, but relatively little has been written about how anxiety affects the family. Researchers often have cited the familial factors involved in anxiety disorders and have focused on issues such as genetic transmission, biological vulnerability, and environmental factors of anxiety, in that children often learn to be anxious like their parents or become "neurotic" as a result of their parents' anxiety. However, usually these researchers are attempting to understand how anxiety disorders are transmitted and contribute to creating another person with an anxiety disorder. Rarely do authors attempt to identify and understand how a person with anxiety affects significant others—family members—and how this effect feeds back to the person with the anxiety (Oakley & Padesky, 1990). This then is the focus of this chapter.

As a clinician, for over 20 years I have had the opportunity to see many patients who have come for the treatment of anxiety. Typically, an individual comes to seek help after months or years of struggling with anxiety. The prospective patient, usually a woman, will complain about various symptoms and express how difficult her distress has been for her. It is the clinician's role to assess what is causing the anxiety and diagnose what type(s) of anxiety disorder, if any, is present so that an effective treatment plan can be formulated. During the assessment and treatment planning phase, the clinician usually focuses on the individual patient who is seated in front of him or her. Depending on the clinician's clinical orientation and discipline (M.D., Ph.D., M.F.T., etc.), he or she may prescribe a drug or recommend some form of therapy (cognitive-behavioral, psychoanalytic, supportive, etc.) for the patient. He or she may try to explain to the patient how the anxiety disorder came about and how the treatment actually works from a technique standpoint.

Unfortunately, a very important piece of information is typically either overlooked or undervalued—and that is the effect and interaction that a person's anxiety disorder has on significant others in his or her life. Many clinicians gather little information from the patient on how the spouse, parents, and/or children experience or react to this person's anxiety symptoms. In addition, the clinician rarely engages family members in the therapy sessions to gather information or to provide feedback about the patient. Basically the family is excluded or extruded from treatment. However, the clinician who attempts to diagnose and treat the anxiety-disordered individual and neglects the family member(s) will achieve fewer and less enduring treatment goals. Further, the practitioner needs to assess the impact on the family or couple and to work with them to help the identified patient. The clinician also must assist them with their concerns as these influence and are influenced by the anxiety problems.

When clinicians speak of getting family members involved with an individual's problems and treatment, they often think that this entails shifting to a marital or family therapy modality. Many individually oriented practitioners are uncomfortable with this perceived shift and instinctively negate the idea of family involvement. In addition, many anxiety-disordered patients resist the concept of family member involvement because they fear that the clinician is implying that their anxiety is rooted in a marital problem or a family conflict. As a result, the proposed spouse/family involvement often is avoided. I do not mean to suggest that marital or family therapy is indicated in all cases; however, the clinician should involve significant family members in some way during the assessment and treatment. This may be in a supportive role for didactic or educational purposes, or as part of the treatment unit. Whatever role the family plays in the treatment, the clinician should not imply that the relationship caused the anxiety; rather, it must be explained that the anxiety has had an impact on significant others who thus are involved already and that they can participate in the quest for resolution of the difficulties.

The severity of the anxiety disorder and the specific diagnostic category are important in determining the appropriateness of marital/family therapy. (The more severe and chronic the disorder, the more likely that the family issues will need to be a greater focus of treatment.) For example, if a woman has developed panic attacks with some mild agoraphobic/avoidant behavior only recently, then it is probably better to treat her individually with perhaps one or two collateral sessions with her husband to help him understand the nature of the problem. However, if she has had a panic disorder for two years and generally avoids many situations and responsibilities, then it is important to involve him (and perhaps the children, depending on their ages). Such involvement will help him to understand her symptoms and to help her. In addition, couple's therapy may be necessary to help determine if and how the relationship contributes to her problems and/or to help him deal with his feelings about her difficulties. If this is not done, not only may it be more difficult for her to work through and recover from her anxiety problems, but even if she does, their relationship may be left with permanent scars that can lead to other serious problems. Clearly researchers and clinicians should pay more attention to the role significant relationships play in the development of anxiety disorders and to the treatment issues that arise from them. Besides understanding the biological factors, cognitive-behavioral, and psychodynamic issues that are involved, the critical importance of relational issues must be recognized to understand and treat anxiety disorders.

ANXIETY DISORDERS AS THEY IMPACT ON THE COUPLE AND FAMILY

Specific Phobias

Specific fears of an object or situations occur in most of the population, but for about 10 percent of people, these fears are termed "disorders" and are called phobias (Myers et al., 1984). The DSM-IV (APA, 1994) defines a specific phobia as a marked and persistent fear that is excessive or unreasonable, cued by the presence or anticipation of a specific object or situation (e.g., flying, hikes, animals, etc.). Exposure to the phobic stimulus provokes an immediate anxiety response, and the person does recognize that the fear is excessive or unreasonable. The phobic situation is avoided or endured with intense anxiety or distress. The avoidance, anticipation, or distress interferes significantly with the person's normal routine. Most people handle their phobias without ever seeking treatment; if and when they do go for help, it is often after years of trying to cope with the problem on their own. These phobias tend to have a less serious impact on the couple or other family members than do other anxiety disorders. However, the relational component still needs to be dealt with. For example, the person who has a phobia about flying clearly will place limits on his or her own mobility and often also on the travel of a spouse and/or other family members. I often will see a "flying phobic" only after the patient has been pressured by the spouse to go for therapy and sometimes only after an ultimatum has been issued. The spouse may believe he or she is not able to go on vacation or travel to see his or her family because of the mate's phobia. The spouse may feel too guilty to go alone and leave the phobic mate home, or the spouse may have developed a counter-dependence in which he or she cannot be apart from the phobic mate. Over the years, not only do everyone's plans become altered, but a certain resentment/pressure dynamic can settle in. The phobic person comes to feel pressured and guilty that he or she cannot fly and the spouse/children feel angry and cheated by the phobic's restrictions. Often an ongoing dynamic of tension develops between the couple as a by-product of the flying avoidance. This interactive pattern also will need to be reviewed and worked through, either before the phobia treatment begins or afterward, to help the couple put the past behind them and enable them each to let go of the mutual resentments related to the phobia.

Panic Disorder and Agoraphobia

The DSM-IV defines Panic Disorder with Agoraphobia as involving panic attacks, which are discrete periods of intense fear or discomfort in which at least four of the following symptoms occur: palpitations, tachycardia, sweating, trembling, choking, shortness of breath, abdominal distress, dizziness, lightheadedness, feelings of unreality or depersonalization, fear of losing control or going crazy, fear of dying, and agoraphobic anxiety about certain situations and places, resulting in their avoidance. This common anxiety disorder may have the most debilitating affect of all the anxiety disorders on the couple/family. The most common scenario is when a woman in her late 20s or early 30s develops panic attacks, characterized by intense physical symptoms such as dizziness, heart racing, gastrointestinal problems, and severe fears that something terrible is going to happen, or that she is going to die or go crazy. These attacks usually come "out of the blue" and cause the person to withdraw from people and situations, want to stay home and/or cling to her husband for safety and support. Initially the husband is also afraid of what is going on, tries to help, and shows concerns and caring. However, when medical tests show "nothing is wrong" and after the husband sees no improvement over time, he becomes frustrated, resentful, "fed up," and withdraws into his own life, leaving his wife feeling more fearful, alone, and depressed.

The second scenario involves the husband who, instead of becoming resentful and withdrawn, becomes overinvolved with his anxious wife, takes over for her in terms of responsibility, and allows or indirectly encourages her to give up and avoid life. He thereby helps her to become very dependent on him emotionally and physically. What appears to be a very loving and caring spouse actually may be a person who is reinforcing his wife's pathological coping mechanisms partly because of his own comfort with her increasing dependency. Many clinicians feel that marital relationships play a role in the development and maintenance of agoraphobia (Goldstein, 1970; Lazarus, 1966). Goldstein and Chambliss (1978) believe that people with low "self-sufficiency" experience ambivalence about wanting to leave their unhappy marriage and that they fear independence. This conflict can create anxiety or panic, which is resolved by avoidance and withdrawal into the home. Nonetheless, other clinical researchers disregard the role that marital relationships play in the development of panic and agoraphobia (Klein, Zitrin, Woerner, & Ross, 1983; Sheehan, Ballanger, & Jacobsen, 1980). These researchers appear to be behavioral in orientation as opposed to dynamic or interpersonal.

Goldstein and Chambliss (1978) proposed that agoraphobia be divided into two types: "complex" and "simple." Complex agoraphobia is considered to be precipitated or compounded by marital conflict. It is associated with additional major problems such as hypochondriasis, generalized anxiety, obsessive-compulsive symptoms, social phobias, and depression. After treatment of the panic and agoraphobia, relapse is frequent, usually related to marital difficulties that are precipitated or made worse by the initial treatment. Simple agoraphobia is different in that it usually occurs after an accumulation of life stress and conflict; that is, traumatic events usually can be reported. Rarely are the other syndromes present in the complex type mentioned. If marital difficulties occur after effective behavior therapy, they rarely are associated with relapse of the patient's agoraphobia.

Several studies in the 1970s suggested that some marriages deteriorate as the agoraphobic wife becomes more independent (Hafner, 1976; Milton & Hafner, 1979). This seems to imply that something in these patients' marriages was a contributing factor to the agoraphobia or that the agoraphobia stabilized the marriage. Holm (1980), who treated agoraphobic inpatients and their spouses in Norway, stated that

> because an agoraphobic woman's symptoms are strongly connected to a specific homeostatic collusion pattern between her and her husband, it is essential to include the husband in treatment. It is important to stimulate his feeling of individuality and bring him to regard his wife's newly won freedom positively. The individuation process is important for both of them; it also helps keep the marriage from being destroyed. Many of the patients who relapse do so because the husband has a difficult time accepting a symptom-free, mature, independent, active, and lively woman. (p. 117)

However, more recent studies have shown that successful treatment has little or no negative impact on spouses and, in fact, leads to more marital happiness (Himaldi, Cerny, Barlow, Cohen, & O'Brien, 1986).

Overall, in my clinical experience, "simple" agoraphobia cases improve with either no spouse or family involvement, or accompanied by the use of a basic strategy of educating the spouse/family members about the nature of the symptoms and how to help with the recovery. In addition, some conjoint sessions to clarify and resolve some of the misunderstandings, fears, guilt, or resentment can be helpful. However, more intense, focused marital or family therapy usually is not essential. In the complex type of agoraphobia, not only is education/information necessary, but ongoing marital or family therapy is vital to understand how the interpersonal relationships may have contributed to the patient becoming agoraphobic and to resolve these issues, if possible.

Studies regarding treatment outcome of agoraphobics reveal a mixed picture of results. There is little evidence that treatment negatively impacts the marital relationship (Carter, Turovsky, & Barlow, 1994). In fact, most investigations have found that the interpersonal relationships of agoraphobics generally remained unchanged after treatment. According to Carter and coworkers, only seven investigations have been done to examine the impact of couple's therapy on the overall treatment of agoraphobia. They state that although

> spousal involvement clearly does not detract from treatment, available studies offer contradictory results as to its effectiveness—considering the importance assigned to so-called faulty interpersonal relationships, it is surprising that none of the studies to date has clearly explicated a specific dysfunctional interpersonal pattern, its relationship to agoraphobia, or its impact on the syndrome. (p. 28)

In summary, although clinicians typically have believed that agoraphobics have or develop significant interpersonal problems that affect the couple or family, there has been a paucity of research to demonstrate what specific interpersonal dynamics play a key role or what type of treatment methods are appropriate and effective. Based on extensive clinical experience and perusal of the literature, I believe that methods ranging from psychoeducation, to intensive marital or family therapy are appropriate and depend on the type of agoraphobia present and the severity and chronicity of the dysfunction. That is, the more acute onset and less severe types can be treated with either no spousal or family involvement or with psychoeducation and/or support groups. Along with Holm (1980), I have found that more severe and chronic types of agoraphobia will require more exploratory and intensive forms of marital or family psychotherapy, so family members can deal with their reactions to the malady and change their perception and actions as the symptomatology abates.

Obsessive-Compulsive Disorder (OCD)

Individuals with OCD are bothered by persistent and recurring thoughts or "obsessions" that are very disturbing. Obsessions are defined by the following:

1. Recurrent and persistent thoughts, impulses, or images that are experienced, at some time during the disturbance, as intrusive and inappropriate and that can cause marked anxiety or distress.
2. The thoughts, impulses, or images are not simply excessive worries about real-life problems.
3. The person attempts to ignore or suppress such thoughts, impulses, or images, or to neutralize them with some other thought or action.
4. The person recognizes that the obsessional thoughts, impulses, or images are a product of his or her own mind (not imposed from without as in thought insertion).

These bad thoughts usually are reflective of some exaggerated anxiety or fears that are not based on objective reality. These individuals have severe and constant doubts about their behavior and usually seek reassurance from others. For example, a common obsession relates to a fear of contamination. Such people constantly worry that they will either be contaminated by or will contaminate someone else with some bodily secretion or some chemical. Often people with obsessions feel compelled to perform some ritual to relieve the anxiety caused by the obsession. For example, a person with "contamination" obsession may compulsively wash his hands or go around the house washing everything that he has touched or spraying all with Lysol. Although the person realizes that the obsession and compulsion make no sense, he cannot stop. Compulsions are defined by:

1. Repetitive behaviors (hand washing, watering, checking) or mental acts (praying, counting, repeating words silently) that the person feels driven to perform in response to an obsession or according to rules that must be applied rigidly.
2. The behaviors or mental acts are aimed at preventing or reducing the stress or preventing some dreaded event or situation; however, these behaviors or mental acts either are not connected in a realistic way with what they are designed to neutralize or prevent or clearly are excessive.

Recent evidence suggests that biological factors may contribute to the development of OCD, although previously it was believed to be caused by family attitudes and experiences (Rappaport, 1989). Whatever the reason, there is a clear tendency for OCD to run in families. At least 3 percent of the population, or 6 million people in the United States, suffer from OCD. Symptoms generally start during young adulthood, and women are more likely to suffer from OCD.

Today professionals who treat OCD generally accept that it is not helpful to speculate about how early childhood experiences or parental attitudes may have contributed to a patient's OCD. For many years, OCD patients were treated with analytic or psychodynamic psychotherapy, the goal being either to uncover an early trauma that led to the patient's fixation (OCD) or to better understand how the patient's family dynamics or individual psychodynamics created the symptom complex. Many patients spent years in these types of traditional treatment and either failed to improve or became worse.

Today, the standard treatment for OCD patients is either behavior/cognitive therapy and/or psychopharmacology. A fair amount of debate exists as to which modality is more effective. While this debate rages on, clinicians often neglect the issue of the effects that OCD has on the interpersonal system. For example, a patient who is afraid to touch his wife because he might contaminate her comes to a clinician's office for treatment. Some psychiatrists would advocate the use of Anafranil (clomipramine); psychologists might try behavior therapy; but neither one might also consider some sort of spousal involvement. In this case, it seems obvious that all clinicians, regardless of their discipline, should involve the spouse at least to gain some information and educate her about OCD and its treatment.

Actually, it would seem that some couple's therapy would be needed to deal with either their premorbid relationship or with the effects that this obsession has had on them. Unfortunately, usually this important component of treatment is omitted. Also unfortunate is the fact that very little research has been done thus far to examine the effects that spousal/family treatment has on the primary treatment of the OCD patient. Since OCD is such a chronic and often debilitating illness, and since it can have such a dramatic impact on the family, significant others should be involved in treatment routinely. Depending on the symptoms manifested by the OCD patient, the spouse or family members' lives are clearly affected.

If the OCD patient is a "checker," the spouse or family may need to wait an extra hour before they can leave for a day at the park or a visit to friends, while the patient is checking all of the light switches. A compulsive washer may not be able to stay in the family room or at the dinner table for more than five minutes between each washing. The hoarder may refuse to let anyone throw out any newspapers, or even the garbage, without at least checking to see if anything was too important to let go of. The patient who is afraid of illnesses spread by blood from chicken or meat may refuse to buy this food and cause everyone in the family to become vegetarian. Clearly then, OCD symptoms typically strain and at times even destroy marital and family relationships. Family members need to be educated, enabled to deal with the patient in a helpful, even therapeutic way, and helped to vent and resolve their own frustrations and resentments. Marriage and family therapy, and/or support groups for family members, are extremely important in resolving rather than perpetuating these issues.

Social Phobia

Marks and Gelder (1966) described a syndrome in which a person becomes very anxious in situations where he or she may be under the scrutiny of others while performing a task. Examples of this are public speaking, eating in public, or urinating in public bathrooms. The key factor is that the patient has a problem only when others are watching, but not in private when doing the same thing. This concept was developed further by other clinicians and offered as an official diagnosis in DSM-III (APA, 1980). Currently, clinicians are expanding the concept of social phobia and proposing that certain other behavioral problems or disorders be considered as social phobias. For example, Barlow (1988) has suggested that sexual dysfunction, particularly erectile dysfunction, is simply another social phobia. "As with urinating in public or throwing a baseball to first base, sexually dysfunctional individuals perform flawlessly in private (solitary masturbation) but their performance deteriorates rapidly in the presence of a sexual partner" (p. 535).

Whether one wants to conceptualize sexual dysfunction as a social phobia or not, it is clear that various types of social phobia can and do have a significant impact on the couple/family. For example, recently I was referred a 30-year-old married female who had "panic attacks" and fears of swallowing her food. As a result, she was having difficulty eating and had begun to avoid eating in restaurants with her husband and friends. Her husband had become increasingly upset and angry with her because he enjoyed dining in fine restaurants and his business success partially depended on taking clients out to dinner. Her fears of eating in public were based on her extreme self-consciousness and concern about others watching her while she ate. She was so apprehensive that she created her own symptoms of swallowing difficulty. Her husband became more irate and intolerant and began to criticize her openly in front of other people, which caused her to want to avoid restaurants further. This example of social phobia clearly demonstrates how the syndrome can have an impact on the couple and how the way in which the spouse deals with it can either help or cause a worsening not only of the social phobic symptoms but also of the marital relationship. This example and the sexual dysfunction illustration clearly point out the need to consider spousal involvement in the treatment of certain types of social phobia.

Treatments of choice basically fall into two types. The first type involves educating the spouse about social phobia and helping him or her help the patient with cognitive and behavioral treatment techniques and goals. For example, in the case of the woman who avoided eating in restaurants, the husband was brought into sessions to help him help her confront her negative self-statements about eating in front of others and to help her gradually go to restaurants, first just with him, then with friends, and finally with business acquaintances. The second modality of treatment involves a more psychotherapeutic intervention in which the husband was helped to express his resentment toward her in a healthier way and she was able to express how she resented always having to "perform" for him and her fear that she would embarrass him.

These two "modalities" of couple's treatment generally are adequate in helping facilitate the individual treatment of the social phobic and to improve the relational aspects as well (Barlow, 1988).

Generalized Anxiety Disorder (GAD)

Generalized anxiety disorder is based on a person's unrealistic or excessive anxiety and worry (apprehensive expectations) about two or more life circumstances—for example, worry about something bad happening to one's child (when there is no danger) or worry about finances (no obvious reason) for a period of six months or longer during which the patient is bothered by these concerns more days than not. Various symptoms are present involving motor tension, autonomic hyperactivity, and vigilance and scanning. Prevalence ranges from 2.5 percent (Anderson, Noyes, & Crowe, 1984) to 4 percent (Barrett, 1981). Most clinicians speak of the GAD patient as the classic "worrier" in that these patients seem to worry about everything. Depending on the severity of their apprehensive expectations, their worrying often significantly interferes with their lives or diminishes their happiness. For instance, a mother who is always worrying that some accident might happen to her child will spend her day, while her daughter is enjoying day camp, anxious and under stress. The only positive emotion she may feel all day is the relief that she experiences when her daughter steps off the bus, unharmed. Similarly, the man who is excessively worried about finances, even when there is no realistic reason, may experience little enjoyment or satisfaction from his financial success and actually be unhappy when he purchases something for his wife or children. In fact, his worry about spending money may not only cause him to be unhappy, but he also may convey to his family that they are causing him "pain" for wanting something that costs money.

These common GAD scenarios clearly demonstrate that the disorder has an impact on family members. The child of the worried mother may feel her mother's unhappiness when going off to camp and, in the long run, may develop either guilt about leaving her mother to engage in normal childhood experiences or may learn to be fearful of harm when there is no real reason for this apprehensiveness. The man who worries excessively about finances may spoil his family's joyful experiences and create a depressive environment in the home, at a time when happiness should be expected.

As with the other types of anxiety disorders, professionals who treat generalized anxiety disorders typically focus on the identified patient and treat him or her with either medication or psychotherapy. I included the two scenarios to stress the negative impact that the GAD patient's worry and behavior can have on the family members and to emphasize the need for treatment of the couple/family's interactive relational systemic issues. Family members should be included in sessions with the GAD patient in order to help them verbalize the feelings and experiences that have accumulated as a result of the patient's behavior. Not only will this enable family members to express and relieve their resentments, but it also will help participants realize how the GAD has affected everyone in a gradual, subtle way. Only then can everyone become involved in supporting one other in changing.

Post-Traumatic Stress Disorder (PTSD)

People who suffer from post-traumatic stress disorder (PTSD) have experienced a traumatic event that is usually outside the range of normal human experience. Victims experience anxiety characterized by increased autonomic activity and cognitive dysfunctions such as loss of concentration and increase in memory problems. In addition, reexperiencing of the traumatic event and a numbing of emotional responsiveness occur. Traumatic events may range from experiences in war (Figley, 1978), to serious injuries from auto accidents, natural disasters (e.g., earthquakes and hurricanes), physical assault (rape and other physical violence), or death of a loved one. Why some people develop PTSD and others do not even when they are involved in the same traumatic events is not yet understood.

The effect that PTSD has on an individual and his or her spouse and family can be devastating. Two cases that I have treated demonstrate how suddenly a family's stability and psychosocial existence can be destroyed and how the interpersonal aspect is so critical in treating PTSD. The first case involved a 40-year-old man who was a very successful professional and a wonderful husband and father. He was actively involved with his children, especially with sports, as he was a physically active man. One day he suffered a broken back and severe internal injuries during the crash of a small plane. Although he survived, he had severe chronic pain, needed metal rods through his shattered spine, and was beset by various other problems that required long-term rehabilitation. He came to me for treatment because he was having severe symptoms of PTSD, including depression, anxiety, flashbacks, insomnia, irritability, and suicidal thoughts. Financial problems evolved because he could not work, and within a few months marital conflicts developed. He and his wife argued about finances, who should pay what bill, children, friends, and other things. He lost his patience with the children and began to fight with his wife, complaining that she was not taking care of things. Within six months, he was considering separation and was not on speaking terms with his teenage son.

Clearly, the stress on all family members was causing a severe deterioration in their relationships; family treatment was initiated. Both problem solving (Epstein & Bishop, 1981; Haley, 1976) and expression of feelings (Satir, 1988) were an integral part in the treatment. As family treatment helped resolve issues they had with each other, the PTSD patient was able to focus more on his recovery, and he made significantly better progress.

The second case involved a woman who was just entering her apartment when she was accosted by two men, tied up, and beaten. Although they did not rape her, they repeatedly threatened to do so. Two months later she was suffering from multiple PTSD symptoms and came to me for treatment. She reported that one of the problems she was having was severe self-doubt and blame, partially because her husband was very critical of her for not noticing that these men had been following her and "How could she have been so blind?" He blamed her for other things, such as wearing flashy jewelry and for being "naive." In order for her PTSD treatment to begin, it was imperative to consider the relational aspect of the diagnosis; in treatment I attempted to help the husband alter his perception of what had happened and realize that he was blaming the victim and that he should stop doing so; I also helped the wife express her resentment toward him for his hypercritical attitude and behavior. In my opinion, if her husband had not been included in the treatment, the patient's PTSD would have worsened despite her individual treatment. In the treatment of PTSD, the clinician needs to be very much aware of such relational issues and how sudden and destructive the PTSD can be on the couple or family.

CONCLUSION

Many advances have been made in recent years in the understanding and treatment of anxiety disorders (Oakley & Padesky, 1990). We have gone from the general term "anxiety neurosis" to specifying various types of anxiety disorders. A better understanding of the biopsychosocial aspects of anxiety disorders and methods for treating these aspects have evolved. In general, cognitive-behavior therapy and/or psychopharmacology are the standard recommended treatment methods. Recently a greater interest in the relational aspects of anxiety disorders has taken place. This chapter has urged clinicians to assess the impact the patient's anxiety disorder has had or is having on the relational aspects of his or her life and to take an aggressive approach in treating the couple or family when working with the anxiety-disordered patient. It is my contention that if clinicians more routinely involved the spouse/family members in treatment, better treatment results would be achieved.

REFERENCES

American Psychiatric Association (1980). *Diagnostic and statistical manual of mental disorders,* (3rd ed.). Washington, DC: Author.

American Psychiatric Association (1994). *Diagnostic and statistical manual of mental disorders,* (4th ed.). Washington, DC: Author.

Anderson, D. J., Noyes, R., Jr., & Crowe, R. R. (1984). A comparison of panic disorder and generalized anxiety disorder. *American Journal of Psychiatry, 141,* 572–575.

Anxiety Disorders Association of America (1991). *Obsessive-compulsive disorder.* Rockville, MD: Author.

Arnow, B. A., Taylor, C. D., Agras, W. S., & Telch, M. J. (1985). Enhancing agoraphobia treatment outcome by changing couple communication patterns. *Behavior Therapy, 16,* 452–467.

Barlow, D. H. (1988). *Anxiety and its disorders.* New York: Gilford.

Barrett, D. (1981). Psychiatric diagnoses (research diagnostic criteria) in symptomatic volunteers. *Archives of General Psychiatry, 49,* 448–454.

Carter, M. M., Turovsky, J., & Barlow, D. H. (1994). Interpersonal relationships in panic disorders with agoraphobia: A review of empirical evidence. *Clinical Psychology: Science and Practice, 1,* 5–33.

Epstein, N. B., & Bishop, D. S. (1981). "Problem centered systems therapy of the family." In A. S. Gurman & D. P. Kniskern (Eds.), *Handbook of family therapy.* New York: Brunner/Mazel.

Figley, C. R. (Ed.). (1978). *Stress disorders among Vietnam veterans: Theory, research and treatment.* New York: Brunner/Mazel.

Goldstein, A. J. (1970). Case conference: Some aspects of agoraphobia. *Journal of Behavior Therapy and Experimental Psychiatry, 1,* 305–313.

Goldstein, A. J., & Chambliss, D. L. (1978). A re-analysis of agoraphobia. *Behavior Therapy, 9,* 47–59.

Hafner, R. J. (1976). Fresh symptom emergence after intensive behavior therapy. *British Journal of Psychiatry, 129,* 378–383.

Hafner, R. J. (1977). The husbands of agoraphobic women and their influence on treatment outcome. *British Journal of Psychiatry, 131,* 289–294.

Haley, J. (1976). *Problem solving therapy.* San Francisco: Jossey-Bass.

Himaldi, W. G., Cerny, J. A., Barlow, D. H., Cohen, S. L., & O'Brien, G. T. (1986). The relationship of marital adjustment to agoraphobic treatment outcome. *Behavior Research and Therapy, 24,* 107–115.

Holm, H. J. (1980). The agoraphobic married woman and her marriage pattern: A clinical study. *Fokus Pa Familien* [Norwegian Journal for Family Therapy], *3,* 106–119.

Klein, D. F., Zitrin, C. M., Woerner, M. G., & Ross, D. C. (1983). Treatment of phobias II. Behavior therapy and supportive psychotherapy: Are there any specific ingredients? *Archives of General Psychiatry, 40,* 139–145.

Lazarus, R. S. (1966). Behavior rehearsal vs. non-directed therapy vs. advise in effecting behavior change. *Behavior Research and Therapy, 4,* 209–212.

Marks, I. M., & Gelder, M. G. (1966). Different ages of onset in varieties of phobias. *American Journal of Psychiatry, 123,* 218–221.

Marsland, D. W., Wood, M., & Mayo, F. (1976). Content of family practice: The data bank for patient care, curriculum and research in family practice—patient problems. *Journal of Family Practice, 3,* 25–68.

May, R. (1979). *The meaning of anxiety.* New York: Washington Square Press.

Milton, F., & Hafner, J. (1979). The outcome of behavior therapy for agoraphobia in relation to marital adjustment. *Archives of General Psychiatry, 36,* 807–811.

Myers, J. K., Weissman, M. M., Tischler, C. E., Holzer, C. E., III, Anthony, J. C., Boyd, J. H., Burke, J. D., Jr., Kramer, M., & Stoltzman, R. (1984). Six-month prevalence of psychiatric disorders in three communities. *Archives of General Psychiatry, 41,* 959–967.

Oakley, M. E., & Padesky, C. A. (1990). Cognitive therapy for anxiety disorders. In M. Hersen, R. M. Esler, & P. M. Miller (Eds.), *Progress in behavior modification* (vol. 25, pp. 12–46). Newbury Park, CA: Sage.

Rappaport, J. L. (1989). *The boy who couldn't stop washing.* New York: E. P. Dutton.

Satir, V. (1988). *The new peoplemaking.* Palo Alto, CA: Science and Behavior Books.

Sheehan, D. V., Ballanger, J., & Jacobsen, G. (1980). Treatment of endogenous anxiety with phobic, hysterical and hypochondriacal symptoms. *Archives of General Psychiatry, 37,* 51–59.

CHAPTER 17

Understanding and Treating Couples with Borderline Disorders

MARION F. SOLOMON, PhD

Understanding the dynamics of borderline disorders and appreciating their effects on interactions between partners can lend a new perspective to the treatment of marital and family conflicts. As we witness growing numbers of people seeking therapy for relationship problems (Sager, Gundlach, & Kremer, 1968), alternative insights and interpretations gain increasing importance. Psychoanalytic literature has correlated early bonding failures with developmental disturbances in relationship patterns enduring into adulthood (Kernberg, 1975; Kohut, 1971, 1977; Masterson, 1981; Scharff & Scharff, 1987; Stern, 1985). These failures may be the product of biological or temperamental deficits that require particularly skillful parenting to overcome, or they may be caused by parents who are themselves dysfunctional. In both cases, the resulting defenses can lead to borderline pathology and a history of problematic relationships. Methods of marital therapy are available for treating both the borderline condition and relationship difficulties that accompany it.

THE BORDERLINE PROFILE

Various forms of borderline pathology are engendered by an accumulation of early experiences that were too painful or too fearful to allow into consciousness. The result of these intolerable experiences is typically twofold: Internally, there is a splitting off of feelings, perceptions, and fantasies; externally, there is a distancing from whatever caused the painful exposure to needs. The essential feature of borderline disorders is a pattern of instability that pervades self-image, mood, and interpersonal relationships beginning by early adulthood and present in a variety of context (Grotstein, Solomon, & Lang, 1985). Often there is an extensive identity disturbance manifested by uncertainty in regard to major life areas, such as long-term goals, career choice, types of friends or lovers, values and principles, and even sexual orientation. Patients often report erratic mood swings in their work and school experiences and many difficulties in familial and social relationships.

Extremely vulnerable borderlines often feel that they are unable to protect themselves from stress or intrusions—in essence, they are hypersensitive and "thin-skinned." As a result of early intrusions by significant others, they feel poorly defended, fully exposed to anyone who chooses to glance their way. They have a high need for an affirming bond with another, along with low frustration tolerance and a proneness to shame and guilt (Lansky, 1993). They may protect themselves against intolerable internal chaos by deadening their emotions or by rageful "dumping."

In therapy, some borderlines deny any awareness of feelings and report a chronic sense of emptiness or boredom. Others evidence a limited range of feelings that includes anger, rage, and/or fury. Some borderline patients maintain a rational, pleasant demeanor and then lash out unexpectedly when an apparently innocuous remark touches an internal wound. Indeed, the therapeutic relationship is often stormy. Therapists are likely to be devalued, at the very least, or therapy terminated abruptly. More often, therapists are confronted by a barrage of difficult behaviors, to which they will have strong countertransference reactions.

The tragedy of these individuals is that although they need so much from others, they are unable to internalize what they receive and often sabotage their relationships when the desired empathy triggers fear rather than comfort. Borderline individuals have never achieved a satisfactory experience of drawing emotional sustenance from others; they are like atoms floating alone in space, constantly trying to connect with someone or something in order to feel grounded and whole. They may try using computers, cars, or houses to fill their emotional vacuity. Severe impulsive behaviors, including suicide attempts, eating disorders, alcohol or drug abuse, sexual promiscuity or perversions, reckless driving, compulsive shopping sprees, and shoplifting may be symptomatic of borderline states.

Interpersonal relationships are usually very important to persons with borderline disorders, because they fear loneliness and feel frantic if they experience abandonment, whether real or imagined. Despite the importance of relationships, however, unstable and intense reactions repeatedly threaten interpersonal connection, as extremes of idealization alternate with disappointment, anger, and devaluation. Borderline individuals often "set up" interpersonal situations to provoke outcomes that confirm their worst fears. They select partners and maintain relationships that are filled with emotional volatility. If the relationship is calm because the significant other will not engage in combat, they do all they can to churn up a crisis. In more severe forms of the borderline disorder, relationships are intense and chaotic—experienced as very painful to both partners and likely to end abruptly, often following substance abuse, sexual abuse, sexual addiction, or violence.

In less severe forms of the disorder, relationships have both strengths and vulnerabilities, and couples may be helped through conjoint treatment. In these relationships, disagreements serve as opportunities to replay pervasive feelings of anger, blame, and vindictiveness. The overt arguments serve as justifications for covert defensive operations that are in place to cope with expected disappointment and abandonment by others.

In response to criticism or intrusiveness by partners, people with such underlying fragility may react with humiliation followed by rage and acting out. Often they can mask these feelings with an aura of cool indifference until something jars their emotional stability. They then defend themselves through verbal or physical aggression, and afterward behave as if the emotional outburst had never occurred. They generally refuse to discuss the incident, expecting the relationship to continue as it was. Partners, friends, and coworkers may find this pattern unnerving. Left with intense reactions, they must withhold expressing their feelings for fear of recreating the emotional outburst or being punished in some way. Thus, relationships in which borderline defensive patterns are pervasive tend to be shallow, distant, self-protective, with general feelings of depression and worthlessness prevailing on both sides.

THE FIRST RELATIONSHIP AS A PROTOTYPE

Each relationship throughout life carries the remnants of earlier interactions. Sander (1987) notes that it is the infant-caregiver system that regulates and organizes the infant's experience of inner states. The development of relationship competencies is therefore a systems competence. Stern (1985) identifies various senses of self from the child's interactions with "self regulating others." Consequently, the relationship with the earliest caregiver establishes patterns that are reenacted in all subsequent relationships. Consider the following case history drawn from my book, *Lean on Me* (1994).

Case History

Ernest was not an easy baby. Highly sensitive to noise, to light, and to being touched, he cried a lot and slept little. He was the fourth of four boys and his parents were beside themselves trying to care for this demanding baby, so different from his brothers. Ernest reacted to almost any stimulation, however nurturing, as an impingement. His mother, despite tending to three older children, offered her child a great deal. She was considered a "natural" at mothering by her family and friends. But no matter how she tried to comfort him, he would cry or push her away.

When a baby like Ernest—a child with special problems—enters the world and the parents do not have the emotional wherewithal to meet all the child's needs, the child's view of his place in the world is dramatically impacted. Such babies apparently experience life as painful. They hurt too much or experience too much sensory overload to be comfortable with the nurturing and caretaking extended to them. Still, these children need to be held and rocked gently, even though they appear unresponsive to the ministrations of their parents.

For adults with this kind of history, bonding in intimate relationships is never easy, just as bonding in infancy was not easy. An ever-present pull toward merger is countered by an ever-present retreat from it. Ernest, for example, handled his strong dependency needs as an adult by finding others who needed him, doing things for them, and making them dependent on him. Although he gives generously to his friends and business associates, he does not trust them and is not able to accept support from them. Because of his early bonding failures, Ernest does not believe that anyone can love him for himself. If a woman is interested in him, it must be for his money or social position. He has not yet healed the wounds from his early experiences. It is extremely difficult for him to maintain a close relationship because of this, even though this is what he wants more than anything.

Ernest's case demonstrates that a failure at the time of primary bonding can result in a lifelong inability to trust or to depend on others. When normal bonding needs are met, remnants of each painful conflict and discomfort do not remain as hindrances in future relationships. Regardless of the success of early bonding, the core need to be united with another human being remains with us as part of our makeup as adults. Problems arise when borderline defenses erupt in times of high stress or when the objects of affection or of narcissistic supplies are absent or insecurely attached.

Individual psychic life originates in an interactional field of infant and mother. Because the core self derives from each person's history of intersubjective transactions, the concept of an isolated individual mind is a theoretical fiction (Stolorow & Atwood, 1992). The internal experience of being differentiated is embedded in a living system (Sander, 1985). As a result, individual experience always manifests itself in relationships to others. In the earliest representations shared by mother and infant, what is represented are structures of interaction, "an emergent dyadic phenomenon" (Stolorow & Atwood, 1992), which cannot be described on the basis of either partner alone.

FUNCTION OF REPRESENTATIONAL MODELS IN ADULT RELATIONSHIPS

From this discussion, we can see how the ways in which partners interpret behaviors and respond to one another is historically conditioned. The internal representations the person brings into a relationship are central in giving meaning to the relational experience. Individuals work hard to maintain and defend their preexisting models, which organize expectations, interpretations, and response patterns. The need of individuals to preserve the representational model strongly conditions every relationship into which the individual enters. Two people will not form a relationship unless the partnership appears—at least initially—to preserve an internal structure that for each of them recalls experiences that are familiar.

Individuals with complementary patterns often marry (Bowen, 1978; Gurman, 1978; Solomon, 1989). After a period of time together, an unconscious fusion can form, with each partner in a relationship fitting into the others' patterns of expectations. In this situation, the internal representations of each partner, although separate, become so interlinked that any aspect of one implies a reciprocal aspect in the other. Consequently marital therapy helps the couple break the fusion that underlies the frozen complementarity. Breaking this fusion requires a profound understanding of its intrapsychic and relational aspects.

To feel secure with a stable, supportive other is a basic need of the infant. Where the other is chronically unavailable, or when life events cause a premature separation, there may be a persistent search for security or a tendency to discard intolerable feelings. Early experiences of terror or danger from loss of security may cause emotions to be split off and transferred outside the self. The borderline patient searches throughout life for another to become the container of intolerable affects.

Babies whose needs are not met emotionally often block out the reality of others. They live in a world designed by themselves, viewing all situations according to their own internal arrangement. They grow up and enter relationships with the expectation that others think and feel as they do.

MAKING A DIAGNOSIS

Borderline has been described as a state, a trait, a condition, a disorder, and a discreet diagnostic category. Grotstein (personal communication) describes "four borders" to the borderline: "On the north is the neurotic border (i.e., obsessional, hysterical), on the south the psychotic border (i.e., severe personality disorder, schizotypal); on the east is the psychosomatic border (what the mind cannot think, the body experiences), and on the west the alexithymic border (an inability to put words to emotions)." Grinker (1977) similarly identifies four borderline subtypes: the psychotic borderline, who engages in inappropriate, nonadaptive behavior, and whose deficient self-identity and reality leads to expressions of anger, negative behavior, and depression; the core borderline, who vacillates in involvement with others, acting out anger, depression, and inconsistent self-identity; those individuals whose adaptive affectedness is characterized by appropriate surface behavior, complementary relationships, and little demonstration of affect or spontaneity; and those whose borders with the neuroses imply anaclyctic depression, anxiety, and whose symptoms closely resemble neurotic, narcissistic disorders.

The problem is exacerbated by the various definitions of the terms and differing treatments for borderline and related narcissistic disorders. Kernberg (1975) suggests supportive psychotherapy rather than analysis for borderlines. Kohut (1977) contends that borderline individuals are unanalyzable, while those with narcissistic pathology can be analyzed. He made a clear distinction between narcissistic and borderline patients, believing the latter too disturbed to benefit from his model of self-psychology. This assumption has been challenged by intersubjective psychologists (Stolorow, Brandchaft, & Atwood, 1987). Increasingly, the two disorders—narcissistic and borderline—are viewed as closely related, and there is now some question as to which is more severe (Grotstein, 1981, 1985; Masterson, 1985). In treating couples, the differentiation between borderlines and other personality disorders is even less clear than it is in individual treatment.

Gunderson, in his description of borderline pathology, identifies it as a discrete category with seven identifying factors (1985). The diagnostic signs include low achievement, impulsivity, manipulative suicide attempts, heightened affectivity, mild psychotic experiences, high socialization, as well as disturbed close relationships and destructive, critical qualities.

According to DSM-IV (APA, 1994), in borderline personality there is a pervasive pattern of instability of self-image, interpersonal relationships, and mood, beginning by early adulthood and present a variety of contexts. There is also a marked and persistent identity disturbance, manifested by uncertainty about several life issues, such as self-image, sexual orientation, long-term goals or career choice, types of friends or lovers to have, or which values to adopt. In addition, persons with borderline disorders experience an instability of self-image and chronic feelings of emptiness or boredom. These persons have a high degree of need for others but generally have interpersonal relationships with fluctuating patterns of closeness and upset with others, characterized by extremes of overidealization and devaluation. They have difficulty tolerating being alone, demand the other's presence, and feel chaotic and sometimes violent when the other withdraws. They often make frantic efforts to avoid real or imagined abandonment.

DSM-IV states that emotional instability among borderlines is common, with marked mood shifts from baseline mood to depression, irritability, or anxiety that can last for minutes, hours or even days. Those with borderline personality disorder (BPD) often display inappropriately intense anger or lack of control of their anger; they have frequent bouts of temper, resulting sometimes in physical fights. The problems are marked by impulsive behavior that may be self-damaging, such as shopping sprees, substance abuse, reckless driving, casual sex, shoplifting, and binge eating. There may be recurrent suicidal threats or gestures, and other self-mutilating behavior (e.g., wrist-scratching) in the more severe forms of the disorder. This behavior may serve to manipulate others, may be a result of intense anger, or may counteract feelings of "numbness" and depersonalization that arise during periods of extreme stress.

Quite often, social contrariness and a generally pessimistic outlook also are observed. Alternation between dependency and self-assertion is common. During periods of great stress, transient psychotic symptoms may occur, but they are generally of insufficient severity or duration to warrant an additional diagnosis of psychosis. People who are prone to borderline defenses also may manifest many narcissistic features. In fact, there is considerable diagnostic overlap in the DSM-IV; associated features of borderline personality disorders include histrionic, narcissistic, and antisocial personality disorders, and in many cases, more than one diagnosis is warranted. A narcissistic subcategory of the borderline disorder can be identified by a grandiose sense of self-importance with an underlying sense of worthlessness (Kernberg, 1975; Stone, 1980). There is a hypersensitivity to the judgments of others, a lack of empathy that is present in a variety of interpersonal contexts, and a pervasive pattern of grandiosity in fantasy or actual behavior that sometimes leads to extraordinary feats of heroism and, occasionally, risky but surprisingly successful endeavors.

MARRIAGE ORGANIZED AROUND PROTECTION OF A VULNERABLE SELF

All marriages bring out infantile feelings. Marriage is the nearest adult equivalent of the bonds between baby and caregiver (Dicks, 1967). Happy marriages allow freedom for deeply repressed feelings to be conveyed without loss of dignity or security (Nadelson & Paolino, 1978). Conversely, in troubled marriages, both the need to express repressed infantile feelings and the awareness that such expression is likely to result in harmful interactions cause regression and defensive reactions. In marriages hampered by borderline defenses, disagreements serve as opportunities to vent repressed infantile rage and vengefulness in the form of blame. The manifest issues serve as justification for primitive defensive operations that bring to the forefront fear of abandonment, of disappointment, and of not being cared for. Demands and a sense of entitlement pervade vulnerable marriages because omnipotent expectations can never be fulfilled.

Marriages in which at least one partner has borderline features are organized around the containment and expression of massive fury and fear and around the collusive exchange of projective defenses that ward off debilitating anxiety and fragmentation experiences. The result is that both members of the couple may be constantly preoccupied with holding themselves together, especially in intimate situations. Feelings of emptiness, futility, depression, and rage abound.

Treating relationship disturbances requires an understanding of the core issues and internal representations of each partner as well as a grasp of the multilevel communications that underlie interactions and intense affect at work when a couple is in a high-stress situation. By having the couple come together from the first session, it is possible to begin to untangle the joint self of the relationship and to clarify the contribution of each partner to the marital collusion. "Cross-complaining" couples defend themselves by attacking each other. Both come into therapy hoping that the therapist will perceive the situation and "straighten out" the partner. Underneath this facade of rationality is often a frightened child expecting to be blamed and attacked.

Those who have done couple's therapy are well aware of the "stubbornness" of the symptomatology that plays itself out in the field of the relationship. Couples generally seek therapy when enmeshed in repetitive, bewildering, painful patterns of interaction. Although some couples leave the sessions and continue the work that emerges in the therapy, others use the therapy sessions as the only safe place to talk about "dangerous" subjects. Some never talk about the sessions at all from one week to the next. Still others use the sessions and their aftermath to play out core issues of jealousy, competitiveness, control, distancing, enmeshment, discounting, or emotional battering. The therapist must be aware of the transferences between partners as well as transference reactions to him or her. The status of these representations determines whether the participants view the therapeutic setting as a safe holding environment for containment and detoxification of projections or as a dangerous territory in which shameful or humiliating feelings will emerge; in the latter case, blame and attack will be the response to their needy, undefended selves. Often they attack the partner in a preemptive bid to avoid anticipated injury by the other.

Identifying Characteristics in Treatment

When couples enter marital therapy, they often begin with a presenting problem that centers around specific issues, such as money or sex. An interactional pattern emerges in the treatment process often representing a collusion between partners. Dicks (1967) described series of presenting patterns of interaction:

1. One of the partners is dominant and aggressive; the other submissive and masochistic.
2. One of the partners is emotionally detached; the other craves affection.
3. There is continuous rivalry between the partners for aggressive dominance.
4. One of the partners is helpless, craving dependency from omnipotent mate; the mate is endlessly supportive.
5. One of the mates alternates between periods of dependency and self-assertion; the other between periods of helpfulness and unsatisfied need for affection. (p. 221)

Destructive Collusions

When both partners have a history of early emotional injury and strong narcissistic defenses, their relationship becomes a collusive means for protecting themselves and each other. A collusion is an unspoken agreement to maintain the consistency of each partner's perceptions. Because of this covert agreement, neither partner is forced to deal with overwhelming negative feelings or extreme conflict. Hiding emotional problems from themselves and each other, the partners create a joyless pretense of safety and security, not a true haven of comfort and love. In this way, one or both partners temporarily may avoid dealing with a serious problem. Instead of helping each other grow and mature, each may use the other to reinforce a distorted view of reality. The collusive contract is maintained because each partner needs to keep destructive forces at bay. Instead of changing and adapting, the relationship relies on static or regressive defensive strategies (Lansky, 1981).

Some relationships contain unrecognized fears left over from infancy, such as fear of abandonment or the terror of destructive fantasies. Partners develop a pattern of interacting based on projecting their doubts and fears onto each other. When difficulties arise, each partner sees the problem as coming from the other. Should their defensive arrangement falter, the vulnerable partner may become irrational, demanding attention or justice with a rage that goes beyond the immediate issues.

In such relationships, communication is not viewed as a way to improve a problematic situation but as a danger that might expose underlying fears of falling apart and being humiliated (Lansky, 1981). Both partners may think of the relationship as a disaster. They conspire, however, to maintain the discomfort by keeping true communication at a minimum. Through years, even decades, of unremitting misery, these collusive, conflictual relationships endure.

INABILITY TO INTEGRATE EMOTIONS

Feelings of intimacy, including tenderness and concern about the welfare and personal growth of a partner, regularly coexist with lustful feelings in those who have the capacity to integrate these strong emotions (Stone, 1980). In people with borderline personality disorders, this capacity to integrate is lacking or enfeebled. This may be because a person who develops such defenses was reared in an environment where there were striking inconsistencies and insufficiencies in the parents' ability to love. In addition, the developing child had no imprint—no pattern for mature integrated loving—to be drawn upon and utilized later. As a result, when we examine the pseudointimate relationships of borderlines, we may find sex unaccompanied by love, or sex and love combined in a way that seems immature: a stifling and possessive or symbiotic partnership, rather than a sexual love between two people who respect and foster each other's needs for continued individuation and evolution (Stone, 1980).

Alongside a low self-image, especially among those who have experienced incest or overt seductiveness within the family, there is a tendency toward sensation seeking. Alternating reactions of idealization and intense need for connection are intertwined with contempt and hatred from feeling misused. Acting-out sexually can make this a self-fulfilling prophecy. This provides a sense of relating without being involved fully in a relationship. Sexuality is marred by borderline defenses, not only by the rapid changing of partners to enhance sexual excitement, but also by a drivenness and impersonality. The combination of loneliness, hunger for attention, indifference to social conventions, and impulsivity—all common qualities in borderline disorders—are sometimes dealt with through the use of alcohol and drugs combined with sexual promiscuity.

A history of incest is not uncommon in borderline patients who appear quite disturbed (Baker-Miller, 1992). The defense patterns in the more disturbed borderlines—denial, disavowal, splitting, devaluation, idealization, and omnipotent control—resemble attitudes of people who have participated in incestuous relations (Stone, 1980). This is not surprising; patients who were subjected to the incestuous impulses of an older family member often respond with a sense of idealization, sexual excitement, and passionate infatuation with that person, at the same time experiencing feelings of contempt, revulsion, and hatred toward the same person who has taken unfair advantage and betrayed a trust. The ambivalence generally exceeds the child's coping abilities, and the resulting defenses can lead to borderline symptoms.

The early fixation of sexual interest gets played out with one partner after another—persecutors who are alternately adored and vilified. This oscillation between adoration and vilification of the other is a recognized part of splitting. In addition, these relationships produce conflicting self-images, including victim and guilty participant. The guilt at having betrayed the parent and self-blame for parental problems often is overpowering.

Love and Hate in the Borderline

Patients with an early history of disturbed relationships are likely to have extremely low self-esteem and are suspicious of the love that others claim to feel toward them, fearing that it cannot be genuine. The result is a constant need for reassurance to maintain a fragile self. Consider the following case.

Case History

Ellen, a patient molested by her uncle from age eight to age ten, was explaining to her husband and the therapist why, even four years after their marriage, she keeps testing her husband's fidelity and level of commitment. Ellen still does not believe that Alex will not abandon her. Although Alex has repeatedly assured her that his love is steadfast, Ellen continues to behave in provocative ways that arouse anger in him. She then desperately begs for forgiveness and assurance that he will not leave her. Alex says he understands and accepts, trying to reassure her even after seeing what she can do at her most difficult. She says that there can never be enough reassurance. "If you tell me at 12:30 that you will be there tomorrow, I will feel wonderful until 12:31 when I begin worrying again. I never feel sure that we have a future, that our relationship will last," she explained. Her need is bottomless.

In another couple, a husband's similar angry, disruptive pattern leads the wife, with her own narcissistic defenses, to disconnect and eventually leave the marriage.

Case History

Darrell and Jill's marriage shows the strains of protecting a fragile self with borderline defenses. In daily life, Darrell and Jill interact quite rationally, discussing their differences and solving their problems. But when Darrell undergoes stress, his unconscious, defensive behavior emerges. He can no longer communicate rationally, and he becomes almost unaware of Jill's existence. When the emotional outburst is over, he returns to normal, except he will not discuss with his wife what has happened. Jill feels more and more removed, withdrawing from her emotional investment in the relationship each time Darrell has one of his "tantrums."

There are periods when Darrell seems so calm, normal, and reasonable that Jill begins to believe that his last eruption was simply an aberration that will never occur again. It is beyond her understanding, but she has said in therapy that one day Darrell will simply snap. She knows that when that happens, she will turn Darrell "off" and leave him. She also knows that if this happens, Darrell will not understand why. Although she is completely frustrated by his inability to discuss the problem, he remains oblivious to the fragility of the situation.

Darrell's defensive maneuvers combine several processes related to borderline defenses. He splits off his rage, suppressing any memory of it to protect himself from the feeling of living with such boiling anger. When a confrontation occurs, he slips into an inability to think, attacking Jill and blaming her, with no realization of what he is doing. Outside the relationship, both partners function at a fairly mature level, because the relationship helps cover extreme dependency, low self-esteem, and general neediness.

In attacking the mate, the borderline partner really is trying to attack anything that threatens the couple's bond and the relationship's continued existence. Without realizing it, the borderline partner can destroy the relationship he or she needs so desperately and will be surprised and defensive if he or she succeeds in driving the partner away.

THERAPEUTIC GOALS

The goal of marital therapy is to produce behavioral changes in functioning within the relationship along with changes inside the partners. An insight-oriented model involving interpretation of feedback helps partners understand how their defensive interactions become self-defeating and block new ways of relating. At the beginning of treatment, the focus is not the content of the disagreements but on how they operate together: what needs are not being met; what hurts, fears, and old wounds are hidden under the barrage of words.

Therapists generally enter the picture at the point where discharge of overwhelming emotions takes the form of mutual blaming or acting out. As the treatment progresses, it is possible slowly to uncover the underlying vulnerabilities. Because borderline and narcissistic defenses are learned ways of protecting a fragile self, healing occurs in part through accepting the reality that blaming another or destructive behavior is used as a protection against humiliation or fear of abandonment.

The well-established ability of borderline patients to impart their intolerable feelings to others raises the risk that the therapist may become intolerant and do something that, though ostensibly rational, actually constitutes a devastating piece of acting out that may doom the treatment to failure. Assigning tasks and giving advice may be the therapist's response to feelings of futility, rage, emptiness, or depression transmitted by the patient. Because of many borderlines' exquisite sensitivity to injury and because of their volatile reactions when they are hurt, advice and assignments often will cause further injury and the reemergence of defenses. Despite the therapist's best intentions, the demand, the outbursts, and the emotional retreats of borderline patients often produce countertransference reactions in the therapist that can lead to withdrawal of patients from therapy. A clinician who constantly tries to elicit emotions from a husband who denies knowing his feelings, or one who tries to investigate a wife's sexual "frigidity" when she has closed off sexuality in the marriage, may end up inadvertently aligning with one partner and cause the mate to feel misunderstood or judged. Rigorous self-observation and self-control on the part of the therapist are necessary precautions.

The Therapeutic Alliance

Psychotherapeutic treatment of borderline relationships requires a special form of therapeutic alliance. In individual, analytically oriented therapy, this alliance evolves so that the observing part of the patient's ego identifies with the therapist in order to modify the pathological defenses being used to ward off internal danger. The ability to ally oneself with rational and caring parts of the therapist requires that the patient have a firm sense of self and a recognition of the therapist as a separate person. Persons with self disorders lack this ability because their object relations are at a primitive, need-gratifying level (Grotstein, 1981).

A major drawback to the development of a working alliance in conjoint therapy for borderline disorders is the greater risk of exposure to emotional injury resulting from insufficiently empathic responses on the part of the therapist or the partner. Things may be said that are hurtful, and the therapist may not always be empathically attuned to the pain of one or both partners. Because the treatment must remain even-handed, one partner may feel neglected and become angry or withdrawn. Conversely, some patients who fear too much closeness may find conjoint sessions less anxiety-provoking than the intensity of the individual therapeutic relationship. They feel understood without fearing that the therapist will expect them to reveal deep emotions.

Utilizing the concepts of transference and countertransference in working with couples, it is possible to see how they relate, not only to the therapist, but also to each other. When a couple comes for therapy, they bring both an intrapsychic system based on their individual histories and an interactive system based on their history of transactions with each other in a "bipersonal transference." The therapist works with both systems in an attempt to clarify what occurs psychodynamically within each partner as well as what occurs between them that exacerbates each partner's internal dysfunctions, leading to disturbances within the marriage (Solomon, 1989). In order to work with the intrapsychic system, it is necessary to be cognizant of the various aspects of transference and countertransference, particularly as they relate to the defenses of projection, introjection, splitting, and projective identification.

When projective identification occurs between mates, unacceptable aspects within the self are unconsciously projected into and considered to be part of the partner, who then seems filled with malevolent feelings. When the internal experience is a painful re-creation of early abandonment fears, the defense may be an emotional withdrawal or an intrapsychic negation of the existence of the other. A borderline-narcissistic defense might include volatility of mood, intense rage, a temporary loss of cognitive functioning, or an acting out of aggressive feelings. Small failures lead to defensive posturing. At this point, there is a chance to mend the failure. By focusing in therapy on the defense as a message of distress and by exploring what is happening at this moment in the relationship to cause the need for such a reaction, it may be possible to follow the threads to the painful affect.

In working through affect the person feels too painful, frightening, or humiliating to stand, it can be brought into focus, faced, and increasingly tolerated. The therapist helps the patient hold and contain toxic affects in the process of detoxification. This is often a difficult, tedious process.

The Many Transferences

Sometimes one or both of the partners choose to have individual therapy with another therapist, in addition to working on the marriage. Other times marital therapy has been recommended by a therapist working with one of the mates. The splitting of the transference implicit in such situations does not appear to be a problem for the marital therapy, as long as it is not a problem between the therapists. The marital therapist should discuss with the couple their feelings about his or her having any contact with the individual therapist. Some clients are pleased with the idea, experiencing it as a parental interest in them or as special treatment. Others seem hesitant, sending a direct or encoded message that they want the individual therapy to be quite separate and private. It is wise to abide by the client's wishes. People have transference reactions to a whole variety of situations at different points in their lives. The transferences in marital therapy are necessarily different from those in individual treatment. Much of the time the focus is on the connections that take place between the partners and between the couple as a unit and the therapist. The transference to the individual therapist is not diluted to any greater extent than it would be by any other close relationship in the patient's life.

Of somewhat greater concern is the issue of how the development of the transference in individual therapy affects the transferences that take place normally between husband and wife. All therapists have had experiences of spouses resenting and even sabotaging the individual treatment in a competitive struggle. The partner who is not in therapy fears that the other will one day come home and say, "I'm well, now I want a divorce." Sometimes individuals do go into therapy and end up getting a divorce. If a change occurs in a system, other parts of the system must change or unconscious structural forces push toward reestablishment of equilibrium at the original level. The therapy is the means to change and growth. The family, if it is not part of the therapeutic process, represents a force of regression and a return toward pathology—it seeks a return to the former homeostatic balance, no matter how dysfunctional.

With respect to conjoint therapy, a more damaging scenario may occur in the context of individual therapy. As the therapist listens to a patient describe his or her mate, there is a tendency to believe that the account is totally accurate and free of transference distortions. It is then easy to reinforce a split between good (therapist) and bad (spouse). As the partner becomes increasingly resentful and competitive, the therapist, patient, and spouse are in a triangulated relationship in which the "identified problem" is kept outside, away from the increasingly functional therapeutic dyad (Bowen, 1978).

Other Crucial Factors in Treatment

It is up to the therapist to provide an atmosphere in which the psychic drama can unfold. Four factors are necessary for this to occur.

Neutrality

In treatment of borderline partners, therapy does not begin with a specific set of rules, exercises, or predetermined expectations that they behave, feel, or act in any specific way. This may sound paradoxical because the couple comes to change something. Investment is a key word in therapeutic situations. The therapist must not be invested in the partner's change for the therapist's own narcissistic ends. The therapist becomes immersed in the session "without memory or desire" (Bion, 1962) and allows the material to emerge as it fits the pattern of the couple. In this way, the internal patterns of each partner and the patterns of interaction are observable very quickly.

The Therapist's Use of Self

The therapist becomes immersed in the patients' subjective reality without feeling threatened by emotions, memories, and fantasies. Paradoxically, the "boundaries" of the therapist's identity need not be rigidly defended. Becoming more "permeable" to primitive messages conveyed from the other does not imply "merger" or loss of self for the therapist, but rather the freedom to make contact with intensely personal parts of the other's experience without needing to impose the normal barriers to such contact. This is in addition to what has been called the "working alliance" or real relationship.

Empathy

Empathy is an awareness of the underlying meaning of the drama as it feels to the participant. The therapist becomes a witness to this potent experience of the patient. No matter how distorted or obsessive the material, it is the patient's reality and it needs to be understood. Giovacchini (1985, p. 59) wrote about "the reasonableness of the unreasonable patient." Empathic attunement occurs at both conscious and unconscious levels. The therapeutic empathy takes place when there is a relaxing of defensive barriers. There is a deep, intimate therapeutic contact that includes images, thoughts, and feelings that arise in relation to a patient, as if the therapist's unconscious speaks directly to the patient's unconscious.

Countertransferential reactions supply news from within about the dynamic interaction of the couple. Sometimes this can involve an experience of surprising, powerful images. Images and dreams give important information. They tell the therapist something for which there does not seem to be words. Empathically attuned therapists often have dreams or images that serve as unconscious clues. Instead of pushing them away when working with someone, the question to ask is "What is the relevance of this message to the therapeutic dyad or triad?"

Often projective identification is connected with powerful emotions, often about things that occurred before there were words that could describe them. In these circumstances, patients do not know their feelings, cannot name them or convey them verbally. They can divulge their experience only nonverbally, and yet they desperately want the therapist to empathize. "Understand what I feel, even though there is no way I can express it to you because I don't have words." That is why images are so powerful: One is communicating in a preverbal language that is conveyed effectively and by means of a contact that bypasses ordinary language.

Primary Therapeutic Preoccupation

Another necessary factor is the provision of an environment in which the patient's psychodynamics can emerge, the "primary therapeutic preoccupation." Winnicott (1965) talked about "primary maternal preoccupation" and observed that there is a similar process in treatment. Primary therapeutic preoccupation means that the therapist is available and "there" on all levels to focus and interact with the patient(s) in that particular hour.

When these four factors are present—empathy, neutrality, use of self as a tool of treatment, and primary therapeutic preoccupation—then the therapy provides what Winnicott called a "holding environment" for the couple that will allow for complete exploration of the life dramas expressed in the therapeutic situation. Transference, countertransference, and projective identification can flourish in the safety of such an environment; to the extent that these are understood instead of being acted out, change becomes possible.

Issues in Ongoing Treatment

Patients tend to re-create old scenarios that play out in therapy and in their marriage. Often these are imprints of interactional sequences originally experienced in the family of origin (Solomon, 1994). For example, someone who grew up expecting others to become angry will behave in ways that are designed to provoke anger. Someone who saw seductive behavior rewarded in the home is likely to utilize seductive mannerisms to get what he or she wants.

The therapist treating a couple must resist being drawn into their collusive pattern and, at the same time, not shame them for their behavior. Instead, both the behavior and the underlying need must be identified. For example, when a woman repeatedly comes for conjoint sessions with a male therapist in short, spare dresses, while her husband complains of his jealousy about other men, the therapist must be aware that the same dynamics are taking place in the treatment setting. The therapist also must be aware that it is not abnormal to find himself responding to the wife's provocations. The danger is in reacting inappropriately to the response. Instead of saying "Your seductive behavior is provoking rage in your husband," the therapist may say, "You behave seductively because you want to be special, buy you are frightened of getting the sexual response that your father gave. You are trying to communicate the things that feel dangerous without continuing to do things that are destructive to you." The wife then has a sense of being understood rather than judged and can respond to the danger, the need to be special, the reaction of her husband, or whatever else emerged in her at that point. Or she may say nothing and thereupon can turn to the husband to see what his response might be to the therapist's comments.

In the treatment of partners who had failures in early childhood, it is crucial not to underestimate the threat of abandonment. Many people have experienced abandonment repeatedly. This occurs not only when parents physically leave the child through death or divorce, but also when a postnatal mother is very depressed and detached, when there are family problems and the parent is unavailable to provide caregiving, or when the child has many needs because of genetic or biological deficits. This experience of felt abandonment is a part of memory that emerges in later relationships.

Independence cannot be risked by spouses in a blaming marriage; the fear of separateness and loss of the object is too great. This is the impasse. Change and growth are necessary, but the fear of dangerous repercussions to the relationship often is neglected by therapists who value change at all costs without full consideration of the role of other factors in emotional growth.

The Midphase of Treatment

Couples therapy with borderline patients is not a short-term treatment. Therapists must be prepared to stay with the treatment through what invariably is a turbulent period. During the midphase of treatment, the goal is to examine the relationship between the intrapsychic and the interpersonal and to provide avenues for modification. This requires a focus on the process rather than on the surface or content of the encounter. Only by taking the time during the session to stop the process and consciously focus with the partners on the minute details of feelings as they emerge—anger or withdrawal, attack or defense—can the cycle of injury and fear be broken.

The "working through" phase begins when the spouses feel safe enough with the therapist that they no longer act "on their best behavior" and instead begin to show their pathology. Some of the at-home arguments now are played out in the sessions. Reframing their behavior as an effort to show the therapist what they live with allows the opportunity to examine the behavior together, to see what pain, what shame, what fears bring out the defenses of each partner. With the help of the therapist, they can look at how the relationship protects them.

Acceptance over time enables spouses to shed their outer defenses and reveal their basic conflicts, which provide the material for depth interpretations. The dysfunctional patterns of attack and counterattack, blame and refutation, hurt and defense, increasingly emerge for examination in the therapy session. The couple is so used to their patterns and processes that they will engage in their usual destructive interaction quite naturally in the therapeutic sessions, provided nothing is done to stop the process. A couple's willingness to fight in front of the therapist may be accepted positively as a sign of a willingness to present their true interactional pattern in order to find ways to change it.

Allowing partners to engage freely in problem behaviors and examining the related processes—the needs and defenses—with each other in detail, while developing alternative responses, is the essence of long-term treatment of marital partners. As the work expands beyond the reality, problem-solving, or behavioral change aspects of shorter-term treatment of the marriage, it reaches the level of disturbed object relations (Slipp, 1984; Scharff & Scharff, 1987). Therapy may remain at this level for a long time, in a slow process of uncovering and treating narcissistic vulnerability, emotional injury, and related defense patterns.

Together, the couple and therapist go through aspects of each partner's sense of being hurt and the recurring regressive sequences that result from repeated disappointments. The spouses are helped to understand their vulnerable reactions and the connections between regressive behavior, perception of narcissistic loss, and subsequent revenge reactions. The therapy repeatedly works through disappointment in one partner, which causes angry reactions, withdrawal, falling apart, and even regression into acting-out behavior. They may be helped to deal with terror of abandonment and its reverse, expressed in emotional distancing.

It is during this phase of therapy that spouses can learn to utilize their observing egos for themselves and for each other. For example, each construes the other's projective defenses against anxiety and rejection as indifference. A couple in such a bind is doomed to endless frustration and unhappiness because, armed with a ironclad expectation of disappointment, each is afraid to relinquish a defensive posture. By pointing out ways each partner regulates self-esteem and self-cohesion for the other, a therapist can model not only an observing ego but an empathic ear. In time, the critical attacks and the belligerent complaints about the partner's defects begin to fall by the wayside as each individual acknowledges a sense of inadequacy and insecurity.

By this point, there may be a greater capacity for supportive empathy. Parallel to this development, partners react less to every lapse of positive responsiveness in each other as if it were an intentional rebuff. Marital therapy supports this process by letting each spouse see the other in a realistic perspective, complete with his or her more vulnerable parts. Once they have learned how to communicate better and how to understand defenses and anxiety, couples can proceed to work on their discrepant views of each other.

In treatment, the issue is presented by saying "I am getting two different pictures from what each of you is saying. People are used to seeing each other in a certain way, and sometimes it is hard to get used to having mates behave differently. If we can understand why both of you get a mixed view of the other, and make sure that what gets communicated is received accurately, we might be able to figure out together things you can do that will make it better for you both."

The goal at this point is not only to raise the question of how each distorts his or her perception of the other but to do so in a way that will help the couple assimilate the information without raising their anxiety level. Thus, it is important to show both partners how logical it is that certain behaviors and interchanges between them naturally cause an increase in anxiety and, therefore, distort how they view one another. As treatment proceeds through the midphase, spouses sometimes regress to behaviors that resemble those that first brought them to therapy. There are many opportunities for old transference patterns to reemerge because the partners spend more time together outside treatment than they do in therapy. Until changes become well ingrained, there is tendency for couples to revert to their old behavior patterns.

Depending on the level the therapy is affecting, the work at this stage may provoke moments of great discomfort and anxiety. People fear change no matter what they may consciously say or think. The known, even when it is painful, often appears safer than the unknown. A client rarely comes into a session saying "I am creating problems in my relationships because of some underlying problem that I have and I wish to make some changes." The partners may want to work on their own individual expectations and distortions, especially the ones that are affecting the relationship, but they are also afraid to do so. Generally, as noted before, both members of the couple come into conjoint therapy because they want the therapist to change their spouse.

Some of the most valuable learning takes place when one of the partners interacts with the therapist just the way he or she does at home. A woman who gets extremely upset with her husband when he violates her expectations or seems not to be paying attention to her will eventually get upset with the therapist in a similar way when he or she makes an error in an intervention, because he or she invariably does make inappropriate responses. For example, Gary was very silent during a session when he had expressed a belief that he and his wife of 13 years, Ann, ultimately would get a divorce. As Ann speculated about what might be going on "in his head" that would make him leave his children, whom he professed to love, the therapist responded with some possible reasons. Gary became enraged with the therapist. "Don't fuck with my mind. You don't know me or how I feel. You aren't even giving me a chance to think this through." Gary's issue became clearer. He could hardly say anything about his wish to find a space for himself in the relationship. Any attempt was met with a barrage of words from Ann, who feared being left. Ann acknowledged that she would do anything, say anything, be anything to keep him tied to the marriage. The harder she tried to figure out what was wrong and how to hold him, the angrier he became and the more he wanted to get out.

When to Consider Termination of Treatment

When partners are able to overcome their need to hide shameful, embarrassing feelings from each other, they can relinquish repression of archaic needs. The therapist assists this process by constantly and continuously reinterpreting interactions to remind the partners of underlying needs. For example, "Of course you are angry. You don't know how to respond when Abe accuses you of being out with other men when you work late. You stopped talking and withdrew because it didn't seem very safe to say anything while you were feeling attacked. Meanwhile, when you don't respond, Abe sees it as confirmation that he must be right."

When both partners can examine their needs during painful or anxious moments, while experiencing grief and loss, or when desirous of praise and approval. Listening to the therapist respond with empathy to the vulnerability and pain that lies below what appears to be a demand or attack eventually will make partners aware of their areas of sensitivity and of the feelings of helplessness arising from unmet needs. The therapist helps the couple to reinterpret anger—to recognize that rage may be based on an inability to assert needs and demands so that they can be met. Each partner must be allowed, as much as possible, to express needs freely in a nonjudgmental, empathic atmosphere. The partner learns to hear the needs hidden behind demands and rage.

When they are more responsive to each other, because they have been observing empathic modeling, partners begin learning methods for giving and receiving responses to previously submerged frightening feelings. They learn how to hear messages that usually are sent only in encoded form. As these messages are received and accepted, the partners can send new communications in a less guarded form. As it becomes less necessary to mobilize defenses against old needs and feelings, a transformation often occurs. *Demandingness can be replaced by an even, consistent assertiveness. Timidity and withdrawal, once needed to protect against shame and embarrassment, are replaced by a willingness to expose high aspirations and deep devotion.*

CONCLUSION

Borderline patients are known to be difficult to treat. Their interactions with anyone with whom they are close tend to be volatile. They expect much, are invariably disappointed, and react with anger, negative behavior, and rapid withdrawals. This is followed by attempts to reconnect because they have a dread of abandonment. When a therapist is the recipient of the projections of a borderline, the treatment can be quite turbulent and often terminates prematurely.

These people who have trouble in a therapeutic relationship often are married and have families. The same difficult relationship patterns are likely to emerge repeatedly. Although borderline disorders may keep relationships in turmoil, separation and divorce is rarely a solution. Intimate partners have unconsciously found each other at approximately the same level of pathology (Gurman, 1978; Gortstein, Solomon, & Lang, 1985). The wounds of the borderline begin in relationships. Healing of wounds requires a reparative relationship. The tendency is to re-create old interactional patterns. If the marriage fails, borderline partners are likely to reenter similar collusively pathological partnerships. Often children then grow up in dysfunctional families, destined to repeat the pattern. Change can happen only when, as the pattern reemerges, the response is different from that of the past. This happens in reparative relationships. The wounds of the past can be healed in the here-and-now of corrective relational experience.

This chapter has attempted to provide a paradigm for therapists engaged in helping people involved in disturbed marital and family relationships. It has described methods of treating borderline couples, encompassing a variety of educational and social supports, to enable people to develop healing and satisfying relationships.

REFERENCES

American Psychological Association (1994). *Diagnostic and statistical manual of mental disorders* (4th ed.). Washington, DC: Author.

Baker-Miller, J. (1992). *Women's growth in connection: New perspectives on psychological development.* Paper presented at the Continuing Education Seminars, Los Angeles, November 6–7.

Beebe, B., & Lachmann, F. (1988). The contribution of mother-infant mutual influence to the origins of self and object representations. *Psychoanalytical Psychology, 5,* 305–337.

Bion, W. (1962). *Learning from experience.* New York: Basic Books.

Bowen, M. (1978). *Family therapy in clinical practice.* New York: Aronson.

Brandchaft, B., & Stolorow, R. (1985). The borderline concept: An intersubjective viewpoint. In J. Grotstein, M. Solomon, & J. Lang (Eds.), *The borderline patient: Emerging concepts in psychodynamics and treatment* (vol. II, pp. 103–126). Hillsdale, NJ: Analytic.

Dicks, H. V. (1967). Marital tension. London: Routledge and Kegan Paul.

Giovacchini, P. L. (1985). The "unreasonable" patient and the psychotic transference. In J. Grotstein, M. Solomon, & J. Lang (Eds.), *The borderline patient: Emerging concepts in psychodynamics and treatment* (pp. 59–68). Hillsdale, NJ: Analytic.

Grinker, R. R. (1977). The borderline syndrome: A phenomenological view in borderline personality disorders. In P. Hartocollis (Ed.), *Borderline personality disorders* (pp. 159–172). New York: International Universities.

Grotstein, J. (1981). *Splitting and projective identification.* New York: Aronson.

Grotstein, J., Solomon, M., & Lang, J. (Eds.). (1985). *The borderline patient: Emerging concepts in diagnosis, etiology, psychodynamics and treatment.* Hillsdale, NJ: Analytic.

Gunderson, J. (1985). Interfaces between psychoanalytic and empirical studies of borderline personality. In J. Grotstein, M. Solomon, & J. Lang (Eds.), *The borderline patient: Emerging concepts in psychodynamics and treatment* (pp. 37–60). Hillsdale, NJ: Analytic.

Gurman, A. S. (1978). Contemporary marital therapy: A critique and comparative analysis of psychoanalytic, behavioral, and systems theory approaches. In T. J. Paolino & B. S. McCrady (Eds.), *Marriage and marital therapy* (pp. 445–566). New York: Brunner/Mazel.

Kernberg, O. F. (1975). *Borderline conditions and pathological narcissism.* New York: Aronson.

Kohut, H. (1971). *Analysis of the self.* New York: International Universities.

Kohut, H. (1977). *Restoration of the self.* New York: International Universities.

Kohut, H. (1984). *How does analysis cure?* Ed. A. Goldberg with P. E. Stepansky. Chicago: University of Chicago.

Lachkar, J. (1985). Narcissistic/borderline couples: Theoretical implications for treatment. *Dynamic psychotherapy, 3*(2), 109–125.

Lansky, M. (1981). Treatment of the narcissistically vulnerable marriage. In M. Lansky (Ed.), *Family therapy and major psychopathology.* (pp. 163–183). New York: Grune & Stratton.

Lansky, M. (1993). Family genesis of aggression. *Psychiatric Annals, 23*(9).

Mahler, M. S., Pine, F., & Bergman, A. (1975). *The psychological birth of the human infant: Symbiosis and individuation.* New York: Basic Books.

Masterson, J. F. (1981). *The narcissistic and borderline disorders: An integrative approach.* New York: Brunner/Mazel.

Masterson, J. F. (1985). *The real self.* New York: Brunner/Mazel.

Nadelson, C. C., & Paolino, T. J. (1978). Marital therapy from a psychoanalytic perspective. In T. J. Paolino & B. S. McCreedy (Eds.), Marriage and marital therapy: Psychoanalytic, behavioral, and systems perspectives (pp. 89–165). New York: Brunner/Mazel.

Sager, C. J., Gundlach, R., & Kremer, M. (1968). The married in treatment. *Archives of General Psychiatry, 19,* 205–217.

Sander, L. (1985). Toward a logic or organization in psychobiological development. In H. Klar & L. Siever (Eds.), *Biologic response styles* (pp. 20–36). Washington, DC: American Psychiatric Association.

Sander, L. (1987). Awareness of inner experience. *Child Abuse and Neglect, 11,* 339–346.

Scharff, D., & Scharff, J. (1987). *Object relations family therapy.* Hillsdale, NJ: Aronson.

Slipp, S. (1984). *Object relations: A dynamic bridge between individual and family treatment.* New York: Aronson.

Solomon, M. (1989). *Narcissism and intimacy: Love and marriage in an age of confusion.* New York: W. Norton.

Solomon, M. (1994). *Lean on me: The power of positive dependency in intimate relationships.* New York: Simon & Schuster.

Stern, D. (1985). *The interpersonal world of the infant.* New York: Basic Books.

Stolorow, R. D., Brandchaft, B., & Atwood, G. E. (1987). *Psychoanalytic treatment: An intersubjective approach.* Hillsdale, NJ: Analytic.

Stolorow, R. D., & Atwood, G. E. (1992). Contexts of being: Intersubjective foundations of psychological life. Hillsdale, NJ: Analytic.

Stone, M. (1980). *The borderline syndromes.* New York: McGraw-Hill.

Tustin, F. (1987). *Autistic barriers in neurotic patients.* New Haven, CT: Yale University.

Winnicott, D. W. (1965). *The maturational process and the facilitating environment: Studies in the theory of emotional development.* New York: International Universities.

CHAPTER 18

Sadomasochistic Interactions

CHERYL GLICKAUF-HUGHES, PhD

The meanings of the concepts of masochism and sadism have changed greatly over time. Furthermore, there has been much debate in the literature as to whether sadomasochism is a unitary phenomena (with sadism and masochism as its two poles) or whether they are two separate albeit at times complementary phenomena.

MASOCHISM: HISTORY OF TERM

Masochism, in particular, "has become one of the most confusing and controversial clinical and diagnostic terms within the psychological literatures" (Glickauf-Hughes & Wells, 1991, p. 53). One reason for this controversy is that, historically, masochism has been defined in terms of the victim's pleasure in pain and has been equated with that which is feminine or female.

The concept of masochism was introduced initially by Krafft-Ebing (1895), who on the basis of his observation of prostitutes described masochism as a sexual perversion in which erotic pleasure was derived from pain. Freud (1905, 1919, 1924) applied the term more broadly (i.e., moral masochism) to include nonerotic pleasure associated with submission and humiliation. In contrast, Reich (1933), Bieber (1966), and Glickauf-Hughes and Wells (1991) do not believe that masochists get pleasure from suffering but rather consider suffering a prerequisite for or a necessary consequence of getting that which they vitally need.

Berliner (1940, 1947, 1958) took a clearly relational approach to the understanding of masochism and viewed it as the love object's sadism and a means of getting love from a vitally needed but critical object (1947). Glickauf-Hughes and Wells (1991) expanded upon Berliner's conceptualization of masochism by viewing it as a learned, pathological way of loving and individuating. A pathological way of loving includes being devoted to critical and rejecting love objects and attempting to win their approval through pleasing and self-sacrifice. The masochistic style of individuating refers to a process of anticipating or projecting the forceful domination of another's will and then resisting this domination through often-unconscious strategies such as passive-aggressiveness. Thus, as psychoanalytic theory has evolved from a drive to an object relations theory, the definition of masochism also has become broader and more relational.

SADISM: HISTORY OF TERM

Sadism, a term used by Krafft-Ebing (1895), originally referred to the wish to inflict pain upon the object of one's sexual desires. Freud (1924) further elaborated upon this construct as a desire to subjugate others. He saw sadism as an element of male aggression and thought that it was part of the underpinnings of male sexuality. Freud perceived two aspects of sadism as: the desire to physically hurt the sexual object and the desire to humiliate the sexual object.

As the object relations school of psychoanalysis developed, sadism (or sadomasochism) was conceptualized as a type of object relationship that defends against object loss (Avery, 1977; Fromm, 1973; Nydes, 1963). "The dynamics of sadomasochism are felt to be centered around the struggle to intimidate a potentially deserting partner into believing that the loss of the object will cause him/her significant pain" (Fiester & Gay, 1991, p. 376).

Bieber (1966) viewed sadism as a response to a threat in general, rather than just to the threat of object loss. He saw sadism as a "defensive, paranoid mechanism in which the victim is a personified representative of a variety of irrationally perceived threats; he must then be dominated, injured, neutralized or destroyed" (p. 263). Bieber believed that in the act of vengeance, the sadistic individual feels a sense of triumph over the extinction of an irrationally perceived enemy.

Finally, Fiester and Gay (1991) believe that with the development of the theory of self-psychology, there was a further understanding of the concept of sadism based on understanding the dynamics of the narcissistic personality (Kohut, 1971, 1977). Within this framework, the sadist is viewed as having early empathic failures leading to inadequate idealization of the object and regulation of self-esteem. This leads to an intense dependency on external objects for a sense of cohesiveness and security. This speculation about the relationship between sadism and narcissism will be elaborated upon further later in this chapter.

THE POLITICS OF PERSONALITY DISORDERS

Over time, sadism and masochism have become not only two of the most confusing but also the most controversial diagnostic terms in the psychological literature. One reason for this controversy is that masochism historically has been equated with that which is female (Deutsch, 1944; Freud, 1924; Gero, 1962; Horney, 1939; Krafft-Ebbing, 1895) and defined in terms of the victim's enjoyment of and need for pain. Critics have thus objected to this term as being both sexist and victim blaming (Caplan, 1984). Franklin (1987), in particular, sees this diagnostic category "as a dangerous weapon that could frequently be misused to blame women, particularly abused women for societal failures" (p. 53).

In response to the sexist and victim-blaming connotations of the term "masochism," alternative, environmentally based explanations have been suggested to describe and explain patterns of traumatic bonding in battered women such as cultural norms that condone violence (Straus, 1977; Walker, 1979), lack of economic resources (MacLeod, 1980), learned helplessness (Seligman, 1975), intermittent reinforcement (Dutton & Painter, 1981), a power imbalance (Dutton & Painter, 1981), and a cyclical pattern in abusive relationships of tension-building, explosive battering and relief, or a loving respite (Walker, 1979).

As masochism has been equated with that which is feminine, sadism has been equated with that which is masculine (Fromm, 1973; Krafft-Ebing, 1895; Schad-Somers, 1982). Gero (1962) noted that "Sadistic acts are identified with the role of the male who is depicted as the cruel attacker who inflicts pain and injury" (p. 331).

Due in part to these concerns, the diagnostic terms "sadistic" and "masochistic" (and even the less inflammatory term, "self-defeating personality disorder") have been eliminated from the DSM-IV (APA, 1994). However, despite these valid criticisms and the fact that research does demonstrate a sex bias in the diagnosis of these disorders (Landrine, 1989), some theorists believe that eliminating the categories masochistic and sadistic deprives clinicians of useful conceptualizations (Glickauf-Hughes & Wells, 1991; Simons, 1987). Young and Gerson (1991), in particular, believe that Caplan's (1984) overview of psychoanalytic theories of masochism is too narrow and does not include contemporary psychoanalytic literature related to masochism such as attachment theory, separation-individuation, object relations theory, and self psychology. They believe that theories of characterological development and theories of trauma and survival (Dutton & Painter, 1981; Walker, 1979, 1984, 1987) need not be mutually exclusive.

Among unresolved problems noted by clinicians is the great difficulty that individuals in abusive relationships have separating from one another (Brennan, 1985; Guyford, 1975, 1983). Many abused women report experiencing violence with their partners prior to making a commitment to the relationship (Dobasch & Dobasch, 1983; Rosenbaum & O'Leary, 1981; Snyder & Fruchtman, 1981).

While instances of the sadistic personality are somewhat rare, particularly in outpatient clinical populations, the self-defeating personality is common in the population (DSM-III-R, APA, 1987). Sadism is commonly mentioned in conjunction with other personality disorders (e.g., narcissistic, borderline, paranoid, antisocial), and sadomasochistic interactions are common in couples (Lawner, 1979), particularly enmeshed couples and those with narcissistic issues and/or disorders (Finell, 1992; Gear, Hill, & Liendo, 1983). This chapter attempts to provide greater clarity to the understanding and treatment of sadomasochistic interactions in couples. Of particular relevance in understanding these dynamics is Klein's (1935) theory on the depressive and paranoid positions.

KLEIN'S (1935) THEORY ON THE DEPRESSIVE AND PARANOID POSITIONS

While this has been subsequently disputed, Klein hypothesized that the origin of the paranoid position is during the first quarter of the oral phase (i.e., the first year of life). When the infant (and later adults) are in the paranoid position, their primary goal is to protect the self from harm from "bad objects." What the individual in the paranoid position most fears is annihilation, loss of the self, and loss of self-esteem.

Infants at this stage of life and adults fixated at this stage relate to others as part rather than whole objects. Others are thus viewed as all good or all bad contingent upon their momentary success at gratifying the individual's needs.

As the individual's primary goal is self-protection and survival, the defenses that the individual uses are those that are particularly effective at accomplishing this goal. These include: projection (especially projection of the bad parts of the self onto the object); projective identification of the bad parts of the self "into" the object (i.e., behaving toward the object so that he or she eventually does manifest the projection); and splitting of the bad and good parts of the self and objects to keep the bad from contaminating the good. What the individual in the paranoid position is willing to give up, if necessary, to protect the self is a good relationship with the object.

Klein postulated that the depressive position emerges in the late oral stage or second quarter of the first year of life; this, too, is disputed. Klein believed that at this stage, infants begin to experience the mother as a whole (good and bad) object with her own needs and feelings. As the mother that gratifies is the same one as the mother that frustrates, infants begin to realize that their rages toward the bad or frustrating mother also hurt the mother that they love and need.

The primary goal of infants at this phase of development (and adults in the depressive position) is preserving the relationship with the object from their own aggression. The individual in the depressive position most fears the loss of the object and the object's love. In order to prevent this loss, several defenses are utilized, including introjection of relational problems and denial of the object's sadism. While such defenses keep the individual from acknowledging bad qualities in the object (which might lead to separation and loss), he or she pays a price in terms of lowered self-esteem.

SADOMASOCHISM: CONCURRENT OR SEPARATE PHENOMENA

There is much controversy in the literature as to whether sadomasochism is a unitary or binary phenomenon. In essence, are sadism and masochism separate entities (Freud, 1924) or two sides of the same coin (Bonaparte, 1952; Brenner, 1959; Freud, 1905; Keiser, 1949)? This complex question is beyond the scope of this chapter to resolve fully. However, before discussing criteria for diagnosis of sadomasochistic interactions, this issue will be addressed briefly.

The thesis herein is that sadomasochism can be unitary or binary, depending on the character structure of the individuals in the sadomasochistic relationship and their level of ego development (i.e., neurotic, preneurotic, or borderline) as described by Kernberg (1975), Horner (1979), Wells and Glickauf-Hughes (1993), and Glickauf-Hughes and Wells (1995). To briefly summarize: (1) the neurotic individual has a cohesive, differentiated sense of self and a fully developed sense of object constancy; (2) the borderline individual has an enfeebled sense of self that is vulnerable to fragmentation and little or no sense of object constancy; and (3) the preneurotic individual has a differentiated sense of self (but poor self-esteem regulation) and incomplete object constancy (i.e., others are seen as integrated, however, self-object functions such as soothing and empathy are not fully internalized). Individuals at the borderline level of ego organization and object relations development tend to manifest the paranoid position, and individuals at the preneurotic and neurotic levels of object relations and ego organization tend to exhibit predominately the depressive position. This follows Klein's (1935) thesis that the depressive position is more developmentally advanced.

Thus, individuals with a narcissistic, paranoid, sadistic, or sociopathic character organization (particularly those with a borderline level of object relations/ego development) mostly manifest the paranoid position and the sadistic role in sadomasochistic interactions. Individuals with a self-defeating character or mixed personality disorder with self-defeating features (particularly those structured at the neurotic or preneurotic level of object relations/ego development) predominately manifest the depressive

position and masochistic behavior in sadomasochistic interactions. While both characters may regress or progress in treatment and manifest the other side of the coin, their
predominant tendency is toward one or the other.

Where the confusion lies is with the hysteroid borderline or "sadomasochistic" personality (Glickauf-Hughes & Wells, 1995; Kernberg, 1975). Because self and object are
undifferentiated and good and bad are unintegrated, hysteroid or sadomasochistic borderlines can manifest behaviors that appear masochistic when paired with narcissistic
individuals (Finell, 1992) and sadistic when partnered with self-defeating individuals
(Glickauf-Hughes & Wells, 1991). However, while sadomasochistic borderlines may
identify with the victim role and feel and behave masochistically, due to their underlying paranoid position dynamics, their partners tend to experience their behavior as abusive or sadistic.

It is thus my contention that there are three subgroups involved in sadomasochistic
interactions. This has in fact been supported by a number of descriptive and observational studies over the last 17 years (Breslow, 1987; Spengler, 1977; Weinberg, Williams,
& Mosher, 1984). The first group, which primarily assumes the depressive position,
generally enacts the masochistic role. The most common character styles observed to
manifest this role are the self-defeating or masochistic-depressive personality and mixed
neurotic disorders with self-defeating features. The second group, which primarily assumes the paranoid position, enacts the sadistic role. The most common character styles
observed to manifest this role are the sadistic, narcissistic, paranoid, and sociopathic
personalities. The final group in which self-other differentiation is most confused manifests sadomasochistic behavior. The most common character style that manifests this
role is the hysteroid borderline personality. In this chapter, dynamics and treatment
considerations are based primarily on couples where each member assumes the
masochistic or sadistic role and predominately has a depressive or paranoid stance in the
world. It is assumed that the dynamics and treatment of sadomasochistic hysteroid patients, while related, have some distinctive characteristics.

RELATIONSHIP OF KLEINIAN POSITION TO CHARACTER STYLE
AND SADOMASOCHISTIC INTERACTIONS

Masochistic Interactions and the Depressive Position

It is the thesis herein that an important factor underlying masochistic interactions is the
predominance in the individual's dynamics of the depressive position as described by
Klein (1935). Thus, the goal of the self-defeating or masochistic character is to preserve the relationship with the love object, however troubled that relationship is.

Glickauf-Hughes and Wells (1991) hypothesize that due to the unpredictable environment in which the masochistic character was raised (with intermittent punishment
and reinforcement), such individuals struggle with anxious attachment. Bowlby (1973)
described anxious attachment as "unusually frequent and urgent attachment behavior"
due to the individual's lack of "confidence that his attachment figures will be accessible and responsible to him when he wants them to be" (p. 213).

One of the major conflict areas for individuals with self-defeating or masochistic
proclivities is thus separation and loss (Avery, 1977; Glickauf-Hughes & Wells, 1991).
Leaving the significant other seems so frightening and painful to masochists that the
pain that they experience in their relationships is considered more endurable than the

pain that they believe they would feel in leaving and facing the ensuing loss of the other. As individuals in the depressive position prefer to sacrifice self-esteem, when experiencing conflict with significant others they tend to rationalize and deny the hurtful or sadistic behavior of the other and to blame themselves for relational difficulties. They believe that if their partner is angry at them, they must be "bad" or defective. For example, one masochistic patient reported that her husband was angry because the cat's litter box was not cleaned. He thus threw the cat against the wall. This patient expressed a great guilt and remorse for provoking his behavior by failing to clean the litter box sooner (Glickauf-Hughes & Wells, 1995). This example echoes the self-blame that is often heard when treating abused spouses (e.g., "I knew he was having a bad day. I should have been more sensitive to him").

Masochistic individuals also blame themselves for relational problems due to a history of being blamed or scapegoated by parents. As the child is so dependent, he or she is motivated to idealize the parent and internalize relational difficulties (Fairbairn, 1952). As Bowlby (1973) stated:

> No child cares to admit that his parent is gravely at fault. To recognize frankly that a mother is unjust and tyrannical or that neither parent ever wanted you is intensely painful. Moreover, it is intensely frightening. Given any loophole therefore, most children will seek to see their parents' behavior in some more favorable light. (p. 315)

However, being raised by parents who make extensive use of projection, projective identification, and splitting and have a propensity to scapegoat their child takes a toll on the child's self-esteem. Furthermore, having failed to receive sufficient empathy and soothing from parents, the masochistic individual remains insecure and thus overly dependent on others for these functions.

A vicious cycle is thus set up in which children develop anxious attachment and unstable self-esteem due to their parents' unpredictable behavior, insufficient use of empathy and containment, and excessive use of projection and projective identification. This keeps them overly reliant on others for maintaining self-esteem through getting critical or rejecting partners to love and approve of them and finding idealized partners to identify with. Both of these propensities often draw masochistic individuals into relationship with narcissistic individuals (Glickauf-Hughes & Wells, 1991, 1995) who, like the masochist's parents, tend to use projection and projective identification. Thus, the cycle continues.

It is the contention here that the motivation behind masochistic behavior in individuals with a self-defeating character is not sexual pleasure (Krafft-Ebing, 1895) or pleasure in pain and humiliation (Freud, 1905) but the belief that painful relationships are the lesser of two evils. The self-defeating individual thus does not enjoy being hurt by a sadistic partner. Rather, he or she believes it is the price that must be paid to gain love and avoid loss. This is exacerbated by the self-defeating character's tendency to idealize the object and rely on the object for narcissistic functions. This tendency of masochistic individuals to have narcissistic issues (e.g., problems in self-esteem regulation) also has been noted by Stolorow (1975).

Sadistic Interactions and the Paranoid Position

Just as depressive dynamics are postulated to be an important underlying factor in masochistic behavior, paranoid dynamics are believed to underlie sadistic behavior. Due

to their impoverished and fragmented sense of self and problems in self-esteem regulation, self-protection in many forms is the main motive of the sadist. Like the hysteroid
personality, the sadist relies on primitive defenses such as splitting, projection, projective identification, and devaluation. Combined, all protect an impoverished self with
fragile self-esteem and enhance the compensatory grandiose self structure.

Much literature relates narcissism to sadism (Finell, 1992; Gear, Hill, & Liendo,
1983; Stolorow, 1975). Fromm (1973) posited that one of the most important sources of
defensive or malignant aggression is the wounding of narcissism and thought that sadistic behavior is quite common in the narcissistic character "for whom even a slight damage will arouse an intense craving for revenge" (p. 274).

The narcissist is very sensitive to slights. When shamed, he or she tends to become
enraged and to devalue and/or become abusive toward others. Thus, many of the proposed diagnostic criteria for or symptoms in sadomasochistic interactions are related to
fragile self-esteem (e.g., pathological jealousy, explosive fights, power struggles) or to
self-enfeeblement and consequent fear of engulfment (e.g, problems with boundaries
and limits, distancer-pursuer dynamics).

Fromm (1973) believed that an important motivation behind sadistic behavior is the
attempt to overcome one's sense of suffering over the realization of one's powerlessness
and separateness. He stated that the core of sadism "is the passion to have absolute and
unrestricted control over a living being . . . to force someone to endure pain and humiliation. . . . [to make] another living being . . . into his thing, his property, while he becomes the other's god" (pp. 288–289). Sadism is thus one solution to the problem of
human existence (i.e., of being dependent, separate, and powerless creatures). "It is the
transformation of impotence into the experience of omnipotence" (p. 290). Fromm also
held that the sadistic character is frightened of everything that is not predictable and certain; frightened by life and particularly by love because they are so uncertain. Sadists
thus can love only those objects that they control. Two areas that are particularly important to control in the other are shame and abandonment.

Lansky (1980), in discussing the dynamics of blaming in couples, believed that the
blaming member of the couple attacks precisely the traits and behaviors in the partner
that threaten the relational bond. "The blamed activities may be sexual, aggressive,
competitive, but they may also be anything including simple independence or going
one's own way—freedom from the dependent and restrictive dyadic relationship." In the
act of blaming, the sadistic individual both asserts aggression and covers over intense
dependency with a facade of self-righteousness and mastery (Lax, 1975). Lansky (1980)
believed that "this exhilarated sense of self-righteousness and mastery lasts only during the act of blaming and serves a defensive function in those in whom humiliation or
desertion is a major issue" (p. 437).

Lansky thought that in the act of inflicting punishment, the avoidance of humiliation is of the utmost importance. In contrast, he believed that for the partner who accepts punishment, "preservation of the relationship at the cost of self-respect . . . is less
anxiety provoking" (1980, p. 438). These two stances are similar to the motivational
aims of the paranoid and depressive position. Lansky further stated that blame, an important aspect of sadistic behavior, serves several important functions, including "the
preservation of self-esteem and reestablishment of the dyadic equilibrium in order to
lock the other back into the relationship when he threatens to go his own way" (p. 446).

Therefore, it is my contention that sadistic behavior is not motivated by getting pleasure by inflicting pain on another per se. Rather, the desire is to compensate for feelings of impotence, shame, and fears of abandonment by attempting to establish absolute

control over another, particularly the other's autonomous behavior. The desire for control in sadists was empirically demonstrated by Breslow (1987). The relationship between sadism and the object's autonomous strivings is demonstrated in a study by Gill (1970), which found that the highest incidence of child abuse is against youngsters between ages three to nine years of age, when the child is still helpless but beginning to have independent strivings.

CRITERIA FOR DIAGNOSIS

Pathological Jealousy and Possessiveness

Because the sadistic partner needs to have absolute control over the masochistic partner (Fromm, 1973) in order to feel a sense of security and self-esteem, the masochistic partner's relationships with others are extremely threatening. The sadistic partner thus has a propensity to be extremely jealous of any meaningful relationship that the masochistic partner has, tends to wrongly interpret the masochist's other relationships as sexual or romantic, and uses extreme measures to control or limit the masochist's relationships (e.g., blaming, jealous rages, punishing, withdrawal, physical violence). One wife thus returned home an hour late from a business meeting to find her husband in a drunken rage and accusing her of infidelity.

Fragile Self-Esteem

Both the masochistic and sadistic partner have nonresilient self-esteem. This is manifested by sensitivity to criticism or slights by the other, blaming and projective defenses by the sadistic partner, and depression, self-recrimination, and introjective defenses (e.g., self-attribution of relational difficulties) by the masochistic partner. The sadistic partner also has a propensity to feel envy in regard to the masochist's positive attributes and accomplishments. Thus, when a husband who worked for the same company as his wife advanced further in his career than she did, the wife became angry, rejecting, and had an affair to punish him.

Frequent Relationship Breakups (and Reconciliations)

Due to the predominance of the primitive defenses mentioned earlier, couples with sadomasochistic dynamics frequently terminate their relationship after explosive fights. However, as both partners are so symbiotically involved and require the other to function as a selfobject to enhance security and self-esteem or as a container in which to project ego—dystonic, fragmented aspects of the self—relationship breakups are fraught with extreme anxiety for both partners. Both the sadist and the masochist "may be securely locked into such a relationship for decades, yet experience themselves on the verge of divorce" (Lansky, 1980, p. 446). Lansky believed that divorce is actually uncommon in these couples, who "may be chronically miserable, yet stay together" (p. 431).

Hostile-Dependent Behavior

One reason for the proclivity of these couples to live either on the verge of divorce or to cycle back and forth between separation and reunion has to do with the preponderance of both hate and the extreme need that each feels for the other. Both sadists and masochists often believe that they cannot live without the other who, however, makes their life miserable. For example, one husband became angry at his wife for going on business trips as her leaving made him cognizant of his great need for her and of his not having control over her behavior.

Power Struggles

Problems with autonomy in both sadists and masochists lead to frequent power struggles in the relationship, which can occur over almost anything, but especially in areas that reflect individuation strivings of one or both partners. The sadist attempts to control the masochistic partner's behavior directly, whereas the masochist attempts to gain power through more passive-aggressive means. The masochist may appear overtly to comply with the partner while covertly defying him or her (Glickauf-Hughes & Wells, 1991). For example, in response to his wife's rejection and attempts to control him, a masochistic husband continually forgot to do the errands he had promised to do.

Intermittent Loving and Abusive Behavior

The literature on both masochism (Glickauf-Hughes & Wells, 1991) and spouse abuse (Walker, 1979) notes a common pattern in which abusive or extremely rejecting behavior is followed by loving, romantic, or conciliatory behavior. Intermittent reinforcement is a powerful contingency pattern in maintaining behavior. Furthermore, such a pattern keeps the masochistic partner believing in the goodness of the object whose love would be forthcoming if only he or she could determine the right thing to do (Glickhauf-Hughes & Wells, 1991). For example, one sadistic partner was extremely romantic and loving after an explosive fight. Another sent his spouse two dozen roses after rejecting her for several weeks.

Victim-Persecutor Dynamics

A common dynamic in sadomasochistic interactions is the belief that the self is a victim and the other is the persecutor. For the masochist, this dynamic commonly is played out with a third party (e.g., friend, therapist) who assumes the role of the rescuer (Horner, 1979). While the sadistic partner's behavior appears more overtly abusive or victimizing, he or she generally justifies this behavior as a response to a felt or imagined injury caused by the masochistic partner. Thus, one sadistic wife believed that her husband deserved her verbal abuse due to his perceived neglect of her.

Distancer-Pursuer Dynamics

Another common aspect of these interactions is distancer-pursuer dynamics in which the sadistic partner (especially those with a narcissistic character) experiences the masochistic partner as engulfing and the masochistic partner experiences the sadistic/narcissistic partner as rejecting (Glickauf-Hughes, 1994). The more that the sadistic/narcissist partner withdraws, the more that the masochistic partner clings and vice versa. In addition to feeling impinged upon, the sadistic/narcissistic partner, like a rapprochement child, also dislikes his or her partner's autonomous activities and thus responds to the partner's independent strivings with possessiveness and behavior that reinstates the symbiotic bond. Thus, while one sadistic/narcissistic husband did not want his masochistic wife intruding upon his activities, he became angry and even more rejecting when she made plans to leave the house, causing her to become insecure about leaving.

Frequent and Extreme Blaming

An important function of blaming in couples is to prevent separation-individuation (Lansky, 1980). The sadistic partner's blaming reinforces the masochist's already low self-esteem and keeps the masochist believing that relational problems are all his or her fault and that no one else would love him or her. The more masochistic/depressed partner feels unentitled to blame the blamer back. Having internalized the blamer's accusations, the masochist often feels responsible for altercations and guilty about being angry.

Problems with Boundaries and Limits

Partners engaged in sadomasochist interactions frequently manifest a variety of problems with boundaries and limits. Due to the use of projective and introjective mechanisms, it is often unclear to both partners where a trait lies (e.g., anger, dependency). Sadists have a tendency to overattribute their own ego-dystonic traits to their masochistic partners, and masochists, in turn, internalize sadists' projections. Both partners tend to push the other's limits (e.g., stay out too late, use a prized possession) and have difficulties in setting and maintaining clear limits. Thus, one masochistic wife who was uncomfortable with her own aggression took a valuable book of her husband's outside on a rainy day, causing him to be enraged (and thus manifest the anger in the relationship).

Explosive Fights

Another extremely important characteristic of sadomasochistic interactions is "fights that become nuclear." Due to problems respecting the other's limits, sensitivity to narcissistic injury, low frustration tolerance, and the use of primitive defenses, arguments quickly and frequently can become explosive (e.g., shouting, threatening divorce, physical abuse, throwing or breaking inanimate objects, making severely disparaging and hurtful statements). Thus, one husband snapped at his wife for interrupting his work and she responded by leaving the house, slamming the door, and staying out all night. The next day he threatened to divorce her.

TREATMENT

"The reality of contemporary practice . . . is that many couples come for help together and prefer to be treated conjointly . . . yet the kinds of difficulties many couples present reflect problems with separation-individuation and seem to call for the kind of reparative intervention that derives from the view of *treatment as a developmental opportunity*" (Applegate, 1988, p. 419). This is particularly the case in the treatment of couples with sado-masochistic interactions.

The treatment model thus recommended for these couples is a multimodal therapeutic approach involving couple's therapy, individual therapy, and moderate use of medication. The couples and individual methods of treatment that are described are based on object relations principles around which there has been a recent rapprochement between individual and systemic intervention (Slipp, 1984). In both individual and couples therapy, therapeutic goals are facilitating insight and providing clients with a corrective interpersonal experience (Glickauf-Hughes & Wells, 1995). The goal of the latter is to provide clients with a developmental second chance (Kohut as cited in Greenberg & Mitchell, 1983) to work through unresolved conflicts, modify psychic structure, and develop more satisfying interpersonal relationships.

Couples Therapy

Lachkar (1992), in describing the treatment of narcissistic/borderline couples who have sadomasochistic interactions, believes that "the therapist must see the couples together before transition into individual therapy to form a safe bond with the couple as a team" (p. 177). She contends that referring these couples to individual treatment too quickly without first helping them understand their couples dynamics and providing them with a framework for understanding their relational conflict often leads them to feel abandoned. Lachkar noticed how these couples' interactions often diminish a sense of individuality and security; she believes that the therapist "should safeguard against this through the provision of boundaries and limitations" (p. 179).

Thus, an important function in therapy of couples with sadomasochistic interactions involves containing the clients' feelings of shame, rage, and abandonment. Bion (1962, 1967, 1970) described containment as a special state in which the mother bears the infant's anxiety and frustration so that the infant feels secure and able to manage these feelings him- or herself. Therapists can provide a sense of containment for couples' feelings in several ways.

Solomon (1985) believed that "in conjoint therapy, couples are helped to formulate messages that more accurately describe their needs, and to receive messages from the partner with fewer distractions. The therapist translates or decodes confusing messages and, in so doing, provides a safe containing environment" (p. 145). Lansky (1980) posited that when treating overreactive, narcissistically vulnerable, blaming couples, therapy must be structured so that communications go through the therapist in the manner described in Bowen (1966). By so doing the therapist becomes a role model for empathic contact.

In addition to clarifying communication and providing empathy, the therapist is able to transmute or change into palatable form the projected or disowned aspects of the self in the communication. Thus, in the example of the husband who became enraged at his wife for ruining his book, the therapist said that she wondered if the wife "might be a little frustrated with her husband for ignoring her lately."

Therapists also provide containment by articulating safe rules for the therapy (e.g., no verbal abuse, threats of divorce, etc.). However, care needs to be taken not to confront either spouse too much, particularly the sadistic one, for "the therapeutic activities of pointing out what the spouses actually do, i.e., describing patterns of communication or action, is often humiliating to the point of endangering treatment" (Lansky, 1980, p. 169).

An important opportunity for containment and transmutation of rage and threats of abandonment occurs in the transferential relationship with the therapist. Lansky (1980) believed that if the therapist is able to "not be put off by the unpleasantness of the perpetual berating [of the therapist] and talk of leaving [therapy], a quite successful therapy progresses in the presence of surface chaos" (p. 452). Finell (1992) concurs that successful treatment of the couple depends on the therapist's ability to handle rage and (the couple's) realization that "their rage is not, in fact, deadly to them or the other" (p. 368).

A second important aspect of treating sadomasochistic couples is fostering the development of the spouses' observing ego or capacity to self-observe their feelings, behaviors, and relational interactions noncritically. Such couples become overwhelmed by affect in general and feelings of shame in particular. In treating narcissistically vulnerable individuals, even interpretation can feel like blaming and cause feelings of humiliation and defensiveness (Lansky, 1980).

Lansky believed that an alternative technique for increasing self-awareness in humiliation-prone individuals is the use of intergenerational constructions described by Bowen (1966). This may be done through use of a genogram or through tracing family-of-origin themes intergenerationally. Lansky observed that helping the patient in such a manner to understand why he or she is sensitive to terror, abandonment, envy, and the like, helps him or her to examine more objectively ego-dystonic aspects of the self as a result of a process rather than a defect in the self. However, caution must be exercised here, as patients with narcissistic vulnerabilities tend to idealize the parent-child relationship (Miller, 1981). Thus, intergenerational explanations must be made in a manner that also empathizes with the patient's parents.

The third important component in treatment is providing the couple with self-object functions that each partner did not receive sufficiently as a child and continues to get from one another unsuccessfully. Solomon (1985) opined that "through the therapist's understanding, empathy, and resulting transmuting internalizations, the individual with narcissistic wounds learns to understand the excruciating sensitivity he or she feels in the face of failure to elicit empathic responses from others" (p. 145). Schwartzman (1984) concurred that the inability of couples to provide admiring or idealized self-object functions for one another is a primary source of marital discord and suggested that in treating "such couples, the therapist may come to function as a self-object for either or both, thereby reestablishing self-cohesion for one or both of the partners" (p. 6). Solomon (1985) offered that "it is possible in conjoint marital therapy to produce changes in the internal structure of the self based upon a patient's increasing ability to tolerate narcissistic frustrations" (p. 145). In contrast, Lansky (1980) and Glickauf-Hughes (1994) believe that when individuals with structural deficits seek such psychological therapy for purposes of making changes in themselves, individual therapy is the treatment of choice to remediate these structural deficits. However, for many individuals, individual treatment is too threatening (Solomon, 1985). Nonetheless, when individuals are open to this process, it is an extremely useful adjunct to conjoint treatment.

Individual Therapy

It is beyond the scope of this chapter to describe in detail individual treatment of those with sadistic or masochistic relational proclivities or individual approaches for remediating defective self structures. However, some general treatment goals for the masochistic (or depressive) partner and the sadistic (or paranoid) partner can be outlined.

In treating individuals who manifest the depressive position and relational masochism, the following treatment goals are often important: (1) increasing resiliency of self-esteem through transmuting internalizations of the therapists' empathy; (2) increasing awareness and appropriate expression of dependency needs and aggression; and (3) completing the development of object constancy to diminish anxious attachment to and extreme separation anxiety from "bad" objects (Glickauf-Hughes & Wells, 1995).

For the partner enacting the sadistic role (with underlying paranoid dynamics), treatment goals include leaning to: (1) differentiate self from objects; (2) resolve splitting;

(3) integrate fragmented aspects of the self (which are projected onto the partner); (4) decrease vulnerability to narcissistic injury; and (5) achieve object constancy. Working with the mechanism of blaming and the underlying feelings of impotence and humiliation are central.

Medication

Due to the sadistic partner's extreme sensitivity to slights and the masochistic partner's tendency toward experiencing depression as a result of loss, the judicious use of antidepressant medication can be an important adjunct to treatment (Friedman, 1991; Lansky, 1980). Serotonin reuptake inhibitors such as fluoxetine (i.e., Prozac™) can be particularly useful since they act to reduce rejection sensitivity (Kramer, 1993).

However, the decision to use medication in combination with therapy can be problematic. Treating the masochistic patient with medication can appear to collude with the couple's stance that the masochist is indeed the identified patient and thus the source of the relational problems. To the "humiliation-prone patient, just the act of being mediated may be experienced as blame and sadistic control by spouse and therapist" (Lansky, 1980, p. 177). Lansky believed, however, that while moderate use of antidepressants can be helpful, antianxiety medication is not useful and that it is important that medication be "an adjunct rather than a central feature in the treatment" (p. 179). An overemphasis on the use of medication with these difficult couples often is indicative of the therapist's countertransference.

Case History

Anne and Jim came to couple's therapy in their sixth year of marriage complaining of frequent, explosive arguments, power struggles, and sexual problems. Despite the tempestuous nature of their relationship, they were very loving and affectionate at times and were extremely attached to one another. Threats of divorce led to depression and feelings of extreme anxiety in both.

Anne was a 31-year-old graduate student in social work. Anne's father was warm, affectionate, extremely immature, and explosive. Anne and her father had engaged in frequent power struggles for as long as she could remember, in which her father would tell her that if she said one more word he would hit her with a belt, and she said "one more word." Anne and her older brother were extremely attached to their severely depressed mother, who was perceived by others as a "pillar of the community" and "a saint." Anne remembers that when she was five years old and her brother was eight, they talked their mother out of a suicide attempt. Despite her love for her mother and her attempts to please, Anne's mother told Anne that she was her "punishment from God."

Jim was a 29-year-old computer programmer with one sister who was seven years older than he. His father died when he was eight years old, and his mother (to whom he was completely devoted) never remarried. Jim thus grew up feeling doted on and completely dominated by women.

Courtship between Anne and Jim was ecstatic. Jim loved and admired Anne's strength and competence and experienced her as someone who would care for and protect him as his mother and sister had. Anne found Jim to be charming and tender and was attracted to his vulnerability. Jim became devoted to her as he had been to his mother and sister and was the first person Anne really felt loved by.

As the courtship period receded, Jim began to have all the negative feelings for Anne that he had not allowed himself to have for his mother and sister. He experienced her as "bossy," controlling, manipulative, and suppressing his true self. As he felt extremely dependent upon her and was terrified that she would abandon him, he was prone to extreme possessiveness including jealous rages and punishing withdrawal in response to Anne's autonomous activities.

   Anne, hoping to recapture Jim's love as she had done with her mother, believed that if only she would do the right things, Jim would adore her again. When she dressed up in hopes of recapturing his sexual and romantic interest, he accused her of infidelity. When she tried harder to be accomplished in her career so that he would be proud of her, he felt envious. When she tried to please him by doing special things for him, he felt impinged upon and manipulated. When she tried to "give him space," he felt abandoned. Like her mother and father, Jim seemed unpleasable; as she had done with her parents, she continued to try to get his love and approval. Needless to say, Anne grew angrier and more resentful by the day, an anger she was only partially conscious of and expressed indirectly. Although Jim was irritable in the mornings, she often was affectionate toward him at that time. In spite of his pathological jealousy, she often stayed out late with her friends. While she would make frequent thoughtful gestures, such as making a special trip to the store to buy his favorite cereal, she would return with the wrong cereal.

   When Anne and Jim entered treatment, they loved, hated, and needed each other and desperately wanted to make their marriage work. While it is beyond the scope of this chapter to give an in-depth account of treatment, some general goals and principles will be outlined.

Couples treatment goals included facilitating separation/individuation, containing and maturing primitive affects, and increasing the capacity to empathize with a separate other. Separation/individuation was promoted by painstakingly helping the couple to sort out projections, introjections, and transference as they occurred as well as to support their attachment to other people, initially the therapist. Primitive affects were contained by responding nonreactively to explosive fights, helping each partner understand the more vulnerable feeling behind the anger, and transmuting projective identifications, particularly those directed at the therapist (i.e., "I wonder if you may have been feeling a little irritated at me lately?"). Empathy was increased in partners by ongoing modeling on the part of the therapist.

   Individual treatment goals for Anne included increasing resiliency of self-esteem, learning to set appropriate limits with Jim's expressions of rage, learning to express her own anger directly, and completing object constancy (including a greater sense of internal security and an increased ability to self-soothe). Individual treatment goals for Jim included gaining a genuine sense of potency, autonomy, and effectiveness in his life; resolving splitting; increasing self-esteem; and integrating ego-dystonic aspects of himself, such as sadness and dependency and resolving his maternal transference. A combined format of individual and couple's therapy was used, alternating each on an every-other-week basis. At one point in treatment, Anne was prescribed fluoxetine (Prozac) for a rather severe depression. Use of medication helped enormously in increasing her capacity to self-soothe and thus set appropriate limits with Jim. While medication also might have been useful for Jim, he experienced the idea of taking medication as weak and shameful and thus the suggestion was not pushed.

CONCLUSION

While sadism and masochism have long been regarded as confusing and controversial phenomena, due to the frequency of occurrence of sadomasochistic interactions in couples, they deserve demystification and clarification. This chapter has attempted to explain the underpinnings of relational masochism and sadism in light of Klein's (1964) theory of the paranoid and depressive positions. Finally, criteria for diagnosing relational sadomasochism have been articulated and a multimodel approach to treatment based on object relations principles has been elaborated briefly.

REFERENCES

American Psychiatric Association. (1987). *Diagnostic and statistical manual of mental disorders* (3rd ed., rev.). Washington, DC: Author.

American Psychiatric Association. (1994). *Diagnostic and statistical manual of mental disorders* (4th ed.). Washington, DC: Author.

Applegate, J. S. (1988). Alone together: An application of separation-individuation theory to conjoint marital therapy. *Clinical Social Work Journal, 16,* 418–429.

Avery, N. D. (1977). Sadomasochism: A defense against object loss. *Psychoanalytic Review, 64*(1), 101–109.

Berliner, B. (1940). Libido and reality in masochism. *Psychoanalytic Quarterly, 9,* 322–333.

Berliner, B. (1947). On some psychodynamics of masochism. *Psychoanalytic Quarterly, 16*(4), 459–471.

Berliner, B. (1958). The role of object relations in moral masochism. *Psychoanalytic Quarterly, 27,* 38–56.

Bieber, I. (1966). Sadism and masochism. In S. Arieti (Ed.), *American Handbook of Psychiatry* (vol. 3, pp. 256–270). New York: Basic Books.

Bion, W. R. (1962). *Learning from experience.* London: Tavistock.

Bion, W. R. (1967). *Second thoughts.* London: Heinemann.

Bion, W. R. (1970). *Attention and interpretation: A scientific approach to insight in psychoanalysis and groups.* London: Tavistock.

Bonaparte, M. (1952). Some biological aspects of sadomasochism. *International Journal of Psycho-analysis, 33,* 373–383.

Bowen, M. (1966). The use of family theory in clinical practice. *Comprehensive Psychiatry, 7,* 345–374.

Bowlby, J. (1973). *Separation: Anxiety and anger.* New York: Basic Books.

Brenner, C. (1959). The masochistic character: Genesis and treatment. *Journal of the American Psychoanalytic Association, 7,* 197–226.

Breslow, N. (1987). Locus of control, desirability of control, & sadomasochists, *Psychological Reports, 61,* 995–1001.

Bromberg, W. (1955). Maternal influences in the development of moral masochism. *American Journal of Orthopsychiatry, 25,* 802–812.

Caplan, P. J. (1984). The myth of women's masochism. *American Psychologist, 39,* 130–139.

Deutsch, H. (1944). *Psychology of women.* New York: Stratton.

Dobasch, R. E., & Dobasch, R. P. (1983). Patterns of violence in Scotland. In R. J. Gelles & C. P. Cornell (Eds.), *International perspectives on family violence* (pp. 147–157). Lexington, MA: Lexington Books.

Dutton, D. G., & Painter, S. (1981). Traumatic bonding: The development of emotional attachments in battered women and other relationships of intermittent abuse. *Victimology: An International Journal, 6,* 139–155.

Fairbairn, W. R. D. (1952). *An object relations theory of the personality.* New York: Basic Books.

Fenichel, O. (1945). *The psychoanalytic theory of neurosis.* New York: Norton.

Fiester, S., & Gay, M. (1991). Sadistic personality disorder: A review of data and recommendations for DSM-IV. *Journal of Personality Disorders, 5*(4), 376–385.

Finell, J. S. (1992). Sadomasochism and complementarity in the narcissistic and borderline personality type. *Psychoanalytic Review, 79*(3), 361–379.

Franklin, D. (1987). The politics of masochism. *Psychology Today, 21,* 52–57.

Freud, S. (1905). Three essays on the theory of sexuality. In J. Strachey (Ed.), *Standard Edition of the Complete Psychological Works of Sigmund Freud* (hereafter *Standard Edition*) (vol. 7). London: Hogarth.

Freud, S. (1919/1955). A child is beaten. In J. Strachey (Ed.), *Standard Edition* (vol. 18). London: Hogarth.

Freud, S. (1924/1961). The economic problem of masochism. In J. Strachey (Ed.), *Standard Edition* (vol. 19). London: Hogarth.

Friedman, R. (1991). The depressed masochistic patient: Diagnostic and management considerations—a contemporary psychoanalytic perspective. *Journal of the American Academy of Psychoanalysis, 19*(1), 19–30.

Fromm, E. (1973). *The anatomy of human destructiveness.* New York: Holt, Rinehart & Winston.

Gayford, J. (1975). Wife battering: A preliminary survey of 100 cases. *British Medical Journal, 1,* 194–197.

Gayford, J. (1982). Battered wives. In R. D. Gelles & C. P. Cornell (Eds.), *International perspectives on family violence* (pp. 123–137). Lexington, MA: Lexington Books.

Gear, M. C., Hill, M. A., & Liendo, E. C. (1983). *Working through narcissism: Treating its sadomasochistic structure.* New York: Aronson.

Gear, M., Liendo, E. C., & Scott, L. (1983). *Patients and agents: Transference-Countertransference in therapy.* New York: Aronson.

Geller, J. (1982). Conjoint therapy: Staff training and treatment of the abuser and abused. In M. Roy (Ed.), *The abusive partner: An analysis of domestic battering* (pp. 198–215). New York: Van Nostrand Reinhold.

Gero, G. (1962). Sadism, masochism and aggression: Their role in symptom formation. *Psychoanalytic Quarterly, 31,* 31–41.

Gill, D. G. (1970). *Violence against children.* Cambridge, MA: Harvard University Press.

Glickhauf-Hughes, C. (1994). Dynamics and treatment of the masochistic-narcissistic couple. *Psychoanalysis and Psychotherapy, 11*(1).

Glickhauf-Hughes, C., & Wells, M. (1991). Current conceptualizations on masochism: Genesis and object relations. *American Journal of Psychotherapy, 45*(1), 53–68.

Glickhauf-Hughes, C., & Wells, M. (1995). *Treatment of the masochistic personality: An interactional object-relations approach to therapy.* New York: Aronson.

Greenberg, J. R., & Mitchell, S. A. (1983). *Object relations in psychoanalytic theory.* Cambridge, MA: Harvard University Press.

Horner, A. (1979). *Object relations and the developing ego in therapy.* New York: Aronson.

Horney, K. (1939). *New ways in psychoanalysis.* New York: Norton.

Keiser, S. (1949). The fear of sexual passivity in the masochist. *International Journal of Psycho-Analysis, 30,* 162–171.

Kernberg, O. (1975). *Borderline conditions and pathological narcissism.* New York: Aronson.

Klein, M. (1935/1964). A contribution to the psychogenesis of manic-depressive states. In M. Klein (Ed.), *Contributions to psychoanalysis, 1921–1925.* New York: McGraw-Hill.

Kohut, H. (1971). *Analysis of the self.* New York: International Universities.

Kohut, H. (1977). *The restoration of the self.* New York: International Universities.

Krafft-Ebing, R. F. (1895). *Psychopathia sexualis.* London: Davis.

Kramer, P. (1993). *Listening to Prozac.* New York: Viking.

Lachkar, J. (1992). *Narcissistic-borderline copules: A psychoanalytic perspective on marital treatment.* New York: Brunner/Mazel.

Landrine, H. (1989). The politics of personality disorder. *Psychology of Women Quarterly, 13,* 325–339.

Lansky, M. (1980). On blame. *International Journal of Psychoanalytic Psychotherapy, 8,* 429–456.

Lawner, P. (1979). Sadomasochism and the imperiled self. *Issues in Ego Psychology, 2*(1), 22–29.

Lax, R. (1975). Some comments on the narcissistic aspects of self-righteousness. *International Journal of Psycho-Analysis, 56,* 283–292.

MacLeod, L. (1980). Wife battering in Canada: The viscious circle. Canadian Government Publishing Center.

Miller, A. (1981). *The drama of the gifted child.* New York: Basic Books.

Nydes, J. (1963). The paranoid-masochistic character. *Psychoanalytic Review, 50,* 55–91.

Painter, S. L., & Dutton, D. (1981). *Patterns of emotional bonding in battered women: Traumatic bonding.* Paper presented at the Canadian Psychological Association Convention.

Reich, W. (1933). *Character analysis.* New York: Simon & Schuster.

Reik, T. (1941). *Masochism in modern man.* New York: Farrar and Rinehart.

Rosenbaum, A., & O'Leary, K. D. (1981). Marital violence: Characteristics of abusive couples. *Journal of Consulting and Clinical Psychology, 49,* 63–71.

Schad-Somers, S. (1982). *Sadomasochism: Etiology and treatment.* New York: Human Sciences.

Schwartzman, G. (1984). Narcissistic transferences: Infreences for the treatment of couples. *Dynamic Psychotherapy, 2,* 5–14.

Seligman, M. (1975). *On depression, development, and death.* San Francisco: Freeman.

Simons, R. C. (1987). Self-defeating and sadistic personality disorders: Needed additions to the diagnostic nomenclature. *Journal of Personality Disorders, 1*(2), 161–167.

Slipp, S. (1984). *Object relations: A dynamic bridge between individual and family treatment.* New York: Aronson.

Snyder, D. K., & Fruchtman, L. A. (1981). Differential patterns of wife abuse: A data based typology. *Journal of Consulting and Clinical Psychology, 49,* 878–885.

Solomon, M. F. (1985). Treatment of narcissistic and borderline disorders in marital therapy: Suggestions towards an enhanced therapeutic approach. *Clinical Social Work Journal, 13,* 141–156.

Spengler, A. (1977). Manifest sadomasochism of males. *Archives of Sexual Behavior, 6,* 441–456.

Stolorow, R. D. (1975). The narcissistic function of masochism (and sadism). *International Journal of Psycho-Analysis, 56,* 441–448.

Straus, M. A. (1977). Sociological perspectives on the prevention & treatment of wife beating. In M. Roy (Ed.). *Battered women: A psychosociological study of domestic violence.* New York: Van Nostram.

Walker, L. (1979). *The battered woman syndrome.* New York: Springer.

Walker, L. (1984). *The battered woman syndrome.* New York: Springer.

Walker, L. (1987). Inadequacies of the masochistic personality disorder for women. *Journal of Personality Disorders, 1,* 183–189.

Wells, M., & Glickauf-Hughes, C. (1993). A psychodynamic-object relations model for training differential diagnosis. *Psychotherapy Bulletin.*

Young, G. H., & Gerson, S. (1991). New psychoanalytic perspectives on masochism and spouse abuse. *Psychotherapy: Theory, Research, and Practice, 28*(1), 30–38.

CHAPTER 19

Persons with Antisocial and Histrionic Personality Disorders in Relationships

WILLIAM C. NICHOLS, EdD

This chapter deals with two personality disorders listed in the current *Diagnostic and Statistical Manual* (DSM-IV) (American Psychiatric Association [APA], 1994). Both Antisocial Personality Disorder (APD) and Histrionic Personality Disorder (HPD) are grouped with other personality disorders under Axis II on the basis of the common features of dramatic, emotional, or erratic behavior (Taylor, 1993). Personality disorders refer to traits or behaviors that are characteristic of the person's long-term and recent functioning. They reflect significant impairment in a person's social or occupational spheres or subjective distress.

The lengthy history of a personality disorder originates during childhood and continues into adulthood. Low self-esteem, stemming from the failure to form meaningful attachments with parents, has long been held to result in dysfunctional adult interpersonal styles (Bowlby, 1977a, 1977b). APD and HPD can be viewed as expressing this inadequate sense of the self as well as significant fears and difficulties in forming close relations with others (Marshall & Barbaree, 1991).

Antisocial Personality Disorder (DSM-IV)

Although recognized and given various names for two centuries, APD was first included in the second edition of the APA's *Diagnostic and Statistical Manual* (DSM-II) in 1968 (Akhtar, 1992).

The current diagnosis requires that an APD individual be at least 18 years of age and have had a diagnosable conduct disorder with the onset occurring before age 15. According to DSM-IV, the individual must evidence "a pervasive pattern of disregard for and violation of the rights of others occurring since age 15," as indicated by at least three of the following:

- Failure to conform to social norms with respect to lawful behaviors, as indicated by repeatedly performing acts that are grounds for arrest.
- Irritability and aggressiveness, as indicated by repeated physical fights and assaults.
- Consistent irresponsibility, as indicated by repeated failure to sustain consistent work behavior or to honor financial obligations.
- Impulsivity or failure to plan ahead.

- Deceitfulness, as indicated by repeated lying, use of aliases, or conning others for personal profit or pleasure.
- Reckless disregard for safety of self or others.
- Lack of remorse, as indicated by being indifferent to or rationalizing having hurt, mistreated, or stolen from another.

This behavior must not occur exclusively during the course of a manic episode or schizophrenia.

Antisocial personality frequently is thought of primarily in relation to lawbreakers and individuals convicted of criminal behavior. The focus on APD in this chapter is not on persons who are in overt conflict with legal authorities or who are confined to prison. Rather, it is broader and includes individuals who manifest antisocial characteristics but still perform adequately. Adequate social functioning, as Akhtar (1992) has indicated and Sutker has demonstrated (Sutker & Allain, 1983), does not rule out the existence of antisocial attitudes and behaviors.

The salient feature of antisocial personalities is their tendency to ignore conventional authority, acting as if social rules and guidelines for self-discipline and cooperative behavior do not apply to them (Millon, 1981). Those whom Millon (1981) refers to as aggressive personalities often find places in society where their hostile and belligerent behaviors are admired rather than punished. They include the conniving and "sharp" businessman, the "competitive" athlete who plays with a reckless disregard for those whom he brutally batters, the hostile and punitive teacher, the callous and calculating attorney, and the demanding surgeon who ruthlessly dominates coworkers. All of these socially responsible and otherwise admirable roles provide the opportunity to act out vengeful hostility under the guise of doing one's job (Millon, 1981).

While trampling over the rights of others, many antisocial personalities initially present a social facade of bland civility and often of sincerity. Unfettered by constraints of honesty, truth, loyalty, or guilt, they may readily and skillfully engage in pathological lying, deception, and swindling. Their charm eventually may disappear as they cease striving to continue the deception because they lose interest in wearing the mask of social acceptability or decide to let others know how clever they have been (Millon, 1981).

What kinds of behavior do individuals manifesting APD exhibit in close and intimate relationships?

Case History

An Antisocial Couple Relationship

Juanita Sayers[1] was hospitalized following an unsuccessful suicide attempt. When Juanita did not keep an appointment, a friend went to find her and called emergency medical services because she was unconscious. The following history emerged:

Reared in impoverished circumstances in the rural Midwest, Juanita began working at age 18 in an automobile plant where her parents had labored for more than 20 years. The work was repetitive, boring, and physically hard. She was compelled to turn over most of her income to her father because the family "needed the money and he wanted it to buy liquor." Juanita was afraid to disobey her verbally and physically abusive father.

---

[1] Pseudonyms have been used throughout this chapter to protect client confidentiality.

Eventually, "tired of all the abuse and being told what to do all the time," she let her father know that she had "a new life." She had met Beau, a bartender who was attentive and flattering and seemed to have a lot of money. After another battering at her father's hands, she left town with Beau.

Beau Sayers had an even less promising background. Deserted by his brutal father when he was in elementary school and expelled from high school for his "wildness," Beau had joined the military. According to Beau, he had bargained his way out of the navy. "They knew I was selling drugs and skin flicks, but they couldn't prove anything, and I had too much on one of the [ship's officers], so I agreed to a [dishonorable] discharge and got out without doing any time." He had lasted a year in a marriage before being divorced because of his "boozing and womanizing."

When they got to Detroit, Beau showered Juanita with attention and a new "sexy" wardrobe and easily talked her into marrying him. He got a job as a bartender and bouncer at a nightclub where Juanita became an exotic dancer. She soon learned that he was pimping for some of the other dancers and distributing cocaine. Without informing Beau, she began to sell prescription drugs that she obtained from a "black market" connection. Enjoying the high lifestyle, she played down the risks involved, saying "I'm smarter than that [i.e., than to get caught]."

The crisis that led to Juanita's hospitalization arose when Beau attempted to get her to "date" a client of the club who was willing to pay handsomely for an evening with her. She refused and violent arguments ensued. Beau took back presents he had given her, took most of her clothes out of their apartment, and renewed his demands that she "date" the man. Juanita promptly took some pills, washing them down with liquor. After being restored to consciousness at the hospital, she asserted that she had not known what else to do, because she could not, and would not, go back home and did not want to have to "be nice to creepy men." She would stay with Beau and they could continue to "make lots of money," she said, but she, and not he, would decide which men "got their hands on" her.

Histrionic Personality Disorder (DSM-IV)

Formerly called Hysteria or Hysterical Personality Disorder, HPD is described in DSM-IV as follows: A pervasive pattern of excessive emotionality and attention seeking, beginning by early adulthood and present in a variety of contexts, as indicated by at least five of the following:

- Is uncomfortable in situations in which he or she is not the center of attention.
- Interaction with others often is characterized by inappropriate sexually seductive or provocative behavior.
- Displays rapidly shifting and shallow expression of emotions.
- Consistently uses physical appearance to draw attention to the self.
- Style of speech is excessively impressionistic and lacking in detail.
- Self-dramatization, theatrical, and exaggerated expression of emotion.
- Suggestibility, that is easily influenced by others or circumstances.
- Considers relationships to be more intimate than they actually are.

What kinds of behaviors do individuals manifesting HPD exhibit in close and intimate relationships?

Case History

A Histrionic Couple Relationship

Striding along with an arm around each other in a walking embrace, the couple made a striking picture as they exited the college football stadium. Nobody could miss the flamboyance of their college color garb, complete with cowboy hats and boots. Both thrust out their chests. His bright shirt was open halfway down his chest, despite the cool autumn air. The seductiveness of her tight blouse and skimpy skirt were enhanced by her hip-swinging walk. Gaily they called out the school yell to people they knew and to people they did not know; their team had won. When there was a response, they acknowledged it with a sweeping gesture much in the manner of monarchs accepting the plaudits of their subjects.

Bob and Gayla Skipper, a couple in their middle thirties, were on the way home to host one of their "patented" postgame parties. Lots of liquor would flow; jokes complete with pantomime, dramatization, and cueing of listeners for applause would pop out of Bob almost nonstop; and Gayla would be persuaded or would volunteer to treat the guests to "a few songs" in her husky and "sexy" tones. The guests would be "simply a few of our closest friends," probably somewhere in the neighborhood of 20 to 30 persons.

Life for the Skippers was basically one ongoing party, at which they usually vied for the limelight. The guests for their year-long schedule of parties constantly changed. Bob, a salesman, continually invited customers and potential customers. Gayla brought in acquaintances she made in the course of her work as a human resources director for a large company and from her "little theater" activities. The Skippers' marital relationship included a significant amount of animated conversation and extensive expressions of endearment.

What neither disclosed to the other was that each occasionally "had a little fun on the side" with a brief extramarital fling. None of the affairs lasted very long or provided much satisfaction after the initial thrill had worn off. Asked how they felt about their partner, each was likely to respond in terms of how the other "loves me very much," "adores me." As a kind of second thought, they would relate unselfconsciously how happy they were, or, on some occasions, how bad things were, always painting themselves as the hero/heroine or victim.

The Skippers' children are virtual caricatures of their parents in their eagerness to please, their seeking for attention, and their shallowness.

RELATIONAL ACTION PATTERNS: AN OVERVIEW

This section briefly summarizes interactional patterns, syndromes, and symptomatology that APD and HPD individuals exhibit in interpersonal relationships.

Common Characteristics

A significant common feature of APD and HPD is their social nature. Unlike some other psychiatric disorders, they require interaction with others for their expression. They share a coping style that predisposes the individuals so afflicted to seek out other persons and to deal with them in social relationships. To contemplate being antisocial or histrionic in isolation generates comparisons to the question of whether there is noise when a tree falls in the forest without anyone around. Somebody else is required in order to fully complete transactions and express the needs and desires inherent in the disorders.

Additionally, individuals with both types of personality can be charming and may be capable of eliciting strong positive reactions from others, particularly during the early stages of an interpersonal relationship. The most common, everyday term for describing these personalities in their interaction with others is, however, "selfish." Self-centeredness is perhaps their most obvious shared attribute. Cloninger's (1978; Cloninger & Guze, 1970; Cloninger, Reich, & Guze, 1975) schema, which has been adapted by Taylor (1993), shows commonality between the disorders by classifying both as high in novelty seeking and low in harm avoidance (i.e., having reckless disregard for personal safety and the safety of others).

The major difference between APD and HPD personalities in the Cloninger schema lies in how they depend on others for rewards. They need others for quite different reasons and relate to others in different ways. Antisocial personalities are rated low in reward dependence whereas histrionic personalities are rated high. This difference is described in detail by Millon (1981). He labeled antisocial personalities as independent in their style of interpersonal functioning and histrionic personalities as dependent.

Active-Independent: The Aggressive Personality

Antisocial personalities who are active in their interpersonal independence (termed "aggressive personalities" by Millon, 1981) believe only in themselves and mistrust others. They do not depend on others for support, nurturance, or success. Propelled by a need to prove their superiority and anticipating that others will be hostile to them, they display a tendency to turn to themselves as the primary source for fulfilling their needs. Distrust of others is a stronger motivator than a belief in their own self-worth. They make a grab for power in order to get it before others can get it and harm, humiliate, or exploit them. Once they get the power, they use it in a vengeful and vindictive fashion, seeking retribution for what they consider past humiliations. Their action constitutes a preemptive strike against the painful treatment they have come to expect. In everyday terms, they have a "chip on [the] shoulder" attitude (Millon, 1981, p. 212). The world is perceived as a hostile place. The drive for power emerges from "a deep well of hate and the desire for retribution and vindication" (Millon, 1981, p. 202).

Active-Dependent: The Gregarious Pattern

Actively dependent in interpersonal relationships, histrionic personalities display a gregarious pattern of relating (Millon, 1981). They lack identity apart from others and must gain approval and nurturance from their fellow creatures. Feeling hollow, they seek emotional supplies indiscriminately from whatever potential sources they may encounter. Not only do they often seek attention inappropriately, but they also have trouble in being satiated and tend to move on to other sources after they get approval from one person.

Histrionic personalities may be quite accomplished in "selling" themselves through their charm and skill in "reading" how to please the other. Unfortunately, they are much less adept and capable in delivering genuine substance to the relationship. Once the other is "hooked," histrionic personalities may withdraw quickly lest their shallowness and inability to deliver become evident. They fear at some level of awareness that others will discover how little they are able to provide in terms of what they flamboyantly promised in return for what they greedily seek. Combine this tendency with the inability of the other person to fill the "bottomless pit" of the histrionic person, and the reasons for the superficiality and often ephemeral nature of the histrionic person's relationships become evident.

At the same time that they may blindly seek approval, esteem, and affection from inappropriate sources, histrionic personalities may exhibit an exquisite sensitiveness to potential rejection. It is virtually impossible to be neutral toward many such personalities without eliciting in them feelings of rejection, failure, dejection, and anxiety. At such points, particularly when new sources of emotional attention and feeding are not readily available, the histrionic personality appears most vulnerable to depression and, consequently, most open to seeking a therapist.

RECENT LITERATURE ON THE DISORDERS

Recent literature on APD and HPD appears to add to the growing case for giving increased attention to the family context in which such persons are reared and to their current family, marital, and other intimate relationship contexts. The relationship itself is a basic part of the functioning of both disorders. Because of the importance of interaction with others in the derivation and continuation of the disorders, inclusion of the relationship/interaction seems essential to an accurate and adequate diagnosis and assessment.

Differential Incidence

Although APD and HPD are found in both males and females, APD is more commonly diagnosed in males and HPD is more frequently diagnosed in females. Differences in the incidence of diagnosed disorders according to gender have long been observed. Twenty years ago, Cloninger and associates (Cloninger, Reich, & Guze, 1975) found APD to be three times more common in men, for example.

Various interpretations have been made of the differences. Taylor (1993) recently speculated that the variations in observed frequency may result from the effects of such gender-related factors as developmental and endocrine influences "on the common pathophysiology" (p. 259). Suggestions have been made for changes to the existing criteria for HPD (Pfohl, 1991). Some recent research, however, suggests that sex biases may be reflected in the diagnosis of these disorders, although not in the diagnostic criteria used in the assessment (Ford & Widiger, 1989).

Etiology

Some experts have suggested that a strong relationship between APD and HPD implies a common etiology expressed differently in men (APD) and women (HPD) (Lilienfield, Van Valkenburg, Larntz, & Akiskal, 1986; Taylor, 1993). The reality of that possibility is far from being demonstrated at this time. Indeed, some widely held explanations of etiology for the two disorders would not support a common etiology.

Antisocial Personality Disorder

An abusive or disruptive childhood has been linked in theory to the later development of APD (Marshall & Barbaree, 1984, 1991). Recent research by Luntz and Widom (1994) has found that abuse and neglect during childhood can be a "significant predictor of the number of lifetime symptoms of . . . and a diagnosis of antisocial personality disorder" (p. 672). These findings tend to support earlier research, such as that of Glueck and Glueck (1956, 1959), which found that antisocial disorder began early in life, continued far into adulthood, and was related to neglect and deprivation of emotional ties. Relatedly, Guze (Guze, Woodruff, & Clayton, 1971) supplied data establishing the child-to-adult continuum of the disorder (Akhtar, 1992). The majority of persons diagnosed with APD had parents who were separated, divorced, dead (with death of one or both occurring during the client's childhood); who had deserted; or who were alcoholic or criminal (Taylor, 1993).

Luntz and Widom (1994) interpret their research as implying that factors other than childhood abuse or neglect also play a role in the development of APD. They do not, however, indicate what might constitute additional factors.

Recognition that early parental rejection may evolve into a long-term cycle of parent-child conflict provides a potential bridge between theories espousing a childhood abuse/neglect explanation and an additional factors explanation of etiology. The initial parental rejection may stem from a negative reaction to the infant's original disposition (i.e., he or she for constitutional reasons may be "cold," testy, resistive, and difficult to manage). Once the infant has been stereotyped as a difficult and miserable human being, reciprocal negative feelings build up into a continuing feud between parent and child (Millon, 1981). Observations of family systems in operation have long provided indications that family-of-origin ties continue to flourish and to affect behavior long after individuals have left home. So-called childhood influences are not confined to tender years and are not necessarily carried solely "inside the head" of a person but continue as ongoing systemic and interpersonal patterns (Bowen, 1978; Framo, 1992; Williamson, 1991).

Persons with APD display a tendency to marry someone with the same characteristics, according to Taylor (1993, citing Guze, 1976). Decades ago, research established homogamy in mate selection in such areas as propinquity (Katz & Hill, 1958), social class (Hollingshead, 1950), ethnic background (Thomas, 1954), and physical and psychological characteristics (Burgess & Wallin, 1944).

Histrionic Personality Disorder

Three features of persons manifesting HPD can be linked to three distinct patterns of parental treatment. As adapted from Millon's (1981) description, parents of children who develop histrionic personalities: (1) seldom punish the child, (2) provide rewards only for the actions they approve or admire, and (3) reward somewhat unpredictably by sometimes failing to reward even when the child acts in an acceptable manner. The consequences of such parental behavior are the creation of behaviors designed essentially to (1) secure rewards, (2) create a sense of competence and acceptance only if others attend to and commend one's actions, and (3) develop a pattern of seeking approval for approval's sake. As with antisocial personalities, the patterns of parent-child interaction in the families of future histrionic adults tend to continue in long-term and often lifelong repetition, carrying over into relationships with peers and children.

CRITERIA FOR RELATIONAL DIAGNOSIS

If a couple meet a specified minimum of the characteristics associated with the particular type of relationship system, diagnosis is applicable to that type of relationship system. Thus, in the cases discussed earlier, Beau and Juanita Sayers qualify as having an Antisocial Relationship Disorder (ARD), according to the following criteria for such designation. Similarly, Bob and Gayla Skipper meet the criteria for an Histrionic Relationship Disorder (HRD).

Antisocial Relationship Disorder (ARD)

For the ARD diagnosis to apply, the following conditions must be met:

A. Both partners at least 18 years of age.
B. A pervasive pattern of disregard for and violation of the rights of each other and/or children, as indicated by at least five of the following:
   1. Failure to conform to social norms with respect to lawful behaviors as indicated by repeatedly performing acts that are grounds for arrest, thereby putting couple or children at risk.
   2. Sexual abuse of children or each other.
   3. Irritability and aggressiveness, as indicated by physical fights or assaults, including child-beating or abuse of family elders.
   4. Consistent irresponsibility, as indicated by repeated failure to sustain consistent work behavior or honor financial obligations, including support for dependents on a regular basis.
   5. Neglect of parental or guardian responsibilities, as indicated by one or more of the following:
      a. Malnutrition of child
      b. Child's illness resulting from lack of minimal hygiene
      c. Failure to obtain medical care for a seriously ill child
      d. Child's dependence on neighbors or nonresident relatives for food or shelter
      e. Failure to arrange for a caregiver for a young child when parent is away from home
      f. Repeated use on personal items of money required for household necessities
   6. Impulsivity or failure to plan ahead, thereby putting the couple and/or children at risk.
   7. Deceitfulness, as indicated by repeated lying, use of aliases, or "conning" others for personal profit or pleasure.
   8. Reckless disregard for safety of the couple or children.
   9. Lack of remorse, as indicated by being indifferent to or rationalizing having hurt, mistreated, or stolen from others.
   10. Lack of sense of right or wrong, no conscience.

Occurrence of antisocial relationship behavior is not found exclusively during the course of schizophrenia or a manic episode.

Histrionic Relationship Disorder (HRD)

For the HRD diagnosis to apply, the following criteria must be met:
A. Both partners at least 18 years of age.
B. A pervasive pattern of excessive emotionality and attention seeking, starting with the beginning of the relationship, as indicated by at least five of the following:
    1. Couple constantly seek or demand reassurance, approval, or praise.
    2. Interaction often is characterized by inappropriate sexually seductive or provocative behavior with children or others.
    3. Rapid shifting and shallow expression of emotions.
    4. Consistent use of physical appearance to draw attention to couple or self.
    5. Style of speech that is excessively impressionistic and lacking in detail.
    6. Self-dramatization, theatricality, and exaggerated expression of emotion.
    7. Suggestibility, that is, couple easily influenced by each other, children, or circumstances.
    8. Relationships considered more intimate than they are in reality.

SUGGESTED USEFUL TREATMENT PLAN/PROTOCOL

Treatment approaches used with personality disorders typically have focused on individuals. Pessimistic statements in the literature regarding the outlook for treatment of persons with antisocial and histrionic disorders must be read with that fact in mind.

Antisocial Relationship Disorder

Many persons with APD are unable to change, according to Millon (1981), because of deeply rooted habits that are highly resistant to change. Only if this kind of personality finds a socially acceptable area in which to channel his or her hostilities and energies can the prognosis be promising. Some experts claim that antisocial personalities are not treatable (Woody, McLellan, Luborsky, & O'Brien, 1985). Others hold that such persons need to be told that their condition is not amenable to treatment, that they are responsible for their actions, and that when they get older they may develop better self-control (Taylor, 1993).

Luntz and Widom (1994) suggest that if interventions are made early enough with abused and neglected individuals who have acquired antisocial characteristics, chronic APD may be avoided in their adulthood. Thus, professionals often seem to conclude that unless antisocial personality characteristics are modified before they become deeply rooted, it is necessary to wait until some kind of middle-age "burnout" occurs.

These personalities seldom think that they need treatment. They may contact a therapist only because of external conditions such as major marital discord, work conflicts, or court referral. On a one-to-one basis with a therapist, they may react as if they are being called on to "submit" to something they do not want. They frequently attempt to outwit and defeat the therapist, either by being openly militant or outwardly congenial but cleverly noncooperative and evasive (Marshall & Barbaree, 1991; Millon, 1981).

Results of group treatment are a bit more promising. Agreeing that the main difficulty in treating APDs is lack of motivation for change, Salama (1988) concluded that they are most likely to benefit from a therapeutic community approach to treatment. In groups led by professionals, these personality types may be disruptive. Sometimes, however, they do pick up useful insights and social skills. Group self-help procedures in which they can discuss their attitudes freely with peers without feeling the conflict they experience facing a professional may help them to acquire some loyalty and sense of group responsibility that may be generalizable to other settings (Millon, 1981).

Family Therapy Approaches

Some guidance for dealing therapeutically with ARD cases is provided by the Beavers Systems Model of family functioning (Beavers & Hampson, 1990). The types of families that produce such personalities are what Beavers terms "severely dysfunctional centrifugal families." Marked by poor boundaries, confused communication, and other deficiencies, these families do not provide strong incentives for children to attach to their family or expectations that they will receive support.

The treatment perspective recommended in this chapter is that of integrative psychotherapy, based on psychodynamic, family systems, and social learning approaches (Kirschner & Kirschner, 1986; Nichols, 1995; Nichols & Everett, 1986). Social learning (behavioral) perspectives and techniques have been demonstrated to be particularly fitting for some antisocial patterns. Couple's therapy is the preferred modality for both ARD and HRD, frequently conducted concurrently with individual therapy. A combination of self-help group treatment and family therapy appears to be more promising with most ARD persons than individual therapies. Family-of-origin work is used with some cases at a later stage, particularly in instances in which it appears possible to secure positive changes at the family system level. Carefully planned skill training should be a part of the regimen for many such persons. This involves especially helping family members to learn to interact and communicate in more adaptive ways (Dumas, 1989).

Working with a family of marital system places the therapist and the clients in a very different position from dealing solely with the antisocial personality on a one-to-one basis. Issues of blame, questions of authority, and other matters that typically prove difficult in individual therapy are minimized by the fact that the focus is on the relationship, the system, rather than on one person. Working directly with family processes also enhances the possibility of dealing directly with conditions and processes that shaped and continue to maintain pathology. Whether it is possible to effect change in the family of origin of the affected persons or not, it may be possible to change the current relationship and thus to provide something of a "corrective emotional experience" in relationships. Such therapeutic interventions as "midwiving a relationship" (Nichols, 1988) seem preferable to individual approaches in attempting to ameliorate the conditions of both an ARD and an HRD.

The therapist's behavior with antisocial clients requires particular attention. Millon (1981) correctly urged the therapist to tolerate the client's less attractive traits as well as possible, remembering the setting from which he or she came. Advocating a mixture of firmness, fairness, and strong authority on the part of the therapist, he suggested that one can provide a helpful model by teaching new attitudes and offering more constructive direction of the client's energies.

Histrionic Relationship Disorder

As in the case of ARDs, persons involved in HRDs seldom seek therapy except when impelled by external forces such as social disapproval or deprivation. Turkat (1990) says that the majority of HPDs present with depression and are no longer motivated for therapy once the mood has lifted.

A somewhat different perspective was given by Millon (1981). Histrionic personalities do have predictable difficulties in sustaining interest in long-term therapy unless their discouraging life experiences continue, he said. Nevertheless, due to their motivation and skill for maintaining relationships, those who enter therapy often have a fairly good prognosis.

Millon (1981) recommended an initial therapeutic intervention of calming down the HPD's tendencies toward overemotionalizing. Next, attention should be given to strengthening a previously successful lifestyle. If therapy goes beyond the brief intervention stage, attention should be given to building self-reliance and the capacity to form more lasting emotional attachments. Group and family therapy are recommended as possible ways to help the client to develop better ways of relating to others (Millon, 1981).

Family Therapy

Most of the previous statements regarding the efficacy of family therapy for individuals manifesting ARD also apply in working with HRD cases. Of particular value is the possibility of helping partners in an histrionic relationship to establish safe boundaries so that they can be helped to negotiate clear communication and predictable interactive systems of reward. In many instances, they can be assisted to realize that their current relationship does not have to embody the capriciousness of rewarding that existed in their family of origin.

With respect to current relationships with the family of origin, Williamson's (1991) approach to reworking the authority relationship between adult clients and their parents may be useful in modifying some of their long-term patterns for dealing with the world.

OUTCOME RESEARCH

Outcome research on individual treatment with APD and HRD is not promising. Both controlled research and clinical research point to "unsuccessful treatment outcomes" (Turkat, 1990, p. 60, citing Liebowitz, Stone, & Turkat, 1986). Reviews of outcomes with APD are particularly pessimistic; some conclude that it is not responsive to any treatment (Taylor, 1993, citing Woody et al., 1985).

There is not much useful information available on intervention with HPD cases (Turkat, 1990). Among the few bright spots is the finding of Winston and coworkers (1994) that active dynamic short-term psychotherapy is beneficial with HPD. The authors found no significant differences between short-term psychodynamic therapy that focused on affect or on brief adaptive psychotherapy that was more cognitive. The improvement was maintained in an average follow-up period of 1.5 years.

Outcome research with ARD and HRD is available mainly from clinical research and by extrapolation from family therapy approaches in which an individual DSM diagnosis was used and marital and family therapy were employed.

Treatment focused on ARD and HRD as interactive systems should provide adequate opportunity to secure reliable outcome data in a relatively short time.

REFERENCES

Akhtar, S. (1992). *Broken structures: Severe personality disorders and their treatment.* Northvale, NJ: Aronson.

American Psychiatric Association (1994). *Diagnostic and statistical manual* (4th ed.). Washington, DC: Author.

Beavers, W. R., & Hampson, R. B. (1990). *Successful families: Assessment and intervention.* New York: Norton.

Bowen, M. (1978). *Family therapy in clinical practice.* New York: Aronson.

Bowlby, J. A. (1977a). The making and breaking of affectional bonds: I. Aetiology and psychopathology in the light of attachment theory. *British Journal of Psychiatry, 130,* 201–210.

Bowlby, J. A. (1977b). The making and breaking of affectional bonds: II. Some principles of psychotherapy. *British Journal of Psychiatry, 130,* 421–431.

Burgess, E. W., & Wallin, P. (1943). Homogamy in social characteristics. *American Journal of Sociology, 49,* 109–124.

Burgess, E. W., & Wallin, P. (1944). Homogamy in personal characteristics. *Journal of Abnormal and Social Psychology, 29,* 475–481.

Cloninger, C. R. (1978). The antisocial personality. *Hospital Practice, 13,* 97–106.

Cloninger, C. R., & Guze, S. B. (1970). Psychiatric illness and female criminality: The role of sociopathy and hysteria in the antisocial woman. *American Journal of Psychiatry, 127,* 303–311.

Cloninger, C. R., Reich, T., & Guze, S. B. (1975). The multifactorial model of disease transmission. II. Sex differences in the familial transmission of sociopathy (antisocial personality). *British Journal of Psychiatry, 17,* 103–137.

Dumas, J. E. (1989). Treating antisocial behavior in children: Child and family approaches. *Clinical Psychology Review, 9,* 197–222.

Ford, M. R., & Widiger, T. A. (1989). Sex bias in the diagnosis of histrionic and antisocial personality disorders. *Journal of Consulting and Clinical Psychology, 57,* 301–305.

Framo, J. L. (1992). *Family-of-origin therapy: An intergenerational approach.* New York: Brunner/Mazel.

Glueck, S., & Glueck, E. (1956). *Physique and delinquency.* New York: Harper.

Glueck, S., & Glueck, E. (1959). *Predicting delinquency and crime.* Cambridge, MA: Harvard University.

Guze, S. B. (1976). *Criminality and psychiatric disorder.* New York: Oxford University.

Guze, S. B., Woodruff, R. A., & Clayton, P. J. (1971). Hysteria and antisocial behavior: Further evidence for association. *American Journal of Psychiatry, 127,* 957–960.

Hollingshead, A. B. (1950). Cultural factors in mate selection. *American Sociological Review, 15,* 619–627.

Katz, A. M., & Hill, R. (1958). Residential propinquity and marital selection: A review of theory, method and fact. *Marriage and Family Living, 20,* 27–34.

Kirschner, D. A., & Kirschner, S. (1986). *Comprehensive family therapy: An integration of systemic and psychodynamic treatment models.* New York: Brunner/Mazel.

Liebowitz, N. R., Stone, N. H., & Turkat, I. D. (1986). Treatment of personality disorders. In A. J. Frances & R. E. Hales (Eds.), *American Psychiatric Association annual review* (vol 5., pp. 356–393). Washington, DC: American Psychiatric Press.

Lilienfield, S. O., Van Valkenburg, C., Larntz, K., & Akiskal, H. L. (1986). The relationship of histrionic personality disorder to antisocial personality and somatization disorders. *American Journal of Psychiatry, 143,* 718–722.

Luntz, B. K., & Widom, C. S. (1994). Antisocial personality disorder in abuse and neglected children grown up. *American Journal of Psychiatry, 151,* 670–674.

Marshall, W. L., & Barbaree, H. E. (1984). Disorders of personality, impulse and adjustment. In M. Hersen & S. M. Turner (Eds.), *Adult psychopathology and diagnosis* (pp. 406–449). New York: Wiley.

Marshall, W. L., & Barbaree, H. E. (1991). Personality, impulse control, and adjustment disorders. In M. Hersen & S. M. Turner (Eds.), *Adult psychopathology and diagnosis* (2nd ed.) (pp. 360–391). New York: Wiley.

Millon, T. (1981). *Disorders of personality: DSM-II: Axis II.* New York: Wiley.

Millon, T. (1987). A theoretical derivation of pathological personalities. In T. Millon & G. L. Klerman (Eds.), *Contemporary directions in psychopathology: Toward the DSM-IV* (pp. 639–669). New York: Guilford.

Millon, T., & Klerman, G. L. (Eds.) (1987). *Contemporary directions in psychopathology: Toward the DSM-IV.* New York: Guilford.

Nichols, W. C. (1988). *Marital therapy: An integrative approach.* New York: Guilford.

Nichols, W. C. (1995). *Treating people in families: An integrative approach.* New York: Guilford.

Nichols, W. C., & Everett, C. A. (1986). *Systemic family therapy: An integrative approach.* New York: Guilford.

Pfohl, B. (1991). Histrionic personality disorder: A review of available data and recommendations for DSM-IV. *Journal of Personality Disorders, 5,* 150–166.

Salama, A. A. (1988). The antisocial personality (the sociopathic personality). *Psychiatric Journal of the University of Ottawa, 13,* 149–153.

Sutker, P. B., & Allain, A. N. (1983). Behavior and personality assessment in men labeled adaptive sociopaths. *Journal of Behavioral Assessment, 5,* 65–79.

Taylor, M. A. (1993). *The neuropsychiatric guide to modern everyday psychiatry.* New York: Free Press.

Thomas, J. L. (1954). Out-group marriage patterns of some selected ethnic groups. *American Catholic Social Review, 15,* 9–18.

Turkat, I. D. (1990). *The personality disorders: A psychological approach to clinical management.* New York: Pergamon.

Williamson, D. L. (1991). *The intimacy paradox: Personal authority in the family system.* New York: Guilford.

Winston, A., Laikin, M., Pollack, J., Samstag, L. W., McCullough, L., & Muran, J. C. (1994). Short-term psychotherapy of personality disorders. *American Journal of Psychiatry, 151,* 190–194.

Woody, G. E., McLellan, A. T., Luborsky, L., & O'Brien, C. P. (1985). Sociopathy and psychotherapy outcome. *Archives of General Psychiatry, 42,* 1081–1086.

CHAPTER 20

Schema-Focused Diagnosis for Personality Disorders

JEFFREY E. YOUNG, PhD and VICKI L. GLUHOSKI, PhD

Interest in defining personality and associated pathology began many centuries ago. Over time, a tradition has evolved that focuses on the intrapsychic nature of personality disorders. This tradition has remained largely unchallenged and continues to be manifested in Axis II of DSM-IV (American Psychiatric Association, 1994). In this chapter we argue that limitations in the Axis II diagnostic approach impair our ability to understand personality pathology comprehensively. More specifically, a diagnostic system is needed that takes into account the relational context of personality.

PERSONALITY CLASSIFICATION: HISTORICAL BACKGROUND

By reviewing classifications of personality and historical trends in personality pathology, we provide a background for understanding the basis for DSM-IV. We discuss criticisms of the current diagnostic system for personality disorders and outline the rationale for diagnosis within a relational context. Young's schema-focused model is described and the utility of this model for personality disorder diagnosis is addressed. Finally, the treatment implications of this proposed diagnostic approach are discussed. It is hoped that this chapter demonstrates the critical need to attend to interpersonal factors in the diagnosis of personality disorders.

What Is Personality?

A number of controversial issues have been raised about assessing and diagnosing personality. Of primary significance is the definition of personality itself. Millon (1981) defined personality as "a complex pattern of deeply embedded psychological characteristics that are largely unconscious, cannot be eradicated easily and express themselves automatically in almost every facet of functioning" (p. 8). Others (Alden, Wiggins, & Pincus, 1990; Costa & McCrae, 1992) have suggested that personality is an individual's unique pattern of cognitions, emotions, and behaviors, particularly within an interpersonal realm.

More specifically, personality can be viewed at several levels of analysis: biologically, including innate temperament; intrapsychically, as a set of defensive maneuvers or as a developing self; behaviorally, as a set of learned behavioral responses; culturally, as a response to social forces; or interpersonally, as an outgrowth of ongoing social relations. Vaillant (1987) argued for just two components of personality: temperament and character. He suggested that temperament reflects inherent biological and genetic processes. For Vaillant, character develops out of early experiences and includes the individual's typical style of responding to his or her environment. Although his model is parsimonious, it may not account for the full range of factors that contribute to each individual's uniqueness.

It is clear that there is no universally accepted definition and classification of personality. Historically, personality has been classified in many ways. These models include temperament, factorial, circumplex, and five-factor approaches.

Temperament Models

The earliest approaches to temperament can be traced to the Greeks and were based on bodily humors; these humors were the forerunners of basic temperaments. The most recent temperament models have been based on underlying endocrine or neuroanatomical structures. (See Millon, 1981, for a review.) Maddi (1968) has proposed that an inherent activity trait determines personality. He identified high-activation individuals who seek stimulation to maintain an elevated behavior level. Low-activation individuals avoid stimulation so that their low level of behavior will not be disrupted. Buss and Plomin (1975) also focused on activity level but argued for four basic temperaments: activity, emotionality, sociability, and impulsivity. All of these recent temperament theorists are attempting to describe inherent biological processes that are manifested in observable behavior. The focus is on the immutable, genetically-based aspects of personality.

Factorial Models

Another recent trend is based on statistical analysis of a broad range of traits, behaviors, and symptoms. In this model, intercorrelations among individual responses, characteristics, and observations are determined. Clusters of descriptors are then derived statistically. Cattell (1965) has identified 16 factors that he believes are primary in determining personality classification. These factors are arranged in bipolar sets and include such variables as low versus high ego strength, submission versus dominance, and dull versus bright. From these 16 factors, Cattell argued that four basic personality types can be identified: high anxious-introversion, low anxious-introversion, high anxious-extraversion, and low anxious-extraversion. However, although these characteristics may cluster together, they are not tied to clinical diagnoses and have limited use for clinicians.

Circumplex Models

Other models of personality have been developed that focus on interpersonal factors. In circumplex models, typically eight interpersonal variables are arranged in a two-dimensional circular space (see Pincus & Wiggins, 1990; Sim & Romney, 1990). These categories are ordered around two underlying orthogonal dimensions: dominance versus submission (the control axis) and nurturance versus hostility (the affiliation axis). The advantage of circumplex models is that they include a wide range of traits, and, thus, numerous clusters of styles can be examined (Gunderson, Links, & Reich, 1991). In addition, the social context of the individual is not neglected but in fact is highlighted.

Five-Factor Models

Costa and McCrae (1990, 1992) argue that personality consists of varying degrees of five factors: neuroticism, extraversion, openness, agreeableness, and conscientiousness. They cite research that supports this model and conclude that these factors are valid, universally observed, have a heritable component, and are stable across time. Others (Hofstee, deRaad, & Goldberg, 1992) have suggested that an integration of the five-factor and circumplex models is the most appropriate and comprehensive system for assessing personality. These theorists have developed ten circumplexes, which they have defined as an abridged big-five-dimension circumplex. This approach is the first attempt to integrate the strengths of established models of personality in a new format.

HISTORICAL TRENDS IN PERSONALITY PATHOLOGY

Although the models just outlined provide rich descriptive information, they have limited utility in determining personality pathology. In this realm, several systems of typology exist.

Character Pathology

The most widely recognized and extensively developed models of personality disorders are psychoanalytic. Freud (1932) proposed that character disorders be classified based on the constructs of ego, superego, and id. He suggested the narcissistic, compulsive, and erotic types, each of which is associated with a dominant ego, superego, and id, respectively. Subsequently, analysts have differentiated character pathology into three types: the oral, anal, and phallic characters, based on the level of psychosexual development at which they are fixated.

Behavioral, Interpersonal, and Social Learning Pathology

Several of the models of personality outlined earlier also address pathology, particularly the circumplex and five-factor models. These approaches emphasize that personality disorders occur within a social context; the expressed behavior is distressing to others but the individual may not view it as problematic (Vaillant, 1987). Pincus and Wiggins (1990) suggest that faulty interpersonal behavior is the defining characteristic of most people with personality disorders. These individuals have inflexible and ineffective patterns of interaction. Their behavior elicits a limited range of responses from others, and thus the pattern is continued.

Gunderson and coauthors (1991) argue that a circumplex model is appropriate for personality disorders; they view pathological personalities as the extreme of naturally occurring traits. Sim and Romney (1990) believe the interpersonal circumplex is suited for diagnosis because these individuals use certain behaviors to an extreme degree and rely exclusively on a few interpersonal action patterns. Both of these factors can be charted within a circumplex model.

Some (Widiger & Frances, 1985) have argued that most personality disorders can be defined easily with a circumplex design. However, Pincus and Wiggins (1990) have found that only six personality disorders can be adequately captured with that model: avoidant, schizoid, dependent, narcissistic, histrionic, and antisocial. They believe that a five-factor model is better suited for describing all personality disorders. Costa and McCrae (1990, 1992) concur. They believe that personality disorders represent an extreme variation of the dimensions of normal personality and suggest that Axis II should include a description of the individual's personality in the five domains. Treatment could then focus on the symptoms and not the underlying personality structure.

Millon (1981) has proposed a classification system based on social learning theory. He suggested a twin-axis model, which represents a combination of temperament and social learning. On one axis is the active-passive dimension of personality. On the second axis is the reinforcement style characteristic of the individual. He distinguished four of these: dependent, independent, ambivalent, and detached reinforcement styles. This four-by-two system leads to eight basic personality types, including passive-dependent, active-independent, and active-ambivalent. The system is based on how the individual goes about gaining rewards and interacting with the environment. These patterns are derived from a variety of social learning sources: feelings and attitudes, behavior control, styles of communication, content of learning, family structure, and traumatic experiences.

Millon suggested three criteria that must be met to diagnose personality pathology: rigid use of coping behaviors, repeated self-defeating cycles, and questionable stability in stressful situations.

CRITIQUE OF DSM-IV, AXIS II

Like many of the models just discussed, Axis II of DSM-IV developed out of a descriptive rather than theoretical or empirical approach. By relying on historically traditional categories rather than a unified theory or on empirical research, its assumptions about the nature of personality disorders remain unconfirmed. By not questioning previous theorists but instead expanding within these existing frameworks, DSM-IV has perpetuated the limitations of earlier models of personality disorders, particularly psychoanalytic classifications.

The approach of DSM-IV has been widely criticized. Many (Benjamin, 1987; Buss & Craik, 1987; Grove & Tellegen, 1991) find fault with the overlapping categories. Because of the shared descriptors, individuals can receive diagnoses of several personality disorders; the categories are not orthogonal. The overlap is systematic, suggesting that these categories do not define discrete disorders. Differentiating among diagnoses thus is problematic.

In addition, there is limited empirical support for the existing categories (Benjamin, 1987; Livesley, Jackson, & Shroeder, 1991). These groupings were developed primarily from clinical observation and are arbitrary. Acceptable standards of reliability and validity have not been demonstrated (Livesley, 1987). The subjective nature of the descriptors contributes to the poor reliability; the criteria are vague, global, and require much inference on the part of the diagnostician. We have had many instances of patients who present with serious, lifelong characterological issues yet who fit none of the present Axis II diagnoses. This is particularly true of patients with more complex, lifelong relationship difficulties.

Alternatives to Axis II

Several theorists have suggested ways to improve personality disorder classification in DSM-IV. Widiger and Frances (1985) argued that personality disorders are not discrete entities. Because they have vague and overlapping boundaries, a categorical approach is inadequate. They proposed that a dimensional model is most appropriate. It offers several advantages: It is less arbitrary, more informative, and represents the continuum between normal and pathological behavior.

Others (Livesley, 1987) have argued that personality disorder criteria must be more specific. Buss and Craik (1987) believed that specific prototypical behaviors associated with each diagnosis must be identified and described. This information should enable clinicians to make more accurate diagnoses and enhance both reliability and validity.

Some researchers have begun to develop scales to determine more accurately how personality disorders should be diagnosed. Livesley, Jackson, and Schroeder (1991) constructed a scale with 100 personality dimensions and derived 16 components. These factors included social avoidance, hypersensitivity, and insecure attachment. They found much similarity between their empirically derived components and the Axis II personality disorders. However, their factors were much more specific and accurate. This work represents an initial and welcome attempt to develop empirically derived diagnoses.

Despite the new trends and possibilities for personality diagnosis just outlined, shortcomings still exist in all of these approaches. We propose that at least six conditions be met for an adequate model of personality diagnosis:

1. Diagnosis of personality disorders should be based on a sophisticated theoretical model of personality dysfunction with empirical support.
2. The relational context of personality pathology should be incorporated into the diagnosis.
3. The model should be more dimensional than categorical.
4. The dimensions should be broad and inclusive enough that they incorporate most major aspects of personality pathology.
5. The model should have treatment implications that guide the therapist.
6. The dimensional model should be subject to modification and adaptation as empirical data emerge from research studies.

The current Axis II personality disorder categories were not derived from extensive research. These disorders were designated somewhat arbitrarily and have questionable validity. Some of the newer models of personality discussed earlier, such as the circumplex and five-factor models, were theoretically derived. However, they were developed to describe aspects of normal functioning. Subsequently, they may not be comprehensive enough to define personality pathology.

YOUNG'S SCHEMA-FOCUSED MODEL

We will demonstrate how Young's schema-focused model (Young, 1990; Young, Beck, & Weinberger, 1993; Young & Klosko, 1993) can help overcome many of the limitations inherent in previous approaches to personality disorder diagnosis. This model represents a broad, clinically based approach to personality dysfunction that can be validated empirically. In addition, interpersonal experiences and their influence on the development and maintenance of personality are essential elements of this model. The remainder of this chapter outlines the schema-focused model and addresses its relation to personality disorder diagnosis. Finally, treatment implications of this approach are discussed.

Conceptual Model

Eighteen early maladaptive schemas (EMSs) are believed to be the defining core of personality disorders. (See Table 20.1.) An EMS is an encompassing theme about oneself and one's interpersonal relationships. EMSs have a cognitive, affective, and behavioral component. These maladaptive schemas are developed early in childhood and expanded throughout one's life. They often reflect a significant amount of dysfunction. Generally they operate outside of awareness, but the individual can be taught to recognize them through diverse techniques.

Three processes are associated with schemas: maintenance, avoidance, and compensation. These processes reflect coping styles that are generated in response to the schema and subsequently serve to reinforce it. Schema maintenance occurs when the individual engages in cognitive distortions and dysfunctional behavior patterns that directly support the early schema. For example, a woman with an abandonment schema

---

Table 20.1   Early Maladaptive Schemas with Domains (Revised January 1995)

Disconnection and Rejection

(Expectation that one's needs for security, safety, stability, nurturance, empathy, sharing of feelings, acceptance, and respect will not be met in a predictable manner. Typical family origin is detached, cold, rejecting, withholding, lonely, explosive, unpredictable, or abusive.)

1. Abandonment/Instability

   The perceived *instability* or *unreliability* of those available for support and connection.
   Involves the sense that significant others will not be able to continue providing emotional support, connection, strength, or practical protection because they are emotionally unstable and unpredictable (e.g., angry outbursts), unreliable, or erratically present; because they will die imminently; or because they will abandon the patient in favor of someone better.

2. Mistrust/Abuse

   The expectation that others will hurt, abuse, humiliate, cheat, lie, manipulate, or take advantage. Usually involves the perception that the harm is intentional or the result of unjustified and extreme negligence. May include the sense that one always ends up being cheated relative to others or "gets the short end of the stick."

3. Emotional Deprivation

   Expectation that one's desire for a normal degree of emotional support will not be adequately met by others. The three major forms of deprivation are:
   A. *Deprivation of Nurturance:* Absence of attention, affection, warmth, or companionship.
   B. *Deprivation of Empathy:* Absence of understanding, listening, self-disclosure, or mutual sharing of feelings from others.
   C. *Deprivation of Protection:* Absence of strength, direction, or guidance from others.

   (Continued)

Table 20.1   *(continued)*

Disconnection and Rejection

4. Defectiveness/Shame

   The feeling that one is defective, bad, unwanted, inferior, or invalid in important respects; or that one would be unlovable to significant others if exposed. May involve hypersensitivity to criticism, rejection, and blame; self-consciousness, comparisons, and insecurity around others; or a sense of shame regarding one's perceived flaws. These flaws may be private (e.g., selfishness, angry impulses, unacceptable sexual desires) or public (e.g., undesirable physical appearance, social awkwardness).

5. Social Isolation/Alienation

   The feeling that one is isolated from the rest of the world, different from other people, and/or not part of any group or community.

Impaired Autonomy and Performance

(Expectations about oneself and the environment that interfere with one's perceived ability to separate, survive, function independently, or perform successfully. Typical family origin is enmeshed, undermining of child's confidence, overprotective, or failing to reinforce child for performing competently outside the family.)

6. Dependence/Incompetence

   Belief that one is unable to handle one's *everyday responsibilities* in a competent manner, without considerable help from others (e.g., take care of oneself, solve daily problems, exercise good judgment, tackle new tasks, make good decisions). Often presents as helplessness.

7. Vulnerability to Harm or Illness (Random Events)

   Exaggerated fear that "random" catastrophe could strike at any time and that one will be unable to prevent it. Fears focus on one or more of the following: (A) *Medical:* e.g., heart attack, AIDS; (B) *Emotional:* e.g., go crazy; (C) *Natural/Phobic:* elevators, crime, airplanes, earthquakes.

8. Enmeshment/Undeveloped Self

   Excessive emotional involvement and closeness with one or more significant others (often parents), at the expense of full individuation or normal social development. Often involves the belief that at least one of the enmeshed individuals cannot survive or be happy without the constant support of the other. May also include feelings of being smothered by, or fused with, others. OR Insufficient individual identity. Often experienced as a feeling of emptiness and floundering, having no direction, or in extreme cases questioning one's existence.

9. Failure

   The belief that one has failed, will inevitably fail, or is fundamentally inadequate relative to one's peers in areas of *achievement* (school, career, sports, etc.). Often involves beliefs that one is stupid, inept, untalented, ignorant, lower in status, less successful than others, etc.

Impaired Limits

(Deficiency in internal limits, responsibility to others, or long-term goal orientation. Leads to difficulty respecting the rights of others, cooperating with others, making commitments, or setting and meeting realistic personal goals. Typical family origin is characterized by permissiveness, overindulgence, lack of direction, or a sense of superiority—rather than appropriate confrontation, discipline, and limits in relation to taking responsibility, cooperating in a reciprocal manner, and setting goals. In some cases, child may not have been pushed to tolerate normal levels of discomfort or may not have been given adequate supervision, direction, or guidance.)

Table 20.1   *(continued)*

Impaired Limits

10. Entitlement/Grandiosity

    The belief that one is superior to other people; entitled to special rights and privileges; or not bound by the rules of reciprocity that guide normal social interaction. Often involves insistence that one should be able to do or have whatever one wants, regardless of what is realistic, what others consider reasonable, or the cost to others; *or* an exaggerated focus on superiority (e.g., being among the most successful, famous, wealthy)—in order to achieve *power* or *control* (not primarily for attention or approval). Sometimes includes excessive competitiveness toward, or domination of, others: asserting one's power, forcing one's point of view, or controlling the behavior of others in line with one's own desires—without empathy or concern for others' needs or feelings.

11. Insufficient Self-Control/Self-Discipline

    Pervasive difficulty or refusal to exercise sufficient self-control and frustration tolerance to achieve one's personal goals or to restrain the excessive expression of one's emotions and impulses. In its milder form, patient presents with an exaggerated emphasis on discomfort-avoidance: avoiding pain, conflict, confrontation, responsibility, or overexertion—at the expense of personal fulfillment, commitment, or integrity.

Other-Directedness

(An excessive focus on the desires, feelings, and responses of others, at the expense of one's own needs—in order to gain love and approval, maintain one's sense of connection, or avoid retaliation. Usually involves suppression and lack of awareness regarding one's own anger and natural inclinations. Typical family origin is based on conditional acceptance: Children must suppress important aspects of themselves in order to gain love, attention, and approval. In many such families, the parents' emotional needs and desires—or social acceptance and status—are valued more than the unique needs and feelings of each child.)

12. Subjugation

    Excessive surrendering of control to others because one feels *coerced*—usually to avoid anger, retaliation, or abandonment. The two major forms of subjugation are:

    A. *Subjugation of Needs:* Suppression of one's preferences, decisions, and desires.

    B. *Subjugation of Emotions:* Suppression of emotional expression, especially anger.

    Usually involves the perception that one's own desires, opinions, and feelings are not valid or important to others. Frequently presents as excessive compliance, combined with hypersensitivity to feeling trapped. Generally leads to a buildup of anger, manifested in maladaptive symptoms (e.g., passive-aggressive behavior, uncontrolled outbursts of temper, psychosomatic symptoms, withdrawal of affection, "acting out," substance abuse).

13. Self-Sacrifice

    Excessive focus on *voluntarily* meeting the needs of others in daily situations, at the expense of one's own gratification. The most common reasons are: to prevent causing pain to others; to avoid guilt from feeling selfish; or to maintain the connection with others perceived as needy. Often results from an acute sensitivity to the pain of others. Sometimes leads to a sense that one's own needs are not being adequately met and to resentment of those who are taken care of. (Overlaps with concept of codependency.)

14. Approval-Seeking/Recognition-Seeking

    Excessive emphasis on gaining approval, recognition, or attention from other people, or fitting in, at the expense of developing a secure and true sense of self. One's sense of esteem is dependent primarily on the reactions of others rather than one's own natural inclinations. Sometimes includes an overemphasis on status, appearance, social acceptance, money, or achievement—as means of gaining *approval, admiration,* or *attention* (not primarily for power or control). Frequently results in major life decisions that are inauthentic or unsatisfying, or in hypersensitivity to rejection.

(Continued)

Table 20.1   *(continued)*

Overvigilance and Inhibition

(Excessive emphasis on controlling one's spontaneous feelings, impulses, and choices in order to avoid making mistakes or on meeting rigid, internalized rules and expectations about performance and ethical behavior—often at the expense of happiness, self-expression, relaxation, close relationships, or health. Typical family origin is grim (and sometimes punitive); Performance, duty, perfectionism, following rules, and avoiding mistakes predominate over pleasure, joy, and relaxation. There is usually an undercurrent of pessimism and worry—that things could fall apart if one fails to be vigilant and careful at all times.)

15. Negativity/Vulnerability to Error (Controllable Events)

    A pervasive, lifelong focus on the negative aspects of life (pain, death, loss, disappointment, conflict, guilt, resentment, unsolved problems, potential mistakes, betrayal, things that could go wrong, etc.) while minimizing or neglecting the positive or optimistic aspects. OR An exaggerated expectation—in a wide range of work, financial, or interpersonal situations that are typically viewed as "controllable"—that things will go seriously wrong or that aspects of one's life that seem to be going well will fall apart at any time. Usually involves an inordinate fear of making mistakes that might lead to financial collapse, loss, humiliation, being trapped in a bad situation, or loss of control. Because potential negative outcomes are exaggerated, these patients frequently are characterized by chronic worry, vigilance, pessimism, complaining, or indecision.

16. Overcontrol/Emotional Inhibition

    The excessive inhibition of spontaneous action, feeling, or communication—usually to create a sense of security and predictability; or to avoid making mistakes, disapproval by others, catastrophe and chaos, or losing control of one's impulses. The most common areas of excessive control involve: (a) inhibition of *anger* and aggression; (b) compulsive *order* and planning; (c) inhibition of *positive impulses* (e.g., joy, affection, sexual excitement, play); (d) excessive adherence to routine or ritual; (e) difficulty expressing *vulnerability* or *communicating* freely about one's feelings, needs, etc.; or (f) excessive emphasis on *rationality* while disregarding emotional needs. Often the overcontrol is extended to others in the patient's environment.

17. Unrelenting Standards/Hypercriticalness

    The underlying belief that one must strive to meet very high *internalized standards* of behavior and performance, usually to avoid criticism. Typically results in feelings of pressure or difficulty slowing down and in hypercriticalness toward oneself and others. Must involve significant impairment in: pleasure, relaxation, health, self-esteem, sense of accomplishment, or satisfying relationships.

    Unrelenting standards typically present as: (a) *perfectionism,* inordinate attention to detail, or an underestimate of how good one's own performance is relative to the norm; (b) *rigid rules* and "shoulds" in many areas of life, including unrealistically high moral, ethical, cultural, or religious precepts; or (c) preoccupation with *time and efficiency,* so that more can be accomplished.

18. Punitiveness

    The belief that people should be harshly punished for making mistakes. Involves the tendency to be angry, intolerant, punitive, and impatient with those people (including oneself) who do not meet one's expectations or standards. Usually includes difficulty forgiving mistakes in oneself or others, because of a reluctance to consider extenuating circumstances, allow for human imperfection, or empathize with feelings.

may choose partners who are cold and unstable and who leave her. The expectation that she will be deserted is thus perpetuated.

Schema avoidance reflects attempts by the individual to avoid activating the schema and its associated affect. In this realm, a person who expects to be rejected may avoid significant relationships because they would activate this belief system and lead to painful dysphoria.

Schema compensation occurs when the individual attempts to overcompensate for the early schema. For example, a successful businessman may push himself relentlessly because he holds an underlying schema of failure. Unfortunately, because these strategies are used to an extreme degree, they may fail and, thus, the underlying schema is supported.

EMSs are believed to originate early in childhood. A developmental aspect of the model proposes that five domains are relevant in defining the schema's origins. The domains include: disconnection and rejection, impaired autonomy and performance, impaired limits, other-directedness, and overvigilance and inhibition. Each domain reflects a core need of children for adaptive psychological growth. The 18 schemas are clustered within these five domains and reflect these broader needs.

Specific Schemas and Schema Domains

As noted, the 18 schemas are grouped into five domains. Each includes a current interpersonal component as well as associated early dysfunctional relationships that served as the origins. These two aspects of the schema model will be outlined here.

The *disconnection and rejection* domain reflects a lack of nurturance and safety in the early environment. As adults, these individuals expect that their need for stability, love, and acceptance will not be met. Individuals in the *impaired autonomy and performance* domain were raised in enmeshed or overprotective environments that did not support the child's independence. These individuals do not believe that they can cope adequately and are excessively reliant on others. Children raised in overpermissive families or who were taught a sense of superiority show *impaired limits*. As adults, they have a sense of entitlement, difficulty with self-discipline, and an impaired ability to consider the needs and rights of others. The *other-directedness* domain develops when children are taught to focus excessively on the desires, feelings, and responses of others, at the expense of their own needs. The parents' needs are viewed as more important than the child's needs. In adult relationships, these individuals focus on satisfying others, or gaining acceptance, while their own needs go unmet. The final domain, *overvigilance and inhibition,* develops in a family context of perfectionism and rigid rules. Such adults are overly controlled and have unrealistic standards that interfere with meaningful relationships.

These domains and their associated schemas can be assessed with several questionnaires. Young (1994) has recently developed the Young Parenting Inventory. Clients rate both their mother and father on 72 items using a six-point scale. These items are clustered around distinct schemas. For example, "withdrew or left me alone for extended periods" is associated with an abandonment schema, while "treated me as if I was stupid or untalented" reflects a failure schema. By identifying typical parental behavior, the early maladaptive schemas often can be uncovered.

The Young Schema Questionnaire (2nd ed.; Young & Brown, 1990) is another instrument for assessing schemas. Clients rate 205 items on how accurately the statements describe them; items are grouped by schemas. Statements include: "I let other people have their way because I fear the consequences" (the subjugation schema) and "No one I desire would want to stay close to me if he/she knew the real me" (the defectiveness schema). In one recent study (Schmidt, Joiner, Young, & Telch, 1995), the factor structure of the questionnaire was found to offer considerable support for the construct validity of most of the schemas Young hypothesized.

Schema Processes: Coping Behaviors

The three schema processes of maintenance, avoidance, and compensation are viewed as the individual's coping attempts. New questionnaires for identifying two of these processes have been developed recently. The Young-Rygh Avoidance Inventory (1994) asks clients to rate their agreement with a variety of statements that assess avoidant behavior. The Young Compensation Inventory (1995) is similarly constructed. Clients respond to such statements as "I get defensive when I'm criticized" and "I am more flirtatious or seductive than the average person." These statements are rated on a six-point scale, indicating their degree of endorsement. Research is under way to determine the psychometric properties of these inventories. All of the schema assessment scales discussed here represent attempts to quantify some of the determinants and correlates of personality pathology. The schema-focused model thus has an advantage in comparison with most earlier approaches to personality in that it is theoretically derived, empirically testable, and has treatment implications.

The Association Between DSM-IV Personality Disorders and Schemas

The schema model outlined here overlaps with many Axis II personality disorders. However, this model is broader in several respects. The schema approach represents a model of personality pathology rather than merely a cluster of descriptors. In addition, it is more specific than Axis II in delineating particular cognitions, affects, and behaviors associated with specific personality pathology. It is also suited for empirical study and validation. Finally, it examines the etiology of personality disorders and discusses their current ramifications, with particular attention to the interpersonal realm.

Some of the character types described in Axis II represent schemas, while others are based on schema processes. For example, Dependent Personality Disorder reflects schema maintenance, in the Impaired Autonomy and Performance domain. Avoidant Personality Disorder represents schema avoidance in the Disconnection and Rejection domain. Narcissistic Personality Disorder is linked to the Entitlement schema, usually as compensation for Defectiveness or Emotional Deprivation. Narcissism thus operates in two domains: Disconnection and Rejection, and Impaired Limits.

SCHEMA-FOCUSED DIAGNOSIS OF PERSONALITY DISORDERS

We now turn to the implications of the schema-focused model for personality diagnosis. We propose that personality pathology be assessed in four areas: core themes, coping styles, emotional disposition, and global level of dysfunction. Each area has several dimensions within it, to be rated separately on a scale from 0 to 100 percent. Until normative data become available, we have set, based on our clinical experience to date, a cutoff score of 75 percent on each dimension (except global level of dysfunction) for it to be considered serious enough to be included in the final diagnostic summary of personality dysfunction for a given patient. (The 75 percent level represents dimensions that are "strongly characteristic" of the patient.)

The first area, Core Themes, represents groupings of early maladaptive schemas based on similar family origins. (See Table 20.2.) Core themes describe the central issues confronted by patients in their early childhood environment. Most of these themes refer to prototypical views of the self and others in relationships, derived from the earliest interactions with parents and siblings at home. These themes generally represent either how the child was treated by the family or how the family wanted the child to perform. They do not necessarily indicate how the child actually behaved at home, but rather the forces imposed on the child by the early environment. (The individual's actual behavior is more a function of two other areas of personality to be discussed later: the child's emotional disposition and characteristic coping styles.) These core themes emerge as areas of sensitivity in relationships. For example, patients with a Subjugation theme become hypersensitive when their partners manifest any attempt to influence or control them.

Table 20.2 is a draft version of the core themes area and comprises a provisional list of central issues that often prove dysfunctional later in life. The table also includes the

Table 20.2   Core Themes

Directions: Rate patient on each of the following themes from 0% to 100% depending on severity of theme over the past ten years. The list below provides descriptions for some of the intervals along this scale.

0% = Not At All Characteristic	75% = Strongly Characteristic
25% = Slightly Characteristic	100% = Very Strongly Characteristic
50% = Moderately Characteristic	

1. *Other-Directedness:* Emphasis on self-denial, people-pleasing; overemphasis on needs and opinions of others. Schemas: Self-Sacrifice, Approval- and Recognition-seeking.

2. *Hypercriticism and High Expectations:* In areas of performance and achievement: perfectionistic, hypercritical, high expectations for achievement; shamed or unloved for inadequate performance. Schemas: Unrelenting Standards, Failure, Vulnerability to Error (Negativity).

3. *Subjugation and Inhibition:* Overcontrolled by others, restrained, emotionally-inhibited, rule-bound, given little freedom of expression. Schemas: Subjugation, Overcontrol, Punitiveness.

4. *Overprotection and Overinvolvement:* Parents overinvolved in life situations, fostering dependence, discouraging autonomy, enmeshing, worried, overconcerned with danger. Schemas: Dependence/incompetence, Vulnerability to harm and illness, Enmeshment.

5. *Disconnection and Rejection:* In area of intimacy and closeness: Child is emotionally deprived, socially isolated, misunderstood; made to feel unlovable, undesirable, bad. Schemas: Emotional Deprivation, Defectiveness, Social Isolation.

6. *Overindulgence:* Without adequate parental limits, spoiled, undisciplined. Schemas: Entitlement, Insufficient Self-Control.

7. *Lack of Safety and Stability:* Mistreated, abused, lied to, betrayed, manipulated, humiliated, abandoned; environment characterized by instability, unpredictability, danger, or inconsistency. Schemas: Mistrust and Abuse, Abandonment.

early maladaptive schemas associated with each core theme. The specific themes that would ultimately appear on this list would be derived from factor analytic studies of inventories such as the ones we have developed (e.g., Young Schema Questionnaire, Young Parenting Inventory). Seven (tentative) core themes are listed, each of which represents one aspect of the demands placed on the child in the early family environment: Hypercriticism and High Expectations, Subjugation and Inhibition, Disconnection and Rejection, Overprotection and Overinvolvement, Overindulgence, Lack of Safety and Stability, and Other-Directedness.

Patients are rated on each core theme on a scale from 0 to 100 percent, depending on how severe the issue has been for the individual during the past ten years. These would be assessed in much the same way that we would evaluate schemas in schema-focused therapy: through questionnaires; through an analysis of specific areas of vulnerability in the life history, especially patterns in relationships; through experiential or projective techniques such as imagery or the Thematic Apperception Test (TAT); and through a description of parent-child and family dynamics in the patient's family of origin.

The second area, Coping Styles, describes patients' characteristic styles of responding to the demands placed on them by the environment. (See Table 20.3.) Whereas the core themes area measures the strength of various early family forces on the patient, coping style assesses the patient's actual interpersonal behavior in response to those forces. For example, in the face of unloving parents (the Disconnection and Rejection theme), one patient learns to cope by overcompensation (impressing people) while

Table 20.3   Coping Styles

Directions: Rate patient on each of the following dispositions from 0% to 100% depending on how pervasive and extreme it has been over the past ten years.

0% = Not At All Characteristic	75% = Strongly Characteristic
25% = Slightly Characteristic	100% = Very Strongly Characteristic
50% = Moderately Characteristic	

1. *Aggression-Hostility: Vents anger* directly and excessively: defies, abuses, rebels, blames, attacks, or criticizes.

2. *Manipulation-Exploitation:* Meets own needs through *covert* manipulation, seduction, dishonesty, or conning.

3. *Dominance:* Controls others through *direct* means to accomplish goals, with little regard for needs or feelings of others.

4. *Overcompensation, Recognition-seeking:* Overcompensates through high achievement, status, grandiosity, attention-seeking, etc.

5. *Stimulation-seeking, Impulsivity:* Risk-taking, action-oriented, novelty-oriented, low impulse control.

6. *Compliance-Dependence:* Reliant on others, seeks affiliation, passive, submissive, excessive desire to be liked, avoids conflict.

7. *Excessive Self-Reliance:* Exaggerated focus on independence; may be caretaker for others; has difficulty depending on others.

8. *Compulsivity-Inhibition:* Perfectionistic, strict order, rule-bound, routinized, closed to new experience, emotionally inhibited.

9. *Psychological Withdrawal:* Copes through addiction, dissociation, fantasy, or other forms of psychological escape.

10. *Social Isolation-Avoidance:* Introverted, uncomfortable with people, schizoid, socially avoidant.

another responds through excessive self-reliance (avoiding dependence on others). When these themes and coping styles persist into adulthood in a dysfunctional manner, we label them personality disorders. Personality disorders, according to our model, represent both the individual's distorted perceptions of the self in relationships, as well as the individual's actual interpersonal behaviors.

We hypothesize that the choice of coping styles for a given individual is a function of both the child's innate temperament and parental modeling. Table 20.3 lists the ten most common dysfunctional coping styles we have observed in patients with significant characterological difficulties. These coping styles comprise elements of most major theories of personality classification, outlined earlier in this chapter. At least one of these ten styles parallels each of the following dimensions identified by other researchers as important: active-passive (Buss & Plomin, 1975; Millon, 1969); introverted-extroverted (Buss & Plomin, 1975; Costa & McCrae, 1992); dependent-independent-detached (Millon, 1969); agreeableness (Costa & McCrae, 1992); openness (Costa & McCrae, 1992); conscientiousness (Costa & McCrae, 1992); dominance-submission (Pincus & Wiggins, 1990); and impulsivity (Buss & Plomin, 1975). These ten coping styles are even more closely related to the factors of personality pathology identified by Livesley and associates (1991).

The ten coping styles parallel the schema processes mentioned earlier. Aggression, manipulation, dominance, recognition-seeking, and stimulation-seeking are all forms of schema compensation; they represent exaggerated attempts by the individual to fight back actively against perceived threats, similar to those they encountered in childhood. Excessive self-reliance, psychological withdrawal, and social isolation-avoidance are examples of schema avoidance; all three may become dysfunctional means of avoiding close relationships. Compliance-dependence and compulsivity-inhibition are examples of schema maintenance; they represent a surrendering of an individual to the demands and expectations of others, rather than an expression of the "true self."

Table 20.3 is a draft version of the coping styles area; the final version will be derived from factor analytic studies of inventories such as the ones we have developed (Young-Rygh Avoidance Inventory, Young Compensation Inventory). As with core themes, patients are rated on each coping style from 0 to 100 percent, depending on how much of the time the individual has utilized each one over the past ten years. Coping styles would be rated in a manner similar to our assessment of schema processes in schema-focused therapy: through questionnaires; through an analysis of behavior patterns in the life history, especially patterns in relationships; through experiential or projective techniques such as imagery or the TAT; through observation of the patient's interaction with the diagnostician or therapist; and through interviews with spouses or family members, when available. Ultimately, norms will be developed for each coping style to determine how far the patient's score deviates from the mean. In the meantime, scores of 75 percent or above are considered clinically dysfunctional; we have observed that most patients score high on more than one coping style.

The third area, Emotional Disposition, measures one important aspect of the patient's temperament that we have found to be uniquely important in assessing an individual's long-term personality functioning. Emotional disposition refers to the patient's predominant mood state. Independent of interpersonal themes and characteristic coping styles, how we experience the world and how others experience us are partially a function of our emotional makeup. As mentioned earlier, historically there have been many classifications of temperament. We have decided not to follow any one of these earlier models, either because they have not been developed specifically as measures of dysfunctional temperaments or because they have not been validated empirically.

We have selected four specific temperaments, drawn from earlier theories, that have proven useful in our own work with characterological patients: *labile, sensitive, irritable,* and *nonreactive.* (See Table 20.4.) Labile usually is associated with highly emotional and erratic patients, such as borderlines. (See the discussion of emotionality in Buss & Plomin, 1975.) Sensitive is a less pejorative label for what has been called the "neurotic" temperament (Costa & McCrae, 1992), characterized by chronic, low-level tension, worry, dysphoria, and insecurity. The irritable disposition refers to elements of the Type A personality: impatience and irascibility. We also hypothesize that irritability may be linked to antisocial and aggressive behavior. The fourth disposition, nonreactive, refers to individuals who are calm and placid, unaffected by emotions, and often unaware of emotions in others. (See Kahn, 1928, for a description of the "athymic" type.)

Patients are rated on each emotional disposition from 0 to 100 percent, with 100 percent representing the extreme of that type. Until we have normative data, scores of 75 percent or above are considered clinically dysfunctional. It is expected that most patients will score high only on one, or at most two, of the four dispositions. At present we assess disposition from observation of the patient, the descriptions of significant others, and the patient's self-report. We are in the process of investigating more reliable measures.

We have found it interesting to create a grid mapping the coping styles and emotional disposition areas together. (See Figure 20.1.) The resulting ten-by-four grid yields 40 potential personality types. To use this grid for a given patient, we list all coping styles and emotional dispositions for which the patient scores 75 percent or higher. We then highlight those cells in the grid corresponding to these high-scoring pairs.

Although it is unclear whether this grid-based typology will prove useful clinically, we find that it provides a link between the traditional system of Axis II categories and the present proposal, which relies primarily on dimensional classification. Thus, most of the Axis II personality disorders are included among the 40 potential personality types in the grid; some Axis II disorders require multiple cells. For example, Borderline Personality Disorder would be classified as Labile disposition, with the Manipulation and Stimulation-Seeking coping styles. These appear as cells 2L and 5L in Figure 20.1. Other hypothetical cells include: 1L for the Antisocial Personality, 8S for the Obsessive-Compulsive Personality, 6S for the Dependent Personality, 3N and 4N for the Narcissistic Personality, and 10I for the Paranoid Personality.

Table 20.4   Emotional Disposition

Directions: Rate patient on each of the following dispositions from 0% to 100% depending on how pervasive and extreme it has been over the past ten years.

0% = Not At All Characteristic	75% = Strongly Characteristic
25% = Slightly Characteristic	100% = Very Strongly Characteristic
50% = Moderately Characteristic	

1. *Labile:* Emotionally extreme, excitable, erratic, inconsistent, intense.
2. *Sensitive:* Dysthymic, worried, empathic, tense, exhibiting chronic, low-level affect, "neurotic."
3. *Irritable:* Short-tempered, impatient, irascible, Type A.
4. *Nonreactive:* Robust, calm, insensitive, unemotional, flat.

EMOTIONAL DISPOSITION → COPING STYLE ↓	LABILE (L)	SENSITIVE (S)	IRRITABLE (I)	NON-REACTIVE (N)
1. AGGRESSION HOSTILITY	1. L	1. S	1. I	1. N
2. MANIPULATION EXPLOITATION	2. L	2. S	2. I	2. N
3. DOMINANCE	3. L	3. S	3. I	3. N
4. OVERCOMPENSATION RECOGNITION-SEEKING	4. L	4. S	4. I	4. N
5. STIMULATION-SEEKING IMPULSIVITY	5. L	5. S	5. I	5. N
6. COMPLIANCE DEPENDENCE	6. L	6. S	6. I	6. N
7. EXCESSIVE SELF-RELIANCE	7. L	7. S	7. I	7. N
8. COMPULSIVITY INHIBITION	8. L	8. S	8. I	8. N
9. PSYCHOLOGICAL WITHDRAWAL	9. L	9. S	9. I	9. N
10. SOCIAL ISOLATION AVOIDANCE	10. L	10. S	10. I	10. N

Figure 20.1   Emotional disposition × coping style.

The final area in which we propose to classify personality dysfunction is Global Level of Dysfunction. The ratings on global level of dysfunction take into account several areas of performance: intimate and family relations; friendship and community ties; career and work performance in relationship to potential; self-sufficiency; and self-esteem. Each patient is rated twice, once for current level of dysfunction and again for average level of dysfunction over the past ten years. Table 20.5 provides tentative reference points along a dimension from No Significant Impairment (0 percent) to Very Serious Impairments (100 percent).

Table 20.5   Global Level of Dysfunction

Rate patient from 0% to 100%. Rate twice: once for current global level of dysfunction and again for average global level of dysfunction during adulthood.
   Reference points follow:

   0 = No significant impairment: No major dysfunction in terms of intimate and family relations; friendship and community ties; career and work performance in relationship to potential; self-sufficiency; or self-esteem. Very high satisfaction ratings from self and others. (Probably does not need treatment or counseling.)

 25 = Mild impairments: Mild overall dysfunction, weighing all of the following factors: intimate and family relations; friendship and community ties; career and work performance in relationship to potential; self-sufficiency; and self-esteem. High satisfaction ratings from self and others. (May not need treatment, except perhaps brief counseling.)

 50 = Moderate impairments: Moderate overall dysfunction, weighing all of the following factors: intimate and family relations; friendship and community ties; career and work performance in relationship to potential; self-sufficiency; and self-esteem. Moderate dissatisfaction ratings from self or others. (Probably appropriate for standard outpatient treatment.)

 75 = Serious impairments: Major overall dysfunction, weighing all of the following factors: intimate and family relations; friendship and community ties; career and work performance in relationship to potential; self-sufficiency; and self-esteem. Low satisfaction ratings from self or others. (Probably appropriate for intensive outpatient treatment.)

100 = Very serious impairments: Very serious overall dysfunction, weighing all of the following factors: intimate and family relations; friendship and community ties; career and work performance in relationship to potential; self-sufficiency; and self-esteem. Very low satisfaction ratings from self or others. (May represent serious threat to own life or that of others; may require hospitalization or incarceration.)

Satisfaction is assessed both from the point of view of the patient and the vantage point of significant others and the community at large. Thus, patients who appear functional to society but who feel highly dissatisfied (such as lonely patients with the excessive self-reliance coping style) would not score high on overall level of functioning. Similarly, patients who feel content themselves but create pain for others (such as patients with the aggression-hostility coping style) would not score high on overall level of functioning.

At this point we evaluate level of dysfunction by the rater's global impression, based on an interview with the patient regarding current and past performance in several areas, as well as an interview with a significant other when possible. In addition, we are exploring scales and inventories to assess interpersonal relations, along with other areas of life functioning, in a more systematic fashion. Until we obtain normative data, we have determined that a patient must receive ratings of at least 50 percent on both current level of dysfunction and average dysfunction over ten years to be classified as having clinically significant personality dysfunction requiring clinical intervention at the present time. Patients who score below 50 percent on ten-year average but 50 percent or above on current dysfunction would be diagnosed with an adjustment disorder but not clinically significant personality dysfunction. Those who score below 50 percent on current level of dysfunction but 50 percent or above on ten-year average dysfunction would be diagnosed with clinically significant personality dysfunction but not currently in need of treatment.

Case History

To offer a better grasp of our schema-focused model of personality diagnosis, a brief case illustration is given. Neil presented in therapy with marital problems, hypochondria, and a history of alcoholism in remission. Like many long-term patients, Neil did not qualify for any of the traditional Axis II personality disorders, and yet he had had a lifelong history of significant dysfunctional behavior linked to characterological themes and coping styles.

His first marriage ended because of his alcoholism and subsequent emotional withdrawal from his wife and children. Now, in his second marriage, Neil became enraged and verbally abusive toward his wife, Flo, whenever she made a suggestion or mild criticism. Paradoxically, the therapist observed early in treatment that Neil's hypochondriacal symptoms would intensify whenever his relationship with his wife seemed calm and peaceful. In the work sphere, his career as an illustrator had been characterized by frequent dismissals as a result of conflicts with superiors, especially women. His pattern was one of deferring to bosses, then at some later point exploding inappropriately at them.

Neil recalled his mother's claim that, unlike his siblings, he was a colicky baby who cried all the time and could not be soothed. Throughout his childhood, Neil was sent away to live with various family members for a few years at a time. Furthermore, when he did live with his parents, Neil's mother was physically and verbally abusive toward him, while his father was rigid and highly controlling. Both had high expectations for achievement and were quite punitive when he failed to live up to them. In addition, Neil would frequently start fights with his peers at school, which would then result in further punishment at home.

Based on assessment interviews and a variety of schema inventories, we diagnosed Neil as follows, using the schema-focused model. Only dimensions scoring 75 percent or above are reported in the first three diagnostic areas:

1. Core Themes:
    Hypercriticism and High Expectations
    Subjugation and Inhibition
    Disconnection and Rejection
    Lack of Safety and Stability
2. Coping Styles:
    Aggression-Hostility
    Psychological Withdrawal
3. Emotional Disposition:
    Irritable
4. Global Level of Dysfunction:
    Current: 50 percent (Moderate Impairment)
    Ten-year Average: 65 percent (Moderate to Serious Impairment)
    Global Personality Diagnosis:
    Clinically Significant Personality Dysfunction
    Currently Requires Treatment

Let us explain how we arrived at this diagnosis. The first area, Core Themes, refers to the central issues Neil confronted as a child and that persisted into adulthood as areas of sensitivity. His responses on the Young Schema Questionnaire and Young Parenting Inventory confirmed the information we had obtained in taking a childhood history. Neil grew up in a household with exceptionally high standards of performance from two highly critical parents (Hypercriticism and Rejection). This theme manifested itself in Neil's relationship to Flo: He was hypersensitive to any criticism from her and then overreacted. The same theme was apparent in his first marriage, in which he constantly perceived himself as unable to meet his wife's high expectations for him. This perception eventually led him to withdraw from her, which in turn led to alcohol abuse.

The second theme, *Disconnection and Rejection,* was the result of the frequent abandonments Neil experienced as a consequence of being sent from relative to relative throughout his childhood. What emerged in discussions with him was that he associated periods of peace and stability with impending abandonment. Thus, whenever his marriage seemed calm, Neil became highly anxious as he awaited the inevitable abandonment. His hypochondriacal symptoms would then be exacerbated, and he would turn to Flo for reassurance and attention, hoping that his needy and diminished state would somehow deter Flo from leaving him.

The last theme, *Subjugation and Inhibition,* reflects the controlling influence of his father. Neil's father punished him for any outward display of anger. Neil thus learned to suppress his anger, which he later vented uncontrollably with his peers. This same pattern expressed itself in both his marriages: He would hide feelings of anger or disagreement, then explode later when he felt he could not allow himself to be taken advantage of any more. These explosions often took the form of verbal abuse. This abusiveness itself had its root in another core theme, Lack of Safety and Stability, and represented Neil's reenacting of his mother's physical and emotional abusiveness toward him.

Turning to the second area, Coping Styles, Neil relied primarily on two mechanisms when he was in conflict. When the core themes were triggered, he would characteristically respond either through aggression and hostility (by verbally abusing people or blowing up inappropriately) or through psychological withdrawal (through alcohol abuse or by detaching emotionally from his wives and children). These mechanisms proved highly dysfunctional: They led to job dismissals; to the breakup of his first marriage, and more recently to the possible dissolution of his second marriage if he continued to explode and act abusively.

The third area of diagnosis, Emotional Disposition, refers to Neil's characteristic mood state, irritability. His mother complained, as noted, that he was a colicky child, difficult to soothe even as an infant. This corresponded with the therapist's own sense that Neil seemed impatient and might easily be set off. This evidence, taken together, led us to diagnose him as irritable in the Emotional Disposition area. This mood state may have been one of the factors contributing to his angry outbursts.

In terms of Global Level of Dysfunction, we rated Neil 50 percent on current level and 65 percent on ten-year average. These ratings reflected primarily his unstable relationship history, his anger and abuse problems, his loss of jobs, and his history of alcoholism. The current rating was not higher than 50 percent because at that time he was employed and married and because his alcohol abuse was in remission. These ratings translated into our global diagnosis: that he had clinically significant personality dysfunction and that he required treatment at the time of the evaluation.

Treatment Implications

Let us turn finally to the treatment implications of schema-focused diagnosis. One of the major advantages of this four-pronged diagnosis is that, unlike most other diagnostic models, it typically has direct implications for treatment. We return to Neil to illustrate this briefly.

Looking first at Core Themes, Neil's four high scores directed the therapist to his major areas of vulnerability and sensitivity in relationships. The therapist was able to point these themes out to Neil and then utilize a variety of cognitive, behavioral, and experiential techniques to help him change them. Neil became better able to identify and anticipate situations in which his schemas (core themes) might be triggered easily and also to understand how he often misinterpreted situations in line with these themes.

Turning to Coping Styles, Neil found the identification of his two primary styles of handling conflict to be extremely useful. They helped him make sense of many aspects of his unhappy life history. Neil was able to see how he tended to react to conflict in one of two extreme fashions: either by withdrawal or by aggression. Once he could see this pattern, the therapist was able to work with Neil and Flo together in couple's therapy to help them work out more adaptive coping strategies when they were in conflict.

As for Neil's diagnosis under Emotional Disposition, it was a relief for Flo to understand that Neil's irritability was probably part of his makeup and that she no longer had to personalize his impatience or irascible moods. Neil had to learn anger management techniques to gain more control over his outbursts. The therapist was able to help Neil become more appropriately assertive, instead of pushing down his needs, so that his anger would not explode unpredictably later. Although it was not necessary with Neil, many patients with troubling emotional temperaments benefit from psychotropic medication to aid in mood management.

By the end of six months of once-a-week schema-focused therapy, Neil had made significant progress in recognizing his core themes and their resulting sensitivities; had incorporated more adaptive coping styles, most of the time, instead of withdrawal and aggression; and had learned to cope better with his irritability so that it did not interfere so much with his interpersonal relationships and job performance. At about the time when his current global level of dysfunction had dropped from 50 to 25 percent, Neil, Flo, and the therapist mutually agreed to discontinue regular therapy sessions.

CONCLUSIONS

Although schema-focused diagnosis is only in its infancy, it potentially meets all six of the criteria laid out for an acceptable model for diagnosing personality pathology. First, schema-focused diagnosis is based on a complex model of personality dysfunction, consistent with current psychological theories; early research suggests that the model has excellent potential to be empirically testable. Second, the schema approach places a high emphasis on the relational context of personality. Core themes and coping styles are predominantly focused on the early interpersonal environment of the child and the ensuing repercussions in adult relationships. Third, the model is primarily dimensional rather than categorical. Patients are rated on all dimensions using a 100-point scale. An attempt has been made, however, through a dual-axis grid, to link schema-based diagnosis with more traditional personality categories such as those on Axis II in DSM-IV.

Fourth, the dimensions covered by schema-focused diagnosis are quite broad and inclusive. They incorporate most of the dimensions previously found to be important in earlier research on personality. By including *core themes, coping styles, disposition,* and *global dysfunction,* the schema model overcomes the limitations of other models, which rarely include more than two of these areas. Finally, this diagnostic system has direct and clear implications for treatment, particularly for therapists working within a schema-focused therapy framework. The schema approach has been applied success-fully to personality disorders for several years, and schema-focused diagnosis is a nat-ural outgrowth of this treatment approach.

In conclusion, schema-focused diagnosis offers a promising new avenue for assess-ing personality dysfunction within a relational context and offers considerable hope for overcoming many of the serious limitations of DSM-IV in this important area.

REFERENCES

Alden, L. E., Wiggins, J. S., & Pincus, A. L. (1990). Construction of circumplex scales for the Inventory of Interpersonal Problems. *Journal of Personality Assessment, 55,* 521–536.

American Psychiatric Association. (1994). *Diagnostic and statistical manual of mental disorders* (4th ed.). Washington, DC: Author.

Beck, A. T., Rush, A. J., Shaw, B. F., & Emery, G. (1979). *Cognitive therapy of depression.* New York: Guilford.

Benjamin, L. S. (1987). Use of the SASB dimensional model to develop treatment plans for per-sonality disorders. I: Narcissism. *Journal of Personality Disorders, 1,* 43–70.

Buss, D. M., & Craik, K. H. (1987). Act criteria for the diagnosis of personality disorders. *Jour-nal of Personality Disorders, 1,* 73–81.

Buss, A. H., & Plomin, R. (1975). *A temperament theory of personality development.* New York: Wiley.

Cattell, R. B. (1965). *The scientific analysis of personality.* Chicago: Aldine.

Costa, P. T., & McCrae, R. R. (1990). Personality disorders and the five factor model. *Journal of Personality Disorders, 4,* 362–371.

Costa, P. T., & McCrae, R. R. (1992). The five factor model of personality and its relevance to personality disorders. *Journal of Personality Disorders, 6,* 343–359.

Freud, S. (1932/1950). Libidinal types. In *Collected Papers* (vol. 5). London: Hogarth.

Grove, W. M., & Tellegen, A. (1991). Problems in the classification of personality disorders. *Journal of Personality Disorders, 5,* 31–41.

Gunderson, J. G., Links, P. S., & Reich, J. H. (1991). Competing models of personality disor-ders. *Journal of Personality Disorders, 5,* 60–68.

Hofstee, W. K. B., deRaad, B., & Goldberg, L. R. (1992). Integration of the big five and circum-plex approaches to trait structure. *Journal of Personality and Social Psychology, 63,* 146–163.

Kahn, E. (1928). *Psychopathischen personlichkeiten.* Berlin: Springer.

Livesley, W. J. (1987). Theoretical and empirical issues in the selection of criteria to diagnose personality disorders. *Journal of Personality Disorders, 1,* 88–94.

Livesley, W. J., Jackson, D. N., & Schroeder, M. L. (1991). Dimensions of personality pathol-ogy. *Canadian Journal of Psychiatry, 36,* 557–562.

Maddi, S. R. (1968). *Personality theories: A comparative analysis.* Homewood, IL: Dorsey.

Millon, T. (1969). *Modern psychopathology: A biosocial approach to maladaptive learning and functioning.* Philadelphia: W. B. Saunders.

Millon, T. (1981). *Disorders of personality: DSM-III: Axis II.* New York: Wiley.

Pincus, A. L., & Wiggins, J. S. (1990). Interpersonal problems and conceptions of personality disorders. *Journal of Personality Disorders, 4,* 342–352.

Schmidt, N. B., Joiner, T. E., Young, J. E., & Telch, M. J. (1995). The schema questionnaire: In-vestigation of psychometric properties and the hierarchical structure of a measure of mal-adaptive schemas. *Cognitive Therapy and Research, 19,* 295–321.

Sim, J. P., & Romney, D. M. (1990). The relationship between a circumplex model of interpersonal behaviors and personality disorders. *Journal of Personality Disorders, 4,* 329–341.

Vaillant, G. E. (1987). A developmental view of old and new perspectives of personality disorders. *Journal of Personality Disorders, 1,* 146–156.

Widiger, T. A., & Frances, A. (1985). The DSM-III personality disorders. *Archives of General Psychiatry, 42,* 615–623.

Young, J. E. (1994a). *Cognitive therapy for personality disorders: A schema-focused approach* (rev. ed.). Sarasota, FL: Professional Resource Press.

Young, J. E. (1994b). *Young parenting inventory.* New York: Cognitive Therapy Center of New York.

Young, J. E. (1995). *Young compensation inventory.* New York: Cognitive Therapy Center of New York.

Young, J. E., Beck, A. T., & Weinberger, A. (1993). Depression. In D. H. Barlow (Ed.), *Clinical handbook of psychological disorders* (2nd ed.) (pp. 240–277). New York: Guilford.

Young, J. E., & Brown, G. (1990). *Young Schema Questionnaire* (second edition). Reprinted in J. E. Young, (1990), *Cognitive therapy for personality disorders: A schema-focused approach* (rev. ed.). Sarasota, FL: Professional Resource Press.

Young, J., & Klosko, J. (1993). *Reinventing your life.* New York: Plume Books.

Young, J., & Rygh, J. (1994). *Young-Rygh avoidance inventory.* New York: Cognitive Therapy Center of New York.

CHAPTER 21

Partner Relational Problems and Affective Disorders

JACKIE K. GOLLAN, MS, ERIC T. GORTNER, MA, and NEIL S. JACOBSON, PhD

Research developments in the field of social psychiatry have sparked enthusiastic interest in conceptualizing individual psychological health within the context of interpersonal relationships. There is strong suggestion that complex interpersonal processes are major determinants of the development, expression, and remission of psychiatric conditions (Burman & Margolin, 1993; Markus & Cross, 1990). Defining psychiatric conditions using a social contextual framework provides a more compatible formulation for studying the development of affective disorders. This is particularly relevant in the area of relationship distress and depression. Having observed a remarkably consistent association between the presence of depression and distressed intimate relationships, investigators have generated research that suggests a unique transactional process between the two conditions. While genetic and biological factors are important in the etiology of affective disorders, they alone cannot predict the timing, expression, and number of symptoms. By placing importance on psychosocial factors, such as interpersonal behavior, we move beyond the limitations of the biomedical model and develop a more compelling explanation of the onset, course, and resolution of affective disorders.

This increase in theoretical and empirical attention has been propelled by reports that relationship distress is a frequent correlate of clinical depression (see Barnett & Gotlib, 1988; Gotlib & Beach, 1995; Gotlib & McCabe, 1990 for research review). Reports indicating that as many as half of the depressed individuals seeking treatment for depression reported serious marital difficulties, and focused on resolving these relational problems in therapy (Gotlib & McCabe, 1990). Similarly, distressed individuals presenting for couple therapy find that their depressive symptoms are integral to their relationship difficulties (Beach, Jouriles, & O'Leary, 1985). Another recent study concluded that the risk of developing depression was ten times greater for individuals experiencing relationship distress, compared to the risk for individuals in a nondistressed relationship (O'Leary, Christian, & Mendell, 1994). Given the high rates of co-occurrence, the presence of distress and depression may be more than a spurious correlation (Beach, Martin, Blum, & Roman, 1993; Beach & Nelson, 1990; Gotlib et al., 1995; Gotlib & Hooley, 1988). This raises questions about etiological development (e.g., Is there a unidirectional relationship, such that one condition causes the other?), and diagnostic specificity (e.g., Is the condition of relational depression diagnostically distinct from relationship distress and depression?) (Burns, Sayers, & Moras, 1994).

The diagnostic value of defining depression within a relational context was recently recognized with the inclusion of the 'Relational Problems' category in the fourth edition of the Diagnostic and Statistical Manual of Mental Disorders (DSM-IV)(American Psychiatric Association, 1994). This category describes situations that involve problematic interactions between parents, children, or siblings that require clinical attention, either because of their direct effect or secondary role in complicating other presenting problems. Depending on clinical importance, the relational difficulty can be designated as a primary diagnosis on Axis I or function as a descriptor and maintain its original placement on Axis IV. One of the diagnoses in this category is Partner Relational Problem, code V61.1. It is defined as follows: "This category should be used when the focus of clinical attention is a pattern of interaction between spouses or partners characterized by negative communication (e.g., criticisms), distorted communication (e.g., unrealistic expectations), or noncommunication (e.g., withdrawal) that is associated with clinically significant impairment in individual or family functioning or the development of symptoms in one or both partners" (APA, 1994, p. 681).

Upon closer examination, this description appears to be conceptually and diagnostically incomplete. First, the experience of relational distress seems to vary among individuals. Some couples report communication difficulties, while others report only experiencing decreased intimacy and unhappiness. Second, clinicians and researchers have yet to outline a definitive set of 'symptoms' of relational distress and, furthermore, to specify the duration and severity of distress that should exist to warrant the diagnosis. Third, the lack of diagnostic clarity, evidenced by the previous two points, complicates questions about primary diagnosis and treatment. This is particularly confusing when an individual presents with a concomitant psychiatric disorder that has a similar clinical presentation to relational distress. For example, it can be difficult to ascertain whether an individual is withdrawing from their partner due to their depression, or due to their dissatisfaction with the relationship, or a combination thereof. Without definitive criteria for distress, clinicians are less able to clearly determine whether relational problems are independent from other conditions. Finally, the lack of diagnostic specificity reduces the standardized use of the diagnosis allowing clinicians and researchers to define situations that qualify as relational distress. Taken together, the current definition reflects the relative scarcity of pertinent and well-controlled research on the interpersonal context of psychiatric disorders, to date.

The purpose of this chapter is to develop a data-based definition of Partner Relational Affective Disorder with preliminary criteria that operationalize this diagnosis. Towards this goal, the first section summarizes what is known about the bidirectional association between relationship distress and the clinical course of depressive illness. This includes a review of the influence of relationship distress during the acute phase of depression, and the effect that such distress has upon treatment response and depressive relapse. We also review studies that examine the impact of depression upon relationship functioning and identify the relationship factors that seem relevant to relational depression. Together, these serve as a suggestive template for diagnostic criteria. In the second section, we suggest a more refined diagnostic definition of Partner Relational Affective Disorder and a preliminary outline of clinical criteria. Our final section presents arguments for and against the usefulness of this diagnosis and comments about strategies for future research.

RESEARCH REVIEW

Several lines of research support the relational distress-depression association, including (1) accounts from longitudinal life-stress studies examining relationship distress as a precursor of depression; (2) descriptions from epidemiological studies documenting relationship stress as a principal correlate of depressive symptoms; (3) reports from prospective work examining predictors of depression and the influence of relationship distress upon the course of depression; (4) observational research on interactional patterns concomitant to affective disorders; and (5) results from psychotherapy outcome research that suggest specific factors that mediate the effectiveness of marital therapy for individuals who present with unipolar depression and relational distress. Since the vast majority of research work has concentrated on unipolar depression, our review focuses on this type of affective disorder. However, information on bipolar disorder is included when available.

Relationship Functioning and the Course of Depressive Illness

Onset

Our review of the data indicates a bidirectional link between relational distress and depression: Relational distress plays a role in the generation of depression and, likewise, depression influences the development of relational distress. Evidence that supports the role of relationship distress as a precursor and a modifier of depressive experience can be found in the life-stress and depression research. The literature indicates that relationship problems are often a source of stress and that relationship factors can buffer or inoculate against stress-induced depression.

In general, the research indicates that depressed individuals experience significantly more social disruption before and during depressive episodes. Individuals often report depression after the experience of an acutely stressful event, such as the sudden loss of a valued relationship through death or marital separation, or during an extended period of stress, like chronic marital discord (Andrews & Brown, 1988; Bebbington, 1987; Costello, 1982; Hirschfeld, 1981; Lewinsohn, Hoberman, & Rosenbaum, 1988; Roy, 1987; Weissman, Leaf, & Tischler, 1988). The results from prospective studies provide the best evidence that individuals in unhappy marriages are at greater risk for depression compared to individuals who are happily married (Brown & Harris, 1978; Markman, Duncan, Storaasli, & Howes, 1987; Monroe, Bromet, Connell, & Steiner, 1986; Munroe & Steiner, 1986; Paykel, 1969; Weissman & Paykel, 1974). In general, these studies found that depressed individuals experienced more social stress like marital difficulties prior to the onset of their depression. Ellicott and colleagues conducted a two year prospective study and found a modest relationship between bipolar illness and life stress (Ellicott, Hammen, Gitlin, Brown, & Jamison, 1990). Results indicated a significant relationship between the highest levels of stress and the likelihood of relapse, in that those with highest stress were four times more likely to relapse compared to subjects with low stress. Another illustration of the robust effect of relational stress on mood is found in Beach and Nelson's (1990) research where marital stress experienced six months after marriage predicted depressive symptomatology one year later. Although one should consider that prospective studies establish temporal order and not necessarily cause and effect relationships, the collective research nonetheless generally supports the idea that relationship stressors can trigger clinical depression.

Complementing these findings, studies on the effect of social support provide additional evidence of the relationship distress-depression connection. A detailed review of the social support research (Cohen & Wills, 1985) indicates that social support has a main and buffering effect on depression, in that individuals who have extensive social support are more likely to be healthy than those without it. Additionally, these individuals are less likely to become depressed when stressed (Gottlieb, 1988). Similarly, most of the available studies note that bipolar subjects' perceptions of social support are ameliorative against the depressive phase of bipolar disorder (Ellicott et al., 1990; Jackson, 1992; Lesser, 1983; Leverich, Post, & Rosoff, 1990). The work on general social support is highly relevant to this review as intimate relationships are reportedly the primary source from which individuals derive social and emotional support. Furthermore, involvement in a satisfying relationship has a prophylactic effect in buffering the individual from the depressogenic effects of stress (Brown et al., 1978; Brown, Bifulco, Harris, & Bridge, 1986). This is documented among many of the prospective studies where social support offered within the context of marriage is associated with a lower risk of depressive symptoms at follow-up assessments (Markman et al., 1987; Monroe et al., 1986). Researchers note that the status of being married per se does not reduce exposure to stress, rather the degree of intimacy and relationship satisfaction, as well as the individual's effective coping style and social competence, function to buffer the individual from the detrimental effects of stress (Kessler & Essex, 1982). Individuals who cannot elicit interpersonal intimacy from their relationship lose a core source of support. The lack of a supportive intimate relationship can potentiate the effects of the stress from the social environment and affect emotional functioning (Schuster, Kessler, & Aseltine, 1990).

In summary, the depressogenic effects of interpersonal stress and the protective role of social support highlight the importance of relational factors in the development of depression. These findings, along with the theoretical understanding of depression within a social/relational context, may help explain the different prevalence rates between men and women. Typically, studies have reported a 2:1 ratio between females and males experiencing unipolar depression (McGrath, Keita, Strickland, & Russo, 1990; Weissman & Klerman, 1985). To explain the disparity, a variety of theorists have proposed that women and men go through different self-definition processes, with women's view of "self" tending to be more relationally focused (Jordan, Kaplan, Miller, Stiver, & Surrey, 1991; Nolen-Hoeksema, 1987). The implication here is that in the face of relational distress, women may be uniquely at risk for depression (Hammen, 1991; Koerner, Prince, & Jacobson, 1994). Though exploration in this area has just begun, research results suggest several formulations. First, the data indicates that women are more overwhelmed by relationship difficulties and seek more social support when depressed than men (Whiffen & Gotlib, 1989). Second, women also appear to be more influenced by the relationship quality than are men (Kessler & McLeod, 1984). Considering these two points, this work begins to outline a more compelling explanation of different prevalence rates and support a relationally specific approach to understanding depression.

Remission and Recovery

One of the more convincing arguments for considering the social context of depressed persons can be found in the results citing the effectiveness of marital therapy of individuals who present with concomitant unipolar depression and relationship distress.

Although the number of well-controlled outcome studies is small, results have generally documented the beneficial effects of marital therapy on treatment of depression (Beach & O'Leary, 1992; Foley, Rounsaville, Weissman, Sholomaskas, & Chevron, 1989; Jacobson, Dobson, Fruzzetti, Schmaling, & Salusky, 1991; Jacobson, Fruzzetti, Dobson, Whisman, & Hops, 1993). A study by O'Leary and Beach (1990) investigated the relative effectiveness of individual cognitive therapy (CT) and behavioral marital therapy (BMT) in the treatment of depression. Thirty-six maritally discordant couples in which the wife was depressed were randomly assigned to marital therapy, cognitive therapy, or a waiting-list control condition. As expected, both types of therapy outperformed the waiting-list control condition in alleviating depressive symptoms. Results also revealed that the marital and individual treatments were equally effective in reducing depressive symptoms. Importantly, only marital therapy decreased relationship discord, which, as will be noted later, may affect longer-term therapy outcomes. Jacobson and colleagues (1991) also compared BMT and CT in the treatment of depression, along with a treatment that combined BMT and CT. Their initial findings indicate that marital therapy for depression may be particularly effective for those couples who identify themselves as distressed and, conversely, less helpful than individual therapy for nondistressed couples. However, when considering the most serious or "truly discordant" couples in the sample, results again suggest that marital therapy is as effective as individual therapy in treating depression and, additionally, is more effective in reducing relational distress (Beach et al., 1995).

It appears that marital therapy affects depressive symptoms in a manner that is different from standard individual treatment. While there is scant literature on the precise mechanisms of change, there is evidence that the effects of marital therapy are derived through direct changes in the marital environment (Beach et al., 1995). That is, relational treatments do not appear to be treating depression through the same mechanisms of change as cognitive therapy (e.g., core schemata or other cognitive processes). Although marital therapy may influence such intraindividual mechanisms, it's unique effect may lie in changes in marital adjustment (e.g., changes in satisfaction and communication) (Jacobson et al., 1991). These findings underscore the significance of relational factors in the treatment of depression. In sum, the extant literature suggests that marital therapy has a unique advantage in addressing the dual problem of depression *and* relationship distress.

Relapse

Given the high rates of recurrence in unipolar and bipolar illnesses, the issue of relapse has proven to be a critical one. One approach in considering the role of relational distress in affecting depressive relapse is to examine the differential recurrence rates for those who have received individual versus couple's treatment of depression. This means that if relational distress uniquely affects probability of relapse and, further, if marital therapies uniquely target such relational distress, then lower relapse rates would be expected in depressed samples that have received marital therapy as opposed to individual treatment for depression. Unfortunately, few studies have investigated the long-term effectiveness of marital treatments for depression. Furthermore, the sample sizes and length of follow-up periods have precluded truly powerful tests to determine if there is, in fact, differential maintenance of treatment effects. Two recent reports of one-year follow-up investigations comparing behavioral marital therapy and cognitive therapy treatments for depression provide some preliminary evidence (Beach & O'Leary, 1992;

Jacobson et al., 1993). The main finding from these studies is that marital treatment produces short-term gains that are on par with Cognitive Therapy. Combining both follow-up studies, of the 17 patients who responded to marital therapy, only one relapsed (Beach et al., 1995). Beach and O'Leary (1992) have also documented that at one-year follow-up, BMT continued to show advantage over CT in terms of marital adjustment. Given that cognitive therapy often is recognized as the treatment of choice for depression, these findings offer compelling evidence for the viability of marital treatment for depression.

Another approach in examining the impact of relational distress on relapse rates is to examine prognosticators of recovery or relapse in clinically depressed samples. One possible reason for the high relapse rate for individuals with major depression, which has been reportedly as high as 50 percent within two years of treatment, is the presence of stressful social circumstances (Belsher & Costello, 1988; Keller, Lavori, Lewis, & Klerman, 1983). Relational factors certainly have been implicated in increasing the vulnerability to depressive relapse. Numerous studies have demonstrated the importance of relationship variables in the course and outcome of treatments for depression. For instance, Hooley and Teasdale (1989) examined the influence of marital support at intake on post-hospital course of depression and found that the level of expressed criticism from the spouse proved to be a predictor of symptomatic relapse for depressed inpatients. Results from McLeod, Kessler, and Landis's study (1992) showed that spouses' positive reactions to partners' depression predicted a more rapid recovery. Similarly, Goering, Lancee, and Freeman (1992) found that the strongest predictor for six month relapse rates was depressed wives' perception of the quality of spousal support. Rounsaville and colleagues (Rounsaville, Weissman, & Prusoff, 1979) discovered that marital distress at the outset of individual treatment for depression predicted poorer treatment response for depressed women. Finally, in a study examining the effects of marital therapy for dysthymia, Waring and Patton (1984) suggested that the presence of a spousal support figure may be "a potent therapeutic factor in treatment" (p. 96).

Collectively, the research suggests several conclusions regarding the role of relational factors in the treatment of depression. First, relational treatments for depression, such as behavioral marital therapy, are at least as effective as individual cognitive therapy when depressed clients suffer from concurrent marital problems. Second, relational treatments are more effective than individual treatments at targeting *both* depression and relationship distress. This aspect becomes more important when we consider the third main conclusion: Relational factors have important predictive influence in both the recovery and subsequent relapse rates for depression.

Depression and the Course of Relationship Distress

So far, the literature review emphasizes the etiological role of a couple's distress. However, it's evident that the direction of effect can be reversed: Depression can impact relationship functioning, which in turn, can exacerbate depressive symptomatology (Gove, Hughes, & Style, 1983). Studies have suggested that (1) depressed individuals behave in a way that discourages social interaction and increases relationship conflict; (2) non-depressed individuals who interact with depressed individuals tend to react and evaluate depressed individuals negatively; and (3) compared to nondepressed couples, the relationships of depressed couples are characterized by higher levels of overt conflict, more withdrawal, and greater negativity.

Social behavior of depressed individuals generally has detrimental effects upon relationship functioning. Compared to nondepressed persons, moderately to severely depressed individuals generally are less skillful socially, less expressive socially, and less engaged interpersonally (Lewinsohn, Mischel, Chaplin, & Barton, 1980; Segrin, 1992). Depressed persons seem to express more hostility and criticism of themselves and others (Hooley, 1986; Hooley & Teasdale, 1989) as well as more sadness and dependency (Blumberg & Hokanson, 1983). Additional evidence of the impact of affective disorders comes from a recent study that compared bipolar and unipolar subjects to matched comparison subjects (Coryell et al., 1993). Unipolar subjects were much more likely to report poorer relationship quality and dissatisfaction with sexual activity. With remission of the depressive episode, both bipolar and unipolar depressed patients reported increased satisfaction with their relationships. Crowther (1985) compared family functioning among depressed, bipolar, anxiety disorder, and alcohol abuse patients and found that depressed patients reported significantly more marital maladjustment than the other psychiatric inpatients.

Marital interaction studies have observed that depressed individuals interact in troubling ways with their nondepressed partners. Couples with one depressed partner are more likely to experience negativity and conflict compared to their nondepressed counterparts (Hautzinger, Linden, & Hoffman, 1982; Hinchliffe, Hopper, & Roberts, 1978). Comparing the ratio of positive to negative exchanges, such couples engage in long and aversive exchanges (Biglan et al., 1985; Nelson & Beach, 1990; Ruscher & Gotlib, 1988), are highly reactive to recent events (Jacobson, Follette, & Revenstorf, 1982), and generate negative appraisals about their partner (Gotlib & Whiffen, 1989; Kowalik & Gotlib, 1987). Related to the last point, it's interesting to note that some couples with a bipolar spouse report little relationship distress (Bauwens, Tracy, Pardoen, Vander Elst, & Mendlewicz, 1991; Fadden, Bebbington, & Kuipers, 1987). It appears that some spouses of bipolar patients make fewer negative spousal attributions about their partner's florid behavior (e.g., their behavior is part of an illness which cannot be controlled), which has less detrimental effects on the relationship.

Only a few studies have expressly tried to separate the dysfunctional couple interaction patterns unique to depression from those that are associated with marital distress (Hautzinger et al., 1982; Linden, Hautzinger, & Hoffman, 1983; Schmaling & Jacobson, 1990; Schmaling, Whisman, Fruzzetti, Truax, & Jacobson, 1991). In general, the research has documented certain behaviors to be more frequent among depressed couples. Women tend to report more depression and more problem-solving difficulties. Additionally, the presence of depression among women seems to reduce or suppress aggressive behavior from their nondepressed partners (Biglan et al., 1985). One recent study (Schmaling, Hops, & Jacobson, 1993) reported that depression was more evident when couples were discussing conflictual topics, but once relationship distress was controlled statistically, depression did not suppress aggressive spousal behavior. In contrast to the previously cited studies, these investigators concluded that marital distress rather than depression was responsible for the dysfunctional interaction patterns found in depressed couples.

The interpersonal burdens inherent in living with a depressed partner can increase the nondepressed partner's susceptibility to depression. Coyne has spearheaded several studies on the social transmission of depression by focusing on nondepressed individuals' reactions to depressed persons. Earlier, Coyne (1976) had examined the behavioral response of nondepressed subjects interacting via telephone with a depressed patient, a nondepressed patient, or a normal control. Results indicated that subjects who had interacted with a depressed patient experienced themselves as more anxious, hostile, rejecting, and depressed. In a later study, Coyne, Kessler, and Tal (1987) noted that 40 percent of the spouses living with a depressed patient were distressed to the point of meeting criteria for clinical intervention.

Collectively, the research to date indicates that depressive symptomatic characteristics play an important role in affecting the quality of relationships and the development of distress. More recent sophisticated tests of the unique effects of marital interaction, using longitudinal design, video technology, and detailed coding systems, have been able to examine closely the potential causal role of depressive behavior in marital discord.

Relational Factors

In describing the literature on relational functioning, three key relationship factors emerges as most relevant to depression. These include poor communication, problem-solving difficulties, and low relationship satisfaction.

Communication

One of the hallmarks of relationship distress in both homosexual and heterosexual relationships is poor communication. (See Clarkin & Miklowitz, in press, for a review of marital and family communication difficulties.) Communication difficulties manifest through lower levels of expressiveness, more vague requests, and higher levels of verbalized hostility (Noller, 1981, 1984). When interacting, these individuals are less likely to be accurate in decoding and comprehending their partner's messages (Sher, Baucom, & Larus, 1990) and are more likely to color their partner's negative comments with more global and stable attributions (Camper, Jacobson, Holtzworth-Munroe, & Schmaling, 1988; Sher, Baucom, & Larus, 1990). Hautingzer and colleagues (1982) have noted that communication between distressed partners is more asymmetrical, with the content of conversations tending to focus on psychological and somatic complaints.

Possibly depression can be understood as related to the communicative aspects of the relationship (Gottman, 1979; Hooley & Hahlweg, 1989; Hooper, Douglas, Hinchliffe, & Vaughan, 1977; Markman, 1979). That is, poor communication is an important precursor of couple distress which is central to the development of depression (Baucom & Epstein, 1990). Linden and colleagues (1983) observed that distress was likely to lead to depression. Couples with one depressed partner used more depression-specific verbal behaviors (e.g., more self-derogatory statements) than their nondepressed counterparts. Sher and Baucom (1993) reported that the presenting levels of depression and distress were correlated with different communication patterns and different assigned meanings. Results indicated that depression was associated with more negative expression by the depressed partner while the nondepressed spouse appeared to have lower understanding of their messages. Research has found that a commonly destructive communication pattern called "demand-withdraw interaction" represents different intimacy preferences between partners (Heavey, Layne, & Christensen, 1993; Jacobson, 1989). Such a pattern can lower intimacy and lead to depression (e.g., Beach, Nelson, & O'Leary, 1988; Hickie, Parker, Wilhelm, & Tennant, 1991). Schweitzer, Logan, and Strassberg (1992) looked at the role of intimacy in depression and found that women who reported low levels of intimacy with their spouses were more likely to become depressed. Similarly, Beach and colleagues (1988) noted that the level of intimacy within the relationship distinguished between distressed couples who were depressed and nondepressed.

Some studies have found that the expression of negative communication per se is not consistently associated with relationship problems, in that the expression of hostility in nondistressed relationships was correlated with later reports of greater relationship satisfaction (Gottman & Krokoff, 1989). However, the overall research indicates that poor communication is particularly important in the development and maintenance of depression.

Problem-Solving Deficits

A second relationship factor strongly associated with distress and depression is the use of ineffective problem-solving strategies to resolve conflict. These strategies are oriented toward resolving differences between couples and are based on the couple's ability to talk about areas of disagreement and their collective willingness to reach viable solutions. Problem-resolution skills are critical to smooth relationship functioning as couples without these skills seem to use strategies, such as confrontation or avoidance, that are relatively ineffective in reducing stress and do not resolve conflict satisfactorily (Gottman, 1993). Observational research on couple communication indicates that poor problem identification and definition and lack of focus is critical in relationship distress and is related to depression (McCabe & Gotlib, 1993).

Relationship Dissatisfaction

A third interpersonal factor linked with depression is relationship dissatisfaction. This factor often develops through couple interaction and is negatively correlated with relationship distress and depression (Merikangas, Prusoff, Kupfer, & Frank, 1985; Olin & Fennell, 1989). Specific complaints of relationship dissatisfaction can be measured using the Marital Satisfaction Inventory (MSI) (Snyder, 1981), the Marital Adjustment Scale (MAS) (Locke & Wallace, 1959) and the Dyadic Adjustment Scale (DAS) (Spanier, 1976). Although at times communication and problem-solving deficits may be subsumed under relationship dissatisfaction, a dissatisfied couple still may have otherwise "normal" communication and problem-solving strategies. Some investigators have noted that the dissatisfaction is correlated with blame attributions and dysfunctional marital beliefs (Townsley, Beach, Fincham, & O'Leary, 1991), while others have found it to be correlated with the unequal distribution of labor in the relationship (Whisman & Jacobson, 1989). In sum, evidence of the importance of dissatisfaction in depression has been well documented (Beach & O'Leary, 1993; Gotlib & Whiffen, 1989; Hooley & Hahlweg, 1989).

Essentially, communication problems, problem-solving difficulties, and relationship dissatisfaction comprise the main aspects of relationship distress. Most individuals experience short-lived feelings of hostility, resentment, and dysphoria about their relationship, but these three relationship factors represent more enduring interpersonal problems, sufficient to influence the development and expression of depression. Two of these interactional variables, problem-solving and communication, represent dyadic coping abilities that, when left unaddressed, lead to escalated conflict and depressive reactions. The third relationship variable, relationship satisfaction, derives from the couple's interaction but reflects the individual's adjustment in the relationship. Collectively, these factors provide a preliminary basis for defining Partner Relational Problems with Affective Disorders.

Diagnosis of Partner Relational Problems with Affective Disorder

Based on our review, we propose the following definition for Partner Relational Problems with Affective Disorder.

A. Individual meets DSM-IV diagnostic criteria for current Major Depressive Episode (APA, 1994, p. 320).

B. Individual meets criteria for Partner Relational Distress as defined below:

There should be the presence of (1) and *either* (2) or (3):

1. Partner(s) identify themselves as needing assistance with their relationship in that they are considering separation or divorce; seriously discussing separation or divorce; in the process of separating or divorcing; legally separated or preparing for legal divorce. (This could be ascertained by using the Marital Satisfaction Inventory (MSI) (Snyder, 1981) to measure the status of the relationship and the individual's preparations for leaving it; and the Dyadic Adjustment Scale (DAS) (Spanier, 1976) to assess relational distress and the degree of relationship commitment.)

    Similar to the diagnostic specifiers used to qualify affective conditions, assessment of relational distress might use specifiers to rate the severity of the current relational distress. Specifiers include ratings as mild, moderate, or severe, or in partial or full remission.

2. Partner(s) report either communication difficulties or problem-solving difficulties. Communication difficulties are similar to the DSM-IV description of Partner Relational Problem where the person reports negative communication (e.g., criticism, expressed hostility), distorted communication (e.g., unrealistic expectations), or absent communication (e.g., withdrawal).

3. Partner(s) report relationship dissatisfaction as measured by conventional cutoff scores indicating relationship dissatisfaction on the Marital Satisfaction Inventory (MSI) (Snyder, 1981), Marital Adjustment Scale (MAS) (Locke & Wallace, 1959) and Dyadic Adjustment Scale (DAS) (Spanier, 1976).

C. Concurrent presence of relational distress, as defined above, and affective disorder.

The following typology specifies whether depression or relationship difficulties is the primary complaint:

Type I: Depression influences relationship difficulties.

Type II: Relationship difficulties influence depression.

Type III: Cannot be determined.

(This allows the clinician to specify which is the primary complaint, and describe whether relationship difficulties contributed to or influenced the expression of the presenting affective condition.)

D. No duration criteria of relationship distress. (This is due to the lack of reliable data on the duration of relationship difficulties.)

CONCLUSION

Several points argue for further development of the diagnosis of Partner Relational Problems with Affective Disorders. First, the empirical literature shows a significant association between relationship distress and depression, in that distress functions as a correlate, precursor, and sequelae of affective disorders. As a result, relational distress is a strong contender in affecting the development and resolution of depressive illness. Second, with the availability of this diagnosis, individuals with concurrent relational distress and depression are given a more accurate classification of the comorbid condition, which helps identify the important features that need clinical treatment. Third, the direction of causality between relationship distress and depression has not been established definitively, but this diagnosis offers a description that can help identify the function of each condition in sustaining the other.

Arguments against the development of this diagnosis are based on the premise that the research has not demonstrated that relationship problems causally influence affective disorders. Though researchers have developed more sensitive designs to locate the source of effect, more research is needed before we can confidently use the depression-distress association to define psychopathology. Several arguments that remind us that this diagnosis is still tentative. First, considering the correlational nature of the research, it is difficult to know whether the above definition we have outlined should include more general or limited clinical diagnostic criteria. While we would like to use criteria with empirical backing, these criteria are accurate only to the degree that research reliably identifies causal factors that link distress and depression. Although the research so far is promising in terms of the relational distress-depression linkage, few definitive statements that can be made regarding the casual impact of relationship distress on depression. As noted earlier, this is a reflection of a research base still in the developing stages. Second, the field has yet to establish reliable methods through which to determine specific criteria for relational distress (e.g., threshold of severity, frequency, and chronicity). Finally, perhaps a more basic incompatibility is that theoretically partner relational diagnosis is defined interpersonally, whereas the current diagnostic system, using the DSM-IV, adopts an intraindividual definition of pathology.

To develop the relational-affective disorder connection, research can start by using more methodologically rigorous designs. This includes using longitudinal, prospective studies designed to examine causal status using more stringent statistical techniques (e.g., sequential modeling). Central questions might focus on the process of etiology and evolution of distress and depression, identify specific factors common and unique to discord and depression, and focus on power and gender factors to examine the asymmetry in couple interactions. From the trends in recent research, it appears that relational research and depression research are likely to become even more closely related. Collectively, the work presented in this chapter forms the foundation from which to develop a more comprehensive and accurate definition of relational problems.

REFERENCES

Andrews, B., & Brown, G. W. (1988). Social support, onset of depression and personality: An exploratory analysis. *Social Psychiatry and Psychiatric Epidemiology, 23,* 99–108.

American Psychiatric Association. (1994). *Diagnostic and statistical manual of mental disorders* (4th ed.). Washington, DC: Author.

Bakan, D. (1966). *The duality of human existence: An essay on psychology and religion.* Chicago: Rand McNally.

Barnett, P. A., & Gotlib, I. H. (1988). Psychosocial functioning and depression: Distinguishing among the antecedent, concomitant, and consequences. *Psychological Bulletin, 104,* 97–126.

Baucom, D. H., & Epstein, N. (1990). Assessment. In D. H. Baucom & N. Epstein (Eds.), *Cognitive-behavioral marital therapy* (pp. 125–241). New York: Brunnel.

Bauwens, F., Tracy, A., Pardoen, D., Vander Elst, M., & Mendlewicz, J. (1991). Social adjustment of remitted bipolar and unipolar outpatients. *British Journal of Psychiatry, 159,* 239–244.

Beach, S. R. H., Arias, I., & O'Leary, K. D. (1986). The relationship of marital satisfaction and social support to depressive symptomatology. *Journal of Psychopathology and Behavioral Assessment, 8,* 305–316.

Beach, S. R. H., Jouriles, E. N., & O'Leary, D. K. (1985). Extramarital sex: Impact on depression and commitment in couples seeking marital therapy. *Journal of Sex and Marital Therapy, 11,* 99–108.

Beach, S. R. H., Martin, J. K., Blum, T. C., & Roman, P. M. (1993). Effects of marital and coworker relationships on negative affect: Testing the central role of marriage. *American Journal of Family Therapy, 21,* 313–323.

Beach, S. R. H., & Nelson, G. M. (1990). Pursuing research on major psychopathology from a contextual perspective: The example of depression and marital discord. In G. Brody & I. E. Sigel (Eds.), *Family Research* (Vol. 2, pp. 227–259). Hillsdale, NJ: Erlbaum.

Beach, S. R. H., Nelson, G. M., & O'Leary, K. D. (1988). Cognitive and marital factors in depression. *Journal of Psychopathology and Behavioral Assessment, 10,* 93–105.

Beach, S. R. H., & O'Leary, K. D. (1992). Treating depression in the context of marital discord: Outcome and predictors of response for marital therapy vs. cognitive therapy. *Behavior Therapy, 23,* 507–528.

Beach, S. R. H., & O'Leary, K. D. (1993). Marital discord and dysphoria: For whom does the marital relationship predict depressive symptomatology? *Journal of Social and Personal Relationships, 10,* 405–420.

Bebbington, P. (1987). Marital status and depression: A study of English national admission statistics. *Acta Psychiatrica Scandinavica, 75,* 640–650.

Belsher, G., & Costello, C. G. (1988). Relapse after recovery from recovery from unipolar depression: A critical review. *Psychological Bulletin, 104,* 84–96.

Biglan, A., Hops, H., Sherman, L., Friedman, L. S., Arthur, J., & Osteen, V. (1985). Problem-solving interactions of depressed women and their husbands. *Behavior Therapy, 16,* 431–451.

Blumberg, S. R., & Hokanson, J. E. (1983). The effects of another person's style on interpersonal behavior in depression. *Journal of Abnormal Psychology, 92,* 196–209.

Brown, G. W., Bifulco, A., Harris, T., & Bridge, L. (1986). Life stress, chronic subclinical symptoms and vulnerability to clinical depression. *Journal of Affective Disorders, 11,* 1–19.

Brown, G. W., & Harris, T. (1978). *Social origins of depression: A study of psychiatric disorders in women.* New York: Free Press.

Burman, B., & Margolin, G. (1993). Analysis of the association between marital relationships and health problems: An interactional perspective. *Psychological Bulletin, 112,* 39–63.

Burns, D. D., Sayers, S. L., & Moras, K. (1994). Intimate relationships and depression: Is there a causal connection? *Journal of Consulting and Clinical Psychology, 62,* 1033–1043.

Camper, P., Jacobson, N. S., Holtzworth-Munroe, A., & Schmaling, K. S. (1988). Causal attributions for interactional behaviors in married couples. *Cognitive Therapy and Research, 12,* 195–209.

Clarkin, J. F., & Miklowitz, D. J. (in press). Marital and family communication difficulties. To appear in T. A. Widiger, A. J. Frances, H. A. Pinkus, & M. First. (Eds.), *DSM-IV sourcebook.* Washington, DC: American Psychiatric Press.

Cohen, S., & Wills, T. (1985). Stress, social support, and the buffering hypothesis. *Psychological Bulletin, 98,* 310–357.

Coryell, W., Scheftner, W., Keller, M., Endicott, J., Maser, J., & Klerman, G. (1993). The enduring psychosocial consequences of mania and depression. *American Journal of Psychiatry, 150,* 720–727.

Costello, C. G. (1982). Social factors associated with depression: A retrospective community study. *Psychological Medicine, 12,* 647–651.

Coyne, J. C. (1976). Toward an interactional description of depression. *Psychiatry, 39,* 28–40.

Coyne, J. C., Kessler, R. C., & Tal, M. (1987). Living with a depressed person. *Journal of Consulting and Clinical Psychology, 55,* 347–352.

Crowther, J. H. (1985). The relationship between depression and marital adjustment: A descriptive study. *Journal of Nervous and Mental Disease, 173,* 227–231.

Ellicott, A., Hammen, C., Gitlin, M., Brown, G., & Jamison, K. (1990). Life events and the course of bipolar disorder. *American Journal of Psychiatry, 147*(9), 1194–1198.

Fadden, G., Bebbington, P., & Kuipers, L. (1987). The burden of care: The impact of functional psychiatric illness on the patient's family. *British Journal of Psychiatry, 150,* 285–292.

Fadden, G. (1989). Pity the spouse: Depression within marriage. *Stress Medicine, 5,* 99–107.

Foley, S. H., Rounsaville, B. J., Weissman, M. M., Sholomaskas, D., & Chevron, E. (1989). Individual versus conjoint interpersonal psychotherapy for depressed patients with marital disputes. *International Journal for Psychiatry, 10,* 29–42.

Goering, P. N., Lancee, W. J., & Freeman, S. J. (1992). Marital support and recovery from depression. *British Journal of Psychiatry, 160,* 76–82.

Gotlib, I. H., & Beach, S. R. H. (1995). A marital/family discord model of depression: Implications of therapeutic intervention. In N. S. Jacobson & A. S. Gurman (Eds.), *Clinical Handbook of Couple Therapy* (pp. 411–436). New York: Guilford.

Gotlib, I. H., & Hooley, J. M. (1988). Depression and marital distress: Current status and future directions. In S. Duck (Ed.), *Handbook of personal relationships: Theory, research, and interventions* (pp. 543–570). Chicester, England: Wiley.

Gotlib, I. H., & McCabe, S. B. (1990). Marriage and psychopathology. In F. D. Fincham & T. N. Bradbury (Eds.) *The psychology of marriage: Basic issue and applications* (pp. 226–257). New York: Guilford.

Gotlib, I. H., & Whiffen, V. E. (1989). Depression and marital functioning: An examination of specificity and gender differences. *Journal of Abnormal Psychology, 98,* 23–30.

Gottlieb, B. H. (1988). Marshalling social support: The state of the art in research practice. In B. H. Gottlieb (Ed.), *Marshalling social support: Formats, processes and effects* (pp. 11–52). Newbury Park, CA: Sage.

Gottman, J. M. (1979). *Marital interactions: Experimental investigations.* San Diego: Academic.

Gottman, J. M. (1993). The roles of conflict engagement, escalation, and avoidance in marital interaction: A longitudinal view of five types of couples. *Journal of Consulting and Clinical Psychology, 61,* 6–15.

Gottman, J. M., & Krokoff, L. J. (1989). Marital interaction and satisfaction: A longitudinal view. *Journal of Consulting and Clinical Psychology, 57,* 47–52.

Gove, W. R., Hughes, M., & Style, C. B. (1983). Does marriage have positive effects on the psychological well-being of the individual? *Journal of Health and Social Behavior, 24,* 122–131.

Hammen, C. (1991). Generation of stress in the course of unipolar depression. *Journal of Abnormal Psychology, 100,* 555–561.

Hautzinger, M., Linden, M., & Hoffman, N. (1982). Distressed couples with and without a depressed partner: An analysis of their verbal interactions. *Journal of Behavior Therapy and Experimental Psychology, 13,* 307–314.

Heavey, L., Layne, C., & Christensen, A. (1993). Gender and conflict structure in marital interaction: A replication and extension. *Journal of Consulting and Clinical Psychology, 61,* 16–27.

Hirschfeld, R. M. (1981). Situational depression: Validity of the concept. *British Journal of Psychiatry, 139,* 297–305.

Hinchliffe, M., Hopper, D., & Roberts, F. J. (1978). *The melancholy marriage.* New York: Wiley.

Hickie, I., Parker, G., Wilhelm, K., & Tennant, C. (1991). Perceived interpersonal risk factors of non-endogenous depression. *Psychological Medicine, 21,* 399–412.

Hooley, J. M. (1986). Expressed emotion and depression: Interactions between patients and high-versus low-expressed emotion spouses. *Journal of Abnormal Psychology, 95,* 237–246.

Hooley, J. M., & Hahlweg, K. (1989). Marital satisfaction and marital communication in German and English couples. Special Issue: Coding Marital interaction. *Behavioral Assessment, 11,* 119–133.

Hooley, J. M., & Teasdale, J. D. (1989). Predictors of relapse in unipolar depressive: Expressed emotion, marital distress, and perceived criticism. *Journal of Abnormal Psychology, 98,* 229–237.

Hooper, D., Douglas, J. F., Hinchliffe, M. K., & Vaughan, P. W. (1977). The melancholy marriage: An inquiry into the interaction of depression: I. Introduction. *British Journal of Medical Psychology, 50,* 113–124.

Hops, H., Biglan, A., Sherman, L., Arthur, J., Friedman, L., & Osteen, V. (1987). Home observations of family interactions of depressed women. *Journal of Consulting and Clinical Psychology, 55,* 341–346.

Jackson, P. B. (1992). Specifying the buffering hypothesis: Support, strain, and depression. *Social Psychology Quarterly, 55*(4), 363–378.

Jacobson, N. S. (1989). The politics of intimacy. *The Behavior Therapist, 12,* 29–32.

Jacobson, N. S., Dobson, K., Fruzzetti, A. E., Schmaling, K. B., & Salusky, S. (1991). Marital therapy as a treatment for depression. *Journal of Consulting and Clinical Psychology, 59,* 547–557.

Jacobson, N. S., Follette, F. C., & Revenstorf, D. (1982). Towards a standard definition of clinically significant change. *Behavior Therapy, 17,* 308–311.

Jacobson, N. S., Fruzzetti, A. E., Dobson, K., Whisman, M., & Hops, H. (1993). Couple therapy as a treatment for depression II: The effects of relationship quality and therapy on depressive relapse. *Journal of Consulting and Clinical Psychology, 61,* 516–519.

Jordan, J. V., Kaplan, A. G., Miller, J. B., Stiver, I. P., & Surrey, J. L. (1991). *Women's growth in connection: Writings from the Stone Center.* New York: Guilford.

Keller, M. B., Lavori, P. W., Lewis, C. E., & Klerman, G. L. (1983). Predictors of relapse in major depressive disorder. *Journal of American Medical Association, 250*(24), 3299–3304.

Kessler, R. C., & McLeod, J. D. (1984). Sex differences in vulnerability to undesirable life events. *American Sociological Review, 49*(5), 620–631.

Kessler, R. C., & Essex, M. (1982). Marital status and depression: The importance of coping resources. *Social Forces, 61,* 484–507.

Koerner, K., Prince, S., & Jacobson, N. S. (1994). Enhancing the treatment and prevention of depression in women: The role of integrative behavioral couple therapy. *Behavior Therapy, 25,* 373–390.

Kowalik, D. L., & Gotlib, I. H. (1987). Depression and marital interaction: Concordance between intent and perception of communication. *Journal of Abnormal Psychology, 96,* 127–134.

Lesser, A. L. (1983). Hypomania and marital conflict. *Canadian Journal of Psychiatry, 28,* 362–366.

Leverich, G. S., Post, R. M., & Rosoff, A. S. (1990). Factors associated with relapse during maintenance treatment of affective disorder. *International Clinical Psychopharmacology, 5*(2), 135–156.

Lewinsohn, P. M., Hoberman, H. M., & Rosenbaum, M. (1988). A prospective study of risk factors for unipolar depression. *Journal of Abnormal Psychology, 97,* 251–264.

Lewinsohn, P. M., Mischel, W., Chaplin, W., & Barton, R. (1980). Social competence and depression: The role of illusory self-perceptions. *Journal of Abnormal Psychology, 89,* 203–213.

Linden, M., Hautzinger, M., & Hoffman, N. (1983). Discriminant analysis of depressive interactions. *Behavior Modification, 7*(3), 403–422.

Locke, H. J., & Wallace, K. M. (1959). Short-term marital adjustment and prediction tests: Their reliability and validity. *Journal of Marriage and Family Living, 231,* 251–255.

Markman, H. J. (1979). Application of a behavioral model of marriage in predicting relationship satisfaction of couples planning marriage. *Journal of Consulting and Clinical Psychology, 47,* 743–749.

Markman, H. J., Duncan, S. W., Storaasli, R. D., & Howes, P. W. (1987). The prediction of marital distress: A longitudinal investigation. In K. Hahlweg & M. Goldstein (Eds.), *Understanding major mental disorder: The contribution of family interaction research* (pp. 266–289). New York: Family Process.

Markus, H., & Cross, S. (1990). The interpersonal self. In L. A. Pervin (Ed.), *Handbook of personality theory and research* (pp. 576–608). New York: Guilford.

McCabe, S. B., & Gotlib, I. H. (1993). Interactions of couples with and without a depressed spouse: Self-report and observations of problem-solving situations. *Journal of Social and Personal Relationships, 10,* 589–599.

McGrath, E., Keita, G. P., Strickland, B. R., & Russo, N. F. (Eds.), (1990). *Women and depression: Risk factors and treatment issues.* Final report of American Psychological Association Task Force on Women and Depression. Washington, DC: American Psychological Association.

McLeod, J. D., Kessler, R. C., & Landis, K. R. (1992). Speed of recovery from major depressive episodes in a community sample of married men and women. *Journal of Abnormal Psychology, 101,* 277–286.

Merikangas, K. R., Prusoff, B. A., Kupfer, D. J., & Frank, E. (1985). Marital adjustment in major depression. *Journal of Affective Disorders, 9,* 5–11.

Monroe, S. M., Bromet, E. J., Connell, M. M., & Steiner, S. C. (1986). Social support, life events, and depressive symptoms: A 1 year prospective study. *Journal of Consulting and Clinical Psychology, 54,* 424–431.

Munroe, S. M., & Steiner, S. C. (1986). Social support and psychopathology: Interrelations with preexisting disorder, stress, and personality. *Journal of Abnormal Psychology, 95,* 29–39.

Nelson, G. M., & Beach, S. R. H. (1990). Sequential interaction in depression: Effects of depressive behavior on spousal aggression. *Behavior Therapy, 21,* 167–182.

Nolen-Hoeksema, S. (1987). Sex differences in unipolar depression: Evidence and theory. *Psychological Bulletin, 101,* 259–282.

Noller, P. (1981). Gender and marital adjustment level difference in decoding messages from spouses and strangers. *Journal of Personality and Social Psychology, 41,* 272–278.

Noller, P. (1984). *Nonverbal communication and marital interaction.* New York: Pergamon.

O'Leary, K. D., Christian, J. L., & Mendell, N. R. (1994). A closer look at the link between marital discord and depressive symptomatology. *Journal of Social and Clinical Psychology, 13,* 33–41.

O'Leary, K. D., & Beach, S. R. H. (1990). Marital therapy: A viable treatment for depression and marital discord. *American Journal of Psychiatry, 147,* 183–186.

O'Leary, K. D., Riso, L. P., & Beach, S. R. H. (1990). Attributions about the marital discord/depression link and therapy outcome. *Behavior Therapy, 21,* 413–422.

Olin, G. V., & Fennell, D. L. (1989). The relationship between depression and marital adjustment in a general population. *Family Therapy, 16,* 11–20.

Paykel, E. S. (1969). Recent life events in the development of depressive disorder. In R. A. Depue (Ed.), *The psychobiology of depressive disorder: Implications for the effects of stress* (pp. 245–262). New York: Academic.

Rounsaville, B. J., Weissman, M. M., & Prusoff, B. A. (1979). Marital disputes and outcome in depressed women. *Comprehensive Psychiatry, 20,* 483–490.

Roy, A. (1987). Five risk factors for depression. *British Journal of Psychiatry, 150,* 536–541.

Ruscher, S. M., & Gotlib, I. H. (1988). Marital interaction patterns of couples with and without a depressed partner. *Behavior Therapy, 19,* 455–470.

Schmaling, K. B., Hops, H., & Jacobson, N. S. (1993). *What's unique about couples with a depressed wife?: An examination of macro-and micro-analytic data.* Paper presented at the meeting of the Association for the Advancement of Behavioral Therapy, Atlanta, GA.

Schmaling, K. B., & Jacobson, N. S. (1990). Marital interaction and depression. *Journal of Abnormal Psychology, 99,* 229–236.

Schmaling, K. B., Whisman, M. A., Fruzzetti, A. E., Truax, P., & Jacobson, N. S. (1991). Identifying areas of marital conflict: Interactional behaviors associated with depression. *Journal of Family Psychology, 5,* 145–157.

Schuster, T. L., Kessler, R. C., & Aseltine, R. H. (1990). Supportive interactions, negative interactions, and depressed mood. *American Journal of Psychiatry, 18,* 423–438.

Schweitzer, R. D., Logan, G. P., & Strassberg, D. (1992). The relationship between marital intimacy and postnatal depression. *Australian Journal of Marriage and Family, 13*(1), 19–23.

Segrin, C. (1992). Interpersonal reactions to dysphoria: The role of the relationship with partner and perceptions of rejection. *Journal of Social and Personal Relationships, 10,* 83–97.

Sher, T. G., & Baucom, D. H. (1993). Marital communication: Differences among maritally distressed, depressed, and nondistressed-nondepressed couples. *Journal of Family Psychology, 7,* 148–153.

Sher, T. G., Baucom, D. H., & Larus, J. M. (1990). Communication patterns and response to treatment among depressed and nondepressed maritally distressed couples. *Journal of Family Psychology, 4*(1), 63–79.

Snyder, D. K. (1981). Empirical validation of the marital satisfaction inventory: An actuarial approach. *Journal of Consulting and Clinical Psychology, 49,* 262–268.

Spanier, G. B. (1976). Measuring dyadic adjustment: New scales for assessing the quality of marriage and similar dyads. *Journal of Marriage and the Family, 38,* 15–28.

Townsley, R. M., Beach, S. R., Fincham, F. D., & O'Leary, K. D. (1991). Cognitive specificity for marital discord and depression: What types of cognition influence discord? *Behavior Therapy, 22,* 519–530.

Waring, E. M., & Patton, D. (1984). Marital intimacy and depression. *British Journal of Psychiatry, 145,* 641–644.

Weissman, M. M., Leaf, P. J., & Tischler, G. L. (1988). Affective disorders in five United States communities. *Psychological Medicine, 18*(1), 141–153.

Weissman, M. M., & Paykel, E. S. (1974). *The depressed woman: A study of social relationships.* Chicago: University of Chicago Press.

Weissman, M. M., & Klerman, G. L. (1985). Sex differences in the epidemiology of depression. *Archives of General Psychiatry, 34,* 98–111.

Whiffen, V. E., & Gotlib, I. H. (1989). Stress and coping in maritally distressed and nondistressed couples. *Journal of Social and Personal Relationships, 6,* 327–344.

Whisman, M., & Jacobson, N. S. (1989). Depression, marital satisfactions, and marital and personality measures of sex roles. *Journal of Marital and Family Therapy, 15,* 177–186.

CHAPTER 22

Assessment of Abusive Spousal Relationships

LENORE E. A. WALKER, EdD

Domestic violence,[1] often called spouse abuse, partner abuse, woman abuse, or simply battered women, is estimated to occur in between 2.5 million to 4 million homes in the United States every year (National Institute of Justice [NIJ], 1994). Some researchers estimate at least twice that number of women are battered; my work suggests that as many as one out of two women are abused during their lifetime (Walker, 1979). If we added estimates from different countries around the world, it becomes understandable why the American Psychological Association's Presidential Task Force on Violence and the Family (APA, 1996) found that domestic violence is so prevalent that it agreed with the past three U.S. Surgeon General's declarations that family violence is an epidemic. Although some estimates from epidemiological studies suggest that an equal number of men and women are battered (Straus, 1993), in fact, the actual reported data shows that only in approximately 5 percent of the reported cases are women abusing men. Mutual arrests account for another 5 percent, placing the total number of women who are known to use violence against a man at approximately 10 percent of known cases. When women do use physical aggression against a man, data show that it is usually in response to violent behavior toward them, often in self-defense. Nonetheless, the stereotypical myth that both parties play a role in the interactive violence often predominates mental health professionals' treatment planning, especially among those family therapists who have minimal training in the area and who minimize the importance the violence has in influencing the behavior of family members (Bograd, 1988; Dell, 1989; Hansen & Harway, 1993).

The understanding of spouse abuse that has been gained during the past 20 years has focused on the dynamics of abuse and the social factors that support or facilitate its occurrence. Emphasis on the criminal nature of assaults has moved the field away from the psychological pathology viewpoint. Intervention approaches have focused on same-gender group and individual programs rather than the traditional marital and family-oriented or individual psychotherapy. Thus, little attention has focused on describing and defining abusive relationships or on mental health diagnosis other than the use of the diagnostic term Battered Woman Syndrome, which also may be used as a subcategory of Post-Traumatic Stress Disorder (PTSD). The heterogeneous distribution of battering behavior across all demographic groups and the complexities of the social

---

[1] Although some researchers and practitioners use the terms "domestic violence" and "family violence" interchangeably, in its most common use, "family violence" is the broader term used when any abuse is found in the family, "domestic violence" usually refers more specifically to partner abuse. The common usage of these terms is used in this chapter.

situation both within the family as well as outside in society contributes to the difficulties of making relational diagnoses. Some researchers are now focusing on one group of batterers who also have mental disorders such as depression, paranoid disorders, and personality disorders. This chapter reviews some of the major theories about domestic violence and how they impact on clinical practices including assessment, diagnosis, intervention, treatment, and prevention. The prevailing viewpoint among advocates for battered women suggests that societal conditions rather than mental health issues should dominate any interventions. However, psychological research suggests that psychological treatment may be helpful in stopping both batterers' use of the violence and abuse itself and the resulting psychological effects for victims. Criteria are developed that differentiate abusive relationships from marital dysfunction and the marital strife that comes from healthy disagreements.

A number of demographic factors appear to define those who are subjected to domestic violence. Most studies have found that men who batter women come from all demographic groups; they are both rich and poor, educated and uneducated, employed and unemployed, and from every racial, ethnic, socioeconomic, and class group. Gelles and Straus (1988) found that their study population had an overrepresentation of the poor, while this author (1984) found that almost one-quarter of participants in a study population came from upper- and middle-class and professional families. It has been suggested that poor and minority women are more likely to come to the attention of the system than those with greater financial and social resources; the former are more likely to need government services, and their male partners are more likely to be arrested and incarcerated for violent crimes (American Psychological Association, 1995). Although poor women often have a great deal of difficulty in leaving an abusive home, ostensibly because of financial conditions, in fact, if they are receiving government benefits, they may have immediate access to greater financial resources to support themselves and their children than do the more affluent middle-class and professional women, who frequently are cut off from any access to the man's finances and also are ineligible for any government financial aid. Even when the court orders temporary or permanent support, batterers frequently continue their control over the woman by refusing to pay the support money as ordered.

Explanations for why women do not leave battering relationships abound. The reasons include the above-mentioned financial difficulties, inadequate social supports, housing problems, fear of losing their children, and fear of being hurt or killed for leaving, which many batterers threaten. Leaving a batterer does not necessarily stop the abuse. Psychological reasons also play a role; battered women often have become dependent on the batterer, do not have the self-confidence and self-efficacy needed to leave a relationship, are not mentally strong enough to deal with continued dangers such as harassment and stalking behavior, and have developed learned helplessness or Battered Woman Syndrome. One of the most common myths is that "It can't really be that bad" or that "The victim really likes to be abused" because of some personality defect in the victim. Holding the woman responsible for staying in the relationship is evidence of the typical, although sometimes subtle, "blaming the victim" that takes place; why should the woman be held the sole responsible party for the termination of the relationship? Even so, the data suggests that most battering relationships do end in divorce, although the divorce may take a long time to obtain and does not necessarily stop the violence. A National Crime Survey report found that 70 percent of the reported domestic violence occurred after separation (Liss & Stahly, 1993).

I have found (1984) that the average battering relationship lasted six years; in 1980, the average marriage in the United States also lasted approximately six years. Most specialists in domestic violence believe that the most dangerous time in a battering relationship is at the point of separation, when serious physical harm or death is more likely to occur, perhaps because of the man's disorganization when threatened with abandonment or because he has no intention of letting the woman leave him if she is alive, as he often states. Yet most therapists minimize and deny the seriousness of the violence that their clients' relationships present. For example, Hansen, Harway, and Cervantes (1991) found that the therapists they surveyed seriously underestimated the level of violence in analog studies based on actual cases, one of which had ended in a homicide. Therapists who reported having a family systems theoretical orientation, were most likely to avoid dealing with the violence and, therefore, were perceived by the victim (and most advocates as well as the researchers) as colluding with the offender. Such therapists reported that they would avoid blaming or holding anyone responsible and deal with the underlying marital conflict and each individual's contributions to the dysfunction while ignoring violence that was clearly escalating. Most theorists and therapists who work with domestic violence victims and perpetrators believe that it is important to use labels that clearly define each person's roles and responsibilities in order for the violent and abusive behavior to be stopped. Sharing responsibility and focusing on each person's contributions to the dysfunction only reinforces the victim's inability to move toward becoming a survivor and perpetuates the batterer's externalizing his anger without facing his own responsibility for using violent behavior no matter what the woman's behavior is.

THEORIES ABOUT DOMESTIC VIOLENCE

A number of different psychological theories help account for the occurrence of domestic violence. The most popular theories all acknowledge the abuse of power and control seen in those who are known abusers, although the role of power and control variables differ from one theoretical orientation to another. The feminist perspective states that domestic violence has its roots in the patriarchal structure of society, including the traditional family structure in which the man expected to have power over the woman (Bograd, 1988). Although men in egalitarian relationships also are known to abuse their female partners, the suggestion is that the closer a couple is to creating an equilitarian relationship, the less likely domestic violence will occur (Pence & Paymar, 1993; Smith, 1990; Yllo, 1993). Lesbian relationships where there is an unequal balance of power between partners also may replicate the heterosexual situation in terms of violence in the relationship (Lobel, 1986). No matter what the specific theoretical orientation's particular emphasis, most agree that there is an abuse of power and control in domestic violence relationships.

Other psychological theories also are used to help explain the causes of domestic violence. For example, cognitive-behavioral and social-learning frameworks look at how aggression, abuse, and violence[2] are learned and transferred to other members of the

---

[2] The terms "aggression," "abuse," and "violence" are used interchangeably in some studies while in others they have very specific meanings. For example, in child abuse studies *abuse* often conveys something less serious than severe *violence,* while *maltreatment* is used to specify psychological abuse and neglect.

family or community. Historical and ecological approaches suggest that violence against women and children always has been present; certain groups become targets when the social conditions facilitate it. The history of men being expected to keep women "in line" behaviorally, even if this entailed use of corporal punishment, is still evident today in many countries, and some religious group's values still promulgate male superiority over women. This history has given rise to what is often referred to as *male entitlement.* The feminist orientation finds this underlying philosophy as facilitating and sometimes even encouraging the use of domestic violence to discipline a woman and get her to do what the man demands. Psychodynamic approaches focus more on the internal psychological processes that create the need to use or accept violence. A systems approach focuses on the interaction between the family members and the shared responsibility for whatever occurs. Sometimes theories are combined, and probably one theoretical approach is not sufficient to explain the complex behavior that takes place within families. (Cf. Walker, 1994, for further discussion.)

A community-based, public health–like model[3] often is applied when a disorder is considered to be at epidemic proportions, and concepts of risk and resiliency are employed for theoretical and practical understanding. In studies of domestic violence, the only risk factor consistently found to exist is if a man has been exposed to or experienced violence in his own childhood family (Hotaling & Sugarman, 1986). Yet millions of children are so exposed every year. Other potentially high risks within this particular population include bullying and intimidating behavior, substance abuse, holding inappropriate sex-role stereotyped views about women, dating those engaged in antisocial behavior, and living in a community with high levels of violent behavior.

Although many community-based programs do not utilize psychological perspectives when designing effective strategies for dealing with domestic violence, preferring to focus on social factors, a psychological approach can help strengthen families by promoting good mental health so that violent behavior is not resorted to as a way to meet needs for power and control over one's life. Furthermore, any comprehensive community-based program intended to deal with domestic violence needs psychologically based intervention programs for men, women, and children who live in homes where abuse has already begun. Offender-specific treatment programs include short-term psychoeducational

---

On the other hand, *abuse,* not *violence,* is used when a child is sexually violated, whether physical or psychological coercion is used to force compliance. In the battering literature, *abuse* and *violence* are used interchangeably although *violence* may be used to specify incidents otherwise described as psychological abuse. The term "aggression" often is used to describe an operationalized definition of abuse and violence in research studies that may not always relate directly to violence in the family. Because it is so difficult to come to an agreement on the exclusive use of one of these terms, the three terms are used interchangeably in this chapter.

[3] The community-based model places psychotherapy as one of many interventions that comprise treatment and prevention. The context within which therapy takes place often includes the necessity for therapists to collaborate with other professionals who are working on different aspects of the same problem. For example, if the legal system is involved, the therapist might be expected to have contact with the attorney to help the client deal more effectively with the legal issues raised. If there are children involved who have been exposed to violence in the home, the therapist may help develop specific high-risk interventions for them with other professionals. Or the therapist may participate in universal nonviolent family promotion efforts, such as an educational program in the local schools. They may need to contact a local battered woman shelter to assist clients further. Such a community-based model calls for the therapist to get out of the therapy office and collaborate with other professionals working in the area of domestic violence.

batterer's groups and long-term psychotherapy groups to help perpetrators stop their violent and abusive behavior. For the more dangerous batterers, these therapy programs may be offered in the jails, often thought of as a tertiary-level care system. Battered women are offered a range of psychological services to help them deal with the aftereffects of abuse, including special self-help or facilitated groups for battered women, victim counseling provided by the courts when charges have been filed, and individual and group psychotherapy. Battered women shelters and safe homes provide a tertiary level of care for those who need to be more protected. Some psychiatric hospitals have a trauma unit that deal with multiply abused women, and battered women often are found there. Some communities also offer family counseling after the violence has been stopped for a time. These treatment programs are described later in the chapter.

DYNAMICS OF BATTERING RELATIONSHIPS

Although the concept of the Battered Woman Syndrome was originally developed from research on the psychological effects of repeated abuse on a woman who also had a special relationship with the abuser, often including dependency, love, and affection (Walker, 1979, 1984), today its meaning has been broadened to include descriptions of the dynamics of battering relationships, particularly when used in the legal system. Research from studying a group of 400 battered women found that many experienced a group of psychological symptoms that appear similar to the Post-Traumatic Stress Disorder diagnosis now listed in the fourth edition of the *Diagnostic and Statistical Manual of Mental Disorders* (DSM-IV) (American Psychiatric Association [APA], 1994). Researchers, practitioners, and instructors who teach and supervise battered women need to understand their stories (and, more recently, those of batterers too), particularly as a way to recognize the pattern when a couple or individuals present for treatment.

Cycle of Violence

Most battering relationships evidence a pattern of violence that can be described as cyclical in nature. This cycle of violence consists of three main phases: (1) a period of tension-building; (2) the acute battering incident or explosion; and (3) a period of loving contrition. An atypical courtship period often precedes the appearance of these three phases and is similar to the phase 3 period of loving contrition in that there is an intensity to the positive and loving behaviors expressed and demonstrated. Thus, often it is difficult to predict that a relationship will turn violent—often it does not occur until after the woman makes a definite commitment to the man—because the telltale behaviors are more easily seen in retrospect than when first occurring. This cycle refutes the psychoanalytic notion of battered women as masochists whose reward is the beating and instead follows learning theories about positive reinforcement in the third phase, often described as the honeymoon period. (See Walker, 1979, 1984, 1989, 1994 for a fuller description of the cycle of violence.) Further study has modified the cycle to describe variations in the third phase of loving contrition. In many relationships, an absence of tension is considered rewarding, whereas in other relationships where the violence has reached life-threatening proportions, the fear of more serious harm is never totally gone. Many women describe these relationships as feeling like they are "walking on eggshells." In most relationships the courtship period sets the stage for the third phase to become a reinforcer. The battered woman typically believes that the "real" man is the one who displayed the kind, loving, nurturing behavior during their courtship and, when he settles down after his explosion of anger, she believes his statements that he really will change and never hurt her again and his pleas that she not leave him.

It is possible to graph the cycle in specific relationships by taking details from four abusive incidents; the first battering incident remembered, the last one that occurred prior to the interview, the worst or one of the worst incidents, and a typical battering incident. By collecting this data, the woman is helped to learn how to avoid more serious physical harm by developing a crisis safety plan. Sometimes a couple's cycle changes over time, usually due to external circumstances. For example, pregnancy and the presence of a young infant in the house may increase the abuse; having teenage children who are acting out or losing one's job also may increase the frequency and severity of the abuse. Serious illness, an arrest with incarceration or an offender-specific intervention program, and individual treatment may cause a decrease in the abuse. In some cases, desistance, or the complete cessation of abuse, occurs simply from the arrest and brief incarceration. Perhaps the man has learned that he can control his violent behavior; understands he will get in more trouble if he persists in using violence; changes his attitudes about being entitled to a woman's services; or gets scared of the consequences. In other cases, the physical violence may decrease or stop while the psychological abuse and control increases. There is very little information about interventions in stopping the pattern of sexual abuse in battering relationships, although it is believed that use of sexual aggression is simply another way to humiliate and, therefore, gain better control over the woman. Although some studies suggest that couples who stay together may become violence-free, there is no way to predict which relationships will escalate and which will not. Therefore, it is wisest to assume the most common pattern: Abuse will escalate in families characterized by domestic violence. *However, it is important for therapists to remain neutral about terminating the battering relationship.* Although we know that the violence usually escalates without intervention, the goal is to help the batterer stop using violence and abuse and to help the victim become safe and a survivor.

Learned Helplessness

Although the cycle of violence helps explain the psychological behavior that keeps abusive relationships together, individuals are affected differently by the repeated cycle, and those reactions may continue to have an affect on them as well as on their families. One social learning theory that provides a useful way to understand battered women's often contradictory-appearing behavior is the *theory of learned helplessness,* first discovered in the experimental animal laboratory by Seligman (1975) and then applied to both college students and other specific groups as battered women (Walker, 1979, 1984). Many battered women advocates do not like the theory primarily because its name suggests perpetuating the myth that battered women are passive and helpless when, in fact, they exhibit many behaviors that are designed to cope with and best protect themselves and their children from abuse. Seligman (1990) has focused on the prevention of learned helplessness through his work on teaching an optimistic view of the world despite adversity in childhood. The concept of learned helplessness holds that women (in this case) who are exposed to random and variable abuse that they believe is inescapable lose the ability to perceive that what they do will make a difference in protecting themselves from the noncontingency between response and outcome in the relationship. The cycle of violence they experience supports this result in that the same behavior may work during one phase and not during another. Thus, battered women begin to concentrate on coping strategies that have the highest prediction of being successful; they do not use many behaviors that have a lower probability of being protective, including terminating the relationship, because they have learned the truth that leaving the batterer does not necessarily stop the abuse.

This theory is attractive in that it assumes the man's violence is learned behavior and therefore it can be unlearned. Furthermore, whatever the victim has learned as survival skills during the relationship can be unlearned when she finally achieves safety. It has at the core a model that permits the restoration of self-efficacy, often labeled as reempowerment by treatment providers (Walker, 1994). My research findings were consistent with the theory that battered women are more likely to develop learned helplessness from the battering relationship, even when they also have experienced sufficient exposure to abuse as a child to cause the same symptomology (1984). Although it often is assumed that the psychological effects of any trauma experienced as an adult will be worse if there has been a history of trauma, I have not necessarily found this in battered women who are exposed to other forms of violence and abuse (1984). Further, many battered women have social and other skills to function without difficulty outside of the battering relationship, which suggests that the areas of psychological problems noted in the assessment of a battered woman may simply disappear once the woman perceives herself or actually becomes safe from further violence and abuse. It is important for therapists to remember that battered women often perceive the legal process and other types of harassment as a continuation of the battering relationship. Often the attempts of others to help the woman are perceived as controlling behaviors and reactivate the traumatic memories of the abuse, even when the actions are not actually intended to be harmful.

BATTERED WOMAN SYNDROME AND OTHER DIAGNOSES

The collection of psychological symptoms that make up the Battered Woman Syndrome are very similar but not identical to those that comprise the diagnosis of Post-Traumatic Stress Disorder (PTSD) (Figley, 1986; Walker, 1994). These include the following reactions normally expected when someone is exposed to trauma.

Anxiety and High Physiological Arousal

- Hypervigilance
- Panic attacks
- Physiological distress
- Startle reaction
- Emotional lability
- Hysteria

Avoidance of the Trauma and Its Effects

- Numbing of feelings
- Depression
- Minimization

- Denial
- Repression
- Dissociation
- Loss of interest in activities

Cognitive and Memory Disturbances

- Confused thinking
- Partial amnesia for some events
- Intrusive memories of some traumatic events
- Nightmares and sleep disorders
- Flashbacks to fragments of memories of previous traumatic incidents
- Perception that the abuse is reoccurring when exposed to a reminder
- Retelling stories about abuse with or without affect and going off on tangents

It is common for some memories of abuse to be forgotten and then later remembered again while other memories become so intense they intrude on the victim's waking and sleeping thoughts. Often victims believe they are reexperiencing the trauma by being exposed to or remembering the abusive events or the feelings aroused by the trauma. Psychophysiological symptoms frequently accompany these traumatic memories. The mechanisms explaining how these memories are stored and recovered are still under investigation (American Psychological Association, 1996).

Some differences between Battered Woman Syndrome and PTSD criteria listed in the DSM-IV (APA, 1994), include; changes in the battered woman's interpersonal relationships caused by isolation, jealousy, overpossessiveness, and intrusiveness by the man that is observed along with his psychological, physical, and sexual abuse. These effects may be compounded in battered women who have been abused in other situations (Walker, 1994). The more isolated the man can keep the woman, the more control he will have over her physical and mental presence. Many battered women come to limit their relationships with family and friends because the man dislikes her having these interactions and she wants to avoid upsetting him. Her goal is to keep him as calm as possible. Today, after various public education campaigns to teach the general population about the seriousness of domestic violence, few battered women believe that all the man's violence is their own fault; rather, they are more likely to understand that using violence is his fault and he can control his behavior. But most battered women also believe that they need to find ways to keep their partner from escalating his abuse or losing his temper. Although battered women often minimize the frequency and severity of battering incidents and it is tempting for a therapist to collude with her when she makes comments such as "It wasn't so bad," in fact, such an attitude perpetuates the myth that women have control over the man's aggressive behavior and can contain it if they are not provocative, when in reality, only the man can stop his violence. Often, it is more helpful to reframe or cognitively restructure the woman's beliefs into a more accurate appraisal that she can take certain steps to help herself and her children become safer from his violence.

It is not uncommon for battered women to have substance abuse problems, either with drugs obtained on the street or by doctor's prescriptions. The numbing of feelings that is associated with Battered Woman Syndrome may be enhanced through the use of these drugs. For some women, particularly those exhibiting high levels of anxiety or depression, carefully monitored psychotropic drugs may help in their healing process. Others probably do not need medication; rather, they need to learn how to strengthen their own psychological resources (Herman, 1992; Walker, 1994). Some battered women have learned to hide their symptoms in front of other people, even family and friends, while others need to tell everyone every detail of what has occurred. Some battered women are more compliant; others have turned their feelings of injustice into anger and hostility that is expressed whenever their feelings get hurt. Most battered women have developed a sensitivity to other people's negative feelings toward them although they rarely read neutrality accurately. Thus, relationships are seen as helpful or harmful; there is nothing in between. Most abused women do not think that anyone really will believe them; the batterers usually have told them this for a long time. Thus, in establishing therapeutic relationships, it is important to validate their stories. Victims have learned how to look as if they are listening and understand when someone is talking to them even when their anxiety is so high it prevents them from really concentrating on the message. Therefore, therapists must make sure they really are being understood.

Many battered women are multiple abuse victims. Some have been physically and/or sexually abused as children (Kirschner, Kirschner, & Rappaport, 1993); some have been sexually assaulted as adults (Herman, 1992), sexually exploited by others in positions of power and authority (Pope, 1994), and/or sexually harassed in school or on the job (Walker, 1994). The more forms of abuse experienced, the more violent it was, the more life-threatening was the experience, and the earlier the experience, the more likely the psychological effects are to be severe and complex. Herman (1992) suggests that a new form of complex PTSD be included in diagnostic systems to enable clinicians to assess these victims properly. Her studies have found that Borderline Personality Disorder (APA, 1994) is not an appropriate diagnostic category because the symptoms presented by women who have been battered repeatedly are more responsive to trauma treatment. Often these clients' manipulation and bouts of anger respond better to reempowerment than to tighter controls (Brown, 1995; Herman, 1992; Walker, 1994).

PSYCHOLOGICAL FUNCTIONING OF BATTERERS

Research has suggested that identification of batterers is far more complex than simply observing the abuse of power in a relationship. Batterers, like the women and children they harm, come from all demographic groups and do not fall into any one particular profile pattern, although they do demonstrate some similar behaviors consistently, such as overpossessiveness, jealousy, disrespect for women in general, insecurities often covered over by bravado, and belief in sex-role stereotypes.

Many feminists who believe that the societal oppression of women (particularly those of racial, ethnic, and cultural diversity or who have been discriminated against because of their lifestyle, sexual orientation, socioeconomic class, or physical disabilities) is a direct factor contributing to the continuing violence against women (Dobasch & Dobasch, 1992) do not accept the different typologies being studied in a variety of recent research studies (Holtzworth-Munroe & Stuart, 1994). Incarceration in jail or prison and psychoeducational programs that deal with anger management, attitudes toward women, and power and control issues are their recommended interventions to make batterers stop their violent behavior (Adams, 1988; Pence & Paymar, 1994; Yllo, 1993). But eliminating the concept of psychotherapy as one possible corrective intervention to pursue may cause theorists to overlook the possibility that there are several typologies of batterers.

New research into batterers suggests that there may be several different ways to create typologies. (See Holtzworth-Munroe & Stuart, 1994, for a more complete review.) Like the mythical battered woman, abusive men were first thought to have sadistic needs that corresponded to the needs of their partners. This theory was replaced by one that labeled all batterers as having a character disorder, usually some form of antisocial personality disorder. O'Leary (1993) describes some of the more recent psychological research that has led to better descriptions of the psychological functioning of abusive men. Dutton and Starzomski (1993) have found three major types of batterers. One type has major mental disorders, particularly depression, paranoia, and borderline personality traits. The other two types include men who are oversocialized in sex-role patterns that disadvantage women and men who engage in other criminal behavior in addition to beating their partners. Sonkin, Martin, and Walker (1985) found that many men who learned to devalue women through their socialization were also angry at women and engaged in dysfunctional thinking, particularly around their inability to believe that they have done anything wrong. They tend to rationalize their abusive acts by believing that they are entitled to make a woman behave in the manner they desire. These men often battered more than one partner, even when the women used different strategies to cope with the abuse. Walker and Sonkin (1994) found that stalking and harassment behavior by batterers is associated with dysfunctional thinking that often reaches obsessive levels and results in compulsive behavior that is both intentionally and nonintentionally annoying, intimidating, and abusive. O'Leary (1993) suggests that different levels of severity in violence relationships can be measured. His studies have found that some abusive relationships remain at a fairly stable level of verbal aggression, while others seem to follow the more typical pattern of escalation to more severe violence.

Gottman and associates (1995) have attempted to study the abuser's physiological correlates within the context of angry conflict in the relationship. Using measures comparable to those found in the literature and developed for use with measuring the physiological responses of other violent criminals, these findings can be important in learning how to sort out batterers for different interventions. For example, learning who will respond to arrest or other legal constraints, who will respond to brief psychoeducational intervention, who needs long-term psychotherapy, and for whom the best intervention is prison may increase treatment efficacy. Sometimes these interventions will be applied sequentially; other times, as with drug and alcohol treatment, they will be concurrent.

Even though the behavior of batterers may appear similar, their individual psychological and physiological processes may vary so much that different treatment methods are necessary to avoid escalating the violence. By studying both the partner's responses and the physiological and psychological processes in the angry batterer during an experimentally contrived conflict situation, Gottman and associates (1995) have found that there are differences in the way batterers experience and process their reaction to conflict and control needs. Their data clearly demonstrates that although both groups of batterers, those whose heart rates accelerated and those whose heart rates decreased during the experiment, were reported to engage in similar violent and abusive acts against their victims, at least two different psychological and physiological processes occurred that differentiated one group from the other. Interestingly, those with lowered heart rates and physiological responses closer to that which is reported for other anti-social and violent criminals were perceived as more dangerous by their partners, and the partner stated she was fearful of further violence should she attempt to terminate the relationship. The application of these preliminary findings to victims would suggest that women who relate to one type or the other can expect different responses from the particular batterer to their reactive behavior, especially with the first five minutes from the beginning of a fight.

The descriptions of criminals with Antisocial Personality Disorder frequently include behaviors that appear calm, calculating, well controlled, and extremely dangerous. The findings of an association of a lowered heart rate and other physiological changes when an argument occurs with this type of person are indeed similar to the findings in studies of those who commit criminal offenses other than woman abuse and adds further support to findings by O'Leary (1993), Dutton and Starzomski's (1993), and others of at least one type of batterer who also exhibits such dangerous behavior. The narcissism and independence of many batterers, including this antisocial personality type, also may contribute to their inability to judge the needs of their partners, and the continued contempt and belligerence often seen in those most intractable to therapy seems to further lower the women's self-esteem (Gottman et al., 1995). Family treatment for these perpetrators would not be appropriate and may even be more dangerous.

Thus, there is no typical batterer and the different types of batterers may not be easy to distinguish from each other or from other men who do not abuse their partners. However, three major typologies have been identified:

1. Those who batter at home motivated by abnormal power and control needs and whose violent and abusive behavior could be stopped with some psychoeducation about anger management and sex-role attitude readjustment (Pence & Paymar, 1993).

2. Those who also have serious psychological problems including depression, dysfunctional thinking and obsessive-compulsive behavior, paranoid disorders, borderline traits, and/or other serious mental disorders and need individual and group psychotherapy (Dutton & Starzomski, 1993; Hamberger & Lohr, 1989; O'Leary, 1993; Saunders, 1992).

3. Those who have committed other crimes as well as assaults within the home and could be labeled Antisocial Personality Disorder. To date there is little effective treatment for this type, and the best intervention is prison (Dutton & Starzomski, 1993; Fagan, Stewart, & Hansen, 1983).

IMPLICATIONS FOR ASSESSMENT AND DIAGNOSIS

Often it is difficult to measure the seriousness of the abusive relationship because of the complex interaction between intentional and unintentional acts, the resulting violence, any injuries, the context within which the violence occurs, and the woman's current and historical physical and mental state. Women can describe differences between batterers or battering incidents from their own fear and other psychological reactions to their partners' abuse, not just the violent acts themselves. This is quite clear in assessing the individual battered woman's *reasonable perception of imminent danger* should she kill the man in what she believes is self-defense (Walker, 1989). Often women describe physiological changes in the man, such as a different look in his eyes, changes in facial features, or a twitch that usually precedes serious violence; they recognize these clues that warn of greater danger. Men, on the other hand, are less able to describe the abusive incidents themselves. Further, unless they committed the acts with the intent to harm the woman, batterers simply do not acknowledge an act as abuse or violence. In addition, both women and men minimize and deny the violence in the relationship when reporting it. If women are asked to give details of violence in front of the batterer, in the therapist's office, the courtroom, or the hospital emergency room, often they are unable or unwilling to explain what has happened for fear of retribution when they leave the safe place and go home and because they do not want to make him angry. Battered women, like other women, are expected to "stand by their man" and not report much "personal" information. For their own safety, that is what they often do.

The clinical and empirical data discussed suggest making the shift from a unidimensional view of batterers (Pence & Paymar, 1993) to an understanding that batterers and battering relationships are multidimensional with differentiating characteristics that are measurable. Further, these differences suggest the need for a "triage" approach to the types of intervention available. This is precisely the arena in which the Gottman and associates' study (1995) focuses our attention. The physiological differences that are measured during interactions by different couples provide strong evidence of different processes that may help explain why some of the current intervention and treatment approaches do not work and why others are more effective with some batterers in stopping the violence.

The methodological problems that arise during attempts to assess and diagnose in battering relationships are formidable. Obviously, it is not particularly difficult to label physical acts of violence as battering. However, sometimes it is quite hard to discern if the acts were committed as part of a domestic violence pattern, if they occurred in self-defense, or if they were in response to something else. The debate about whether women or men hit more is an example of distracting the focus from the essence of the domestic violence relationship by getting lost in counting the physical acts of violence. Women's violent acts against men should not be overlooked; however, it is important to know the context within which domestic violence occurs, including the pattern of physical, sexual, and psychological abuse. Measuring this context is difficult, and men and women can be expected to differ in their perceptions and explanations. (See Chapter 24.)

The measurement of a *cycle of violence* often provides information for the understanding of the behaviors that occur during the tension-building and loving-contrition phases, in addition to the acute battering incident. So too does the *concept of learned helplessness,* which can be measured on seven factors characteristic of the battering relationship (Walker, 1984, 1994). These include learned helplessness variables from the relationship and from childhood, and lethality assessment variables.

Learned Helplessness Variables from the Relationship

1. The pattern of the violence often escalates in frequency and severity and follows the cycle.
2. Sexual abuse and coercion occur within the relationship.
3. Power and control factors, including intrusiveness, overpossessiveness, jealousy, and isolation, occur.
4. Direct and indirect threats to kill the woman and her family.

   5. Psychological torture using the Amnesty International definition including
- a. verbal aggression with humiliation and name-calling
- b. denial of powers
- c. induced debility
- d. monopolizing perceptions
- e. mind control
- f. threats to kill
- g. isolation
- h. drugs or alcohol
- i. occasional indulgences

   6. Violence correlates including abuse
- a. against other people
- b. against children
- c. against pets
- d. toward inanimate objects

   7. Alcohol and drug abuse

Learned Helplessness Variables from Childhood Experiences

   1. Witnessing or experiencing abuse in the childhood home.

   2. Victim of sexual abuse or molestation as a child.

   3. Critical factors of noncontrol such as
- a. early parent loss through death
- b. separation or divorce of parents
- c. frequent moves
- d. alcohol and/or other drug abuse by one or both parents
- e. trauma in family

   4. Rigid traditionality, sex-role-stereotyped behaviors, or fundamentalist religious beliefs.

   5. Chronic health problems.

Assessment of lethality is also important. The following factors have been found to be important in the research and were compiled by Walker and Sonkin (1994). However, the best predictor of future violence is past behavior. It is essential to remember that these are predictors of group behavior that place everyone in the group in a higher risk pool; there are no statistically reliable and valid predictors for specific individuals.

Lethality Assessment Variables

   1. Frequency of man's use of violence is escalating.

   2. Severity of man's violence is escalating.

   3. Frequency of alcohol intoxication and drug use.

   4. Man's threats to harm children.

   5. Man's threats to kill the woman or others.

   6. Man's forced or threatened sex acts.

7. Man's or woman's suicide threats or attempts.
8. Weapons kept in the home or easily accessible and have been used in fights.
9. Psychiatric impairment of man or woman.
10. Proximity of man and woman—how close do they both work and live.
11. Man's need for control of contact around children.
12. Current life stresses in man's and woman's lives.
13. Man's past criminal history.
14. Man's attitudes toward violence, especially violence against women.
15. Presence of new relationships for man or woman.

Sometimes it is possible to infer the presence of battering when diagnosing Battered Woman Syndrome or PTSD in a victim. More often such inferences are used to support the woman's credibility. Of course, many of the symptoms in the PTSD diagnostic criteria also may be found in other disorders, although the presence of the pattern along with an abuse history supports the assessment of domestic violence. Using the PTSD diagnosis to help determine treatment goals for female victims usually is the best way to help them to become survivors of the violence. It also gives victims a way to think about what has happened to them without feeling as if they are crazy, which is what most batterers threaten will happen to them. Some battered women do have other mental health diagnoses, the most common being panic disorders and depression that go beyond the typical PTSD symptoms. If a battered woman has emotional problems that come from the abuse or from other sources, she should not be denied access to competent therapists. These problems need to be treated individually or in group therapy.

IMPLICATIONS FOR TREATMENT

The following implications for treatment come directly from the acceptance of the fact that domestic violence is the responsibility of the man who commits the violence. Family or couple's treatment is not recommended until he has been in offender-specific therapy and has stopped all abuse. It is also recommended that the battered woman deal with her own personal issues in individual or group therapy prior to entering couple's therapy. Sometimes both the woman's and the man's therapists conduct the couple's treatment, making sure each has his or her own advocate. The following checklist (Walker, 1993b) helps therapists know when family therapy is appropriate.

Family Therapy Checklist

The batterer:

- Accepts all responsibility for his violent behavior.
- Stops all stalking and harassing behavior.
- Stops all obsessional thinking and compulsive behavior.
- Learns skills to manage his control needs.
- Learns ways to manage anger and conflict.
- Has addressed his own family-of-origin issues.
- Learns new sex-role socialization patterns.

Implications for Batterer's Treatment

The implications of the new research on violent and aggressive men for therapists are enormous. For example, the Gottman and associates' study (1995) found that battered women in relationships with the "increased heart-rate men" who overtly displayed more emotion, especially anger, were more likely to divorce than those who were in relationships with the "lower heart-rate men" who displayed less emotional reactivity. This second group fits the description of batterers described as "cold" and "intimidating" men who systematically control through bullying, cruel, and antisocial behavior. Although this finding makes some intuitive sense, as it indicates a more stable relationship that is less likely to come apart than one that is emotionally chaotic, the level of contempt and belligerence still prevents the development of a strong, loving, nonfearful, and nonviolent pattern of interaction, even if the couple stays together.

The early popularity of psychoeducational programs that deal directly with a batterer's anger as well as his sense of entitlement from sex-role-socialized norms that suggest women must meet men's needs (Pence & Paymar, 1993) has waned. These programs are being supplemented and replaced by a variety of different interventions and treatment programs. The Sherman and Berk (1983) Minnesota police experiment that found that batterers desisted in continued use of violence after arrest has been replicated, and the findings suggest a more complex relationship between arrest and offender-specific treatment programs. Most communities now encourage mandatory arrest and at least an overnight stay in jail followed by interventions such as reduction of bond if the assessment of the man's potential use of violence is low and he attends offender-specific psychoeducational programs (Sherman & Berk, 1983). The replication studies suggest that some interventions appear to cause greater violence in a few men while others have had better success than predicted. For example, batterers who have a job and community status are more likely to respond to arrest and treatment than are those who are unemployed and/or are not concerned about their reputation. It is also important to remember that there has been little follow-through by judges after arrest and conviction on domestic violence assault charges when the terms and conditions of probation are disregarded, so it is difficult to say what the success might be if the proper protocols actually were implemented.

Gottman and coworkers (1995) have begun an important discussion of the implications of their findings for treatment. For example, they discuss the fact that a treatment program based on the assumption that all batterers lack impulse control could be a mismatch for both the therapist and the client for those batterers who have excellent control over when they do and do not choose to use aggression. In their group of men with the lowered physiological reactivity, the subjects could be said to be overcontrolling their impulses. The role of drug and alcohol abuse for either the perpetrator or the victim and the role of an individual battered woman's behavior also must be considered when treatment is planned. Some batterers are know to relate to a woman in a particular way in order to get her to interact. It must be assumed that there are other personal and external factors not yet discussed or studied that may impact on domestic violence in any particular relationship. The literature suggests a variety of interesting hypotheses for further research. For example, why do some batterers use certain strategies under some conditions, such as conflict, but not at other times (Margolin, John, & Gleberman, 1988)?

It is estimated that approximately 20 percent of the known batterers have committed other types of crimes besides assault in their homes (Dutton & Starzomski, 1993;

Holtzworth-Munroe & Stuart, 1994). Although they have not been studied previously, some men who come to the attention of the courts and mental health professionals for reasons other than domestic violence, appear to emerge from this group. Many of these men commit the most dangerous and serious violent acts against their partners. Some have the obsessive thinking that underlies continued stalking and harassment behavior, especially after the woman attempts to terminate the relationship.

New treatment programs to deal directly with the batterer who is also a stalker by helping remedy obsessive and dysfunctional thinking are now available, although they are not yet in wide use (Walker & Sonkin, 1994). This treatment approach uses a cognitive-behavioral model with both the victim and the perpetrator, but in separate therapies with separate therapists. This format may make it easier for the couple to relate better to one another after treatment; during the often-difficult process of divorce; around custody or visitation issues, which are so problematic with this population; or while trying to rebuild the relationship. An intervention that holds promise is to use these antistalking programs along with electronically monitoring the abuser and sending reports to the courts and appropriate law enforcement personnel should there be any violations of restraining orders.[4]

Treatment for Battered Women

Treatment for the woman is designed to help her survive by staying as safe as possible. The goals of survivor therapy, which is based on feminist therapy along with trauma theory, include safety, reempowerment, validation, exploring options, cognitive clarity and judgment, making her own decisions, and healing trauma effects. Walker (1994) describes the treatment issues and techniques that can be used to help the woman heal. Feminist therapy principles are used that respect the power differential between therapist and client as well as promote egalitarian relationships, while still maintaining proper boundaries between the two. The areas that seem to be the most damaged include body image and sexuality, anger and rage, intimacy, compliance and confrontation, and manipulation for power and control. Some of the techniques for dealing with these issues can be viewed in the video Survivor Therapy.[5] It is important to remember that sometimes a self-help group is sufficient for many battered women who need to be with others like themselves to heal.

IMPLICATIONS FOR PREVENTION

Family therapists often can prevent the transmission of violence from one member of a family to the next generation by identifying risk factors and promoting nonviolent ways of resolving conflict. The deliberate increase in positive interactions within the family helps reduce the incidence of child abuse; such a program of increasing positive interactions may reduce the risk of domestic violence also. Prevention programs can include

---

[4] Both the perpetrator stabilization and victim empowerment programs and the electronic monitoring are available from a Boulder, Colorado, company, BI, Inc. This antistalking program is currently being written by Walker and Sonkin (1994) for use with or without the electronic monitoring; publication is expected soon.

[5] This videotape is available from Newbridge Communications in New York City. It is one in their series on master therapists.

attempts to educate the general population as well as specific short-term interventions that are designed to work with high-risk groups. For example, some adolescent girls exposed to domestic violence are known to become more depressed if their mothers leave their fathers. Teaching teenagers how to recognize the cues of overcontrolling behavior is another way to promote nonviolent relationships. Children who exhibit bullying behavior in school or in the community can be encouraged to join a group that deals with better ways to gain positive power and control. Universal prevention programs such as education about sex-role socialization patterns and the disadvantages of behavioral stereotyping for women (as well as for men) or sermons from religious leaders on the negative impact of violence in the family are important ways to reach the entire population, not just targeted high-risk groups. Obviously, intervention with young children who have been exposed to parental fighting and violence will help prevent the abuse from being transmitted from one generation to another. Boys who witness their fathers batter their mothers are 700 times more likely to use violence in their own lives. When the boy also has been abused himself, he is 1,000 times more likely to use violence (Kalmuss, 1984).

CONCLUSION

In summary, identification and assessment of abusive spousal relationships need to be done in two major steps. First, an abuse history must be taken, looking at the dynamics of the battering relationship. Using the cycle of violence, learned helplessness factors, and the lethality checklist as a guiding model, the dynamics of a particular relationship can be clearly discerned. Second, the evaluation of the effects from domestic violence also must be assessed in the individual members of the family. The presence of Battered Woman Syndrome, Post-Traumatic Stress Disorder, or other mental health problems such as depression and anxiety also need to be measured using standard psychological interviews, protocols, and standardized testing when necessary. The batterer's behavior and personality characteristics must be assessed using standardized testing and clinical interviews so that it can be compared to the typologies suggested. Finally, children who have been exposed to or who have experienced violence in their homes must be assessed and referred for intervention programs designed to prevent the family violence from being transferred to and internalized for acting-out later by the next generation.

REFERENCES

Adams, D. (1988). Treatment models of men who batter: A profeminist approach. In K. Yllo & M. Bograd (Eds.), *Feminist perspectives on wife abuse* (pp. 176–199). Newbury Park, CA: Sage.

American Psychiatric Association. (1994). *Diagnostic and statistical manual of mental disorders* (4th ed.). Washington, DC: Author.

American Psychological Association. (1996). *APA presidential task force on violence and the family report.* Washington, DC: Author.

Bograd, M. (1988). Power, gender and the family: Feminist perspectives on family systems therapy. In M. A. Dutton-Douglas & L. E. A. Walker (Eds.), *Feminist psychotherapies: Integration of therapeutic and feminist systems* (pp. 118–133). Norwood, NJ: Ablex.

Brown, L. S. (1995). *Subversive dialogues.* New York: Basic Books.

Dell, P. (1989). Violence and the systemic view: The problem of power. *Family Process, 28,* 1–14.

Dobasch, R. P., & Dobasch, R. E. (1992). *Women, violence and social change.* New York: Routledge.

Dutton, D. G., & Browning, J. J. (1988). Concern for power, fear of intimacy, and aversive stimuli for wife abuse. In G. T. Hotaling, D. Finkelhor, J. T. Kilpatrick, & M. Straus (Eds.), *New directions in family violence research* (pp. 113–121). Newbury Park, CA: Sage.

Dutton, D. G., & Starzomski, A. J. (1993). Borderline personality in perpetrators of psychological and physical abuse. *Violence and Victims, 8,* 327–337.

Figley, C. (Ed.) (1986). *Trauma and its wake.* New York: Brunner/Mazel.

Gelles, R., & Straus, M. A. (1988). *Intimate violence: The causes and consequences of violence in the American family.* New York: Simon & Schuster.

Gottman, J. M., Jacobson, N. S., Rushe, R. H., Wu Short, J., Babcock, J., La Taillade, J. J., & Waltz, J. (1995). The relationship between heart rate reactivity, emotionally aggressive behavior, and general violence in batterers. *Journal of Family Psychology, 9.*

Hamberger, L. K., & Lohr, J. M. (1989). Proximal causes of spouse abuse: A theoretical analysis for cognitive-behavioral interventions. In P. L. Caesar & L. K. Hamberger (Eds.), *Treating men who batter: Theory, practice, and programs* (pp. 53–76). New York: Springer.

Hansen, M., & Harway, M. (Eds.) (1993). *Battering and family therapy: A feminist perspective.* Newbury Park, CA: Sage.

Hansen, M., Harway, M., & Cervantes, N. (1991). Therapists' perceptions of severity in cases of family violence. *Violence and Victims, 6,* 225–235.

Hart, B. (1988). Beyond the "duty to warn": A therapist's "duty to protect" battered women and children. In K. A. Yllo & M. Bograd (Eds.), *Feminist perspectives on wife abuse* (pp. 234–248). Newbury Park, CA: Sage.

Herman, J. L. (1992). *Trauma and recovery.* New York: Basic Books.

Holtzworth-Munroe, A., & Stuart, G. L. (1994). Typologies of male batterers: Three sub-types and the differences among them. *Psychological Bulletin, 116,* 476–497.

Hotaling, G. T., & Sugarman, D. B. (1986). An analysis of risk markers in husband and wife violence: The current state of knowledge. *Violence and Victims, 1,* 101–124.

Kalmus, D. (1984). The intergenerational transmission of violence in the family. *Journal of Marriage and the Family, 46,* 11–19.

Kirschner, S., Kirschner, D. A., & Rappaport, R. (1993). *Working with adult incest survivors.* New York: Brunner/Mazel.

Liss, M., & Stahly, G. (1993). Child custody and visitation issues for battered women. In M. Hansen & M. Harway (Eds.), *Battering and family therapy: A feminist perspective.* (pp. 175–187). Newbury Park, CA: Sage.

Lobel, K. (Ed.) (1986). *Naming the violence: Speaking out about lesbian battering.* Seattle: Seal.

Margolin, G., John, R. S., & Gleberman, L. (1988). Affective responses to conflictual discussions in violent and non-violent couples. *Journal of Consulting and Clinical Psychology, 56,* 24–33.

National Institute of Justice. (1994). Report on victims of domestic violence. Washington, DC: U.S. Department of Justice.

O'Leary, K. D. (1993). Through a psychological lens: Personality traits, personality disorders, and levels of violence. In R. J. Gelles & D. R. Loeske (Eds.), *Current controversies on family violence* (pp. 7–30). Newbury Park, CA: Sage.

Patterson, G. R. (1982). *Coercive family processes.* Eugene, OR: Castaglia.

Pence, E., & Paymar, M. (1993). *Working with men who batter: The Duluth model.* New York: Springer.

Pope, K. (1994). *Sexual feelings in psychotherapy.* Washington, DC: American Psychological Association Press.

Seligman, M. P. (1975). *Learned helplessness: On depression, development and death.* New York: Wiley.

Selgiman, M. P. (1990). *Learned optimism.* New York: Wiley.

Sherman, L. W., & Berk, R. A. (1984). The specific deterrent effects of arrest for domestic assault. *American Sociological Review, 49,* 261–272.

Smith, M. D. (1990). Patriarchal ideology and wife beating: A test of a feminist hypothesis. *Violence and Victims, 5,* 257–273.

Sonkin, D. J., Martin, D., & Walker, L. E. (1985). *The male batterer.* New York: Springer.

Straus, M. A. (1993). Physical assaults by wives: A major social problem. In R. J. Gelles & D. R. Loeske (Eds.), *Current controversies on family violence* (pp. 67–87). Newbury Park, CA: Sage.

Walker, L. E. (1979). *The battered women.* New York: Harper & Row.

Walker, L. E. A. (1984). *The battered woman syndrome.* New York: Springer.

Walker, L. E. A. (1989). *Terrifying love: Why battered women kill and how society responds.* New York: Harper/Collins.

Walker, L. E. A. (1993a). The battered woman syndrome is a psychological consequence of abuse. In R. J. Gelles & D. R. Loeske (Eds.), *Current controversies on family violence* (pp. 133–152). Newbury Park, CA: Sage.

Walker, L. E. A. (1993b). *Survivor therapy: Clinical assessment and intervention workbook.* Denver, CO: Endolor Communications.

Walker, L. E. A. (1994). *Abused women and survivor therapy: A practical guide for the psychotherapist.* Washington, DC: American Psychological Association.

Walker, L. E. A. (1995). Current perspectives on men who batter women: Implications for intervention and treatment to stop violence against women. *Journal of Family Psychology, 9.*

Walker, L. E. A., & Sonkin, D. J. (1994). *Jurismonitor stabilization and empowerment programs.* Denver, CO: Endolor Communications.

Yllo, K. A. (1993). Through a feminist lens: Gender, power, and violence. In R. J. Gelles & D. R. Loeske (Eds.), *Current controversies on family violence* (pp. 47–62). Newbury Park, CA: Sage.

CHAPTER 23

Sexual and Gender Identity Disorders in a Relational Perspective

WILLIAM R. STAYTON, ThD

Sex therapy, in its beginnings as a discipline by William Masters and Virginia Johnson, was framed in relational terms. In their book *Human Sexual Inadequacy,* they said "there is no such thing as an uninvolved partner in any marriage in which there is some form of sexual inadequacy" (1970, p. 2). Even though some sexual dysfunctions, such as female orgasmic disorder, can be treated on an individual basis, it is still important to engage in relational sex therapy if she is partnered, so that she can become orgasmic with her partner as well as by herself.

The effects of a sexual dysfunction on a relationship cannot be overstated. Performance fears, anxiety, and low self-esteem often are direct results of a person feeling like a failure in the bedroom. Depression is common in either or both partners as they cannot get turned on or feel they can satisfy their partner. On the other hand, when positive sexual functioning begins to occur, it can help the entire relationship to blossom, just as resolving some of the marital discord can promote a more relaxed and satisfying sexual interaction.

Since 1970, not only has much more been learned about sexual function and dysfunction, but the field of sex therapy has expanded to include a much wider range of sexual issues that affect sexual function and dysfunction, such as sex therapy with persons with disability, both physical and mental, and gender identity issues.

Although the fourth edition of the Diagnostic and Statistical Manual of Mental Disorders (DSM-IV) (American Psychiatric Association [APA], 1994) does not use relational diagnoses, this chapter follows the DSM-IV individual diagnostic categories for the sexual and gender identity disorders. Following a discussion of healthy sexual function, we turn to the treatment issues transforming DSM-IV categories into a relational context. The final section of this chapter addresses gender-related issues and their effect on the couple relationship.

HEALTHY SEXUAL FUNCTION: MALE AND FEMALE

In the last 30 years, much data has emerged about healthy sexual functioning in both the male and the female in both the medical and behavioral sciences. The skilled marital/sex therapist can incorporate the information that is now available into his or her clinical practice. There have been three major contribution streams to our overall understanding and knowledge of adult sexual response.

Masters and Johnson

William Masters and Virginia Johnson certainly should be credited with beginning the modern movement toward our understanding of the sexual response cycle. They divided the sexual response cycle into four phases: excitement (or arousal), plateau, orgasm, and resolution. In their seminal book, *Human Sexual Response* (1966), they detail these phases of the response cycle for both men and women. These phases are depicted in Figure 23.1.

Sexual arousal and response are natural to everyone from birth to death. They are not experiences that happen at adolescence and end with menopause, but rather occur to be enjoyed and experienced throughout the life cycle.

Helen Singer Kaplan

Another major contribution to our understanding of sexual function comes from Helen Singer Kaplan (1974, 1979, 1983). She described sexual response in a triphasic model consisting of desire, excitement, and orgasm. In discussing her differences with Masters and Johnson's model, she combined their excitement and plateau stages as describing different degrees of her vasodilatory excitement phase. She believed that the resolution stage of Masters and Johnson merely refers to the absence of sexual arousal. (See Figure 23.2.)

In Kaplan's book *Disorders of Sexual Desire* (1979), one point that is very clear is that it is natural to have sexual desire. Thus Kaplan discussed all the factors that contribute to the inhibition of sexual desire: medication, relational problems, sexual abuse, the effects of illness and disease. As is true in the DSM-IV, we will not be concerned here with desire-phase disorders due to the "effects of a substance (e.g., a drug of abuse, a medication) or a general medical condition." Among the major psychological contributors to sexual desire disorders are childhood sexual abuse, rape, negative attitudes toward sexuality, low self-esteem, religious orthodoxy, and relational problems. Later in this chapter we look at some behavioral suggestions that can be helpful to couples working through problems in this phase.

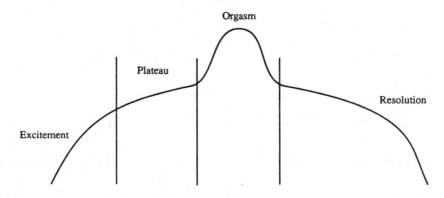

Figure 23.1   Masters and Johnson, sexual response cycle.

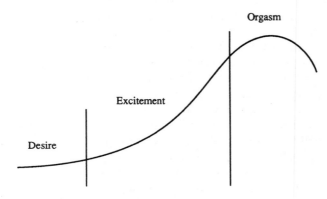

Figure 23.2   Kaplan, triphasic model.

David M. Reed

A most important contribution to our knowledge base in clinical sexology comes from the Erotic Stimulus Pathway (ESP) theory of David M. Reed (Stayton, 1989, 1992). The ESP theory enhances our understanding and treatment of the sexual dysfunctions. Reed divides the sexual response cycle into four phases, which correspond to those of Kaplan and Masters and Johnson. (See Figure 23.3.)

For many people, these phases are learned developmentally. The first phase is the Seduction phase. In this phase a person learns how to get aroused sexually and how to attract someone else sexually. Seduction gets translated into memories and rituals. For example, the adolescent may spend much time on personal appearance, choice of clothes, and mannerisms. These can enhance positive self-esteem if the adolescent likes the way he or she feels. If the adolescent feels good about the way he or she looks and feels, then attracting another person will be much easier. As the adolescent gets older, these positive feelings get translated into sexual desire and arousal. These seductive techniques get programmed into the brain and can be activated later on in life.

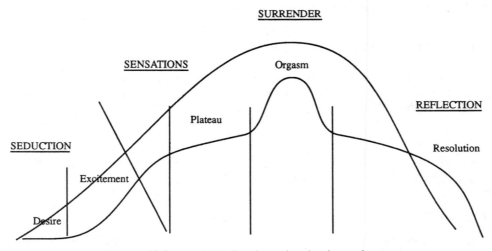

Figure 23.3   David M. Reed, erotic stimulus pathway.

The second stage of ESP is the Sensations phase. In this phase, the different senses can enhance sexual excitement and ideally prolong the plateau phase. The early experiences of *touch* (holding hands, putting arms around a loved one, etc.) become very important. The sense of *vision* (staring at a loved one, holding an image of him or her when absent, etc.) is a way of maintaining interest and arousal. *Hearing* the loved one in intimate conversation or over the telephone becomes very important. Hearing the sounds of a partner responding to sexual stimulation can be titillating. The *smell* of the loved one, either a particular scent he or she is wearing or the sexual smell, brings additional excitement. Finally, the *taste* of a food or drink or the taste of the loved one becomes very important to the memory and fantasy of the loved person. All of these senses get translated sexually into extending the excitement into a plateau phase, which makes one want to continue the pleasurable moment over a longer period of time.

All of these seduction and sensation experiences are the psychological input to the physiology of sexual response. They are the precursors to sexual climax and orgasm.

The third phase is the Surrender phase. According to Reed, orgasm is a "psycho-physiological surprise." The psychodynamic issues surrounding orgasm are power and control. The person with orgasmic dysfunction may be in a power struggle with him- or herself or with the partner or with the messages received about sex. Overcontrol or undercontrol are important issues that can affect the person's orgasmic potential and the ability to allow all of the passion to be expressed.

The final phase is Reflection. How does the person feel immediately after the experience? If the person feels it was a positive experience in that he or she liked the way he or she felt during the sexual episode, the reflection will create a positive feedback situation that will affect future desire. If it is negative, then that will diminish future desire, at least regarding that specific partner, if not for sex itself. Because the reflection phase is central to the whole experience, especially the first time a person has sex, it is important that the first sexual experience not be traumatic; otherwise it can have a negative effect on future sexual encounters. For example, if a person has been sexually abused or raped, it can take years for him or her to be able to experience sex in a positive way. The effects of early negative sexual experiences can be manifested later in lack of sexual desire, vaginismus or dyspareunia, orgasmic disorders, sexual orientation confusion, gender dysphoria, low self-esteem, and erotophobia.

ETIOLOGY OF SEXUAL DYSFUNCTION

> Human sexual response consists of a complex orchestration of emotional and hormonal influences, via the autonomic nervous system, to trigger basic reflexes. Any agent that alters metabolism, stimulates or depresses the central nervous system, or locally influences anatomy or physiology is likely to affect sexual functioning. (Satterfield & Stayton, 1980, p. 23)

Certainly stress, emotional well-being, relational issues, and general health all affect one's attitudes about sexual intimacy and functioning.

Organic Factors

The responsible clinician will want first to rule out any possibility of organic, physiological, or chemical factors in the sexual dysfunction. Different emotional and physiological illnesses, neurological disorders, use of illicit drugs and/or medications, or psychotropic drugs can have a profound impact on raising or lowering sexual desire or function. A complete physical examination for each person should be urged or even required at the beginning of treatment to rule out or correct this type of etiology.

Individual Psychodynamics

When Masters and Johnson (1970) first presented their material on sexual inadequacy, it was believed that over 90 percent of sexual dysfunction was psychologically caused. Performance anxiety was believed to be the chief culprit. Analysts thought that most sexual dysfunctions were the result of unresolved psychological issues, such as unresolved Oedipal wishes. Other causes of sexual dysfunction were thought to be borderline personality disorder, obsessive-compulsive personality disorders, anxiety disorders, and depression. While it is true that all of these can have an impact on sexual function, they are certainly not the only factors to be evaluated by the clinician.

The Relationship

It is common for marital therapists to believe from their own clinical experience and from familiarity with the sex therapy literature that most sexual problems are due to significant relationship problems. Hostility, battles for power and control, poor communications, and excessive dependency needs are all known to be incompatible with sexual intimacy and good functioning.

For sex therapy to be successful, such relationship problems need to be worked through. Otherwise the behavioral suggestions recommended later in this chapter will not work and can even increase marital discord.

Sociocultural and Religious Factors

According to the classic cross-cultural studies on sexuality by Ford and Beach (1951) and Marshall and Suggs (1971), the United States is one of the most sexually repressive cultures in history when compared with both ancient and other contemporary societies. Both Kaplan and Masters and Johnson held that religious orthodoxy has played a major part in the widespread sexual dysfunction of our day. Guilt, fear, and the denial of sex as pleasure have resulted in much sexual inhibition.

In the past few decades widely held sex-role stereotypes (males as aggressive; females as passive; etc.) have been challenged. Cultural imprinting or conditioning (males pressured to perform quickly; females conditioned not to stimulate the male directly, etc.) are considered to be important factors in creating sexual dysfunction.

TREATMENT OF SEXUAL DYSFUNCTION

Assuming that the physiological, cultural, and relational issues are understood and have been dealt with, the couple may then be ready for the treatment of the specific sexual dysfunction. It is important that both partners want to overcome the sexual problem and have the time, between therapy sessions, to implement the suggestions that follow. If a heavy travel or work schedule precludes their having time together, the clinician may want to postpone the active sex therapy program until the couple has sufficient time to devote to each other between sessions.

One of the lessons to be learned is that a couple must intentionally give time to nurturing their sexual relationship and not relegate sex to an addendum to an already exhausting day and busy schedule. Many couples experienced satisfying sexual relations during the dating, courtship, and early marital phase, because time was allocated to this aspect of their lives together.

Another issue for many people is that they were not taught to be good lovers. While we are all born sexual and with the capacity for sexual response, we are not born lovers. In our all-too-often sexually repressive and sex-negative culture, being a good lover is a matter of learning new attitudes and skills; sex therapy can provide a good education into the "how-to" of being a lover. A sexual dysfunction can be overcome by learning good information and practicing the techniques of being a considerate and passionate lover. Sex therapy, then, should be informative, fun, and erotically rewarding for the couple.

Sexual Desire Disorders

The desire disorders (Kaplan, 1979) correspond with Reed's seduction phase. In any given case, it must be determined when seduction takes place; in the present or in the past? Treatment of two types of sexual desire disorders will be discussed: hypoactive sexual desire and sexual aversion. These disorders must create enough distress and interpersonal difficulty for the couple for both members to be motivated to change.

Lack of desire may be lifelong or may have been acquired; that is, desire may have been there once, but then have diminished for some reason. A lack of desire may be generalized, that is, it is experienced in every situation; or it may be situational, that is, occurs only in certain situations. For example, one may have desire on vacation but not at home in familiar surroundings. Or one may lack lustful feelings with the long-term partner but feel aroused by others. The dysfunction may be due only to psychological factors or to a combination of psychological and disease, organic, or chemical factors.

Hypoactive Sexual Desire Disorder

In this disorder there is a lack of desire for sexual activity and often an inability to experience sexual fantasies. A psychiatrist, Sheldon Kule, in the MedPro video *Loving Better Series,* volume 5, has suggested several exercises that can be helpful in overcoming this disorder.

First, discuss or have each partner write out each one's turn-ons and turn-offs. It is best to have each one do this individually, so that they are not influenced by their partner's reaction. Have them discuss this in the therapy session. It may be that a partner may have to go back years to a time when he or she did experience sexual desire.

Second, ask each one to write out a "want ad" regarding their partner. They need to do it with the same enthusiasm and creativity they would use if they wanted to sell a home. Imagine that they want to sell their partner. What could they say that would make others want to "buy" their partner? For example:

> For sale, my partner, who is passionate, exciting, very attractive, desirable, and extremely interesting. He/she is a great lover and could turn on any partner easily. etc.

They then share their want ad with their partner in the therapy session.

Third, have the couple each take a book on sex such as Alex Comfort's *Joy of Sex* (1972) and go through the index, considering each subject. If there is no interest in discussing a particular subject, it should be crossed out. If there is some curiosity in knowing more about the subject, the couple should underline the item. If there is great wonderment and an interest in discussing or experiencing the item, it should be circled. The marked items should then be shared with each other in the therapy session.

These exercises may at first glance seem superficial, but they can produce a tremendous amount of helpful material for the clinician. It may be better to treat the desire issue with these exercises after going through all the exercises that follow in the next sections on arousal and orgasmic disorders. The goal is to build seduction through positive rituals and memories that can aid in promoting desire and arousal.

Fantasy can be encouraged through either making up fantasies on the spot with the help of the clinician or through reading books on sexual fantasies, such as Nancy Friday's *My Secret Garden* (1973).

Sexual Aversion Disorder

Sometimes there is an aversion to or avoidance of kissing, touching, and genital sexual contact. It is important to discuss what the client's experience is as each gets near his or her own or partner's genital area. Using a picture or genital model can be helpful. Clients should discuss their feelings about and experience of observing or touching the model.

As clients become more comfortable talking about and observing the picture or model, they then can transfer this experience over to their partner in the privacy of their own space. They should not have to go any further than observing and/or touching genitals without the goal of stimulation. Stimulation can be added as comfort increases. If the issue of previous trauma or abuse comes up, then these have to be dealt with in therapy.

Sexual Arousal Disorders

Female Sexual Arousal Disorder

Women who have difficulty getting aroused sexually have difficulty lubricating and feeling erotic genitally. There is little or no genital swelling. The therapist can recommend lubricants, such as K-Y Jelly or Astroglide, which can be bought over-the-counter and utilized instead. Postmenopausal women who have vaginal dryness or thinning of the vaginal walls also can benefit from the use of a lubricant, such as Replens (Winthrop Laboratories). However, usually a psychological component needs to be addressed also. The analog to this condition in males is known as erectile disorder. The treatment is similar, so both are covered in the next section.

Male Erectile Disorder

If the male has difficulty gaining or maintaining an adequate erection suitable for sexual activity, he suffers from erectile disorder. When a man presents with erectile dysfunction, it is important to first have him evaluated by a physician. Even though a physician may be able to treat the erectile capability through some medical intervention, it is still valuable to evaluate the effect of the erectile disorder on the couple's relationship.

Currently there are four possibilities of medical intervention.

1. Testosterone injections, if the testosterone levels are low. These can be very helpful in both increasing desire and erectile capability.

2. Use of yohimbine, a natural ingredient from the bark of the yohimbe tree. This can be obtained from a health food store or by prescription from a physician under the name Yocon or Aphrodyne. Several studies indicate that yohimbine helps both desire and erection ability.

3. Penile injections (self-administered) are an excellent means for achieving full erections. These have to be obtained from a physician and usually consist of a combination of Prostaglandin E1, Papaverine, and phentolamine Regitine. Research seems to indicate that it is safe with no long-range scarring or other problems. The injections are painless, but giving oneself an injection in the penile area may not have aesthetic appeal.

4. The vacuum pump is a device that is put over the penis to create a vacuum, then blood is drawn into the penis by the pump. When an erection is attained, a rubber band is put over the base of the penis to hold the blood in. The pump is also a prescription item and can be obtained through a physician.

A number of other medical interventions probably will be available within the next few years.

These options should be supplementary to sex therapy, which can help greatly with the relational issues that may occur as a result of the dysfunction. For example, it is common for the nondysfunctional partner to feel her partner is no longer attracted to her or that he may be interested in someone else. He may have lost his confidence in himself or believe that he is no longer attracted to his partner. Both may feel powerless and fearful. Even though he may have regained his erectile capability through a medical intervention, if the interpersonal issues are not treated, sexual desire may still be affected.

Some simple pleasuring exercises can increase or enhance the arousal process. Masters and Johnson called these exercises sensate focus.

Nongenital Pleasuring.   When a person starts dating, often as an adolescent, genital sex usually is not involved, at least in the beginning. Feelings are self-focused; that is, the person focuses on what he or she is experiencing as touch is given and received. How we experience ourselves is very important to both desire and arousal. These experiences then can lead to genital arousal later on.

First, it is important to have a couple sensually touch each other over their entire body, except for the genital and breast areas. This is often difficult, because when the couple is experiencing sexual difficulties, one or both often take on spectator roles and try to think about what is going on in their partner's head. When this occurs, they lose the focus on their own pleasure as participants.

Genital Pleasuring.   Once each member has been able to focus on his or her own pleasurable experiences, then they can move to exploring the breasts and genitals and determine which touches are pleasurable, threatening, or irritating. What most couples do not realize is that different areas on the breasts and genitals can be more erotic and sensitive than other spots. The couple is then instructed to caress the breasts and genitals in a very sensual way in order to produce arousal. If either of the partners experiences arousal, then they may go on to noncoital orgasm, unless the dysfunction is orgasm related.

Before trying intercourse when he is able to gain an erection consistently, the man should deliberately lose his erection by having his partner stop stimulating him. Once his erection has gone down, his partner should then restimulate him until he has another erection. The important lesson here is that if there has been no orgasm, he can lose his erection several times and regain it with further erotic stimulation. Too often a man believes that if he loses his erection once, the experience is over for him. This is not true.

After the man has accomplished losing and regaining an erection, it is beneficial if his partner can stimulate him while he is lying on his back and then mount him and just hold his penis near the labia and clitoris. When she does this and he holds the erection, she should then insert the penis into her vagina without doing any thrusting, so that he can experience being contained in her vagina without stimulation. He will then lose his erection and she should restimulate him erotically. When he gets an erection again, she should put his penis into her vagina and begin slowly thrusting. They should continue this exercise until they are having satisfying intercourse.

If these exercises do not work, using another means of achieving erection should be considered to help the man gain back his erectile confidence, such as the injection method. A major psychodynamic issue that develops in erectile dysfunction is performance anxiety. If the client cannot relax into the exercises, then the addition of the injection or the vacuum pump may help accelerate therapy and the couple's success. A number of books on the process offer other good suggestions (Heiman & LoPiccolo, 1988; McCarthy & McCarthy, 1993; Morganstern & Abrahams, 1994; Stubbs & Saulnier, 1988; Zilbergeld, 1992).

Orgasmic Disorders

Psychodynamically, the issues involved in orgasmic disorders partially center around power and control, either within the individual and/or the couple dynamics. Other problems that occur with orgasmic disorders involve the inability to relax, let go, and let the tension of the sexual response take over. The fears involved in being vulnerable, or of failure, or even the fear of success can affect one's orgasmic potential. It is important for the therapist to address these issues in the course of sex therapy.

Female Orgasmic Disorder

If the female client has never been orgasmic, then it is best to start this phase of the treatment with her alone. If it is acceptable within her moral value system, she should begin with self-exploration and stimulation. This will help her to experience her own sexual response cycle without having to perform in front of her partner. The books *For Yourself* (Barbach, 1976), *Sex for One: The Joys of Selfloving* (Dodson, 1987), or *Becoming Orgasmic: A Sexual and Personal Growth Program for Women* (Heiman & LoPiccolo, 1988) are very helpful resources to have the client read regarding masturbation and orgasm. A vibrator also can be a useful aid in helping the woman experience her orgasmic potential. Once she has become orgasmic, it is easier for her to share with her partner the type of touch that helps her to have an orgasm. As she develops her orgasm response, she can then introduce the experience into intercourse by masturbating or using a vibrator while the penis is inside her. She should not get discouraged if orgasm does not occur during the first few lovemaking encounters. It takes time, patience, and comfort.

Male Orgasmic Disorder

I have never known a male who has never had an orgasm. Generally, the clinician will see a male who cannot have an orgasm with intercourse. This is also a fairly rare occurrence. Such cases occur most often with a man who has difficulty giving himself easily in a relationship. It is most helpful to have him masturbate with his partner, so that she can experience him having an orgasm. Then during intercourse, when either is ready for their orgasm, he should withdraw and masturbate until he feels himself on the brink of orgasm and again insert his penis in the vagina. The goal is to have him experience having an orgasm and ejaculating inside the vagina. Once this occurs, it is easier for him to get to the point of orgasm through intercourse. A lot of patience and practice are needed for this dysfunction. If the man works on his ability to give of himself generally to the relationship, it will help him to be able to have orgasm vaginally.

Premature Ejaculation

Premature ejaculation has been successfully treated with both the "stop-start" method and the "squeeze" technique. My preference is the "stop-start" method (Masters & Johnson, 1970; McCarthy, 1989). After the man is aroused, his partner should stimulate (masturbate) him until he reaches the point where he feels as if he is almost ready to ejaculate. He should signal his partner, who then stops any further stimulation until the feeling of ejaculatory inevitability subsides. The partner can then start restimulating until he reaches that point when he feels he is going to ejaculate; then the partner stops again. This should be done three or four times, and then he should go ahead and have an ejaculation. This process should be repeated several times a week until the client is able to hold back ejaculating for as long as he would like. He should then try intercourse, using the female superior position, going through the same process. When his penis is in her vagina, she should begin moving up and down on the penis, until he feels he is going to ejaculate. Then she should stop until he loses that feeling, and then she should start moving up and down again. This should be repeated several times, and then he should go ahead and have an orgasm. With patience and practice, this method will work.

It is also possible to treat premature ejaculation with a small dose of fluoxetine (Prozac) (Morganstern & Abrahams, 1994). Combining the use of this drug with the exercises can bring about more rapid results.

Sexual Pain Disorder

When a client suffers from dyspareunia (painful intercourse) or vaginismus (inability to have a penis inserted into the vagina because of spasms), it is best for the relational therapist to refer the client to a specialist, such as a gynecologist, who is trained to help with these dysfunctions, or to a certified sex therapist. To find a certified sex therapist, contact the American Association of Sex Educators, Counselors and Therapists (319-895-8407) or the American Board of Sexology (202-462-2122).

GENDER IDENTITY DISORDERS

An increasingly important area in sex and marital therapy is working with clients where there is a gender identity disorder.

Diagnosis: The Gender Spectrum

Most people never question their gender identity as a male or a female. Each person, however, is on a gender spectrum. According to Money (1980; Money & Tucker, 1975), by the age of two or two and a half, everyone goes through a process of coding masculine and feminine attitudes, feelings, and behavior. Those that are coded as congruent with one's own gender are coded positive (+). Those that are coded negative (−) are appropriate for the other gender. Figure 23.4 diagrams the process of coding.

Using the male as an example (although it could be just as well a female by inserting Joanne on traditional end of continuum and Joe at the transsexual end of the continuum), we can see that gender lies along a continuum from a traditionally coded male to where the biological male has coded mostly feminine attitudes, feelings, and behaviors, which is known as transsexualism. In the center of the continuum is the man who codes both masculine and feminine attitudes, feelings, and behaviors as positive. This person is a transvestite, which means that he needs to code eroticism and/or relaxation as positive, so that he must cross-dress or fantasize being cross-dressed in order to get eroticized or relaxed.

If a male codes between the traditional and the transvestite, he is considered androgynous, which means that be blends masculine and feminine but does not need to dress in order to express his feminine side. His masculinity is also not threatened by the blending.

If the male codes between the transvestite and transsexual end of the continuum, then he needs to see a gender therapist. The Harry Benjamin International Gender Dysphoria Association can provide the name of the nearest gender therapist (707-938-2871). While the transgendered person often wants to go for surgical reassignment, usually it is not appropriate, because he still has enough masculine coding that he probably would not adjust well to being a female in this society.

Identification (+)
Complementation (-)

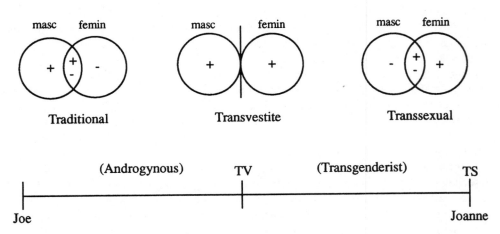

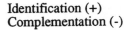

Source: From W. E. Stayton, *Religious belief systems and sexual health*, in R. M. Green (Ed.), *Religion and sexual health: Ethical, theological, and clinical perspectives* (p. 208). The Netherlands: Kluwer Academic Publishers. Copyright © 1992 by Kluwer. Reprinted with permission.

Figure 23.4   Stayton, gender spectrum.

Treatment Issues

Individual

It is important that the gender-dysphoric client see a therapist who can help him or her identify where he or she is on the gender spectrum and work through the consequences of any choices to be made on family members, vocation and career, and community.

Relational

If the client is a transvestite, it is important that his or her partner know about it, because it is such an important part of who he or she is. The vast majority of transvestites are heterosexual, but usually a partner's first concern is that he or she is gay. When this concern is alleviated, the partner may question her or his own orientation. It is important to reassure the partner that her or his partner is not gay, nor is her or his gender or orientation in question.

Ideally, once the partner of a transvestite understands the dynamics of transvestism, she or he will be able to accept the partner's erotic response to cross-dressing and let it be a pleasurable experience for both of them. It is best if it is just considered as a "different" turn-on rather than some deep-seated psychological problem. All people have different things that turn them on erotically. Most are harmless and nonthreatening, such as particular clothing, a romantic video, flowers, the ocean or a mountain stream, silk sheets. Cross-dressing is similar, although "different" from the usual or expected, but it need not to be threatening or a turn-off.

If the partner cannot accept this "difference," then the couple must negotiate among the options. First of all, transvestism cannot be cured, but it can be controlled. Is it all right for the partner to cross-dress in private, so that no one else is involved? Is it acceptable to cross-dress on a special occasion, such as Halloween? Can the partner agree to allow cross-dressing magazines in the home? A large selection of magazines are available, including *Tapestry Journal* (617-899-2212) and *International Tran Script* (610-640-9449).

If cross-dressing is not acceptable under any circumstances, then the transvestite has to make a decision regarding the marriage. The cross-dressing may be a compulsive behavior that the person feels no power to control. If the cross-dressing occurs at times of stress and tension, then the couple will need to keep those times to a minimum.

Another issue that can create anxiety is how far the cross-dressing will go. Will the client be satisfied with cross-dressing at home? Will he or she want to go out in public? Will he or she want to cross-dress more often than what seems reasonable? Will it lead him or her to want to be a transsexual? These are all important and serious questions.

A final concern is centered around the children. Should the children know, or is it best to keep the cross-dressing from them? My experience has been that children can handle "differences" very well, especially if the parents are comfortable. I find it best to talk with the children about a parent's transvestism either before puberty or in late adolescence or adulthood. Puberty is such a difficult transition time itself that the young adolescent has enough to work through with his or her own issues.

For the majority of transvestites, once the cross-dressing is "out of the closet," they want to cross-dress a lot. Just as a person who finds a new food desires it often, once he has had enough, he will eat the food on a more reasonable basis. The transvestite, in the beginning, may want to cross-dress very often, but once the newness of being "out of the closet" is over, the cross-dressing occurs on a more reasonable proportion of time.

There are organizations that provide support systems for partners of transvestites. The Renaissance Education Association (610-975-9119) or PARTNERS: A Newsletter for Couples (210-438-7604) can provide resources.

Regarding transgenderist and transsexual partners, relationships become increasingly complicated. Often the male in such a relationship is fantasizing being a female making love to a female. Technically, this is called "male lesbianism." The partner has to decide whether she can enter into a lesbian relationship if her partner does indeed desire to go for genital reassignment surgery. The transsexual partner may desire to be in a heterosexual relationship with a man as a woman. I have couples who have divorced, but maintained a good working relationship because of their children, and I have worked with couples who decided to stay together in a lesbian relationship.

The illustration has been male. While not seen as often, we could have a partnered female-to-male transsexual. In this case, she would have been having sex with her male partner as a male (or gay relationship in her head). If in a lesbian relationship, she may have been heterosexual in her fantasy of the sexual part of the relationship. Although complicated, these issues need to be resolved in relational therapy.

CONCLUSION

This chapter attempted to explain the issues involved in sexual dysfunctions within the context of one's significant relationships. While the majority of time, the dysfunction is a problem in the sexual response cycle of the couple, it also can be a problem that goes beyond sexual function to issues around gender dysphoria of one of the partners. Important issues need to be addressed in marital therapy within the framework that goes beyond DSM-IV and considers the relational system. Therapy suggestions as well as resources have been offered.

REFERENCES

American Psychiatric Association. (1994). *Diagnostic and statistical manual of mental disorders* (4th ed.). Washington, DC: Author.

Barbach, L. (1976). *For yourself: The fulfillment of female sexuality.* Garden City, NY: Doubleday.

Comfort, A. (1972). *The joy of sex.* New York: Crown.

Dodson, B. (1987). *Sex for one: The joys of selfloving.* New York: Harmony Books.

Ford, C. S., & Beach, F. A. (1951). *Patterns of sexual behavior.* New York: Harper Colophon.

Friday, N. (1973). *My secret garden.* New York: Pocket Books.

Heiman, J., & LoPiccolo, J. (1988). *Becoming orgasmic: A sexual and personal growth program for women.* Englewood Cliffs, NJ: Prentice-Hall.

Kaplan, H. (1974). *The new sex therapy.* New York: Brunner/Mazel.

Kaplan, H. (1979). *Disorders of sexual desire: And other new concepts and techniques in sex therapy.* New York: Brunner/Mazel.

Kaplan, H. (1983). *The evaluation of sexual disorders: Psychological and medical aspects.* New York: Brunner/Mazel.

Marshall, D. S., & Suggs, R. C. (1971). *Human sexual behavior.* New York: Basic Books.

Masters, W., & Johnson, V. (1966). *Human sexual response.* Boston: Little, Brown.

Masters, W., & Johnson, V. (1970). *Human sexual inadequacy.* Boston: Little, Brown.

McCarthy, B. (1989). Cognitive-behavioral strategies and techniques in the treatment of early ejaculation. In S. R. Leiblum & R. C. Rosen, (Eds.), *Principles and practice of sex therapy: Update for the 1990s* (pp. 141–167). New York: Guilford.

McCarthy, B., & McCarthy, E. (1993). *Sexual awareness: Enhancing sexual pleasure.* New York: Carroll & Graf.

Money, J., & Tucker, P. (1975). *Sexual signatures: On being a man or a woman.* Boston: Little, Brown.

Money, J. (1980). *Love and love sickness: The science of sex, gender difference, and pair-bonding.* Baltimore: Johns Hopkins University.

Morganstern, S., & Abrahams, A. (1994). *Overcoming impotence: A doctor's proven guide to regaining sexual vitality.* Englewood Cliffs, NJ: Prentice-Hall.

Satterfield, S., & Stayton, W. (1980). Understanding sexual function and dysfunction. In W. R. Stayton (Ed.), *Topics in Clinical Nursing, 1*(4), 21–32.

Stayton, W. R. (1989). A theology of sexual pleasure. In W. R. Millar (Ed.), *American Baptist Quarterly, 8(2),* 94–108.

Stayton, W. R. (1992). Religious belief systems and sexual health. In R. M. Green (Ed.), *Religion and sexual health: Ethical, theological and clinical perspectives* (pp. 203–218). The Netherlands: Kluwer Academic Publishers.

Stubbs, K. R., & Saulnier, L. A. (1988). *Romantic interludes: A sensuous lovers guide.* Larkspur, CA: Secret Garden.

Zilbergeld, B. (1992). *The new male sexuality.* New York: Bantam.

CHAPTER 24

Relationship Conflict—Verbal and Physical: Conceptualizing an Inventory for Assessing Process and Content

ARTHUR M. BODIN, PhD, FAClinP

WHY DEVELOP A RELATIONSHIP CONFLICT INVENTORY?

The purposes for developing a Relationship Conflict Inventory (RCI) include to:

1. Help therapists and patients target the areas of greatest conflict.
2. Allow accumulation of normative data on both Verbal and Physical Conflict to help patients and their therapists discern what part of the conflict spectrum a couple occupies and the degree to which the partners concur in viewing their relationship conflict.
3. Have a hierarchical scale for assessing the severity of both Verbal and Physical Conflict—potentially useful in forensic as well as clinical and research applications.
4. Have a scale for assessing the *processes* of conflict as well as the *content* of conflict.
5. Have a scale for assessing both the frequency and distress level of various kinds of conflict.
6. Make possible the inclusion of relationship conflict as a diagnostic category in DSM or other classification systems.
7. Provide a concise but broad and sensitive inventory for measuring changes in relationship conflict.

SCOPE OF THE PROBLEM

It will come as no surprise to anyone experienced in working with families that research has shown the major factor in divorce is problematic communication. This was recently confirmed by Parker and Drummond-Reeves (1993), who state that "marital communication was found to be the primary problem area contributing to relationship deterioration and dissolution in Bradford's study (Bradford, 1978) and in the current study. In the original study, 75% of the sample identified communication as the primary problem as compared to 95% in the current study."

With or without divorce, violence is an extremely serious and widespread problem. This is why the RCI includes items addressing Physical Conflict. Here are some recent prevalence figures on family violence:

> Some of the commonly reported figures are those of Gelles and Straus (1989) which indicate that 1 out of every 6 wives reports that she has been hit by her husband at some point in her marriage. In 6 cases out of 1,000 the attack takes the form of a severe beating, and in 2 cases out of 1,000 the attack involves the use of guns or knives.
>
> Estimates were made that 8.7 million couples experienced at least one assault during 1985 (Straus & Gelles, 1988). The same researchers estimate that in 3.4 million households, the violence had a relatively high risk of causing injury. However, it is said that less than 1 out of every 250 spouse assaults is reported (Steinmetz, 1977), therefore, the statistics are likely to be considerably higher than those listed above. (Harway & Hansen, 1994, p. 2)

STIMULUS FOR THIS WORK

Task Force on Family Diagnosis

When the Division of Family Psychology of the American Psychological Association formed its Task Force on Family Diagnosis led by Florence Kaslow in 1987, I was pleased to be one of its original members. At an early meeting we considered seeking inclusion of some relationship diagnoses in the fourth edition of the *Diagnostic and Statistical Manual of Mental Disorders* (DSM-IV) (American Psychiatric Association, 1994), by adapting concepts already developed by such leading thinkers in the family field as Robert Beavers and David Olson. Ted Millon sat in on one of our meetings as a consultant. His experience in contributing significantly to the development of the Axis II categories of the DSM-III and III-R gave him a lot of credibility. He made one particularly memorable point: "If you are to have a chance of getting any relational diagnoses accepted into the DSM-IV, then whatever you submit must use the format employed in DSM criterion sets." Specifically, our criterion sets must be lists of observable signs or subjective symptoms, either present or absent. In other words, each criterion must be in the form of a binary choice, not a continuum, and not something even farther from the DSM context, such as a circumplex with an optimal midrange zone between two undesirable zones conceived as opposite qualities at their respective ends of the same continuum.

Millon's remarks caused us to go back to the drawing board and brainstorm to create a list of relationship dimensions we thought were important and potentially definable in terms of sets of binary criteria. I proposed that relationship conflict be one of the concepts from which we would attempt to develop new diagnoses, and I volunteered to attempt to describe this diagnostic category by developing a set of criteria, each of which could be determined to be either present or absent.

RELATIONSHIP CONFLICT: AN OVERVIEW

It Takes Two to Tangle!

The determination of whether a statement about a relationship is true or false can be fraught with complications not encountered in diagnosing an individual by deciding whether specific signs or symptoms are present or absent. Specifically, the situation in a relationship diagnosis (the focus here will be on couples so as to have a consistent frame of reference) presents three possibilities: (1) the partners agree there is a problem in the relationship, (2) the partners agree there is no such problem, and (3) one partner feels there is such a problem but the other does not concur. It is essential to acknowledge that if *either* partner feels there is a problem in the relationship, then there *is* one, and the disagreement of the other partner simply adds a "metaproblem." I had already reflected upon this point in the course of almost two and a half decades of working with families, and I had been fascinated repeatedly by the puzzle of how to conceptualize a relationship in which one partner says there is a significant problem and the other says (in the case of the man), "Everything's fine—she's just a chronic malcontent!" I had found it useful to respond to such a man along the following lines: "Let me see whether I understand you correctly: You feel everything is fine. Jane is distressed by what *she* describes as a problem. Are you saying that her distress is all right with you—it isn't a problem for you to have an unhappy wife?" Usually such men begin to backpedal, saying something like "I guess not exactly; I hadn't thought about it that way." The woman in this situation is likely to say that her partner can't stand conflict, won't talk about the relationship except to blame her, won't talk about his feelings, and tries to deny that there is any problem—engaging in the wishful thinking that ignorance is bliss. But his remaining ignorant *after* she has described to him what she feels is a problem adds another level of distress. Once she has told him what is bothering her, she regards his continuing to deny that there is a problem as imperviousness, and it makes her all the more miserable. My experiences with and reflection about this problem have led me to conclude that it is useful to adopt the view that if one person says there is a problem, then there *is* a problem. It may not be precisely and completely described by the one who says a problem exists, since there is the commonly overlooked additional layer of a "metaproblem" in the further problem about whether there is a problem at all. It is useful to take the view that now we have two problems. Whether you count these as two problems or as different levels of the same problem makes no difference in answering the question "Is there a problem?" Either way, there is *at least one* problem.

Blame: The Sound of One Hand Clapping

Our temptation to blame our partner for conflict in the relationship may stem in part from failure to recognize the tautology inherent in the conviction that we are right and the partner is wrong. Of course we believe in our *own* view and are tempted to think it right—unless we have acquired the following views. It is vital to distinguish between two distinct domains: the domain of fact and the domain of opinion or taste. It is possible in matters of fact, such as the height of a table, to be right or wrong, and usually to be proven so. It is not possible in matters of opinion or taste, however, to be right or wrong. Failure to draw this distinction often results in one person saying to another about a matter of opinion or taste, "You're wrong!" The recipient of such a communication is likely to feel disconfirmed, rejected, invalidated, hurt, depressed, and/or angry. Later, in discussing "Content Conflict," we shall return to this distinction between fact and opinion and discuss conflicts over *which* categorization is appropriate.

Indeterminacy: An Unanswerable Question about Which Hand Clapped Louder

When a relationship is extremely symmetrical in that its participants are inflexibly engaged in a pattern of exchanging equivalent behaviors, the resulting pathology is one of hypercompetitiveness (Watzlawick, Beavan, & Jackson, 1967). This can result not only in the "I can do anything better than you can" pattern, but also in a tendency to want to make sure that the partner gets at least as much blame as *you* do for a conflict. While there are extreme cases in which it is clear that one partner is more responsible for the conflict or some manifestation of it than the other—such as in cases of physical partner abuse—in many instances the situation is and must be dealt with as systemic and characterized by *shared* responsibility. Recognition of this fact causes us to laugh at a cartoon of a husband and his wife, who is responding to the opening question by the marriage counselor: "Of course I know what trouble is—*him!*" In instances in which one or both spouses show great determination to assign all blame to the other, I have found it useful to place between them a little coffee table with the game called Labyrinth on it. The game consists of a rectangular wooden box with a knob on each of two adjacent sides controlling the movement of a panel suspended within the rectangular opening of the box. This panel has a series of numbered holes at each point in a maze, past which the player (ordinarily one person) attempts to cause a steel ball to roll without falling through any of the holes. My modification of this game is to ask each partner to control just *one* knob and thus only one of the two directions of tilt. Of course the ball falls through either the first or second hole, at which point I ask the couple, "Who caused the ball to fall?" Perhaps they catch the mischievous twinkle in my eye, for most partners grasp immediately the impossibility of determining any sensible answer to that question other than "We both did." Or "Neither of us did it alone." Or "Either of us might have prevented it!"

The foregoing demonstration of the indeterminacy of the relative contributions of the partners when things go amiss in a mutually controlled sequence of events is not in itself sufficient. I also try to get the partners to become profoundly disinterested in the question of blame and to focus their competitiveness, instead, on the question "*Who has the power to make things better?*"

Process and Content: Two Sides of the Conflict Coin

Virginia Satir's Differentiation between Process and Content

Some distinctions between process and content were given by Satir in response to my interviewing her on this topic in about 1965. Perhaps the simplest distinction is that *content* is *what* is being discussed while *process* is *how* it is being discussed. Some couples have conflict about process, some have conflict about content, and some have conflict about both—either sequentially or simultaneously. Some even become confused about what they are arguing about, so that one partner may be trying to resolve something about content, while the other is trying to resolve something about process. Thus, the two are talking about different facets of their conflict, and perhaps only one of them or maybe neither grasps this disparity.

Derailing Content by Directing Attention to Process

The book *Translations from the English* (Smith, 1958) contains a cartoon showing a couple arguing. The caption indicates what the speaker is saying; the subcaption (in parentheses) indicates what the speaker is really thinking. The caption reads, "It isn't *what* you said, Dear; it's *how* you said it!"; the subcaption reads, "It isn't *how* you said it; it's *what* you said!" This cartoon stimulated me to wonder how many times in real life one partner interrupts the *content* of a discussion to complain about the *process*—thus changing the subject from *what* was being said to *how* it was being said. This occurs frequently among couples, and the second topic may generate so much heat that they never get back to the original topic. This sequence may constitute an unconscious or even a conscious stratagem for avoiding a topic one does not wish to discuss. What at one level appears to be a failure to get back to the original topic may, at a second level, constitutes success in avoiding that topic, thus rewarding the process-sensitive topic changer. At a deeper level, however, the success in avoiding the topic constitutes a source of discontent for the partner who brought up the original topic, only to have his or her stream of thought aborted by a diversion. It is hardly any solace to the original speaker that the diversion may have been unwitting; in fact, that may make it all the more difficult to deal with, since the diversionary action may itself be earnestly denied.

Process Conflict: Forms of Conflict

To develop the RCI, I first reviewed the many forms of dysfunctional communication I had read about in the collected early papers of the Mental Research Institute (MRI) in Palo Alto, California (Jackson, 1968a, 1968b), in *Conjoint Family Therapy* (Satir, 1964), in *Pragmatics of Human Communication: A Study of Interactional Patterns, Pathologies and Paradoxes* (Watzlawick et al., 1967), and in *The Self and Others: Further Studies in Sanity and Madness* (Laing, 1961). I focused particularly on those types of dysfunctional communication that impressed me when I read about them, observed them, heard them described clinically, or experienced them in my family of origin or adult family. I listed about 20 such examples and then put them in the form of descriptive statements that the respondent could either check or not check. These statements were intentionally cast in a form which did not assign blame, but allowed the partners to indicate independently whether they felt this particular form of conflict had occurred *in their relationship*. By keeping the items indeterminate regarding assignment of blame or relative personal contribution, it was thought more candid responses would be elicited precisely because the items did not call for specifying individual and arguably "blameworthy" behavior; rather, they asked only about the nature of the interaction.

Since the criterion sets being developed needed to be based on DSM-III-R (American Psychiatric Association, 1987) type binary items, it seemed possible for me to get out of the interviewer role by developing a self-report inventory. As I tried out this first draft with couples and individuals starting therapy with me, they provided many useful suggestions, not only about wording the questions more clearly but also about new items worth including. For example, one woman said, "You don't have in here how I torture my husband! I tell him, 'If you ever do such and such again, something *TERRIBLE* will happen!'" Her suggestion was shaped into a vague all-purpose threat item.

Verbal Conflict

The 23 Verbal Conflict items developed seemed to be categorizable into six areas for the purpose of devising the type of criteria used in the DSM format. Each of these six areas was given a brief title, though these headings were removed in later versions. A rough hierarchical progression of Verbal Conflict categories is evident, proceeding from virtually ubiquitous and less serious, to more unusual and more serious items. These categories are:

A. Communication Difficulties (6 items)
B. Arguments (6 items)
C. Painful/Deteriorating Relationship (6 items)
D. Distancing (2 items)

E. Intimidation (2 items)

F. Separation (1 item)

Physical Conflict

The first 23 items covered a spectrum of levels of Verbal Conflict, clustered in a roughly ascending hierarchy of seriousness. Seriousness of Physical Conflict fell into the same number of levels as did those in the section on Verbal Conflict. These six levels, each with one item, have been designated:

A. Physical Coercion/Intimidation

B. Indirect Aggression

C. Physical Abuse (level I)

D. Physical Abuse (level II)

E. Physical Abuse (level III)

F. Use of Weapons (beyond the levels) (level IV)

In both the Verbal Conflict and Physical Conflict sections of the RCI, the items were kept in roughly ascending order of hierarchical levels. The reason they were not scrambled was to avoid the shock and defensiveness likely to result from encountering early in either section of the RCI high-level items about Verbal or Physical Conflict.

Initially each Physical Conflict level contained only one item, but the Research Committee at the MRI suggested that *each level also might contain a second and more critical version,* defined in the same way as its less critical version but with more than one occurrence. In recognition of the ascending significance of increasing levels of Physical Conflict, two additional variations in defining them were included. The first consisted of increasing the retrospective time frame covered by the items from 6 months to 24 months as the items ascended the scale of severity of violence. The second consisted of introducing a continuum of decreasingly stringent criteria for defining the existence of a pattern as the items increased in their severity of violent conflict. Thus, with these two innovations combined, the existence of a pattern at the low end of the scale would be defined as more than three occurrences over the past 6 months; a pattern at the high end of the scale would be defined as two or more occurrences over the past 24 months.

In defining the forms of conflict as *verbal* and *physical,* description of the latter as *violent* conflict was avoided. During the Vietnam War, a prominent minister was quoted as having appeared to be justifying mob violence by implying that it is equivalent and hence a natural response to "institutional" violence. He seemed to have intentionally blurred the distinction between Verbal Conflict and Physical Conflict, thus appearing to justify the latter as an understandable and perhaps inevitable result of the former. I was surprised that he would contribute to the increasing incivility of society by blurring rather than maintaining what I believe is a sacrosanct distinction. The metaphoric use of the word "violence" could contribute to the rationalizations of those who engage in Physical Conflict, whether in the form of riots or spouse abuse. Instead, it is important to maintain one of the gains of civilization, namely that we expect people to conduct their conflicts with words rather than with blows or weapons. To blur this distinction is evil, since it contributes to the escalation of primitive forms of conflict against which societies have struggled as they have evolved.

Gender Differences in Threshold Labeling of Physical Conflict?

By delineating in a hierarchy of increasingly severe levels of Physical Conflict it may be possible to discern gender differences in labeling the thresholds for each level. Based on my clinical experience of over 30 years with countless couples, it appears that more often than not the woman will describe interaction in more physically violent terms than does the man. A particularly vivid demonstration of this occurred when one woman telephoned me late at night to say that her husband had hit her. During their session the next morning, the wife said he "hit" her, but the husband said he "shoved" her. I asked the husband to demonstrate exactly what he had done but in extreme slow motion and without actually making any bodily contact. He demonstrated how he had placed his hand against her shoulder and pushed her backward onto the bed. At the conclusion of his demonstration she said, "See, he hit me!" He said, "See, I shoved her!" I understood at that moment more vividly than I ever had in the past how men and women may label the same actions with different words. I reflected about this aloud, speculating that the nearly universal experience of males during elementary school and junior high school is to be part of or at least witness to some fistfights on the playground, thus acquiring the mental set to define "hitting" as entailing a closed fist connecting with another person's body with a distinctive sound of impact. The experiences of females during the same time period appear not to restrict their definition in the same way; rather, they may categorize even those actions resulting in *silent* impact as falling within the definition of hitting. In discussing this definitional difference with a couple, it is important not to make light of the experience of either one. However this husband chose to label his action, it was interpreted by his partner as menacing and frightening.

Menacing: Symbolic Violence or Symbolic Verbal Conflict

Upon further reflection on the items used to describe the various levels of Physical Conflict, I became uneasy about the possibility that I too might have slipped into the same blurring of the boundary between Verbal and Physical Conflict as the minister had. What I actually had done was place psychological coercion or intimidation in the superordinate category called "Verbal Conflict" and physical coercion or intimidation in the superordinate category called "Physical Conflict." What I meant by physical coercion or intimidation was any verbal or physical action referring to, implying, seeming to menace with, or directly threatening physical abuse. Such words or actions induce fear of physical pain or harm. Such fear is gender-linked, according to a recent study showing that "Only wives were fearful during violent and nonviolent arguments" (Jacobson et al., 1994, p. 982).

The items that appeared to fall between Verbal and Physical Conflict seemed easier to conceptualize after I discussed with Murray Straus the details of scoring the Conflict Tactics Scale (Straus, 1979). He pointed out that although he had viewed these "in-between" kinds of items as falling outside the scope of those items he scored as physically violent, he had created a special category for them called "symbolic violence." I then realized that what I had done was not the same as blurring the boundary between Verbal and Physical Conflict. Like Straus, I had discerned a gray area that was *verbal* or *gestural* in its mode of delivery but that clearly referred to or threatened *Physical* (violent) Conflict. I had placed these items under the *Physical Conflict* category because they seemed designed to produce the same effect (fear) as Physical Conflict without actually resorting to it—unless the symbolic violence failed to produce the desired effect.

Content Conflict: Topics of Conflict

All of the questions initially developed were geared to tap both Verbal and Physical Conflict; they were about the *process* of conflict. Next some questions about the *content* of conflict were promulgated. Although it took three years to develop the 35 items of the *process* section (23 on Verbal Conflict, 12 on Physical Conflict), it took only three days to develop the 82 items of a *content* section for the next version of the instrument, titled the "Relationship Conflict Inventory." These items are arranged into nine *content* clusters:

1. Activities
2. Change
3. Characteristics
4. Communication
5. Habits
6. Preferences
7. Relationships
8. Responsibilities
9. Values

Conflict over Facts vs. Opinions

Sometimes the topic over which a couple will argue is *whether* a particular assertion is a fact or an opinion. As noted in *The Invented Reality* (Watzlawick, 1984), we construct our individual realities by our interpretations of events. In this process of personally constructing our realities, a fact can get transformed into an opinion, or the passage of time can transform a fact into an opinion because people may recall events differently, even if they interpreted them the same way initially. Thus, a couple might disagree about what a particular person said at a party the previous night, and the topic of their disagreement is *now* in the realm of opinion; if they had made a tape recording of the conversation, then the statement could be reviewed and its content would be in the realm of fact. With or without a tape recording, the exact content of the statement *was* in the realm of fact at that time but was transformed (by the unreliability of memory) into the realm of opinion by the time the couple decided to discuss the matter. It is easy for a couple to overlook the subtlety of such a transformation and become incensed with each other's insistence that what seems like a fact could have drifted into the domain of opinion.

RELATIONSHIP CONFLICT: A SELECTIVE REVIEW OF THE LITERATURE

Level of Analysis

Levels of analysis were described in "Conjoint Family Assessment: An Evolving Field" (Bodin, 1968). Individual, conjoint, and combined approaches (Bauman & Roman, 1966; Bodin, 1966; Ferreira, 1963; Ferreira & Winter, 1965; Levy & Epstein, 1964; Strodtbeck, 1951) were distinguished.

Individual Data

Data can be obtained from individuals who are in a relationship, regardless of whether their partners also provide data. These data can be analyzed according to gender, for example, to obtain separate norms for males and for females.

Paired Data

Data can be obtained from couples and can be analyzed to ascertain the degree of agreement between the male and the female and whether one gender reports more conflict than the other gender—for reasons such as denial, sensitivity, or differences in what each learned to label as conflict (threshold differences).

Individual data can be gathered about individual actions or about interaction. Actual interactional data is more difficult to obtain. The RCI elicits individual data *about* interaction. Intracouple comparisons can be made if the partners provide parallel data.

Process Conflict: Forms of Conflict

Verbal Conflict

The concepts of Verbal Conflict are well described in *An Anthology of Human Communication: Text and Tape* (Watzlawick, 1964), *Conjoint Family Therapy: A Guide to Theory and Technique* (Satir, 1964), and *Pragmatics of Human Communication: A Study of Interactional Patterns, Pathologies and Paradoxes* (Watzlawick et al., 1967). Instruments to measure the processes of Verbal Conflict include the Conflict Tactics Scales (CTS) (Straus, 1979), the Problem Solving Communication Scale of the Marital Satisfaction Inventory (MSI) (Snyder, 1979), the Styles of Conflict Inventory (Metz, 1993), the Kansas Marital Conflict Scale (KMCS) (Eggeman, Moxley, & Schumm, 1985), the Interpersonal Conflict Scale (ICS) (Hoskins, 1981, 1983), the Partner Abuse Scale: Non-Physical (PASNP) (Hudson, 1990a), the Non-Physical Abuse of Partner Scale (NPAPS) (Garner & Hudson, 1990a), the Abusive Behavior Inventory Partner Form (Shepherd & Campbell, 1992), and the ten-item Communication Scale from *PREPARE/ENRICH* (Olson, Fournier, & Druckman, 1986). An example of a true interactional measure is the Marital Interaction Coding System III (Weiss & Summers, 1983). Some attention has been given to conflict not restricted to people in an ongoing relationship. This broader focus characterizes the Test of Negative Social Exchange (TENSE) (Ruehlman & Karoly, 1991) and the Aggression Questionnaire (Buss & Perry, 1992) with four aggression factors yielded by factor analysis, physical aggression, verbal aggression, anger, and hostility.

Except for the observational rating scales of actual interaction, the Aggression Questionnaire, and at least one version of the Conflict Tactics Scales (the one I used for validation), the instruments just listed are specific regarding who did what to whom. Thus, a person taking one of these instruments may feel put on the spot, as these instruments can arouse defensiveness and, hence, underreporting because of their inherent though perhaps incidental elicitation of blame—including self-blame. While specific responsibility for different components of the interactions often must be addressed in therapy, the individuals in the system may be more forthcoming if they are allowed to "ease into" the topic of conflict by being asked only what happened in the relationship rather than who did what to whom. The specifics can, of course, be vital, but can be elucidated in later discussions.

Physical Conflict

Physical Conflict has been much discussed in the literature (Connors & Harway, 1995; Frieze & Browne, 1989; Gelles & Straus, 1989; Harway & Hansen, 1994; Straus, 1983; Straus, Gelles, & Steinmetz, 1980). Instruments to measure Physical Conflict include the Conflict Tactics Scales (Straus, 1979), the Partner Abuse Scale: Physical (PASPH) (Hudson, 1990b), the Physical Abuse of Partner Scale (PAPS) (Garner & Hudson, 1990b), the Abusive Behavior Partner Form (Shepherd & Campbell, 1992), and the Aggression Questionnaire (Buss & Perry, 1992). These instruments, except for the Aggression Questionnaire and at least one version of the Conflict Tactics Scales, assign blame by focusing on who did what to whom.

FROM CRITERION SET TO INVENTORY: AN EVOLUTIONARY PROCESS

Marital Conflict Inventory

To obtain the kind of dichotomous data being sought, a set of items that could be checked off was developed. This format, however, provides no way of detecting skipped items.

Relationship Disorder with Verbal and/or Violent Conflict

Shift to Focus on Relationships Rather Than Marriages: Broadened Applicability

Shifting the focus and title from marriages to relationships made it possible to include unmarried heterosexual couples (such as those living together, engaged couples, and divorced couples); same sex couples; parent-child relationships (with some modifications); sibling relationships; and lateral, vertical, and diagonal work relationships. The modifications required for the last three entail, for example, removal of items about sex. The only modified version I have attempted so far is a sibling form, which is a truncated version of the subsequent Relationship Conflict Inventory with dual Likert scales and was designed for use by a school counselor who was doing research on programs to reduce sibling conflict. Such forms might be useful in parent education and in conflict reduction programs in schools or the workplace. With considerable additional work, a parent-child form could be developed to define more operationally the criteria for reporting child abuse. By the same token, the couple relationship version of the form could prove useful in spouse abuse prevention programs, the treatment of battered spouses, and the treatment of batterers.

Shift to True/False Format

The checklist format lacks the fail-safe provision of presenting at least one alternative that must be checked. Asking the respondent to "check those items that apply" sounds simple but elicits no clue as to whether an unchecked item was left blank because it did not apply or because the respondent was rushing and did not see it. A third possibility also exists; specifically, that the respondent saw the item but decided not to respond. All three of these possibilities (or at *least* the first two) were taken care of by shifting to the True/False format. Along with this shift came the clustering of items into categories arranged somewhat hierarchically; the use of longer retrospective time frames for items referring to more serious types of conflict; and the use of a *sui generis* category indicating a uniquely higher level of seriousness for actual use of a weapon. The True/False format lent itself to the development of DSM-like criterion sets for both Verbal and Physical Conflict. Finally, departing from the DSM tradition, a numerical scoring system for Verbal and Physical Conflict was created to which weights were assigned on an a priori basis (see Figure 24.1). The scoring by raw item counts of conflict [level] categories based on criterion sets (top of figure), and by weighted item counts (bottom of figure) can be compared by empirically determining which scoring version correlates best with related measures such as the Conflict Tactics Scales (Straus, 1979).

Relationship Conflict Inventory

Once it became clear that the DSM-IV would contain only one facet of the work of the Coalition on Family Diagnosis, namely the Global Assessment of Relational Functioning (GARF) Scale (American Psychiatric Association, 1994, Appendix B, pp. 758–759) spearheaded by Lyman Wynne—and only as a supplementary scale—there was no further reason to stick with a binary or True/False format. I was now free to use a more sensitive Likert scale format. Despite the fact that some people favor a 6-point Likert scale so as to force the respondent out of a neutral position, this did not seem to do justice to people's psychological experience—which may be excruciatingly ambivalent *or* neutral—so I opted for a 7-point Likert scale format.

Once having decided to sensitize the RCI through Likertization, the problem of using an a priori weighting was solved by turning the weightings over to the respondents. To further sensitize the instrument, two dimensions were given to respond to frequency of occurrence and distress level (see Figure 24.2, pp. 384–385).

A 7-point *frequency* scale was developed that proved identical to the one used by Straus in the Conflict Tactics Scale (1979). I was pleased at this and decided it would be a distinct advantage to use the same frequency scale used in the instrument most vital for validating the RCI. There is a challenge in this 7-point scoring since some of the scale points represent a range of frequencies; thus, the score can be either the single digit of the Likert scale or the midpoint of the frequency range. Which one will correlate best with related measures is a question that can be answered empirically.

REDEFINING, DECONSTRUCTING, ABANDONING, AND TRANSCENDING A CRITERION SET

Redefining Relationship Disorder with Verbal and/or Violent Conflict: Lowering the Threshold and Extending the Range—The Next Stage

Once it became clear that the DSM was not going to incorporate a new relationship disorder category except for the GARF and supplementary scales regarding spousal or child abuse, I lowered the threshold at the bottom end and extended the range at the top end, creating six levels of Verbal Conflict and six levels of Physical Conflict:

1. Absent
2. Mild
3. Moderate

Code # _____   Date: _____
04/19/94
Respondent: _____

RELATIONSHIP CONFLICT INVENTORY (Preliminary Version)
SCORE SHEET (2 types of scoring presented)
Arthur M. Bodin, Ph.D., © 1994

Verbal and Physical Conflict Categories Based on Raw Item Counts

I.   VERBAL CONFLICT: Criteria for severity of verbal conflict:

- It takes 3 items to meet each of the first three criteria – A, B, C.
- It takes 1 item to meet each of the last three criteria - D, E, F.

0 - Absent   No criteria from A - F are met.
1 - Mild   1 criterion from A - F is met.
2 - Moderate   2 criteria from A - F are met.
3 - Strong   3 criteria from A - F are met.
4 - Severe   4 criteria from A - F are met.
5 - Extreme   5 criteria from A - F are met.

II.   PHYSICAL CONFLICT: Criteria for severity of physical conflict:

0 - Absent   No criteria from A1, B1, C1, D1, E1, or F1 are met.
1 - Mild   1 criterion from A1, B1, or C1 is met.
2 - Moderate   1 or 2 criteria from A2, B2, and/or C2 are met, or:
                2 criteria from A1, B1, and/or C1 are met.
3 - Strong   3 criteria from A1, B1, C1, A2, B2, and/or C2 are met.
4 - Severe   1 or more criteria from D1, E1, and/or E2 are met.
5 - Extreme   1 or more criteria from D2, F1, and/or F2 are met.

Verbal and Physical Weighted Scores Based on Weighted Item Counts

I.   Scoring for Verbal Conflict:

		Factor	X	Number of Items	=	Score	Max.
A.	Communication Difficulties	3		_____		____	18
B.	Arguments	3		_____		____	18
C.	Painful/Deteriorating Relationship	5		_____		____	30
D.	Distancing	5		_____		____	10
E.	Psychological Coercion/Intimidation	8		_____		____	16
F.	Separation	8		_____		____	8

Verbal Conflict Score:.............................. ____   100 (max.)

II.   Scoring for Physical Conflict:

		Factor	=	Score	
*	A1. Physical Coercion/Intimidation	6		____	*
	A2. A pattern of the above	8		____	
*	B1. Indirect Aggression	6		____	*
	B2. A pattern of the above	8		____	
*	C1. Violence (Level I)	10		____	*
	C2. A pattern of the above	14		____	
*	D1. Violence (Level II)	14		____	*
	D2. A pattern of the above	18		____	
*	E1. Violence (Level III)	18		____	*
	E2. A pattern of the above	24		____	
*	F1. Use of weapons	22		____	*
	F2. A pattern of the above	28		____	

Physical Conflict Score:.............................. ____   100 (max.)

Combined Verbal and Physical Scores:...... ____   200 (max.)

*   Include this item in the total only if the next item does not apply.

Figure 24.1   Relationship Conflict Inventory (preliminary version).

4. Strong
5. Severe
6. Extreme

Deconstructing Relationship Disorder with Verbal and/or Physical Conflict: Acknowledging the Albatross of A Priori Arbitrariness

Because of the arbitrariness of an a priori weighting system, a shift was made to Likert scales with the ratings determined by the respondents.

Abandoning Relationship Disorder with Verbal and/or Physical Conflict: Transforming a Crude Dichotomy into a Nice Continuum

In shifting to dual Likert scales, it became evident that a 1 to 7 format was not psychologically congruent with people's inner experience. Specifically, one patient indicated— and I agreed—that it seemed jarring to designate that there were *no* instances of conflict of a particular type in the past year and/or that there was *no* distress associated with such conflicts by circling a "1." Rather, it seemed more logical to designate the absence of any occurrences or any distress by circling a "0." Moreover, it was important to get the polarity right by designating higher frequencies and distress levels of conflict with *higher* numbers and by designating the *absence* of conflict by "0."

Transcending Relationship Disorder with Verbal and/or Physical Conflict: Achieving Multidimensionality

By shifting from the binary mindset of determining whether particular signs and symptoms exist and, as a result, whether relationship disorder with verbal and/or violent conflict exists, I was free to adopt the nonidentical twin dimensions of frequency and distress level of different examples of conflict. This innovation makes it feasible to characterize some couples as having frequent conflict with low levels of distress, other couples as having infrequent conflict with high levels of distress, some couples as having frequent conflicts with high levels of distress, and some pairs as having infrequent conflicts with low levels of distress! This kind of conceptualization allows greater realism and subtlety in describing couples than declaring them merely to have or not to have "relationship disorder with or without verbal and/or physical conflict."

PRACTICAL PLANS AND PERSPECTIVES

The DSM's Organismic Focus and Implicit Interactional Categories

Embarrassing Chinks in the Armor

One objective of the Task Force on Classification and Diagnosis of Division 43 of American Psychological Association, and of the multiorganizational Coalition on Family Diagnosis, was to try to have some relational diagnoses included in the DSM-IV. One of the points we called attention to was the fact that the supposedly organismic focus of the DSM-III-R already contained at least two diagnoses that were basically relational. One of these was Oppositional Defiant Disorder, since it implicitly acknowledges oppositional defiance *to* some other person and hence is explicitly a systemically oriented

Relationship Conflict Inventory
Arthur M. Bodin, Ph.D., © 1994

PROCESS SECTION

INTRODUCTION: The purpose of this inventory is to get a "picture" of conflict in your relationship <u>during the past 2 months</u> by learning how many times and with what level of distress you experienced each of the "Forms of Conflict" with your partner listed below.

INSTRUCTIONS:
1. If this form of conflict has <u>ever</u> occurred, circle Y (for Yes); if this form of conflict has <u>never</u> occurred, circle N (for No).
2. Circle the <u>one letter</u> below that best reflects the number of times each form of conflict occurred <u>in the past two months</u>.
3. Circle the <u>one number</u> that best describes your level of distress for each form of conflict <u>at the time of its occurrence</u>.

PART I: VERBAL CONFLICT

FORMS OF CONFLICT:	Ever?	How Many Times (in the past 2 months) 0 Times / 1 Time / 2 Times / 3-5 Times / 6-10 Times / 11-20 Times / 20+ Times	Distress Level (at the time of occurrence) No distress / Very slight distress / Slight distress / Moderate distress / Great distress / Very great distress / Extreme distress
3. The focus gets sidetracked and we don't get back to the original topic.	Y N	a b c d e f g	0 1 2 3 4 5 6
6. Talking includes direct or indirect put-downs or insults.	Y N	a b c d e f g	0 1 2 3 4 5 6
12. The focus of at least one partner is on blaming the other, rather than on solving the problem.	Y N	a b c d e f g	0 1 2 3 4 5 6
16. Conflicts escalate.	Y N	a b c d e f g	0 1 2 3 4 5 6

384

PART II: PHYSICAL CONFLICT

29. At least one partner reports feeling fear about safety because of some verbal and/or physical threat(s) or action(s) by the other.

    Y N   a b c d e f g   0 1 2 3 4 5 6

31. At least one partner reports that angry actions have occurred, such as punching a wall, breaking dishes, kicking, throwing, or smashing something.

    Y N   a b c d e f g   0 1 2 3 4 5 6

CONTENT SECTION

INTRODUCTION: The purpose of this inventory is to get a "picture" of conflict in your relationship during the last 2 months by learning how many times and with what level of distress you experienced conflict with your partner about each of the "Topics of Conflict" listed below.

INSTRUCTIONS:

1. If this topic of conflict has ever occurred, circle Y (for Yes); if this form of conflict has never occurred, circle N (for No).
2. Circle the one letter below that best reflects the number of times each form of conflict occurred in the past two months.
3. Circle the one number that best describes your level of distress for each form of conflict at the time of its occurrence.

TOPICS OF CONFLICT:

	Y	N	a	b	c	d	e	f	g		0	1	2	3	4	5	6
21. Willingness and/or ability to talk about how we communicate.	Y	N	a	b	c	d	e	f	g		0	1	2	3	4	5	6
40. Furnishing, decorating, landscaping.	Y	N	a	b	c	d	e	f	g		0	1	2	3	4	5	6
49. Balance of separateness/togetherness (i.e., desire to spend time together).	Y	N	a	b	c	d	e	f	g		0	1	2	3	4	5	6

Figure 24.2 Sample items from the new dual Likert version of the RCI.

Copyright 1994 by Arthur M. Bodin. Printed with permission.

diagnosis. The other is Separation Anxiety Disorder, since it implicitly refers to anxiety about separation *from* somebody, thus making this category too, inherently systemic in its focus.

Political Problems of Turf and Tenacity

Task Force and Coalition members were informed that these two diagnoses were well established within the domain of child psychiatry and were disorders of individuals, and that there would be considerable resistance to reconceptualizing them. Even as we sowed the seeds of paradigm shift, we were inundated with the triumph of tradition.

Accepting DSM's Rejection as an Invitation to Growth

From Diagnosis by Dichotomies to Categorization by Continuum

As already indicated, the rejection of the concept of relational diagnosis for Axis I inclusion in DSM-IV provided me with the sense of freedom to shift to more subtle and realistic measurement methods that could capture *and reflect* different levels of conflict frequency and distress, rather than just blur these dimensions in arriving at a statement of whether the couple does or does not suffer from "relationship disorder with verbal and or physical conflict." It also helped give impetus to this book.

From Diagnosis Alone to Diagnosis and Outcome Measurement

The rejection of relational diagnoses for inclusion in the main body of DSM-IV, along with the rise of managed health care, provided the impetus for another shift. Instead of focusing exclusively on diagnosis, the Coalition has decided to expand its focus to include outcome measurement. This new focus is expected to prove increasingly important in the cost-conscious context of managed health care, not only in application to outcome measurement but also in attempts to generate guidelines based on research about the number of sessions required to achieve a certain level of results (the dose-effect curve) with particular types of therapy, with specific frequency and distress levels of couple conflict, and even by some specific therapists.

Shortening the Focus of the "Retrospectiscope" from 12 Months to 2 Months

Once the decision had been made to adjust the Relationship Conflict Inventory so that it would be useful for outcome measurement as well as for diagnosis, it became clear that looking back over the past year was too long a time frame. In view of the brevity of much or even most therapy in this age of limits imposed by managed care, two months seemed like a reasonable time frame. Three months was probably longer than most therapy would last, and one month seemed like too short a time frame for complete behavior cycles to unfold, such as drinking-violence-begging for forgiveness-"honeymoon"-tension buildup-and drinking again.

Pilot Study of Dichotomous Data

Small Sample Using the Inventory for Relationship Disorder with Verbal and/or Physical Conflict

In a talk about avoiding conflict with customers that I presented to a group of electrologists, I asked how many were in a continuing relationship. I then asked how many of those would be willing to remain behind to participate for about 20 minutes in some research on relationship conflict. Twenty-one people stayed and completed the instrument, and rated their degree of couple satisfaction/dissatisfaction on a 7-point scale. The relationship between conflict and dissatisfaction in the ratings these 21 people made of their relationships was found by calculating Spearman's rank order correlation coefficient, which was .74, significant at the .001 level. What this crude pilot study suggests is a strong association between relationship conflict and relationship dissatisfaction, the former accounting for more than half the variance of the latter.

Larger Sample with Criterion Measures

Verbal and Physical Conflict Categories

In order to follow the Yes/No style of the DSM criterion sets, criteria were developed for both Verbal and Physical Conflict ranging from Absent to Extreme, with intermediate steps of Mild, Moderate, Strong, and Severe. Thus, the scores for both Verbal and Physical Conflict were arrayed on a 6-point scale.

Results

Data were collected over a two-year period from a larger group of respondents using the binary (True/False) version of the Relationship Conflict Inventory. Separate analyses were conducted for females and males, correlating both Verbal and Physical Conflict scores on the RCI with Verbal and Physical Conflict scores on the Conflict Tactics Scale (Straus, 1979), the Global Distress and Problem Solving Communication Scales of the Marital Satisfaction Inventory (Snyder, 1979), and the Cohesion and Adaptability Scales of the FACES II (Olson, Portner, & Bell, 1982). Although all the research participants (nonclinical sample) completed all the instruments, only some of the patient participants (clinical sample) completed all of the instruments. Thus, different correlation coefficients have different ns. These data will be presented in a future manuscript but are mentioned to give an impressionistic glimpse of the results.

Correlations with RCI Verbal Conflict Scores

Females' RCI Verbal Conflict scores' Pearson product moment correlation coefficients with all of the other pertinent variables just mentioned achieved two-tailed significance levels of $p < .001$, with ns ranging from 29 to 33. Correlation coefficients for the males on these same variables were remarkably similar to those of females except for the correlation between Verbal Conflict on the RCI and Verbal Conflict on the Conflict Tactics Scales, which had a significance level of only $p < .05$, $n = 21$. All the other correlation coefficients for the males showed significance levels of $p < .001$, ns ranging from 15 to 21, except for the correlation between RCI Verbal Conflict and FACES II Cohesion with $p < .01$, $n = 15$. All correlation coefficients involving Cohesion and Adaptability are, of course, in the negative direction.

Correlations with RCI Physical Conflict Scores

RCI Physical Conflict scores for females were compared with CTS Physical Conflict, MSI Global Distress and Problem Solving Communication, and FACES II Cohesion, and Adaptability scores. The resulting correlation coefficients were all significant; three were at the .01 level and two were at the .001 level, with ns ranging from 29 to 34. These same variables yielded a strikingly different pattern for the males. Specifically, the correlation of the RCI Physical Conflict score with the Conflict Tactics Scales Physical Conflict score was significant with $p < .001$, $n = 20$. However, all of the other correlation coefficients were low, none of them reaching significance. This pattern may have resulted from some combination of: (1) relatively low n (15 to 16), (2) the denial factor, (3) the definitional threshold factor, and (4) the fact that Physical Conflict was not claimed to be present as ubiquitously as Verbal Conflict. The data showed that when we restricted our attention to those participants who came in as couples, the males and females reported about the same amount of Verbal Conflict, but the males reported far less Physical Conflict. This finding could be due either to denial or to the now familiar definitional differences seen clinically, which typically set male thresholds higher than female thresholds for what actions get labeled "hitting."

Additional Validity Support from Demographic Data

The correlations between RCI data and Conflict Tactics Scales data all support the validity of the RCI, as does the fact that Verbal and Physical Conflict scores for females and Verbal Conflict scores for males achieved a consistent pattern when point-biserial correlations were calculated with the nominal demographic data indicating why each individual was tested. Specifically, those in therapy for family problems (clinical subsample) and those tested for research purposes only (nonclinical sample) achieved point-biserial correlations that were positive and significant for the clinical sample, and negative and significant for the nonclinical sample, all ps $< .01$, and half the ps $< .001$. The male Physical Conflict scores failed to reach significance, though they were in the right direction. Not surprisingly, the clinical subsample (who were in therapy but not for family problems) had point-biserial correlations in an intermediate and nonsignificant range.

Pattern of Unique Contributions of the RCI

Correlation coefficients were computed for subjects who had completed the RCI, the Conflict Tactics Scales, and each of the other variables, and a multiple regression was used to test the significance of the unique contribution of the stronger predictor (RCI or Conflict Tactics Scales) over the weaker predictor of the other variables. There were 16 such comparisons of how well the RCI acted as a predictor variable versus how well the Conflict Tactics Scales acted as a predictor variable. Ten of these comparisons were significant at the .05 level—nine at the .01 level—all favoring the RCI. Because the probability level was not specified in advance, one can use only the .05 level correlations. Using the binomial expansion, the probability associated with at least 10 out of 16 comparisons being significant at the .05 level is less than 1 in 100 million, rather unlikely under the null hypothesis. This does not necessarily suggest that the RCI is a better measure than the Conflict Tactics Scales. Rather, it may be that the greater number and subtlety of the Verbal Conflict items on the RCI (in comparison to Verbal Conflict items of the Conflict Tactics Scales) makes the former correlate better with the Global Distress and Problem Solving Communication Scales of the Marital Satisfaction Inventory and with the Cohesion and Adaptability Scales of the FACES II.

Another way of viewing the RCI in comparison with the Conflict Tactics Scales is that the kind of conflict measured by the former has more in common with the other relationship measures. One might, therefore, regard the Conflict Tactics Scales as tapping a narrower domain than the RCI, but the pattern was not in evidence for the males in regard to Physical Conflict. This could reflect both the smaller number of males in this sample *and* the pronounced relative rarity of the males admitting that any actual or symbolic violence had occurred. Subsequent research with the revised dual Likert scale version of the RCI will be needed to clarify whether the RCI—in that format—or the CTS has relatively low ability to evoke from male respondents reports of physical relationship conflict or relatively high ability to evoke evidence of male denial of physical relationship conflict.

Moving from the True/False version to the dual Likert scale version of the RCI may capture evidence of male awareness of Physical Conflict in their relationship but may show that males report lower frequency and distress levels than females. Whether this would constitute denial by the males or exaggeration by the females is not a simple question. The males are not necessarily rating their *own* violence, since the RCI asks merely whether various types of Physical Conflict have occurred *in the relationship* rather than whether such types have been *carried out by the male*. Also, the observation offered earlier that males seem to have a higher threshold for what they label as "Physical Conflict" may be a significant part of the explanation for this discrepancy, whittling away some possible temptation to attribute denial to the males or exaggeration to the females!

Future

Data have now been gathered for two years using the newer version of the Relationship Conflict Inventory—with dual Likert scales, a section on content, the retrospective time frame shortened from 12 to 2 months, and the reading level lowered from eleventh grade to less than eighth grade for the Process Section and to fifth grade for the Content Section. Several additional instruments were administered in gathering the data on the "Likertized" Relationship Conflict Inventory. These data remain to be analyzed. Validation data from more diverse demographic samples and reliability data have yet to be gathered and analyzed. Two publications have mentioned the availability of the RCI, which can be provided for researchers and clinicians who are willing to participate in gathering additional validation data or who are simply curious (Aldarondo & Straus, 1994; Harway & Hansen, 1994).

Treatment Implications

Can Taking the RCI Be Therapeutic?

A number of patients have told me spontaneously that taking the RCI was beneficial to them. They stated that it helped them by putting into words experiences they have had and by implying to them that many others have had similar experiences. A colleague gave me the same feedback about his use of the RCI with a battered woman.

Initial Assessment and Outcome Measurement

The areas of interest the RCI is designed to illuminate at the start and at the finish of therapy (initial assessment and outcome measurement, respectively) include the following:

- How frequent is each kind of Verbal and Physical Conflict according to each partner?

- How intense is the distress from each kind of Verbal and Physical Conflict according to each partner?
- How similar are the frequency and distress ratings of the partners across the spectrum of Verbal and Physical Conflicts?
- Does either partner report more frequent conflict of any kind, which the other partner seems either to be unaware of or motivated to deny?

The RCI can probably be made more sensitive for brief therapy progress and outcome measurement by shortening the retrospective time frame from 2 months to 1 month. Doing this makes it important to add a new Yes/No column to mark beside each item to show whether that Form or Topic of conflict *ever* occurred. This last addition, long used by Straus (1979), supplements the 1 month time frame by reaching back further to capture low base-rate events which may, indeed, be particularly important.

Treatment Planning

A focused overview of relationship conflict likely to flow from the RCI, particularly in discussing it with the couple, includes accurate and applicable information about the following:

- Do the partners acknowledge and attempt to account for differences in their views, and do they argue about such differences or seek accommodation? Observing the process of their response to mutual feedback provides information about whether they are ready to begin discussing *content* conflict (substantive differences) or whether they must first discuss *process* conflict and substitute better processes of conflict resolution.
- Which kinds of Verbal and Physical Conflicts have high initial priority because of their frequency and/or distress levels, *and/or because of their potential for emotional or physical destructiveness?*
- Which *process* conflicts need to be addressed before the couple can discuss matters calmly enough to achieve accurate mutual understanding and the goodwill to move forward?
- Which *content* areas are most pressing or distressing and can now be addressed as examples of substantive conflict resolution that the therapist can observe and use as a basis for offering immediate coaching through pithy, tactful hints provided on line in real time?

Treatment Implementation

The problematic processes pinpointed by the RCI provide illumination for the therapist to aim interventions not only where the light is good but also where the interactional problems are. Thus, according to what is illuminated by the RCI, the therapist can focus on helping the partners appreciate the importance of and gain skill in:

- Communicating in a confirming way *and* avoiding disconfirming both the partner and oneself;
- Harnessing escalation as a second-nature signal to suspect the possible existence of an unrecognized misunderstanding;

- Checking back with each other through paraphrasing the partner's point as powerfully as they can, so as to detect and correct misunderstandings; and
- Using appropriate steps on a "hierarchy of conflict resolution techniques" ranging from "agreeing to disagree," flipping a coin, taking turns, meeting the other person part way, catering to the one who cares more, and bargaining, to "principled negotiation" (Fisher & Ury, 1981), with its win-win spirit.

CONCLUSION, INVITATION, AND HOPES

I have attempted to present a clear conceptual model for assessing the *processes* (verbal and physical) and the *content* of relationship conflict. I hope readers have gained an appreciation of the possibilities this model offers and an interest in the progress of validating the revised dual Likert scales version of the RCI.

I invite you to contact me to receive a copy of the RCI or to explore possibilities for participating in its validation—for example, through data collection—or to discuss other research applications, such as outcome studies.

Arthur M. Bodin, Ph.D.
Senior Research Fellow, MRI
555 Middlefield Road
Palo Alto, CA 94301-2124

Phone:(415) 328-3000
Fax:(415) 328-4334

Finally, I hope that this work will contribute to something beyond mere clarity in conceptualizing relationship conflict by making it easier for therapists to "know the score" and, with its guidance, to help couples find not only the words but also the music as they seek to create harmony in their relationships.

REFERENCES

Aldarondo, E., & Straus, M. (1994). Screening for physical violence in couple therapy: Methodological, practical, and ethical considerations. *Family Process, 33*(4), 430.

American Psychiatric Association. (1987). *Diagnostic and statistical manual of mental disorders* (3rd ed.). Washington, DC: Author.

American Psychiatric Association. (1994). *Diagnostic and statistical manual of mental disorders* (4th ed.). Washington, DC: Author.

Bauman, G., & Roman, M. (1966). Interaction testing in the study of marital dominance. *Family Process, 5*(22), 230–242.

Bodin, A. M. (1966). *Family interaction, coalition, disagreement, and compromise in problem, normal and synthetic family triads.* Unpublished doctoral dissertation, State University of New York, Buffalo.

Bodin, A. M. (1968). Conjoint family assessment: An evolving field. In P. McReynolds (Ed.), *Advances in psychological assessment* (Vol. 1, pp. 223–243). Palo Alto, CA: Science and Behavior Books.

Bradford, L. (1978, April). *The death of a dyad.* Paper presented at the meeting of the Central States Speech Association, Chicago, IL.

Buss, A. H., & Perry, M. (1992). The Aggression Questionnaire. *Journal of Personality and Social Psychology, 63*(3), 452–459.

Connors, J., & Harway, M. (1995). A male-female abuse continuum. *Family Violence and Sexual Assualt Bulletin 11*(1 & 2), 2933.

Eggeman, K., Moxley, C., & Schumm, W. R. (1985). Assessing spouse's perceptions of Gottman's Temporal Form in marital conflict. *Psychological Reports, 57,* 171–181.

Ferreira, A. J. (1963). Decision making in normal and pathologic families. *Archives of General Psychiatry, 8,* 68–73.

Ferreira, A. J., & Winter, W. D. (1965). Family interaction and decision making. *Archives of General Psychiatry, 13,* 214–223.

Fisher, R., & Ury, W. (1981). *Getting to yes: Negotiating agreement without giving in.* Boston: Houghton-Mifflin.

Frieze, I. H., & Browne, A. (1989). Violence in marriage. In L. Ohlin & M. Tonry (Eds.), *Family violence* (pp. 163–218). Chicago: University of Chicago.

Garner, J. W., & Hudson, W. W. (1990a). Non-physical Abuse of Partner Scale (NPAPS). In W. W. Hudson, *WALMYR assessment scales scoring manual* (p. 45). Tempe, AZ: WALMYR.

Garner, J. W., & Hudson, W. W. (1990b). Physical Abuse of Partner Scale (PAPS). In W. W. Hudson, *WALMYR assessment scales scoring manual* (p. 46). Tempe, AZ: WALMYR.

Gelles, R. J., & Straus, M. A. (1989). *Intimate violence: The causes and consequences of abuse in the American family.* New York: Simon & Schuster.

Harway, M., & Hansen, M. (1994). *Spouse abuse: Assessing and treating battered women, batterers, and their children.* Sarasota, FL: Professional Resource Press.

Hoskins, C. N. (1981). Psychometrics in nursing research: Construction of an interpersonal conflict scale. *Research in Nursing and Health, 6,* 243–249.

Hoskins, C. N. (1983). Psychometrics in nursing research: Further development of the Interpersonal Conflict Scale. *Research in Nursing and Health, 6*(2), 75–83.

Hudson, W. W. (1990a). Partner Abuse Scale: Non-physical (PASNP). In W. W. Hudson, *WALMYR assessment scales scoring manual* (p. 43). Tempe, AZ: WALMYR.

Hudson, W. W. (1990b). Partner Abuse Scale: Physical (PASPH). In W. W. Hudson, *WALMYR assessment scales scoring manual* (p. 44). Tempe, AZ: WALMYR.

Jackson, D. D. (Ed.). (1968a). *Communication, family and marriage.* Palo Alto, CA: Science and Behavior Books.

Jackson, D. D. (Ed.). (1968b). *Therapy, communication and change.* Palo Alto, CA: Science and Behavior Books.

Jacobson, N. S., Gottman, J. M., Waltz, J., Rushe, R., Babcock, J., & Holtzworth-Munroe, A. (1994). Affect, verbal content, and psychophysiology in the arguments of couples with a violent husband. *Journal of Consulting and Clinical Psychology, 62,* 982.

Laing, R. D. (1961). *The self and others: Further studies in sanity and madness.* London: Tavistock.

Levy, J., & Epstein, N. B. (1964). An application of the Rorschach test in family investigation. *Family Process, 3,* 344–376.

Metz, M. E. (1993). *Manual for the styles of conflict inventory.* Palo Alto, CA: Consulting Psychologists Press.

Olson, D. H., Fournier, D. G., & Druckman, J. M. (1986). *PREPARE/ENRICH counselor's manual.* Minneapolis, MN: Life Innovations.

Olson, D. H., Portner, J., & Bell, R. Q. (1982). *FACES II: Family adaptability and cohesion evaluation scales.* St. Paul, MN: Family Social Science, University of Minnesota.

Parker, B. L., & Drummond-Reeves, S. J. (1993). The death of a dyad: Relational autopsy, analysis, and aftermath. *Journal of Divorce & Remarriage, 2,* 116.

Ruehlman, L. S., & Karoly, P. (1991). With a little flak from my friends: Development and preliminary validation of the test of negative social exchange (TENSE). *Psychological Assessment, 3,* 97–101.

Satir, V. (1964). *Conjoint family therapy: A guide to theory and technique.* Palo Alto, CA: Science and Behavior Books.

Shepherd, M. F., & Campbell, J. A. (1992). The Abusive Behavior Inventory: A measure of psychological and physical abuse. *Journal of Interpersonal Violence, 7*(3), 291–305.

Smith R. P. (Pictures by Macdonard, R.) (1958). *Translations from the English.* New York: Simon & Schuster.

Snyder, D. K. (1979). *Marital satisfaction inventory (MSI) administration booklet.* Los Angeles: Western Psychological Services.

Steinmetz, S. (1977). Wife-beating, husband beating: A comparison of the use of physical violence between spouses to resolve marital fights. In M. Roy (Ed.), *Battered women: A psychosocial study of domestic violence* (pp. 63–67). New York: Van Nostrand Reinhold.

Straus, M. A. (1979). Measuring intrafamily conflict and violence: The Conflict Tactics (CT) Scales. *Journal of Marriage and the Family, 41,* 75–88.

Straus, M. A. (1983). Ordinary violence versus child abuse and wife beating: What do they have in common? In D. Finkelhor, R. J. Gelles, G. T. Hotaling, & M. A. Straus (Eds.), *The dark side of families: Current family violence research* (pp. 213–234). Newbury Park, CA: Sage.

Straus, M. A., & Gelles, R. J. (1988). How violent are American families? Estimates from the National Family Violence Resurvey and other studies. In G. T. Hotaling, D. Finkelhor, J. T. Kirkpatrick, & M. A. Straus (Eds.), *Family abuse and its consequences: New directions in research* (pp. 14–36). Newbury Park, CA: Sage.

Straus, M. A., Gelles, R. J., & Steinmetz, S. K. (1980). *Behind closed doors: Violence in the American family.* New York: Doubleday/Anchor.

Strodtbeck, F. L. (1951). Husband-wife interaction over revealed differences. *American Sociological Review, 16,* 468–473.

Watzlawick, P. (1964). *An anthology of human communication: Text and tape.* Palo Alto, CA: Science and Behavior Books.

Watzlawick, P., Beavan, J. H., & Jackson, D. D. (1967). *Pragmatics of human communication: A study of interactional patterns, pathologies and paradoxes.* New York: Norton.

Watzlawick, P. (1984). *The invented reality: Contributions to constructivism.* New York: Norton.

Weiss, R. L., & Summers, K. J. (1983). Marital Interaction Coding System III. In E. E. Filsinger (Ed.), *Marriage and family assessment* (pp. 85–116). Beverly Hills, CA: Sage.

CHAPTER 25

Intrafamily Child Sexual Abuse

TERRY S. TREPPER, PhD and DAWN M. NIEDNER, PhD

One of the most troubling of the possible relational diagnostic categories is that of intrafamily child sexual abuse. Although recent extensive media attention may have led to an exaggerated public sense of the frequency of occurrence, most epidemiological studies suggest the problem is indeed a major mental health concern (Finkelhor, Hotaling, Lewis, & Smith, 1990; Russell, 1983, 1986).

Few would argue with the fact that the problem is serious, both in terms of the immediate severe crisis for the family and the long-term consequences to the child victim. While there are certainly resilient individuals who overcome intrafamily child sexual abuse (cf. Wolin & Wolin, 1993), a great deal of evidence suggests that many victims experience serious social and psychological problems in later life, including sexual dysfunction and adjustment problems (Wyatt, 1991), eating disorders (Jones & Emerson, 1994; Waller, 1993), personality disorders (Waller, 1993), and substance abuse disorders (Barrett & Trepper, 1992a).

It is particularly disconcerting for therapists who work with intrafamily child sexual abuse to use the DSM-IV for diagnosis (APA, 1994). While it is sometimes possible to provide an authentic diagnosis for the individual family members involved—usually the offending family member, the victim, and sometimes a nonoffending parent—oftentimes no member displays the criteria for an Axis I or II disorder (Marshall & Eccles, 1991). More important, the complexities of the interactional patterns that occur within incestuously abusing families, and that come to make the families vulnerable to abuse, are largely ignored by focusing on the individual psychopathology of the family members involved.

It would be far more useful, in terms of research, diagnosis, and treatment, to understand intrafamily child sexual abuse as a larger-system phenomenon worthy of a relational diagnosis. The purpose of this chapter is to offer the rationale and conceptual framework for the relational diagnosis of intrafamily child sexual abuse, to offer specific criteria for the diagnosis, and to suggest how designating this diagnosis may lead to improved therapeutic outcomes.

FAMILY CHARACTERISTICS IN INTRAFAMILY CHILD SEXUAL ABUSE

In the past two decades a great deal of attention has focused on the etiology, maintenance, and long-term consequences of intrafamily sexual abuse. Interestingly, even though by definition incestuous abuse occurs within the family, most of the previous literature has focused on the offending family member and child victim only. However, recently there has been increasing interest in the characteristics of families in which there is intrafamily abuse. Theoretical explanations are being given about the characteristics of abusing families, some based on clinical experience (Alexander, 1985; Anderson & Shafer, 1979; Dietz & Craft, 1980; Justice & Justice, 1979; Pelletier & Handy, 1986; Ribordy, 1989; Stevens, 1992; Tierney & Corwin, 1983; Trepper & Barrett, 1986, 1989); some based on retrospective studies of adult "survivors" of childhood intrafamily sexual abuse (Alexander & Lupfer, 1987; Carson, Gertz, & Donaldson, 1991; Harter, Alexander, & Neimeyer, 1988; Kirschner, Kirschner, & Rappaport, 1993; Yama, Tovey, & Fogas, 1993); and a few that have systematically examined family characteristics in cases of ongoing incestuous abuse (Dadds, Smith, Webber, & Robinson, 1991; Faller, 1991; Levang, 1989; Trepper, Niedner, Mika, & Barrett, 1995).

Despite the paucity of research on the family characteristics of incestuously abusing families, some factors have emerged. What follows is a summary of what has been consistent in the literature and what we have found in our clinical population of intact, incestuously abusing families over the last 15 years (Trepper & Barrett, 1989; Trepper et al., 1995).

Socioenvironmental Factors

It has been hypothesized that a number of socioenvironmental factors exist that will make families more vulnerable to intrafamily child sexual abuse (Doe, 1990; Tierney & Corwin, 1983; Trepper & Barrett, 1986, 1989). Recent empirical studies have confirmed that family environments characterized by high levels of stress are indeed more vulnerable. For example, Gordon (1989) found that among incestuously abusing fathers, there is a significant amount of drug and alcohol abuse, of marital problems, and of insufficient income. It has traditionally been suggested that social isolation of families increases their vulnerability to being abusive (de Chesnay, Marshall, & Clements, 1988; Finkelhor, 1978, 1980a); this has been confirmed with our clinical population, where 79 percent of the families were identified as moderately or extremely socially isolated.

Transgenerational Patterns of Abuse

It is commonly reported that being abused as a child, either sexually or physically, increases individual offenders' vulnerability to later abuse. Most studies show that while the majority of adult offending family members were not sexually abused as children (Kaufman & Zigler, 1987), offending parents' perceptions of having been abused as children does increase their vulnerability to being abusive (Parker & Parker, 1986). A more recent study found that about one-third of offending fathers and stepfathers, and over half of the nonoffending mothers, were sexually abused as children (Faller, 1989). In our clinical population, about one-third of both offending and nonoffending parents reported having been sexually and/or physically abused, although almost one-fourth of the offending fathers did not know whether they had been sexually abused, leading us to conclude that our numbers may be low.

Family Structure

Most of the empirical literature on family structural variables in intrafamily child sexual abuse suggests that incestuous families are more dysfunctional than other clinical population families and than nonclinical families. Specifically, incestuously abusing families have been shown to have poor communication (Levang, 1989); low spousal intimacy and unequal marital power distribution (Carson, Gertz, & Donaldson, 1991; de Chesnay, Marshall, & Clements, 1988); poor emotional responsiveness (Carson et al., 1991); inadequate conflict-resolution skills (Dadds et al., 1991; Hoagwood & Stewart, 1989; Madonna, Van Scoyk, & Jones, 1991); and weak generational boundaries (Carson et al., 1991).

Most of these variables also were found to be present in our clinical sample. In the majority of these families, leadership was limited and erratic. Roles were generally unclear or shifted often. The marital relationships were generally poor, with almost 90 percent displaying either moderate or extreme emotional separateness, 66 percent reporting the marriages unsatisfying; only 7 percent of couples reported their sexual satisfaction as very high. With regard to communication, a whopping 92 percent of the families exhibited negative communication patterns and 32 percent rated overall communication as extremely poor and incongruent.

One of the more unclear family structural variables is that of cohesion, or the degree of emotional bondedness in a family. Some studies have found incest families to display a high degree of enmeshment, where emotional bondedness is extreme, individual autonomy is stifled, and privacy and independence are discouraged (Hoagwood & Stewart, 1989; Madonna et al., 1991). Others have found the opposite, with incest families scoring low in cohesion (Carson et al., 1991; Dadds et al., 1991). It has been suggested that both extremes on cohesion are common with incest families (Carson et al., 1991; Trepper & Sprenkle, 1988), in keeping with Olson's circumplex model (Olson, Russell, & Sprenkle, 1983).

In summary, then, there is a great deal of evidence that intrafamily child sexual abuse can be considered a relational diagnosis. While there are certainly individual psychopathological factors that contribute to a family's vulnerability to abuse, including the obvious, pedophilia, these do not adequately explain the entire incest phenomenon. The reason is that, unlike specific individual diagnoses such as dysthymia or schizophrenia, intrafamily child sexual abuse must involve other family members for it to exist. The patterns of vulnerability that are present in families, coupled with the typical course of response to its discovery, suggest a pattern or syndrome in and of itself, separate from individual psychopathologies. In this case, the whole is greater than the sum of its parts.

COMMON INTERACTIONAL PATTERNS

The field is just beginning to understand the complex patterns involved in intrafamily child sexual abuse. A number of specific family interactional patterns, sequences, and styles are emerging from clinical research. Here we focus on two such patterns that seem to be consistent in and across most incestuously abusing families.

Family Abusive Style

Four broad categories of family abusive style have been identified by Larson and Maddock (1986): affection exchange, erotic exchange, aggression exchange, and rage expression. These categories, although not always mutually exclusive, are generally distinct and have proven reliable in the assessment of intrafamily child sexual abuse (Trepper & Barrett, 1989).

Affection Exchange

The affection-exchange family appears to outsiders as very loving and caring. There is a great need for and expression of nurturance, especially by the offending family member and child victim, and the sexual episodes seems to occur partially as a result of this high need for affection. Rarely is any physical abuse present with this style family, and most family members wish to remain together after the abuse is made known. The child victims in affection-exchange families often will recant their stories rather than "tear up the family" or see the offending family member face a jail sentence. This is the most common type, with 62 percent of our clinical population falling into this category.

Erotic Exchange

The erotic-exchange family is one where many, if not most, interactions are sexualized. These families elevate sexuality to a libertine philosophy; part of that philosophy may include viewing intrafamilial sex as liberating. An erotic-exchange family would be one where pornography is openly displayed, where nudity is expected, and where explicit sexual comments are passed across generations. Erotic-exchange families can be involved in organized family sexual activities, such as shared group family sex (family "swinging"). Mother-son sexual abuse is more common with this family style than with the other three. This type of family is relatively uncommon, appearing as the primary family abusive style in only 8 percent of this clinical study population.

Aggression Exchange

The intent of the sexual interaction between family members in the aggression-exchange family is hostile. There is much anger, expressed hostility, and negative interactions in aggression-exchange families. Physical abuse is often present, and the sexual abuse is usually an extension of that. For example, after an argument has escalated it is not uncommon for a father to sexually abuse his daughter, as a form of punishment and humiliation. Sibling incest occurs most often within this family abusive style, especially between an older brother and younger sister. The aggression-exchange family is found 16 percent of the time in our clinical sample.

Rage Expression

Although the rage-expression family gets the most media attention, it is actually one of the least common, with only 8 percent of our study population falling into that category. It is the most dramatic and usually results in the worst long-term consequences for child victims. The abuse occurs with much concomitant physical abuse, often quite sadistic. This type of abuse never appears to be consensual, but instead seems like a violent rape. The offending family members display the most serious psychopathology, including psychotic disorders, which are fairly uncommon in the other three types.

Patterns of Denial

Denial is usually described as an individual defense mechanism. However, over the years our treatment team has described patterns of denial that are commonly present in intrafamily child sexual abuse (Barrett, Sykes, & Byrnes, 1986; Barrett & Trepper, 1992b, 1992c; Trepper & Barrett, 1989). These types of denial can be present in only one family member; all family members may express one type of denial; or all members may express a different type. The function of each type of denial is primarily to separate the person psychologically from the devastating reality that he or she has engaged in behavior that violates one of our society's strongest taboos.

Denial of Facts

With denial of facts, a family member or members challenge the reality of the abuse even though all evidence supports its veracity. Either the abuse itself or the details of the abuse may be challenged. Offending parents usually deny facts directly, as do the nonoffending parents ("She just lied about it! She never did like him."[1]) The child victim can deny facts by changing the story or recanting her claim to protect the family. In our clinical sample, 32 percent of offending parents, 13 percent of nonoffending parents, and 11 percent of the victims denied facts at intake.

Denial of Awareness

Denial of awareness occurs when a family member states that although the abuse probably did occur, he or she was not aware of it at the time. An offending parent might state that he was intoxicated at the time. ("I guess I did it if she said so, I mean she wouldn't lie, but I do have this drinking problem, and I was drunk at the time . . .") A nonoffending parent might say that the abuse may have occurred, but she wasn't aware of it, "didn't hear" or "didn't remember" when her daughter told her it had happened. A victim can deny awareness by claiming that she was asleep at the time or by saying that she didn't know what was happening was sexual in nature. (We have had victims who were repeatedly penetrated make this claim.) In our clinical sample, at intake, 15 percent of the offending parents, 13 percent of the nonoffending parents, and 6 percent of the victims denied awareness of what had transpired.

Denial of Responsibility

Denial of responsibility occurs when a family member who accepts the facts of the abuse and was aware of its occurrence displaces the responsibility from the offending family member and places it someplace or on someone else. The offending parent, for example, may state that, although he did repeatedly fondle his stepdaughter, she was "seductive and seemed to like it." A nonoffending parent might blame herself ("If I had only given him sex when he wanted it.") or blame her daughter ("You don't know how she can be, she tried to get him excited, just to get back at me!"). And the victim herself may deny appropriate responsibility (i.e., not place the responsibility on the offending family member) by assuming her own personal responsibility. ("If I just hadn't asked him the question, none of this would have happened.") In our clinical population, 17 percent of offending parents, 21 percent of nonoffending parents, and 9 percent of victims denied the appropriate responsibility.

---

[1]The statements found in this section are actual client quotations.

Denial of Impact

Family members might accept the facts, report awareness, and express appropriate responsibility but still deny the impact of the abuse. With this type of denial, a family member reduces or dismisses the seriousness of the abuse or its potential consequences. For example, an offending or nonoffending parent might say, "It was only fondling," or "Intercourse only happened a couple of times," or "She seems to be doing fine now." The victim can deny impact by stating "I don't really care if it happened" or "It was no big deal." In our clinical population, 22 percent of the offending parents, 23 percent of the nonoffending parents, and a large 33 percent of victims denied impact at intake.

FEATURES, COURSE, PATTERNS, AND CRITERIA FOR DIAGNOSIS

We believe, based on the previous review of clinical and empirical evidence, that intrafamily child sexual abuse can be considered a relational diagnosis in and of itself, and even lends itself to the format found in the DSM. What follows is our rendition of the essential features of this particular relational diagnosis for this first volume containing such a typology.

Diagnostic Features

The essential feature of intrafamily child sexual abuse is that one or both parents engaged in sexual behavior with one or more children in the family. Intrafamily child sexual abuse also may include any nonconsensual sibling sexual behavior (Kaslow, Haupt, Arce, & Werblowsky, 1981) or any sibling sexual behavior where one sibling is from a different childhood "generation." A childhood generation refers to the subjective feeling the child has that another child is approximately his or her age, rather than that there is any specific age difference.

Finally, intrafamily child sexual abuse also may include sexual activity between an adult member of the extended family (such as a grandfather or aunt) and a child member of the family. Intrafamily child sexual abuse is not limited to biologic or "blood" relatives but refers to any "functional" family member—for example, a stepfather, a mother's long-term live-in boyfriend, or a very close family friend who may be identified by the family as "almost like family."

Any behavior that was intended to stimulate the child sexually or in which a child was used to stimulate the offending family member would be considered abusive. This would include vaginal, oral, or anal intercourse; fondling, caressing, or kissing a child in a sexual manner; encouraging the child to masturbate in front of the offending family member, or the family member masturbating in front of the child; encouraging the child to engage in sexual acts with others; or purposely exposing the child to erotic or pornographic materials (Russell, 1984).

The family usually comes to professional attention through the child protective service system. Most often the child has confided in a teacher, friend, or outside relative, who reports the abuse. The family often will seem more distressed by the intrusion into their lives by the social service system than by the sexual abuse. In fact, it is extremely common for the child either to recant altogether or to deny the impact of the abuse when he or she realizes how angry or distraught the family has become following the public allegation. It is equally common for the nonabusing parent and the other members of the family to be angry more with the child for disclosing the abuse than with the abusing parent for perpetrating it.

Associated Descriptive Features

Even though intrafamily child sexual abuse sometimes involves only a single episode, more often it involves a gradual increase in the frequency, duration, and severity of the sexual acts themselves (Meiselman, 1978; Trepper & Barrett, 1989). Often other members of the family, including the nonabusing parent, know about the abuse but for a variety of reasons may deny its occurrence when openly confronted, making diagnosis difficult. The family dysfunctional patterns that make them vulnerable to intrafamily child sexual abuse are often what supports the secrecy and denial. Some associated family systemic characteristics include lack of family cohesion, a highly patriarchal structure, inflexibility to change, poor marital relationship, and poor communication. What distinguishes intrafamily child sexual abuse from pedophilia, incestuous type, is the complex and systemic family patterns that often include all members of the family in the origin and maintenance of the abuse.

Associated Mental Disorders

Some, although not most, adult family members who incestuously abuse may be pedophiles. Other paraphilias, such as voyeurism or exhibitionism, may also predispose an individual to engage in those paraphilias with a child family member (Abel et al., 1988). In rare cases a predisposing disorder is hypoactive sexual desire disorder. Antisocial Personality Disorder (APA, 1994; see also Chapter 19) also may be associated with intrafamily child sexual abuse. In the case of sibling abuse, Conduct Disorder often is associated. (See Chapter 14.) The nonabusing parent often displays a passive-dependent personality disorder.

A number of mental disorders that occur as a consequence of being abused include Conduct Disorder in childhood or adolescence; alcohol and/or drug abuse; dissociative disorders; mood disorders; Post-Traumatic Stress Disorder; sexual disorders, especially Sexual Aversion Disorder and Sexual Arousal Disorder; and Borderline Personality Disorder (Brown & Anderson, 1991; Cahill, Llewelyn, & Pearson, 1991; Chu & Dill, 1990; McLeer et al., 1988). However, the majority of both incestuously abused children and adults who were sexually abused as children do not have primary Axis I diagnosable disorders (Sirles, Smith, & Kausama, 1989). Recent evidence suggests that the overall quality of family functioning and of parenting skills ironically may mediate against the development of mental disorders among victims of intrafamilial sexual abuse (Harter, Alexander, & Neimeyer, 1988; Parker & Parker, 1991).

Associated Symptoms and Physical Examination Findings

Children who have been sexually abused may become symptomatic; a physical examination or laboratory findings may reveal a sexually transmitted disease. Of course, the abusing family member also should be examined for evidence of a sexually transmitted/

transmittable disease, as should other family members who may have had sexual contact with that individual. In addition, the child may show physical signs and trauma to the genitalia, breasts, buttocks, and anus.

Prevalence, Incidence, and Risk

Approximately 27 percent of the women in our study population were sexually abused as children, 29 percent of those by family members; 16 percent of men were sexually abused as children, 11 percent of those by family members (Finkelhor et al., 1990). Sibling incest is the most common form of intrafamily sexual abuse (Finkelhor, 1980b; Kempe & Kempe, 1984). Father-daughter and stepfather-stepdaughter sexual encounters account for three-fourths of all reported cases of intrafamily child sexual abuse (Kempe & Kempe, 1984). Sexual abuse is five times more likely in reconstituted families (Finkelhor, 1980a), and 17 percent of adult women raised by a stepfather are sexually abused by him before age 14 (Russell, 1986). And although they are less common, father-son, mother-son, and mother-daughter abuses are being reported in increasing numbers (Chasnoff et al., 1986).

Course

Intrafamily child sexual abuse usually begins gradually and increases in frequency, duration, and severity of abuse for a number of years. Children are most at risk between the ages of 10 to 14 (Finkelhor, 1980a). The abuse typically will continue until the child discloses it to a person outside the family, is able to stop it herself, or is old enough to leave home. In some cases, the abuse ends when the child reaches another childhood "generation" (e.g., he or she was abused in prepubescence but it ends when she reaches adolescence).

Complications and Consequences

Common later complications include marital problems, divorce, suicide attempts, eating disorders, running away, problems in school, adolescent promiscuity and other acting-out behaviors, and/or becoming sexually abusive and perpetuating the cycle.

Differential Diagnosis

If the sexual abuse has occurred without any concomitant family involvement (e.g., there is no denial of facts, awareness, responsibility, or impact by other family members), or if there is evidence that the abusing adult is primarily or exclusively sexually aroused by children, then a diagnosis of Pedophilia, incestuous type, would be more appropriate, or may be an additional individual diagnosis for the abusing family member.

Diagnostic Criteria: Intrafamily Child Sexual Abuse

At any time one or both parents, an extended family member, or sibling who is from at least one childhood generation above engaged in sexual behavior with one or more children in the family in at least one of the following ways:

1. Had vaginal, oral, or anal intercourse with the child or adolescent.
2. In any way made the child or adolescent engage in oral or manual sexual stimulation.
3. Fondled, caressed, or kissed the child or adolescent with a sexual intent and/or it was perceived by the child to have a sexual intent.
4. Encouraged the child or adolescent to masturbate in front of the adult, or the adult masturbated in front of the child.
5. Encouraged the child or adolescent to engage in any sexual behaviors with another person, whether a child or adult.
6. Purposely exposed the child or adolescent to erotic or pornographic materials.
7. Forced the child to bathe or shower with them, another adult, or a sibling from a different age generation.
8. Purposely walked nude in front of the child or exposed his or her genitals to the child with the intention of arousing the child and/or against the child's wishes.
9. Engaged in voyeuristic behavior with the child as the object.

TREATMENT CONSIDERATIONS

Historically, intrafamily child sexual abuse has been treated with primarily individually oriented psychotherapy, often with each member of the family receiving therapy from a different clinician. Given this review of intrafamily child sexual abuse as a relational diagnosis, it would certainly seem that it would be appropriate to treat incestuously abusing families using a relational treatment model. Indeed many now are calling for systemically oriented therapy (Babins-Wagner, 1991; Fish & Faynik, 1989; Madonna & Berkovitz, 1990; Regina & LeBoy, 1991; Silovsky & Hembree-Kigin, 1994; Trepper & Barrett, 1989).

A number of systemic models have been proposed and are being used by family-therapy trained clinicians (Babins-Wagner, 1991; Furniss, 1987; Gelinas, 1988; Giarretto, 1978; McCarthy, 1990; Orenchuk-Tomiuk, Matthey, & Christiansen, 1990; Ribordy, 1989; Trepper & Barrett, 1989). While each model is somewhat different, there are some common characteristics. Most models: (1) are integrated from a variety of formal family and individual therapy schools; (2) use multiple methods of intervention, including family, individual, couple, and group therapy; (3) are ecosystemic in that they demand inclusion of all involved external systems in the treatment, such as protective services and legal, judicial, and school systems.

What separates these programs most from traditional social service interventions is the heavy emphasis on family therapy as part of the multiple-systems therapy. The family therapy component usually includes the following:

1. Extensive restructuring of the family unit so that intergenerational boundaries are strengthened and maintained.
2. Encouraging a more egalitarian style and reducing the commonly extreme hierarchical differences among family members.
3. Reducing intrafamily enmeshment and isolation while encouraging independence and privacy.

4. Improving communication among family members and especially reducing secrecy.

5. Marital relationship enrichment, including sex therapy if needed.

6. Helping family members increase their general coping mechanisms.

7. Inculcating respect for the taboo against incest and fostering awareness of the damage it causes to all involved.

Although few empirical outcome studies on systemically based treatment models for intrafamily child sexual abuse exist, what has been done has offered promise (Silovsky & Hembree-Kigin, 1994). General empirical evaluations have found extremely low recidivism rates after treatment (Giarretto, 1978; Trepper & Barrett, 1989; Trepper & Traicoff, 1985). While these program evaluations have been positive, further research using controlled clinical trials is needed to better evaluate the effectiveness of these programs.

REFERENCES

Abel, G. G., Becker, J. V., Cunningham, S., Rathner, J., Mittleman, M. S., & Rouleau, J. L. (1988). Multiple paraphilic diagnoses among sex offenders. *Bulletin of the American Academy of Psychiatry and the Law, 16,* 153–168.

Alexander, P. C. (1985). A systems theory conceptualization of incest. *Family Process, 24,* 79–88.

Alexander, P. C., & Lupfer, S. L. (1987). Family characteristics and long-term consequences associated with sexual abuse. *Archives of Sexual Behavior, 16,* 235–245.

Alter-Reid, K., et al. (1986). Sexual abuse of children: A review of the empirical findings. *Clinical Psychology Review, 6,* 249–266.

American Psychiatric Association (APA). (1994). *Diagnostic and statistical manual of mental disorders* (4th ed.). Washington, DC: Author.

Anderson, C. M., & Shafer, G. (1979). The character-disordered family: A community treatment model for family sexual abuse. *American Journal of Orthopsychiatry, 49,* 436–445.

Babins-Wagner, R. (1991). Development and evaluation of a family systems approach to the treatment of child sexual abuse. *Journal of Child and Youth Care, Fall,* 103–128.

Barrett, M. J., & Trepper, T. S. (1992a). Treating drug-dependent women who were also victims of childhood sexual abuse. *Journal of Feminist Family Therapy, 3,* 127–146.

Barrett, M. J., & Trepper, T. S. (1992b). Treatment of denial in families where there is child sexual abuse. In C. LeCroy (Ed.), *Case studies in social work,* (pp. 57–68). Belmont, CA: Wadsworth Publishing Co.

Barrett, M. J., & Trepper, T. S. (1992c). Unmasking the incestuous family. *Family Therapy Networker, 16,* 39–46.

Barrett, M. J., Sykes, C., & Byrnes, W. (1986). A systemic model for the treatment of intrafamily child sexual abuse. *Journal of Psychotherapy and the Family, 2,* 67–82.

Brown, G. R., & Anderson, B. (1991). Psychiatric morbidity in adult inpatients with childhood histories of sexual and physical abuse. *American Journal of Psychiatry, 148,* 55–61.

Cahill, C., Llewelyn, S. P., & Pearson, C. (1991). Long-term effects of sexual abuse which occurred in childhood: A review. *British Journal of Clinical Psychology, 30,* 117–130.

Chasnoff, I. J., Burns, J., Schnoll, S. H., Burns, K., Chisum, G., & Kyle-Spore, L. (1986). Maternal-neonatal incest. *American Journal of Orthopsychiatry, 56,* 577–580.

Chu, J. A., & Dill, D. L. (1990). Dissociative symptoms in relation to childhood physical and sexual abuse. *American Journal of Psychiatry, 147,* 887–892.

Carson, D. K., Gertz, L. M., & Donaldson, M. A. (1991). Intrafamily sexual abuse: Family-of-origin and family-of-procreation characteristics of female adult victims. *Journal of Psychology, 125,* 579–597.

Dadds, M., Smith, M., Webber, Y., & Robinson, A. (1991). An exploration of family and individual profiles following father-daughter incest. *Child Abuse and Neglect, 15,* 575–586.

de Chesnay, M., Marshall, E., & Clements, C. (1988). Family structure, marital power, maternal distance, and paternal alcohol consumption in father-daughter incest. *Family Systems Medicine, 6,* 453–462.

Dietz, C. A., & Craft, J. L. (1980). Family dynamics of incest: A new perspective. *Social Casework, 61,* 602–609.

Doe, T. (1990). Towards an understanding: An ecological model of abuse. Special issue: Abuse. *Developmental Disabilities Bulletin, 18,* 13–20.

Faller, K. C. (1989). Why sexual abuse? An exploration of the intergenerational hypothesis. *Child Abuse and Neglect, 13,* 543–548.

Faller, K. C. (1991). Polyincestuous families: An exploratory study. *Journal of Interpersonal Violence, 6,* 310–322.

Finkelhor, D. (1978). Psychological, cultural, and structural factors in incest and family sexual abuse. *Journal of Marriage and Family Counseling, 4,* 45–50.

Finkelhor, D. (1980a). Risk factors in the sexual victimization of children. *Child Abuse and Neglect, 4,* 265–273.

Finkelhor, D. (1980b). Sex among siblings: A survey report on its prevalence, variety, and effects. *Archives of Sexual Behavior, 9,* 171–194.

Finkelhor, D., & Hotaling, G. T. (1986). Sexual abuse in the National Incidence Study of Child Abuse and Neglect: An appraisal. *Child Abuse and Neglect, 8,* 22–33.

Finkelhor, D., Hotaling, G. T., Lewis, I. A., & Smith, C. (1990). Sexual abuse in a national survey of adult men and women: Prevalence, characteristics, and risk factors. *Child Abuse and Neglect, 14,* 19–28.

Fish, V., & Faynik, C. (1989). Treatment of incest families with the father temporarily removed: A structural approach. *Journal of Strategic and Systemic Therapies, 8,* 53–63.

Furniss, T. (1987). An integrated treatment approach to child sexual abuse in the family. *Children and Society, 2,* 123–135.

Gelinas, D. J. (1988). Family therapy: Critical early structuring. In S. M. Sgroi (Ed.), *Vulnerable populations: Evaluation and treatment of sexually abused children and adult survivors* (pp. 51–76). Lexington, MA: Lexington Books.

Giaretto, H. (1978). Humanistic treatment of father-daughter incest. *Journal of Humanistic Psychology, 18,* 17–21.

Gordon, M. (1989). The family environment of sexual abuse: A comparison of natal and stepfather abuse. *Child Abuse and Neglect, 13,* 121–130.

Harter, S., Alexander, P. C., & Neimeyer, R. A. (1988). Long-term effects of incestuous child abuse in college women: Social adjustment, social cognition and family characteristics. *Journal of Consulting and Clinical Psychology, 56,* 5–8.

Hoagwood, K., & Stewart, J. M. (1989). Sexually abused children's perception of family functioning. *Child and Adolescent Social Work Journal, 6,* 139–149.

Jones, W. P., & Emerson, S. (1994). Sexual abuse and binge eating in a nonclinical population. *Journal of Sex Education and Therapy, 20,* 47–55.

Justice, B., & Justice, R. (1979). *The broken taboo: Sex in the family.* New York: Human Sciences Press.

Kaslow, F. W., Haupt, D., Arce, A. A., & Werblowsky, J. (1981). Homosexual incest. *Psychiatric Quarterly, 53,* 184–193.

Kaufman, J., & Zigler, E. (1987). Do abused children become abusive parents? *American Journal of Orthopsychiatry, 57,* 186–191.

Kempe, R. S., & Kempe, C. H. (1984). *The common secret: Sexual abuse of children and adolescents.* New York: W. H. Freeman & Co.

Kirschner, S., Kirschner, D. A., & Rappaport, R. L. (1993). *Working with adult incest survivors.* New York: Brunner/Mazel.

Larson, N. R., & Maddock, J. W. (1986). Structural and functional variables in incest family systems. In T. S. Trepper & M. J. Barrett (Eds.), *Treating incest: A multiple systems perspective* (pp. 27–44). New York: Haworth.

Levang, C. A. (1989). Father-daughter incest families: A theoretical perspective from balance theory and GST. *Contemporary Family Therapy: An International Journal, 11,* 28–44.

Madonna, J. M., & Berkovitz, T. (1990). Prescribing the system: An example of paradox in incest treatment. *Journal of Family Psychotherapy, 1,* 39–50.

Madonna, P. G., Van Scoyk, S., & Jones, D. P. (1991). Family interactions within incest and nonincest families. *American Journal of Psychiatry, 148,* 46–49.

Marshall, W. L., & Eccles, A. (1991). Issues in clinical practice with sex offenders. *Journal of Interpersonal Violence, 6,* 68–93.

McCarthy, B. W. (1990). Treatment of incest families: A cognitive-behavioral model. *Journal of Sex Education and Therapy, 16,* 101–114.

McLeer, S. V., Deblinger, E., Atkins, M. S., Foa, E. B., et al. (1987). Post-traumatic stress disorder in sexually abused children. *Journal of the American Academy of Child and Adolescent Psychiatry, 27,* 650–654.

Meiselman, K. C. (1978). *Incest: A psychological study of causes and effects with treatment recommendations.* San Francisco: Jossey-Bass.

Olson, D. H., Russell, C. S., & Sprenkle, D. H. (1983). Circumplex model of marital and family systems: VI. Theoretical update. *Family Process, 22,* 69–83.

Orenchuk-Tomiuk, N., Matthey, G., & Christiansen, C. P. (1990). The resolution model: A comprehensive treatment framework in sexual abuse. *Child Welfare, 69,* 417–431.

Parker, H., & Parker, S. (1986). Father-daughter sexual abuse: An emerging perspective. *American Journal of Orthopsychiatry, 56,* 531–549.

Parker, S., & Parker, H. (1991). Female victims of child sexual abuse: Adult adjustment. *Journal of Family Violence, 6,* 183–197.

Pelletier, G., & Handy, L. C. (1986). Family dysfunction and the psychological impact of child sexual abuse. *Canadian Journal of Psychiatry, 31,* 407–412.

Ray, K. C., Jackson, J. L., & Townsley, R. M. (1991). Family environments of victims of intrafamily and extrafamily child sexual abuse. *Journal of Family Violence, 6,* 365–374.

Regina, W. F., & LeBoy, S. (1991). Incest families: Integrating theory and practice. *Family Dynamics of Addictions Quarterly, 1,* 21–30.

Ribordy, S. C. (1989). Treating child sexual abuse from a systemic perspective. *Journal of Psychotherapy and the Family, 6,* 71–88.

Russell, D. E. H. (1983). The incidence and prevalence of intrafamily and extrafamily sexual abuse of female children. *Child Abuse and Neglect, 7,* 133–146.

Russell, D. E. H. (1984). The prevalence and seriousness of incestuous abuse: Step-fathers vs. biological fathers. *Child Abuse and Neglect, 8,* 15–22.

Russell, D. E. H. (1986). *The secret trauma: Incest in the lives of girls and women.* New York: Basic Books.

Silovsky, J. F., & Hembree-Kigin, T. L. (1994). Family and group treatment for sexually abused children: A review. *Journal of Child Sexual Abuse 3,* 1–20.

Sirles, E. A., Smith, J. A., & Kausama, H. (1989). Psychiatric status of intrafamilial child sexual abuse victims. *Journal of the American Academy of Child and Adolescent Psychiatry, 28,* 225–229.

Stevens, G. D. (1992). Family characteristics of incest victims. *TCA Journal, 20,* 19–31.

Tierney, K. J., & Corwin, D. L. (1983). Exploring intrafamily child sexual abuse: A systems approach. In D. Finkelhor et al. (Eds.), *The dark side of families* (pp. 101–127). Beverly Hills, CA: Sage.

Trepper, T. S., & Barrett, M. J. (1986). Vulnerability to incest: A framework for assessment. *Journal of Psychotherapy and the Family, 2,* 13–25.

Trepper, T. S., & Barrett, M. J. (1989). *Systemic treatment of incest: A therapeutic handbook.* New York: Brunner/Mazel.

Trepper, T. S., Niedner, D., Mika, L., & Barrett, M. J. (1995). *Family characteristics of intact sexually abusing families: An exploratory study.* Manuscript submitted for publication.

Trepper, T. S., & Sprenkle, D. H. (1988). The clinical use of the circumplex model in the assessment and treatment of intrafamily child sexual abuse. *Journal of Psychotherapy and the Family, 4,* 93–111.

Trepper, T. S., & Traicoff, E. M. (1985). Treatment of intrafamily sexuality: Conceptual rationale and model for family therapy. *Journal of Sex Education and Therapy, 11,* 18–23.

Waller, G. (1993). Association of sexual abuse and borderline personality disorder in eating disordered women. *International Journal of Eating Disorders, 13,* 259–263.

Wolin, S. J., & Wolin, S. (1993). *The resilient self: How survivors of troubled families rise above adversity.* New York: Villard Books.

Wyatt, G. E. (1991). Child sexual abuse and its effects on sexual functioning. *Annual Review of Sex Research, 2,* 249–266.

Yama, M. F., Tovey, S. L., & Fogas, B. S. (1993). Childhood family environment and sexual abuse as predictors of anxiety and depression in adult women. *American Journal of Orthopsychiatry, 63,* 136–141.

CHAPTER 26

Relational Components of the Incest Survivor Syndrome

SAM KIRSCHNER, PhD and DIANA A. KIRSCHNER, PhD

According to Russell's landmark study (1986), a substantial percentage of the female population, as high as one in five, has been subjected to an incestuous experience at some point in childhood. Most of these victims have been sexually abused before the age of 14 years. Other studies, most notably one by Porter (1986), have claimed that one boy out of six will have been sexually victimized by the age of 16, although the incidence for incest has not been established.

Because incest occurs during childhood, the victim is especially vulnerable to being traumatized for life. An increasing number of investigators have concluded that the victim's later maturation and development will be adversely affected. Browne and Finkelhor (1986) have reported that about 40 percent of all survivors of child sexual abuse end up requiring psychotherapy in adulthood.

There is also an emerging awareness among clinicians in both inpatient and outpatient settings that a substantial number of their clients are incest survivors. Studies have found that between 25 and 44 percent of all outpatients are survivors (Briere, 1984; Rosenfeld, 1979; Spencer, 1978; Westermeyer, 1978). Similar results were obtained by Emslie and Rosenfeld (1983) in their study of hospitalized children and adolescents. They found that 37.5 percent of all nonschizophrenic girls and around 8 percent of the boys had been incestuously victimized.

It has become increasingly clear that a host of symptoms is generally related to the complex of experiences surrounding the incest. These symptoms include: low self-esteem; anxiety disorders and chronic depression; eating disorders; drug and alcohol abuse; borderline personality disorder; sexual dysfunction; and abusive marital and/or incestuous relations in the family of creation. We have tried to classify the most common problems brought into therapy by survivors into four areas: interpersonal, cognitive, emotional, and physical/somatic. While other classifications are possible, we have attempted to simplify the task here by presenting those issues that most often motivate incest victims to seek psychotherapy.

While survivors do not have to present with serious psychopathology in all four areas, they often will fall on a continuum of moderate to high dysfunction in all categories. This nexus of problems from the four areas and their interaction effects form the incest survivor syndrome.

Incest in and of itself is a relational disorder, a breakdown of normal family functioning. In its wake, the survivor is left with a host of relational problems. This chapter focuses on findings from research and clinical studies that describe survivors' devastating interpersonal difficulties. These relational problems include fear of intimacy or commitment in love relationships, domestic violence or incest in the family of creation, hypervigilance and anxiety in parenting, and sexual dysfunction.

The next section of the chapter outlines some of the interlocking cognitive, emotional, and physical/somatic symptoms that are common to this clinical population. The third section addresses some assessment issues and delineates formal diagnostic criteria for the incest survivor syndrome. These criteria include both individual and interpersonal problems common to survivors.

The last section presents treatment considerations with a focus on the use of integrated individual, marital, and family therapy as the treatment of choice for survivors in committed relationships. It includes the therapy outcome research that supports this treatment approach to deal with the anxiety and depressive disorders that often bring survivors into treatment.

INTERPERSONAL ISSUES

Survivors often come to therapy with interpersonal issues as their primary concern. Numerous studies have shown that female survivors, in comparison with survivor controls, are severely conflict-laden, experience rage and ongoing hostility to both their parents, and hold all women in contempt. Courtois's data (1979) indicated that 79 percent of her female sample reported moderate to severe problems relating to men. Against this backdrop it is understandable that a substantial percentage of these women are unable to commit to an intimate relationship. Three studies have corroborated that female survivors were less likely to get married than nonsurvivors (Courtois, 1979; Meiselman, 1978; Russell, 1986). The data in these studies ranges from a high of 40 percent to a low of 30 percent of the women never having been married.

The most pervasive problems faced by survivors in relationships are around issues of intimacy. Lundberg-Love, Crawford, and Geffner's data (1987) showed that 89 percent reported an inability to trust people, while 86 percent had difficulties dealing with close relationships. Meiselman's study (1978), comparing female survivors with a group of controls, showed that 64 percent of survivors reported conflict and fear with spouses and lovers as compared with 40 percent of the controls. Many survivors also become victims of domestic violence in their families of creation, especially if they had been physically abused in childhood.

Because of their lack of trust and the accompanying feelings of fear and anger, survivors have severe difficulties in allowing significant others, especially partners, to nurture or give to them. They will either rigidly maintain the caretaking role in the relationship or distance themselves. Often they will complain, especially in couple's work, that their partner does not attend to them, but, when the therapist intervenes to rectify the situation, the survivor tends not to cooperate. The survivor's inability to be in the cared-for role stems from both a fear of being dependent and the terror of being hurt again.

Another factor that contributes to the dynamics of rigid roles in the couple is the survivor's basic belief that she or he is unlovable and not worthy of being cared for. Thus, survivors often choose someone who is not very loving and who also perceives them as unworthy of being treated well. While that belief system persists, transactional work with the couple will not be successful.

Survivors who are able to marry and have children often experience severe anxieties in relation to their children. They will play out their fears of being abused by being hypervigilant over their children's safety, both in going to or coming home from school, fears about strangers hurting them, and about their safety after being put to sleep. Survivors often become highly anxious about their spouses or partners becoming perpetrators either because they have chosen a potential or actual perpetrator or because they have generalized their fears to include all men. About 30 percent of all survivors actually re-create the family drama in which their own children are victims of incest (Kaufman & Zigler, 1987).

Some survivors do present with children in treatment who have been either physically or sexually abused. These children, in turn, often are referred because of school truancy, serious acting out in school, or by the police.

Another serious consequence of incest is sexual revictimization. The study by Lundberg-Love and coworkers (1987) found that 50 percent of their sample had been sexually revictimized. Other studies also have concluded that survivors are at serious risk to be raped or to be victimized in nonconsenting sexual experiences. For example, in Russell's study (1986), 68 percent of the survivors had been victims of either rape or attempted rape. Revictimization often brings survivors into treatment as they seek to understand why they are always being hurt.

In the past 15 years, a number of clinically based studies have corroborated what clinicians have seen in their consulting rooms: the devastating consequences of incest on later adult sexual functioning (Briere, 1984; Herman, 1981; Lundberg-Love, 1990; Meiselman, 1978). These studies have shown that as many as 87 percent of women studied reported sexual problems. Studies using nonclinical samples also reveal that survivors as young as college age score significantly lower on a measure of sexual self-esteem than controls (Finklehor, 1979). Courtois (1979) indicated that up to 80 percent of nonpatient survivors reported sexual difficulties.

We have found it useful, following Sprei and Courtois (1988), to classify six types of sexual dysfunction that often are given by survivors as reasons for entering either individual or couple's therapy. These are: desire disorders, arousal disorders, orgasmic disorders, coital pain, frequency and satisfaction difficulties, and qualifying information (Schorer, Friedman, Weiler, Heiman, & LoPiccolo, 1980).

In the study by Lundberg-Love and others (1987), 67 percent of female survivors experienced an aversion to sex. Briere (1984) reported that 42 percent of his sample experienced low sexual desire. These studies suggest that incest victims have been negatively conditioned to sexual activity. As with other learned responses, these behaviors can be difficult to extinguish if they are not understood in the context of the incest. Maltz and Holman (1987) have observed that since the sexual abuse probably constituted the child's first experience with sex, negative conditioning in survivors is very strong.

Kirschner, Kirschner, and Rappaport (1993) observed that arousal disorders are common to both male and female survivors and are present among both homosexuals and heterosexuals. In female survivors, arousal problems manifest themselves as lubrication difficulties, including no lubrication at all. If intercourse is then attempted, pain is sure to follow. Many couples (or individuals) who present in sex therapy with this problem are usually unaware of the symptom's connection with an incest history.

Orgasmic disorders are also common to both male and female survivors. Problems with retarded ejaculation or a total inability to achieve orgasm occur frequently among men. In women, survivors may be able to achieve orgasm only through solitary masturbation. Even manual stimulation by a spouse often will fail to bring the woman to orgasm. In many women solitary masturbation may be experienced as the only safe way to enjoy sexual activity (Courtois, 1988).

Survivors often are referred by their internists or gynecologists because of severe coital pain, vaginismus, or dyspareunia (Courtois, 1988; Kirschner, Kirschner, & Rappaport, 1993). These symptoms can prevent the couple from having sex even though the survivor may very much want to do so. It is not surprising then that the Lundberg-Love's study (1987) found that 56 percent of their sample reported unsatisfactory sexual relationships. But as Courtois (1988) has noted, many widely divergent patterns exist in terms of both frequency and satisfaction. Clearly, some survivors enjoy normal sexual relationships with their partners.

Qualifying information is what Courtois (1988) refers to in describing other variables that affect sexual functioning. These include flashbacks, memories, and other intrusions that are triggered by sex. Dissociation and derealization also can occur during sex; these are adaptive in the sense that the survivor is at least able to be physically present. Unfortunately, these states may preclude any sexual enjoyment for either the survivor or her or his partner.

Another sexual problem that has been written up and documented recently is that of sex addiction. Carnes (1991) has reported that 81 percent of his sample of male and female sex addicts were sexually abused as children. Of these, 33 percent of the men and 42 percent of the women had been abused by their mothers or fathers. The pattern of incest leading to sex addiction and possibly to further incest has been identified only recently and requires further study.

In addition to interpersonal problems, adult incest survivors also suffer moderate to severe dysfunction in the cognitive, emotional, and physical-somatic realms. All of these individual problems tend to impact on survivor's relationships with significant others.

COGNITIVE PROBLEMS

The most pervasive difficulty with which survivors struggle are issues in self-esteem and self-concept. Poor self-esteem and self-references that are chronically negative are commonly reported. Survivors also believe that they are inherently "bad" because there is something fundamentally wrong with them. Two separate studies, one by Herman (1981) and one by Lundberg-Love (1990), reported that nearly 100 percent of their female survivors felt stigmatized, damaged, and/or irreparably branded.

Survivors also share a predominant belief that they are unlovable. Whether this faulty belief stems from feelings of guilt or self-blame over the incest is unclear. Nevertheless, as a group, survivors, despite evidence to the contrary from spouses, lovers, children, and therapists, continue to persist in their belief that they are unlovable and bad.

Survivors also may suffer from learning difficulties and poor attention spans. These disabilities often begin in childhood or early adolescence when the abuse is taking place. As adults, the cognitive problems may manifest as gaps in memories, childhood amnesia, thought disorders, or enduring concentration and learning difficulties.

Several studies have validated the clinical observation that most survivors suffer from some degree of dissociative disorder. Browne and Finklehor's excellent review of the literature (1986) concluded that dissociation is a long-term consequence of incest.

Briere (1984) reported that 41 percent of his sample experienced dissociation, 33 percent derealization, and 21 percent had out-of-body experiences. Lundberg-Love, Crawford, and Geffner's study of survivors (1987) found that 61 percent of their sample exhibited dissociative symptoms.

Another manifestation of the dissociative disorder is a form of psychological splitting. The survivor develops two distinct aspects of self-representation, a "good me" and a "bad me." In certain cases, the "good me" will overcompensate for the shameful existence of the "bad me" through overachievement and/or perfectionism. In its extreme form, the splitting process may result in Multiple Personality Disorder, that is, the birth of a host of distinct personalities of various ages and different genders. Putnam (1989) found that about 85 percent of patients with the diagnosis of Multiple Personality Disorder had a history of sexual abuse.

EMOTIONAL PROBLEMS

Survivors often come to therapy with symptoms of anxiety and depression (Briere & Runtz, 1985). Nightmares, night terrors, insomnia, and fears of sleeping alone are typical symptoms. Nightmares and night terrors usually are recurrent in nature with basic themes of being chased, hunted, captured, or suffocated. Survivors who are also parents may have fears of being alone at night as well as manifest extreme vigilance over the children when they are sleeping.

Some survivors present with fears of losing their loved ones, especially their partners. Others will report that they are afraid of being killed or annihilated even in situations where there is no imminent danger. These fears often are expressed as having arisen in night terrors or nightmares. Those clients who are torn between fears of abandonment and annihilation often will present as lethargic, depressed, and almost paralyzed.

According to a study by Briere and Runtz (1986), survivors are much more likely to consider or attempt suicide. They are also much more prone to self-mutilating behaviors using cigarettes or razor blades. These activities reflect the underlying depression and lack of a desire to live that are characteristic of this population.

Still another category of emotional reaction to the incest is a persistent and pervasive feeling of shame (Fossum & Mason, 1986). Survivors often will report feelings of wanting to hide from the world or that they do not deserve to live. Other survivors suffer from chronic guilt over almost anything, especially enjoyment. Their children's successes, spending money, or pleasure over eating are sources of or triggers to experiences of guilt. These feelings come out early in treatment and are not repressed or even suppressed as they are with many other types of clients.

PHYSICAL/SOMATIC DISORDERS

Survivors also will complain of many physical disorders. Common symptoms are gastrointestinal disorders, chronic tension, migraines, insomnia, chronic itching or pain in the vaginal area, and nausea (Lundberg-Love, Crawford, & Gefford, 1987; Sedney & Brooks, 1984; Walker et al., 1988). Unlike some writers who see these as psychosomatic complaints or as conversion symptoms (e.g., Courtois, 1988), we prefer to view the disorders as physical reactions to extreme stress in the same way we view ulcers.

Two other types of serious physical problems often bring survivors into treatment: eating disorders and drug or alcohol abuse. For example, Lundberg-Love and coauthors (1987) found that 53 percent of their sample suffered from eating disorders, while Cornelius (1991) reported that 61 percent of the women treated at the Renfrew Center, (a center for treating eating disorders) had been sexually abused as children.

Many clinicians, including Courtois (1988), have confirmed our clinical experience that incest often occurs in the context of an alcoholic family. Virkkunen (1974) and Meiselman (1978) found that up to 50 percent of incest fathers could be considered alcoholic. As children of alcoholics, survivors are at great risk of becoming chemically dependent. As many as four out of ten survivors abuse or have abused drugs and/or alcohol. Lundberg-Love and associates (1987) found that 42 percent of their sample were substance abusers, and this group tended to abuse more than one type of substance. Similarly, Briere (1984) found that 27 percent of his female survivors had a history of alcoholism and 21 percent, a history of drug abuse as compared with 11 percent and 2 percent nonsurvivors, respectively. Herman's study (1981) of incest victims reported that 35 percent abused drugs and alcohol.

We also have seen a substantial minority of family cases in which the husbands are survivors of sexual abuse and are themselves both perpetrators and alcoholics. In some of these cases, the spouse also may be a survivor who is not an abuser herself but functions as a codependent partner. In many instances, this entire pattern of the weak and codependent woman and the alcoholic man who abuses their daughter may represent the intergenerational transmission of alcoholism, codependency, and sexual abuse. Two different reports of male perpetrators (Kaufman & Zigler, 1987; Pelto, 1981) have shown that between 30 to 50 percent of them were either sexually abused or witnessed incest between their fathers and sisters.

Etiological Considerations

The specific relationship between early traumas and the later development of psychopathology in survivors continues to be investigated (Lundberg-Love, 1990; Nash, Sexton, Haralson, & Lambert, 1993; Rieker & Carmen, 1986; Weaver & Clum, 1993). Nevertheless, an emerging body of research is confirming that survivors appear to be a distinct clinical population (Lundberg-Love, Marmion, Ford, Geffner, & Peacock, 1992; Nash et al., 1993). These studies have shown that survivors of child sexual abuse can be distinguished from clinical nonsurvivor populations on the Minnesota Multiphasic Personality Inventory (MMPI).

On the other hand, some researchers are challenging the belief that it is simply child sexual abuse that causes later psychopathology. Sexual abuse occurs in the context of highly dysfunctional family dynamics. Several authors, including Follette, Alexander, and Follette (1991) and Harter, Alexander, and Neimeyer (1988), have urged researchers to consider *all* the variables that may impact on the pathogenic consequences of sexual abuse, including social and economic factors as well as family of origin dynamics. In their view, the long-term sequelae of childhood sexual abuse are mediated in part by the context in which the abuse has occurred. Indeed, Nash and coworkers (1993) found that sexual abuse by itself is *not* associated with psychological distress independent of the effects of perceived family environment. The family-of-origin dysfunction, therefore, may be as responsible for survivors' lingering interpersonal, cognitive, emotional, and physical/somatic symptomatology as the abuse itself.

ASSESSMENT ISSUES

The concept of the *incest survivor syndrome* has been developed as a useful guide to clinicians who work with victims of incest. In our experience, survivors who come for treatment suffer dysfunction in every major aspect of their lives. Even those patients who may have successful careers are apt to be unable to enjoy that success and/or live in tremendous fear of abandonment or annihilation. This group of survivors, in particular, often will ask how it is possible that events which occurred so many years ago could so profoundly influence them today. How, then, can we understand the onset and intractability of the syndrome and its apparent relationship to the incest trauma?

As we discussed earlier, survivors have been subject to extreme conditions of stress. As children, they grew up in families in which they could not exert control over their parents' behavior, especially the perpetrators', or ultimately over their own boundaries and space. Some survivors lived in unpredictable conditions, not knowing when they would be violated next or if they or others would be beaten. Calof (1987) has described these unpredictable conditions as reflecting intermittent reinforcement in which the child is loved one day and abused the next, under similar contingencies. As a consequence, many survivors lived in fear and developed the condition of "learned helplessness."

Indeed, Seligman's experiments shed light on the stressful conditions under which abused children live and their subsequent reactions to those stressors. Seligman (1975) created an experimental situation in which dogs were trained to avoid being shocked by learning to jump from one compartment to the next. Then he raised an impenetrable barrier that made it impossible for the dogs to jump and hence avoid the electric shock. Over time he observed that the dogs exhibited increased passivity, decreased performance, isolation, and an apparent loss of motivation. Garber and Seligman (1980) observed that even when the painful shock was absent, neither the passage of time nor reexposure to the same situation seemed to ameliorate the helplessness or the depression.

When we compare Seligman's experimental conditions with those endured by many abused children, we can see the similarities: The subjects are trapped, have no control over the situation, and are powerless to stop their oppressors. Seligman's observations of the lab animals' behavior also have several important commonalities with the reports of adult incest survivors: persistent and enduring feelings of intense fear, helplessness, and dysphoria.

Survivors' reactions to the trauma meet the criteria set forth in DSM-IV (APA, 1994) for Post-Traumatic Stress Disorder (PTSD). As indicated earlier, research has shown that survivors suffer from flashbacks and recollections of the trauma, and may have: numbing of affect; feelings of isolation or detachment; dissociative disorders or psychogenic amnesia; hypervigilance; difficulties falling asleep; and symptoms of anxiety and depression. All of these symptoms are part of the criteria for PTSD in DSM-IV. In sum, there can be little doubt that the extremely stressful situations surrounding the incest (including the familial control, denial, and enforced silence) create intolerable psychological conditions for the victim. Over time, these conditions give rise to the reactions that typify the incest survivor syndrome.

Briere (1984) has called for a diagnosis of post-sexual abuse syndrome, and Courtois (1988) has argued convincingly that PTSD should be used as the principal Axis I diagnosis or as a secondary diagnosis to survivors' other symptoms. (See Courtois's excellent review of the literature on PTSD and the incest trauma.) We also believe that the evidence is compelling for considering a PTSD diagnosis alongside the diagnosis for one or more of the client's other symptoms. For incest survivors, we suggest the PTSD diagnosis of "incest survivor syndrome."

It is important for practitioners to consider a dual diagnosis when treating clients who are incest survivors and who present with other symptomatology too. Contemplating a dual diagnosis will remind both the clinician and the client (or client family) that the presenting difficulties are responses to and legacies of an intolerable situation. And normalizing the client's symptoms and depathologizing the survivor are integral parts of a successful treatment plan. The dual diagnosis view, then, helps to facilitate the normalizing process for all treatment participants including the therapist.

Diagnostic Criteria for the Incest Survivor Syndrome

Following the work of Courtois (1988), Ellenson (1985, 1986) and Lundberg-Love (1990), we have suggested the following criteria for the incest survivor syndrome: The person has experienced a sexualized event or series of events in childhood or adolescence that occurred in interaction with family members who are adult(s) or older child(ren); this experience falls outside the range of normal physical contact, caretaking, and/or exploration. This sexual abuse includes incestuous events involving parents, older siblings, stepparents, or other members of the extended family. The trauma may include threats to the child's life or physical integrity and may be accompanied by physical violence, rape, or torture. The sexual abuse is committed by someone who is older, has more authority, and/or has some coercive power over the victim.

A. The sexual abuse is reexperienced in at least *one* of the following ways:
    1. Recurrent and intrusive distressing recollections of the abuse either before, during, or after sexual contact.
    2. Recurrent distressing nightmares in which the person, his or her children, or family members are hurt or killed.
    3. Recurring illusions of an intruder or malevolent person in the house.
    4. Recurring visual, auditory, or olfactory hallucinations that involve partial reliving of the abuse.
    5. Recurring obsessions that include impulses to harm one's child or that one's child is in danger.
    6. Dissociative episodes and flashbacks.
    7. A history of sexual revictimization.
B. The survivor also shows persistent avoidance of stimuli associated with the sexual abuse or numbing of affect and general responsiveness (not present before the sexual abuse) as indicated by at least *three* of the following:
    1. Psychogenic amnesia or an inability to recall the period of time surrounding the sexual abuse or important details of the traumatic abuse.
    2. Feelings of detachment, estrangement, or mistrust of significant others.
    3. Restricted range of affect—for example, unable to experience or express loving feelings with significant others.
    4. Numbing of sensation in genital areas and an inability to experience sexual pleasure.

5. Arousal disorders (in both men and women).
6. Orgasmic disorders (in both men and women).
7. Coital pain, vaginismus, or dyspareunia in women.
8. Avoidance of places, situations, or activities that arouse recollections of the sexual abuse.
9. In young children, regression to an earlier developmental stage or the loss of recently acquired skills (e.g., toilet training or verbal skills).

C. In addition, the survivor shows persistent symptoms of increased arousal (not present before sexual abuse) as indicated by at least *two* of the following:

1. Difficulty falling or staying asleep (insominia).
2. Unexplained agitation, irritability, or outbursts of anger.
3. Hypervigilance over his or her children's safety (e.g., separation anxiety that may manifest itself at bedtime or when the child is going or coming home from school).
4. Panic disorders, with or without agoraphobia; the fear of being alone.
5. Other phobias or avoidance behaviors.
6. Generalized anxiety disorder.
7. Self-mutilating behaviors, suicidality, and suicide attempts.

D. Duration of the disturbance (symptoms in A, B, & C) is more than one month.

Associated Features

Symptoms of depression and anxiety are common and in some instances may be sufficiently severe to be diagnosed as an Anxiety or Depressive Disorder in addition to the diagnosis for incest survivor syndrome. Survivors often describe persistent and painful feelings of shame as well as expressing guilt about pleasurable activities when most people would not. Adult survivors may have histories of eating disorders and/or substance abuse. There may be persistent physical symptoms such as chronic nausea, migraines, vaginal pain, or gastrointestinal disorders that may be diagnosed as Somatization Disorder. A diagnosis of Dissociative Disorder or Multiple Personality Disorder may also be warranted.

Age at Onset

The disorder can occur at any age, including childhood.

Course of Disorder

Some of the symptoms may begin immediately or soon after the sexual abuse. Delayed onset is also common, with symptoms developing after a latency period of months, years, or even decades following the traumatic event(s).

TREATMENT ISSUES

No single approach, be it cognitive-behavioral, psychodynamic, or family systems, can by itself deal with the multiproblem presentations of survivors. Rather, the breadth of their individual and interpersonal problems calls for a comprehensive and integrative treatment plan (Kaslow, Haupt, Arce, & Werblowsky, 1981). The plan would be considered to be technically eclectic and would include techniques from various therapeutic perspectives, organized around the goal of maximizing change (Beutler, 1989; Kaslow, 1981; Kirschner & Kirschner, 1986; Lazarus & Messer, 1991).

In this treatment schema, each of the four major problem areas presented by survivors would be addressed. For example, survivors' fears, phobias, and other cognitive distortions would require cognitive/behavioral work. The clinician might use psychodynamic, gestalt, and other emotive work in order to facilitate the memory retrieval process. The practitioner might need to treat the anxiety and depressive disorders with a course of antianxiety or antidepressant medications, along with psychodynamic techniques and anger-releasing gestalt role play. The survivors' physical/somatic complaints might call for relaxation training, biofeedback, and any necessary drug and alcohol treatment. Finally, the survivors' interpersonal problems would require couple's and family therapy targeted to help their sexual and intimate relationships with their partners, their parenting of children, and their relationships with members of the family of origin.

Additionally, since the survivor syndrome shows consistent patterns of anxiety and depression (Lundberg-Love et al., 1987; Sedney & Brooks, 1984), inclusion of the spouse/partner in the whole treatment process may be beneficial for the survivor who is in a committed relationship. There is considerable support in treatment outcome research for including the spouse in treatment for anxiety disorders (Jacobson, Holtzworth-Munroe, & Schmaling, 1989; Marten & Barlow, 1993) and depression (Jacobson et al., 1989). Barlow, O'Brien, and Last, (1984), found that including spouses in treating agoraphobics was more effective than individual therapy in terms of symptom relief and positive effect on measures of the patients' social, work, and family functioning.

Conversely, not including spouses in treating survivors may either hurt the relationship or negatively affect the partner. Hafner (1977), Milton and Hafner (1979), and others have found that successful individual therapy of married female agoraphobics is associated with deteriorating marital relations and/or the emergence of psychiatric symptoms in the husband. Coyne (1987) found similar results with married depressives who were treated individually.

Following these research findings, we have developed an integrated approach for treating incest survivors that combines cognitive-behavioral, psychodynamic, and systemic treatment modalities. For married clients or those in committed relationships, the therapy process can contain up to seven components, which may or may not occur sequentially. Each of the components may be adapted for use in briefer treatment formats. The treatment components are:

1. Individual sessions with the survivor in which traumatic memories are recovered and emotions are ventilated.

2. Joint sessions with the survivor's partner in which symptoms are reframed and normalized.

3. Individual and conjoint meetings in which cognitive restructuring, in vivo exposure, desensitization, relaxation training, and other cognitive-behavioral techniques are used to help alleviate presenting symptomatology.

4. If appropriate, preparing the survivor and partner for sessions with the family of origin through behavioral rehearsal, role playing, and assertiveness training.

5. If appropriate, family therapy sessions in which the survivor meets with the surviving parents and siblings and discusses the details of the abuse and its effects.

6. Follow-up family sessions and contacts via letter to effect reparation, forgiveness, and resolution.

7. Marital therapy sessions in which sex therapy techniques and communications skill-building training are emphasized; or, for single survivors, working on dating and building relationships.

In this approach, partners are brought in from the outset of treatment as therapeutic allies to help the survivor deal more effectively with the incest trauma. The goal of this strategy is to create a corrective transactional experience for the survivor in which two important people, spouse and therapist, are in a constructive alliance with the survivor. (See Kirschner, Kirschner, & Rappaport, 1993, for a full description of the treatment approach.)

CONCLUSION

Incest survivors often present in therapy with a variety of interpersonal difficulties, including fear of intimacy or commitment in love relationships, domestic violence or incest in the family of creation, hypervigilance in parenting, and sexual dysfunction. In addition, survivors tend to suffer from cognitive, emotional, and physical symptomatology. These problems and the interactions between them form the incest survivor syndrome. Because incest has powerful consequences on the victim, a diagnosis of incest survivor syndrome as well as a diagnosis of the presenting complaint needs to be made. A dual diagnosis will assist the clinician, the patient, and his or her family in normalizing the presenting problems and in depathologizing the survivor.

The multiplicity of survivors' problems calls for an integrative treatment approach that is technically eclectic, including, among other strategies and techniques, contextual/relational, cognitive/behavioral, psychodynamic, and family systems work. Additionally, treatment of those in committed relationships should include their spouses or partners.

REFERENCES

American Psychiatric Association (1994). *Diagnostic and statistical manual of mental disorders* (4th ed.). Washington, DC: Author.

Barlow, D. H., O'Brien, G. T., & Last, C. (1984). Couples treatment of agoraphobia. *Behavior Therapy, 15,* 41–58.

Beutler, L. E. (1989). The misplaced role of theory in psychotherapy integration. *Journal of Integrative & Eclectic Psychotherapy, 8,* 17–22.

Briere, J. (1984, April). *The effects of childhood sexual abuse on later psychological functioning: Defining a post-sexual abuse syndrome.* Presented at the third National Conference on the Sexual Victimization of Children, Washington, DC.

Briere, J., & Runtz, M. (1985, August). *Symptomatology associated with prior sexual abuse in a non-clinical sample.* Presented at the annual meeting of the American Psychological Association, Los Angeles.

Briere, J., & Runtz, M. (1986). Suicidal thoughts and behaviors in former sexual abuse victims. *Canadian Journal of Behavioral Science, 18,* 413–423.

Browne, A., & Finkelhor, D. (1986). Impact of child sexual abuse: A review of the literature. *Psychological Bulletin, 99,* 66–77.

Calof, D. (1987, March). *Treating adult survivors of incest and child abuse.* Workshop at the Family Therapy Networker Symposium, Washington, DC.

Carnes, P. (1991). *Don't call it love: Recovery from sexual addiction.* New York: Bantam.

Cornelius, C. (1991, April). PE. *Shape,* pp. 81–83.

Courtois, C. A. (1979). Characteristics of a volunteer sample of adult women who experienced incest in childhood and adolescence. *Dissertation Abstracts International, 40A,* 3194A.

Courtois, C. A. (1988). *Healing the incest wound.* New York: Norton.

Coyne, J. C. (1987). Depression, biology, marriage, and marital therapy. *Journal of Marital and Family Therapy, 13,* 393–407.

Ellenson, G. S. (1985). Detecting a history of incest: A predictive syndrome. *Social Casework, 66,* 525–532.

Ellenson, G. S. (1986). Disturbances in perception in adult female incest survivors. *Social Casework, 67,* 149–159.

Emslie, G. J., & Roenfeld, A. A. (1983). Incest reported by children and adolescents hospitalized for severe psychiatric problems. *American Journal of Psychiatry, 140,* 708–711.

Finkelhor, D. (1979). *Sexually victimized children.* New York: Free Press.

Follette, V. M., Alexander, P. C., & Follette, W. C. (1991). Individual predictors of outcome in group treatment for incest survivors. *Journal of Consulting and Clinical Psychology, 59,* 150–155.

Fossum, M. A., & Mason, M. J. (1986). *Facing shame.* New York: Norton.

Garber, J., & Seligman, M. E. D. (1980). *Human helplessness: Theory and application.* New York: Academic.

Hafner, R. J. (1977). The husbands of agoraphobic women and their influence on treatment outcome. *British Journal of Psychotherapy, 131,* 289–294.

Harter, S., Alexander, P., & Neimeyer, R. A. (1988). Long term effects of incestuous child abuse in college women: Social adjustment, social cognition, and family characteristics. *Journal of Consulting and Clinical Psychology, 56,* 5–8.

Herman, J. (1981). *Father-daughter incest.* Cambridge, MA: Harvard University.

Jacobson, N. S., Holtzworth-Munroe, A., & Schmaling, K. B. (1989). Marital therapy and spouse involvement in the treatment of depression, agoraphobia, and alcoholism. *Journal of Consulting and Clinical Psychology, 57,* 5–10.

Kaslow, F. W. (1981). A dialectic approach to family therapy and practice: Selectivity & synthesis. *Journal of Marital and Family Therapy, 7,* 345–351.

Kaslow, F., Haupt, D., Arce, A. A., & Werblowsky, J. (1981). Homosexual incest. *Psychiatric Quarterly, 53,* 184–193.

Kaufman, J., & Zigler, E. (1987). Do abused children become abusive parents? *American Journal of Orthopsychiatry, 57,* 186–191.

Kirschner, D. A., & Kirschner, S. (1986). *Comprehensive family therapy.* New York: Brunner/Mazel.

Kirschner, S., Kirschner, D. A., & Rappaport, R. (1993). *Working with adult incest survivors: The healing journey.* New York: Brunner/Mazel.

Lazarus, A. A., & Messer, S. B. (1991). Does chaos prevail? An exchange on technical eclecticism and assimilative integration. *Journal of Psychotherapy Integration, 1,* 143–158.

Lundberg-Love, P. K. (1990). Adult survivors of incest. In R. T. Ammerman & M. Hersen (Eds.), *Treatment of family violence: A sourcebook.* New York: Wiley.

Lundberg-Love, P. K., Crawford, C. M., & Geffner, R. A. (1987, October). *Characteristics and treatment of adult incest survivors.* Presented at the annual meeting of the Southwestern Psychological Association, New Orleans.

Lundberg-Love, P. K., Marmion, S., Ford, K., Geffner, R., & Peacock, L. (1992). The long-term consequences of childhood incestuous victimization upon adult women's psychological symptomatology. *Journal of Child Sexual Abuse, 1,* 81–102.

Maltz, W., & Holman, B. (1987). *Incest and sexuality.* Lexington, MA: Lexington Books.

Marten, P. A., & Barlow, D. H. (1993). Implications of clinical research for psychotherapy integration in the treatment of the anxiety disorders. *Journal of Psychotherapy Integration, 4,* 297–311.

Meiselman, K. (1978). *Incest: A psychological study of causes and effects with treatment recommendations.* San Francisco: Jossey-Bass.

Milton, F., & Hafner, R. J. (1979). The outcome of behavior therapy for agoraphobia in relation to marital adjustment. *Archives of General Psychiatry, 36,* 907–911.

Nash, M. R., Hulsey, T. L., Sexton, M. C., Haralson, T. L., & Lambert, W. (1993). Long-term sequelae of childhood sexual abuse: Perceived family environment, psychopathology, and dissociation. *Journal of Consulting and Clinical Psychology, 61,* 276–283.

Pelto, V. L. (1981). Male incest offenders and non-offenders: A comparison of early sexual history. *Dissertation Abstracts International, 42*(3-B), 1154.

Porter, E. (1986). *Treating the young male victim of sexual assault.* Syracuse, NY: Safer Society Press.

Putnam, F. (1989). *Diagnosis and treatment of multiple personality disorder.* New York: Guilford.

Rieker, P., & Carmen, E. (1986). The victim-to-patient process: The disconfirmation and transformation of abuse. *American Journal of Orthopsychiatry, 56,* 360–370.

Rosenfeld, A. A. (1979). Endogamic incest and the victim-perpetrator model. *American Journal of Diseases of Children, 133,* 406–410.

Russell, D. (1986). *The secret trauma: Incest in the lives of girls and women.* New York: Basic Books.

Schorer, L. R., Friedman, J. M., Weiler, S. J., Heiman, J. R., & LoPiccolo, J. (1980). *A multi-axial descriptive system for the sexual dysfunctions: Categories and manual.* Stony Brook, NY: Sex Therapy Center.

Sedney, M. A., & Brooks, B. (1984). Factors associated with history of childhood sexual experience in a nonclinical female population. *American Journal of Child Psychiatry, 23,* 215–218.

Seligman, M. E. D. (1975). *Helplessness: On depression, development and death.* San Francisco: Freeman.

Spencer, J. (1978). Father-daughter incest. *Child Welfare, 57,* 581–589.

Sprei, J., & Courtois, C. A. (1988). The treatment of women's sexual dysfunctions arising from sexual assault. In J. R. Field & R. A. Brown (Eds.), *Advances in the understanding and treatment of sexual problems: Compendium for the individual and marital therapist.* New York: Spectrum.

Virkkunen, M. (1974). Incest offenses and alcoholism. *Medical and Scientific Law, 14,* 124.

Walker, E., Katon, W., Harrop-Griffiths, J., Holm, L., Russo, J., & Hickok, L. (1988). Relationship of chronic pain to psychiatric diagnoses and childhood sexual abuse. *American Journal of Psychiatry, 145,* 75–80.

Weaver, T. L., & Clum, G. A. (1993). Early family environments and traumatic experiences associated with borderline personality disorder. *Journal of Consulting and Clinical Psychology, 61,* 1068–1075.

Westermeyer, J. (1978). Incest in psychiatric practice: A description of patients and incestuous relationships. *Journal of Clinical Psychiatry, 39,* 643–648.

CHAPTER 27

Dissociative Identity Disorder in Relational Contexts

WILHELMINA S. KOEDAM, PhD

Dissociative Identity Disorder (DID), (formerly multiple personality disorder (MPD)) as defined in the DSM IV (American Psychiatric Association, 1994) establishes the following criteria as necessary for the diagnosis of dissociative identity disorder:

- The presence of two or more distinct identities or personality states (each with its own relatively enduring pattern of perceiving, relating to, and thinking about the environment and self).
- At least two of these identities or personality states recurrently take control of the person's behavior.
- Inability to recall important personal information that is too extensive to be explained by ordinary forgetfulness.
- The disturbance is not due to the direct physiological effects of a substance (e.g., blackouts or chaotic behavior during alcohol intoxication) or a general medical condition (e.g., complex partial seizures). Note: In children, the symptoms are not attributable to imaginary playmates or other fantasy play (p. 230).

DID has been alluded to in religious belief systems, carvings and other artworks, and behaviors as far back in time as cave paintings. Shamanistic transformation and possession states have been illustrated in paintings or handed down in stories from one generation to the next. Between 1880 and 1920 a large number of cases of DID were reported in the United States and France. Dissociative process and DID were generally accepted and researched during this era; the writings of Janet (1890) reflect this fact.

From 1920 to 1970 there was a trend toward decreased interest in and reporting of the DID phenomena. Putnam (1989) postulates that the arrival of behaviorism, public criticism of the phenomena and research on MPD, acceptance of psychoanalytic theory, and the increased interest, popularity, and acceptance of the diagnosis of schizophrenia all contributed to this decline in interest in DID. However, Putnam reports that since the 1970s, there has been a marked increase in the diagnosis, treatment, research, and acceptance of the phenomena of DID and dissociative processes.

Although recently there has been a dramatic rise in the amount of research, and number of books, journal and popular magazines articles, and television shows about Dissociative Identity Disorder, most of the focus to date has been on the individual who manifests DID. Little information has been provided on the effect of this disorder on significant others. Therefore, this chapter focuses on the issues of DID in relational contexts. First the theoretical basis for the development, symptomology, characteristics, and demographics of Dissociative Identity Disorder are reviewed. Then relational issues in terms of breach of trust and boundary violations in significant relationships and the subsequent consequences of this breach are explored. A theoretical basis and framework for the efficacy of concurrent individual and family therapy is presented, as are treatment strategies and clinical considerations.

THEORETICAL BASIS FOR THE DEVELOPMENT OF DID

The individual who develops dissociative identities has a number of predisposing factors and unique personality characteristics. The pathological use of dissociative process as a means to protect and defend oneself psychologically in the presence of overwhelming traumas is the cornerstone of the development of DID. Childhood trauma is linked to 97 percent of all reported DID cases; 68 percent of these cases reported incidence of incest. Other types of sexual, emotional, and physical abuses are reported in the National Institute of Mental Health survey (Putnam, 1989). Additional predisposing factors reported by Braun and Sachs (1985) include an "inborn capacity to dissociate" wherein the individual has the capacity to incorporate information and keep this information in a separate cognitive structure, which often results in the same person reporting unawareness of this information. The person may be unaware of the unconscious influence of the alternate personality on his or her behavior. Additionally, the individual may have no awareness of his or her behaviors during a dissociative state. One young woman in my practice reported that she would wake up on the beach in the early hours of the morning with her clothing disheveled and "know" that her sexual alter personality had engaged in sexual behavior the night before. She also stated that she has a variety of clothing in her closet that she does not recall purchasing although the tags are still on the items. She "knows" various alter identities shopped at different times, choosing specific fashion looks to express themselves. These patients often have no recall or memory of events and statements made while in a dissociative state. One patient I worked with stated that she would often sit on the couch on a Sunday afternoon and when she would become aware of herself again it might be midnight or later. She reported no memory of events, hearing the phone ring, or using the rest room during these hours. She said that it was disconcerting when friends told her they had called a number of times and wondered where she was. She also reported having no recollection of conversations with friends during this dissociative period, although they refer to comments she apparently made during these episodes.

Other predisposing factors reported by Braun and Sachs include a good "working memory," above-average intelligence, and creativity (1985). A good "working memory" is perceived as critical, as the experiences and information the alter personalities are exposed to need to be maintained in memory in separate and distinct forms. Individuals with DID may score poorly on standardized IQ tests, as different alters may manifest themselves during the testing (i.e., a child alter may not do well on the Wechsler Adult Intelligence Scale-Revised [WAIS-R], as that alter has not been present while the adult alters are learning specific information). Braun and Sachs postulate that intelligence is the ability to adapt to one's environment. Therefore, the ability to create new and distinct personalities as a result of being exposed to intolerable anxiety, physical pain, and trauma is a clear indicator of above-average intelligence. This is especially true in light of the possibility that, under the same set of circumstances, most individuals may exhibit psychotic decompensation. The third factor Braun and Sachs highlighted is creativity. These individuals tend to be artists, poets, and composers who have the innate ability to create art as well as alter personalities to help them cope (in Kluft, 1985).

Putnam (1989) discusses the theory that all individuals are born with the potential for dissociative personalities. As a baby develops from infancy onward, he or she exhibits various states of consciousness and awareness. According to Putnam, in normal development these discrete states become personality states that transition smoothly into an integrated personality. More states develop but the transition between states seem to "smooth" out so they are no longer discrete; rather, they consolidate into an integrated personality. In addition, Putnam mentions studies that indicate that high hypnotizability evident in children allows them to dissociate more readily than adults do. Therefore, if hypnotizability is associated with the ability to dissociate to cope with stress, then it would follow that young children are more likely and can more easily access this hypnotic or dissociative state to cope with overwhelming trauma. The capacity for fantasy found in children in the form of projecting personalities on objects and situations and creating imaginary companions is a fertile ground for the creation of alternative personalities to endure the abuses the child is experiencing (Putnam, 1989). Ross (1989) lists a number of theories regarding the etiology of DID, including a psychoanalytic model; an autohypnotic model that discusses the hypnotizability factor proposed by Braun, Sachs, Putnam, and Kluft; a social learning model; neurological theories; feminist analysis; divided consciousness models; state-dependent learning; and state-of-consciousness or mood models (Braun & Sachs, 1985; Kluft, 1985; & Putnam, 1989).

The social learning model is of particular interest as it takes into account the interactions in abusive families during the formation of DID in children. Social cues, role demands, punishment, consequences, reinforcers, and denial or neglect are important factors to be considered (Ross, 1989). Ross (1989) summarizes Kluft's four-factor theory of DID:

- DID patients are good dissociators.
- They use dissociation to cope with trauma.
- The form and structure of the DID may vary depending on the individual's temperament and other nonabuse experience.
- The abuse was chronic and there was insufficient love and nurturance to heal the emotional wounds.

I would add another factor, the ego strength of the individual before the occurrence of abuse. In my clinical experience, this appears to have bearing on whether an individual will develop DID. When one sees the range of trauma evident in clinical practice and then begins to assess which individuals exhibit DID symptomology and which do not, given similar levels and amount of trauma, the factor of the individual's premorbid ego strength or the clinician's theory about it may be another predisposing factor to examine when assessing patients. Without comparing or judging the level of trauma, it is interesting to note that some patients with a long history of frequent severe abuse—emotional, sexual, or physical—may not evidence DID, given they survive the abuse. Rather, these patients present with other dysfunctional patterns—an eating disorder, major depression, borderline personality disorder, chemical dependency, and others. On the other hand, I have encountered individuals with one episode of abuse who evidence DID. Other factors, such as age of occurrence, severity of the incident, and the damage incurred, must be considered in addition to premorbid ego strength.

Inconsistent, frequent, chronic, and unpredictable exposure to traumatic abuse is a major factor in the development of DID. This abuse can take many forms, such as incest; sexual molestation by a nonfamily member; physical, verbal, and/or emotional abuse; torture; neglect; extreme poverty; witnessing extreme violence or death; ritual or cult abuse; and war experiences. The individual who has a good dissociative capacity and experiences these incredibly horrifying chronic, unpredictable, inconsistent abuses compartmentalizes these events, memories, and associations, thus creating amnestic barriers. The memories and experiences of one compartment or memory will have no "co-consciousness" of the information held in the other memory compartments, and the person therefore processes information from one memory box independently from that of the other memory boxes. As the abuse continues, these similar memory compartments may become linked so that they become related based on a specific theme. A set of behavioral responses that is uncommon for the child may be the result of the personality fragment, or alter, trying to create an adaptive response between the linked memory compartments. For example, an angry alter may act out in response to perceived threats. The host or original personality may have no awareness, understanding, or explanation for the "new" behavioral response. If the personality fragment continues to experience the same or similar traumatic environment or episodes, this personality fragment develops a "life history." This life history encompasses information and emotional responses the host personality is unaware of and is the basis for the emergence of a new personality or alter (Sachs, Frischholz, & Wood, 1988). Putnam (1989) states that dissociative states of consciousness are recognized as adaptive responses to acute trauma for the following reasons:

- They are a mechanism for escape from reality.
- Dissociative process contains the traumatic events and feelings associated with those events outside of normal consciousness.
- Detachment of the self so the trauma is experienced by someone else or a depersonalized self.
- Analgesia (p. 53).

Putnam further elaborates that in these dissociated states, there is a specific sense of self that is repeatedly reentered in order for the child to escape from the trauma or to perform certain behaviors that he or she normally would be incapable of doing, such as tolerating the incest being committed or hurting other children and animals. Consider the case of a child who was forced to participate in ritualistic cult practices with a stepfather. This child created an alter who participated in the cult rituals. She (her participatory alter) was forced to sacrifice animals and babies after being told (and believing) that her family would come to harm or death if she did not participate. Since this behavior was so foreign, intolerable, and incomprehensible to her, she created the participatory alter to perform these acts. Putnam postulates that each time the child enters these specific dissociative states, memories, emotions, and behaviors become "state-dependently bound" to that specific state, building a "life history" for that alter personality (p. 54).

Braun and Sachs (1985) discuss "perpetuating factors" contributing to the development of DID. The first perpetuating factor proposed is the "personal component," which is the use of dissociative identities to reduce and defend against stress and anxiety. As this process successfully reduces the stress and anxiety, the reinforcing nature of this coping device causes the individual to use the dissociative process as the primary form of defense. "Interpersonal factors" relate to the patient's family dynamics. The response the patient created to cope with the dysfunctional dynamics may be subject to subsequent "stimulus generalization." As the abuse continues and the individual creates an alter to cope in a specific emotional or psychological pattern with the abuse or situational variables, the host personality may respond to other similarly perceived situations by switching to that alter personality. This generalization may become so diffuse that the host personality may respond in maladaptive ways to any real or imagined stimuli. The third factor that may perpetuate the development of DID is the "situational variable," which is defined as direct exposure to trauma and/or the indirect effect of societal attitudes, pressures, and normative behavior adopted by significant others—family members or caregivers. Clinicians who seek to understand the symptomology, characteristics, and demographics of individuals who manifest DID must study the perpetuating factors contributing to the development of DID in the individual.

SYMPTOMOLOGY CHARACTERISTICS AND DEMOGRAPHICS OF DID

DSM-IV (APA, 1994) describes DID as a failure to integrate various aspects of identity, memory, and consciousness. The personality states are experienced as having a distinct personal history, self-image, and identities. These identities (alters) also may have names and characteristics that differ from the primary or host identity. These identities can take control sequentially at the expense of one another and may deny knowledge of one another or engage in open conflict. DSM-IV further describes those with DID as having frequent gaps in memory for personal history, both past and present. The passive personalities have more constricted memories while the more aggressive, controlling, or "protector" identities have more comprehensive memories. The various identities "switch" or transition due to psychological distress, and the process may take seconds, with physiological indicators manifested during the transition from one alter state to another. Putnam (1989) discusses some of the manifestations of "switching" with physical and psychological observations. Changes in posture, motor activity, body language, and facial expressions as well as voice and speech alterations and dramatic differences in dress, grooming, and makeup is quite common. While the alters are switching, a rapid fluttering of the eyelids, a facial twitch, or a grimace may be observed. In addition, body shudders or postural changes may be evident as well as reports of dizziness and severe headaches. At times the individual will go into an unresponsive or trancelike state, with a blank expression on the face. Once the switch occurs, the new personality may need time to "ground" by touching his or her face, temples, a chair or couch, looking around the room, shifting posture, or closing or covering their eyes and just communicating orally or in writing. Psychological changes are manifested by a sudden unexplained shift in affect or an apparent change in the individual's level of maturity, such as engaging in childlike gestures. The thought processes may reflect either abstract or concrete levels of understanding depending on the age of the alter. This switch can be illustrated by the case of a professional in her early 30s. She began the second session by discussing current life issues. She then began to rub her head and complain of pain in her head. Shortly thereafter she removed her eyeglasses and started in a childlike voice that she "did not wear these" (eyeglasses). She then removed her watch, earrings, and rings. She repeated this sequence of events in each subsequent session prior to her "four-year-old" coming out and beginning to work in the session. It is interesting to note that this patient did not wear glasses when she was four, nor was she permitted to wear any jewelry.

According to the DSM-IV, the highest incidence of reporting of this disorder occurs in the United States. Females are three to nine times more frequently diagnosed than males. Ross (1989) suggests that males are underreported by clinicians as they are more likely found in the penal and judicial system rather than in the clinician's office. The DSM-IV states that when females are compared to males who have been diagnosed with DID, females have an average of 15 or more identities while males have an average of eight identities (APA, 1994).

Ross (1989) identifies ten diagnostic "clues" for DID. When these diagnostic parameters occur together the diagnosis of MPD, DID is warranted. Ross states that 100 percent of patients who present with these criteria have classical MPD (DID):

- History of childhood sexual and/or physical abuse
- Female sex
- Siblings
- Age 20 to 40
- Blank spells
- Voices in the head or other Schneiderian symptoms (first-order symptoms for schizophrenia, such as hearing voices, talking, arguing, or screaming in their heads, passive influence phenomena or believing they are "made" to engage in specific behaviors)
- DSM III-R criteria for borderline personality are met or nearly met
- Previous unsuccessful treatment
- Self-destructive behavior
- No thought disorders
- Headache

Individual behavioral manifestations of DID include psychiatric, neurological, and medical symptoms. These individuals tend to receive many diagnoses in the course of their medical treatment and do not tend to respond well to standard psychiatric treatments. Putnam (1989) highlights commonly reported symptoms, such as depression and mood swings. The host personality, who generally presents for treatment, typically exhibits low self-esteem, reports feeling overwhelmed, anhedonic, and has a negative outlook toward life.

Additional difficulties include problems with concentration, fatigue, sexual dysfunction, and crying spells. Sleep disorders usually include recurring nightmares and frightening hypnogogic phenomena. Dissociative symptoms are a cornerstone in individuals who have DID. Time loss and amnesia are the most common dissociative symptoms manifested, although difficulty with recall and memory disturbance are also common. Anxiety and phobic reactions in the host personality often trigger switching to alter personalities. Substance abuse and eating disorders are found frequently in this population of patients. Hallucinatory process, which is rarely reported, appears to be experienced in the form of "voices in my head" that berate, belittle, or command the individual's thoughts or actions. Visual, olfactory, tactile, and autoscopic hallucinations also occur; these are sometimes referred to as "body memories." Putnam (1989) further suggests that DID patients do not evidence a real thought disorder but rather a phenomenon of rapid switching in which no one personality or identity is stabilizing enough to appear coherent and integrated in behavior. He proposes that rapid cycling may be the process of various alters struggling to gain executive control. Suicidal behavior is very common in DID patients, as is self-mutilation. If a DID patient becomes too overwhelmed, catatonic behavior is not uncommon.

Regarding neurological and medical symptoms patients report headaches that cannot be relieved by standard analgesics (Putnam, 1989). Seizurelike behaviors and loss of consciousness are sometimes present. Sensory and motor disturbances as well as cardiorespiratory, gastrointestinal, and bowel disorders as well as gynecological or reproductive system discomfort are often found in the medical histories of this patient population. One patient reportedly spent years seeing physicians and various specialists for treatment of unexplained numbness. No physiological finding accounted for this phenomenon. During our therapeutic work, she recovered the physiological memory that she used to "numb" her body so she would not feel what her perpetrator was doing to it while he was having incestuous relations with her.

Besides being beset by this multitude of medical symptoms and psychological difficulties, the patient with DID usually is attempting to cope within a close social structure such as family, friendships, school or work, and neighborhood settings. These social situations may cause innumerable difficulties for the individual as well as the people in his or her life. In settings outside the home, many DID patients apparently create specific identities or alters who engage in specific sets of behaviors that are appropriate to that setting; for examples, a patient may develop an attorney, secretary, or teacher alter to cope with the work setting. The patient may create an adult social alter to meet expected social demands. For example, one patient I worked with created a "Sarah" alter to represent Sarah Bernhardt so she could "act" in any social setting and no one would know that other child or adult alters were present.

The family or home setting is where the individual's alter identities are most likely to come out. The following sections highlight the issues of family members coping with these identities and their behavioral pattern.

INTERACTION PATTERNS AS A CRITICAL DYNAMIC IN THE DEVELOPMENT OF DID IN FAMILY SYSTEMS AND RELATIONSHIPS

The most painful and difficult reality that a child may have to face in his or her development is when there is a fundamental breach of trust and of emotional, physical, and sexual boundaries by a significant person in the child's life. When someone the child is raised to "expect" to protect, love, nurture, and care for him or her and therefore trusts implicitly violates the child, the emotional damage to the youngster may be catastrophic. Although this chapter's focus is primarily on family relationships, it is important to consider the scope of other trusting relationships that are abrogated and that can contribute to the development of DID as a coping strategy for dealing with overwhelming feelings of anxiety, betrayal, abandonment, and pain. The following is a representative list indicating the types of significant others whose violation of the child's trust and sense of safety can cause the child, given the aforementioned characteristics and perpetuating factors, to use dissociative process or DID to cope:

- Father
- Mother
- Siblings
- Extended family members such as grandparents, uncles, aunts, cousins, etc.
- Stepparent
- Educator
- Clergy member
- Neighbors
- Medical personnel
- Friends of, parents, siblings, child
- Child care workers, day care teachers, nannies, baby-sitters, etc.
- Teachers
- Scout leaders, coaches

Once this method of coping becomes the primary defense mechanism for dealing with anxiety-provoking situations and stimulus generalization occurs, it seems difficult for the individual to learn other coping mechanisms without therapeutic intervention. Unfortunately, many of these people tend to seek out emotional, sexual, and physical relationships with others who are similar to those encountered in either the traumatizing period of their lives or their dysfunctional family of origin. Conversely, they may totally avoid relationships and close human connections in an effort to create a feeling of safety. The choice of similar abusive relationships and environments serves to perpetuate the use of dissociative process. It also continues to embroil the individual in self-destructive patterns that perpetuate the damage to the person's mind and body.

The patients that I have treated who isolate and avoid close interpersonal relationships tend to use dissociative process and interactions with the alter personalities to fill the lonely void in their interpersonal life. The interaction with alter personalities is possible only if the personalities are aware, or "co-conscious," of each other's presence in the individual's personality structure. These patients will often function for a number of hours per day at work or school but will quickly retreat to their homes and spend most of their time "alone." The journals these patients bring to treatment often reflect conversations with other alters, which is evident by different handwriting, personality style, and grammatical and spelling levels. In addition, the journal entries read as distinct interactions; comments and questions are followed by responses from various alters personalities. As one treats these individuals in session and then reads the journals, the unique style and characteristics of each alter is clearly evident.

For patients who are involved in new relationships or families, individual therapy with adjunctive family or significant other therapy may be indicated in order to maximize the individual's functioning, safety, and success in individual therapeutic work. As many spouses, significant others, and children have no preparation for dealing with the unique behavioral manifestations of DID, oftentimes these families are in constant states of crisis. Family therapy in conjunction with individual therapy can create an atmosphere of trust and understanding that will facilitate the DID patient taking risks to try to establish a healthy relationship. The coping methods designed and created in both types of therapy will help build self-esteem, reduce crises, and enhance the functioning of the family.

THEORETICAL BASIS FOR CONCURRENT INDIVIDUAL AND FAMILY THERAPY FOR PATIENTS DIAGNOSED WITH DID

Minuchin's theory (1974) of family structure proposes that the family has an invisible set of functional demands that organize the interaction of the members through transactional patterns. These patterns regulate the family member's behavior. Within this structure is a hierarchy of power and mutual expectations of behavioral interactions between particular family members. In this way the system maintains its homeostatic balance. Similarly, Trepper and Barrett (1986) discuss the "family style" as the pervasive enduring pattern of interaction a family displays.

When the family of origin's dysfunction, enmeshment, abuse, and neglect coalesce to force an individual family member to resort to developing DID to survive the traumatizing psychological or physical reality, the disorder is rarely recognized in the abusive family. If the abuse occurs outside of the family of origin, the perpetrator often intimidates the child in a variety of ways to maintain his or her silence. Therefore, the family of origin may have no knowledge of the event and have no inkling as to the development of the alter identities. Often, these alters become a hidden, secret way for the traumatized and abused individual to cope.

When these individuals create a new family structure by marrying, having children, risking close friendships, or engaging in monogamous relationships with significant partners if they are homosexuals or lesbian, the impact of the disorder on the new family or relationship structure is profound. These partners have to evolve a new structure reflecting the needs of its participants. Based on the plethora of psychological symptoms, behavioral patterns, and medical problems, individuals with DID evidence significant others in the DID person's life must learn to cope with a wide range of problems unique to this disorder.

Family members' responses to the unique characteristics of each alter affect the family structure, interactions, relationship expectations, and equilibrium. The emergence of these alter identities changes the family dynamics as the other members respond to the alter personality's unique emotive and physical presentations. Developmental aspects of alters who represent different ages (i.e., child alters) may force fluid family adaptations to the developmentally based needs, demands, safety issues, and cognitive development of the alter present. Alter personalities who represent particular emotions, such as anger, may create management and safety issues for the patient as well as for the significant others present while that alter is in executive control of the individual. The family as a unit as well as the individuals within the family constantly are forced to adjust and adapt their behaviors, responses, and responsibilities to the alter in executive control at the moment. Conversely, alters may emerge in order to adapt to the existing family structure or changes in the family dynamics. The family may represent a source of stasis for the DID patient, as this patient has little or no internal stasis, especially if he or she is subject to rapid switching.

Another concern is how the family deals with the "secret" of having a member who has DID in terms of disclosure to neighbors, extended family, and friends. The new family may represent the first opportunity for the individual to experience safety. Given this hopeful reality, the need for individual as well as family therapy becomes clearer.

TREATMENT STRATEGIES AND CLINICAL CONSIDERATIONS

The five "major phases" for the successful treatment of DID presented by Sachs, Frischholz, and Wood (1988) include family participation. These phases include:

1. Once a diagnosis is established, educating the individual and family members about the diagnosis and its function as a coping style is helpful in creating more understanding and tolerance in the home or group. Gaining dissociative information from family members helps validate the diagnosis. Asking the family to contribute suggestions for coping styles for the patient and the family as a unit may enhance the functioning of the DID patient as well as the family itself.

2. Identification of alter identities and personality fragments, including their purpose and function by the individual and family members, increase the understanding of the dynamics of the patient and the subsequent effect the alters have on the family structure.

3. Memory work around the trauma experience by the various alter identities is necessary in order to work out the emotional confusion that the stimulus generalization and its effects have transferentially on the therapist, spouse, family members, and significant others. The inclusion of family members in this phase of treatment allows differentiation between current people in the patient's life and the patient's past abusers.

4. Family member support during integration of the identities, may aid the patient working through the fear of the loss of an alter personality with a specific coping function and allow that coping mechanism to be incorporated in the unifying personality. This family support may enable the individual to maintain the integration or cooperation of the alters and create a stable homeostatic environment for all concerned.

5. Learning alternative coping mechanisms to help the individual maintain integration or cooperation of the alters is essential in the process of therapy. The coping mechanisms include cognitive and experiential techniques for resolving internal conflicts, reduction and management of stress, and improvement in communication skills with significant others. Family participation and cooperation can reduce the risk of family crisis that may cause the individual to create a new alter or resurrect an old one.

A number of specific treatment and intervention strategies merit attention here. Teaching the individual and family members to recognize alter states and specific triggers that tend to elicit switching is a valuable aid for the family as members will be able to anticipate the behaviors of the emerging alter. This will then enable them to support the individual in engaging in alternative behaviors or situations to establish internal and external safety. An example of this is supporting the individual in turning the television off when there is a movie, news program, or documentary with components that will trigger emotional reactions or painful memories.

The therapist can model adaptive ways of interacting with the alter identities to enhance communication while the person is in an alter state. The aim here is to maintain safety for the individual as well as facilitate the return of the "host" personality. For instance, the therapist or family member, communicating to a child alter that "children" are not supposed to drive a car, or take medications, or cook without help from an adult, suggesting to the alter not to engage in this behavior or alternatively, allow an adult actor to emerge who will engage in these "adult" behaviors.

Another technique is teaching the spouse or child not to expect an alter to respond in a rational way to reason. The alter usually represents an intensified fragment of personality. A family member trying to get an angry alter to listen to "reason" and resolve an issue is likely to fail. It is generally more useful to contain any potential damage or acting out until that alter has switched back to the host personality before dealing with the issue.

Adaptive strategies for dealing with a family crisis can be facilitated by the individual, the therapist, and family members by preparing and agreeing in advance what type of interventions are acceptable. The patient may agree to give a family member permission to call the therapist under certain conditions even if the alter, in executive control during a crisis, states he or she does not want the therapist contacted. In this way the other alters feel that they have been in control in determining acceptable interventions.

Phone management of DID alters and family members include the anchoring of alters and attempting to reestablish the adult or host personality in executive control. Also, therapists must establish phone limits with the patient and the family to create clear appropriate boundaries around calling between sessions.

Ensuring safety in the family system is critical for the entire family. Safety includes psychological, emotional, verbal, and physical comfort for all concerned. When a family is able to define, delineate, and discuss the parameters around internal and family safety, the members then are able to function in a more balanced sate. Family boundary definitions, their maintenance and adherence to these boundaries, are critical for the appropriate functioning of the family.

Another method of creating understanding and trust within the family is preparing everyone for possible hospitalizations. This is crucial to help facilitate the successful course of hospitalization, if the need is compelling. Family coping plans, in case the individual with DID will be absent from home for a period of time, are critically important. In addition, demystifying the fear around a psychiatric facility will aid in decreasing the fear and negative impact on the family structure.

Couple counseling regarding marital and sexual issues is often essential. Survivors of sexual abuse need help in identifying sexual concerns and the connection between past abuse and present sexual dilemmas. This includes creating new healthier sexual attitudes and behaviors with their partner (Maltz, 1993). Often individuals with DID express concern that their child alters "come out" when the adult is engaging in a consensual sexual encounter. When this occurs, the child alter may abreact during the sexual encounter. Strategies for dealing with child alters in such cases are vital. Some examples include educating the child alter on sexual issues in an age-appropriate manner and formulating strategies so he or she is not present when the adult is engaging in adult, consensual, loving, safe sexuality.

In a series of articles Benjamin and Benjamin discuss various rational and group treatment paradigms for partners and parents of DID clients. They postulate that a group model functions as an opportunity for partners and parents to share issues and concerns in a supportive, empathic, and safe milieu (Benjamin & Benjamin, 1994a). In a subsequent article they discuss the emergence of the "common themes" characteristic of these unique groups. A representative list includes concerns regarding types of behaviors that are deemed acceptable around DID clients, dealing with people outside the family, spiritual issues, how to avoid becoming a "therapist" family member, parenting, and sexual issues (Benjamin & Benjamin, 1994b). Benjamin and Benjamin (1994c) found that classifying types of marital partners into seven categories—new abusers, caretakers, "damaged goods," obsessive, paranoids, schizotypal roommates, and closet dissociatives—enabled them to gain a much clearer perspective on the marital context and homeostatic process. Parenting issues for these couples are of paramount concern. They discuss the critical importance of a family treatment model, play therapy, and hypnosis for treating a child with dissociative process and the power of family participation in aiding the treatment. They also believe that the treatment of the "child-parent subsystem in dissociative family" is likely to decrease the likelihood of transgenerational dysfunction in families with a DID parent (Benjamin & Benjamin, 1993). As the couple engages in marital therapy, the focus on appropriate, safe, well-planned supportive parenting strategies can greatly enhance the couple's relationship and the family transactions. Another author supports the concept of family and partner treatment but suggests that these treatments be conducted by a treatment team rather than by one therapist engaging in both individual therapy with the DID client and couple's or family counseling with the family (Chiappa, 1994). Several excellent books are targeted at helping partners of DID clients cope with the multitude of issues inherent with this type of relationship; these include works by Davis (1991), Gil (1992), and Glaber (1991).

Many Voices publishes articles submitted by individuals with DID. A recent issue that focused on parenting included a piece written by Tammy and parts (1994, pp. 2–3), which gave a list of tips for parents who have either an ego-state disorder or DID. The following is a summary of this contribution:

- Explain your "down days" to your child and distinguish between the parent's individual issues and the child's behavior so the child will recognize it is not his or her fault that the parent is distressed.
- Do not give detailed abuse stories as the specifics may traumatize the child.
- If the child insists on knowing the details of the history of the abuse the parent suffered, agree on a designated age when the child will be told, such as 18 years old.
- Let the child know that DID is not contagious (as other medical disorders may be).
- Demystify weekly therapy sessions either by having the child participate in an actual session or by play-acting a session so the child understands what it is. Also, make the therapist's name a household word.
- Discuss DID in comfortable, natural settings rather than a formal serious family meeting if the child is young.
- Create intra- and interfamily as well as social boundaries that are clearly defined.
- Allow the child to make his or her own choices around relationships with those who abused the parent as long as there is no danger of abuse to the child.
- Do not make DID the entire focus of the household; attempt to normalize DID as much as possible so the child can depend on the parent. Normalize the family with typical family outings and events. Also focus on good feelings, when they are part of the day's experience.

- Prepare the child to deal with the myths and fears of uninformed people who may be encountered.
- If hospitalization is necessary, show the child the facility if possible, and maintain contact with the family based on the family's schedule needs.
- Do not be mysterious about oneself. Inform the child about some of the issues and triggers to facilitate understanding.
- Tell the child good memories.

A multitude of clinical considerations are entailed in treating DID individuals and their families to maximize functioning. Issues surrounding physical and psychological safety, intervention strategies, interpersonal concerns with family members as well as outside contacts are important factors in this treatment. In addition, adaptive strategies designed by the individual and the family are critical for coping with treatment. Some of the suggestions raised previously if the DID person needs hospitalization illustrate this fact. The family must be prepared to deal with the patient's process of integration. It often includes grief work around the loss of alters, which the family must be able to support and understand. Often it is difficult for significant others to fathom the difficulty the DID individual faces in "giving up" a significant alter. In one case a DID patient was initially appalled when she acknowledged her multiplicity during a session and became quite angry with the therapist for proposing the diagnosis. As her treatment progressed and two of the alters, a four-year-old and a four-year-old mute, began to merge spontaneously, this patient called in crisis, crying that it felt like one of the "twins" was leaving. This caused her great pain, as the mute alter was the one who not only held the key to the memory of what had happened to her but was also a "companion" to the verbal four-year-old alter. The family could not understand why the patient was upset that the spontaneous integration occurred. Family and therapist support is imperative for the patient to deal with the "loss" of alters who played a critical role in their emotional and physical survival.

CONCLUSIONS

It is clear that adjunctive, concurrent family and couple's counseling is vital for maximizing the functioning of the individual with DID. This fact is especially significant considering the issue of stimulus generalization that affects the perceptions of and interactions with significant others in the person's life. The treatment strategies discussed highlight the critical need and value of participation by family members in the DID patient's treatment. The potential for decreasing the risk of transgenerational psychological damage to the children of DID patients, the increased potential of ensuring safety for both the DID patient and his or her family members, and the heightened possibility of maximizing the functioning of the individual and therefore of the family system are a few examples of the tremendous contribution family therapy can make in the treatment of DID.

By including the family and significant others in concurrent family therapy, risk management of the individual is enhanced as there is an informed, intervention-ready support system in the individual's daily life. Creating a predictable homeostasis for the individual and family can be invaluable for fashioning an atmosphere that will be conducive to the integrative process as well as to potentially decreasing the length of individual treatment necessary.

Overall, perceiving DID as a diagnostic syndrome with both intrapsychic and interpersonal ramifications seems to dictate the inclusion of family members and significant others in the treatment. Couple's and/or family therapy appear to be powerful and positive strategies for increasing the potential for a successful therapeutic outcome.

REFERENCES

American Psychiatric Association. (1994). *Diagnostic and statistical manual of mental disorders* (4th ed.). Washington, DC: Author.

Benjamin, L. R., & Benjamin, R. (1992). An overview of family treatment in dissociative disorders. *Dissociation, 5*(4), 236–241.

Benjamin, L. R., & Benjamin, R. (1993). Interventions with children in dissociative families: a family treatment model. *Dissociation, 6*(1), 54–65.

Benjamin, L. R., & Benjamin, R. (1994a). A group for partners and parents of MPD clients. Part I: Process and format. *Dissociation, 7*(1), 35–43.

Benjamin, L. R., & Benjamin, R. (1994b). A group for partners and parents of MPD clients. Part II: Themes and responses. *Dissociation, 7*(2), 104–111.

Benjamin, L. R., & Benjamin, R. (1994c). A group for partners and parents of MPD clients. Part III: Marital types and dynamics. *Dissociation, 7*(3), 191–196.

Braun, B. G., & Sachs, R. G. (1985). The development of multiple personality disorder predisposing, precipitating, and perpetuating factors. In R. P. Kluft, *Childhood antecedents of multiple personality* (pp. 38–64). Washington, DC: American Psychiatric Press.

Chiappa, F. (1994). Effective management of family and individual interventions in the treatment of dissociative disorders. *Dissociation, 7*(3), 185–190.

Davis, L. (1991). *Allies in healing.* New York: Harper Perennial.

Gil, E. (1992). *Outgrowing the pain together.* New York: Dell.

Glaber, K. (1991). *Ghosts in the bedroom: A guide for partners of incest survivors.* Deerfield Beach, FL: Health Communications.

Janet, P. (1890). *The major symptoms of hysteria.* New York: Macmillan.

Kluft, R. P. (1985). *Childhood antecedents of multiple personality.* Washington, DC: American Psychiatric Press, Inc.

Maltz, W. (1993). The therapists' page. In W. Lynn (Ed.) *Many voices* (pp. 4–5). Cincinnati, OH: MV Co.

Minuchin, S. (1974). *Families and family therapy.* Cambridge, MA: Harvard University.

Putnam, F. W. (1989). *Diagnosis and treatment of multiple personality disorder.* New York: Guilford.

Ross, C. A. (1989). *Multiple personality disorder diagnosis, clinical features and treatment.* New York: Wiley.

Sachs, R. G., Frischolz, E. J., & Wood, J. I. (1988). Martial and family therapy in the treatment of multiple personality disorder. *Journal of Marital and Family Therapy, 14*(3), 249–259.

Tammy & parts. (1994). Tips for better parenting with DID. In *Many voices* (pp. 2–3). Cincinnati, OH: MV Co.

Trepper, T. S., & Barrett, M. J. (1986). *Treating incest: A multimodal systems perspective.* New York: Haworth.

CHAPTER 28

Mood Disorders and the Family

GABOR I. KEITNER, MD, IVAN W. MILLER, PhD, and CHRISTINE E. RYAN, PhD

This chapter provides an overview of what is known about families of patients with unipolar and bipolar disorders. It is unnecessary, given the focus of this book and its likely audience, to reiterate the significant role that the psychosocial environment plays in the course and outcome of major psychiatric disorders. One of the goals of this volume is to provide a more empirically driven recognition of the ways in which interpersonal problems interact with illnesses. Professionals interested in couples and families are well aware of the importance of this interaction. Knowledge about family interactional processes in patients with illnesses, however, has not been articulated clearly enough to gain acceptance in the wider medical and mental health community, in part due to a lack of clarity about the populations we study and/or a consistent conceptual framework within which to frame our findings.

POPULATION DIAGNOSES

For this chapter, our focus is on two groups of patients with mood disorders: major depressive disorder and bipolar disorder. In contrast to most of the literature, it concentrates on patients at the more severe end of the mood disorders spectrum.

The important diagnostic feature of a major depressive episode is the stability and duration of the symptoms that make up the illness. The symptoms must be present for at least two weeks and represent a change from the person's previous functioning. One of the symptoms must be either a depressed mood or a global loss of interest in pleasure. Other symptoms may include the following: change in weight, insomnia or hypersomnia, psychomotor agitation or retardation, feelings of worthlessness or excessive guilt, difficulty concentrating, and recurring thoughts of death. These symptoms must cause clinically significant distress or impairment in social, occupational, or other areas of life functioning.

In bipolar disorder, episodes of depression alternate with manic episodes. Mania consists of a distinct period of abnormally and persistently elevated expansive or irritable mood lasting at least one week. Some of the associated symptoms during this period include inflated self-esteem or grandiosity, decreased need for sleep, increased talkativeness, flight of ideas or racing thoughts, distractibility, increased activity levels, and excessive involvement in pleasurable activities that have a high potential for painful consequences. Again, these disturbances must be sufficiently severe to cause marked impairment in occupational functioning, usual social activities, or relationships with others.

434

The key issues in these diagnostic formulations are the clusters of symptoms, their stability, and their duration. In some reports, there is a tendency to diagnose populations using instruments that assess a mood state at one given point in time (the Beck Depression Inventory [Beck et al., 1961]) or to ignore the duration criterion. As a consequence, patients with adjustment disorders and personality disorders, who by definition may have unstable moods, are assumed incorrectly to be patients with defined mood disorders. Furthermore, combining milder cases of the illness with their more severe manifestations tends to obscure interactional patterns that may be most representative of the disorder.

FAMILY FUNCTIONING IN MAJOR DEPRESSIVE DISORDER

In this chapter, we emphasize what is known about families with a member having a mood disorder. Much more has been published on couples issues in this population. (See Chapter 21.) From our perspective, the distinction between couples and families is quite arbitrary. We define families as all members of a social group living under the same roof. This could include couples, traditional families, extended families, or even friends living together. It is important to assess and involve those significant others in the patient's social field who have an ongoing relationship with the patient and are in a position to be impacted by or to influence his or her illness.

Recent reviews of the functioning of families of patients with major depressive disorder are available (Keitner & Miller, 1990; Keitner, Miller, & Ryan, 1993, 1994). There is consistent evidence in both outpatient and inpatient populations that an episode of major depression is associated with significant family dysfunction (Hinchliffe, Hooper, Roberts, & Vaughan, 1975; Keitner, Miller, Epstein, Bishop, & Fruzzetti, 1987; Merikangas, Prusoff, Kupfer, & Frank, 1985). A wide range of family functions are disturbed during the acute episode. Communications, problem-solving, and role functioning are especially likely to be dysfunctional.

Depressed inpatients are found to have significantly more marital and family maladjustment than diagnostically mixed comparison groups (Crowther, 1985; Miller, Kabacoff, Keitner, Epstein, & Bishop, 1986). Depression also has been found to be more problematic for marriages than either rheumatoid arthritis or cardiac illness (Bouras, Vanger, & Bridges, 1986).

In general, family functioning improves as the depression remits. Nonetheless, families of patients with major depression still are noted to exhibit more problematic functioning, even at remission of the depression, than do control families (Keitner et al., 1987; Krantz & Moos, 1987; Merikangas et al., 1985). The family dysfunction present during the acute episode does not appear to be merely a reaction to the stress of the illness. Ongoing monitoring and support for families of patients with depression may be necessary even after the acute episode has subsided.

The relationship between family functioning and the course of the depressive illness is of particular clinical and theoretical interest. In general, improvement in family functioning is associated with improvement in depressive symptomatology and a shorter duration of the depressive episode (George, Blazer, Hughes, & Fowler, 1989; Goering, Lancee, & Freeman, 1992; Keitner et al., 1987; McLeod, Kessler, & Landis, 1992; Swindle, Cronkite, & Moos, 1989).

Clearly, many factors besides family functioning or interpersonal relationships affect the course of an illness. Swindle and coworkers (1989) found the presence of preintake medical conditions and family conflicts persistent predictors of poor long-term outcome. In a one-year follow-up study, we found several factors associated with nonrecovery, including longer inpatient hospital stay, earlier age of depression onset, poor family functioning, greater number of previous hospitalizations, and comorbidity (Keitner, Ryan, Miller, & Norman, 1992). Of these five risk factors, however, only one, family functioning, is amenable to psychosocial intervention.

We attempted to explore whether poor family functioning was caused by a more severe depression or whether it aggravated the depressive illness already present. We studied "functional" and "dysfunctional" families in order to see how clinical and psychosocial characteristics of depressed patients from these families compared to each other and to see if the course of illness in these groupings was different over a one-year follow-up period (Miller et al., 1992). With a single exception (neuroticism), a dysfunctional family was not significantly associated with severity or other parameters of the patients' depression. This study suggests that the social environment in which the depression evolves, in and of itself, independent of the depressive symptoms and the severity of the depression, has a significant modifying effect on the evolution of that depressive episode.

The presence of persistent family dysfunction, especially high levels of criticism, is strongly related to the likelihood of relapse (Hooley, Orley, & Teasdale, 1986; Hooley & Teasdale, 1989; Vaughn & Leff, 1976a). Depressed patients, in fact, tend to relapse at even lower levels of criticism than do schizophrenic patients.

One dissenting report (Veiel, 1993) cautions against assuming that family and social support is invariably beneficial. Veiel found that among recovered nonworking women, a large network of supportive relatives was associated with a greater likelihood of the recurrence of depressive symptoms and a lower likelihood of further recovery from depression. Veiel suggests that these women may face an overload of emotional demands from family members who may pressure prematurely the person who, although recovered, is still vulnerable.

FAMILY FUNCTIONING IN BIPOLAR DISORDER

There is significantly less research on the functioning of families with a member with bipolar disorder than for those with major depression. Beginning in the 1950s, a number of investigators observed that families of bipolar patients have significant problems (Ablon, Davenport, & Gershon, 1975; Janowsky, El-Yousef, & Davis, 1974; Wadeson & Fitzgerald, 1971). While these early studies were based on clinical impressions, more recent studies (Mayo, O'Connell, & O'Brian, 1979; Miklowitz, Goldstein, Nuechterlein, Snyder, & Mintz, 1988; Miller, Keitner, Epstein, Bishop, & Ryan, 1991), using more empirical methods of assessing family functioning, also have documented impairments in families of bipolar patients during the acute episode. In one such study we found significant impairment in all areas of family functioning except in the capacity to communicate with each other (Miller et al., 1991). Almost 60 percent of these families reported unhealthy functioning, twice the percentage usually found in nonclinical families.

Frank, Targum, and Gershon (1981) reported that family functioning in patients with bipolar illness may return to normal levels when the illness remits. Three other studies, however (Ablon et al., 1975; Davenport, Adland, & Gold, 1979; Mayo et al., 1979), found continued family impairment, even after remission from the acute episode.

As a follow-up to our acute phase study and in order to explore the relationship between family functioning and the course of bipolar illness, we reviewed hospital records five years after the initial episode to determine the number of subsequent readmissions for bipolar patients. The results indicated that poorer overall family functioning was significantly correlated with number of readmissions. Patients with families who were judged to be unhealthy had more than twice the number of readmissions than did patients from "healthy" families (Miller et al., 1991). This study suggests that relapse and rehospitalization in bipolar disorder is related to the level of family impairment. Miklowitz and coworkers (1988) also found that high expressed emotion and pathologic affective style measured during the acute episode predicted relapse at a nine-month follow-up period.

Despite the limitations of available studies, findings are consistent in suggesting that, as with patients with schizophrenia and major depression, families of bipolar patients have significant levels of impairment, and the level of family impairment is related to the course of the bipolar disorder.

SPECIFICITY OF FAMILY DYSFUNCTION

It would be theoretically elegant and clinically reassuring if specific areas of family functioning were related to particular psychiatric illnesses. Similar to the historic search for specific intrapsychic conflicts in different psychosomatic disorders, the quest for simplistic interactional models continues. There is little evidence to support such models. Despite many commonalities, individuals are as different from each other as are their families and their illnesses.

Nonetheless, only so many broad areas of family interactional styles that can be conceptualized and measured reasonably. Given the large number of disorders with psychosocial correlates, it would indeed be surprising if particular areas of family functioning could be preferentially related to specific disorders. The issue is further confused by the numerous different conceptual frameworks used to describe families and the variety of instruments used to measure their functioning.

Even when the same measure is used, such as the Family Assessment Device (Miller, Epstein, Bishop, & Keitner, 1985), a complex picture of family issues and conditions emerges. Different aspects of family life appear to be problematic for different conditions, such as major depression, schizophrenia, substance abuse, bipolar disorder, and adjustment disorders (Miller et al., 1986). Compared to nonclinical families, families of patients with major depression reported poorer family functioning during the acute episode in general functioning, problem solving, communication skills, roles, and affective involvement (Keitner et al., 1987). Families with members having a chronic illness (recruited from oncology, rheumatology, and gastroenterology clinics) were noted to have a particularly high prevalence of unhealthy communication skills, poor affective involvement, and problems in behavioral control (Arpin, Fitch, Browne, & Corey, 1990). Communications, roles, and behavioral control dimensions were found to be important for families of patients who had had a stroke (Evans, Bishop, Matlock, Stranahan, & Noonan, 1987). In the families of adolescents with alcohol and drug abuse, problems in affective responsiveness and role functioning were associated with higher levels of substance abuse (McKay, Murphy, Rivinus, & Maisto, 1991). Clearly there is much overlap, in addition to the differences.

No current evidence exists for a prototypical type of family functioning related to either major depression (Keitner et al., 1995) or bipolar disorder. The role of the family is undoubtedly important in impacting on the length of the episode and the likelihood of relapse. Each family, however, needs to be assessed for its own unique strengths and weaknesses in relation to the particular manifestations (age of onset, symptom clusters, duration, frequency of episodes, and severity) of the illness. An attempt to evaluate the specific family's response to the particular nature of their patient's illness, although perhaps more complicated for the therapist, is nonetheless likely to result in more realistic and appropriate treatment for that family.

EMPIRICAL ASSESSMENT OF FAMILIES

A major problem in elucidating characteristic family interactional patterns in various psychiatric and medical conditions is the lack of agreed-upon instruments to assess marital and family functioning.

Some instruments are well validated and psychometrically tested (Epstein, Baldwin, & Bishop, 1983; Locke & Wallace, 1959; Moos & Moos, 1981; Snyder, Wills, & Keiser, 1981; Vaughn & Leff, 1976a). Other instruments were not primarily designed or validated to assess family functioning, although some of their subscales have been used for that purpose (Weissman, 1975). Still others were designed for a particular study and do not have much psychometric support (Targum et al., 1981; Waring et al., 1981). Family instruments range from questions concerning general satisfaction (Locke & Wallace, 1959; Spanier, 1976) to schedules assessing multiple aspects of family life (Epstein et al., 1983; Moos & Moos, 1981; Olson et al., 1982; Snyder et al., 1981). It is unclear whether the same or similar family processes are being measured by these instruments and to what extent findings from different studies can be pooled.

A second problem in the assessment of families is that few studies actually have attempted to evaluate family functioning using external raters. Most studies have used perceptions of family members as a reflection of their families' functioning. (A significant exception are studies assessing expressed emotion with the Camberwell Family Interview [Vaughn & Leff, 1976b].) Few have attempted to observe and rate families using trained interviewers (Hinchliffe et al., 1975; Hooley et al., 1986); fewer still have tried to observe patients in their own home environments (Hops et al., 1987).

Attempts at consensus conferences by principal investigators of the various scales have occurred but, not surprisingly, have failed to reach meaningful agreements. Our Family and Mood Disorders Research Program uses the McMaster Model of Family Functioning (MMFF) as a conceptual model for assessing and treating families. Apart from our vested interest in the evolution and development of this model, we find that it provides a consistent organizing framework not readily available by patching together components from different models.

The McMaster Model of Family Functioning (Epstein, Bishop, & Baldwin, 1982) is a clinically oriented, systemic model of family functioning that delineates the structural and organizational properties of the family group and important transactional patterns found among family members. In addition to this broadly based conceptual model, we have developed two instruments that provide empirical assessments from both an intrafamily point of view (the Family Assessment Device) as well as from an external observer (the McMaster Clinical Rating Scale). A well-delineated model of therapy, the Problem-Centered Systems Therapy of the Family (PCSTF) (Epstein & Bishop, 1981) also has been formulated and is currently undergoing research evaluation. The combination of all three elements—an overriding conceptual framework, the availability of assessment instruments from an intra- and extrafamilial point of view, and a well-defined therapeutic program—provides internal consistency and potential for empirical validation and replication that is unusual in the field.

The Family Assessment Device (Epstein et al., 1983; Miller et al., 1985) is a 60-item, self-report instrument developed to assess the dimensions of the MMFF, including problem solving, communication, roles, affective responsiveness, affective involvement, behavioral control, and overall functioning. Briefly, problem solving reflects the family's ability to resolve problems and the steps they go through to do so. Communication refers to the effectiveness, extent, clarity, and directness of information exchanged in the family. The roles dimension describes the efficacy with which family tasks are allocated and accomplished. Tasks include those associated with provision of resources (food, clothing, shelter), nurturance and support, the development of life skills, and maintenance and management of the family system (e.g., housekeeping, yardwork, bills, health issues, power, decision making). Affective responsiveness assesses the ability of family members to respond with appropriate emotion, encompassing feelings of welfare (joy, love, concern, tenderness, affection) and emergency (sadness, depression, anger, fear). Affective involvement refers to the quality of interest, concern, and investment that family members have for each other. Behavioral control describes the standards and latitudes for behavior. Overall functioning is self-evident.

The FAD is completed by each family member over the age of 12 and provides information on each of the six basic MMFF dimensions, plus a general functioning evaluation. The FAD is appropriate for clinical screening and research investigations. It has adequate test-retest reliability, low correlations with social desirability, and moderate correlations with other self-report measures of family functioning, and it differentiates significantly between clinician-rated healthy and unhealthy families. Cutoff scores for identifying healthy and unhealthy families have been developed and have adequate sensitivity and specificity (Miller et al., 1985). A psychometric study of the FAD (Kabacoff, Miller, Bishop, Epstein, & Keitner, 1990) found that the scale reliabilities were favorable and that the hypothesized factors structure of the FAD was supported. This study also supported the use of the FAD to include families with a medically disabled member.

The McMaster Clinical Rating Scale (MCRS) was developed to provide an interview rating of family functioning along with the dimensions of the McMaster Model. The MCRS can be completed either by a rater who observes a suitable, in-depth family interview or by the clinician who carries out such an assessment.

Each rating is made on a seven-point scale. A rating of 1 is given for the most ineffective or disturbed functioning, and a rating of 7 represents the most effective or healthy functioning. A manual for the MCRS defines each dimension, explains the scaling system, and outlines concise, accurate description for points 1, 5, and 7 on the scales. These descriptions, couched in operational and behavioral terms, describe the type of functioning that should be present to qualify for a score in the various levels.

Overall, the MCRS appears to have acceptable psychometric properties for continued research, use, and development (Miller et al., 1994). It demonstrates good inter-rater reliability and rater stability. It can be used effectively by relatively naive raters as well as by experienced family therapists. Correlations among dimensions are moderate and consistent with theory.

There are significant correlations (0.40–0.60) between most of the scales of the MCRS and the FAD, indicating a moderate level of overlap between these two methods for measuring the dimensions of the McMaster Model. In contrast, with the exception of the Beavers Model (Beavers & Hampson, 1990), previous studies have found little generalizability across different methods of family measurement (Olson, 1985). This higher degree of correspondence between self-report and observer ratings obtained using the MCRS and the FAD most likely reflects the McMaster Model's emphasis on behavioral description and operationalization of constructs based on clinical observation of families.

In an attempt to further standardize the assessment data on which clinical ratings are made, we have developed the McMaster Structured Interview of Family Functioning (McSIFF) (Bishop, Epstein, Keitner, Miller, & Zlotnick, 1987) to elicit appropriate information about the McMaster Model dimensions. This interview is currently being validated. Preliminary results suggest that it is useful in research, teaching, and clinical practice.

FAMILY TREATMENT FOR MOOD DISORDERS

Major Depressive Disorder

Few studies have evaluated the effectiveness of family interventions in the treatment of patients with mood disorders. Marital therapy has been assessed more extensively and found to have a positive outcome in the treatment of depression, especially if it has been accompanied by marital distress (Beach, Whisman, & O'Leary, 1994).

One study of inpatient family treatment for patients with schizophrenia and affective disorders has been reported (Glick et al., 1985, 1991; Haas et al., 1988; Spencer, Glick, & Haas, 1988). These investigators randomly assigned patients to family treatment composed of six psychoeducational family meetings over a five-week hospital stay or no family intervention. All other treatments, including pharmacotherapy, were held constant.

At discharge from the hospital, the positive effect of the family intervention was limited to female patients with affective disorders and their families. At 18-month follow-up, the therapeutic effect was restricted to female patients with schizophrenia or "major affective disorders," whereas the effect on male patients was minimal or "slightly negative."

Anderson and colleagues (1986) randomly assigned inpatients with affective disorders and their families to either a multiple family group with a process orientation, emphasizing support and self-help, or to a psychoeducational group, emphasizing information about the illness. Both types of family groups were found to be useful and desirable. Families receiving the psychoeducational program, however, were more satisfied with their experience.

Our research group is in the process of assessing the effectiveness of adding family therapy and/or cognitive-behavioral psychotherapy to standard pharmacotherapy for patients with major depression. We are interested in the question of which patients, with what kind of deficits, can most benefit from which combination of treatments.

Bipolar Disorder

Even fewer studies have assessed the effectiveness of adding a family treatment to pharmacotherapy for bipolar disorders. In a retrospective evaluation, Davenport, Ebert, Adland, and Goodwin (1976) compared the response of bipolar patients in three types of aftercare: couple's psychotherapy group, lithium maintenance clinic, or community-based aftercare. This research group found that patients in the couple's psychotherapy condition had fewer instances of rehospitalization or marital failure and better social and family functioning than patients in the other treatment conditions. However, confidence in these results is qualified by the lack of random assignment to groups and by significant differences in patient characteristics prior to treatment.

Miklowitz and Goldstein (1990) reported a pilot study of a behavioral family management approach to aid families of bipolar manic patients. This treatment was well accepted by patients and families, and the rate of relapse at a nine-month follow-up was lower than obtained in a naturalistic follow-up of bipolar patients from the same facility receiving only medication management. While this study provides preliminary support for the efficacy of this family intervention, it is limited by the small sample, lack of randomized control groups, and short follow-up interval.

Our research group has conducted a pilot study on the effectiveness of family treatment for bipolar disorder (Miller, Epstein, Keitner, & Bishop, 1991). Subjects for this study consisted of patients recently admitted to a psychiatric hospital with a diagnosis of bipolar mania. Patients were randomly assigned to one of two treatment conditions: standard treatment (hospital milieu, semistructured pharmacotherapy protocol, and clinical management sessions) or family treatment (standard treatment plus family therapy). Assessments were done prior to and at the end of treatment. In addition, rehospitalization data were collected for two years after discharge. Ten families completed this pilot project. At the end of treatment, those in the family treatment condition reported greater improvement in family functioning than did families in the standard treatment condition.

Ninety-two percent of the patients in this pilot study met criteria for full or partial recovery by the end of treatment. The patients in the family therapy condition had a higher proportion of patients who made a full recovery (56 percent) than did patients in the standard treatment condition (20 percent). Conversely, there were no differences in mean severity of manic or depressive symptoms at the end of treatment, with patients in both treatment conditions manifesting significantly improved symptom levels from pretreatment.

Although this pilot study was terminated after the end of the active treatment phase, a chart review of hospital records for a two-year period following the end of the randomized treatment phase indicated that patients entered into the family treatment condition had approximately half the readmissions (mean = 0.6) than patients entered into the standard treatment (mean = 1.3). While this difference was not statistically significant due to small sample size, it does represent a medium-large effect size (0.70) and is congruent with the effect sizes obtained in other pilot studies of family treatment of bipolar disorder and schizophrenia.

Based on this pilot data, our research group is now funded to study the efficacy of adding two types of family interventions—psychoeducational intervention and family therapy—to standard treatment composed of pharmacotherapy plus clinical management in a larger group of bipolar patients. We are subdividing families of bipolar patients into "dysfunctional" and "functional" groups in order to explore the treatment response of these two types of families to the three treatment conditions.

In summary, the preliminary evidence from the few available studies of both unipolar and bipolar patients suggests that adding a family intervention is likely to enhance recovery and to diminish the likelihood of relapse. It should be stressed that the question is not whether family therapy or psychotherapy or pharmacotherapy is most effective in the treatment of mood disorders, but rather how to determine which combination of these treatments is most effective for which particular patient at which point in time.

The Problem-Centered Systems Therapy of the Family

The Problem-Centered Systems Therapy of the Family (PCSTF) (Epstein & Bishop, 1981) has several characteristics that make it particularly relevant both for clinical and empirical investigation of the effectiveness of family treatment for patients with mood disorders. This comprehensive method of family therapy is based on a well-developed theoretical model, the McMaster Model of Family Functioning. It is a highly structured treatment that has been described extensively. Procedures to train and evaluate new therapists have been developed and tested (Byles, Bishop, & Horn, 1983). This multidimensional systems-oriented treatment allows the integration and coordination of a number of different treatment approaches depending on the specific clinical presentation. It is a short-term intervention that can be delivered in a cost-effective manner. A conference sponsored by the National Institute for Mental Health on family therapy research recommended PCSTF as one of the three most promising treatment models for family therapy research (Gurman, 1988).

The main features of the PCSTF are an emphasis on current problems; an active, directive stance by the therapist; a collaborative therapeutic relationship; a focus on behavioral and cognitive change; an open, straightforward therapeutic stance by the therapist; use of homework; and time-limited treatment. An important element is a careful and complete assessment of all dimensions of family life. Treatment should not begin until the family is understood comprehensively. The focus is on family strengths as opposed to family pathology so that, for example, the therapist may accept strategies that families have effectively worked out (as long as these are not dangerous), regardless of the therapist's own bias.

The major stages of treatment are assessment, contracting, treatment, and closure. Each treatment stage incorporates a number of substages and general strategies. The PCSTF treatment model hypothesizes that these "macro"-stages of therapy are the most important focus for treatment, rather than the idiosyncratic maneuvers and styles of various therapists.

There is good evidence to suggest that, at a minimum, all families of patients with mood disorders should be assessed. For many families, the assessment may be sufficient in and of itself to identify strengths and to resolve uncertainties and minor conflicts. These assessment sessions also may be used to provide information concerning the illness and support for the family to continue to cope as effectively as possible.

However, for patients with more significant family dysfunction, additional family interventions may be helpful and essential.

Combined Psychopharmacological and Psychosocial Treatment for Mood Disorders

Thirty years ago, a major concern in psychiatry was whether drugs could be integrated successfully into the psychosocial treatments of patients with mood disorders. Today, the pendulum appears to have swung in the opposite direction, and biological therapies have become the dominant treatment modality. With development of new, and perhaps better, pharmacological treatments for mood disorders, the current question for many psychiatrists is whether to "bother" integrating psychosocial treatments with pharmacological treatment. Yet more useful theories in medicine reflect a "biopsychosocial" model of illness (Engel, 1977), which assumes that all diseases have biological, psychological, and social factors influencing their development and progression. It follows, then, that providing treatments that impact on each area in a patient's illness should maximize therapeutic effectiveness.

Concerns about the possible negative effects of combining psychosocial and psychopharmacological treatments—such as drugs interfering with psychotherapy—focusing on symptoms rather than underlying issues, providing symptomatic relief (thereby decreasing patient motivation), or increasing magical reliance on the therapist and fostering dependency have proven to be unwarranted (Conte, Plutchik, Wild, & Darasu, 1986). However, combining treatments may offer genuine positive benefits. Medications may increase the effectiveness of psychotherapy by making the patient more accessible and by decreasing symptoms that may impede the patient's ability to profit from psychotherapy (concentration, motivation, energy, anxiety). Medication compliance may be improved by psychosocial treatments. Family interventions may change the patient's environment by decreasing stress and disruption for him or her, in addition to improving treatment compliance.

Unfortunately, there are no well-established criteria to guide which particular combination of treatments is most appropriate for any individual patient. As noted, our research group currently is studying these issues. Until more definitive data becomes available, clinicians are faced with three options.

The first is to provide all treatments for all patients. This would ensure, at the least, that those patients who could benefit from combined treatments would receive optimum care. However, this method might prove not only expensive but, if not done correctly, actually harmful by unsettling areas in patients' lives that are not problematic or are in functional equilibrium.

An alternate approach is to provide sequential treatment trials. In this case, the therapist would start with one treatment modality, such as pharmacotherapy. If this by itself does not work after a reasonable amount of time, the next treatment would be used, say family therapy. This approach is problematic because of the excessive amount of time demanded for treatment trials, uncertainty about which treatment approach to begin first, and uncertainty as to which treatment really is effective.

The third option, the one that we favor, is to try to determine which combination of treatments is most appropriate for a given patient and then to provide that combination from the beginning. The soundest way to determine this is a comprehensive assessment of the psychological, biological, and social aspects of each patient's current presentation and life situation.

Biological assessments should include determining the presence of comorbid medical illnesses, family history of mood disorders and treatment responsiveness of family members, and the presence of neurovegetative signs and symptoms. Psychological assessments should include an evaluation of current conflicts, dysfunctional attitudes, personality styles, and the meaning of the illness for the patient. Social assessments should include an evaluation of current life stressors, availability of social supports, and quality of family functioning.

Not all patients have problems in all these domains. It is the clinician's responsibility to provide an assessment thorough enough to determine which areas of the patient's lives are most problematic and to match treatments most likely to address those areas.

CONCLUSION

There is substantial research support for taking the social context of mood disorders into consideration in anticipating the outcome of these illnesses and in planning treatment. The impact of depression and mania on family life and family relationships is substantial, both during the acute episode and over the course of the illness. The way a family copes, in turn, influences the course of the illness both in duration and tendency to relapse.

If the family system is so integrally involved in depression and manic illness, it follows that family interventions increasingly should become part of standard treatment approaches. Research support for this assumption, however, is not yet available. Few family therapy studies have been reported for this population, and published studies are not unequivocally supportive. Outcome studies evaluating the effectiveness of combining pharmacotherapy with psychosocial treatments, including family therapy, are currently under way and are sorely needed to guide clinical practice.

In the interim, it seems reasonable to suggest that, at a minimum, a patient's social system, particularly relationships with significant others, should be assessed on a routine basis. Many patients with mood disorders do not require family therapy. But most families would benefit from a thorough individual and relational assessment, sharing of mutual concerns, and psychoeducational information about the illness and available treatment options.

Patients and families with more significant dysfunction are likely to benefit from ongoing family intervention. This intervention, however, should be provided as an integrated part of a total treatment program. The combination of pharmacotherapy, psychotherapy, and family therapy, as indicated, represents current state-of-the-art treatment for mood disorders.

REFERENCES

Ablon, S., Davenport, Y., & Gershon, E. (1975). The married manic. *American Journal of Orthopsychiatry, 45,* 854–866.

Anderson, C. M., et al. (1986). A comparative study of the impact of education vs. process groups for families of patients with affective disorders. *Family Process, 25,* 185–205.

Arpin, K., Fitch, M., Browne, G. B., & Corey, P. (1990). Prevalence and correlates of family dysfunction and poor adjustment to chronic illness in specialty clinics. *Journal of Clinical Epidemiology, 43,* 373–383.

Beach, S. R. H., Whisman, M. A., & O'Leary, K. D. (1994). Marital therapy for depression: Theoretical foundation, current status, and future directions. *Behavior Therapy, 25,* 345–371.

Beavers, W. R., & Hampson, R. B. (1990). *Successful families: Assessment and intervention.* New York: Norton.

Beck, A., et al. (1961). An inventory for measuring depression. *Archives of General Psychiatry, 4,* 561–571.

Bishop, D. S., Epstein, N. B., Keitner, G. I., Miller, I. W., & Zlotnick, C. (1987). McMaster Model of Family Functioning Structured Interview. Available from Brown University Family Research Program, Butler Hospital, 345 Blackstone Boulevard, Providence, RI 02906.

Bouras, N., Vanger, P., & Bridges, P. K. (1986). Marital problems in chronically depressed and physically ill patients and their spouses. *Comprehensive Psychiatry, 27,* 127–130.

Byles, J., Bishop, D., & Horn, D. (1983). Evaluation of a family therapy training program. *Journal of Marital and Family Therapy, 9,* 299–304.

Conte, H., Plutchik, R., Wild, K., & Darasu, T. (1986). Combined psychotherapy and pharmacotherapy for depression. *Archives of General Psychiatry, 43,* 471–479.

Crowther, J. H. (1985). The relationship between depression and marital maladjustment: A descriptive study. *Journal of Nervous and Mental Disorders, 173,* 227–231.

Davenport, Y., Ebert, M., Adland, M., & Goodwin, F. (1976). Couples group therapy as an adjunct to lithium maintenance of the manic patient. *American Journal of Orthopsychiatry, 47,* 495–502.

Davenport, Y., Adland, M., & Gold, P. (1979). Manic depressive illness: Psychodynamic features of multigenerational families. *American Journal of Orthopsychiatry, 49,* 24–35.

Engel, G. (1977). The need for a new medical model: A challenge for biomedicine. *Science, 196,* 129–136.

Epstein, N. B., Baldwin, L. M., & Bishop, D. S. (1983). The McMaster Family Assessment Device. *Journal of Marital and Family Therapy, 9,* 171–180.

Epstein, N. B., & Bishop, D. S. (1981). Problem-centered systems therapy of the family. In A. S. Gurman & D. P. Kniskern (Eds.), *Handbook of family therapy* (pp. 444–482). New York: Brunner/Mazel.

Epstein, N. B., Bishop, D. S., & Baldwin, L. M. (1982). McMaster Model of Family Functioning: A view of the normal family. In F. Walsh (Ed.), *Normal family processes* (pp. 115–141). New York: Guilford.

Evans, R. L., Bishop, D. S., Matlock, A. L., Stranahan, S., & Noonan, C. (1987). Predicting poststroke family function: A continuing dilemma. *Psychological Reports, 60,* 691–695.

Frank, E., Targum, S., & Gershon, E. (1981). A comparison of nonpatient and bipolar patient-well spouse couples. *American Journal of Psychiatry, 138,* 764–768.

George, L. K., Blazer, D. G., Hines, D. C., & Fowler, N. (1989). Social support and the outcome of major depression. *British Journal of Psychiatry, 154,* 478–485.

Glick, I., et al. (1985). A controlled evaluation of inpatient family intervention, I: Preliminary results of the six-month follow-up. *Archives of General Psychiatry, 42,* 882–886.

Glick, I. D., Clarkin, J. F., Haas, G. L., Spencer, J. H., Jr., & Chen, C. L. (1991). A randomized clinical trial of inpatient family intervention, VI: Mediating variables and outcome. *Family Process, 30,* 85–99.

Goering, P. N., Lancee, W. J., & Freeman, S. J. J. (1992). Marital support and recovery from depression. *British Journal of Psychiatry, 160,* 76–82.

Gurman, A. (1988). Issues in specification of family therapy interventions. In L. C. Wynne (Ed.), *The state of the art in family therapy research: Controversies and recommendations* (pp. 125–138). New York: Family Process Press.

Haas, G., Glick, I., Clarkin, J., et al. (1988). Inpatient family intervention: a randomized clinical trial. II: Results at hospital discharge. *Archives of General Psychiatry, 45,* 217–224.

Hinchliffe, M., Hooper, D., Roberts, F. J., & Vaughan, P.W. (1975). A study of the interaction between depressed patients and their spouses. *British Journal of Psychiatry, 126,* 164–172.

Hooley, J. M., Orley, J., & Teasdale, J. D. (1986). Levels of expressed emotion and relapse in depressed patients. *British Journal of Psychiatry, 148,* 642–647.

Hooley, J. M., & Teasdale, J. D. (1989). Predictors of relapse in unipolar depressives: Expressed emotion, marital distress and perceived criticism. *Journal of Abnormal Psychology, 98,* 229–235.

Hops, H., Biglan, A., Sherman, L., et al. (1987). Home observations of family interactions of depressed women. *Journal of Consulting and Clinical Psychology, 55,* 341–346.

Janowsky, D., El-Yousef, M., & Davis, J. (1974). Interpersonal maneuvers of manic patients. *American Journal of Psychiatry, 131,* 250–255.

Kabacoff, R. I., Miller, I. W., Bishop, D. S., Epstein, N. B., & Keitner, G. I. (1990). A psychometric study of the McMaster Family Assessment Device in psychiatric, medical, and nonclinical samples. *Journal of Family Psychology, 3,* 431–439.

Keitner, G. I., & Miller, I. W. (1990). Family functioning and major depression: An overview. *American Journal of Psychiatry, 147,* 1128–1137.

Keitner, G. I., Miller, I. W., Epstein, N. B., Bishop, D. S., & Fruzzetti, A. E. (1987). Family functioning and the course of major depression. *Comprehensive Psychiatry, 28,* 54–64.

Keitner, G. I., Miller, I. W., & Ryan, C. E. (1993). The role of the family in major depressive illness. *Psychiatric Annals, 23,* 500–507.

Keitner, G. I., Miller, I. W., & Ryan, C. E. (1994). Family functioning in severe depressive disorders. In L. Grunhaus & J. F. Greden (Eds.), *Severe depressive disorders* (pp. 89–110). Washington, DC: American Psychiatric Association.

Keitner, G. I., Ryan, C. E., Miller, I. W., & Norman, W. H. (1992). Recovery and major depression: Factors associated with twelve-month outcome. *American Journal of Psychiatry, 149,* 93–99.

Keitner, G. I., Ryan, C. E., Miller, I. W., Kohn, R., Bishop, D. S., & Epstein, N. B. (1995). Recovery and major depression: The role of the family. *American Journal of Psychiatry, 152,* 1002–1008.

Krantz, S. E., & Moos, R. H. (1987). Functioning and life context among spouses of remitted and nonremitted depressed patients. *Journal of Consulting and Clinical Psychology, 55,* 353–360.

Locke, H. J., & Wallace, K. M. (1959). Short marital adjustment and prediction tests: their reliability and validity. *Marriage and Family Living, 21,* 251–255.

Mayo, J., O'Connell, R., & O'Brian, J. (1979). Families of manic depressive patients: Effect and treatment. *American Journal of Psychiatry, 136,* 1535–1539.

McKay, J. R., Murphy, R. T., Rivinus, T. R., & Maisto, S. A. (1991). Family dysfunction and alcohol and drug use in adolescent psychiatric inpatients. *Journal of American Academy of Child and Adolescent Psychiatry, 30,* 967–972.

McLeod, J. D., Kessler, R. C., & Landis, K. R. (1992). Speed of recovery from major depressive episodes in a community sample of married men and women. *Journal of Abnormal Psychology, 101,* 277–286.

Merikangas, K. R., Prusoff, B. A., Kupfer, D. J., & Frank, E. (1985). Marital adjustment in a major depression. *Journal of Affective Disorders, 9,* 5–11.

Miklowitz, D., & Goldstein, M. (1990). Behavioral family treatment for patients with bipolar affective disorder. *Behavior Modification, 14,* 457–489.

Miklowitz, D., Goldstein, M., Nuechterlein, K., Snyder, K., & Mintz, J. (1988). Family factors and the course of bipolar disorder. *Archives of General Psychiatry, 45,* 225–231.

Miller, I. W., Costello, E., & Keitner, G. I. (1993). Major depression. In C. Last & M. Hersen (Eds.), *Adult behavior therapy casebook* (pp. 33–46). New York: Plenum.

Miller, I. W., Epstein, N. B., Bishop, D. S., & Keitner, G. I. (1985). The McMaster Family Assessment Device: Reliability and validity. *Journal of Marital and Family Therapy, 11,* 345–356.

Miller, I. W., Epstein, N. B., Keitner, G. I., & Bishop, D. S. (1991, July). *Family treatment for bipolar disorder.* Presented at the meeting of the Society for Psychotherapy Research, Lyon, France.

Miller, I. W., Kabacoff, R. I., Epstein, N. B., Bishop, D. S., Keitner, G. I., Baldwin, L. M., & van der Spuy, H. I. J. (1994). The development of a clinical rating scale for the McMaster Model of Family Functioning. *Family Process, 33,* 53–69.

Miller, I. W., Kabacoff, R. I., Keitner, G. I., Epstein, N. B., & Bishop, D. S. (1986). Family functioning in the families of psychiatric patients. *Comprehensive Psychiatry, 27,* 302–312.

Miller, I. W., Keitner, G. I., Epstein, N. B., Bishop, D. S., & Ryan, C. E. (1991, November). *Family functioning in bipolar disorder.* Presented at the meeting of the Association for the Advancement of Behavior Therapy, New York.

Miller, I. W., Keitner, G. I., Whisman, M. A., Ryan, C. E., Epstein, N. B., & Bishop, D. S. (1992). Depressed patients with dysfunctional families: Description and course of illness. *Journal of Abnormal Psychology, 101,* 637–647.

Moos, R. J., & Moos, B. S. (1981). *Family environment scale manual,* Palo Alto, CA: Consulting Psychologists.

Olson, D. H. (1985). Commentary: Struggling with congruence across theoretical models and methods. *Family Process, 24,* 203–207.

Olson, D. H., McCubbin, H., Barnes, H., Larsen, A., Moxen, M., & Wilson, M. (1982). *Family inventories.* Unpublished manuscript.

Snyder, D. K., Wills, R. M., & Keiser, T. W. (1981). Empirical validation of the Marital Satisfaction Inventory: An actuarial approach. *Journal of Clinical Psychology, 49,* 262–268.

Spanier, G. B. (1976). Measuring dyadic adjustment: New scales for assessing the quality of marriage and other dyads. *Journal of Marital and Family Therapy, 38,* 15–28.

Spencer, J., Glick, I., & Haas, G. (1988). A randomized clinical trial of inpatient family intervention. III: Effects at 6-month and 18-month follow-ups. *American Journal of Psychiatry, 145,* 1115–1121.

Swindle, R. W., Cronkite, R. C., & Moos, R. H. (1989). Life stressors, social resources, coping and the 4-year course of unipolar depression. *Journal of Abnormal Psychology, 98,* 468–477.

Targum, S. D., Dibble, E. D., Davenport, Y. B., et al. (1981). The Family Attitudes questionnaire: Patients' and spouses' views of bipolar illness. *Archives of General Psychiatry, 38,* 562–568.

Vaughn, C. E., & Leff, J. P. (1976a). The influence of family and social factors on the course of psychiatric illness. *British Journal of Psychiatry, 129,* 125–137.

Vaughn, C. E., & Leff, J. P. (1976b). The measurement of expressed emotion in families of psychiatric patients. *British Journal of Social and Clinical Psychology, 15,* 157–165.

Veiel, H. O. F. (1993). Detrimental effects of kin support networks on the course of depression. *Journal of Abnormal Psychology, 102,* 419–429.

Wadeson, H., & Fitzgerald, R. (1971). Marital relationship in manic-depressive illness. *Journal of Nervous and Mental Disease, 153,* 180–204.

Waring, E. M., McElrath, D., Mitchell, P., et al. (1981). Intimacy and emotional illness in the general population. *Canadian Journal of Psychiatry, 26,* 167–172.

Weissman, M. M. (1975). The assessment of social adjustment: A review of techniques. *Archives of General Psychiatry, 32,* 357–365.

CHAPTER 29

Substance Abuse and Addictive Personality Disorders

THEODORE G. WILLIAMS, MD

Today, no mental health professional would doubt that substance abuse is one of the primary health care concerns in the United States. Statistics compiled by the Children of Alcoholics Foundation reveal that alcoholism and alcohol abuse alone cause 100,000 American deaths annually. Over 6 percent of the U.S. population is involved in other drug dependence. Twenty-eight million children are affected, 7 million under the age of 18 years. Health care costs related to substance abuse are estimated at $140 billion a year (Webb & Fabean, 1994).

In spite of the fact that addiction to alcohol and drugs can be traced back to a few thousand years B.C. and the American Medical Association (AMA) first classified alcoholism as a disease in 1956, the controversy over whether alcohol and drug dependencies are diseases or self-destructive, out-of-control behaviors persists to this day (Webb & Fabean, 1994). This controversy confuses everyone involved, including families, treatment professionals, and payers for treatment.

Alcoholics Anonymous (AA), the originator of self-help programs that are now generally considered the most successful approach in maintenance of long-term recovery from addictions (Webb & Fabean, 1994), has not clarified the controversy. AA had its origins in Bible study and prayer groups and soon evolved into the current "12-step" guides for achieving sobriety. Initially the emphasis was on controlling negative behaviors, correcting character "defects," and seeking spiritual identification in recovery (Alcoholics Anonymous, 1976; Mooney, Eisenberg, & Eisenberg, 1992). (More on AA follows later in this chapter.)

Although treating professionals often speak about the disease model of addiction, there is no universally accepted disease model. Believing that drug addiction (including alcoholism) is a result of a biomedical or psychobiological process, many researchers and other medical professionals argue that chemical dependency is legitimately classified as a "disease." Contributing to this argument is the observation that drug dependency fits into the long-held disease model of having an agent (drug), a host (human), and a specific progressive course (at least for alcohol dependency). Goodwin and Warnock (1991) point out that there remains a "turf battle" between the proponents of the disease model and those who believe chemical dependency does not meet criteria for a disease.

HISTORICAL MODELS FOR ADDICTION

Disease Model

Prior to the AMA's declaration in 1956 that alcoholism is a disease, heavy drinking was considered immoral behavior. A "disease model" was pioneered by E. M. Jellinek (1952, 1960). Amazingly, Jellinek's model is still the basis for the medical model, and the treatment of chemical addiction in the United States falls within the realm of medicine. The key elements in the Jellinek model, based on alcoholism as the substance, are: (1) a loss of control over one's drinking, (2) progression through four distinct stages (pre-alcoholic, prodromal, crucial, and chronic), and (3) ultimate death if left untreated. Jellinek also classified subtypes of alpha, beta, gamma, delta, and epsilon of alcoholism. This theoretical model has become a standard paradigm for understanding the progressive course of alcoholism in the United States and also has been applied to dependency on other drugs. Figure 29.1 illustrates his stages of progression as well as steps through rehabilitation and recovery.

More recently, researchers have explored the genetics of chemical dependency with the goal of showing that addicts/alcoholics are somehow biologically different from non-addicts. Studies of brain neurotransmitters (Blum et al., 1990; Noble, Blum, Ritchie, Montgomery, & Sheridan, 1991) have found strong evidence of a genetic basis for alcoholism but have been challenged by other researchers. Currently, no unequivocal biological difference between alcoholics and nonalcoholics has been identified (Doweiko, 1993).

Compulsive Behavior Model

Numerous researchers and clinicians believe that chemical dependency has its basis in personality patterns that may even predict future substance abuse. Much of this view relates to the substance abuse as a compulsive behavior related to seeking an escape from life's trials. Horney (1964) viewed substance abuse as a reflection of emotional pain through which the individual attempts to blot out the anxiety he or she is experiencing. Khantzian (1985) suggested that individuals are drawn to narcotics to control internal feelings of rage and aggression. Bradshaw (1988) believed that all compulsive behavior reflects an individual's attempt to escape the shame experienced in the family of origin.

Hoffman, Loper, and Kammeier (1974), in a series of research projects using the Minnesota Multiphasic Personality Inventory (MMPI), attempted to identify a preexisting "alcoholic personality." A study of 38 males before and after chemical dependency treatment revealed a tendency toward impulsive behavior, but no other significant pathology.

In her book *Treating the Alcoholic: A Developmental Model of Recovery* (1985), Brown noted that the chemical a person uses provides an illusion of control over the harsh painful feelings encountered in life. In summarizing the schools of thought regarding the psychology and personality of substance abusers, Kaufman (1994) reviews issues of excessive dependency, illusion of power, temporary resolution of psychological pain, gender difference, effect intolerance, and dysfunctional family systems.

ADDICTIVE PERSONALITY DISORDER

Although research has not delineated a clear "addictive personality," and there is no such personality disorder listed in the fourth edition of the *Diagnostic and Statistical Manual*

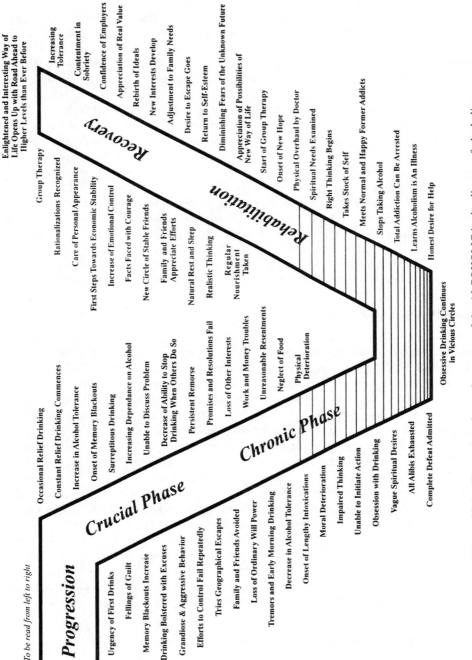

To be read from left to right

Progression

Occasional Relief Drinking

Urgency of First Drinks
Constant Relief Drinking Commences
Fellings of Guilt
Increase in Alcohol Tolerance
Memory Blackouts Increase
Onset of Memory Blackouts
Drinking Bolstered with Excuses
Surreptitious Drinking
Grandiose & Aggressive Behavior
Increasing Dependance on Alcohol
Efforts to Control Fail Repeatedly
Unable to Discuss Problem
Tries Geographical Escapes
Decrease of Ability to Stop Drinking When Others Do So
Family and Friends Avoided
Persistent Remorse
Loss of Ordinary Will Power
Promises and Resolutions Fail
Tremors and Early Morning Drinking
Loss of Other Interests
Decrease in Alcohol Tolerance
Work and Money Troubles
Onset of Lengthy Intoxications
Unreasonable Resentments
Moral Deterioration
Neglect of Food
Impaired Thinking
Physical Deterioration
Unable to Initiate Action
Obsession with Drinking
Vague Spiritual Desires
All Alibis Exhausted
Complete Defeat Admitted

Crucial Phase

Chronic Phase

Obsessive Drinking Continues in Vicious Circles

Rehabilitation

Realistic Thinking
Regular Nourishment Taken
Natural Rest and Sleep
Family and Friends Appreciate Efforts
New Circle of Stable Friends
Facts Faced with Courage
Increase of Emotional Control
First Steps Towards Economic Stability
Care of Personal Appearance
Rationalizations Recognized
Group Therapy

Physical Overhaul by Doctor
Spiritual Needs Examined
Right Thinking Begins
Takes Stock of Self
Meets Normal and Happy Former Addicts
Stops Taking Alcohol
Total Addiction Can Be Arrested
Learns Alcoholism is An Illness
Honest Desire for Help

Recovery

Enlightened and Interesting Way of Life Opens Up with Road Ahead to Higher Levels than Ever Before

Increasing Tolerance
Contentment in Sobriety
Confidence of Employers
Appreciation of Real Value
Rebirth of Ideals
New Interests Develop
Adjustment to Family Needs
Desire to Escape Goes
Return to Self-Esteem
Diminishing Fears of the Unknown Future
Appreciation of Possibilities of New Way of Life
Start of Group Therapy
Onset of New Hope

Figure 29.1   The progression and recovery of the ALCOHOLIC in the disease of alcoholism.

450

of Mental Disorders (DSM-IV) (American Psychiatric Association [APA], 1994), this clinician, in over 20 years of psychiatric practice devoted primarily to the treatment of alcoholics, drug addicts, and other compulsive behaviors, has observed behaviors and attitudes that are almost universal in alcoholics/addicts who present for treatment. These include impatience, impulsivity, emotional immaturity for their developmental and chronological age, superficial sense of entitlement, gradiosity, false sense of control, intolerance for dysphoric mood, self-deception, and, of course, the defense mechanisms of denial, rationalization, projection, and minimization. Additionally, the addict exhibits a distorted view of adult living, usually shunning responsibilities, seeking a caretaker, lying regarding drug-using habits—and often other areas of his or her life—unavailability for interpersonal nurturing and intimacy, and emotional isolation.

In spite of no generally recognized "addictive personality," Nakken (1988), wrote convincingly:

> The foundation of the addictive personality may be found in all persons. It's found in a normal desire to make it through life with the least amount of pain and the greatest amount of pleasure possible. It's found in our negativism and our mistrust of others and the world, whether our pessimism is big or small, valid or not valid. There is nothing wrong with this part of us; it is natural for all of us to have these beliefs to some degree. It's when these beliefs control one's way of life, as they do in addiction, that people get into trouble.

There are people who do not know how to have any healthy relationships and who have been taught not to trust anyone—primarily because of how they were treated while they were growing up; they never learned how to connect positively.

Nakken described the pattern of addicts' thinking that continually supports and reinforces their internal belief system. Also, every time addicts choose to act out in an addictive way, they are saying to themselves one or more of the following:

- "I don't really need people."
- "I don't have to face anything I don't want to."
- "I'm afraid to face life's and my problems."
- "Objects and events are more important than people."
- "I can do anything I want, whenever I want, no matter who it hurts" (p. 27).

Eventually, addiction begins to create what the person is trying to avoid—pain. Then addicts seek relief by moving further into the addictive process.

THE ADDICTIVE PROCESS

All addictions, from a psychological viewpoint, have in common the out-of-control and aimless searching for wholeness, happiness, and peace through a relationship with an object or event (Brown, 1985). The object is to achieve this through a desired mood change. Addiction is seductive because the desired mood change (via the chemical) is predictable and can be obtained rapidly. It substitutes for interpersonal nurturing so that the addict has the illusion of nurturance through avoidance and can delay facing serious life issues. The addiction eventually becomes the primary emotional relationship;

it is to an object (the substance) that is more dependable than people are. Thus, people become one-dimensional objects to manipulate. As the addiction progresses, the addict's compulsive dishonesty leads him or her to mistrust others and he or she becomes more isolated. Eventually, addicts treat themselves as they treat others, as objects, and an emotional breakdown ensues. The addictive personality remains part of these people for life. On some level this type of personality will always be searching for an object or some type of event with which to form an addictive relationship. People with this personality constellation always will hold the illusion that some object or event can nurture them. This underlying drive toward a need for an addictive relationship becomes the core of treatment and, ultimately, of recovery from addiction.

A FAMILY-CENTERED DISORDER

Clearly, the behaviors of the addict have a marked effect on others in his or her life, especially those most intimately involved, namely, family members (including nonmarried partners and friends). The family can be viewed as a system that adapts to the consistently chaotic and usually demanding behavior of the addict/alcoholic (Ackerman, 1983). The family system changes to accommodate him or her. Fear is operant, everybody "walks on eggshells" (Freiberg, 1991), roles are reversed, power and responsibilities are redistributed.

Some family members, especially children, may experience position and power for the first time as the addict member abdicates responsibilities (Williams, 1984). Wegscheider (1981) outlined "survival roles" often adopted by members of a chemically dependent family system. These include the chief enabler, the family hero, the family scapegoat, the lost child, and the family mascot. Figure 29.2 outlines the function and price of each role.

Without family treatment and resolution of the chemical dependency problem, these roles often accompany the family member into adult life and/or other relationships. In adapting to parental chemical addiction, the family acquires a new homeostasis, dysfunctional as it may be. Family members often cling to this fragile balance in order to maintain some stability. Generally, they resist change even when the addict member "sobers up," mistrusting his or her future sobriety and unwilling to relinquish the power they have acquired. So, a paradox exists (Doweiko, 1993): The family is unhappy with the addiction problem but may be comfortable with the redistribution of power and responsibility that eventuated because of it.

Case History

Teen "Superhero"

The following case is illustrative of the type of dynamics and functioning frequently encountered in an alcoholic and his or her family system. The strength of roles within the addictive family and the resistance of the system to change became dramatically apparent to this therapist several years ago in working with an addictive family. The father was referred for evaluation because his drinking problem was beginning to show up on his job. Assessment of the family revealed that the wife/mother was an ambulatory schizophrenic who sometimes took psychotropic medication and often drank with her husband. There were three children: a 14-year-old boy; a nine-year-old daughter who was mentally retarded, living at home and attending a special school; and a six-year-old daughter. The

ROLE	FUNCTION/RESPONSIBILITY	PRICE
Chief Enabler	Shelter the addict from consequences of behavior (usually spouse)	Martyrdom
Family Hero	Family's self-worth Family Counselor (often eldest child)	Compulsive Drive
Family Scapegoat	Divert attention from the drug problem by inappropriate behavior	Self-destructive Behavior (often addiction)
Lost Child	Escape by emotional and physical separation	Social Isolation
Family Mascot	Divert attention from the drug problem by humor	Immaturity and/or emotional illness

Source: Data adapted from S. Wegscheider (1984), *Another chance: Hope and health for the alcoholic family* (Palo Alto, CA: Science and Behavior Books).

Figure 29.2 Survival roles in the addict family.

roles the family members had assumed became evident quickly. Both parents had functionally abandoned their parental responsibilities except that the father was on active duty in the U.S. Navy; this thereby assured them of a paycheck. The son was managing the household, caring for his retarded sister, ensuring that she was ready for the school bus daily, doing the grocery shopping, and preparing most meals for his siblings as well as being sure they were clean and adequately clothed. He was an A student, had nearly reached the level of Eagle Scout, had a newspaper delivery route and a girlfriend, and played on a school athletic team. He was clearly the family "superhero." The older daughter was the family "mascot" and the younger daughter the "lost child."

As attempts at family therapy progressed, most impressive was the son's resistance to giving up power and to changing roles, much more so than other family members. Therapy was interrupted by several crises, including the wife/mother's psychiatric hospitalization; little progress was made before the husband/father's discharge from the navy.

"CODEPENDENCY"

In spite of the popularity of the term "codependency" in the past ten years, particularly in 12-step programs (e.g., "Codependents Anonymous"), there is no standard definition, nor has it been accepted as a legitimate DSM-IV psychiatric diagnosis (American Psychiatric Association, 1994). Wegscheider-Cruse and Cruse (1990) defined codependency as "a pattern of painful dependency on compulsive behaviors and on approval from others in an attempt to find safety, self-worth, and identity." Other meanings might include trying to help another when the assistance actually contributes to hurting or disabling him or her and/or oneself. Codependents believe in the illusion that they can stop the pain if they can get the addict to stop acting out.

Some generally accepted codependent behaviors include:

- Difficulty identifying and expressing feelings
- Difficulty in forming and maintaining relationships
- Difficulty adapting to change
- Rigidity and perfectionism
- Feeling overly responsible for the behaviors and feelings of others
- Constant need for approval from others to feel good
- Indecisiveness
- Feelings of powerlessness over life
- Martyrdom and blaming
- Holding others responsible for one's feelings and emotions
- Making excuses and lying for the addict (covering consequences of behavior)
- Denying problems ("keeping up a front")
- Perpetuating crises
- Losing a sense of self
- Being angry about giving help

In short, a codependent needs the addict to depend on him or her. Of course, not all of these behaviors are present and visible in a codependent at any one time. However, it is important to view the scope of these behaviors and comprehend the extent of the possible psychological damage experienced by persons who are closely connected to the addict/alcoholic over a period of time.

Several cautions are in order. Being caring, nurturing, and courteous are not, in and of themselves, codependent behaviors. These are essential in healthy relationships; it is when they become excessive and unidimensional that they move into the codependent behavior realm. Further, not everyone who is involved in an ongoing relationship with an addict is codependent. Only those who have suffered significant hardship as a result of the nature of the relationship should be considered codependent to the addict.

CHRONIC EMERGENCY LIVING

Usually the only consistency in the addict family is chaos and inconsistency. Adult members may react with legitimate psychological problems, including mood and anxiety disorders, adjustment disorders, somatoform disorders, sleep disorders, sexual disorders, eating disorders, and, in some extreme cases, Post-traumatic Stress Disorder. Owings-West and Prinz (1987), in their review of the impact of parental alcoholism on the psychological development of children, concluded that parental alcoholism contributes to a number of behavioral problems, including poor academic performance and inattentiveness. Children of substance abusers may experience school phobia (separation anxiety), disruptive behavior disorders, tics, and elimination disorders. Some children become addicted to the excitement and unpredictability of living in an addict home and may become involved in fire-setting, shoplifting, or other antisocial behaviors. Others may get caught up in protecting the family and become overly serious, mature, and well organized. Childhood personality and behavior factors found by Brook, Whiteman,

Gordon, and Cohen (1986) to be associated with later substance abuse include rebelliousness, lack of social skills, and aggression. Parental substance use is consistently associated with adolescent marijuana use (Penning & Barnes, 1982). Webb (1989) contended that the adolescent raised in an alcoholic home spends so much time and energy meeting basic survival needs that he or she does not have the opportunity to establish a strong sense of personal identity.

Children of alcoholics often blame themselves for their parent's drinking (Freiberg, 1991) and become stuck in feelings of guilt and shame. This factor was a major contributory one to the formation and success of the ACOA (Adult Children of Alcoholics) self-help groups (Colette, 1990). However, Blau (1990) points out that when ACOA was formed in the early 1980s, it focused on help for survivors of extreme abuse. Over the years the term "abuse" has become blurred, and in his opinion the tendency to blame parents for everything has become "a national obsession."

While growing up in an addictive family, a person learns addictive beliefs and "addictive logic" (Nakken, 1988). Addictive parents exhibit "crazy-making" behaviors, one minute loving and concerned, the next minute acting like irresponsible children. The child changes along with the parent(s) in an attempt to stay connected. The insecurity resulting from this instability leads the child to feel different from peers, experiencing more self-doubt, confusion, and a craving to know what is normal. Often a sense of doom follows them into adulthood, sometimes feeling worse if things are going well, fearing something bad will happen soon. Good times cannot be trusted in addictive families. Members look for distractions to nourish themselves, thus often initiating an addiction of their own. Addicts teach addiction. Family members learn "addictive logic," to deny the chaos; to lie and say the problem does not exist so as not to betray the family. "To survive in an addictive system, children learn to deny their healthy responses that tell them they are in danger; they have to keep increasing these dishonest coping skills because the insanity and the illness keep progressing" (Nakken, 1988, p. 79). Clinicians everywhere have seen how this pattern takes its toll on countless individuals who grow up in addictive families.

SUGGESTED CRITERIA FOR RELATIONAL DIAGNOSIS OF ALCOHOLIC/ADDICT FAMILIES

It is the author's experience (Williams, 1984) that many addictive family members are in need of psychological treatment but do not meet criteria for a DSM-IV Axis I diagnosis. With an understanding of the psychosocial dynamics of the addictive process and the reactive patterns of family members and other persons intimately involved with alcoholics/addicts, the following criteria for relational diagnosis are proposed. The primary DSM-IV Axis IV psychosocial and environmental problem is *difficulty in intimate involvement with a heavy substance abuser* (including alcohol, illicit, and licit drugs). Generally, as it now exists, there would be no coexisting DSM-IV Axis I or Axis II diagnosis. It is suggested that *seven of the 13 characteristic behaviors need to be present in some or all family members to establish the proposed relational diagnosis.*

1. Markedly diminished interest in one or more significant activities (pleasure, job).
2. Decreased attention, concentration, memory, distractibility, indecisiveness.
3. Self-imposed social avoidance and isolation with decreased effectiveness.

4. Depressed mood that persists more than seven days.

5. Irritability or excessive anger (may include explosiveness).

6. Complaints of low energy, fatigue, apathy, feelings of hopelessness, worthlessness, guilt.

7. Pervasive pessimistic attitude.

8. Motor tension (restlessness, shakiness, dizziness, shortness of breath).

9. Excessive complaints of physical symptoms/illness (e.g., headaches, diarrhea, upset stomach).

10. Excessive worry, anxiety, fear (continuous for at least one month; may include panic attacks, sleep disturbance, mild paranoia).

11. Evidence of persistent involuntary or compulsive behaviors to alleviate anxiety (e.g., alcohol and/or drug abuse, eating disorders, rituals, stuttering, tics).

12. Significant deterioration in daily habits (grooming, diet, hygiene, motivation).

13. Onset of high risk, self-endangering behaviors.

TREATMENT FOR THE ADDICTIVE FAMILY

Treatment for the addictive family usually starts with intervention into the addict's disease. The first step is detoxification. Obviously, this requires the addict's cooperation. It is best accomplished in a medical setting for safety reasons (avoidance of medical complications, withdrawal seizures, delirium tremens) and complete assessment (medical, psychological, and psychiatric). Intoxication or withdrawal from alcohol, narcotics, psychostimulants (cocaine and methamphetamine), hallucinogens, and infinite combinations often can mimic psychoses, mania, or severe depression. Psychoactive drugs also may mask underlying DSM-IV Axis I diagnoses. Once detoxification is complete and the addict is cooperative, the family members should become involved in rehabilitation and recovery (for themselves as well as the addict). Sometimes the process starts before detoxification, if family members are involved in an intervention to motivate the addict to accept treatment.

The most widely used technique for formal intervention was developed for the treatment of alcoholism at the Johnson Institute in Minneapolis, Minnesota, and has been adapted for use with all addictions (Johnson, 1980). In this technique available family members and other persons most meaningful in the addict's life (e.g., friends, employer, physician, clergy) are coached by a therapist/counselor to confront the addict with their observations and concerns. Each member of the intervention "team" must present specific details of how the addiction has hurt and negatively affected them in other ways with a nonjudgmental, nonhostile approach and reassure the identified patient of their caring and concern. Liepman, Nirenberg, and Begin (1989), in examining the impact of formal family intervention, showed a much higher rate of alcoholics entering treatment following this kind of intervention.

For the addict, current "state-of-the-art" treatment beyond detoxification involves intensive education on the psychological, biological, and social aspects of the disease. Generally, individual and group education and counseling are utilized with the goal of breaking through the addict's defense mechanisms, which have allowed him or her to continue on a self-destructive course. Figure 29.1 illustrates the steps for successful rehabilitation and recovery. Total abstinence from the chemicals formerly abused has been the most widely accepted model in the United States for many years. Treatment approaches involving controlled alcohol or drug use in alcoholics/addicts (Hester & Miller, 1989) and aversion therapies (Rimmele, Miller, & Dougher, 1989) have not been widely accepted, and their reported results have been challenged.

In recent years the traditional 28-day inpatient rehabilitation programs, which were popular in the late 1970s and 1980s, have dwindled in utilization and size due to funding restrictions in the era of managed health care. The current trend is toward enrollment in day treatment or outpatient counseling programs soon after detoxification (Webb & Fabean, 1994).

For several decades the backbone of long-term recovery has been the self-help "12-step" program of Alcoholics Anonymous (Emrick, Torrigan, Montgomery, & Little, 1993; Kaufman, 1994; Webb & Fabean, 1994). This model has been adapted to the formation of other groups to include Narcotics Anonymous, Cocaine Anonymous, Overeaters Anonymous, Marijuana/"Pot Smokers" Anonymous, Adult Children of Alcoholics (ACA and ACOA), Pills Anonymous, Sexaholics Anonymous, Sex Addicts Anonymous, Sexual Compulsives Anonymous, Alanon and Alateen (for significant others), and several others. This author recently discovered what may be the limit of this phenomenon: TOWA: "The Other Woman's Anonymous" group.

These groups all follow the 12-step program as presented in the "Big Book" of AA, entitled *Alcoholics Anonymous* (1976). These 12 steps involve progression from recognizing one's powerlessness over the addiction, recognizing a higher power, turning one's will over to one's higher power ("God as we understand him"), taking inventory of wrongs to others, making amends, living in total honesty, sharing, and supporting others in their recovery. Major strengths of the 12-step programs are the multiplicity of support meetings held daily in most communities, which supply camaraderie, identification with other recovering addict/alcoholics, and personal sponsorship by a member more senior in the recovery process. Significantly, AA does not talk about a "cure." Rather, paramount in the AA philosophy of recovery is the concept that although a person may be sober and abstinent, he or she must keep in the forefront of thinking that he or she will always be an addict and must guard against relapse. AA and similar 12-step recovery groups stress anonymity, nonallegiance with any other organizations, minimal nonprofit administration, and total self-support.

The past decade has seen more interchange between the fields of addiction treatment and family therapy. Involvement of family members in the treatment of substance abusers, adult and adolescent alike, is now considered a key factor in successful long-term recovery (Friedman & Granick, 1990; Kaufman, 1992). Feldman (1992) emphasizes the synergism between family therapy and individual therapy for the substance abuser. He states that family therapy is the best way to promote interpersonal changes, and intrapsychic individual change often may be blocked by family dysfunction.

Kaufman (1985) outlined four different types of family systems in which alcoholism is a major problem. They require different family therapy interventions, all of which stress the interaction between family dynamics and the dynamics of alcoholic behavior.

In the Functional Family System (the family with an alcoholic member), generally, one member is in the early stages of alcohol dependency and the family is still functioning harmoniously. Therapeutic intervention usually can be limited to educative approaches involving only the nuclear family.

In the Neurotic Enmeshed Family System (the alcoholic family), drinking behavior is grossly disruptive to family life leading to the patterns described earlier in this chapter. Explicit family psychotherapy usually is required, often with multiple generations of those involved in the enmeshed neurotic relationships.

The Disintegrated Family System (the alcoholic temporarily separated from the alcoholic family) often represents a later stage when the family system has collapsed and is marked by estrangement and separation. Any chance of reconstitution can occur only after several months of rehabilitation of the alcoholic member. Some contact between the alcoholic and family members should be made to explore the possibility of reunification and to establish new, healthier roles and relationships.

The Absent Family System (the alcoholic permanently separated from the family) often is at the end stage of alcoholic deterioration, with little or no family contact. Social contacts have deteriorated to include only drinking partners, who offer minimal real support. The goal of intervention is not to reconstitute the family but rather to help the alcoholic develop new social support systems. Partial institutionalization may be required (e.g., "halfway houses").

Figure 29.3 illustrates the emotions and behaviors (source unknown) during the progression and recovery in the addictive family. With professional help and usually full family involvement and the ongoing support of the "12-step" programs, a better-functioning family system can emerge. Of course, not all family members may progress at the same rate. Members with a higher number of the characteristics for diagnosis of a Relational Disorder may need more intensive treatment. It is not uncommon for family members to sabotage recovery so as to keep the familiar dysfunctional system in balance, thereby maintaining roles of power and avoiding the risk of uncertain change.

THERAPY OUTCOMES

Until recently, studies of results of marital/family therapy with addictive families have focused mainly on alcoholic families. Areas studied include therapy to initiate change in the alcoholic, therapy to stabilize change in the alcoholic, behavioral counseling and contracting, multiple-family and couple's group therapy, and therapy during long-term maintenance of sobriety (O'Farrell & Cowles, 1989). Recent studies of treatment outcome in families with drug problems are generally positive.

There is considerable research support for the efficacy of family involvement in group treatment of substance abusers. Kaufman (1992) reports a marked decrease in recidivism of adolescent drug abusers when family members are involved in multiple-family and couple's group treatment. The Netherlands study at the University of Nijmegen (Romijn, Platt, Schippers, & Schaap, 1992) reports that success was most evident when a significant improvement in positive communication occurred during family therapy. Galanter (1994) describes network therapy as a treatment approach that also includes a group of people close to the addict (beyond the family) to provide effective support for rehabilitation.

It is not within the scope of this chapter to review the many techniques of family therapy that have been adapted to or created for the treatment of addict families. Interestingly, McCrady (1986) noted that approaches to family therapy often do not take into account the stage of the addictive behavior. By considering the different roles of family

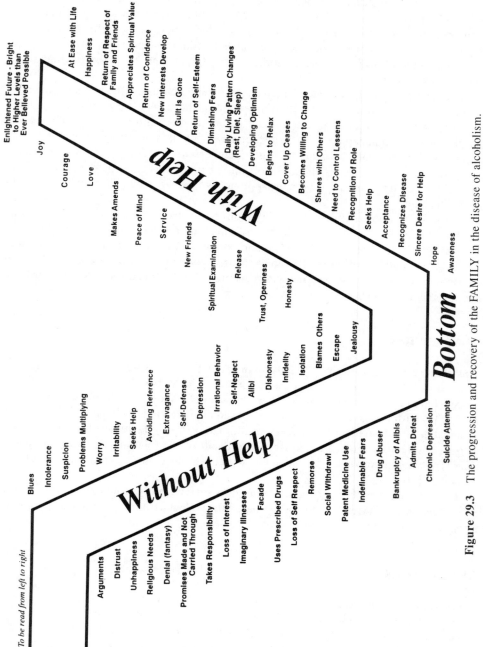

Figure 29.3 The progression and recovery of the FAMILY in the disease of alcoholism.

members at different stages of individual change, the effectiveness of family-involved treatment may be improved.

In the past decade there has been increased recognition of the prevalence of comorbid psychotherapy in addicted populations. Minkoff (1994) outlines historical and economic reasons for the past separation of treatment for addictions and other psychological disorders. He details programmatic approaches to "dual-diagnosis" treatment that require some modification of standard addiction treatment approaches for psychiatric patients and vice versa.

A critical area involves the use of psychotropic medication with substance abusers. In the experience of this author, "12-step" programs have been very slow to accept the use of nonaddictive antidepressant and antipsychotic medications. There is increasing enlightenment and acceptance as the effectiveness of such medications are becoming well known. Individual treatment of family members who meet criteria for a Relational Diagnosis of Addict Families should involve psychotherapies and psychotropic medications (if indicated) plus the treatment approaches involving the addict member as described earlier.

The most effective treatment for addict families involves the engagement of the addict and family members in long-term treatment. This requires many months of professional involvement, beginning with intervention and detoxification followed by intensive education, group and/or individual therapies, pharmacotherapy, if indicated, rebuilding of relationships, and support systems with acceptance of the need for indefinite involvement of the addict in active recovery.

CONCLUSION

This chapter has outlined the relationship of alcoholism and drug addition to family systems. Models of addiction, characteristics of the addictive personality, and the addictive process have been reviewed. Emotional and behavioral responses of family members were elucidated with the goal of justifying proposed characteristic behaviors for the establishment of relational diagnoses in persons intimately involved with alcoholic/addicts and who have suffered significant hardship as a result of the relationship over a period of time. Treatment approaches for alcoholic/addict families and outcome studies were reviewed briefly.

It is clear that members of addictive families suffer greatly from dysfunctional family systems, which often become perpetuated through generations when therapeutic intervention is lacking.

REFERENCES

Ackerman, R. J. (1983). *Children of alcoholics: A guidebook for educators, therapists, and parents.* Holmes Beach, FL: Learning Publication.

Alcoholics Anonymous. (1976). New York: Alcoholics Anonymous World Services.

American Psychiatric Association. (1994). *Diagnostic and statistical manual of mental disorders* (4th ed.). Washington, DC: Author.

Blau, M. (1990). Toxic parents, perennial kids: Is it time for adult children to grow up? *Utne Reader, 42,* 60–65.

Blum, K., Noble, E. P., Sheridan, P. J., Montgomery, A., Ritchie, T., Jagadeeswaran, P., Nogami, H., Briggs, A. H., & Cohen, J. B. (1990). Allelic association of human dopamine D2 receptor gene in alcoholism. *Journal of the American Medical Association, 263*(15), 2055–2060.

Bradshaw, J. (1988). *Bradshaw on the family.* Deerfield Beach, FL: Health Communications.

Brook, J. S., Whiteman, M., Gordon, A. S., & Cohen, P. (1986). Dynamics of childhood and adolescent personality traits and adolescent drug use. *Developmental Psychology, 22,* 403–414.

Brown, S. (1985). *Treating the alcoholic: A developmental model of recovery.* New York: Wiley.

Doweiko, H. E. (1993). *Concepts of chemical dependency* (2nd ed.). Belmont, CA: Wadsworth.

Emrick, C. D., Torrigan, J. S., Montgomery, H., & Little, L. (1993). Alcoholics Anonymous: What is currently known? In B. S. McCrady & W. R. Miller (Eds.), *Research on alcoholics anonymous* (pp. 41–76). New Brunswick, NJ: Rutgers Center for Alcoholic Studies.

Feldman, L. (1992). *Integrating individual and family therapy.* New York: Brunner/Mazel.

Freiberg, P. (1991). Panel hears of families victimized by alcoholism. *American Psychological Association Monitor, 22*(4), 30.

Friedman, A. S., & Granick, S. (Eds.). (1990). *Family therapy for adolescent drug abuse.* Lexington, MA: Lexington Books.

Galanter, M. (1994, January/February). Using family and peer support to improve treatment outcome. *The Counselor,* 10–14.

Goodwin, D. W., & Warnock, J. K. (1991). Alcoholism: A family disease. In R. J. Frances & S. I. Miller (Eds.), *Clinical textbook of addictive disorders* (pp. 122–137). New York: Guilford.

Hester, R. K., & Miller, W. R. (1989). Self-control training. In R. K. Hester & W. R. Miller (Eds.), *Handbook of alcoholism treatment approaches* (pp. 141–149). Elmsford, NY: Pergamon.

Hoffman, H., Loper, R. G., & Kammeier, M. L. (1974). Identifying future alcoholics with MMPI alcohol scales. *Quarterly Journal of Studies on Alcohol, 35,* 490–498.

Horney, K. (1964). *The neurotic personality of our time.* New York: Norton.

Jellinek, E. M. (1952). Phases of alcohol addiction. *Quarterly Journal of Studies on Alcohol, 13,* 673–674.

Jellinek, E. M. (1960). *The disease concept of alcoholism.* New Haven, CT: College and University Press.

Johnson, V. E. (1980). *I'll quit tomorrow* (rev. ed.). San Francisco: Harper & Row.

Kaufman, E. (1985). Family therapy in the treatment of alcoholism. In E. B. Bratter & G. G. Forrest (Eds.), *Alcoholism and substance abuse: Strategies for clinical intervention* (pp. 376–397). New York: Free Press.

Kaufman, E. (1994). *Psychotherapy of addicted persons.* New York: Guilford.

Kaufman, P. (1992). Family therapy with adolescent substance abusers. In E. Kaufman & P. Kaufman (Eds.), *Family therapy of drug and alcohol abuse* (2nd ed., pp. 63–71). Needham Heights, MA: Allyn and Bacon.

Khantzian, E. J. (1985). The self-medication hypothesis of addictive disorders: Focus on heroin and cocaine dependence. *American Journal of Psychiatry, 142,* 1259–1264.

Liepman, M. R., Nirenberg, T. D., & Begin, A. M. (1989). Evaluation of a program designed to help family and significant others to motivate resistant alcoholics into recovery. *American Journal of Drug and Alcohol Abuse, 15*(2), 209–221.

McCrady, B. S. (1986). Family in the change process. In W. R. Miller & N. Heather (Eds.), *Treating addictive disorders: Processes of change* (pp. 305–318). New York: Plenum.

Minkoff, K. (1994). Models for addiction treatment in psychiatric populations. *Psychiatric Annals, 24*(8), 412–417.

Mooney, A. J., Eisenberg, A., & Eisenberg, H. (1992). *The recovery book.* New York: Workman.

Nakken, C. (1988). *The addictive personality: Understanding compulsion in our lives.* New York: Harper/Hazelden.

Noble, E. P., Blum, K., Ritchie, T., Montgomery, A., & Sheridan, P. J. (1991). Allelic association of the D2 dopamine receptor gene with receptor-binding characteristics in alcoholism. *Archives of General Psychiatry, 48,* 648–654.

O'Farrell, T. J., & Cowles, K. S. (1989). Marital and family therapy. In R. K. Hester & W. R. Miller (Eds.), *Handbook of alcoholism treatment approaches* (pp. 183–205). Elmsford, NY: Pergamon.

Owings-West, M., & Prinz, R. J. (1987). Parental alcoholism and child psychopathology. *Psychological Bulletin, 102*(2), 204–281.

Penning, M., & Barnes, G. E. (1982). Adolescent marijuana use: A review. *International Journal of the Addictions, 17*(5), 749–791.

Rimmele, C. T., Miller, W. R., & Dougher, M. J. (1989). Aversion therapies. In R. K. Hester & W. R. Miller (Eds.), *Handbook of alcoholism treatment approaches* (pp. 128–140). Elmsford, NY: Pergamon.

Romijn, C. M., Platt, J. J., Schippers, G. M., & Schaap, C. P. (1992). Family therapy for Dutch drug users: The relationship between family functioning and success. *International Journal of the Addictions, 27*(1), 1–14.

Webb, R. T., & Fabean, A. (1994, October). The evolution of endurance of the 12-step approach. *Family Therapy News.*

Webb, S. T. (1989). Some developmental issues of adolescent children of alcoholics. *Adolescent Counselor, 1*(6), 47–48, 67.

Wegscheider, S. (1981). *Another chance: Hope and health for the alcoholic family.* Palo Alto, CA: Science & Behavior Books.

Wegscheider-Cruse, S., & Cruse, J. R. (1990). *Understanding codependency.* Pompano Beach, FL: Health Communications.

Williams, T. G. (1984). Substance misuse and alcoholism in the military family. In F. W. Kaslow & R. I. Ridenour (Eds.), *The military family* (pp. 73–97). New York: Guilford.

CHAPTER 30

Eating Disorders and Their Impact on Family Systems

PAULA LEVINE, PHD

While a great deal has been written about the impact of the family system on the development of an eating disorder, very little has been written about the impact of the eating disorder on the development of a family. The DSM-IV (APA, 1994) includes refusal to maintain a minimally normal body weight, intense fear of gaining weight, disturbance in the perception of one's body shape or size, and amenorrhea for at least three cycles in postmenarcheal females as the essential diagnostic criteria for Anorexia Nervosa. Other associated features include symptoms of depression, obsessive-compulsive thoughts and behaviors, feelings of ineffectiveness, and restrained emotional expression. Nowhere in the DSM-IV is the relational component mentioned.

For a diagnosis of Bulimia Nervosa, the DSM-IV includes recurrent episodes of binge eating; compensatory methods of purging to prevent weight gain such as vomiting, laxative abuse, and fasting, episodes occurring at least twice a week for three months; and self-evaluation excessively influenced by shape and weight as the essential diagnostic criteria. Associated features include symptoms of depression, symptoms of anxiety, and drug or alcohol abuse. Once again, the relational component of this eating disorder that both erupts in and disrupts family functioning is nowhere mentioned.

A new and still-controversial diagnostic category, termed "Binge Eating Disorder" (BED) was considered for inclusion in the DSM-IV and then rejected (Spitzer et al., 1992). The diagnostic criteria for BED include recurrent episodes of binge eating and a sense of lack of control during the episodes (APA, 1994).

Because anorexia, bulimia, and binge eating disorder are complicated biopsychosocial disorders that are rooted at least partially in the family-of-origin system, this chapter seeks to include the relational component of these eating disorders and develop a criteria set that will reflect relevant relational issues. Other etiological components include bio-genetic and sociocultural factors, individual personality predispositions, body dissatisfaction and dieting history, and life stressors such as puberty, loss, and threats to self-esteem.

What effect does a child who is starving herself have on the family system? What is the impact of her denial, her lies, and her relentless pursuit of thinness? What effect does an adolescent who binges and purges have on the family system? What is the impact of her secrecy, her mood swings, and her nighttime forays into the family kitchen? What effect does the adult who binges without purging, who continually gains weight and turns to food for comfort, have on a new marriage? Conversely, how does the family originate and/or react to these disorders? Can we make any generalizations about families and marriages and how the system impacts the youngster, the adolescent, or the adult?

REVIEW OF THE LITERATURE

The literature contains many more theories and speculations about how family dynamics contribute to the development of an eating disorder than how eating disorder dynamics impact on the family system. Research by both Bruch (1973) and Minuchin (Minuchin, Rosman, & Baker, 1978) with over 100 families of anorexia nervosa patients revealed a parental psychological profile with the following four components: (1) overprotectiveness and enmeshment, including overconcern with dieting and fears of being fat; (2) overconscientious perfectionism; (3) lack of emotional expressiveness; and (4) too little decision making by and too much control over the anorexic child.

Sargent, Liebman, and Silber (1985) saw anorexia nervosa as a powerful interpersonal phenomenon, more influenced by than influencing family disorganization and dysfunction. As basic systems theorists, they saw dysfunctional family patterns forming a chain of circular causality in which every action is a reaction to other actions, and change in one family member affects other members. They described many of the same family phenomena as did Bruch (1973) and Minuchin and coworkers (1978) that maintain and reinforce the anorexic syndrome—enmeshment, overprotectiveness, rigidity, and lack of conflict resolution—and they highlight the specific aspects of family interaction that need to be altered by family therapy in order to assist the family in resolving the symptoms.

Root, Fallon, and Friedrich's study (1986) described three types of bulimic families: perfect, overprotective, and chaotic (dysfunctional). In the perfect family, bulimia becomes a perfect way to belong and to rebel at the same time. In the overprotective family, bulimia becomes a way to separate and create boundaries. In the chaotic family, bulimia becomes a way to capture temporary nurturance in order to fill the emptiness. In a study by Pike and Rodin (1991), it became evident that mothers placed direct pressure on their daughters to be thin as a precursor of their bulimia.

Schwartz, Barrett, and Saba (1985) hypothesized that bulimic symptoms can function in a family system as an excuse for not performing well, as the "passive" rebellion of a person who cannot rebel more directly against intrusive parents, as a way to protect the patient's parents or marriage by providing a focus that distracts them from their conflicts, and/or as an attempt to get nurturant attention or to demonstrate the severity of problems in a family that denies any problem and/or in which siblings are extremely competitive. They believed that most cases of bulimia fit into one or another combination of these hypotheses and that certain themes are present in almost all families with a bulimic member.

Madanes's (1984) marital therapy with symptomatic spouses reflected a strong relational point of view. She wrote about the issue of balancing power and of the incongruent hierarchies that result when the symptomatic spouse is simultaneously inferior and superior. In the case of the bulimic wife, Madanes saw the vomiting as a metaphor for both her submissiveness and her rebellion, or, as I often say to my patients, a metaphor for both "compliance and defiance." Her marital therapy, which consisted of a series of artful and paradoxical interventions, resulted in not only a reduction in binging and purging but also a rebalancing of power in the relationship so that the wife would not have to express either her power or her helplessness through bulimic symptomatology.

Finally, Schwartz (1995) has recently introduced a new way of thinking about and changing the human condition called the internal family systems (IFS) model. IFS combines systems thinking with what Schwartz calls "the multiplicity of the mind"—the idea that we all contain many different beings. Schwartz and his colleagues have done a great deal of work with bulimic clients and their families using the ISF model. They have moved from a traditional structural/strategic model to what they call a "parts" model; once relevant parts are identified and engaged, they are given labels, such as the Striver, the Evaluator, the Asserter, the Caretaker, and so forth. Schwartz believes that some parts of a person are forced into extreme and destructive roles; for example, a bulimic's parents may have stressed the importance of pleasing others and looking good, while shaming her when she showed anger. As a result, she allows the part of her that wants the approval of others to dominate while the part that needs to assert herself gets excluded. IFS would address this polarization of parts and challenge the part that plays the self-destructive role.

The literature just alluded to is about the impact of the family system on the development of an eating disorder rather than vice versa. Yet it is clear that when someone develops an eating disorder, whether it is anorexia, bulimia, or binge eating, it is a sign that something is wrong with both the individual *and* the family.

For example, if the family is preoccupied with food, weight, and dieting, and values perfectionism and high achievement, it is likely that the approval-seeking child, in a desperate measure to both "fit in" and achieve autonomy, will develop an eating disorder. The pursuit of thinness will win the approval of her weight-conscious parents while at the same time giving her a weapon with which to rebel: "No one can force me to eat." In the chaotic family, the weight gain that results from binge eating disorder will protect the individual from her emotional pain while at the same time allowing her to "take up more room" in the family, which might cause them to pay some attention.

As early as 1978, when Minuchin coined the phrase "the anorectic family," he was attempting to describe the interpersonal transactions that organize the behavior of family members and their dysfunctional patterns, and the feedback circularity by which family members constrain each other. He knew that "the identified patient was an active participant in the process of which there are no victimizers or victims, only family members involved in the small details of every day living." But, even in his eloquence, he felt "trapped by words" (Minuchin et al., 1978, p. 51).

THE IMPACT OF THE EATING DISORDER ON THE FAMILY SYSTEM

Less "trapped by words" in 1994, as relational diagnosis is coming of age, there has still been very little written on the impact of the eating disorder on the family or couple systems, an impact that is essential to understand if we are to make a truly relational diagnosis. No matter how the family dynamics and reactions perpetuate the eating disorder and no matter how the eating disorder upsets the family and keeps members overly focused on the individual, precisely this circularity, this "perpetual motion," is what we are attempting to describe.

This chapter addresses the impact of individuals with eating disorders on the following aspects of family life: (1) the initial impact of the discovery, including reactions to denial and secrecy, feelings of guilt and shame, feelings of fear and anxiety, and thoughts about how the family might have contributed; (2) the impact on the family's communication, including intimacy and marital, parent-child, and child-child tensions; (3) the impact on control and power issues, including problem solving and decision making; (4) the impact on everyday situations, including mealtimes, shopping, vacations, interaction with extended family, and family involvement in therapy; and (5) the impact on the family's spirituality.

STUDY OF THE CHARACTERISTICS OF A FAMILY WITH AN EATING-DISORDERED MEMBER

In order to study these family characteristics and tasks, I created a standardized interview schedule[1] that was mailed to 30 families of identified patients who either had been or still are in treatment with me. Of the 30 mailed, 18 were returned, representing 16 families. (One family returned three questionnaires, one from the mother and one from each of two female siblings.) Six identified patients were diagnosed with anorexia and ten with bulimia; of the ten with bulimia, six indicated that a combination of anorexia, bulimia, and binge eating disorder had at some point existed either simultaneously or sequentially.

Since binge eating disorder (BED) was not an exclusive diagnosis for any one of the 16 sample members, and since it was not included in DSM-IV as a separate diagnostic category, I will confine my remarks to anorexia and bulimia and base them on the questionnaire data as well as my own clinical experience. Since no spouses of married patients returned the questionnaire, I will concentrate on family interaction in which the eating-disordered member is a child. Nonetheless, treatment issues related to marriage will be addressed later in the chapter.

This sample of eating-disordered female patients currently range in age from 17 to 30 years, with some families remembering the age of onset as early as six, seven, and eight. This confirms recent findings that the precursors of eating disorders, dieting and body dissatisfaction, are developing in younger and younger populations (Mellin, Irwin, & Scully, 1992). The majority are still students, ranging from eleventh grade to graduate school, including being in law school, social work programs, and doctoral programs in psychology. Of those who work, two are teachers, one is a social worker, and one is a dietitian. In all cases but one, both parents are still alive, but in four out of 16 of the parents' marriages, there has been a divorce. In every case but two, the parent answering the questionnaire was the mother; in one case, both parents answered; and in another, the boyfriend. Eleven of the 16 women had one older or one younger sibling; one had two older siblings; two had two and three younger siblings respectively; and two were "only" children.

Because the questionnaire data did not really distinguish between anorexia and bulimia in any of the aspects of family life that follow, "eating disorders" will be the generic term utilized unless otherwise indicated.

---

[1] For a copy of the questionnaire, write directly to the author: Paula Levine, Ph.D., 111 Majorca Ave., Suite B, Coral Gables, FL 33134.

ASPECTS OF FAMILY LIFE

Impact of the Discovery

There was no common pathway to how or when the eating disorder was discovered. Responses ranged from suspicions that began very early: "She showed an unusual interest in dieting/weight loss and started to eat carefully in second grade" (anorexia), and "At about the age of eight she was terribly unhappy and stole money from home to buy food" (bulimia), to surprises later in life when "our older daughter told us," or "I saw her in a new nightie and gasped, 'What have you done to yourself?'"

After suspicion and discovery, there is often denial. In some families, the problem is the patient's denial; in others, it is the parents': "My husband and I noticed our daughter's anorexia despite her denial and secrecy . . . we saw it as a problem and wanted to help her . . . we sent her to a psychologist and years later, she admitted that she had 'fooled the shrink.'" One mother said, "I knew what was happening immediately but my husband denied it, stating that our daughter had great eating habits and self-control. I fought everyone to get her help but he remained in denial and said that I was trying to destroy her." Finally—and is it any wonder?—some parents, particularly mothers, sought help for themselves.

In addition to the suspicion, shock, denial, and secrecy, often feelings of guilt and shame arise. I was surprised at the wide range of responses that this question yielded, from "we do not feel any shame, guilt or embarrassment . . . we only feel concerned and caring for our daughter . . . we love her," to "I feel guilt and shame knowing that my values contributed to her disorder and great sadness that her way of dealing with the issues was so harmful to herself." One mother was "very open about the problem," while another was "made to promise by her son that his friends would never know about his sister's eating disorder." Some disclaimed feelings of embarrassment—"I was never embarrassed . . . I don't care who knows"—but readily owned feelings of guilt and shame: "I feel guilt for alcoholism during her early formative years and resignation that nothing can give back to her the missed security."

The feelings of fear and anxiety expressed were universal and did not differ between the anorexic and bulimic respondents despite the fact that anorexia is a more life-threatening and sometimes fatal illness. Fears of all kinds were expressed: "She's not eating enough . . . Is this a genetic problem? . . . Will she die? . . . Will she ever recover? . . . How will she cope at college?" One mother wrote, "We all fear for our daughter's life. Her social life and quality of life is always in danger. Her disease totally affects each of us—how we enjoy our lives and how we act toward her." Another wrote, "We are extremely concerned for her well-being—fear for her health and have grave concern about it getting out of control."

In summary, the range of reactions to the discovery of an eating disorder was broad with no one particular emotion prevailing. Families reacted with shock, shame, disappointment, anger, guilt, worry, devastation, sadness, disorientation, panic, fear, concern, and relief. Clearly the discovery stirs up all kinds of emotions in family members who might otherwise have remained disengaged. Both brothers and fathers pay attention to their sisters and daughters in a very different way once an eating disorder has been identified. The eating disorder may serve the purpose, at least initially, of (finally) giving her a voice and role in the family.

Most universally voiced are the thoughts about how family members might have contributed to the eating disorder. Four variables addressed repeatedly were:

- High emphasis on achievement/perfection
- Overconcern with beauty/appearance/thinness
- Parental dieting behavior
- Attention-seeking behavior and low self-esteem

Each will be addressed separately.

High Emphasis on Achievement

Such an emphasis flooded the questionnaire responses. For example, "All of our girls are high achievers; the patient pushes herself the most to excel and succeed above everyone else; achievement problems with our older two daughters—both of whom had eating disorders—may have contributed to the younger daughter's problems; there was a high emphasis on achievement by her father, owner of the ballet school at which I taught and our daughter danced. He constantly reminded her that she had to be thin for ballet and if she didn't get A's in school, her ballet classes were forbidden."

Child psychiatrist Sargent (1986) wrote that excessive reliance upon external achievement in families with eating-disordered individuals might guarantee a sense of worth in the family, but it repeatedly fails because the connections among family members are tenuous. Because there is often a dramatic and rapid fluctuation between over-involvement and abandonment (particularly in "chaotic" families), Sargent posited that all family members are left feeling both isolated and without a sense of self.

Overconcern with Beauty, Appearance, and Thinness

Typical responses were: "Our family may have spent too much time on perfection and talking about weight. Maybe we focused too much on appearance and superficial behaviors." Several mothers agreed that they were overly concerned about appearance and admitted to spending time reinforcing their daughters' beauty, in several cases to compensate for their daughters' outspoken feelings of low self-esteem. Unfortunately, even with more equal rights and opportunities for women than our society has ever known before, young girls still are often prized for their beauty and thinness, while womanhood itself still is often devalued within the family by both father and mother. This leaves daughters without a sense of trust in their bodies and with limited ability to rely upon their parents. With the overemphasis on appearance and the pursuit of thinness in our culture, it is young girls' inner attributes that are most in need of attention.

Parental Dieting Behavior

Dieting behavior of parents received a great deal of attention, and several repeated responses are worthy of note. Many mothers admitted to dieting and an overconcern with their daughter's weight: "Weight was always too important to myself and my husband. Our daughter always seemed unhappy with her body and I wanted to help her to be thinner since thinner was 'definitely better'!" One mother said, "I had a weight problem in both my teenage and my adult life. My daughter saw me diet at 600 calories a day . . . this was the same time that I saw my daughter's concern and obsession with weight begin." Another said, "My daughter doesn't know this, but I used to make myself throw up to lose weight." One mother wrote, "My husband and I have very good self-control about food. I'm able to eat what I want and stop before overeating. He is very disciplined and competitive. Our daughter saw his behavior and interpreted it in her own way in her own lifestyle."

What this last quote highlights is the often-overlooked role of fathers in these eating-disordered scenarios. Despite books such as *Father Hunger* (Main, 1991), which emphasizes the yearning that young girls have for their father's involvement in their lives and the too-frequent myths that somehow excuse or rationalize his absence, mother blaming is still prevalent in the clinical literature. In cases of eating disorders, pathologically narcissistic mothering is seen as a primary cause. Object relations theory speaks specifically of inappropriate attention to the infant's inner states (Bruch, 1973), the support of clinging behavior in the separating phase, and a failure in empathy (Masterson, 1977). All of these theories see the mother as the chief reason for the daughter's failure in an important developmental task, that of separation/individuation, the securing of an autonomous self. Nonetheless, fathers are by no means "blameless." Some pointed quotes follow on how fathers, according to their wives, may have contributed to the problem.

One mother wrote, "My husband is very heavy. We all worry about him, but he hasn't yet admitted that he may have a problem other than weight. On one occasion he suggested that short skirts and bobby socks appeared to cut her height and made her legs look heavier. He suggested some other style, but she heard none of this—only the criticism." This goes back to a point made earlier about a daughter's limited ability to rely on her parents, particularly when "constructive criticism" is being offered by the father from whom she yearns for more attention to her inner attributes and beauty and who himself is extremely overweight. In another family, the obese father constantly reminded his daughter that she had to be thin for ballet. And in another, "There was constant clashing over eating patterns between my husband and myself, when my husband would persuade the children to join him in eating rich desserts following a large meal. My husband loved to eat and would persistently press others to join him. He was extremely critical of my cooking. Dinnertime was not pleasant."

The last variable that many families mentioned in speculating how the family dynamics might have contributed to the eating disorder was the *degree of attention required by and paid to the child* and how this attention interacted with too much or too little self-esteem. The common theme seemed to be that this particular child required and received more attention than any of the others and yet ended up with lower self-esteem. One family with an only child felt that while the parents had not contributed to the problem, their daughter put too much pressure on herself to overachieve; "We have been at a loss as to why she has such low self-esteem (which she admits) . . . and she doesn't seem to be aware of, or believe, how beautiful she is naturally. We've always been very loving and supportive of her. As an only child, I suppose there could be too much attention, but it's not because of too little attention." Another mother wrote that "We do not feel that our eating behavior or too little attention had anything to do with it. Self-worth was low and although we reinforced her beauty—she never believed us."

Whenever the literature describes the personality profile of the young girl who might be "at risk" for the development of an eating disorder, such traits as perfectionism, high need for approval from others, denial of inner needs, and low self-esteem invariably are mentioned. When self-esteem is too rigidly tied to external attributes such as body weight, shape, and appearance, rather than to a more balanced set of attributes that include both inner and outer sources of self-worth, it is not difficult to understand how some young females take on the relentless pursuit of thinness as the promised answer to all of their problems. Once the youngster becomes invested in the pursuit of thinness or a more perfect body shape, a parent can say or do little to reverse the course of action, if what are really at stake are the youngster's core feelings of self-worth. Parents who have always been attentive become stymied, wondering why this disorder happened in the first place. This is truly an example of circularity: The more attention the child demands, the more the parents give, out of desperation, guilt, fear, and love. But the child hears nothing because it is validation that she is seeking, and what she is getting is "you would be so much more beautiful if you just gained (or lost) a few pounds; just put on a few pounds and we'll shop for anything you want; the boys will be falling at your feet if you just fill out a little."

That the identified patient develops symptoms in order to get attention has always been a stalwart hypothesis of systems theory. Minuchin (1978) said that "the concentration on the sick child's symptoms maximizes her self-appraisal . . . illness may become her identity card" (p. 61). Now, support for the "identified patient/attention" hypothesis is coming from even larger systems theory, from sociocultural studies supporting the fact that young women in our country are badly in need of attention, that they are being cheated, invalidated, and robbed of their voices. The groundbreaking research of Carol Gilligan and Lynn Mikel Brown (1992) on women's psychology and girls' development found that up until the age of 11 or 12, girls are clear, confident and courageous, aware of their own feelings, perceptive about relationships, unafraid of differences and conflicts, and willing to say what is on their minds. Then, as if there had been no women's movement in the last 25 years or perhaps, more appropriately, no real "movement for women," young girls absorb society's messages about how women "are supposed to be": good, nice, caring, self-sacrificing, soft-spoken, and ladylike—in short, perfect. They become confused: If they do speak their minds, they fear losing relationships that are important to them; if they do not, they fear they will lose themselves. Eventually, fear of losing (the approval of) others is replaced by rage at having lost themselves, a rage that all too often surfaces later as depression and eating disorders.

What Gilligan and Brown discovered in their Harvard study has been validated in two recently published books, *School Girls* (Orenstein, 1994) and *Failing at Fairness: How America's Schools Cheat Girls* (Sadker & Sadker, 1994). Orenstein and Sadker and Sadker observed what Gilligan and Brown coined as "the tyranny of the nice and kind" in classrooms all over the country. Orenstein studied eighth graders to find out why "young women dumb themselves down" and why they choose to sacrifice high self-esteem for being popular, pretty, polite, and not too smart. She was not surprised that many young women, particularly those who put pressure on themselves to succeed and be "not too smart" at the same time, feel anxious; she hypothesizes that this anxiety has led to a sharp increase in eating disorders among young women.

In summary, the self-esteem of young girls in this country is at its zenith by the age of eight and thereafter begins to plummet. Are eating disorders, therefore, a desperate cry for attention, a way to excel and be noticed without really succeeding, or a way to cope with the self-imposed pressure to achieve, excel, and succeed, goals that are apparently at odds with society's strong messages to conform, sacrifice, and win approval? No doubt all of these are equally good explanations for the increase in eating disorders among young girls in our society.

Impact on Communication

Responses were quite varied in terms of the perceived impact of the eating disorder on family communication. Some families felt they grew closer and more supportive of each other; others felt that the strong disagreement and constant strain were destroying their communication. Many did distinguish between parent-parent, parent-patient, and patient–other children relationships. For example, "As parents, we really supported each other; with the patient it was difficult because we could not reach her; with the patient and her sister communication was very poor." A few mothers reported that their daughters' communication "opened up a little" with their fathers, but in most cases, this phenomenon was a much-welcomed outcome of family therapy. One mother captured the ongoing angst that exists in her family's communication: "We use every means of communication . . . we shout, we talk, we write, we withhold our speech and our thoughts. No stone is left unturned in an attempt to solve, rescue, help ourselves and the patient."

Minuchin and associates (1978) wrote that siblings support, isolate, scapegoat, and teach each other while at the same time developing patterns for negotiating, cooperating, and competing. According to the questionnaire data, any or all of these occurred depending on when and how the eating disorder had interrupted the family life cycle. In some cases, siblings were extremely supportive; in others, they felt threatened and resentful. About the concern and attention lavished on the identified patient, one parent said: "My son was initially very angry because he could see how upset we were and he couldn't understand why she had a problem since he felt she had had a great and comfortable life. He later began to understand more."

Responses to the question on intimacy were very vague; several expressed that there had been no impact, which is dubious. Others felt that the eating disorder actually "pulled us together. We all cared so much about her and were deeply affected by her erratic behavior." In some cases the eating disorder helped the family focus on feelings, not food, and become more supportive of one another. It has been suggested that at least one of the systemic functions of an eating disorder is to help the family get together by giving it a single focus (Schwartz et al., 1985). In at least some respondent families, this hypothesis was validated.

Others admitted to tension in the marriage, none more graphically than one mother who wrote "parent to parent, we continue to fight over her problem due to our frustration and inability to help her. The wedge between us will never heal. Our marriage almost failed due to the stress and accusation of blame. We've weathered it but the disappointment and emotional trauma will always remain."

Impact on Control and Power

There was general agreement that the family member with the eating disorder had acquired the power. This finding is interesting in light of the previous discussion about young girls losing their voice in today's society; how much have eating disorders become a metaphor for the need for young women to "take back their voice"? Is the eating disorder a symbolic way to say "Notice me . . . let me be powerful and excel at something, and if I don't succeed at what I expect of myself, or what I am expected to do, at least love, notice, and give power to my perfect—or perfectly thin—body"?

Impact on Everyday Situations (Mealtimes, Shopping, Vacations, Extended Family, Family's Involvement in Therapy)

Families of anorexics singled out mealtimes as particularly grueling: "Our daughter first determined our mealtimes and restaurant choices, and then avoided eating with us to be with her friends." One mother stated, "I even started to eat more myself trying to show her that I didn't value thinness anymore." Parents of bulimics wrote about the wild swings from "eating only fat-free foods to eating everything in sight." One parent felt defeated "in buying her favorite foods, cooking for her, taking her to nice restaurants—and then she'd 'get rid of' the product of all our money and efforts." One boyfriend wrote that he "found himself watching her take seconds and thirds at dinnertime, not knowing if she was really hungry or just starting a binge."

About shopping, several mothers said it "just wasn't fun anymore." Many expressed frustration and helplessness as they watched their daughters disappear into the fitting rooms and reappear "looking like a bag of bones" yet asking insistently "Do I look fat. . . . Would you tell me the truth if you thought I looked fat?" The mother of a bulimic wrote that "her daughter hated shopping and would refuse new clothes, telling me that I was spoiling her—she wouldn't wear them and I had no idea if they even fit . . . she was always losing and gaining."

In families of anorexics, some wrote that vacations were nonexistent for quite a while. Others wrote about making sure that the right foods would be available as well as the necessary exercise facilities. With some bulimics, vacations became "out-of-control binge-fests"; "on vacations she ate and ate, was always hungry, and would take every opportunity to finish my meal as well." Clearly everyday situations such as mealtimes, shopping, and vacations become joyless, tension-filled, and emotionally charged events.

Surprisingly, the majority of responses indicated that extended family was not significantly involved in either the development or the consequences of the eating disorder. In particular, families of bulimics stated that the extended family had not been informed. Because anorexia is so much more visible than bulimia, families of anorexics did express significant degrees of alarm and concern. Extended family intrusiveness, which I expected might be more apparent in some of the questionnaire responses, was absent. In some cases, what was expressed was that the extended family members simply "did not care"; I doubt that such was really the case. I think that the helplessness expressed by nuclear families is heard and felt by members of the extended family and they simply do not know what to say or do, and so they do very little.

Except for the occasional concern about the financial burden of treatment or the distance traveled in order to see the therapist, all families unanimously agreed that the impact of treatment on the family was a positive one: "Once we got her into treatment we didn't have to play the role of detective as much. . . . It was a much-needed relief"; "Our daughter's treatment has definitely helped, and group and family sessions have brought many problems into the open. Her individual therapy has helped her which directly affects the family"; and "We've all basically enjoyed the education. We still have many questions and concerns and desperately need and want more feedback for a better daily life." No one mentioned the time involved or the impact of multiple appointments with therapists, nutritionists, and physicians, because in almost every case, the families believed that at least some improvements had been made and they felt that their daughters were less at risk and more safely on a road to recovery.

Impact on The Family's Growth and Spirituality

As to whether an eating disorder fostered psychological growth in other family members, many acknowledged years of denial and/or a dysfunctional family system and admitted that "I never would have sought help for myself if it hadn't been for my daughter. The eating disorder opened all our eyes." Most families described a heightened level of awareness not only as a result of the eating disorder per se but also because of the treatment interventions and education received. Several recognized the function of the eating disorder as a catalyst for change in the family system, although these kinds of insights were more likely to occur as a result of rather than prior to psychological treatment. Some families, having recognized the link between the eating disorder and the family's high expectations for achievement and success, lowered their expectations and even encouraged their daughters to enter less stressful academic programs or professions. Others talked about giving their daughters "more options, becoming more loving and flexible, less rigid and less critical." Still others talked about the eating disorder alerting them to the need for more, improved and/or new communication among family members.

Most families did not answer the question on spirituality other than to agree that their hopes had been elevated and that they were feeling much less hopeless and pessimistic. No one expressed the belief that the illness had any particular spiritual meaning, such as "all things happen for a reason."

CRITERIA SET FOR RELATIONAL DIAGNOSIS

In order for a relational diagnosis to be present, the family must meet seven of the following 12 criteria:

1. Upon discovery of the eating disorder, there is evidence of suspicion, denial, and secrecy in the family, as well as denial on the part of the patient, who initially might refuse to seek treatment.
2. Upon discovery of the eating disorder, family members experience feelings of guilt, shame, and embarrassment.
3. As the eating disorder continues, the family is kept in a fearful and anxious state and the patient may respond by eating less or eating, binging and purging more.
4. The family places a high emphasis on achievement and perfection. The patient responds by wanting to excel and win approval and, therefore, acquires either the "thinnest" or the most "perfect" body shape possible.
5. There is overconcern with beauty, appearance, and thinness in the family, and the patient develops an eating disorder in order to accomplish and live up to these particular family expectations.
6. The parents have weight problems themselves, are weight conscious and/or dieters, and put direct pressure on their children to be thin.
7. The patient's low self-confidence and low self-esteem contribute to her excessive need for attention, and the parents, already anxious and frightened by the eating-disordered behavior, lavish the attention.
8. Communication patterns in the family are changed, with members becoming either more or less supportive of each other since the onset of the eating disorder. The patient realizes that the changes are somehow due to her eating-disordered behavior.

9. Intimacy patterns in the family change with the onset of the eating disorder, with the patient feeling guilty about the havoc she has created or the resentment from other siblings.

10. The eating disorder begins to control the household, family members "walk on eggshells," and the eating-disordered member begins to feel her sense of newfound power.

11. Decision making may improve in the daughter's favor, usually not by choice but by force. Other family members feel both defeated and proud of their newfound ability to be more accepting, creative, and flexible.

12. Everyday situations such as mealtimes, shopping, and vacations are severely disrupted with the eating-disordered member feeling a combination of guilt, relief, and power.

TREATMENT PLANS AND PROTOCOL

A comprehensive treatment plan should include individual, family, and group therapy whenever possible as well as nutritional counseling and, particularly with anorexia, regular appointments with a physician. Because irrational belief systems are so central to the symptomatology of all eating disorders—such as "I must be thin in order to be happy; I can't eat what I want to without gaining weight; the only way I'm in control is when I'm dieting"—a cognitive-behavioral perspective should be a major underpinning of the treatment protocol.

Also central to the eating-disorder diagnosis is the individual's overall sense of personal ineffectivenesss, profound feelings of emptiness, role confusion, body dissatisfaction, and low self-esteem. (For this symptom complex, the perspective represented by the writings of the Stone Center, a highly respected women's collective at Wellesley College [Jordan, Miller, Stiver, & Surrey, 1991], and also of Kim Chernin, 1985 and Gilligan & Brown, 1992 are relevant because they emphasize the importance of a woman developing her own voice, a voice that comes from discovering her own individual and relational identity.)

Work with the patient's family must include paying attention to the way this family values the importance of thinness, pressures its members to conform, and robs its members of their rights to individuality. Family treatment must encourage the parents, siblings, and spouses of the patient to hear and understand what she is saying and help her express her needs and get them met without resorting to an eating disorder.

In six out of the 16 patient families who responded to the questionnaire, a strong part of my work included confronting and restructuring an enmeshed mother/daughter relationship and a detached father/daughter relationship. All too frequently I heard, "My mother is my best friend; my father and I don't get along." One mother summed up the family interactional patterns quite succinctly: "There was too much emphasis on thinness, a lack of involvement by her father, too much involvement by me. I think she loves me very much and tried too hard to please me, because she felt I needed it so badly." In all these cases, I recommended, particularly to the fathers, that they read *Father Hunger* (Main, 1991) as a homework assignment.

Group therapy is encouraged because there is substantial evidence, especially for the treatment of bulimia, that it is facilitative of change and recovery. The sociocultural component of the illness is also something that can be handled cogently in group.

Finally, a word about married patients with an eating disorder, whom Vandereycken, Koge, and Vanderlenden (1988) referred to as the "forgotten" group. Despite the fact that research about the occurrence of anorexia or bulimia nervosa in married patients is scarce (Levine, 1988; Woodside, Brandes, Scheleter-Wolfstrom, & Lackstrom, 1993), Vandereycken and coworkers ponder a possible interaction between the eating disorder and the marital relationship. His studies (Vandereycken et al., 1988) indicate that men who are married to an anorexic or bulimic patient evidence psychosocial problems more often than "normal" males in an unproblematic marriage. However, he claimed that the direction of the influence—the cause/consequence issue—remains unclear. Spouses of anorexics or bulimics quite often report dissatisfaction with their marital sexual relationships, whereas the patients themselves appear to minimize these aspects while emphasizing more distress in their general social life. The discrepancy between the patients' and the husbands' appraisal of the affective quality of their relationship may be indicative of communication problems or a lack of marital intimacy, but, said Vandereycken and coworkers, these are only hypotheses to be substantiated by further comparative research.

In general, it is recommended that the "well" spouse be involved in the treatment program from the outset. The husband may learn to help the patient gain control over eating problems and must certainly avoid a "parental" role, treating his partner as a "sick child." I urge marital therapy, with a focus not only on the eating problems but also on the relational issues associated with the disorder. I focus on the couple's mutual expression of their thoughts and feelings and try to teach them how to communicate and solve interpersonal problems more effectively.

Marriages have an established circularity and transactional pattern around the eating disorder in many of the same ways as families do (Levine, 1988). It is important to treat the eating disorder and the family system at the same time in order to establish freedom for both the eating-disordered member to recover and for the family to move beyond denial, guilt, and fear. Many families can and do move from too high expectations, too much enmeshment, and too many tension-filled days and nights, to a healthier, more creative, and more flexible way of functioning.

REFERENCES

American Psychiatric Association. (1994). *Diagnostic and statistical manual of mental disorders* (4th ed.). Washington, DC: Author.

Bruch, H. (1973). *Eating disorders: Obesity, anorexia nervosa and the person within.* New York: Basic Books.

Chernin, K. (1981). *The obsession: Reflections on the tyranny of slenderness.* New York: Harper & Row.

Chernin, K. (1985). *The hungry self: Women, eating and identity.* New York: Harper & Row.

Gilligan, C., & Brown, L. M. (1992). *Meeting at the crossroads: Women's psychology and girls' development.* Cambridge, MA: Harvard University.

Jordan, J. V., Miller, J. B., Stiver, I. P., & Surrey, J. (1991). *Women's growth in connection: Writings from the Stone Center.* New York: Guilford.

Levine, P. (1988). "Bulimic" couples: Dynamics and treatment. In F. W. Kaslow (Ed.), *The family therapy collections: Couples therapy in a family context* (vol. 25, pp. 89–103). Rockville, MD: Aspen.

Main, M. (1991). *Father hunger: Fathers, daughters and food.* Carlsbad, CA: Gurze Books.

Madanes, C. (1984). *Strategic family therapy.* San Francisco: Jossey-Bass.

Masterson, J. F. (1977). *Primary anorexia nervosa in borderline personality.* New York: International Universities.

Mellin, L. M., Irwin, Jr., C. E., & Scully, S. (1992). Prevalence of disordered eating in girls: A survey of middle-class children. *Journal of the American Dietetic Association, 92,* 851–853.

Minuchin, S., Rosman, B., & Baker, L. (1978). *Psychosomatic families: Anorexia nervosa in context.* Cambridge, MA: Harvard University.

Orenstein, P. (1994). *School girls.* New York: Doubleday.

Pike, K., & Rodin, J. (1991). Mothers, daughters and disordered eating. *Journal of Abnormal Psychology, 100,* 198–204.

Root, M. P. P., Fallon, P., & Friedrich, W. N. (1986). *Bulimia: A systems approach to treatment.* New York: Norton.

Sadker, M. T., & Sadker, S. (1994). *Failing at fairness: How America's schools cheat girls.* New York: Scribner.

Sargent, J. (1986). Family therapy interventions for anorectics and bulimics. *Family Therapy Today, 1,* 1–3.

Sargent, J., Liebman, R., & Silver, M. (1985). Family therapy for anorexia nervosa. In D. M. Garner & P. E. Garfinkel (Eds.), *Handbook of psychotherapy for anorexia nervosa and bulimia* (pp. 257–279). New York: Guilford.

Spitzer, R. L., Devlin, M., Walsh, B. T., Hassin, D., Wing, R., Marcus, M., Stunkard, A., Wadden, T., Yanovski, S., Agras, S., Mitchell, J., & Novas, C. (1992). Binge eating disorder: A multi-site field trial of the diagnostic criteria. *International Journal of Eating Disorders, 11,* 191–203.

Schwartz, R. C. (1995). *Internal family systems therapy.* New York: Guilford.

Schwartz, R. C., Barrett, M. J., & Saba, G. (1985). Family therapy for anorexia nervosa. In D. M. Garner & P. E. Garfinkel (Eds.), *Handbook of psychotherapy for anorexia nervosa and bulimia* (pp. 280–307). New York: Guilford.

Vandereycken, W., Koge, E., & Vanderlenden, J. (1988). *The family approach to eating disorders: Assessment & treatment of anorexia nervosa & bulimia.* New York: PMA Publications.

Woodside, D. B., Brandes, J., Schekter-Wolfson, L., & Lackstrom, J. (1993). *Eating disorders and marriage: The couple in focus.* New York: Brunner/Mazel.

CHAPTER 31

Evil in Human Personality: Disorders of Doing Harm to Others in Family Relationships

ISRAEL W. CHARNY, PhD

Knowingly or unknowingly, the science and profession of psychology (and all mental health disciplines) has to choose between adopting a philosophical value that honors adjustment to any and all forms of societal organization as the sine qua non of psychological health versus a standard of mental health based on how well persons organize themselves for maximum protection and fulfillment both of their own and other people's lives. The first definition will condone psychological health as successful adjustment to and performance of state-mandated roles in Nazi, Stalinist, or Cambodian Killing Field societies. The second standard will call for a combination of maximum efforts to stay alive and also keep others alive under all conditions, including a murderous totalitarian society, and also will include a readiness to engage in acts of protest, resistance, and rescue of human life.

The issues and dilemmas are obviously not simple; nor are they susceptible to naive, childlike solutions based on innocent beliefs in goodness or justice. Indeed, because of the complexity of the subject, it may well be necessary to organize a multidimensional framework that will differentiate between people's adjustments to a variety of situations in which political systems have taken various degrees of command over their lives as opposed to democratic societal contexts in which people are relatively free. (See Rummel, 1992, 1994, on comparative analysis of genocide by democratic and nondemocratic societies.) Perhaps we need to adjust our definitions of psychological health under societal conditions of grave coercion, deprivation, and disorganization such as unsafe, violent, or criminally infested communities, war, genocide, massive ecological trauma, and fascist governments. (See Connor, 1989, on how an almost complete reversal of rules of evidence takes place in barbaric societies; Charny, 1982, and Staub, 1992, on the sequence of steps in the unfolding of genocidal societies.) Ullman and Krasner (1975), in a thoughtful discussion of obedience by Nazis living in a concentration camp society took the position that so long as one was responding "accurately and successfully to his environment and not breaking its rules . . . he would not be labeled abnormal" (p. 16). Others, including this writer, and Coleman, Butcher, and Carson (1984) disagree and propose as the criterion for normality whether the behavior fosters "the well-being of the individual and, ultimately, of the group" (p. 15).

There are major implications to the value standard adopted by psychology not only in extreme conditions of war and holocaust, but in every aspect of the psychopathology of everyday life. Thus, in family situations where one parent is dominating the emotional space of the family and is emotionally or physically abusive toward one or more members, a choice has to be made between a concept of psychological health that calls for adjusting to domination and abuse or fighting against it. Adjusting to domination in effect promotes codependency, while fighting it costs considerable tension and perhaps certain dangers to the continuation of the marriage or family. (For discussions of the role of the "second" parent as a bystander to rejection of a child by the first parent, see Blitz, 1993; Charny, 1972.)

Similarly, in many workplaces one must choose between degrees of obeisance, conformity, and "bystanderism" to noxious personalities or organizational structures that are doing obvious harm to workers within that system or to clients served by it. Thus, a resident in psychiatry or clinical psychology in a department where the management and leadership style is authoritarian, derogatory, and humiliating faces complex choices. Should s/he participate blindly in the system, engage in open "resistance"—with all its attendant political risks to his/her career—or conform minimally while "protecting" his/her inner resistance to the department policies and deferring expressing them openly until later, when one has more power and choices of alternatives? Not to make a choice of any sort is to fall into a deadly emotional-moral captivity that suppresses major aspects of a person's self-awareness, energy, aliveness, and capacity for self-fulfillment.

The same kinds of considerations arise with regard to responses even in democratic countries that have embarked on policies of stifling human rights or have undertaken unjust wars. At such a time, I believe, an emotionally healthy person has to choose to define him- or herself as standing against the then-prevailing governmental/societal directive and also against the public consensus. (See a series of studies of evil in the context of Israeli life where, in the Milgram tradition, subjects were asked if they approve or would personally comply with orders to harm others: Charny, 1990; Charny & Fromer, 1990a, 1990b, 1992.)

In this chapter, I introduce two main subjects on the diagnosis of evil in human personality based on a definition of evil as doing harm to human life—to actual survival and with respect to the basic quality of life. The first subject is an overall proposal to evaluate every patient/person both in terms of degrees of what I call disorders of pseudocompetence, invulnerability, and doing harm to others as well as in terms of what I call disorders of incompetence, vulnerability, and personality weakness. Whereas the former disorders introduce to formal mental health diagnosis a systematic perspective on the harm people do to *others,* the latter refer largely to traditional diagnoses of disorders in functioning of the self. The second subject is the specific application of this frame of reference to disorders in marital, family, and parenting relationships. A detailed classification is presented here for the first time, with special interest directed to the concepts of disorders of doing harm to others in marital, family, and parenting relationships. Finally, in order to give more meaning to this preliminary presentation of a radical point of view, I briefly introduce concepts of the treatment of evil, since ultimately the point of diagnosis is to lead to new corrective and therapeutic possibilities.

I note with regret that this chapter will not treat several other important subjects of evil including what I call disorders of excessive power strivings (Charny, in press); disorders of surrender of one's identity to fusion, obedience, and conformity to others; disorders of criminal exploitations, abuse, cruelty, torture, and murder of others; and disorders of prejudice, persecution, and genocide. Regrettably, the subject of evil human behavior is vast. I trust, however, that this chapter will stand as a coherent entry both into the subject as a whole and into the subject of doing harm in family relationships.

RESPECT FOR HUMAN LIFE AS A CATEGORICAL IMPERATIVE AND THE BASIS OF THE CHOICE TO DO OR NOT TO DO HARM TO SELF OR OTHERS

The diagnostic frame of reference proposed herein takes as a guiding value a concept of the sacredness of life, both for oneself and for all other human beings. It is my opinion that this value is implicit in the basic philosophy of science and certainly in the specific science of psychology: It is a statement that the purpose of all knowledge is to promote healthier lives for all human beings. (See Masserman, 1990, on the three fundamental needs of all humans—physical vitality and longevity, interpersonal security, and existential faith.) The information-developing process in science follows in the great tradition of objective inquiry, free of prior assumptions or ideological dictates, and must reach the highest standards of impartiality and accuracy. But the reason why such scientific work is being done in the first place, the definitions of its purposes, and the way the investigation is conducted need to be grounded in a value ethic of devotion to protecting human life. (For a relevant discussion of the governing narrative in scholarship, see Des Pres, 1986.)

I believe that there is a direct line from this statement of respect for life as the quintessential value principle for all science to psychological definitions of normal and abnormal behavior. Those behaviors that are defined as disordered are those that do serious harm to the ability and prospects of human beings to live safely and securely—with adequate food, shelter, biological and emotional security, and dignity. Disturbed, dysfunctional, or disordered behaviors are behaviors that do harm to human lives; these behaviors can be divided into the two categories of doing harm to *oneself* and doing harm to *others*. Accepting respect for human life as a categorical imperative is the basis for analyzing human choices, conscious and unconscious, to do or not to do harm to one's own life or to others; whereas psychologically healthy people protect and enhance lives, psychologically unhealthy people do harm. (Shafransky, 1990, calls for recognition and identification of both evil "deeds and, perhaps, persons" [p. 1].)

Traditionally, mental health concepts have focused largely on disorders of the first of these two types—namely the variety of dysfunctions a person suffers because he or she imposes such suffering on him- or herself or falls victim and is unable to overcome hurt imposed by others (e.g., having been neglected or unloved by parents). The sufferer becomes unable to make an effective adjustment to reality or to find pleasure in the reality of life, and the emotional or mental disturbance tends to take on "a life of its own" as a pathology.

Many other types of behaviors have been examined by psychiatry where people are affecting the lives of others in a disturbing way, but a close look shows that in these cases, too, much of the heuristic meaning and justification of psychiatric diagnoses of people whose disturbing behaviors is hurting others have derived, ultimately, from a focus on the suffering that the person is causing to and bringing down on him or her *own self*, or as a result of the problems caused the person by the suffering or disordered dysfunctional status induced in the other party. Rarely is the focus on the harm being done to *others*.

Thus, many situations in which harm is done to others are subsumed in traditional psychiatric diagnosis under the category of personality disorders. The general diagnostic criteria for a Personality Disorder in DSM-IV specifies that "the enduring pattern leads to clinically significant distress or impairment in social, occupational, or other important areas of functioning" (American Psychiatric Association [APA], 1994,

p. 633). The overriding emphasis in traditional psychiatric diagnosis is on how the life of the doer—the perpetrator—is damaged; only thereby does the person "earn" a diagnosis of psychiatric disorder.

HIDDEN EVIL IN INTERPERSONAL RELATIONSHIPS IN THE FAMILY

Evil is manifest not only in oppression, persecution, and harm. Countless ways of invasion, exploitation, insult, and humiliation, when developed and lived out as continuous ways of relating, contribute to the destruction of the spirit, security, and natural self-love of others. These behaviors are evil. Moreover, while these behaviors can be delivered through words and gestures that are obviously malevolent, they also can be delivered in concealed forms of ostensible concern, involvement, and wishes to help. This generates a further problem for victims who are tricked into succumbing to manipulations without realizing that they are being trapped and abused; in fact, it creates a second kind of evil. (This theme is explicated in Miller's, 1981, 1983, work on how parents induce emotional disturbances in children by demanding that they grow and perform for the parents. Also, see Peck, 1983, for examples of nasty expectations of failure, distress, and suicide of loved ones on the part of "caring" parents or relatives.) A man, for example, can eat away at the dignity of his wife by being so nice, logical, protective, and helpful that she can be driven even crazier than if she had an openly abusive spouse who snarled and erupted into vicious acts of abandonment, dismissal, and contempt (Charny, 1992; Willi, 1982).

Many people disguise the issues of evils even when they apply for therapeutic help, and many clinicians do not help because they do not know how to think or ask about evil. While patients' complaints may imply recalcitrance, non-cooperation, negativism, disconnection, or worse in another family member, most often both patient and therapist tend to start with the unhappiness or difficulty in functioning—that is, the distress that is being experienced and being caused by forces in the relationship—and do not make clear observations about *who is hurting whom*. Rarely are presenting problems and definitions of therapy discussed in terms of the difficulties and harm that one family member is doing to others; for example, therapy would be requested because "S/he is betraying me" (rather than "I am being betrayed by him/her"), "S/he is not talking with me" (rather than "I am all alone"), "S/he is rejecting our child" (rather than "Our child is being rejected or is showing symptoms of emotional stress").

Not infrequently, the situation is truly complicated by the fact that both forces are operating within the suffering person him- or herself, suffering induced by one's own emotional weakness along with suffering caused directly by insult, abuse, or harm being done by another. Often because the victim is so obviously hurting him- or herself, the insult and injury being done by the other remain well disguised. At times, the victim(s) and even the perpetrator may not consciously know that there is a persecutor.

The denial and repression of manifest aggressive sexual abuse, which the victim dissociatively cuts off from conscious knowledge and hides collusively from the conscious attention of other family members, is well known today (Herman, 1992). But other kinds of damaging behaviors take place in family relationships that, while not traditionally considered exploitative, insulting, abusive, or wrong, are prime causes of suffering, regression, and decompensation in other family members. For example, I have previously referred to what I have called "'I'm all right Jack' personalities" (Charny, 1986), namely partners who forever claim to be happy, comfortable, and "good," with nary a scar or burden of anxiety, depression, guilt, uncertainty, or error. It turns out that such people, while looking good and functioning effectively, and avowedly the most mentally healthy and competent persons around, dump an inordinate share of the tasks of concern, fear, and uncertainty on others in their family. They generally establish themselves in a superior-to-inferior position by having others in the family so upset that they must seek mental health assistance. There is no way in traditional psychological diagnosis to spot these kinds of confident people. They can be identified as disturbed only if their denials of upset are recognized while around them other family members react either properly or overreact with upset to objective familial problems.

A recent lone clarion call about "the *illusion* of mental health" by Shedler, Mayman, and Manis (1993) has emphasized that many people who look healthy on standard mental health scales are *not* psychologically healthy. This illusory portrait is based on defensive denial of distress. "People in the defensive group would be characterized by a need to see themselves as well adjusted, *despite* vulnerability, presumably, they preserve a belief in their 'adjustment' by disavowing much of their emotional life, and so have little awareness of their needs, wishes, and feelings" (p. 1117). Peck (1983) has observed that evil is confusing and that it frequently triggers in clinicians experiences of confusion (which, in a way, becomes a diagnostic cue). He observed further, "Knowing so little about the nature of evil, we currently lack the skill to heal it" (p. 67); he proposed that evil must be made the subject of scientific investigation.

DISORDERS OF PSEUDOCOMPETENCE, INVULNERABILITY, AND DOING HARM TO OTHERS

In an effort to create a framework for diagnosis of psychopathology as both doing harm to others and/or to oneself, I have proposed a new framework for diagnosis of Disorders of Pseudocompetence, Invulnerability, and Doing Harm to Others (Charny, 1986).

For the most part, existing psychiatric disturbances may be called Disorders of Incompetence, Vulnerability, and Personality Weakness. In the face of life's challenges, and the anxiety they produce, exaggerated weakness and disavowals of potential competence, strength, and mastery can reach a point where persons are designated as "mentally ill"; they are unable to function in society. When the same range of familiar psychiatric conditions takes the form of burdens inflicted on *other* human beings, interfering with their well-being, these conditions can be seen as Disorders of Pseudocompetence, Invulnerability, and Doing Harm to Others.

Becker (1973) has written eloquently on how much human evil derives from denials of one's mortality—and by extension all weaknesses. As stated in previous work (Charny, 1986):

> Disorders of pseudocompetence represent reactions to universal anxiety about life and death through disavowals of one's weaknesses and demonstrations of one's pseudomastery at the expense of other people. The dread of normal human weakness and needs is repressed through various degrees of overstriving, and inflated sense of oneself, claims of power over others, exploitation and manipulation . . . denials of others' human rights and lives, abuses, cruelty, and actual destruction. (pp. 146–147)

No change in existing definitions of psychopathology is required to add disorders of pseudocompetence. I am merely proposing adding a dimension to existing theory by rotating conventional definitions of disturbances of the person on their axis toward their counterpart statements of the same degree of disturbance a person induces or forces on others. This change seems to make simple good sense, and it is not unlike other theoretical advances in science where an existing known principle has proven to yield hidden extended meanings when turned over or reversed.

One example of a particularly hidden form of doing harm to others in relationships is when one person takes on a role of the accomplished *giver* who is virtually always in charge of providing the financial, organizational, or even emotional resources of encouragement, optimism, and happiness in a relationship system. Others in the family inevitably pale by comparison to these grand paragons of economic, logistical, and emotional organization and support. Most often, one or more significant others in the worlds of these all-around providers are seriously emotionally inhibited, disorganized, or incompetent. A complementary pattern is established between the competent, munificent giver/provider and the other party as emotionally restricted, perhaps emotionally "stingy" or bitter, and generally unable to give of him- or herself.

Another variation of unlimited giving and its consequent infantilization and degradation of others is the personality that takes on the role of *know-it-all*. People tend somehow to feel sullied and tired in the presence of know-it-alls because they cannot possibly keep up with them.

Another variation on the theme of hidden styles of humiliating, exploiting, and abusing others in intimate relationships involves the pursuit, cultivation, and collection of power over others. Some spouses convey without question that they were born to lead in the marital relationship, as do any number of parents who claim royal powers over their children. In each home there obviously must be lines of distribution of power. While these generally are unequal and imperfect in some ways, in too many homes some people truly rule the relationships, becoming the superior one and master of their followers. It must be noted that in such situations, family relationships are produced that are consciously entirely satisfactory to the participants. Yet psychodynamic and systemic analyses show that these are complementary relationships of overcompetence at the expense of assigned incompetence to others; such relationship patterns breed many variants of breakdown in functioning and despair in the incompetent as well as failures in the overall relationship for both parties (Charny, 1987).

In all of these types of relationships, harm is done to others largely *unwittingly* and *unconsciously*. Let us now turn to the many instances of overt domination, exploitation, and emotional and physical abuse of members of one's families.

Mental health concepts do address the abusive person as problematic and disturbed to some extent. In traditional psychiatry (American Psychiatric Association, 1994), several of the personality disorders, such as Narcissistic Personality Disorder and Antisocial Personality Disorder, refer to some qualities of contempt, domination, and abuse of family members. Yet based on the traditional definitions of symptoms, there is a greater interest in proving these personality characteristics cause the *patient* distress and discomfort than in explaining the meanings and transactions between this person and the victimized relatives. The interpersonal, ethical, and relational meanings even of decidedly interpersonal manifestations of disturbance fade into a secondary position.

In family therapy, as compared to conventional individual therapy, the situation is somewhat different. The abuses done to others in a family are more likely to be treated as actions by disturbed individuals and to be defined as the focus of treatment. Also, the focus generally is treatment defined in systemic terms that include both victimizer and victim in interlocking roles, and it is recognized that all the parties to the abuse, perpetrators and victims alike, are being victimized by a disturbance in the quality and integrity of the relationship.

Unfortunately, even within its own ranks, family therapy has failed to produce a systematic classificatory system for diagnosing disturbed and harmful relationships, and within the larger mental health community, family therapy does not enjoy any serious status as a source of diagnostic characterizations of mental and emotional disturbances and personality disorders. (Obviously this volume represents a welcome thrust toward sorely needed new concepts and frameworks of additional diagnoses. See also Kaslow, 1993.) The result is that, overall, in the mental health system, the bona fide "patients" mostly have continued to be those who are the suffering victims.

There is always an available diagnosis for the *victims* in their weaknesses. A child who is being cursed and humiliated by parents can assume a "patient" role when evidence of his or her low self-esteem is reported by the school, but no available diagnosis exists for the parent who speaks to that child disparagingly and in disgust. There is a bona fide diagnosis for a spouse who wishes to escape the blaming and domination of a mate when the upset is translated into psychosomatic disturbances and/or he or she requests marital counseling in order to get out of the bad marriage, but there is hardly a DSM category or a comparable relational diagnosis in the family therapy literature for the demeaning and disparaging spouse.

Another source of avoidance of issues of abuse in the family has emerged paradoxically in family therapy from the very intent to develop systemic thinking; namely, many family therapists have taken understanding abuses in systemic terms as a basis for avoiding defining in individual terms the perpetrator(s) and their behavioral and moral *responsibility* for the execution of the abuse, as if the latter now derive from a unified field of forces and can no longer be attributed to a single individual (Charny, 1994).

The avoidance of defining perpetration of evil as a disturbance in its own right reaches its bizarre extreme in the classic literature on child abuse-violence to the child. According to the prevailing definitions, the majority of parents who abuse children are *not* emotionally disturbed. This (incorrect) conclusion then is used as a basis for telling the parents that their unfortunate behaviors are obviously deriving from some human weakness or are a repetition of their own violent upbringing, but since they are not mentally or emotionally disturbed, it will not be that difficult to teach them how to overcome this weakness. While a noble cause has thus been served by a wise device for teaching people how to stop an abusive behavior chain, it is utter nonsense to ignore the fact that anyone who seriously abuses his or her child is seriously disturbed.

DISORDERS OF DOING HARM TO OTHERS IN MARITAL, FAMILY, AND PARENTAL RELATIONSHIPS

Table 31.1, created by Blitz and Charny (Blitz, 1993) as an extension of Charny's (1986) earlier classification, presents a schema for understanding and diagnosing disorders of pseudocompetence and invulnerability in doing harm to others in marital, family, and parental relationships. Each frame of reference is juxtaposed with counterpart styles of disturbance that are based on incompetence, vulnerability, and personal weakness.

In every case the clinician is encouraged to think about both what kinds of harm a person is doing to him- or herself *and* what is being done to others in the intimate

Table 31.1 Disorder of Incompetence and Pseudocompetence in Marital, Family, and Parental Relationships

Disorders of Incompetence, Vulnerability, and Personal Weakness	Consequent Marital Disorders of Incompetence, Vulnerability, and Personal Weakness	Consequent Family Disorders of Incompetence, Vulnerability, and Personal Weakness	Consequent Parenting Disorders of Incompetence, Vulnerability, and Personal Weakness
Reactions to anxiety through exaggerated disavowals of competence, mastery, and strength	Reactions to anxiety through exaggerated disavowals of competence as a spouse	Reactions to anxiety through exaggerated disavowals of competence in family organization and executing family tasks	Reactions to anxiety through exaggerated disavowals of competence as a parent
	Pronounced vulnerability in interactions with spouse	Pronounced vulnerability in interactions with family members	Pronounced vulnerability in interactions with child(ren) and/or other parent
	Position of weakness in marital relationship	Position of weakness in family relationships	Position of weakness in parent/child relationships
Neurosis: Inability to enjoy oneself and life	Inability to enjoy oneself as a member of a couple and to enjoy the spouse relationship	Inability to enjoy oneself as a member of a family and to enjoy family relationships	Inability to enjoy oneself as a parent and to enjoy the child(ren) and other parent
Renunciation of power over self	Renunciation of power or the right to assert self with one's spouse	Renunciation of power or the right to assert one's self with family members	Renunciation of power or the right to assert one's self with child(ren) and/or other parent
	Inability to make demands of spouse	Inability to make demands of family members	Inability to make demands of child(ren) and/or other parent
Excessive demands of self	Excessive demands of self in spouse relationship	Excessive demands of self in family relationships	Excessive demands of self in parental relationships
	Position of a sufferer in the marital relationship	Position of a sufferer in family relationships	Position of a sufferer in parenting relationships
	Low self-esteem as a spouse	Low self-esteem as a family member	Low self-esteem as a parent
	Neurotic worry and concern about spouse	Neurotic worry and concern about family members	Neurotic worry and concern about child(ren) and/or other parent

	Spouse	Family members	Parent/Child
Personality and behavior disorders: Characterological restriction or exaggeration in style of experiencing, or disturbances in ability to delay needs expressed in repeatedly self-destructive behavior	Disordered regulation of one's needs in the marital relationship, especially oversensitivity and childish demands for gratification in marital relationship	Disordered regulation of one's needs in the marital relationship, especially oversensitivity and childish demands for gratification in family relationships	Disordered regulation of one's needs in the marital relationship, especially oversensitivity and childish demands for gratification in relationship with child(ren) and/or other parent
Identity cryatalizes around upset and hurt self	Repeatedly upset and hurt by spouse	Repeatedly upset and hurt by family members and family life	Repeatedly upset and hurt by child(ren) and/or other parent
Demeaning of self	Repeatedly humiliated and blamed by spouse	Repeatedly humiliated and blamed by family members	Repeatedly humiliated and blamed by child(ren) and/or other parent
Narcissistic overconcern with self	Repeatedly overdemanding and pressuring of spouse for own needs	Repeatedly overdemanding and pressuring of family members	Repeatedly overdemanding and demanding of child(ren) and/or other parent
Abuse of oneself and self-punishment	Abuse of oneself as a spouse emotionally, verbally, sexually, or physically	Abuse of oneself as a family member emotionally, verbally, sexually, or physically	Abuse of oneself as a parent emotionally, verbally, sexually, or physically
Damaging seriously one's life opportunity	Chronic inability to achieve intimacy	Chronic inability to achieve intimacy with family members	Chronic inability to achieve intimacy with child(ren) and/or other parent
	Potential growth & development as a spouse seriously blocked	Potential growth and development as a family member seriously blocked	Potential growth and development as a parent seriously blocked
Psychosis: Breakdown of ability to function in the ordinary world	Breakdown of ability to function as a spouse in the ordinary everyday world	Breakdown of ability to function as a family member in the ordinary everyday world	Breakdown of ability to function as a parent in the ordinary everyday world
Extreme inability to function	Extreme inability to function with spouse	Extreme inability to function with other family members	Extreme inability to function with child(ren) or as a parent
Irreversible self-destruction, e.g., suicidal	Irreversible self-destruction, e.g., being driven crazy in response to one's spouse, or being driven to suicide	Irreversible self-destruction, e.g., being driven crazy in response to other family members, or being driven to suicide	Irreversible self-destruction, e.g., being driven crazy in response to parental role and/or the need to function with child(ren) or other parent, or being driven to suicide

(Continued)

485

Table 31.1 (continued)

Disorders of Pseudocompetence, Invulnerability, and Doing Harm to Others	Consequent Marital Disorders of Pseudocompetence, Invulnerability, and Doing Harm to Others	Consequent Family Disorders of Pseudocompetence, Vulnerability, and Doing Harm to Others	Consequent Parenting Disorders of Pseudocompetence, Invulnerability, and Doing Harm to Others
Reactions to anxiety through exaggerated disavowals of incompetence, vulnerability, and weakness	Reactions to anxiety through exaggerated avowals of pseudocompetence as a spouse	Reactions to anxiety through exaggerated avowals of pseudo-competence in family organization and executing family tasks	Reactions to anxiety through exaggerated avowals of pseudocompetence as a parent
	Pronounced pseudoinvulnerability in interactions with spouse	Pronounced pseudoinvulnerability in interactions with family members	Pronounced pseudoinvulnerability in interactions with child(ren) and other parent
	Position of pseudostrength, control and power in marital relationship	Position of pseudostrength, control and power in family relationships	Position of pseudostrength, control and power in parent/child relationships
Neurosis: Disturbing others' enjoyment of themselves and life	Disturbing others' enjoyment of the marriage and of the spouse relationship	Disturbing others' enjoyment of the family and of family relationships	Disturbing child(ren)'s enjoyment of being a child in a family and/or the other spouse in parenting
Denial of weakness and vulnerability	Denial of weakness and vulnerability as a spouse in the marital relationship	Denial of weakness and vulnerability as a family member in family relationships	Denial of weakness and vulnerability as a parent in relationships to child(ren) and/or other parent
	Excessive demands made of spouse	Excessive demands made of family members	Excessive demands made of child(ren) and/or other parent
Claiming power over others	Claiming power over spouse	Claiming power over family members	Claiming power over child(ren) and/or other parent
	Bystander, accomplice or source of (perpetrator) emotional suffering of spouse	Bystander, accomplice or source of (perpetrator) emotional suffering of family members	Bystander, accomplice or source of (perpetrator) emotional suffering of child(ren) and/or other parent
	Excessively high self-esteem as a spouse	Excessively high self-esteem as a family member	Excessively high self-esteem as a parent
	Lack of worry and concern about spouse	Lack of worry and concern about family members	Lack of worry and concern about child(ren) and/or other parent

	Marital relationship	Family relationships	Parenting
Personality and behavior disorders: Characterological style of repeatedly disappointing, intruding on or upsetting others or exploitation and hurting of others	Disturbing other's ability to achieve and maintain effective regulation of needs in the marital relationship	Disturbing others' ability to achieve and maintain effective regulation of needs in family relationships	Disturbing other's ability to achieve and maintain effective regulation of needs in parenting child(ren) and/or in the relationship with other parent
Disappointing and upsetting	Repeatedly disappoints, upsets, hurts spouse	Repeatedly disappoints, upsets, hurts family members	Repeatedly disappoints, upsets, hurts child(ren) and/or in the relationship with other parent
Demeaning and dehumanization of other	Repeatedly humiliates and blames or relates to spouse with contempt and devaluation	Repeatedly humiliates and blames or relates to family members with contempt and devaluation	Repeatedly humiliates and blames or relates to children and/or other parent with contempt and devaluation
Narcissistic overconcern with self at expense of others	Repeatedly overdemanding and pressuring of spouse for own needs at expense of other	Repeatedly overdemanding and pressuring of family members at expense of others	Repeatedly overdemanding and pressuring of child(ren) and/or other parent at expense of others
Exploitation of others, abuse of others and cruelty	Abuses spouse emotionally, verbally, sexually, or in actual physical abuse	Abuses other family members emotionally, verbally, sexually, or in actual physical abuse	Abuses child(ren) and/or other parent emotionally, verbally, sexually, or in actual physical abuse
Damaging seriously other's life opportunity	Chronic inability to achieve intimacy with mate	Chronic inability to achieve intimacy with family members	Chronic inability to achieve intimacy with child(ren) and/or other parent
	Potential growth and development of spouse seriously blocked	Potential growth and development of family members seriously blocked	Potential growth and development of child(ren) and/or other parent seriously blocked
Psychosis: Damages others' ability to function in the ordinary everyday world	Damages ability of spouse to function in the ordinary everyday world	Damages ability of other family members to function in the ordinary everyday world	Damages ability of child(ren) and/or other parent to function in the ordinary everyday world
Incapacitates and destroys ability to function	Extreme incapacitating and destroying of spouse's ability to function	Extreme incapacitating and destroying of family members' ability to function	Extreme incapacitating and destroying of child(ren) and/or other parent's ability to function
Irreversible destruction of others—e.g., driving other to suicide, murder, patricide, matricide, filicide	Irreversible destruction of spouse—e.g., driving other to suicide or murder	Irreversible destruction of other family members—e.g., driving others to suicide or murder	Irreversible destruction of child(ren) and/or other parent—e.g., driving others to suicide or murder

An extension of Charny's (1986) model for a revised psychiatric classification which includes both disturbances to self and doing harm to others (Developed by Israel Charny & Pnina Blitz.)

© 1995 Israel W. Charny. Institute on the Holocaust & Genocide, Jerusalem, Israel family network. If people who are hurting other family members are understood to be suffering from feelings of inadequacy, and the therapy is focused on dealing with these feelings, the present conception suggests that therapy is better served by remaining focused on *both* the difficulties in handling personal anxiety for the perpetrator and the truths about what he or she is doing to others. Such a combination does not lead to treating the assaults and insults to others so that they become as if unreal and as if "only" derived from the first, for example, not treating a wife for her rejection of her husband but only for her inadequacy feelings since these generate the chain of rejection. Such a combination *calls on people to take responsibility for what they are doing to others.* Thus the approach is more true to the commonsense facts and realities that are taking place in people's lives, including the guilt that decent people feel, even if unconsciously, at the wrong they are doing others. This guilt can be tapped in order to generate behavior changes. It also should be addressed in order to help the perpetrator deal with his or her own inadequacies and personal regrets.

The diagnosis of the degree of disorder is based on an objective appraisal of the degree of damage that has been and is being done to oneself and by the perpetrator to others in the family as well as intentions to damage self or significant others. The classification of disorders is arrayed along the familiar and traditional continuum of degrees of disturbances embodied in neurotic disorders, personality and behavior disorders, and psychotic disorders. Throughout the entire continuum, one judges the extent to which a person is taking away the self-esteem, joy of life and well-being, power, security, and ultimately perhaps life itself either of the self or of the spouse, other family members, or children.

On the diagnostic continuum, the neurotic range of disturbance refers to generation of an overall level of malaise, vulnerability, and restriction of competence in the self and/or others. The level of disturbance is one of attrition of spirit, disturbed mood, and loss of well-being, or disabling anxiety. A person suffering a neurotic level of personality disturbance in marital relationships is unable to enjoy him- or herself as a member of the couple or systematically intrudes on and disturbs the spouse's enjoyment of the self in the relationship by being insensitive to the other's needs, denying his or her own personal limitations or faults, or demands explicitly that the spouse be the servant of his or her demands. Neurotic disorders in family relationships similarly involve an inability to enjoy oneself as a member of a family, or disturbing others' enjoyment of family relationships. Neurotic parenting involves an inability to enjoy oneself as a parent, to enjoy the children and/or the other parent, or disturbing the child's enjoyment of being a child in the family, or disturbing the other parent in parenting.

Personality and behavior disorders refer to other more severe and chronic damaging of the spirit and life opportunities, either of the self or of family members. In traditional diagnosis of disturbances of personal incompetence, the personality-disordered person is unable to be stable and productive in life; generally some excessive demands for immediate self-gratification are evident. In assessing personality disorders of doing harm to others, we see the person hurting, frustrating, and driving family members crazy with unreliability, irresponsibility, unkept promises, squandering of resources, and imposing the shame of failures and malfeasance on the dignity of the family. Such cases include those in which verbal demeaning reaches ruinous levels, actual exploitation of family members by absconding with financial resources, and physical abuse— including the incest that is discovered with great frequency in virtually all cultures.

The psychotic range of disorders refers to such severe damages as those that render the person or other family members incapable of functioning in the reality of life. This includes mental breakdowns of family members and their being relegated to roles of mentally ill people, criminal roles, and becoming subject to the punishment system of society, tragic ends of lives in suicides, and cases of murder in families.

I use the term "psychosis" not to refer to the standard disorders of hallucinations and delusions, but to the farther end of the continuum of the harms people do to themselves or others that result in one or more persons becoming unable to live or to enjoy life. This definition of psychosis includes but is not limited to conditions where a person is what is popularly called "crazy," but rather evaluates whether the right to life or the capacity to live have been or are brought to a full stop, and a human being who might have enjoyed a rewarding life in dignity is forced out and relegated to actual or virtual nonpersonhood or nonexistence. A psychotic level of doing harm to one's spouse is defined as damaging in an ultimate way the spouse's ability to function, such as by driving him or her truly crazy or so demoralizing the spouse that he or she succumbs to major illness, or murdering the spouse. A psychotic way of doing harm to one's family is defined as causing severe damage to their functioning, driving them to suicide, or murdering them. A psychotic level of doing harm in one's parenting is defined as destroying children's ability to function, incapacitating the other parent's ability to function, driving children to suicide, or murdering them.

THE TREATMENT OF DISORDERS OF EVIL

We are only beginning to think about how to treat disorders of evil. In Peck's (1983) important and touching (best-selling) book, *People of the Lie,* where he sensitively defines disorders of evil, the previously rational, learned, psychodynamically oriented therapist then takes off on a flight into the shamanic and occult when he offers religious exorcism as the only way to treat evil people.

It should be understood that herein I address the possible treatment only of those people who are still within the reach of our invitation as psychotherapists to dialogue with us and/or with members of their families when our goals are to address the reality of their evil actions. Even many of those who come to therapists will spurn our efforts to "join" with them and create a sincere therapeutic alliance, and will turn away authentic clarifications of the harm they are doing to others. Sadly, we are currently unable to prescribe psychotherapy for those who are irretrievably committed to destruction of others; there are many such persons in the sad vale of tears of this world. We are not treating the Hitlers, Khoumenis, Machiavellis, and Saddam Husseins; they do not perceive that they need help, nor do they allow us to approach them.

Nonetheless, by treating some number of everyday evil people, we can try to lay a new moral groundwork and contribute to the development of new knowledge about fighting against, standing up to, and containing evil.

FOUR TECHNIQUES FOR PSYCHOTHERAPEUTIC ENGAGEMENT OF EVIL

Facing Evil for What It Is: Identifying Patterns of Destruction of People's Lives Accurately and Forthrightly

One theme that emerges from a relatively wide range of religious, philosophical, and some clinical psychotherapeutic literature is that both the *reality* of evils all about us in human life and also the *potential* of evil within every one of us need to be met with greater consciousness and awareness (Browning, 1992; Charny, 1982; Girard, 1977; Mowrer, 1961). In treating victims of evil, the recognition that evil is a natural part of the human condition can help them come to terms with the reality of the evils that have befallen them, both personally or as members of collectives, in order to go on living. The recognition of evil also provides a true and inspirational way to spot one's own potential for evil, to address it, and to contain it.

In my opinion, conventional individual and family psychotherapies err by not viewing evildoing people for what they are; rather these treatments try, by traditional techniques, to invite them to speak of their hurt, loss, and yearning with the vain hope that they then will be transformed into socially positive and constructive creatures. Many participants in such therapies in effect sit and mock their naive, innocent, and essentially impotent therapists; in their unconscious experience if not consciously, they enjoy a triumph of their power over their therapists. These therapists do not recognize that these people need to be confronted with what they are doing and, *if possible,* pushed to do better. The point is not to credit these evil people with goodness or kindess, but to identify and reduce the harm they are doing others. A common error of a psychotherapist is to treat evil people too respectfully and generously, avoiding confrontation, challenge, correction, or provocation with the expectation that they will respond quid pro quo to the decency offered them.

Evil augments its power considerably by a combination of the perpetrator's concealment of it and by the victims' innocence and denial of evil's existence. Those who have been emotionally abused or rejected should at least have the advantage of knowing what has happened to them. Parental messages, in particular, have enormous power in shaping the mental health and illness of children for many years of their lives; inner expectations of wishes that the child die have been seen as central in fomenting serious psychiatric disorders in children (Anthony & Benedeck, 1970; Blitz, 1993; Charny, 1980; Roth, personal communication, 1994). People who tend to be "innocents" often are caught unaware by nastiness, scheming, malevolence, power manipulations, and outright destructiveness and are its victims at work and in the community and society. Thus, innocent people may not understand why they feel so bad and unsteady in work environments where evil leaders degrade people's ability to work and advance.

Most difficult of all is the acknowledgment of *our* own evil to others. Those who must become accountable for the grave hurt and harm they are doing to others generally offer intense resistance in therapy; often they try to dismiss the therapist or render him or her impotent to continue. However, in many instances this resistance can be penetrated constructively to get the person to acknowledge the dread part of the self that he or she has been denying.

Meeting Evil and Responding to It with Firmness and Power

Once evil is identified for what it is, the therapist's task is twofold; first the evil actions must be identified for what they are, in order to call forth an organization of will and strategy to fight back against the destructive force; second, the patient must be assisted to conduct the battle against the evil. These two tasks must occur whether the evil to be combatted is coming from others or when the evil is centered in the patient. In the former case, the therapy must move from the time-honored position of commiserating with hurt, loss, and emotional injury to an activist position of mobilizing protest and anger against the people who are hurting the patient and helping to plan the most effective counterattack possible. In the latter case, the therapist must move to a moral therapeutic analysis that the patient is doing harmful things to other people.

Case History

In the second year of family therapy for a now 16-year-old boy who a year before had made a serious suicide attempt, the boy was signaling newly emergent desires to grow. For many years, this boy had treated himself as a pleasure-loving, tension-escaping free spirit. Given his new readiness to learn, the therapist asked the parents to arrange for private tutoring, yet months went by with the father subtly sabotaging the process and failing to engage a tutor, and then the father also announced he was ending the boy's therapy. In the showdown that took place, the therapist designed the therapeutic dialogue to lead to critical feedback to the father that he was reluctant to have his son gain new strength for himself because it served the father's purposes to keep the boy weak.

Limiting and Containing Evil That Cannot Be Fought and Confronted

While many times evil cannot be fought and overcome, a variety of steps still may be taken to contain its spread and influence. Again, the first therapeutic task is recognition of harmful actions, whether by the patient to others or by others to him or her.

There are tyrannical or very weak parents whose behavior cannot be modified in family therapy—even if for a time they agree physically to participate in the treatment process. Many times therapists will have no choice but to advise adult or late teen-age children to leave or reduce contact with one or both such parents. In certain job situations one is doomed to be humiliated and exploited, and no amount of competence or good will, self-assertion or politicking, will change the situation; if one can leave such a post, it is wise to do so; so long as one cannot, there are a variety of ways with which to build an inner strength through use of healthy inner aggression against the sources of insult.

The concept of containing evil also pertains to containing one's own evil actions to others in those situations and times when one is not yet able really to overcome one's inner dynamics of wanting to hurt and damage the other(s).

Case History

A teenager showing psychotic symptoms was on the verge of being hospitalized. An incident developed where the boy spoke back rudely to his father and the latter, although so concerned with getting his son to feel better and avoid hospitalization, went crazy and wildly smashed some of the boy's possessions. Years before, this father too had suffered a period of sudden immobilization at work following a narcissistic injury. Without his knowledge, his son's current breakdown was reminiscent to him of his own, and his fury at his son's impotence was the thrust of rage both at his own impotence as well as at his own father, who had very much sought to keep all of his sons far smaller than he was, so that he could rule the roost and dote on his superior feelings.

It was far too early in therapy to analyze this family pattern aloud, but it was not too early to tell the father of the teenage patient that he must commit himself to containing any and all violent eruptions that pushed up in him.

Giving People Who Are Evil Alternative Positive Ways to Act and Showing Them How

The ideal therapeutic goal is to transform evil actions against other people into positive alternatives. When this is possible, therapists and patients together truly experience a heartwarming triumph of good over bad, and that transformative experience often takes on historical milestone meanings that can warm and inspire people for years to come.

Parents who themselves were unnourished, rejected, or manipulated in their childhoods can set in motion a tragic and disastrous chain of psychopathological development in a child, up to and including psychosis and autism, and then be genuinely shocked and alarmed to see their child deteriorating (Charny, 1980). When mobilized in a family therapy process, many of these parents will give a great deal of themselves to arrest and correct the serious damages to their child's development that they do not want to occur; they will enter into an authentic inner dialogue with the forces in them that, unknowingly, sought to freeze out the child and deny it warmth, and even life, just as they, the parents, once had suffered.

Thus, too, many family cutoffs and incidents of family violence originate in legitimate and necessary waves of anger and hatred that arise in the emotional machinery of a person and then erupt in overt expressions of violence. It is possible to teach many people that while their aggressive feelings are legitimate, their overt acts of harmful violence to others are not. The therapist teaches once-violent people that they will be happier with themselves as decent people if they commit to learning how to control their anger and express it in legitimate communications even of intense displeasure and anger, but not in acts of actual violence that do harm to the physical being of the other (Bach & Wyden, 1969). Clinical experience shows that even people who are bona fide psychiatric patients with poor impulse control can be brought down from states of agitated threats of violence, even giving up weapons they are holding, to recommit themselves to a therapy process that will seek real justice for their angry feeling, but without any overt harm being done to anyone (Charny, 1967).

Within a family, frequently it is possible to guide people who are harming others into an entirely different constructive orientation. Often this can be done with a collusive unit within a family, such as where two parents, two siblings, or even a total family group have conspired, generally unconsciously, to scapegoat and injure or punish a family member. (Ivan Nagy's work on uncovering the map or ledger of ethical balances in families is relevant here [Boszormenyi-Nagy & Spark, 1973].) Insofar as the therapist is able to break up the collusive unit and win over someone in the family—and preferably more than one person—to seeking justice for the previous victim, a good deal of help for the previously harmed person is likely.

CONCLUSION

In the diagnostic framework presented of looking both at how people feel for themselves and at how they impact on and affect other people's functioning and well-being, the integrity of relationships becomes no less important than the capacity to function.

The basic meaning in this extended schema of diagnosis, which looks at the impacts of people's behaviors on their significant others, is that the basis for psychiatric diagnosis is not only the ability to remain functional, or avoid dysfunction, but also the ability to support the functioning and avoidance of dysfunction of intimates. The meta-meaning of this point of view is that *psychological health also includes the maintenance of a basic respect, equality, wholesomeness, and integrity in relationships with one's family intimates.*

This concept of diagnosis calls for a paradigmatic shift from a kind of self-centered or narcissistic involvement only with a given human being's ability to function without being disturbed, crazy, and dysfunctional, to looking at relationships with other human beings and the extent to which a person is facilitating, supportive, and creative in the true sense of generating and standing by the creation of life for others (Buber, 1953). *Disturbance is seen when one cultivates dispair, sorrow, and incompetence either in one-self or in one's spouse, family group, children, or partner in parenting.*

I believe this is a more noble and at the same time more down-to-earth an true-to-life basis for psychiatric diagnosis that fits everyday observations of human beings as to who is emotionally responsible and effectively healthy and who is not, not only to one-self but to the people with whom they are connected.

REFERENCES

American Psychiatric Association. (1994). *Diagnostic and statistical manual of mental disorders* (4th ed.). Washington, DC: Author.

Anthony, E. J., & Benedeck, T. (1970). *Parenthood: Its psychology and psychopathology.* Boston: Little, Brown.

Bach, G. R., & Wyden, P. (1969). *The intimate enemy: How to fight fair in love and marriage.* New York: Morrow.

Becker, E. (1973). *The denial of death.* New York: Free Press.

Blitz, P. (1993). *Parental collusions in destructiveness towards a child as a cause of subsequent psychiatric and emotional disturbance.* Unpublished master's thesis, Bob Shapell School of Social Work, Tel Aviv University.

Boszormenyi-Nagy, I., & Spark, G. N. (1973). *Invisible loyalties.* Hagerstown, MD: Harper & Row.

Browning, C. (1992). *The path to genocide: Essays on launching the Final Solution.* New York: Cambridge University Press.

Buber, M. (1953). *Good and evil.* New York: Scribner's.

Charny, I. W. (1967). The psychotherapist as teacher of an ethic of nonviolence. *Voices: The Art and Science of Psychotherapy, 3,* 57–66.

Charny, I. W. (1972). Parental intervention with one another on behalf of their child: A breaking-through tool for preventing emotional disturbance. *Journal of Contemporary Psychotherapy, 5,* 19–29.

Charny, I. W. (1980). Recovery of two (largely) autistic children through renunciation of maternal destructiveness in integrated individual and family therapy. In L. R. Wolberg & M. L. Aronson (Eds.), *Group and family therapy 1980* (pp. 250–281). New York: Brunner/Mazel.

Charny, I. W. (1982). *How can we commit the unthinkable?: Genocide, the human cancer.* Boulder, CO: Westview.

Charny, I. W. (1986). Genocide and mass destruction: Doing harm to others as a missing dimension in psychopathology. *Psychiatry, 49*(2), 144–157.

Charny, I. W (1987). "Marital trap analysis"—Incompetence, complementarity and success traps: Identifying potential future dysfunctions based on a couple's current collusive agreements. *Contemporary Family Therapy, 9*(3), 163–180.

Charny, I. W. (1990). To commit or not commit to human life: Children of victims and victimizers—all. *Contemporary Family Therapy, 12*(5), 407–426.

Charny, I. W. (1992). *Existential/dialectical marital therapy: Breaking the secret code of marriage.* New York: Brunner/Mazel.

Charny, I. W. (1994). Psychological and ethical responsibility in systemic thinking. *The International Connection* (International Family Therapy Association), *7*(1), 7–8.

Charny, I. W. (in press). A personality disorder of excessive power strivings. *Israel Annals of Psychiatry.*

Charny, I. W., & Fromer, D. (1990a). A study of the readiness of Jewish/Israeli students in the health professions to authorize and execute involuntary mass euthanasia of "severely handicapped" patients. *Holocaust and Genocide Studies, 5*(3), 313–335.

Charny, I. W., & Fromer, D. (1990b). The readiness of health profession students to comply with a hypothetical program of "forced migration" of a minority population. *American Journal of Orthopsychiatry, 60*(4), 486–495.

Charny, I. W., & Fromer, D. (1992). A study of the attitudes of viewers of the film "Shoah" towards an incident of mass murder by Israeli soldiers (Kfar Kassem, 1956), *Journal of Traumatic Stress, 5*(2), 303–318.

Coleman, J. C., Butcher, J. N., & Carson, R. C. (1984). *Abnormal psychology and modern life* (7th ed.). Glenview, IL: Scott, Foresman.

Connor, J. W. (1989). From ghost dance to death camps: Nazi Germany as a crisis cult. *Ethos, 17*(3), 259–288.

Des Pres, T. (1986). On governing narratives: The Turkish-Armenian case. *The Yale Review, 75,* 517–531.

Girard, R. (1977). *Violence and the sacred.* Baltimore: John Hopkins University. (Originally published in Paris in 1972 by Editions Bernard Grasser, *La violence et le sacre.*)

Herman, J. L. (1992). *Trauma and recovery.* New York: Basic Books.

Kaslow, F. (1993). Relational diagnosis: Past, present and future. *American Journal of Family Therapy, 21*(3), 195–204.

Masserman, J. H. (1990). The dynamics of world concordance. *Journal of Contemporary Psychotherapy, 20*(3), 155–161.

Miller, A. (1981). *Prisoners of childhood: The drama of the gifted child and the search for the true self.* New York: Basic Books.

Miller, A. (1983). *For your own good: Hidden cruelty in child-rearing and the roots of violence.* New York: Farrar, Straus, Giroux.

Mowrer, O. H. (1961). *The crisis in psychiatry and religion.* New York: Van Nostrand.

Peck, M. S. (1983). *People of the lie: The hope for healing human evil.* New York: Simon & Schuster.

Roth, D. (1994, personal communications). Two unpublished studies at Hadassah Hospital, Mount Scopus, Jerusalem of parental expectations in teenage obesity and teenage suicide attempts.

Rummel, R. J. (1992). Power kills; absolute power kills absolutely. Special Issue 38, *Internet on the Holocaust and genocide* (by the Institute on the Holocaust and Genocide, Jerusalem). 12 pp.

Rummel, R. J. (1994). *Death by government.* New Brunswick, NJ: Transaction.

Shafransky, E. P. (1990). Evil: A discourse on the boundaries of humanity. *Journal of Pastoral Counseling, 25*(1), 1–8.

Shedler, J., Mayman, M., & Manis, M. (1993). The illusion of mental health. *American Psychologist, 48*(11), 1117–1131.

Staub, E. (1992). *The roots of evil: The origins of genocide and other group violence.* New York: Cambridge University.

Ullman, L. P., & Krasner, L. (1975). *Psychological approach to abnormal behavior* (2nd ed.). Engelwood Cliffs, NJ: Prentice-Hall.

Willi, J. (1982). *Couples in collusion.* New York: Aronson.

CHAPTER 32

Chronic Illness and the Family

JOAN C. BARTH, PhD

The chronic illness of an individual affects the entire system in which he or she exists. For example, not only does an individual have cancer, the entire family does. This chapter on chronic illness provides some questions a therapist might ask each member of a system in which someone is suffering from a chronic illness, describes the dynamics of such families, and provides possible strategies for helping them mobilize and cope.

Chronic illness is like gravity. It always exists. It is a state of being in poor health for a prolonged period of time. Unlike acute medical emergencies, chronic illnesses sometimes worsen while at other times they may improve or remain stable. People diagnosed with cystic fibrosis, diabetes, Huntington's disease, arthritis, and other chronic illnesses are aware that they will continue to have those illnesses over time.

However, if the person has an acute medical emergency, the event happens and survival of the event marks its cessation. Those who have a heart attack and survive are relieved that the pain they felt is over. Nonetheless, heart attack survivors frequently feel they may have another attack at any time, or they may have angina or hyperfibrillation. Cancer may worsen. A person who had cancer never is designated "cured." He or she may be in "a state of remission." In other words, medical opinion may perceive the cancer as lying dormant, ready to reappear at any time. Those having strokes—cerebrovascular accidents—have an acute event—the stroke—but its aftereffects are chronic. In these instances, the patient and family often feel they are living under a cloud, uncertain when the next episode may occur and perhaps coping through the use of denial or of preventive measures, including medication and lifestyle changes, or by becoming preoccupied by fear and anxiety. The question frequently asked is whether the focus should be on the patient or the patient and his or her family. Doherty and Baird (1987) believe in what they call "family-centered medical care," which "is concerned with the impact of the illness on the family and of the family's responses and intervention strategies on the patient." In the case of chronic illness, therapists usually are consulted because the family has difficulty handling the emotional issues the illness brings to the surface. Their physician or other health care practitioner may make the referral particularly if he or she recognizes the impact of the illness on the family.

This chapter focuses on the relational impact of chronic physical illness rather than acute physical illness and on specific methods therapists can use to discuss the resulting systems issues in each therapy session. Table 32.1 shows a way to determine who is in the chronically ill person's system and where the person is in his or her own life. It is designed to provide therapists with a graphic chart to accompany questions they might ask each member of that person's system. The questions may provide a kind of road

Table 32.1 Family Information

Family System of _____

Name	Age	Sex	Occupation/ School Grade	Live with Patient	Relationship	Frequency of Contact	Comments

map for the therapist to follow when working with such a system. (Table 32.2 presents the questions in their entirety.)

The questions help one ascertain at what life-cycle stages individual members of the family system are. It is important to assess at what nodal point each family member is when chronic illness occurs. If the family is at the centripetal stage—when it is recently formed and inner-directed—rather than at the centrifrugal stage—when it is more settled and outer-directed (Combrinck-Graham, 1985)—the chronic illness may have more or less importance. Because development of chronic illness occurs in different ways and at different stages of the life cycle, it is important to know at what stage each member is. Some illnesses are present at birth; others develop in childhood, adolescence, adulthood, or old age. For example, Huntington's disease, a genetic illness, does not usually surface until the person is in his or her 40s.

The entire family as well as close others outside the family are affected by any chronic illness that appears in a family member, whether its appearance surfaces at birth or develops later in life. It is important to realize that carriers of illnesses from birth know no other way of being. It is their parents and others who consider them impaired. To them, normalcy is having the condition they were born with.

Table 32.2   Questions Asked of Chronic Illness Systems

1. What were the first symptoms you noticed? What did you do?
2. Whom did you first tell?
3. Who was the first professional you saw?
4. a. What happened?
    b. Diagnostic tests? Did you go alone or take someone with you? Who?
5. a. What was the original diagnosis?
    b. Is it still that?
    c. How did you feel when you first heard the diagnosis?
6. Does anyone else in the family have the chronic illness you do? If so, what one word would you use to describe him or her?
7. What lifestyle changes have you had to make?
8. How have you educated yourself about your disability?
9. a. How do you remain hopeful?
    b. Whom do you feel you can count on for support?
    c. What kind of support and encouragement do you need most?
10. Do you have any major concern?
11. How has the illness changed your:
    work?
    marriage?
    view of the medical system?
12. What have you learned because of your disability?
13. Do you grieve any losses caused by your physical illness?
14. How have you adapted to your situation?
15. What is the prognosis and how do you feel about it?
16. Are there any questions I should have asked and have not?

Bowen (1978) said that medicine and individual psychotherapy both make a point of not divulging confidential information. Yet family therapists do not believe that issues that affect the entire family should be dealt with only by the person who has the diagnosis. By encouraging discussion among all the family members about how the illness affects each of them and what role they want to play in the caregiving system, the family therapist helps them understand that illness is not a private affair. Kerr and Bowen (1988) encouraged family therapists to put questions back into the group rather than answer them themselves. Certain kinds of questions elicit certain kinds of responses (Wright & Leahey, 1994). I find that asking specific questions of particular ethnic groups creates much discomfort. For example, asking a white, Irish-American male what his medical diagnosis is may result in an angry response. It can be helpful for a therapist to express what his or her own feelings would likely be if a similar situation should happen (McGoldrick, Pearce, & Giordano, 1982).

Many physical illnesses are chronic—Alzheimer's, arthritis, cancer, diabetes, various heart diseases, multiple sclerosis, retinitis pigmentosa, AIDS. Some losses of vision or deafness and most accident-produced injuries remain unchanged. If a person incurs an injury in an accident, usually the injury is immediate but the resulting disability is chronic.

Controversy as to whether certain conditions are mental or physical continues. Since all illnesses have some psychosomatic component (from the Latin *psyche* meaning *mind* and *soma* meaning *body*), I believe the controversy is meaningless. However, to those who differentiate between mind and body, some conditions that have heretofore been considered mental are now considered physical. Schizophrenia and depression are two illnesses currently treated extensively with medication alone. The use of drugs such as fluoxetine (Prozac), serta line (Zoloft), and paroxetine (Paxil) has wrought remarkable changes in depressed persons (Gitlin, 1990; Markowitz, 1991; Wynne, 1988). So too have lithium and monoamine oxidase (MAO) inhibitors with schizophrenics (Patterson & Magulac, 1994; Sotsky, 1992).

Obesity is also controversial. At issue is whether diets are harmful and provide few long-term benefits and whether they are ineffective for certain individuals. Does obesity have a genetic component? Families are accustomed to certain lifestyles, which may include eating familiar foods in familiar ways. To change that lifestyle requires being different from the family. A family member may not want to use that option, or the family may resist and sabotage such a visible form of differentiation.

"Obesity should be treated as a chronic disease, not a character weakness." So says Michael Weintraub, M.D., director of the U.S. Food and Drug Administration (FDA) (1994). Because it may be a chronic disease, therapists must help the family view being overweight as something the sick person does not do to be stubborn and must consider what his or her own values are concerning weight. In considering personal values, therapists will find drawing a genogram of the sick person's family of origin useful. On it should be listed all chronic diseases in the family, including such things as poor eyesight and bad teeth. Various computer software programs on drawing genograms are available, such as MacGenogram for the Macintosh and AutoGenogram for the IBM. Books also are available (Kerr & Bowen, 1988; McGoldrick & Gerson, 1985).

Physicians dealing with chronic illnesses often neglect systemic issues. They are expert in handling the physical ramifications of illness and release their patients after the crisis is over. Yet it is important for patients to receive updates on the current situation. For example, a couple may consider the prohibition on having sex immediately after a heart attack to be a general one. There needs to be some update on the situation at least every three months—is it now permissible and presumably safe? Keeping to a diet regimen or an exercise routine also needs periodic professional monitoring.

Some illnesses that formerly ended in death after a short time, such as AIDS, no longer forecast a short life span for the patient and have come to be considered chronic illnesses. Unless the therapist stays aware of the latest treatment, he or she models a rigid, dated attitude that the family may emulate. Staying abreast includes reading about alternative therapies (Brigham, 1994; Sadler & Hulgus, 1992). House, Landis, and Umberson (1988) give a good explanation of how social relationships and health are interdependent. So does Rolland (1984, 1994a, 1994b). Moradi (1994) wrote an article about sick children and how the family is part of the treatment plan. Because education occurs in the therapist's office, he or she should be aware of the current treatments for each of the illnesses his or her patients develop and share that information with the family members. The therapist can recommend books for laypersons to read and videotapes to watch. Entries in the reference list followed by an asterisk are particularly useful for laypeople. Some books are: The Aids Book (Hay, 1988), The Diabetic's Book (Biermann & Toohey, 1981), Epilepsy and the Family (Lechtenberg, 1984), Why Me? (Porter & Norris, 1985), Multiple Sclerosis (Donsbach & Alselehen, 1993), Cystic Fibrosis (Harris & Super, 1987), Mainstay (Strong, 1988), A Whole New Life (Price, 1994), Living with Chronic Illness (Register, 1987), Migraine (Sacks, 1985), We Are Not Alone (Pitzele, 1986), Catching My Breath (Brookes, 1994), The Body Speaks (Griffith & Griffith, 1994), and When a Loved One Is Ill (Felder, 1990). Some classic films, now available on video, include *Cries and Whispers, Love Story, A Woman Under the Influence,* and *Beaches.* Other choices can be made by conferring with local librarians about what is available and appropriate.

The therapist must model ways for the family to discuss the illness with one another, with health care professionals, and with other concerned nonfamily members. Patients often need help in asking for more information about their illness. They may need to be more assertive with their physician. The therapist can be a role model of such behavior.

In a family I worked with, the mother had been diagnosed with multiple sclerosis (MS). She received medical attention but her husband and children did not know how to deal with the illness. They believed they had to act casually about taking care of her but, in fact, resented that pretense. I asked them some questions (see Table 32.2) they had not addressed before. I asked my usual first question: "Tell me about the first time you noticed any symptom that told you something was wrong." Then I sit back and listen, modeling the way the family or spouse should listen—without interruption. I let each person spin out the story, as he or she sees it. (All questions need to be answered by each member of the family. Family members often notice something the patient is unaware of—such as easy fatigue, grumpiness, or weakness. To ask each family member the questions continues to model that this illness affects the entire family, not merely the patient.)

The mother told me about the fall day when she had first noticed her malady:

> I jumped on my bicycle after teaching an aerobics class. I usually bicycled the 15 miles home after class. That day, I stopped to pick up a soda can that someone had thrown out of a car window. (I am always amazed at people who don't care about keeping the environment clean.) As I jumped down, I noticed that my right foot flapped onto the ground. At the end of my ride, I turned into our driveway and pedaled up its long incline. At the three-car garage, I jumped off my Rockhopper and again noticed my foot flapping onto the ground.

As that week went by, I found it harder to ignore the slight symptoms I was experiencing. After all, I had lived with a mother who had MS and was very aware of its symptoms. When I had double vision and numbness in my hands, I knew I needed medical attention.

But the first thing was to tell my husband what was happening. And I agonized about how to do that. Did it mean the end of my independence? What would he say? What did I want from him?

Question 2 is related to this: "Who was the first person you told about your medical suspicions?"

The wife in a couple I was seeing for sexual dysfunction swept into my office saying that her husband had thrown an article in a medical newsletter from my waiting room at her. The article was about prostate cancer. He announced, "That's the surgery I have to have next." It was the first time his wife knew of her husband's physical problem. The reason for their sexual dysfunction had an underlying physical cause that the wife and I were ignorant of. Her husband saw prostate problems as a sign of weakness on his part and did not want to tell his wife of the symptoms that had developed. He had seen a urologist and scheduled surgery but had not figured out a way to tell his wife of the impending event.

Sometimes the hardest part of having a chronic illness is telling the most significant person in your life what your suspicions are. In my clinical practice I find that is especially difficult for males.

Questions 3 and 4 discuss the first professional consulted and the outcome.

The experience of consulting an outside expert can be comforting or upsetting. Cousins (1989) said that the day after diagnosis is often the worst day in a person's life. Not only does a person consult a professional in a crisis, but the prescribed action is made on the basis of the prevailing condition. Because of the evolution of most chronic illnesses, both the patient and the patient's system change. That change affects the lifestyle of both.

A case in point is diabetes. Initial diets for diabetics are stringent. After time, most diabetics who have lost weight and exercise regularly can have an occasional drink or a sugary dessert. The diabetic may know this, but others around him or her may be over-solicitous about rigidly following the original diet. Difficulties between those in the system may result.

The therapist must get such information into the open. Only in the safety of the therapy setting do some patient's families feel confident that any questions are possible. In the neutral setting of a therapist's office, a family often feels able to express feelings that have been taboo elsewhere.

I believe a drawing of the human body should be placed before the patient in the therapist's office. On this drawing the affected organ or body part can be indicated. Also diet and exercise forms should be written out and copied for significant persons who are affected by the illness. The value of such papers is twofold: They give the sick person a visual sense of his or her malady, and they authenticate to the involved family member that this is truly a physical problem. Often, unless a symptom is noticeable, others do not believe it is a "real" problem. For example, because an MS patient walks without limping on a sunny morning, the expectation may be that the same ease is available at night or on a rainy day.

The fifth question has three parts: what was the original diagnosis, is it still that, and how they felt on first hearing that diagnosis.

A former client says that her original diagnosis was influenza. When she worsened appreciably, the physician who had diagnosed her remanded her to the emergency room of the local hospital. In fact, she had a rare illness that required intravenous (IV) antibiotic treatment or death would have occurred in 24 hours.

Question 6 asks whether anyone else in the family has the patient's chronic illness. If the patient has seen someone else with the same symptoms, he/she may be alert to the initial signs that he/she, too, has the illness. This is especially true with genetic illnesses. An illness that members of the family have watched worsen is often an illness anticipated by other family members. Hearing about current treatments of such illness, may be helpful. It also may be different from what it was a few years earlier.

Question 7 covers the lifestyle changes that were made because of the illness. Because chronic illness requires change from the entire family, each member's lifestyle will have been altered, either slightly or significantly. Each participating member in the session must answer Question 7. One couple took turns getting up during the night with their asthmatic daughter. In that way, both changed their lifestyle similarly. A wife who cooked a special diet for her husband who had diabetes said she could not stay with her parents for three weeks because her husband needed her.

Having the list of questions I ask handy (Table 32.2) keeps me on track. The family or couple who see me refer to my list are helped as well. They feel safer because the session is more controlled and not as loose—it is less psychological and more medical. When a session seems more spontaneous, some members may become more careful about revealing their feelings. The list of questions in my hand makes the family feel safer.

The answers given by the client with MS, whom I discussed earlier, were significant. In answer to Question 8 regarding how she obtains more information about her illness, she answered:

> When I went to the hospital, I spent as much time in the medical library as possible. I read everything I could get my hands on about MS. Any researcher's name I came across three or four times, I contacted. I asked others who had no medical background about the illness. That meant asking at my local health food store about alternative medical personnel known in my area. I also asked members of various churches what healing groups existed there. I left no stone unturned to get information.

All people with chronic illness need to feel hopeful; that they will not lose their sight or hearing or their ability to walk, that they will not develop unbearable pain, that their money will not run out. The elderly frequently express worry about whether they will be a burden on loved ones. Question 9 encourages discussion of these issues.

A support group devoted to the patient's illness can be valuable and provide a sense of optimism for the patient and his or her family. Such support groups may be available through local hospitals or in individual therapists' offices. Clients or therapists can telephone 1-800-336-GENE at the Alliance of Genetic Support Groups to discover available groups and to get more information on specific illnesses.

A support group may be made up of participants in various stages of an illness. Sometimes persons in initial stages of an illness are "turned off" by those in more advanced stages (Rolland, 1994b). They do not want to hear what happens in the final stages of their illness. In assembling support groups, therapists should try to gather together people who are in the same stages of an illness.

One woman with a chronic illness said: "Never have a person support you who is fatalistic about your illness." She felt that unless chronically ill people surround themselves with others who believe improvement is possible—including the therapist and other professionals—it is harder for them to contend with the illness.

When working with a family unit, it is useful to add two parts to Question 9. First I ask who can be relied on for support. Some people in the patient's milieu cannot be counted on. Formerly supportive people may be resentful that the person is not as independent as he or she used to be or that he or she needs help for things that previously could be done without assistance. In one case a man who did not have to do any of the household chores before his wife developed arthritis had to do some things she could no longer manage—open jars, knead bread, vacuum rugs, and mop floors. The wife struggled over asking for his help because he gave it so grudgingly.

The third part of Question 9 talks about what kind of support and encouragement the ill person needs most. Those with a chronic illness usually know what kind of support and encouragement makes them feel more hopeful. Others in the system often need to be helped with this question. Frequently they do not think the identified patient needs support and encouragement. A therapist might say "If I were you . . ." completing the sentence with the perceived need. An example is the therapist saying, "If I were you I'd need to hear 'good show' or something." Articulated help may be different from one ethnic group to another and from gender to gender. Some ethnic groups—the Irish, for example, and many women—do not believe it is all right to express any of their own needs in the face of someone who is "really sick."

Patients often express fear of further change in the partner and in the health of the main caregiver in response to Question 10, about major concerns.

> Angie makes my breakfast, packs my lunch kettle with food for lunch and two snacks. After leaving the plant, I stop at the Legion to see the guys and then pick up our mail at the post office. When I get home, I change and go for an hour walk. Angie has my dinner ready. After we eat, I go in and watch television and fall asleep. Angie cleans up and makes my lunch and snacks for the next day. She'll pack them in my lunch kettle in the morning. I couldn't be well without her.

The quote is from a man who has diabetes. He fears that his wife is not taking care of her own health. His major concern is about his caregiver and what will happen to him if she becomes incapacitated. Her major concern is how she can tend to her parents and mother-in-law as well as her husband.

Children's major concern may be what path their parent's illness may take. Children are rarely told many facts about the illness for fear they will worry too much. On the contrary, Bowen (1978) says that silence about the illness creates more consternation. One family where the mother had died of cancer needed to discuss her illness and death several years later. Neither the father nor the mother had discussed cancer with the children while she was struggling with it. After her death the father did not bring up the mother's illness with his children. They thought they had caused the mother to become ill and to die.

Question 11 discusses how the illness has changed the patient's work, marriage, and view of the medical system.

Some people who have a chronic illness are penalized by the work setting. They may lose their jobs, especially if they have cancer or AIDS. People with these diseases may choose not to tell anyone at work of their medical condition because of the feared reaction. They may choose to leave the work setting entirely; the nature of the work itself may make the work too difficult for them to perform; or they may no longer be able to perform their jobs within the allotted time. Others in the system may have to make work accommodations to transport the loved one for chemotherapy sessions, diagnostic tests, or prescribed treatment (Landau-Stanton, Clemons, & associates, 1993).

I leave plenty of time to discuss work issues because the impersonality surrounding work makes the answers about how the illness has affected the marriage easier to handle. In fact, sometimes when discussion becomes too difficult, speaking about work deescalates the tension. One client said: "After the children left home, my development of heart disease gave us a focus. We discussed how to become vegetarians and give up drinking and smoking. For a time we had to forgo sex, and when we resumed it we discussed what was happening. That was different for us."

"Actually, the chronic illness improved our marriage." That's how Lester speaks of his illness. Norman's response to his wife's MS is very different: "We used to travel a lot. Now Regina gets too tired to sightsee and I don't want to see places alone. Staying home is boring and having nothing to do is also. Since Regina has gotten ill our marriage is awful. And it will get worse. I'm not sure I'll stay. Regina is not the woman I fell in love with."

Few options seem possible in cases like Norman's. It may be of some comfort to have a place where the unsayable can be said—the therapist's office (Rolland, 1984, 1994a, 1994b). Because the therapist may be at a different level of sophistication, he or she may have to demonstrate that even the harshest facts can be discussed. These facts may include helping someone in the bathroom, cleaning up vomit, deciding on tube feeding for an Alzheimer's patient, and wanting to leave the relationship.

The healthy person often makes decisions without conferring with the disabled partner. For instance, the healthy person may decide where the patient can visit safely. One woman who broke her back and became paralyzed said to her husband who was making decisions for her: "I broke my back, not my brain."

When chronic illness surfaces, a marriage undergoes much strain. Some people with chronic illnesses curtail sexual activity because of pain, weakness, or fatigue. Changing roles from that of lover to caregiver is not easy. When the chronically ill person appears to be nearing death, the partner may choose to distance him- or herself to make the final separation easier. A caregiver who feels he or she has become the prisoner of the patient may experience much resentment.

Family members are asked how the illness has changed their view of the medical system. One person responded: "I have to assess which medical people have helped me. At one time I had 17 doctors. I decided who really helped me and fired the others."

In talking about the medical system, discussion may center on whether the patient and other family members feel comfortable dealing with the primary care professional. Techniques suggested by Barth (1993) for choosing a physician or other health care professional may prove helpful. Siegel (1986) stated, "Give the doctor a hug." This is increasingly difficult under managed care when choices of providers are limited.

Therefore, the patient needs to be more assertive about his or her needs to the health care practitioner. Those needs are more consistently met by a practitioner who believes in Family Systems Medicine. "Family systems medicine is concerned with processes in any group that make a significant health difference in its members' lives" (Ransom, 1989). It is imperative that patients decide what information they want to receive. A list of questions needing answers should be made up before medical visits. Before taking a long trip on a superhighway, the driver checks a map to determine which exit is closest to the proposed destination. The same is true before visiting a health care practitioner. The patient must decide if this practitioner will help him or her arrive at the destination desired. In order to make that assessment, I suggest that relevant questions be written out before the appointment. Unless there are clear answers to each of these questions, the patient should not consult that doctor again. Anyone in the system who has questions should add them to the list. One person I interviewed told me she had learned to bring a notebook to the hospital. She asked all professionals who saw her to sign in with their name and what they did. I believe such a notebook also should contain the patient's comments about each procedure given.

Question 12 asks what people have learned because of their disability. The answer is brief for some: "Patience," "Fortitude," "To have a sense of humor." Others are likely to reveal more: "All of us are vulnerable. We may be the picture of health one day and have a chronic illness the next." "How independent I was. I liked to do everything for myself. Now I need help. I've learned to ask for assistance. It has not been easy." Another comment, "You can find almost anything by using your phone," showed how a patient was beginning to take more responsibility for herself.

That leads to Question 13, whether the person grieves any losses caused by the physical illness? A response from a woman with rheumatoid arthritis who went to college in the 1960s said she missed being able to play her guitar. Her husband missed the two of them singing together while she played.

Driving, running down the beach, swimming, standing up long enough to cook a meal, lifting a coat onto a hanger, getting in and out of a car alone, eating chocolate, and playing tennis are a few of the losses cited by those having a variety of chronic illnesses. Some of the losses and fears expressed by those involved with them, include having to shop alone, not dancing together, being the only parent who can pick up a child, and having no hope for a better tomorrow.

Therapists can help families grieve together. Grieving separately can ultimately cause further distance in a system already wracked with stress (Kubler-Ross, 1969). Some sessions need to be with the person who has the chronic illness. Others need to exclude that person and be just with the others. "I don't want to hurt him. He has enough to face," one wife told me of a husband who had constant pain from disintegrating hip bones. She told me his illness made her future look bleak. In order to get her to speak of her years to come, I asked her how she could design a happier future. Did it have to include her seeing herself as prime caregiver? I asked her what she would do if this illness was not a part of her life. As a result of those questions she began to take more responsibility for her own future.

To Question 14, on how the person has adapted to the situation, that same woman said she needed to create a life of her own. She planned to attend social events alone because her husband rarely had the stamina to attend them. She was active in political organizations because there were many people there. She went skiing, not only because she liked it but it was an activity where her husband was not in attendance. She needed to get away from him altogether at times.

Question 15 concerns the prognosis and how people feel about it. Some patients and their families want to discuss the future, while others refuse to deal with the coming events. Their method of dealing with issues is by denying their existence. It is respectful to let the family lead the way about how they wish to deal with the coming events. A doctor who was seeing a patient with cancer who did not want to talk about her impending death advised a family member to ask the patient when she would be going home. He felt that the patient would then ask him about her prognosis. Instead she told the relative the day she would be leaving the hospital. It was the day of her death.

The open-ended final question asks whether any questions should have been asked that were not. It has resulted in a variety of additional questions, such as: "How can I face the future?" "How do I enjoy good days when I know bad ones will reoccur?" "How do I tell people to stop asking me health questions?" "When can I invite a friend to spend the night?" "What did I do to deserve this?"

Many of the questions I ask have no answers but need to be asked nonetheless. They can be asked in a therapist's office. The therapist can demonstrate that all issues can be discussed there. It is useful to some families if the therapist says, "It is very hard to talk about this. I need your help." Exposing one's own clumsiness in dealing with life-changing events can be helpful to the family and also to the therapist. Therapists often describe feeling "burned out" by families who are dealing with chronic illness. It is important that they model for families that chronic illness is a difficult situation; by doing so, they eliminate symptoms in themselves and in family members.

CONCLUSION

Chronic illness affects not only the individual who develops it but also the entire unit connected with that individual. Chronic illness may arrive any time during the family developmental cycle and has a different impact on each member. The therapist who sees such a family unit must model by his or her questions an openness in conversing about the chronic illness that the system may lack.

Table 32.2 lists specific questions for therapists to ask family members. The reference list includes helpful books and video tapes for clients and their significant others. In chronic illnesses, the therapist often is also the educator, the clarifier, and resource specialist the system requires.

REFERENCES

Barth, J. (1993). *It runs in my family: Overcoming the legacy of family illness.* New York: Brunner/ Mazel.

Biermann, J., & Toohey, B. (1981). *The diabetic's book.* Los Angeles: Tarcher.

Bowen, M. (1978). *Family therapy in clinical practice.* New York: Aronson.

Brookes, T. (1994). *Catching my breath: An asthmatic explores his illness.* New York: Times Books/Random House.*

Brigham, D. D. (1994). *Imagery for getting well: Clinical applications of behavioral medicine.* New York: Norton.

Bruckheimer-Martell, B., Midler, B., & Jennings-South, M. (Producers), & Donoghue, M. A. (Director). (1968). *Beaches.**

Combrinck-Graham, L. (1985). A developmental model for family systems. *Family Process, 24*(2), 139–150.

Cousins, N. (1989). *Head first: The biology of hope.* New York: Dutton.

Doherty, W. J., & Baird, M. A. (Eds.). (1987). *Family-centered medical care: A clinical casebook.* New York: Guilford.

Note: Entries followed by an asterisk (*) are particularly useful for laypeople.

Felder, L. (1990). *When a loved one is ill: How to take better care of your loved one, your family, and yourself.* New York: NAL Books.*

Gitlin, M. (1990). *The psychotherapists guide to psychopharmacology.* New York: Free Press.

Griffith, J. L., & Griffith, M. E. (1994). *The body speaks: Therapeutic dialogues for mind-body problems.* New York: Basic Books.*

Harris, A., & Super, M. (1987). *Cystic fibrosis: The facts.* New York: Oxford University.*

Hay, L. L. (1988). *The AIDS book: Creating a positive approach.* Santa Monica, CA: Hay House.*

House, J. S., Landis, K. R., & Umberson, D. (1988). Social relationships and health. *Science, 241,* 540–545.

Kerr, M. E., & Bowen, M. (1988). *Family evaluation.* New York: Norton.

Kubler-Ross, E. (1969). *On death and dying.* New York: Macmillan.

Landau-Stanton, J., Clemons, C. D., & associates. (1993). *AIDS, health, and mental health: A primary source book.* New York: Brunner/Mazel.

Lechtenberg, R. (1984). *Epilepsy and the family.* Cambridge, MA: Harvard University.*

Markowitz, L. M. (1991). Better therapy through chemistry. *Family Therapy Networker, 15*(3), 22–31.

McGoldrick, M., Pearce, J. K., & Giordano, J. (Eds.). (1982). *Ethnicity & family therapy.* New York: Guilford.

McGoldrick, M., & Gerson, R. (1985). *Genograms in family assessment.* New York: Norton.

Minsky, H. (Producer), & Hiller, A. (Director). (1970). *Love Story.*

Moradi, S. R. (1994). Involving the family in the evaluation and treatment of the child patient: A psychodynamic approach. *Contemporary Family Therapy, 16*(5), 363–379.

New World Pictures (Producer), & Bergman, I. (Director). (1973). *Cries & Whispers.*

Patterson, J. E., & Magulac, M. (1994, April). The family therapist's guide to psychopharmacology: A graduate level course. *Journal of Marital & Family Therapy, 20*(2), 151–173.

Pitzele, S. K. (1986). *We are not alone: Living with chronic illness.* New York: Workman Publishing.*

Porter, G., & Norris, P. A. (1985). *Why me?* Walpole, NH: Stillpoint Publishing.*

Price, D. (1994). *A whole new life: An illness and a healing.* New York: Macmillan.*

Ransom, D. (1989). Development of family therapy and family theory. In C. N. Ramsey, Jr. (Ed.), *Family systems in medicine* (pp. 18–35). New York: Guilford.

Register, C. (1987). *Living with chronic illness.* New York: Macmillan.*

Rolland, J. (1984). Psychosocial typography in family systems. *Family Systems Medicine, 2*(3), 245–261.

Rolland, J. (1994a). In sickness and in health: The impact of illness on couples' relationship. *Journal of Marital and Family Therapy, 20,*(4), 327–347.

Rolland, J. (1994b). *Families, illness, and disability: An integrative treatment model.* New York: Basic Books.

Sacks, O. (1985). *Migraine: Understanding a common disorder.* Berkeley: University of California.*

Sadler J., & Hulgus, Y. (1992). Clinical problem-solving and the biopsychosocial model. *American Journal of Psychiatry, 149,* 1315–1323.

Shaw, S., Ruban, L. (Producers), & Cassavetes, J. (Director). (1974). *A Woman Under the Influence.*

Siegel, B. S. (1986). *Love, medicine & miracles.* New York: Harper & Row.

Sotsky, S. (1992). Commentary: Integration of pharmacotherapy and a psychiatric perspective. *Family Process, 31*(2), 114–116.

Strong, M. (1988). *Mainstay: For the well spouse of the chronically ill.* Boston: Little, Brown.*

Weintraub, M. (1994). Diet pills. *Women's Health Advocate Newsletter, 1*(7), 1.

Wright, L. M., & Leahey, M. (1994). Calgary family intervention model: One way to think about change. *Journal of Marital and Family Therapy, 20*(4), 381–395.

Wynne, L. (1988, May-June). Changing view of schizophrenia and family interventions. *Family Therapy News,* 3–4.

CHAPTER 33

Panic Disorder and the Family

JOSÉ E. de la GANDARA, MD and ANGELA PEDRAZA, MD

Panic is a combination of fear with a cluster of physiologic symptoms appearing suddenly, capable of reaching such intensity that the individual may misinterpret its source, often thinking that death may be imminent or that an unpredictable dangerous outcome, often undefinable, is about to take place. When no physical explanation of the symptomatology can be found and the frequency of these unexpected episodes increases, criteria for the diagnosis of Panic Disorder may be met. The impact of this disorder on the patient, and the family, can be devastating.

Closely associated to Panic Disorder is another psychiatric disorder known as agoraphobia. This is a phobic condition that frequently does not allow the patient to function or interact with others in public facilities or crowded places, and it predisposes the occurrence of panic attacks.

In this chapter we further elaborate on definitions, epidemiology, etiology, diagnosis, differential diagnosis, treatment, prognosis, and biopsychosocial aspects of the disorder, including its effects on the patient, individual family members, and family dynamics.

HISTORY

Panic Disorder is a nosological entity that was first included by the Task Force of the American Psychiatric Association (APA) developing the third edition of the *Diagnostic and Statistical Manual of Mental Disorders* (DSM-III) (1980). Subsequent revision of the third edition (DSM-III-R) in 1987 and the latest fourth edition (DSM-IV), published in 1994, have modified and attempted to clarify the criteria for diagnosis, but essentially it has remained the same. Both editions make a distinction between panic disorder presentation with and without agoraphobia.

Panic Attacks

Panic attacks are a syndrome consisting of acute, unexpected, unpredictable, relatively short-lived, very uncomfortable episodes of intense anxiety characterized by a cluster of symptoms and an unjustified, often undefinable fear that sometimes reaches irrational magnitude. The fear can be specific, such as in the cases where people think that they are going to lose their mind or they may experience fear of an impending doom. Frequently, however, the panic attack manifests itself as an undefinable fear of the unknown.

The most common symptoms that can be identified in a panic attack include: palpitations, pounding heart, accelerated heart rate, shortness of breath, feelings of choking, aphonia, changes in the tone of voice, chest pain or discomfort, nausea, abdominal distress, dizziness, unsteadiness, lightheadedness, faintness, and diarrhea. Other symptoms include: increased sweating, giddiness, trembling, hot or cold flashes, feelings of unreality (derealization), self-detachment (depersonalization), fears of losing control or going crazy, fears of dying, numbness or tingling sensation, and chills (Kaplan & Sadock, 1991).

The DSM-IV definition of panic attack requires a minimum of four concomitant symptoms developing abruptly and reaching maximum intensity within ten minutes of initiation (APA, 1994). Clinically, however, in many cases, less than four symptoms are elicited in the history on examination, and the time elapsed since the initiation of the first symptom may be difficult to ascertain. Frequently at the time of the interview, patients are overwhelmed by the unexplainable physical symptoms they are experiencing and so skeptical of the potential psychiatric nature of their condition that they are unable to describe, remember, or separate each individual symptom or know the amount of time elapsed from the onset of the first symptom to the presentation of the complete syndrome. In the majority of cases, it is ten minutes or less. The symptoms start to dissipate within 15 minutes to one hour of initial presentation. In rare cases the symptoms persist for longer.

A panic attack may be triggered by a number of external environmental circumstances and situations or may be internally, unconsciously, and unwillingly generated in a stimuli-free environment for individuals who are susceptible. They may even occur in sleep during non-REM (rapid eye movement) sleep stages, particularly between stages II and III, according to findings in Thomas Uhde's Sleep Laboratory at the National Institute of Mental Health. Sleep latency preceding the sleep-related attacks was found to be elongated in contrast with nights in which no attacks took place, and patients with panic manifest an abnormal increase in anxiety related to sleep deprivation, when compared to normal subjects (Roy-Byrne, Mellman, & Uhde, 1988).

In a large number of cases, panic attacks are associated with the presence of phobias. Frequently it is the phobic situation that triggers the presentation of the syndrome (Denboer, Westenberg, & Verhoen, 1990; Kovinsky et al., 1994; Roy-Byrne & Cowley, 1988; Ushiroyama et al., 1992).

Agoraphobia

Agoraphobia is defined by DSM-IV (APA, 1994) as anxiety about being in places or situations from which escape might be difficult or embarrassing, or in which help may not be available in the event of having a panic attack or panic symptoms. Agoraphobic fears typically involve characteristic clusters of situations, such as being outside of the home alone; being in a crowd or standing in a line; being on a bridge; or traveling in a bus, train, or automobile. It has been suggested that the diagnosis of specific phobia be considered if the avoidance is limited to one or only a few specific situations; or social phobia should be considered if the avoidance is limited to social situations. This seemingly unspecified reference to symptom clusters and the suggestion that other related diagnostic entities be considered sets the stage for an additional requirement regarding differential diagnosis of agoraphobia versus other mental disorders, such as social phobia; specific phobias limited to a single situation, such as avoidance of riding in elevators, escalators, or airplanes; obsessive-compulsive disorder in which the individual avoids dirt or touching potentially dirty objects because of obsessive fear of contamination; Post-Traumatic Stress Disorder, in which there is avoidance of stimuli the individual associates with the severe stressor that may have originated the activation of the disorder of separation anxiety disorder and manifested by avoidance of leaving home or relatives due to the anxiety that such action provokes.

Agoraphobia is recognized as an individual nosological entity in DSM-IV under the diagnosis Agoraphobia without History of Panic Disorder. While panic attacks are described specifically, they are not considered an individual codable entity, probably because they are made up of a cluster of symptoms that are common to a number of psychiatric as well as nonpsychiatric conditions.

EPIDEMIOLOGY

Panic disorder is a disease of worldwide distribution that will afflict at least one out of every 75 individuals during their lifetime (National Institute of Health [NIH], 1991). Other authors set the lifetime prevalence of the disorder at 1.5 to 2 percent of the population (Kaplan & Sadock, 1991). The female-to-male ratio of panic disorder with agoraphobia is thought to be 2:1. The mean age of presentation is 25 (Kaplan & Sadock, 1991). A NIH consensus conference, however, reports that the middle teens and early adulthood are the most common age of onset, although it acknowledges that the onset may occur at any time (NIH, 1991).

To illustrate the wide range of variability in age of onset, an article by Hassan and Pollard (1994) reported a group of 13 cases with initial onset at ages 60 or older. Thirty other patients over the age of 60 were also reported to continue to experience panic disorder with a younger original age of onset.

Agoraphobia is estimated to have a lifetime prevalence of 0.6 percent. Approximately one-third of the individuals with panic disorder also have agoraphobia (NIH, 1991). According to the same sources, at least 66 percent of patients with agoraphobia also suffer from panic disorder (Kaplan & Sadock, 1991; NIH, 1991). Agoraphobia has a mean age of onset in the mid 20s', and its appearance is commonly reported to occur following a traumatic event (Kaplan & Sadock, 1991). Patients with agoraphobia tend to have a more severe and complicated course of illness (NIH, 1991).

ETIOLOGY

Although the etiology of panic disorder is not known, a few theories have been postulated in an effort to find an explanation for the disorder. The theories range from biological to psychological. In the next few paragraphs we attempt to present the most important hypotheses.

Biological Theories

In the last few years researchers have succeeded in creating a model for panic attack that allows them to study its phenomenology by provoking a paniclike syndrome while infusing sodium lactate intravenously to predisposed individuals (Roy-Byrne & Cowley,

1988). An interesting finding that may prove helpful in understanding the pathophysiology of panic disorder is that patients who are successfully receiving treatment with alprazolam (Xanax) or imipramine (Tofranil) do not experience the symptomatology of the syndrome when rechallenged with sodium lactate infusion.

In addition to sodium lactate, hyperventilation, carbon dioxide inhalation, yohimbine, caffeine, isoproterenol, and a number of other panicogenic drugs that have been studied in the last few years (Kaplan & Sadock, 1991; Roy-Byrne & Cowley, 1988). One of those other drugs is Norplant, a subdermally implanted contraceptive containing levonogestrel, a synthetic progestin (Wagner & Berenson, 1994). Other orally administered contraceptives also are included in the ever-increasing literature of agents reported to induce panic attacks (Deci et al., 1992; Ushiroyama et al., 1992).

The efficacy of tricyclic antidepressants, monoamine oxidase inhibitors, and certain benzodiazepines in the treatment of panic disorders, now apparently also duplicated by the selective serotonin reuptake inhibitors (SSRI), has opened the way to the emergence of different but closely related theories to explained pathogenesis of panic disorders. Some of these compounds selectively inhibit the reuptake of either norepinephrine or 5-OH triptamine (serotonin) and others inhibit both, with a greater or lesser inhibitory balance ratio between one and the other neurotransmitter.

Two different theories have been postulated based in the uptake inhibitory properties. Both theories implicate the locus coeruleus directly or indirectly. One postulates that the locus coeruleus, which is the principal noradrenergic-containing nucleus in the brain, is involved in anxiety. The other postulates the serotonergic neuronal system's involvement in anxiety disorders and panic disorders specifically (Denboer, Westenberg, & Verhoeven, 1990).

Benzodiazepines receptor research work with anxiolitic and anxiogenic compounds affecting the benzodiazepine receptors such as colecistokynin (CCK), a usually inert peptide that provokes panic attacks in patients but not in normal controls, suggests that this receptor may be a key to the up- and down-regulation of anxiety states. Preliminary evidence cited in the literature from unpublished work of Roy-Byrne and Veith suggests that panic patients may be less sensitive to the catecholamine-reducing effects of benzodiazepines. Indeed the characteristic response of panic patients but not normal controls to CCK indicates the possibility of an imbalance in the sensitivity of the benzodiazepine receptor.

Psychodynamic Theories

In psychoanalytic theory, panic attacks are explained as being an unsuccessful defense against anxiety-provoking impulses. According to this view, the initial anxiety against which the patient consciously tried to defend him- or herself without success is now perceived as an unconscious overwhelming threat or fear that takes the new form of the multiple somatic symptoms characterizing the panic syndrome. Agoraphobia, on the other hand, is explained in psychoanalytic theory as the fear a child has of being abandoned. The defense mechanisms used are repression, displacement, avoidance, and symbolization.

Behaviorists theorize that anxiety is a learned behavior resulting from either parental modeling or classic conditioning. They believe that panic attacks and agoraphobia develop simultaneously or that agoraphobia may even precede the development of panic attacks (Kaplan & Sadock, 1991).

DIAGNOSIS

The diagnosis of Panic Disorder is made on the basis of preset current arbitrary parameters that have been revised since the syndrome was first defined by DSM-III (APA, 1980). The current criteria are established by DSM-IV (APA, 1994) and require that the following three conditions be met:

I.   The presence of both 1 and 2 below:
   1.   Recurrent unexpected panic attacks.
   2.   At least one of the attacks has been followed by a minimum of one month of either persistent concern about having additional attacks, or worry about the implication of the attack or its consequences, such as losing control, having a heart attack, fears of going crazy, and/or a significant change in behavior related to the attack.

II. The absence of the conditions specified in 3 and 4 below:
   3.   The panic attacks are not due to the direct physiological effects of a substance such as medications or recreational drug abuse or a general medical condition such as hyperthyroidism.
   4.   The panic attacks cannot be explained by the presence of another predominant mental disorder such as social phobia, other phobias, obsessive-compulsive disorder, post-traumatic stress disorder, separation anxiety disorder, etc.

III. Absence or presence of agoraphobia for the diagnosis of panic disorder without agoraphobia (300.01) or panic disorder with agoraphobia (300.21), respectively.

DIFFERENTIAL DIAGNOSIS

A thorough medical workup is indicated to rule out physical illnesses. Ruling out medical etiology can be a very challenging task, however, due to the multiplicity of organ systems implicated through symptoms that may be present in panic attacks, many of them mimicking symptoms resulting from a host of medical illnesses and vice versa.

Sheehan, Ballinger, and Jacobson (1986), reported that in one sample group studied, all of the patients with panic disorder have previously consulted a physician at least once about this distress. Seventy percent of them had seen ten or more physicians in relation to their symptoms (Ashok & Sheehan, 1987). One could therefore easily conclude that by the time these patients enter the mental health system and are examined by a psychiatrist, they are fairly well worked up and most medical illnesses have been ruled out. That could be a dangerous assumption in light of the rapidly changing crisis of financing health care.

Discussion

Panic disorder is a very difficult disorder to diagnose, requiring ample interviewing skills, clinical expertise, and experience. As with all other psychiatric disorders, an accurate diagnosis is the cornerstone of successful treatment intervention both psychopharmacologically and psychotherapeutically. Unfortunately, many patients suffer the disorder for years, functioning only marginally. Their treatment addresses only some of their anxiety symptoms, they do not receive the appropriate care, and they are misdiagnosed in busy emergency rooms, by primary care physicians, or by mental health professionals who lack the time and/or expertise necessary to diagnose and treat such cases.

Agoraphobia is said to accompany panic disorder in over 60 percent of the cases. It is thought that many patients develop agoraphobia as a result of classical conditioning, after experiencing a panic attack in a public place, such as a supermarket. Patients developing agoraphobia tend to have a more severe and complicated course of illness.

Psychopharmacologic Intervention

The psychopharmacologic treatment of panic disorder has been carefully studied, particularly in protocols approved by the Food and Drug Administration, which are designed to establish the safety and efficacy of new compounds and of currently approved compounds in order to gain additional approval for their use in panic disorder with and without agoraphobia and agoraphobia without panic disorder.

The compounds studied include benzodiazepines, tricyclic antidepressants, monoamine oxidase inhibitors, SSRI, atypical antidepressants, azospirone group compounds, beta blockers, calcium channel blockers, and antiseizure medications.

The literature contains many case studies and anecdotal reports representing successes and failures using a number of other compounds. Of the benzodiazepine group, alprazolam (Xanax), which is classified among the most potent compounds in this chemical group, was the first one approved for panic disorders. Two other high-potency benzodiazepines, lorazepam (Ativan) and clonazepam (Klonopin), also have proven to be effective in panic disorders.

Of the tricyclic group, the most studied is imipramine (Tofranil), which has shown significant efficacy over placebo and compared favorably with other compounds in several clinical trials. While all the tricyclics, including desipramine (Norpramin), one of imipramine's metabolites, are said to have antipanic properties, a recently published study claims that chlomipramine (Anafranil), the only tricyclic with strong serotonin reuptake inhibitory properties, is superior to imipramine for this indication (Modigh, Westberg, & Erickson, 1992).

Of the SSRI group, fluvoxamine has been studied specifically for this indication through at least one clinical trial sponsored by a multicenter pharmaceutical company. In other independent individually designed studies, fluoxetine (Prozac), paroxetine (Paxil), and sertraline (Zoloft) also have been reported to be effective in the treatment of panic disorders (Hoehn-Saric, McCleod, & Hipsley, 1993). In our clinical experience, all three above-mentioned, approved SSRI antidepressants have proven clinically effective when used for the maintenance of patients with panic disorder. Other compounds also have been reported in the literature to be efficacious, including the anxiolitic buspirone (Bu Spar) and the antiepilectics carbamazepine (Tegretol) and valporic acid (Depakene).

Psychotherapeutic Intervention

It is generally understood and accepted that the efficacy of traditional psychodynamic psychotherapy is poor and quite inadequate in the treatment of panic disorder, although some authors still list insight-oriented psychotherapy as a beneficial alternative, because it helps the patient understand the unconscious meaning of the anxiety and the symbolism of the avoided situation, the need to repress impulses, and the secondary gain of the symptoms (Kaplan & Sadock, 1991).

Increasingly, however, experts in the field have endorsed a combination of cognitive and behavioral therapy accompanied by other useful therapeutic techniques, such as breathing exercises, guided imagery, and relaxation training, to replace psychodynamic psychotherapy in the treatment of this disorder. Cognitive-behavioral psychotherapy supplemented by these above techniques has been demonstrated to be at least as effective as psychopharmacologic treatment options alone. The consensus of experts indicates that medication will enhance the effectiveness of psychotherapy while, reciprocally, psychotherapy enhances the effectiveness of psychopharmacologic treatment schemes (Mavissakalian, 1990). Lesser (1991) cites some advantages of this treatment approach over psychopharmacological treatment, including absence of side effects, chemical dependence, and dose finding. Improvement derived from cognitive-behavioral treatment may be longer lasting than the improvement derived from psychopharmacological treatment strategies (Marks & O'Sullivan, 1988).

Cognitive-behavioral therapy of panic disorder is a modified application evolved from the original therapeutic strategies developed by Beck for treating depression (Beck, Rush, Shaw, & Emery, 1990) and later applied to anxiety disorders, phobias, and personality disorders (Beck, Emery, & Greenberg, 1985).

A case presentation (Persons, 1992) described the evaluation and successful treatment outcome using cognitive therapeutic techniques of a 29-year-old woman suffering from panic disorder that was manifested after the birth of her first and only child. Persons emphasized the importance of the formulation and a thorough understanding of the patient's lifetime psychodynamic history. Also stressed is the need, whenever relevant, to understand the psychodynamics of the patient's significant other fully, to help better understand the dynamics of the couple as a whole and its effects on each individual.

The efficacy of cognitive therapy has been demonstrated in numerous recent studies, including those designed to compare the efficacy of psychopharmacologic intervention versus the psychotherapeutic approach. At least one (Klosko, Barlow, Tassinary, & Cerny, 1990) clearly shows comparable efficacy. A recent article reveals the results of a study carried out at the University of Iowa comparing fluvoxamine, cognitive therapy, and placebo in 75 outpatients with moderate to severe panic disorder. The study was a placebo-controlled, double-blind, multicenter clinical trial to compare safety and efficacy of fluvoxamine versus placebo. A cognitive therapy balanced treatment cell was added in the individual site. In this study, both fluvoxamine and cognitive therapy appeared to be better than placebo; when both active treatment modalities were compared to each other, fluvoxamine was found to be significantly superior to both cognitive therapy and placebo. It should be noted that this was a relatively short-term study (Black et al., 1993).

It is generally agreed, however, that the best treatment approach not only for panic disorder with or without agoraphobia but also for other anxiety-related disorders is a combination of the cognitive-behavioral approach plus psychopharmacologic intervention rather than either one of the two approaches alone (Beck, 1992; Beck et al., 1985; Beck et al., 1990; Pruitt, 1992; Wright & Thase, 1992).

Besides the individual psychotherapeutic modalities just discussed, group therapy, supportive groups, and/or marital and family therapy with a problem-oriented approach can be of significant value in the overall treatment of panic disorder with or without agoraphobia.

PROGNOSIS

Uncomplicated, recent-onset panic disorder with and without agoraphobia and agoraphobia without panic disorder are treatable conditions with good prognosis when accurately diagnosed and properly managed. As with many other psychiatric conditions, however, comorbidity, chronicity, lack of education, lack of compliance, and prejudice complicate the picture and make prediction of treatment outcome less reliable. The prognosis obviously is affected by comorbity with substance abuse, such as alcohol abuse, recreational drug abuse, and caffeine, or with personality disorders or other psychiatric, medical conditions that may cause the patient to be unreliable in treatment followup or that prevent or limit the administration of medication, psychotherapy, or both forms of treatment.

Chronicity is a poor indicator no matter why it occurs. Chronic illness of any kind and chronic mental illness in particular has a powerful effect on us. While chronic illness in the absence of psychobehavioral pathology may strengthen character, chronic mental illness presupposes at least some maladaptive behavior, which in turn reflects the existence and preponderance of pathologic defense mechanisms. It is a very difficult task to reverse years of pathological learned behavior resulting from the application of abnormal defense mechanisms to compensate for a condition that exists constantly to a greater or lesser degree. For these reasons, we submit that chronic panic disorder, while not impossible to treat, has a guarded prognosis.

Education, compliance, and prejudice are factors affecting the treatment outcome. All three are interrelated and cause patients to misinterpret what is happening. Therefore they may not be able to provide the clinician with a reliable history that will help him or her arrive at an accurate diagnosis, they may misjudge the improvement, or they may think that a cure has been achieved and therefore abandon treatment or deny the existence of any difficulties for fear of ridicule and discrimination upon admitting to such "weakness or flaw in character." Much education and change in societal attitudes are required to overcome those obstacles in the treatment of mental disorders and particularly panic disorder.

IMPACT OF PANIC DISORDERS IN THE FAMILY

Psychosocioeconomic Aspects

Panic disorder's socioeconomic impact is of great consequence not only to the patient but also to other family members and to marital relations. Panic disorders rank very high among psychiatric disorders and anxiety disorders in their disruptive consequences to the patient and immediate family members. Their scope of influence reaches to the extended family and society. With a mean presentation of 25 years of age, the disorders strike at a time when the individual, on the average, is reaching the most productive period in his or her life, placing the sufferer at a distinct disadvantage from other individuals in the same age group.

Implications to the Patient

In addition to the obvious pain and suffering of the individual afflicted with panic disorders and the devastating experience of its distinct symptomatology, he or she also must endure psychological pain resulting from the social implications of his or her re-actions to the symptoms. This is particularly true of those individuals who develop pho-bic conditions, including the most ominous, agoraphobia.

Individuals afflicted with this disorder see the routine of life disrupted by frequent routine or emergency visits to the physician's office and the emergency room believing that they are about to or have suffered a heart attack or some other life-threatening con-dition from which they may die. Often they are unable to drive or to ride an elevator, an airplane, a train, or other means of public transportation to attend any kind of activi-ties where groups of people will congregate, from grocery stores and shopping malls to religious services or political or entertainment rallies. They must abstain from a vari-ety of common situations in modern life due to their fears. Patients thus begin to use avoidance as a pathological defense mechanism; if it persists, it confines them to the re-strictive walls of their own home. Individuals consequently see themselves as limited in their ability to function in society. Their ability to perform productive work, to apply their talents, and even to exercise limited financial independence are all profoundly af-fected by their illness. Such a predicament exerts lasting effects on the individuals' psy-chological and mental state and personality, in addition to the disorder itself.

Implications to Society

Besides losing the productive participation of the patients, society also is overburdened directly or indirectly by the cost of the wasteful use of resources, such as overutiliza-tion of medical services or expensive emergency room services. The lack of financial independence of such individuals also has an effect on society; after depleting the fam-ily's financial resources, incapacitated individuals often have to apply for disability or early retirement and have to utilize state or federal financial, health, and nutritional assistance programs in order to exist.

Implications to the Family

The family is gravely affected as a result of the illness. In spite of the high incidence of comorbid psychiatric conditions that are found to coexist with panic disorder, in many instances individuals affected are normal if not outstanding members of society. Their life and that of their family will suffer a tremendous upheaval in a variety of psy-chosocioeconomic spheres as a result of the illness.

A recently published article reveals the results of a multicenter prospective study carried out in five tertiary care center hospitals, each located in five different areas of the United States (Kovinksy et al., 1994). The study focuses on the impact of serious illness on patient's families. To evaluate the impact of illness on the family, patients and/or their surrogates were questioned regarding the frequency of adverse caregiving activities that became essential and the economic burden encountered. More than half of the families reported at least one severe caregiving or financial burden and the in-vestigators concluded that many families of seriously ill patients experienced these bur-dens and their accompanying stress and distress.

Other studies focusing on similar questions corroborate these findings. Patrick and coworkers (1992) and Pruncho and Potashnick (1989) focus on the relationship between the patient's illness and the health of family members as reflected in the increased uti-lization of health-related services by family members. Oppenheimer and Frey (1993) report the results of a study of patients in 52 families conducted using DSM-III-R (APA, 1987) criteria. They were classified into three groups, including major depression, panic disorder, and a nonclinical control group. Family processes were examined using self-report measures and a structured interview. The results suggested that compared to depressed and nonclinical control families, panic disorder families had unresolved life-cycle issues, were enmeshed, used triangulation, and failed to resolve conflict. These findings indicate that dysfunctional family processes may be involved in the expression and maintenance of panic disorders. The data suggest the need for family and marital therapy in addition to the previously discussed psychopharmacologic and cognitive-behavioral treatment approaches for panic disorder.

Case History

The following history is that of a patient that has been followed in our office for the past five years, with the diagnosis of Panic Disorder with Agoraphobia.

The patient is a 43-year-old married female, who stated during her first visit that she experienced her first panic attack at age 26, while shopping at a mall. Her panic attack symptoms include palpitations, shortness of breath, hot flashes, hand tremors, fears of death, "heavy feeling in her head," and feelings of depersonalization. The attacks at the onset of her illness were unexpected, and the symptoms lasted 15 to 20 minutes. She consulted her primary care physician, who concluded after a medical workup, there was no "physical" reason to justify her symptomatology. Benzodiazepines were prescribed. She reported that at age 31 her panic attacks increased in frequency and she developed agoraphobia, which was manifested by fears of going to the stores and fears of driving. These symptoms created significant impairment in her ability to function at home and at work. It was at that time that she was referred to psychologist and psychiatrist for consultation.

The patient has been stable on 150 mg imipramine at bedtime and 0.25 mg alprazolam a day as needed for anxiety, with almost complete resolution of her panic attacks. She remained however, with anticipatory anxiety, and this symptom was prevalent in her daily activities, which in turn affected her relationship with her family. Her daughters were becoming fearful of separating from their mother because of her fears of dying. The patient's symptomatology also was suggestive of the possibility of a heart attack. Her husband believed she was a "hypochondriac," since there was no physical abnormality to justify her symptoms, and felt overwhelmed and helpless in relieving her anxiety. Psychotherapy sessions with her husband and children were recommended to process her illness and their interaction as a family. Her husband was educated about her disorder and his limitations in relieving her anxiety but of the significant benefit of being supportive of her complaints, reassuring that her symptoms would subside and that she would not die from a panic attack. During subsequent visits it became apparent that incorporating this patient's family in the care plan provided a better treatment outcome for her and her family than would have occurred without this intervention.

CONCLUSION

In this chapter we have discussed various biopsychosocial aspects of panic disorder, treatment strategies for the patient, and the emotional and socioeconomic burden the disorder causes for the patient, the individual family members, and the family as a whole. Before we conclude, however, we wish to emphasize our belief that as in many other psychiatric disorders, while the focus of psychopharmacologic and psychotherapeutic treatment is on the patient, overall management of the disorder requires attention to and specific forms of interventions toward the family members individually, the couple, and the entire family. The full range of therapies should include psychopharmacologic, individual supportive, and cognitive-behavioral therapy, plus couple, family, and group therapy, separately or in combination, to maximize treatment efficacy for all family members.

REFERENCES

American Psychiatric Association. (1980). *Diagnostic and statistical manual of mental disorders* (3rd ed.). Washington, DC: Author.

American Psychiatric Association. (1987). *Diagnostic and statistical manual of mental disorders* (3rd ed., rev.). Washington, DC: Author.

American Psychiatric Association. (1994). *Diagnostic and statistical manual of mental disorders* (4th ed.). Washington, DC: Author.

Ashok, R., & Sheehan, D. V. (1987). Medical evaluation of panic attacks. *Journal of Clinical Psychiatry, 48,* 309–313.

Beck, A. T. (1992). Cognitive therapy and psychiatric practice. *Psychiatric Annals, 22*(9), 449–450.

Beck, A. T., Emery, G., & Greenberg, R. L. (1985). *Anxiety disorders and phobias: A cognitive perspective.* New York: Basic Books.

Beck, A. T. et al. (1990). *Cognitive therapy of personality disorders.* New York: Guilford.

Beck, A. T., Rush, A. J., Shaw, B. F., & Emery, G. (1990). *Cognitive therapy of depression.* New York: Guilford.

Black, D. W. et al. (1993). A comparison of fluvoxamine, cognitive therapy, and placebo in the treatment of panic disorder. *Archives of General Psychiatry, 50*(1), 44–50.

Bradwejn, J., Meterissian, G. B., & Koszycki, D. (1988, May 10). *Cholecistokinin induced panic in panic disorder.* Presented at the 141st annual meeting of the American Psychiatric Association, Montreal, Canada.

Deci, P. A. et al. (1992). Oral contraceptives and panic disorder. *Journal of Clinical Psychiatry, 53,* 163–165.

Denboer, J. A., Westenberg, H. G. M., & Verhoeven, W. M. A. (1990). Biological aspects of panic anxiety. *Psychiatric Annals, 20*(9), 494–500.

Hassan, R., & Pollard, A. (1994). Late life onset of panic disorder: Clinical and demographic characteristics of a patient sample. *Journal of Geriatric Psychiatry and Neurology, 7,* 86–90.

Hoehn-Saric, R., McLeod, D. R., & Hipsley, P. A. (1993). Effect of fluvoxamine on panic disorder. *Journal of Clinical Psychopharmacology, 13*(5), 321–326.

Kaplan, H. I., & Saddock, B. J. (1990). *Handbook of clinical psychiatry.* Baltimore: Williams & Wilkins.

Kaplan, H. I., & Saddock, B. J. (1991). *Synopsis of psychiatry* (6th ed.). Baltimore: Williams & Wilkins.

Klosko, J. S., Barlow, D. H., Tassinary, R., & Cerny, J. A. (1990). A comparison of alprazolam and behavior therapy in the treatment of panic disorder. *Journal of Consultation and Clinical Psychology, 58,* 77–84.

Kovinsky, K. E. et al. (1994). The impact of serious illness on patient's families. *Journal of the American Medical Association, 273*(23), 1839–1844.

Lesser, I. M. (1991). The treatment of panic disorders: Pharmacologic aspects. *Psychiatric Annals, 21*(6), 341–346.

Marks, I. & O'Sullivan, G. (1988). Drugs and physiological treatment for agoraphobia, panic and obsessive compulsive disorders: A review. *British Journal of Psychiatry, 153,* 650–658.

Mavissakalian, M. (1990). Differential efficacy between tricyclic antidepressants and behavior therapy of panic disorder. *Clinical Aspects of Panic Disorder.* New York:Wiley-Liss.

Modigh, K., Westberg, P., & Erikson, E. (1992). Superiority of chlomiprimine over imipramine in the treatment of panic disorder placebo controlled trial. *Journal of Clinical Psychopharmacology, 12*(4), 251–261.

National Institute of Health. (1991, September 25–27). *Consensus Development Conference,* (2).

Oppenheimer, K., & Frey, J. (1993). Family transitions and developmental processes in panic disorders patients. *Family Process, 32,*(3), 341–352.

Patrick, C. et al. (1992). Serious physical illness as a stressor: Effects of family use of medical services. *General Hospital Psychiatry, 14,* 219–227.

Persons, J. B. (1992). A case formulation approach to cognitive-behavior therapy: Application to panic disorder. *Psychiatric Annals, 22*(9), 470–473.

Pruitt, S. D. (1992). Cognitive therapy: Efficacy of current applications. *Psychiatric Annals, 22*(9), 474–478.

Pruncho, R. A., & Postashnick, S. L. (1989). Caregiving spouses: Physical and mental health perspectives. *Journal of American Geriatric Society, 37,* 697–705.

Roy-Byrne, P. P., & Cowley, D. S. (1988). Biological aspects of panic disorder. *Psychiatric Annals, 18*(8), 457–463.

Roy-Byrne, P. P., Mellman, T. A., & Uhde, T. W. (1988). Biological findings in panic disorder. *Journal of Anxiety Disorders, 2,* 17–19.

Ushiroyama, T. et al. (1992). A case of panic disorder induced by oral contraceptive. *Acta Obstetrica and Gynecological Scandinavica, 71,* 78–80.

Wagner, K. D., & Berenson, A. B. (1994). Norplant associated major depression and panic disorder. *Journal of Clinical Psychiatry, 55*(11), 478–480.

Woods, S. W. et al. (1988, May 10). *Benzodiazepine receptors antagonist effect in panic disorder.* Presented at the 141st annual meeting of the American Psychiatric Association, Montreal, Canada.

Wright, J. H., & Thase, M. E. (1992). Cognitive and biological therapies: A synthesis. *Psychiatric Annals, 22*(9), 451–457.

PART III

The Future of
Relational Diagnosis

CHAPTER 34

Recurrent Themes Across Diagnoses

FLORENCE W. KASLOW, PhD

Over 95 percent of the authors agree that we definitely need a taxonomy of relational diagnosis. Authors of the two chapters that take a different position, Chapters 7 and 8, on social constructionism and narrative therapy were purposely invited to make certain that the antilabeling/antidiagnosis stance was represented and becomes part of the ongoing dialogue. Nonetheless, given the widespread support from authors and myriad other colleagues drawn from the gamut of mental health and health professions for the importance of the creation, validation, and dissemination of a nosology of relational disorders, one of the questions that has arisen as this volume has shaped up is whether we should continue to lobby for inclusion in future Diagnostic and Statistical Manuals (DSMs) or should we move toward a parallel, complementary, and separate manual? At this time there is little unanimity in the answer to this perplexing query.

My own predilection after carefully reading, editing, and digesting all of the chapters is that it is not an either/or debate but a both/and situation. For a DSM to become a truly comprehensive and inclusive manual of both individual and relational disorders, it would have to grow to mammoth size, and its substantive task and terrain—including the patient population to be diagnosed utilizing its categories—would have to undergo a radical shift. This volume is written from a biopsychosocial perspective, in which interpersonal and contextual factors are considered central and significant. As DSM has become increasingly biologically based, the major thrusts of the two categories of disorders may not be all that compatible. Another key variable is that DSM conceptualizes within a framework of pathology and mental illness; in relational diagnosis, there is an effort to depathologize and look at dysfunctional patterns through a lens that maximizes the possibilities of growth and change toward greater health. Relational diagnosis is based on a more flexible and optimistic worldview; less geared to thinking in terms of an "illness" that is long-term and, perhaps, unchangeable. Some authors think that suggested treatment protocols that have been clinically matched to particular diagnoses and validated for such purposes through outcome research should be considered for inclusion in the future. However, it would have to be specified that these are *guidelines only* and should be tailored to the particular patient's personality, symptoms, relational pattern presentation and concerns, and treating therapist's "style" and range of therapeutic strategies—or we risk causing the very straitjacket and narrowing of options that we believe current protocols lead to.

When we began working on this project, we had some sense of its enormity and complexity. As we completed this volume, we came to realize that creating a topology of relational diagnoses is a gargantuan task and will always be a "work in progress." Our admiration for all of the time, thought, research, and clinical and writing effort invested in the preliminary work preparatory to the publication of various DSMs and *International Classification of Diseases* has mounted, and we commend everyone involved for their achievement. Even the task of deciding what merits inclusion is difficult; as indicated in Chapter 1, the diagnoses included should be neither so broad that all behaviors and interaction patterns fall under the rubric of disorder or dysfunction and the healthy respect for perceiving a wide range of behaviors as normal is lost, nor should they be so narrow that too few qualify for needed programs, needed therapy, or insurance reimbursement. Wherever possible, patients/clients should be involved in co-constructing the diagnostic understanding.

The legal ramifications of diagnosis are manifold. Chapter 7 points out that a therapist may be sued *for* labeling or diagnosing; this has come to pass in cases, for example, in which therapists have been accused of evoking false memory syndromes (Loftus, 1994). Conversely, *failure to diagnose* and to do so *accurately* also can lead to malpractice charges or ethics complaints. Consider, for example, the clinician who does not assess correctly the severity of a person's depression when doing family therapy, because he or she eschews the idea of an identified patient and does not utilize psychological testing as a tool either for accruing objective data in determining or verifying a clinical diagnosis. In addition, because this therapist basically opposes the use of medication, he or she does not like to refer patients for pharmacological evaluation, which could result in the prescription of antidepressant medication. If the patient suicides and the family sues, the therapist may be found "guilty" for not practicing according to the principle of generally accepted standard of care of the mental health professions. Obviously, we are all sanctioned by our respective professions to practice through our state regulatory and licensing boards, and ultimately ethics boards and legal bodies do have authority over what we do. This may be a "damned if you do, and damned if you don't" double-bind dilemma (Watzlawick, 1963) for therapists, and it is posited here that the way to best protect one's patients and oneself is to engage in careful and accurate assessment and to modify the formulations over time to reflect improvement (or deterioration). Only then can the best possible treatment be offered.

Several authors have highlighted the importance of having a model as the context in which various diagnoses are formulated. This is congruent with the position espoused in Chapter 1, which states that within the science of classification, especially as it is utilized in taxonomies of human behavior, underlying models are essential. It seems important to reiterate here that three major types of models currently are extant in the study of mental health and mental illness: the hierarchical, the multiaxial (see, e.g., Chapter 21 on partner relational problems and affective disorders) and the circumplical. The latter is clearly illustrated in Chapter 5 on assessment and treatment using the circumplex model and Chapter 6 on integrating individual and interpersonal approaches to diagnosis within a structural analysis of social behavior (SASB) and attachment theory model. The validity and efficacy of both of these circumplical models are well documented in the research literature and have achieved recognition and widespread utilization both in the United States and abroad. Circumplex models seem particularly well suited to the conceptualization of family diagnosis since they allow for and even encourage delineation of overlapping variables and foster consideration of multifaceted, complex system elements.

Chapter 20 presents an elegant, comprehensive, schema-focused model for assessing personality disorders in a relational context; the authors seem to encompass elements of all three models as their route to ensuring that all relevant factors are taken into consideration.

Authors of several chapters deal mainly with the interaction of physical illness and emotional factors, and all take a holistic biopsychosocial approach consistent with the current mainstream of thought in the family systems medicine field. Chapter 9 presents a viable approach to treating patients who have physical ailments and who are experiencing relational distress in primary care medical settings. The authors urge on-site collaboration of primary care physicians and family clinicians to maximize benefits to patients and believe involvement of the patient's significant others often is essential to enhance the recovery process.

This is congruent with the groundswell of activity that has led in the past decade and a half to the movement called collaborative family health care (CFHC). McDaniels and colleagues at the University of Rochester Medical School, notably Lyman Wynne, Tom Campbell, and David Seaburn, and other luminaries in family systems medicine, such as Don Bloch, William Doherty, Mac Baird, and John Rolland, have played leadership roles (Dym, 1995). Chapter 15 reaches very similar conclusions, although the authors' work emanates from a pediatric medical care setting. They dramatically portray the dilemmas faced by the child patients, how a serious illness impacts on the family, and how family attitudes also influence the child's perception of and ability to cope with the malady and the hospital setting. Chapter 32 extends the portrait that emerges from Chapters 9 and 15 even further and more vividly when Barth analyzes the effect the chronic illness of an adult has on his or her family. She succinctly elucidates the most pressing questions to be asked and kinds of information to be provided by the therapist, whom she believes also assumes an educative function vis-à-vis the physical and emotional aspects of the illness and the changes that are likely to accompany its management—including stress, uncertainty, altered lifestyles, and increased financial costs. Clearly, no long-term physical illness can be viewed as affecting one person only; it has consequences for and effects on all members of the intertwined, interdependent family unit.

Another trend in the past decade and a half has been the growing recognition, replacing some denial and myopia, that all family systems exist in their own idiosyncratic milieu that is multidetermined by their biological and sociocultural heritage; their racial, religious, and ethnic roots; their educational background; and their economic status. This realization has expanded our concepts of what is normative. Earlier literature in the United States in the family therapy field was based predominantly on the white middle- and upper-middle-class family. One notable early exception was the work on *Families of the Slums,* about inner-city black families, a now-classic volume written by Minuchin, Montalvo, Guerney, Rosman, and Scheemer (1967). Socioeconomic and other demographic variables influence what family members consider acceptable and "normal" behavior, how they cope with deviance from their expectations and their standards, why they come to and for treatment, how they present themselves and their problems, how they relate to the therapist, and what their preconceptions are about what therapy is, how it will be conducted, and what the therapy will do to and for them.

Although I think all of the contributing authors consider the variables just mentioned in their assessment, treatment, and research activities, the issue is of such magnitude for relational diagnosis that several chapters specifically address the ethnic component of families. Thus Chapter 10 and Chapter 11 bring the ethnic and cultural context of relational diagnosis and treatment into the foreground, thereby ensuring that these significant variables will not be minimized or ignored. (Due to space limitations it was not possible to include chapters on several other large ethnic population groups that re-side in this country; nonetheless, we believe these two chapters highlight the issues.)

In the past, a sizeable body of literature has accumulated on families with a schizo-phrenic member and the reciprocal impact of the family's behavior on the mentally ill member and of the impact of his or her affliction and disturbed behavior on family members. Because recent books and articles that consider psychoeducational and other approaches for helping families cope with a schizophrenic member (Anderson, Reiss, & Hogarty, 1986; Falloon, Boyd, & McGill, 1984) and that analyze the interactional cor-relates of expressed emotion in the families of schizophrenics (Miklowitz, Goldstein, Falloon, & Doane, 1984) have covered this material so well, we did not include a chap-ter on this topic. Of course, in the next, more inclusive volume, which will serve as a manual, schizophrenia in a relational context will be one category.

Because they have received less focal attention in the family literature, anxiety dis-orders, mood disorders, and eating disorders seemed to warrant our attention. These have been discussed as they affect different subsystems of the family and across the several generations, with consideration given to etiology as well as to assessment, and treatment. Thus Chapter 12 presents a gripping depiction of child and adolescent de-pression. The authors strip away any blinders that readers may still wear regarding whether childhood depression really exists. Chapter 21 describes the interconnectedness of affective disorders and partner relational conflicts. Chapter 28 draws heavily on a re-search base in its appraisal of mood disorders and the family. Its authors identify the course of the illness and reiterate the intertwining of biological with psychological fac-tors and features. These chapters on affective disorders plummet us into the sad and often pessimistic weltanschauung of the depressed family.

Authors of the two chapters on anxiety disorders approached the topic from slightly different perspectives. Chapter 16 is quite psychological in tenor; the author uses DSM-IV criteria sets as a starting point and then places the various anxiety disorders primar-ily in the context of the couple—recommending various psychotherapeutic interventions to lessen the sometimes paralyzing and always stressful impact of obsessive-compulsive behaviors and agoraphobia and the often debilitating effect of panic attacks on self and others. In Chapter 33, de la Gandara and Pedraza, biological psychiatrists who also con-duct psychopharmacological research, also start with the DSM-IV criteria sets and then make a very strong case for using medication in addition to verbal therapies for certain illnesses, such as severe panic disorder. They posit, as does Rosen, that when the index patient, who sometimes must be identified to get treatment improves, the marriage changes—often in a positive direction—and the family system becomes less chaotic and volatile. For example, children who see a parent with a full-blown panic attack rushed to the hospital emergency room because it is feared he or she is having a coro-nary, only to return home mystified as to what happened, are frightened and uncertain when such a terrifying event may occur again. When these attacks are brought under control, the family experiences less fear, there is less need to "walk on eggshells," so the stress level decreases, as does the contention, and the home atmosphere is calmer and more stable.

Chapter 30 deals with eating disorders, covering the panoply of causative factors as well as what features need to be taken into account when arriving at a diagnosis of anorexia, bulimia, or a combination of the two disorders. Levine also paints the ele-ments of eating disorders in bright colors so that their damaging impact on the self, al-most always female, and her significant others is very vivid. Levine also subscribes to the importance of understanding contributory relational factors, of accurate diagnosis being a necessary precursor to the best possible treatment, and to a multipronged treatment approach that might include individual, couples, family, and/or pharmacological interventions.

PROGNOSTICATING OR CRYSTAL BALL GAZING

Discussion of the future of relational diagnosis is based more on trend watching, conjecture, and some hopes for the future rather than on scientific "facts" or outcome research, since these do not exist prospectively.

Given the expansion of managed care and other third-party payer systems in the United States and comparable government-covered health/mental health benefit plans in other countries, several distinct trends related to relational diagnosis and family systems therapy approaches are likely to continue and grow stronger.

The social constructionists and those who use narrative therapy approaches, such as Australian White (1989) and New Zealander Epston (White & Epston, 1990) will expand their sphere of influence, mainly among those who believe that, as Gergen, Hoffman, and Anderson state in Chapter 7, diagnosis may be dangerous, implying that its tendency to be static and rigid may be antithetical to the very change we are trying to help clients achieve.

Since language shapes and even becomes the person's reality, as Andersen also attests in Chapter 8, labeling makes the range of possibilities in therapy too narrow, makes the therapist/client relationship too unequal, and, in this view, disempowers rather than empowers consumers of services in terms of restoring or rechanneling their lives and behaviors. Post-modern approaches have a great deal of appeal to those who like stories and metaphors, and this style of doing therapy may be more fun than more conventional modes. Emotionally these approaches are likely to attract those who are essentially anti-establishment, who place a high value on their own and others' independence, and who dislike being rule-bound. Since many of us become therapists because we treasure being self-directed and free to intervene as we choose, rather than as we are told we must by some computer-generated protocol or managed care case manager, these approaches have some compelling features. Much process and outcome research needs to be conducted regarding the effectiveness of social construction and narrative approaches before the more scientifically oriented theorists and clinicians will adopt these approaches as part of their treatment armamentarium. But they are an important antidote to the very structured behavioral approaches that fall at the opposite end of the pendulum, and they keep the field more firmly connected to its humanitarian roots.

Psychodynamic, object relations, contextual (Boszormenyi-Nagy & Spark, 1973), and other long-term therapies (Kaslow, Kaslow, & Farber, in press) will continue to be utilized by those treating patient couples and families when the patients: (1) want to understand why they act and feel as they do—and seek to acquire greater insight and awareness of self and others; (2) are extremely distressed and/or have deeply ingrained characterological problems and need long-term treatments; or (3) when the therapist believes one of these modalities has distinct advantages over the others for achieving the desired therapeutic goals.

In this book, chapters such as those on child and adolescent depression (Chapter 12), on couples with borderline disorders (Chapter 17), on those who have sadomasochistic interactions (Chapter 18), and on persons with anti-social and histrionic personality disorders in relationships (Chapter 19) are written primarily from a psychodynamic and/or object relations perspective (Slipp, 1988), because the authors think these are best suited to these specific patient populations. Inherent in such choices is a belief that sound treatment can be planned and implemented only if it is based on a carefully formulated relational diagnosis that must remain dynamic and flexible, so that it can be modified as new information emerges and/or as changes occur in the attitudes and actions of the therapy participants. This is a fundamental principle held by over 95 percent of this volume's authors.

Clinicians who have or will become involved in being providers within various third-party payer systems will be obligated to assign a diagnosis to all those whom they are treating. As pointed out in Chapters 1, 2, and 4, for a diagnosis to be not only accurate but ethically correct, it must truly reflect the reasons the patients are coming to therapy and the actual treatment interventions being utilized. Thus if an adult survivor of intrafamily childhood incest (Chapter 26) is being seen individually at first and presents with depression and/or a dissociative identity disorder (Chapter 27), this would be coded on Axis I of DSM-IV (APA, 1994). Although the patient and the therapist are dealing with distress that eventuated from a disturbed and destructive relationship system, the perpetrator(s) are not physically present, and it is the internalized or introjected objects and memories that are being dealt with. However, if the individual reaches the point in his or her therapy when it is jointly deemed appropriate and essential for the parents and perhaps other members of the family of origin to be invited to become involved, and if they agree to more than a one-session "consultation," a shift is made to family therapy and must be so indicated (Chapter 26).

Ideally, all those being seen will be enumerated on the billing sheet, the family system will be mentioned as the unit being treated, and no one specific person will be identified as the index patient. (See Chapter 3.) We will have modifiers for dysfunctional family patterns such as mild, moderate, and severe and will be able to indicate that the major issue is delayed resolution in adulthood of trauma caused by intrafamilial child sexual abuse.

Ultimately a nosology of relational diagnosis will gain widespread acceptance because it is a concept whose time definitely has come. As more and more researchers, theoreticians, and clinicians utilize the concepts set forth herein, conduct the research to validate and refine them, and utilize them in clinical laboratories, we will garner the data and the momentum necessary to launch an all-out effort to convince third-party payers that outpatient (as well as some inpatient) family diagnosis and treatment is cost-effective, and better for many patients, and should be reimbursed. Along with this, we will need to convey to trainees, colleagues in other related disciplines, and insurers that we utilize criteria to determine when individual, couple, family, or group therapy, or a combination of several of these, constitutes the treatment of choice.

Brief therapies (Budman, 1981; de Shazer, 1985; Gustafson, 1986) and behavior therapies (Wilson, Franks, Kendall, & Foreyt, 1987) are likely to continue to be favored by third-party payers, who place a much higher priority on cost containment than on treatment efficacy and quality of care. These approaches also are apt to gain more adherents from therapists who believe in and/or are more comfortable with being here-and-now oriented and problem and/or solution focused, and who do not believe that delving into the past and into the multigenerational transmission process (Bowen, 1978; Kaslow,

1995; McGoldrick & Gerson, 1985) is essential. Diagnoses will be arrived at quickly and will be deemed essential for the behavior therapists, as the treatment will be initiated predicated on the specific diagnosis.

Much initial assessment utilized in formulating the diagnosis will be done by using test batteries and/or pencil-and-paper inventories, most of which will be scored by computer. Those wishing to access a computer printout of the treatment plan matched to a specific diagnostic code will be able to do this from several sources, such as some managed care companies, a computer program designed for this purpose, or perhaps even a manual of relational diagnosis that incorporates treatment recommendations. It is hoped that such crucial ingredients in the therapy process as (1) therapist judgment based on being the only one (or team) who actually see(s) the patients and therefore knows them better than an insurance clerk or a computer can, and (2) therapist ability to relate empathically and holistically to each patient as a person and not as a symptom complex or syndrome, will not be negated or relinquished as part of the field, voluntarily or involuntarily, agrees or submits to becoming increasingly mechanized, depersonalized and dehumanized.

One segment of clinicians will continue to believe that a salient, even sacrosanct, aspect of therapy is the patient/therapy relationship and that principles of confidentiality, privacy, privilege, and informed consent are, and should be, enduring. Because they believe that sending detailed reports to third-party payers can violate these principles and further, that neither an insurance clerk nor another professional who has never seen the patient can verify a diagnosis or determine how long and what kind of treatment is warranted, they will stay out of the managed care enterprise and instead gear their services to the shrinking, but still viable, private-fee-paying clientele. They will do meaningful assessments, from which they will formulate diagnoses and treatment plans, because they are committed to offering their patients the best quality of care they can and these steps are, to them, an essential part of the therapeutic process. (See Chapter 13, on LD and ADHD, Chapter 20, on Personality Disorders in a Relational Context, and Chapter 23 on Sexual and Gender Identity.) All relevant factors will continue to be considered in a kaleidoscopic assessment. In their conceptualizations, as in that discussed in Chapter 6, how one can shift between and encompass intrapsychic and interpersonal variables becomes crystal clear.

Those authors who have been courageous enough to develop criteria sets tend to utilize quantifiable measures such as severity, frequency, chronicity, and length of time condition is experienced (duration) as specifiers in delineating characteristics of a disorder. (See Chapter 12 to determine the presence of depression in children and adolescents; Chapter 13 to ascertain if a child has a learning disability or attention deficit hyperactivity disorder; Chapter 14 to assess whether a diagnosis of Oppositional Behavior or Conduct Disorder should be made; and Chapter 26 to determine whether someone is manifesting incest survivor syndrome.) This is consistent with the efforts of many authors to build on the familiar groundwork supplied in the criteria sets appearing in DSM-III-R (APA, 1987) and DSM-IV (APA, 1994). It seems wise to move with and from the familiar format utilized in diagnosing individual mental disorders to the more uncharted terrain of assessing and diagnosing complex relational disorders. In doing the latter, serious consideration of the circular rather than linear causality of relational patterns and the impact and consequences of most relational problems catapults relational diagnoses to a different level of analysis.

The qualifier "most" has been inserted because the authors who have contributed chapters dealing with intrafamily violence and abuse also posit some linear causation, believing that perpetrators must be held accountable for their behavior and should not be allowed to blame someone else for making them erupt and act abusively. As a dramatic example of the nonculpability of the victim, it is impossible to imagine even the purest of systems theorists purporting that a two-year-old is equally culpable when sexually abused by her father. This theme of responsibility for one's hurtful behavior and its deleterious short-term and long-term ramifications, as these apply in assessment, diagnosis, and treatment, is underscored in the Relationship Conflict Inventory in Chapter 24, as well as in Chapters 22, 25, 26, and 27. Chapter 29, on the interpersonal aspects of substance abuse and addictive personality disorders, is laced with the same theme of responsibility, while still giving credence to the viability of the disease model of addiction; for recovery really to be under way and continuous, the addicted person must not only take responsibility for no longer using any drugs or alcohol but must also, according to 12-step program philosophy, attempt to make amends for the hurt inflicted while he or she was inebriated or "stoned" and/or diverted from normal family and job involvement.

Perhaps one of the most disturbing chapters in the book is Chapter 31, on the evil character and its devastating effects. It also may prove to be one of the most controversial. Charny has written about the kinds of individuals who rarely come to therapy because they do not perceive themselves to be disturbed. In their (usually male) manipulativeness, grandiosity, and contempt for the feelings, wishes, person, and property of others, they blame whatever they perceive to be wrong on others. A seasoned marital therapist who has studied marital love and hate (Charny, 1972) and is a recognized world authority on genocide (1982, 1990), Charny documents the existence of a category of personality that exceeds the borderline, the antisocial, or the psychopathic personality, although these people may have many characteristics in common with them. Their motive often is destructive; they are capable of committing or causing/ordering others to commit barbaric acts of torture and murder; they are excessively power driven; and they totally lack a conscience. When individuals inadvertently choose such a person as a partner, when families sense one of their members is malevolent and "wicked," and when societies allow this type of person to ascend to a top leadership position, often mass denial of what really is happening occurs. It is too horrible to recognize, and so efforts are made to pacify the aggressive, destructive perpetrators of heinous acts—the intentionally abusive husband, the "bad seed" intolerable adolescent who enjoys being destructive, or the political leader of a country seeking to destroy certain religious or ethnic minority groups, to annex neighboring countries, or to wage war to satisfy his megalomania. If we can accept Charny's entry into the realm of a diagnostic category and not continue to relegate evil to a religious concept only, we can help the world understand that such malevolent people do exist. We might be able to heighten individuals' ability to recognize such people and avoid getting involved with them; at a family level, we might be able to help them to seek assistance at the early phase of concern over an unusually and chronically destructive member; and at a societal level, we might be able to help them to take measures to remove someone from power if it becomes clear that his xenophobia, insensitivity, grandiosity, and megalomania are leading the group or country on a course of devastation, even annihilation.

It is prognosticated that the mental health community will continue increasingly to turn to a family-based relational perspective to facilitate and enrich the comprehension and treatment of personal and interpersonal dysfunctional patterns. As we sharpen our diagnostic categories and the tools for relational assessment and expand the database of qualitative and quantitative findings on process and outcome research, treatment methodologies will be selected and focused more carefully. Family practitioners and researchers, through our various organizations, will have the data we need to convince legislators and third-party payers that family therapy is a cost-effective and efficacious modality and merits inclusion in all reimbursement schemes. The big push for this will crescendo in the next few years. We will encourage recognition of the fact that diagnoses also have meaning to patients and their self-concepts and, therefore, utilize these judiciously rather than in an authoritative or cavalier manner.

And soon after this volume is published and we start to receive constructive input from our readers, we hope to begin work on Volume II—perhaps a manual of relational disorders—to offer a language that has achieved high consensus in categories that will be delineated in a more uniform manner, so that more meaningful dialogues can occur among and between therapists, their patients, and those of significance in the larger ecosystem. The schema that has begun to emerge will be validated, expanded, and refined and will enable therapists and researchers in the international family of family therapists and researchers finally to have a nosology of family diagnosis that is applicable across geographical and cultural boundaries.

REFERENCES

American Psychiatric Association. (1983). *Diagnostic and statistical manual of mental disorders* (3rd ed. rev.). Washington, DC: Author.

American Psychiatric Association. (1994). *Diagnostic and statistical manual of mental disorders* (4th ed.). Washington, DC: Author.

Anderson, C. M., Reiss, D. J., & Hogarty, E. E. (1986). *Schizophrenia and the family.* New York: Guilford.

Boszormenyi-Nagy, I., & Spark, G. (1973). *Invisible loyalties.* New York: Harper & Row. (Reprinted 1984. New York: Brunner/Mazel.)

Bowen, M. (1978). *Family therapy in clinical practice.* New York: Aronson.

Budman, S. H. (1981). *Forms of brief therapy.* New York: Guilford.

Charny, I. W. (1972). *Marital love and hate.* New York: Macmillan.

Charny, I. W. (1982). *How can we commit the unthinkable? Genocide: The human cancer.* Boulder, CO: Westview.

Charny, I. W. (1990). Marital therapy and genocide: A love of life story. In F. W. Kaslow (Ed.), *Voices in family psychology* (vol. 1, pp. 69–90). Newbury Park, CA: Sage.

de Shazer, S. (1985). *Keys to solution in brief therapy.* New York: Norton.

Dym, B. (1995, April). Is systems thinking coming to health care? *Family Therapy News,* 3.

Falloon, I., Boyd, J., & McGill, C. (1984). *Family care of schizophrenia.* New York: Guilford.

Gustafson, J. P. (1986). *The complex secret of brief psychotherapy.* New York: Norton.

Kaslow, F. W. (1995). *Projective genogramming.* Sarasota, FL: Professional Resource Press.

Kaslow, N. J., Kaslow, F. W., & Farber, E. W. (in press). Theories and techniques of marital and family therapy. In M. B. Sussman & S. K. Steinmetz (Eds.), *Handbook of marriage and the family* (vol. 2). New York: Plenum.

Loftus, E. F. (1994). The repressed memory controversy. *American Psychologist, 49*(5), 443–445.

McGoldrick, M., & Gerson, R. (1985). *Genograms in family assessment.* New York: Norton.

Miklowitz, J. D., Goldstein, M. J., Falloon, I. R. H., & Doane, J. A. (1984). Interactional correlates of expressed emotion in the families of schizophrenics. *British Journal of Psychiatry, 144,* 482–487.

Minuchin, A., Montalvo, B., Guerney, B. G., Rosman, B. L., & Scheemer, F. (1967). *Families of the slums.* New York: Basic Books.

Slipp, S. (1988). *The technique and practice of object relations family therapy.* Northvale, NJ: Aronson.

Watzlawick, P. (1963). A review of the double bind theory. *Family Process, 2,* 132–153.

White, M. (1989). The externalizing of the problem and the reauthoring of lives and relationships. In *Selected Papers.* Adelaide, Australia: Dulwich Centre Publications.

White, M., & Epston, D. (1990). *Narrative means to therapeutic ends.* New York: Norton.

Wilson, G. T., Franks, C. M., Kendall, P. C., & Foreyt, J. P. (1987). *Review of behavior therapy* (vol. 2). New York: Guilford.

Author Index

Subject Index

John Dewey Library
Johnson State College
Johnson, Vermont 05656

DATE DUE

1/5/98		
MAR 0 2 1998		
DEC 12 1998		
1/10/2000		
4/17/00		
6/16/00		
OCT 2 9 2003 ill		

Demco, Inc. 38-293